ENTERPRISE ARCHITECTURE
USING THE ZACHMAN FRAMEWORK

ENTERPRISE ARCHITECTURE
USING THE ZACHMAN FRAMEWORK

Carol O'Rourke
Neal Fishman
Warren Selkow

THOMSON
COURSE TECHNOLOGY™

Australia • Canada • Mexico • Singapore • Spain • United Kingdom • United States

Enterprise Architecture Using the Zachman Framework

Carol O'Rourke, Neal Fishman, Warren Selkow

Executive Editor:
Jennifer Locke

Product Manager:
Alyssa Pratt

Development Editor:
Lisa Ruffolo

Production Editor:
Lesley Rock, Viewtistic

Marketing Manager:
Jason Sakos

Associate Product Manager:
Janet Aras

Editorial Assistant:
Christy Urban

Text Designer:
GEX Publishing Services

Cover Designer:
Rakefet Kenaan

WHERE WHO

What WHEN

HOW Why

BRIEF CONTENTS

WHERE WHO WHEN
What Why
HOW

TABLE OF CONTENTS

FOREWORD TO ENTERPRISE ARCHITECTURE USING THE ZACHMAN FRAMEWORK

by Clive Finkelstein

I first learned of this book in December 2001 at the annual ZIFA Forum (Zachman Institute for Framework Advancement) in Scottsdale, Arizona. ZIFA is an annual conference of practitioners of the Zachman Framework for Enterprise Architecture. I have spoken at ZIFA over the years about some of the enterprise architecture projects with which I have been involved.

My good friend Warren Selkow, along with Carol O'Rourke and Neal Fishman, drew me aside to tell me they were writing a book to teach the concepts of enterprise architecture using the Zachman Framework.

They told me the book was intended for many audiences. It was to be a university text for undergraduates and graduates, but they also wanted to address the community college level. Furthermore, the text was for business, government, and defense organizations. This was an extremely ambitious undertaking!

As they described the book, I became intrigued. The scale of what they were planning had never been attempted before, yet the text was sorely needed. When they asked me if I would write the Foreword, I accepted immediately, as my curiosity had been whetted. As they sent me each chapter to review, the significance of the book emerged. They were succeeding in their ambitious objective. So now that the book is complete, what is my opinion?

This is a brilliant book! It introduces the concepts of enterprise architecture with humor, using lessons from history. The subject is enormously important, but before this book was written, enterprise architecture was presented in a very abstract way. This made the importance and power of enterprise architecture difficult to communicate.

Enterprise architecture is a rigorous way of thinking about any problem or problem domain. The Framework concepts are simple, but its application is powerful. The

Framework shows how complex problems can be resolved using enterprise architecture by considering all the *perspectives* and *aspects* that must be addressed to understand each specific problem or domain:

- **Perspectives** enable a problem domain to be viewed through the eyes of all of the people who need to be involved: the *planner, owner, designer, builder, subcontractor, and functioning enterprise*. These people and their different interests must all be understood if the result that is produced is to address their various needs.
- **Aspects** are the questions that must be asked to understand each problem domain. These questions are: *what, how, where, who, when*, and *why*. They need to be asked from each person's perspective.

Since the dawn of computers, many application systems have been developed at a great financial cost, yet the majority of applications do not successfully address the needs of the business. This is due to the complexity of most enterprises and the complexity of systems development. The problems are endemic. Above all, the problem is due to the inability of business people and IT people to communicate effectively. The Zachman Framework for Enterprise Architecture brings clarity and understanding to all.

The Framework enables business people to ensure their requirements are met from a business perspective, without requiring them to become technology experts. The Framework enables IT people to understand the business needs from an IT perspective and does not require them to become business experts. The Framework helps business and IT people communicate effectively by considering complex problems from each person's perspective in terms of the six aspects: *what, how, where, who, when*, and *why*.

The Zachman Framework of Enterprise Architecture enables senior business managers to be sure that all requisite business controls needed for corporate governance and accountability can be implemented. The Framework helps ensure that the systems, when built by IT, address the needs and responsibilities of each person who should be supported. The Framework provides a clear way to ensure all requirements are addressed, providing a roadmap for business survivability and success.

This is not a dry technical text. In these pages, Carol O'Rourke, Neal Fishman, and Warren Selkow have written a book that not only informs and instructs, but also entertains! This is why I love it. Not just for the book's importance, but because it is fun to read.

The Purpose of the Book

The book is an invaluable aid for teaching, but has also been written for self-study. It does not require prior knowledge of computers or information technology. The text is intended to be used in many disciplines, including Business Administration, Business Management, Computer Science, Information Systems, Information Technology, and Organizational Management.

For these reasons, it is an excellent book for all who need to understand and manage the planning, design, and construction of any complex endeavor. It teaches its readers how to think and solve complex problems.

In business, government, and defense organizations, this book leads business managers and their business experts—at all management levels—through the use of enterprise architecture using the Framework. It teaches them to think about the planning, design, and establishment or restructuring of any complex enterprise. The book teaches experienced IT staff how to think about the planning, design, and construction of systems (manual or automated) that are needed to support the enterprise. Such IT staff includes CIOs, CTOs, IT managers, information engineers, enterprise engineers, business process reengineers, systems analysts, business analysts, data analysts, process analysts, data administrators, project managers, and many others.

The authors have done their work well. This book will be read and used widely by all of their projected audiences.

The Structure of the Book

Each chapter is structured in several teaching sections. Each section is introduced first with Learning Objectives that indicate the concepts being presented. After covering each section, Review Questions are presented to test understanding of the subject matter. In a formal education environment, these can be assigned to students as exercises for completion.

Chapter 1 introduces John Zachman, the originator of the Zachman Framework for Enterprise Architecture. The chapter provides a short overview of enterprise architecture to establish context.

It is in Chapter 2 that the book draws you in and its beauty starts to emerge. This chapter provides a glimpse of the gems of knowledge that lie ahead in later chapters. The authors have turned to history to introduce their messages. Every problem must be examined in terms of the six aspects: *what, how, where, who, when,* and *why.*

They start with the pyramids of Egypt. These structures are wonders of engineering. Together, Carol O'Rourke, Neal Fishman, and Warren Selkow take us into the mind of Imhotep, the architect of the Great Pyramid. In their hands, the enormity of the task that Imhotep faced comes to life.

We join him as he grapples with problems of planning, designing, and construction using the available technologies of his time. We soon realize that he also must develop systems for project management, resource management, and accounting— so that he can administer all aspects of this massive *project.*

My reaction on reading this was WOW! What a great way to introduce the thinking encouraged by enterprise architecture. As Chapter 2 unfolds, the power of the approach becomes evident as we continue our journey through history.

The authors move us forward thousands of years to the Cathedral of Chartres, built in the twelfth century. This cathedral was the first of the great Gothic cathedrals. They take us to the Manhattan Project, where we consider the problems associated with the design and construction of the atomic bomb. This brought World War II to an end, but also ushered in the Nuclear Age. From there, we move to Levittown and the construction of housing for the U.S. veterans returning from World War II. Each of these was a complex project, involving new problems that had to be resolved. Each project is introduced using the six aspects of the Framework.

We move forward to the Apollo mission: to land a man on the moon by the end of the 1960s. Chapter 2 finally closes with the design and construction of the first all digitally designed plane: the Boeing 777.

Whereas Chapter 2 took us through the perspective of the *planner,* Chapter 3 moves us through the perspective of the *owner.* Each succeeding chapter takes us through the remaining perspectives: *designer* (Chapter 4), *builder* (Chapter 5), *subcontractor* (Chapter 6), and the *functioning enterprise* (Chapter 7).

In Chapter 3, we learn about different types of organizations from the perspective of the *owner*. We consider the 1999 Ford Mustang Cobra automobile. We discuss the NYSE (New York Stock Exchange) and the dot-com enterprises and their demise in the stock market downturn of 2000. We look at public education, Coca Cola, Walt Disney, Movie Outpost, Keane, Cascade Engineering, and Equifax. These case studies help us to understand issues with which the *owner* must be aware. Each is considered in terms of *what*, *how*, *where*, *who*, *when*, and *why*.

Chapter 4 takes us into the mind of the *designer*. We learn about the role of the *designer* at Lockheed, in designing an aircraft capable of flying at a sustained speed of Mach 3. We discuss the roles of people in meetings as a way of understanding the different types of personalities and people that a *designer* must consider in her design solution. We see how Covey's Seven Habits can help the *designer*. We discuss the impact of office politics and the importance of metrics and life cycles in design.

Chapter 5 uses Napoleon's disastrous march on Russia in the winter of 1812 to introduce the importance of environment and topography to the *builder*. The *builder* must ensure that design criteria are satisfied under all circumstances. The impact that the design of the Roman chariot had on NASA, centuries later, when building the space shuttle, demonstrates the longevity of design decisions that can affect the *builder*. A project at Abbott Laboratories also illustrates the need to meet all design criteria. Rules, standards, units of measure, metrics, statistics, and tradeoffs are also considered from the perspective of the *builder*. Examples are drawn from Oracle and from the .NET initiative of Microsoft. The danger of the *builder* changing the design—without first having that change reviewed by the *designer*—is discussed by considering the collapse of floating walkways in the atrium of the Hyatt Regency Hotel in Kansas City, with its consequent terrible loss of life.

Chapter 6 addresses the technical issues of systems development that are important to the *subcontractor*. Parallels are drawn to the artistic nature of the *subcontractor's* task within the enterprise and show how current object-oriented approaches, patterns, extreme programming practices, and long-term thinking can be applied naturally to the Framework. This chapter illustrates that art is an important part of computer science.

With Chapter 7, the authors present the *functioning enterprise* perspective and the Zachman Framework for Enterprise Architecture in its entirety. At this point, you will already understand the clarity of thought behind the Framework. By using the Framework, you will appreciate its effectiveness in resolving both complex and simple problems.

The book concludes by discussing the authors' extension to implementing the Framework in Chapter 8.

I wholeheartedly recommend this book to you. It is an outstanding introduction to the concepts and benefits of the Zachman Framework for Enterprise Architecture. When you complete the book, you will be well prepared to apply these principles to understand and resolve any complex problem that you may encounter in the future.

Clive Finkelstein,
Perth, Western Australia
January 3, 2003

Clive Finkelstein

Clive Finkelstein is acknowledged worldwide as the "Father" of Information Engineering and is managing director of Information Engineering Services Pty Ltd in Australia. Clive is the author of a number of books, including:

- *Information Engineering*, James Martin and Clive Finkelstein, Savant Institute, Carnforth: UK (1981)
- *An Introduction to Information Engineering*, Clive Finkelstein, Addison-Wesley, Sydney: Australia (1989)
- *Information Engineering: Strategic Systems Development*, Clive Finkelstein, Addison-Wesley, Sydney: Australia (1992)
- *Building Corporate Portals with XML*, Clive Finkelstein and Peter Aiken, McGraw-Hill, New York: NY (2000)

His forthcoming book is titled *Building and Delivering Enterprise Architecture for Enterprise Integration: Methods, Techniques, and Technologies.*

Clive Finkelstein is an internationally renowned consultant and instructor, with completed projects for defense, government, and commercial organizations in most industries worldwide. These projects have included enterprise architecture using enterprise engineering and information engineering methods and involved various technologies—including metadata, XML, Web services, corporate portals, and enterprise application integration (EAI).

Many of his papers and projects are available online at *www.ies.aust.com/ ~ieinfo/*, with his courses at *bne002i.webcentral.com.au/catalogue/visible/ default.shtml*. He can be contacted at *cfink@ies.aust.com*.

PREFACE

"All my life I've wanted to be someone; I guess I should have been more specific."
— *Lily Tomlin (b. 1939), Comedian*

Purpose and Goals

The goal of *Enterprise Architecture Using the Zachman Framework* is to build an understanding of the concepts of enterprise architecture and of a classification schema you can use to view an organization holistically. The Zachman Framework provides a vehicle to guide you through the comprehensive process of thinking, reasoning, and communicating effectively about any issue, problem, or opportunity.

Because today's marketplace continues to change rapidly, enterprise architecture should be used to lend order to the process of investing resources during the organization's evolution. The Zachman Framework is a tool for managing and communicating the vast amount of information needed to make broad decisions, those that enable the organization to be competitive.

The Framework is a schema for classifying and organizing the topics related to managing the enterprise, as well as to the design, development, and manifestation of the enterprise. Through this classification and organization of topics, the Framework can assist the organization in becoming more accountable and responsive. This textbook shows how enterprise architecture considers the design and operation of an organization from many aspects, perspectives, and disciplines.

This textbook explains how the *enterprise* in enterprise architecture can apply to a business, government agency, family, or individual. The enterprise becomes the scope of reach. Businesses must evolve constantly to meet the demands of the marketplace and stay competitive. A government agency must change constantly to meet the needs of society. Families and individuals must change constantly as they go through different phases of life. Change is inevitable.

The textbook shows that successful adaptation to a changing environment in any domain or context requires integration, alignment, and responsiveness. Most people are motivated to be contributing members of the organizations for which they work and the families in which they are members. Most people want to make a difference, no matter how small or insignificant that difference may appear. The Zachman Framework can represent many things to many people. Overall, the Framework enables people to make a difference.

The Framework has been adopted by the United States and Canadian governments as the mandatory framework for completing information technology architectures. The Framework is also used by the Australian Department of Defense. The Framework has been taught successfully at Evergreen State College in Washington and progressive high schools like Forest Hills Northern in Michigan. The Framework has been used to apply enterprise architecture successfully in many commercial companies, including Boeing, Glaxo Wellcome, and British Airways.

Information technology is a complex undertaking and relies heavily on people to make the technology work. The Zachman Framework is built on the premise of getting people to work successfully. Problems facing the enterprise today are becoming more complex. New technologies have received isolated successes; however, many enterprises continue to struggle with the same issues and problems.

Technologies such as Java, integrated development environments, and the Internet are all powerful tools, providing an opportunity for many wonderful results. However, people, not technology, are the lynch pins that create a successful enterprise. The Zachman Framework helps pull together people and technology to create a successful, competitive enterprise.

Audience

This textbook is designed for use by people in business and academics. The textbook's focus is on business and information technology; however, many examples illustrate how the Framework can be applied in all avenues of life. These examples show how the Framework establishes rules of behavior needed to establish communication links.

When used in a collegiate setting, undergraduate or graduate students focusing in the following areas will find this text helpful:

- Business Administration
- Business Management
- Computer Science
- Information Systems
- Information Technology
- Organizational Management

The text, which can be used for a full course or only a portion of a course, gives students the foundation they need to think holistically and to make appropriate decisions for any size endeavor, from a small project to an entire enterprise, using the Zachman Framework. Students will learn how to create an enterprise architecture by asking the right questions and paying attention to detail.

Early exposure to the topic of enterprise architecture in introductory classes, such as principles of information systems, principles of management, information and communication infrastructures, and organizational communication courses, is beneficial to students and enables them to focus holistically on an enterprise. Being able to study and learn in subsequent courses from both an IT and business perspective is also beneficial. Enterprise architecture is also an essential topic for graduate or undergraduate courses in management science, business enterprise, strategic business solutions, as well as strategy and business policy.

In addition, the text is intended as a reference for professionals in:

- Business and IT communities
- Continuing education programs
- In-house training

This textbook was developed for motivated individuals who want to learn from the past to prepare for the future. The book addresses the needs of a broad audience. Students need to understand how what they are learning and doing fits into the overall plan of the business. Students need to learn about both business and technology in order to be successful in their careers.

Besides students and their academic institutions, the business and information technology communities also need printed materials related to enterprise architecture and the Zachman Framework for Enterprise Architecture.

The reader is not assumed to have any prior knowledge; however, experience in any of the following could be helpful:

- Analysis
- Modeling
- Programming

How the Book Came to Be

The origins of this book go back to the summer of 1997. Wanting to present her progressive computer science students with an experiential education connected to the business world, Carol O'Rourke approached Keane, Incorporated, which opened a branch office in Western Michigan in 1996.

Keane's business is built upon three synergistic services that cross the plan, build, and manage spectrums: business consulting, application development and integration, and application development and management outsourcing. The Western Michigan branch office was interested in contributing to the community and the educational/business partnership began.

Neal Fishman, senior principal consultant with Keane at the time, volunteered to become part of this innovative partnership and visited Carol's Forest Hills Northern High classroom daily to share his business and computer expertise. The original goal of the partnership was for a business professional to work with students doing Visual Basic programming. However, a colleague of Carol's decided a similar experience would be beneficial to her students as well. Neal then agreed to teach C++ and Java at the other district high school.

The high school students produced an automated employee evaluation software tool for Keane's branch office and presented the tool at the branch's quarterly meeting. An additional benefit resulted when Neal suggested introducing the concepts of the Zachman Framework for Enterprise Architecture.

Through this partnership, the authors learned that students need to understand three concepts to be successful in their careers. They should understand how what they are learning and doing in the classroom or organization fits into the overall plan of the business. They need to learn about both business and technology. They need to see a bigger picture of how enterprises operate and manage change.

Carol continued teaching and learning about the Framework and became convinced an enterprise architecture textbook focusing on the Zachman Framework would help better deliver these important concepts. She contacted Neal, who agreed that more printed materials are needed not only for academic institutions, but also for the business and information technology community.

Carol and Neal decided to tackle the writing project. Neal suggested that Warren Selkow, a friend from the Business Rules Group, would add a valuable dimension to the author team. Carol and Neal then contacted their colleague, Warren, who agreed to join the team.

The result is a textbook that teaches you how to become a systems thinker who asks *what*, *how*, *where*, *who*, *when*, and *why* to create a shared understanding of the organization. The concepts presented in this text allow you to focus on real issues and reduce complexity to a total of 36 cells—enterprise architecture expressed in a picture that is a six-by-six classification schema.

You learn how businesses work and how software gets developed, and you are given a tool that can be used to facilitate communication to prevent the disjoin that sometimes occurs. With knowledge of the Framework, you will be better equipped to assist individuals and organizations in making appropriate decisions that allow and encourage adaptability, integration, alignment, accountability, and responsiveness, resulting in a competitive advantage for the enterprise.

Organization and Approach

Enterprise Architecture Using the Zachman Framework is organized into three parts, followed by appendices, a glossary, and an index.

Although every chapter contains fundamental information leading the reader to an understanding of the six-by-six classification schema illustrated inside the text's cover, the Framework is not mentioned explicitly in Part II prior to Chapter 7. The reader is encouraged to think holistically about problems by using the six interrogatives of the English language and focusing on six different perspectives to create a shared understanding.

Using this method of inquiry, the reader discerns the patterns of forces or events that eventually affect decisions for the enterprise. If this knowledge and understanding are formalized and maintained in models and documents, the enterprise can improve continually and change its dynamics in the marketplace because it has a shared knowledge and understanding. The textbook expands the reader's ability to think abstractly and use systems thinking through the use of stories, analogies, and metaphors.

Outstanding Features

This book is distinctive, addressing enterprise architecture exclusively and offering a tool to manage and communicate the voluminous and disparate amounts of information needed by the enterprise to compete successfully in the changing marketplace. The Zachman Framework for Enterprise Architecture provides a logical schema that can be used to define and control all the interactions and relationships taking place in the enterprise. The reader learns to use this Framework to create a shared knowledge of the organization by providing clarity in communication so enterprise resources can be invested wisely.

The entire writing project has been developed using the Framework. Many sections of the book are broken down into six parts—six interrogatives. Through this pattern, the reader is guided in learning how to use this Framework for thinking through complex problems, reasoning, decision-making, and making a difference in the enterprise.

Fastpath

 Some instructors may choose to use this book as part of an existing course. To facilitate a shortened presentation of course content, a Fastpath has been created through the book. The Fastpath generally includes the introduction, two sections, and the synthesis and summary for most chapters, capturing the main ideas of the Zachman Framework. Special icons (as shown on the left) indicate where each critical component of the Fastpath begins and ends. Students are invited to read material outside the Fastpath to gain a more complete understanding.

 The Fastpath allows the text to be easily integrated with almost any business course and makes a great bundle with systems analysis and design texts, as well as project management texts.

Learning Objectives

Each chapter begins with a statement of the learning objectives phrased as actions the reader will be capable of after reading the book. These learning objectives help the reader focus on the main ideas. The instructor can use the learning objectives to guide discussion and measure the degree of accomplishment of these objectives by using the Review Questions and Discussion Topics provided in each chapter.

Questions to Contemplate

These questions guide the reader in thinking about how the stories and analogies apply to the enterprise today. The Questions to Contemplate also guide the reader toward main concepts in the section. Instructors can use them as an instructional aid to assist the reader in thinking holistically about the content and in transferring this knowledge to different situations.

Sidebars

Additional points of interest are supplied in sidebars. These information boxes contain additional information, interesting facts, related topics, or further detailed explanations of material covered in the chapter.

Chapter Activities

Synthesis and Chapter Summary. The synthesis provides a combination of ideas and elements to enable the reader to form a complex, whole meaning of chapter content. Similarly, the Framework enables people to form a complex, shared knowledge of the organization through a combination of many ideas and elements categorized and stored. The summary is a necessary and useful tool that reviews topics covered previously.

Review Questions. Students can test their knowledge of the material covered in the chapter by answering the review questions. Most review questions simply reinforce basic concepts and terminology introduced in the sections, while others ask the students to transfer their understanding of section content to different scenarios.

Discussion Topics. Instructors can use the discussion topics to increase student understanding through classroom discussions. Students can check their overall understanding of chapter material by responding to these discussion topics after reading the material. While some of these discussion topics measure the students' holistic understanding of the chapter, others ask the students to explain how the concept applies to other situations in business and information technology.

Critical Thinking. The critical thinking exercises often encourage students to explore the community outside the four walls of their classrooms. Students can discover how the topics they are studying in the classroom apply to businesses today. Research topics encourage students to seek a variety of sources for information. Students practice using appropriate verbal and written communication skills while exploring, comparing, analyzing, discussing, and sharing the information gathered with other class members.

Glossary. At the end of the book is an alphabetical list of many terms and meanings that were mentioned throughout the text and indicated by bold formatting.

Teaching Tools

Enterprise Architecture Using the Zachman Framework is accompanied by three ancillaries. When used in an academic setting, these teaching tools can be used by the instructor to enhance classroom instruction: an Instructor's Manual, a Test Bank, and PowerPoint presentations.

Instructor's Manual. The purpose of the Instructor's Manual is to support the instructor and enhance the student's learning experience. The manual contains a sample course syllabus, course outlines, lecture notes, and key terminology. Every chapter includes an outline of key concepts, learning objectives, Questions, to Contemplate, and solutions to Review Questions as well as suggested responses for Discussion Topics.

Course Test Manager (CTM). An electronic Test Bank allows the instructor to create and customize a measurement tool by selecting questions from any section of the book. The instructor can preview the test, or export and print the test. The Test Bank contains multiple choice, true/false, short answer, and essay questions. The CTM program allows students to take their tests at the computer and have their scores calculated electronically.

If desired, the instructor can generate statistical information on individual, as well as group, performance.

Classroom Presentations. Microsoft PowerPoint presentations have been created for each chapter in the book to provide a resource for classroom instruction. These slides can be used for delivery of chapter material and also can be made available to students for review purposes.

CD INCLUDED WITH THIS BOOK

This book includes a CD with a collection of unabridged articles, reference materials, and chapters from the Introduction module of the eBook written by John Zachman. Information is also provided for purchasing the complete eBook, which is called *The Zachman Framework for Enterprise Architecture: Primer for Enterprise Engineering and Manufacturing*. The eBook is published by Zachman Framework Associates and Metadata Systems Software, Inc. Materials on the CD provide an excellent resource for learning more about the subject matter of this textbook. Questions or comments associated with the CD should be directed to *support@ZachmanInternational.com*.

ACKNOWLEDGEMENTS

Enterprise Architecture Using the Zachman Framework is really the synergistic product of a team of people. Creating a quality product requires the collaborative effort of many individuals who, in their various ways, contributed to our inspiration, confidence, perseverance, and determination to complete this project. At the beginning of any book, it is appropriate to acknowledge those who have influenced its development.

We are particularly indebted to our mentor, John Arthur Zachman, who has shaped our ability to think, reason, and communicate effectively about any issue, problem, or opportunity. We hope to make a difference in the lives of the individuals who read our book, as John has made a difference in our lives.

We would like to thank our many friends and colleagues for their discussions and contributions to this book, including Joel Brandon, Jim Redman, Don Morris, Cathrine Blicher, Joe Takarski, Dr. Steve Raskin, Linda Nadeau, Fred Keller, Keri Anderson-Healy, Dr. Robert Deutch, Jane Gietzen, Dr. Nilas Young, Constance Zachman, Thomas Schipp, Linnea Reuterdahl, Ron Ross, Dr. Jeffrey H. Frank, Michael Eulenberg, Tom Hokel, Ana Calderón, Les Dlabay, Dave Barrett, and John McNeilly. We would also like to express our thanks to those who have taken the time to write and tell us where these concepts have led them and how the Framework has helped them. We want to express our sincere appreciation to Clive Finkelstein for writing the foreword to our book.

We gratefully acknowledge all the professionals at Course Technology who helped teach us how to put a book together. The authors want to thank Jennifer Locke, Managing Editor—without her support and enthusiasm, we never would have been able to publish this book. She believed in this effort when it was not much more than a rough set of ideas coupled with a lot of enthusiasm. We are truly grateful for all of her confidence in the project. We also want to thank Lisa Ruffolo, our Development Editor, who painstakingly edited our work and always kept us connected to the pulse of our readers. She made contributions of the most fundamental kind to the clarity of content, the structure of chapters, and the details of paragraphs and sentences.

In addition, the authors would like to thank the following individuals at Course Technology who did a prodigious job in shepherding the manuscript through its last phases and supervising its production: Alyssa Pratt, Product Manager and Lesley Rock, Production Editor. We would also like to acknowledge Janet Aras, Associate Product Manager, who assisted in the completion of the Instructor's Manual.

We would like to thank our reviewers who were generous with their time, liberal with their encouragement, and on target with their criticism. These people contributed greatly in unique ways to the rigor of the ideas and the process of writing them down: Michael Bartolacci, Pennsylvania State University; Jay Lightfoot, University of Northern Colorado; Mark R. Nelson, Rensselaer Polytechnic Institute; David Olsen, Utah State University; David Ozag, Gettysburg; Peter Ross, University at Albany; Anne Marie Smith, La Salle University.

We are grateful to our former and current students; many of them have continued to give encouragement of the most essential kind to our writing and teaching efforts. They have provided us with the invaluable opportunity to learn from their insights and have encouraged us and believed in this writing project from the start.

Finally, we want to express our deep appreciation for the continuous support and encouragement of our families who have supported us as we worked simultaneously at our full-time positions and on this book. Donna, Betty, Damon, Seth, Carissa, Ashton, Emily, Chelsea, Jim, Erin, Michael, Brian, and Shannon have had to do with less of us while we worked night after night and many long weekends on this project. We also want to especially thank our children, who have tolerated our absences and distractions while we were busy writing. Without their cooperation, we would not have been able to complete this book successfully. Thank you for your patience. Here is our *functioning enterprise*.

Carol O'Rourke
Neal Fishman
Warren Selkow

PHOTO CREDITS

Figure 1-11 courtesy of Steelcase
Figure 2-2 © 2003 PhotoDisc/Getty Images
Figures 2-8 and 2-11 courtesy of Jeffery Howe
Figure 3-10 courtesy of Movie Outpost
Figure 3-13 courtesy of Keane, Incorporated
Figures 3-15, 3-16, 3-17, 3-18 courtesy of Cascade Engineering
Figure 3-22 courtesy of Equifax, Incorporated
Figure 4-7 photo courtesy of GlassSteelAndStone.com
Figure 4-11 © Copyright 2002 NBA Entertainment. Photo by NBAE/Getty Images.
Figure 4-23 © 2003 PhotoDisc/Getty Images
Figure 5-4 © Eyewire/Getty Images
Figure 6-1 © Araldo de Luca/CORBIS
Figure 6-13 courtesy of M & M Mars
Figure 6-14 courtesy of Meijer
Figure 6-16 (photo on left) and Figure 7-85 © 2003 PhotoDisc/Getty Images
Figure 6-16 (photo on right) © Eyewire/Getty Images

DEDICATION

To my proudest achievements...Erin Camille, Michael James, Brian Patrick, and Shannon Therese
Carol M. O'Rourke

To my children...Emily and Chelsea
Neal A. Fishman

To the ones I love...Donna, Damon, Seth, Carissa, Ashton, Mother, Father, and Murray
Warren L. Selkow

ABOUT THE AUTHORS

Carol O'Rourke has held a variety of positions in the educational community including classroom teacher, department chairperson, grant writer, and systems engineer curriculum materials developer. As a business education instructor, she was instrumental in enabling Forest Hills Public Schools to become a Microsoft Certified Training Site. Carol is a Microsoft Certified Systems Engineer and a Microsoft Certified Trainer. She has successfully taught enterprise architecture using the Zachman Framework in her high school classes. She has served in a number of leadership roles throughout the business community and brings a variety of workplace experiences to students. As an educator, she is heavily involved in developing and implementing innovative approaches to education through community partnerships. Carol has been a speaker at state and national conferences. She currently serves as a member of the International Society of Business Educators, the North-Central Business Education Association, and the Michigan Career Pathways Regional Planning Group. She is a member of the World Wide Institute of Software Architects, DAMA Michigan Chapter, and the Association for Computing Machinery. She holds a bachelor's degree from Illinois State University and a master's degree from Michigan State University. When she is not teaching, she enjoys running, playing the piano, and attending her children's events.

Carol can be reached via e-mail at *carol@eabook.info*.

Neal Fishman is a senior enterprise architect. He has been involved in many aspects of information technology and has developed many unique perspectives throughout his career. He has spoken at conferences in North America, Australia, and Europe and has had numerous articles appear in information technology publications. Neal is a distance-learning instructor for the University of Washington's certificate program in data resource management. In addition to teaching the Framework at UW, he has taught the Framework at the high school level in Michigan. Neal is certified by IBM as a DB2 developer and database administrator. Neal is a former technology editor for the Data to Knowledge Newsletter and has served on the IEEE IDEFobject Standards Committee. He currently serves as a member of the Business Rules Group. He is an ExperNet expert for Giga, a practicing member of the World Wide Institute of Software Architects, a member of the IEEE, and a former board member of the DAMA Atlanta Chapter. He attended college in England and graduated with a degree in Computer Studies. Currently, he devotes much of his professional time preaching the gospel of Zachman. "Thou shalt horizontally and vertically integrate at excruciating levels of detail, less thou not be able to effectively manage change and compete." Outside of work, Neal enjoys playing the guitar, playing soccer, and watching his two daughters grow up.

Neal can be reached via e-mail at *neal@eabook.info*.

Warren Selkow's career in the data processing industry covers a broad spectrum. He has performed a host of jobs, from programmer to sales representative to DBA to business consultant. His wide range of experience gives him a distinctive outlook on information technology. The companies he has worked for include NCR, Honeywell, Cap Gemini, and IBM. His client companies include organizations in almost all industries. During the past few years, he has been actively engaged in using the Zachman Framework as a baseline measure and guide in performing large reengineering and business process optimization projects. He is an original member of the Business Rules Group, a former member of Guide's Application Development Joint Project, a former board member of the Warehousing, Repository, Architecture, and Design Users' Group, and a member of DAMA San Francisco Chapter. Warren received his undergraduate degree from Temple University, and his master's and doctoral degrees from the University of Pennsylvania.

Warren can be reached via e-mail at *warren@eabook.info*.

Additional information regarding this book may be found at *www.eabook.info*.

What WHERE WHO
HOW WHEN
Why
?

REASONS PART 1

"All truly wise thoughts have been thought already thousands of times;
but to make them truly ours, we must think them over again honestly, till they
take root in our personal experience."

— Johann Wolfgang von Goethe (1749–1832),
Poet, novelist, and dramatist

INTRODUCTION

The English language contains over 600,000 words[1] and is still growing. If you count scientific nomencla-

ture, our language may exceed one million words. Its grammatical rules are complex, and the complexity

is compounded by synonyms, homonyms, and regional dialects. Despite the size of the English language,

it has become universal, and most people who speak it live contented lives building and using a vocabu-

lary that contains between one and two percent of the available lexemes (words).

1

A S I D E

William Shakespeare created the literary device of the aside. In many Shakespeare plays, actors pause during a scene, step out of the sphere of dramatic action, and deliver an aside. The aside presents background information that the audience needs so they can understand what is happening or why.

After delivering the aside, the actor steps back into the sphere of drama and the dialogue continues as if the aside has not been delivered. The authors of this text believe that if an aside was good enough for William Shakespeare, it is good enough for us.

THE MANY VIRTUES OF ENGLISH

As a language, English is often unexamined despite its many paradoxes. After all there is no egg in eggplant, nor ham in hamburger. A pineapple contains no trace of either an apple or a pine. Writers write, but fingers do not fing, and grocers do not groce.

English makes it difficult to determine that farms produce produce; that a soldier might desert his dessert in the desert; that since there is no time like the present, it is time to present the present. That people bank on the bank by the bank.

In what language do people recite at a play and play at a recital? Ship by truck and send cargo by ship? Have noses that run and feet that smell? How can a slim chance and a fat chance be the same, while a wise man and a wise guy are opposites? If you have a bunch of odds and ends and get rid of all but one of them, what do you call it?

English was invented by people, not computers, and it reflects the creativity of the human race (which, of course, is not a race at all).

Outside of English teachers, journalists, and linguists, most people rarely use the word interrogative. It means a word or form used to ask a question.

The English language contains six interrogatives: *what*, *how*, *where*, *who*, *when*, and *why*. With these six words, any English-speaking person can pose a question, probe for answers, reason, contemplate, and communicate.

To communicate effectively, it is not just a matter of what you say, but also how you say it. You have probably heard your mother say that phrase to you a thousand times. When talking with other people, you need to understand how others perceive what you say. What matters is their perception of what you are saying, not yours.

Interrogatives and perception…together they provide a strong basis for understanding all the things life throws your way. Most of this book focuses on handling interrogatives and perceptions.

Rudyard Kipling explores the role of interrogatives and perception in a poem that is part of a short story called "The Elephant's Child," published in 1902 in the book *Just So Stories*.

> I keep six honest serving-men:
> (They taught me all I knew)
> Their names are *What* and *Where* and *When*
> And *How* and *Why* and *Who*.
> I send them over land and sea,
> I send them east and west;
> But after they have worked for me,
> I give them all a rest.
> I let them rest from nine till five.
> For I am busy then,
> As well as breakfast, lunch, and tea,
> For they are hungry men:
> *But different folk have different views:*
> I know a person small—
> She keeps ten million serving-men,
> Who get no rest at all!
> She sends 'em abroad on her own affairs,
> From the second she opens her eyes—
> One million *Hows*, two million *Wheres*,
> And seven million *Whys*!

Endnotes

[1] The 20 volume, second edition of the Oxford English Dictionary contains over 615,000 word definitions.

UBIQUITY: UNDERSTANDING THE ZACHMAN FRAMEWORK

"Friend, do not keep your knowledge to yourself; we are a large party; and any benefit which you confer upon us will be amply rewarded."
— *Plato (427 B.C.E.–347 B.C.E.), Philosopher*

LEARNING OBJECTIVES

After completing Chapter 1, you will be able to:

1. Describe the similarities between the meaning of the term framework and the Framework.
2. Describe the physical layout of the Zachman Framework for Enterprise Architecture.
3. List all the aspects depicted by columns in the Framework.
4. Discuss how understanding can be affected when individuals communicate using different primitives and composites.
5. Discuss the importance of viewing the enterprise from six different perspectives.
6. List three ways from which enterprise architecture considers the design and operation of a business.
7. Discuss how a model can help change something that is implicit into something that is explicit.
8. Discuss how an architecture can be described with words, pictures, models, and diagrams.
9. Describe what is meant by proof.
10. Describe how the Zachman Framework can assist the organization in managing change.
11. Explain why alignment and integration are important to the enterprise.

1.1 INTRODUCTION

This book is about the **Zachman Framework for Enterprise Architecture**. The **Framework's** primary purpose is to provide a classification schema for **artifacts**[1] that describes the various types of designs used to create and deploy computer software.

The Framework is very versatile. A business or organization of any size can use the Framework, whether the organization runs its business with one computer program or one hundred thousand computer programs. In fact, the Framework applies to every facet of an

information technology (IT) project. Information technology includes the products, services, facilities, and resources used to support an organization's computing or automation needs. For an IT project, the Framework is neutral to **methodology**, technology, programming language, and coding style.

At this point, it may seem a little far-fetched to think of the Framework as ubiquitous, or omnipresent. But in due course, you will discover that the Framework exists in everything you do, not only IT projects. When you thoroughly understand the Framework, you can become more effective in everything you do. This means *everything*. This statement is not made lightly. An explanatory discussion follows, so you will have the opportunity to agree or disagree.

You might have some preliminary questions, such as who is Zachman? What is **enterprise architecture**? Is the Framework the same thing as the Zachman Framework for Enterprise Architecture? What does the term *framework* actually mean? What if you do not want something neutral, then what? What does *everything* mean in this context?

Chapter 1 provides answers to these questions. You will learn how to use this book effectively to gain more information about the Framework.

1.1.1 John Zachman

The Framework was originated by a mild-mannered intellect named John Arthur Zachman. Zachman was born in Toledo, Ohio and, after graduating from Northwestern University, served as a line officer in the U.S. Navy. Zachman's business career began with IBM and flourished for more than 26 years.

After stumbling upon the Framework,[2] Zachman spent many years proving his theories and solidifying the rules of the Framework. He started the Zachman Institute for Framework Advancement (ZIFA), a company dedicated to helping corporations from all over the world with issues regarding his Framework and the state of the art in enterprise architecture. As a testament to the significance of his Framework, IBM (in its *Systems Journal* magazine[3]) cited his work along with 21 other papers as a turning point in the history of IBM's computing history.

Appendix A includes a complete biography of John Zachman.

1.1.2 Enterprise Architecture

Some might think of enterprise architecture as a blueprint for a Federation spaceship piloted by Captains James T. Kirk and Jean-Luc Picard in the popular television shows *Star Trek* and *Star Trek: The Next Generation*. In the context of this book, enterprise architecture involves blueprinting a business. See Figure 1-1.

In general terms, an **enterprise** is a business or organization formed to produce a product or provide a service. An **architecture** is the design of any type of structure, whether physical or conceptual, real or virtual.

The senior executives of a business determine the boundary of its enterprise. Should the enterprise include every department and every employee? What about vendors, suppliers, partners, government agencies, and the environment? Should these also be considered part of the enterprise? A business might need to think of its enterprise beyond the realm of its legal domain. The business might also need to split into smaller discrete units and regard each one as its own enterprise.

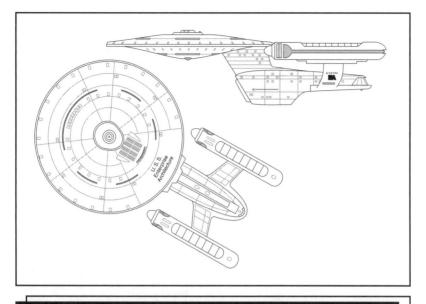

| Figure 1-1 | A different kind of enterprise architecture |

For many businesses, the enterprise is big, too big, and a complete picture of all its parts remains hidden from any single individual—including the **chief executive officer (CEO)**, the highest-ranking member of an organization. In practice, enterprise architecture is often limited to blueprinting activities within an information technology group. To determine whether that is good or bad, take a moment to picture yourself as a CEO, and then ask yourself the following question: "Should vendors, suppliers, partners, government agencies, and the environment also be considered part of the enterprise?"

Enterprise architecture creates the ability to understand and determine the continual needs of **integration**, **alignment**, change, and responsiveness of the business to technology and to the marketplace. You understand and reason, in part, by building **models**—special types of blueprints. A blueprint typically contains shapes or pictures, which have pre-defined meanings. See Figure 1-2.

However, the essence of enterprise architecture is much more than a series of models. Behind each model lie the policies, processes, and procedures through which each area or organization of the enterprise can articulate interests, exercise rights, meet obligations, and mediate differences for the collective whole (i.e., the enterprise).

With so much activity in the enterprise, gathering and organizing all the information critical to understanding and managing the whole business becomes difficult. You are probably familiar with the phrase *changing at the speed of the Internet*. This phrase means that most competitive businesses need to react faster, and the reaction needs to be thoughtful, not a knee jerk reaction.

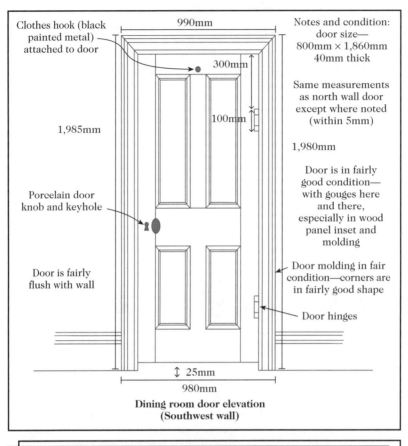

Clothes hook (black painted metal) attached to door

990mm

Notes and condition: door size— 800mm × 1,860mm 40mm thick

Same measurements as north wall door except where noted (within 5mm)

300mm

100mm

1,985mm

1,980mm

Door is in fairly good condition— with gouges here and there, especially in wood panel inset and molding

Porcelain door knob and keyhole

Door molding in fair condition—corners are in fairly good shape

Door is fairly flush with wall

Door hinges

↕ 25mm

980mm

Dining room door elevation (Southwest wall)

Figure 1-2   Example of a blueprint

Because businesses are so active and changing so quickly, they need new types of disciplines to successfully move from forming a concept to introducing that concept to the marketplace. The time required to accomplish this is getting shorter and shorter.

If corporations are struggling to rapidly bring new products into today's competitive marketplace with all the available technology at hand, future challenges will be even greater. After all, businesses need to find ways to adapt and change at even faster rates. This is why the Zachman Framework for Enterprise Architecture is so important. The Framework can help an enterprise manage change and evolve to stay ahead of the competition.

The Zachman Framework differs from other architectural framework tools in its independent, holistic view of the enterprise. The Zachman Framework is neutral with respect to methodology, process, and technology, including the breadth of **scope**—the boundary of concern for the enterprise—to handle all areas of the enterprise. This is true even when deliverable products are not software oriented.

When **external influences** change, the Zachman Framework remains the same. In other words, the Framework is independent of the artifacts classified by the Framework. The artifact may change as the result of an influence, but the Framework itself will not change.

1.1.3 Key Terms

alignment	Framework
architecture	information technology
artifact	integration
chief executive officer	methodology
enterprise	model
enterprise architecture	scope
external influence	Zachman Framework for Enterprise Architecture

1.1.4 Review Questions

1. What is meant by the phrase *blueprinting a business*?
2. What is the primary purpose of the Framework?

3. In the context of the Framework, what is an artifact?

SECTION 1.2 THE ZACHMAN FRAMEWORK FOR ENTERPRISE ARCHITECTURE

The Framework[4] is the key to understanding enterprise architecture. Therefore, it is also the key to understanding the dynamics of an organization. A framework is a set of assumptions, concepts, values, and practices that constitutes a way of viewing reality.[5] Zachman's Framework is organized as 36 cells arranged in a six-by-six matrix—six rows and six columns. It is a two-dimensional **schema**, used to organize the detailed representations of the enterprise, as shown in Figure 1-3.

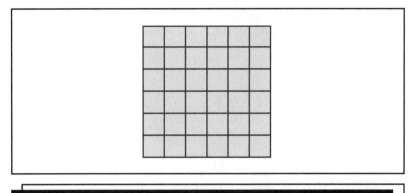

Chapter 8 of this book presents an extension that transforms the Framework into a three-dimensional schema called Zachman DNA. DNA[6] is an acronym for **Depth iNtegrating Architecture**. Zachman DNA combines the architectural representations and the activities, disciplines, and infrastructures required to make a business work.

This three-dimensional schema uses an unchanged two-dimensional schema (six-by-six), and adds an unlimited number of depth segments. Each depth segment mirrors the six-by-six arrangement of the two-dimensional schema, as shown in Figure 1-4.

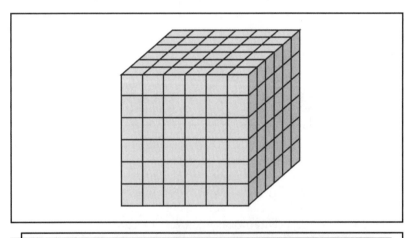

Figure 1-4   *Six-by-six-by-n: Three-dimensional schema*

The six rows of the Framework represent six **perspectives**, as viewed by the **planner, owner, designer, builder, subcontractor**, and **functioning enterprise**. You will learn that these six perspectives represent a comprehensive view of the enterprise. The Framework's six columns represent different **aspects: things, processes, connectivity, people, timing**, and **motivation**. See Figure 1-5. You will also learn that these six aspects represent a comprehensive picture of the enterprise.

	Things	Processes	Connectivity	People	Timing	Motivation
Planner						
Owner						
Designer						
Builder						
Subcontractor						
Functioning enterprise						

Perspective

—————— Aspect ——————

Figure 1-5   *Labeled two-dimensional schema*

PERSPECTIVES

A perspective is the result of an ordered logical method used to break an issue or topic into unique viewpoints or frames of reference.

Planner—one who establishes the universe of discourse; the background, scope, and purpose of the enterprise

Owner—the recipient or user of the enterprise's end product or service

Designer—the engineer or architect who acts as an intermediary between what is desirable (by the owner) and what is technically and physically achievable

Builder—general contractor who oversees the production of the end product or service

Subcontractor—one responsible for building and assembling the parts for the end product or service

Functioning enterprise—the physical manifestation of the end product or service

(continued)

ASPECTS

An aspect is the result of an ordered logical method used to break an issue or topic into defined basic parts.

Things—lists, important items, material composition, and databases; these are associated with the **interrogative** *what*

Processes—specifications, transformations, and software; these are associated with the interrogative *how*

Connectivity—locations, communication, networks, and hardware; these are associated with the interrogative *where*

People—workflows, operating instructions, and organizations; these are associated with the interrogative *who*

Timing—life cycles, events, state transitions, and schedules; these are associated with the interrogative *when*

Motivation—**strategies**, desired results, and means of achievement; these are associated with the interrogative *why*

These initial definitions will be expanded to explain broader issues in this and later chapters.

The intersecting perspectives and aspects yield a **cell**. To understand this concept, you can start with the idea of building a scatter diagram. You would begin by establishing an *x*-axis and a *y*-axis. See Figure 1-6.

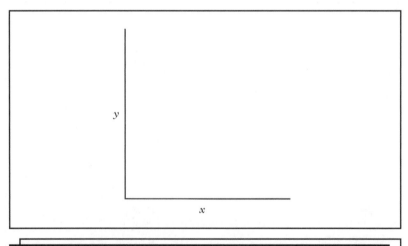

Figure 1-6   x-*axis and* y-*axis*

Now you can plot the first and second points on the diagram. See Figure 1-7.

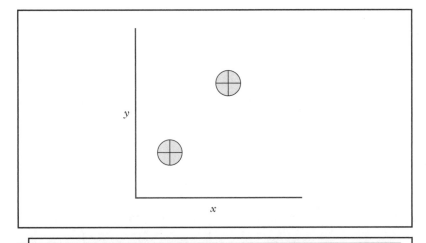

Figure 1-7   *Two plotted points on the scatter diagram*

The plotted points on the scatter diagram represent two different intersections of a point on the *x*-axis with a point on the *y*-axis. If the Zachman Framework classification schema is overlaid on the scatter diagram, the intersecting points lie in a cell or on the border of two or more cells. See Figure 1-8.

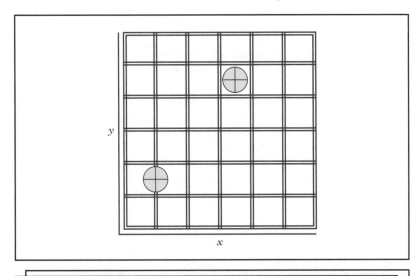

Figure 1-8   *Mapping cells and intersections*

The *y*-axis represents a perspective on the Framework. The *x*-axis represents an aspect on the Framework. The abstraction that results from the intersection is either a **primitive** or a **composite** topic that should be expressed and communicated within the enterprise. For example, if an intersecting point combines the *owner perspective* with the *people aspect*, you may want to create an organization chart, which is an abstract representation of the physical organizations within an enterprise. The artifact, the organization chart, is a primitive abstraction, a single topic for discussion. See Figure 1-9.

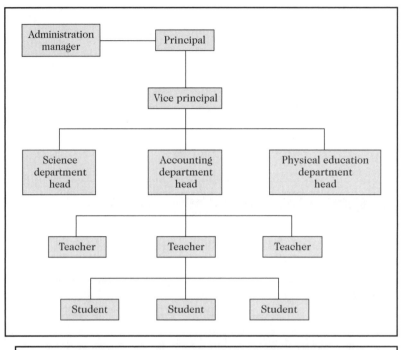

Figure 1-9 *Organization chart for an educational institution*

A composite abstraction is an artifact that combines two or more topics and is illustrated in Figure 1-10. If an intersecting point combines the *subcontractor perspective* with both the *things aspect* and the *processes aspect*, you may want to create an object-oriented program, such as one written in C++. Figure 1-10 contains C++ code that combines data with programming logic. The technique is called encapsulation. Encapsulation is the ability to hide data within a class and make it accessible only through methods. Additionally, a programmer can hide methods from a user.

An abstraction is a representation of the real thing in an artifact, and the artifact is the result of the intersection between a perspective and an aspect. However, there may be more than one possible abstraction for each intersection. The number of abstractions is based on personal preferences, industry standards, personal experience, and the subject being modeled.

For example, a model could be created to illustrate after-school activities a student can participate in during the week. One abstraction might show football, baseball, basketball, band, orchestra, and painting activities. Another more generic abstraction of the same thing might show only sports, music, and art.

```
#include <iostream.h>
class one_datum {
   int data_store;
public:
   void set(int in_value);
   int get_value(void);
};
void one_datum::set(int in_value) {
   data_store = in_value;
}
int one_datum::get_value(void) {
   return data_store;
}
int main() {
one_datum dog1, dog2;
int piggy;

dog1.set(12);
dog2.set(-13);
piggy = 123;
cout << "The value of dog1 is " << dog1.get_value() << "/n";
cout << "The value of dog2 is " << dog2.get_value() << "/n";
cout << "The value of piggy is " << piggy << "/n";
}

// Result of execution
// The value of dog1 is 12
// The value of dog2 is -13
// The value of piggy is 123
```

Figure 1-10   *Encapsulation in a C++ program*

While viewing a single perspective (row) having six aspects (columns), the number of primitive and composite abstractions can be expressed as the equation $2^c - 1$, where c equals the number of columns. This means there are a total of six primitive abstractions[7] and 57 composite abstractions.

As you can see, there are hundreds of possible combinations in the entire Framework.

The Framework helps you organize all of this information. If you have ever had a conversation with someone, but did not understand each other because you were talking at cross purposes, each of you might have been using a different primitive or composite view of the subject. For example, *I'm sorry Professor Kappelman; I thought the assignment was optional*.

The Framework can help everyone mentally align and focus on a given topic or issue. When two people are communicating about alignment in the enterprise, one person may be describing a business requirement and the other may be trying to determine language syntax in a computer program. Both people are trying to address the same issue of alignment, but in a different way.

Although the Framework was born many years ago, it is as relevant today as when it was discovered in 1982. You can be certain that the Framework will also be relevant tomorrow. Some who failed to understand its insight declared the Framework a *legacy architecture* and think the Framework is unable to support

object-oriented techniques. Others say the *Framework is theoretical and cannot be practical*. In this discipline, however, theory is practical.

Leonardo da Vinci (1452–1519), the Italian Renaissance artist, once said *"Quelli che s'innamorano senza scientia sono come il nocchiere che entra navilio senza timone e bussola e che mai ha certezza dove si vada."* [8]

Da Vinci's quote could also suggest that a solid theoretical foundation would also be important to the practice of enterprise architecture. The Framework is based on sound scientific theory and has proven to be practical in many public, private, and government organizations. [9]

THE U.S. GOVERNMENT GETS IN ON ENTERPRISE ARCHITECTURE

Executive Order 13011, Federal Information Technology, established the **Chief Information Officers (CIO)** Council as the principal interagency forum for improving practices in the design, modernization, use, sharing, and performance of agency information resources.

The CIO Council began developing the Federal Enterprise Architecture Framework in April 1998. The CIO Council strategic plan, dated January 1998, guided by priorities of the **Clinger-Cohen Act** of 1996, directed the development and maintenance of a Federal Enterprise Architecture to maximize the benefits of information technology within the government.

According to this strategic plan, architectures for selected high-priority, cross-agency business lines, or segments, will be developed to populate the Federal Enterprise Architecture. The Federal Enterprise Architecture Framework provides a sustainable mechanism for identifying, developing, and documenting architectural descriptions of high-priority areas built on common business areas and designs that cross organizational boundaries.

The Zachman Framework has been selected for Level IV of the Federal Enterprise Architecture Framework.

DEPARTMENT OF HOMELAND SECURITY

The Homeland Security Act of 2002 merged 22 federal agencies, creating the new Department of Homeland Security. The formation of the security department was part of the largest federal reorganization since World War II and was given an IT budget exceeding $2 billion for fiscal year 2003.

Homeland Security director, Tom Ridge, wants to use IT to align and integrate the procedures and systems of the previously separate agencies. To accomplish this, CIO, Steve Cooper, plans to backbone all IT initiatives with a national *enterprise architecture*.

1.2.1 Writing Systems

The purpose of any writing system is to denote and communicate thought. During the creation of a writing system, the sequence, sounds, and words are agreed upon. However, before the writing system is agreed upon, it is generally arbitrary in nature. Early symbol sets, or denotations, were entirely arbitrary. It would be ludicrous to believe the early inventors of the denotation set determined at the outset which character had to come before or after any other character. This may also have applied to the character shape.

Early teachers of the symbol set may have noticed that if every teacher taught the symbol set the same way, their students had an easier time learning the set and communicating the sound and meaning of each character. This would have made it possible to teach by rote, without the students either understanding or appreciating what they learned. The need to teach removed the arbitrariness.

Arbitrariness is also removed when the English alphabet is taught to toddlers. Those early lessons remain with us for a lifetime. Who can recite this alphabet without singing the ABC song? Depending upon your generation, you may sing that song to Mozart's 1780 classic hit K.265, better known today as *Twinkle, Twinkle Little Star,* or possibly you imitate Sesame Street's Big Bird.

In the beginning, the sound each character represented had to be communicated. Then characters were combined to form words that illustrated complex sounds. The next extension was to combine established words with other words to produce a sentence that communicated an even more complex thought.

The result was the formalization of a written language—a tremendous leap forward for the advancement of the human species. The written language represented the difference between **implicit** and **explicit** communication. Implicit communication means talking, while explicit communication means recording thought. This concept would have wide-ranging ramifications and would establish how large groups would be educated in the future.

After letters and words formalized the language, other rules had to be created, including those in the following list:

- Produce a standard form or picture of each character.
- Create a standard spelling for each word.
- Establish standard pronunciations of each letter and each word.
- Institute standard meanings of each word.
- Set up standard rules for the use of words.

Without these rules, the language could not be explicit, and the value of the written language as a communications tool would be worthless. The term for rules that describe other rules is **metarules**. The word **meta** is a prefix that means *about* and is used to describe characteristics of the suffix.

These rules allowed people to form new disciplines to create and study meanings (dictionaries), pronunciation, and syntax (grammar rules). Grammar rules forced the creation of punctuation. The practice and use of words, punctuation, and grammar forced a standard formalization, which allowed people to establish pedagogy, the science of teaching.

After the pedagogues figured out how to teach the alphabet, they could apply similar methods of teaching to other subjects. Writing systems changed what was implicit to language that was explicit. They facilitated communication of thought. Pedagogy expanded the concept of *explicit* by creating the understanding that teaching requires a method.

According to James Hackett, CEO of Steelcase, Inc., the learning environment in a school and the working environment in an enterprise can be similar at times. Steelcase leads the $33 billion global office furniture industry with fiscal 2001 revenue of $4 billion. Founded in 1912 and headquartered in Grand Rapids, Michigan, Steelcase serves customers around the world through its over 800 dealer locations, approximately 20,000 employees, and global manufacturing capabilities.

Hackett says:

> *Most people can recall how the alphabet usually circled the walls of their elementary school classrooms. This visual display of the writing system can still be seen in the classroom today. A similar display of a writing system can be seen at Steelcase. Known in industry as "information persistence," this visual display is used in rooms where product development teams work. Designs of products are kept on display around the room so that team members can learn about what they are trying to put together.*

This daily exposure, or *information persistence*, like the alphabet on an elementary school classroom wall, facilitates shared communication of thoughts and references.

THE STEELCASE PYRAMID

A *celebration of innovation* is Steelcase's own description of its Corporate Development Center (CDC). Architects reverted to the basic design of a time-tested structure to help Steelcase executives streamline operations, improve efficiency, and reduce development time for new products.

Visual (explicit) and verbal (implicit) communications are emphasized—from the four corner entrances that open into a striking atrium with a five-story pendulum sculpture suspended over a reflective pool, to the extensive use of escalators. This building is structurally designed to foster communication between its occupants. See Figure 1-11.

(continued)

Figure 1-11   *Steelcase's CDC — known as the Pyramid*

Rules had to be established to facilitate shared communication. Shared communication is a basic concept of education. Once the concepts of formalization and method of instruction were well established, new disciplines could be created.

The new disciplines had at their core the notion that implicit ideas could be made explicit. Once an idea was made explicit, the idea could be debated, thought about, and proved or disproved. This formalization of language enabled the advancement of civilization and eventually allowed the development of such breakthroughs as the scientific method, which provided the means to offer proof.

Writing systems started out as pictures on cave walls in places such as France and Italy, and over many millennia evolved into alphabets. Today, some ideas are so complex, it is once again helpful to use explicit pictures to communicate implicit thought. Pictures are often referred to as models. A model typically contains shapes that have pre-defined meanings for the domain. Not surprisingly, teachers of modeling have developed similar rules for the alphabetic counterparts:

- Produce a standard form or picture of each shape.
- Create a standard spelling for using shapes.
- Establish standard pronunciations for each shape.
- Institute standard meanings of each shape.
- Set up standard rules for the use of shapes.

Explicit language in the form of written words or models can be further articulated and governed through the use of **metalinguistics** and **metamodels**. Metalinguistics is the study of interrelationships between language and other cultural behavior, such as writing left to right in Germanic languages, right to left in Hebrew, and top to bottom in Chinese. Metamodels are the models that describe other models. For example, a model of motivation should include ends, means, influences, assessment, and values.

Writing systems and the constructs of meta that describe them have allowed mankind to advance. Every science and art has required its own language and symbol set to make certain that all the implicit ideas of that science could be made explicit.

Every discipline has its own symbol set to express ideas. Physicists could not do their work without their seemingly arcane symbol set. Architects could not design a single building of any kind without their own special set of symbols.

The use of each of these unique writing systems creates specific models, such as a chart of accounts. As shown in Figure 1-12, a natural science formula is every bit a model as is a blueprint or an engineering specification drawing. Even an entire language is a model because a language formally represents ideas and objects. All models are visual representations of something. If thoughts change the implicit to the explicit, a model is being created.

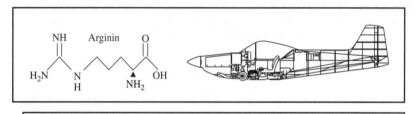

Figure 1-12   *A natural science formula and an aircraft blueprint*

If you parse a sentence, you can see the model of the language. See Figure 1-13. The longer and more complex the sentence, the more the language model will be revealed. Many models create a shorthand notation. Einstein's model and formula for the Theory of Relativity is terse: $E=MC^2$.

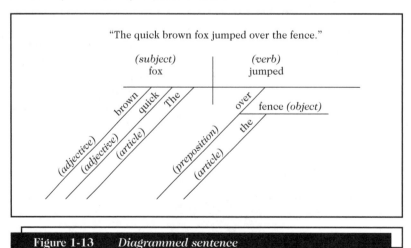

Figure 1-13   *Diagrammed sentence*

Sometimes ideas are so abstract that the language cannot adequately describe the idea. In this case, a picture is required. When describing how to construct an airplane, a picture is worth *thousands* of words. The picture is also a model because it takes an implicit idea and manifests it physically and renders it explicitly. Figure 1-14 shows other types of models: an Egyptian hieroglyphic, a modern hieroglyphic (the Zachman Framework), a picture of a wooden structure, and a typical list.

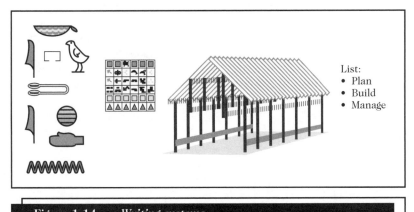

Figure 1-14   Writing systems

Enterprise architecture uses many different writing systems, including the following:

- An alphabet-based language for lists, notes, labels, and supplementary descriptions
- Pictures and models to help explain the complex
- Other specialized writing systems, depending on the domains being expressed

Computer programming languages illustrate one of the writing systems used in the enterprise, as well as entity-relationship diagrams and network wiring schemas. Figure 1-15 shows an entity-relationship diagram.

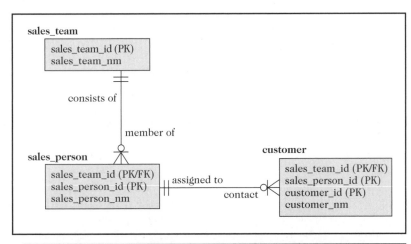

Figure 1-15   Entity-relationship diagram

Enterprise architecture is about effective, consistent communication among work groups to establish a finished product and to facilitate revisions and future enhancements to that product. Techniques for an enterprise architecture pedagogy are related to techniques for making ideas, concepts, and designs explicit. Simply stated, enterprise architecture is a means to organize, communicate, and manage IT and business operations.

The advantage of following the Zachman Framework for Enterprise Architecture is that if you elect not to make something explicit, the same metarules can be applied to govern implicit forms, such as conversation. The metarules also apply to explicit forms that have a very limited life span, such as markings on a whiteboard or chalkboard.

1.2.2 Key Terms

aspect	metamodel
builder	metarule
cell	motivation
Chief Information Officer	object-oriented technique
Clinger-Cohen Act	owner
composite	people
connectivity	perspective
Depth iNtegrating Architecture	planner
designer	primitive
explicit	process
functioning enterprise	schema
implicit	strategy
interrogative	subcontractor
meta	thing
metalinguistics	timing

1.2.3 Review Questions

The following questions relate to Section 1.2:
1. How many rows, columns, and cells does the Zachman Framework for Enterprise Architecture contain?
2. What are the similarities between the Framework and the term *framework*?
3. What do the rows and the columns of the Framework represent?
4. What is the result of the intersection between a perspective and an aspect?
5. What is the difference between a primitive and a composite?

6. When was the Zachman Framework discovered?

The following questions relate to Section 1.2.1:
1. According to the CEO of Steelcase, Inc., how can the environments of a school and the workplace be similar?
2. What is the purpose of a writing system?
3. Explain how writing systems are used in enterprise architecture.
4. How did formalization of a specific written language enable the advancement of humans?

Humanity has established many great and worthwhile professions for individuals to pursue: doctors to heal the sick, lawyers to represent the innocent, and teachers to educate students. Many people believe the field of information technology is a worthy professional career, and have worked toward making it a recognized profession.

Professional people, especially doctors, often abide by a code of ethics, such as the Hippocratic Oath. Essentially, the oath means *Above all, do no harm.* Unfortunately, there is no IT equivalent, although enterprise architecture and the Zachman Framework for Enterprise Architecture represent reasonable doctrine for keeping a business healthy and for not knowingly harming a business.

Thomas Edison (1847–1931) once said, "The doctor of the future will give no medicines but will interest his patients in the care of the *human frame*, in diet and in the cause and prevention of disease." You have the potential to be a *doctor of the future*. Your patient will be the business that engages you as an employee or consultant. You will care for the *business frame*—you will have the power and the knowledge of the Framework.

By learning and understanding each cell in the Framework, you can reason why things work and why things fail. More importantly, you can help prevent or minimize failure. The *diet* is knowledge. The *cause and prevention of disease* involve the ability to communicate and understand the basics of science, humanity, business, and technology. These are the primary ingredients for a happy and healthy business life.

The developer of chiropractic, Bartlett Palmer (1881–1961), D.C., Ph.C., wrote the following creed for chiropractors. After you complete Part II of this book, return to this creed, and see if you can rewrite it for yourself in the context suitable of enterprise architecture. The creed may become your personal mission statement for your professional life.

> *Because I honor the inborn potential of everyone to be truly healthy*
> *Because I desire to help the newborn, the aged, and those without hope*
> *Because I choose to care for the patient with the disease and not the disease*
> *Because I wish to assist rather than intrude; to free rather than control*
> *Because I know doctors do not heal*
> *Because I know the body can heal itself*
> *Because I have been called to serve others*
> *Because I want to make a difference*
> *Because every day I get to witness miracles*
> *Because I know it is right*

The ability to think and reason is helpful when learning enterprise architecture. To make thinking and reasoning about something easier, it helps to classify what you are learning or discovering. Classification is something we all learned in kindergarten; for example, Figure 1-16 shows two objects that are the same.

Figure 1-16 *Butterflies*

However, the two objects shown in Figure 1-17 are different.

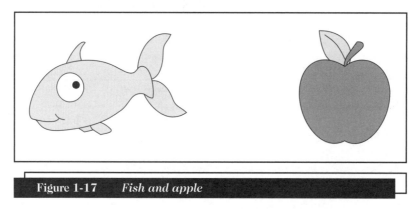

Figure 1-17 *Fish and apple*

Figure 1-18 shows objects that are different, but have similar qualities—they are all forms of travel.

Figure 1-18 *Forms of travel*

A skilled **enterprise architect** not only thinks out of the box, but wonders why you need the box. You have probably used an automated teller machine (ATM) to get cash or find your bank account balance. Putting a plastic card into a machine and entering a four-or five-digit personal identification number (PIN) has become second nature for most people.

To think in terms of abstraction, consider the purpose of the plastic card and PIN—to identify someone. Use that purpose as you explore alternatives and exploit or invent technology.

You may ask yourself a series of *what if* questions to determine if a plastic card is the best way to identify someone. How about a retina scan, a fingerprint scan, a voice recognition system, or a facial scan? *What if* we used a facial scanner and could identify people even before they reached the machine? *What if* when people approached the machine, a voice from the ATM greeted them and asked if they wanted their *usual*—because the machine kept track of how they used their accounts?

Thinking about abstractions can lead to additional ideas. For example, the Oakland Airport near San Francisco is installing a security camera system that analyzes the faces of customers and compares them to existing pictures of either wanted felons or possible terrorists. The use of a security camera is being taken one step further.

In the business world, software that involves evolving abstract ideas needs careful thought and planning. According to a report produced by The Standish Group,[10] only 23 percent of IT projects deliver completed software on time and on budget, with all features and functions as originally specified. The report further stated that 30 percent of completed and working projects are over budget, over the time estimate, and contain fewer features and functions than initially specified. Finally, the report highlighted that the remaining 47 percent of projects are cancelled before completion.

These are dismal statistics. There is only a 23 percent chance of software being delivered as promised. From the other perspective, there is a 77 percent chance of getting either nothing or a minimal return on the investment in time, resources, and manpower. This indicates that much more diligence should be applied to developing and deploying software.

Consider also that software is only a point-in-time solution. The software must be nursed, changed, and improved over time, even as its perceived value and success dwindles even further. In addition, the cost of the originally delivered software escalates due to maintenance costs. Maintenance costs cover the following tasks:

- Fixes required by changes in the business
- Fixes required for software defects
- Fixes needed to add new interfaces to other IT systems

Computer games for machines such as Nintendo and Playstation are point-in-time solutions. Multiple versions of popular games like Donkey Kong, Pac Man, and Tomb Raider demonstrate the concept of point-in-time solutions. If a game could continually satisfy and challenge you, the game makers would not need to create new editions or versions. But, the more you play, the more your skills probably improve, and you may get bored. You are likely to turn to a different game to maintain your enjoyment level.

Businesses get bored too. They never keep the marketplace the same for very long. A business must make sure its employees and customers are always motivated. When customers, competition, or legislation force a corporation to rethink its approach to business, the corporation creates new requirements for its computer systems. Each time a computer system is installed, the system is a point-in-time solution. The computer system's useful life span is only as long as it takes for a new requirement to be defined, built, and tested.

Most companies in the **Fortune 1000** have changed their CEOs or senior executives during the past five years. With each new executive comes a new **vision**, strategy, and point-in-time initiatives. With the dramatic and traumatic changes in corporate leadership and the corporate mergers, acquisitions, and partnerships that usually accompany those changes, how does information technology respond? According to The Standish Group's statistics, not very well.

Why is this? Current business literature is full of ideas and practices on strategy, managing change, and developing software. Yet in practice, most miss the mark, according to The Standish Group. Otherwise, the statistics would report a far different picture. What is missing? A sense of architecture, science, and communication, and their practical application to an enterprise.

This book illustrates how business works, how software is developed, and how the two usually work at cross purposes. Business and technology need to move from the **Information Age** to an Age of Knowledge and Understanding. You need effective architecture, science, and communication. You need **thought leaders** and **systems thinkers** who are not constrained by past bad habits. These leaders and thinkers must understand both business and information technology.

This book provides a Framework for such thought leaders and systems thinkers. It provides you with a holistic view of the corporate enterprise. The book illustrates how the Framework can be applied to many life situations, not just business and information technology.

Many abstract ideas in this book are made concrete by using metaphors and analogies. Hopefully you find this approach to be an entertaining and useful way to start thinking in terms of abstraction.

Keep this thought in mind: To see is to know. To *not* see is to guess.

1.3.1 The Management Imperative

To set direction, a business establishes a vision, which is a set of missions, objectives, strategies, tactics, and implementations. Ultimately, business direction is constrained by the laws of nature (science and physics), the marketplace (**supply chain** and perceived customer desires and needs), and regulatory bodies (legislative **mandates**).

To successfully bring a product or service to the marketplace, executive management (the *owner*) determines what is offered and the terms of that offering. The owner delegates the responsibility for the design of the offering and how the offering is taken to the marketplace. Others are charged with figuring out the process of manufacturing and production. Still others construct the offering. And finally, others make the offering an actual product or service.

The final product or service is constrained by the scope of the project, as envisioned by the *owner, designer, builder*, and construction team. All view their work from different perspectives. All face different problems.

The English language provides six interrogatives that establish a mutual understanding among any group. The *planner, owner, designer, builder*, and *subcontractor* can integrate knowledge and understanding by answering the questions *what, how, where, who, when,* and *why*.

Answering these questions can improve the success rate of both business operations and the software that supports those operations. If the shared knowledge and understanding are formalized and maintained in models and documents, a corporation can continually improve and change its dynamics in the marketplace.

1.3.2 Establishing Proof

Earlier, the Framework's primary purpose was cited for use in information technology. Additionally, the Framework's ubiquity was declared, meaning that the Framework has use beyond information technology and can be applied to everything. Without further definition or evidence, a belief that the Framework is applicable to all we do in our personal, academic, and professional lives would require an act of faith.

Some common concepts can be proven time and time again. For example, an apple falling from a tree always falls down, even in the southern hemisphere. The force that brings the apple to the ground is gravity. Yet we cannot see gravity, and we cannot directly touch gravity as we can touch the apple. To a kindergartner, the effects of gravity may seem more like magic (possibly an act of faith) than a law of physics.

Proofs are based on the scientific method. The scientific method dictates that you can create an experiment to test any discipline or problem set. If the results of the experiment vary or change, you can conclude that one of the variables in the experiment changed. The scientific method was created to demonstrate and help explain observations regarding the underlying physics or science.

SCIENTIFIC METHOD

The great philosopher, Aristotle (384 B.C.E.–322 B.C.E.) was the first to espouse the need for the scientific method, but it was not until the ninth century that the first physical mathematicians in Baghdad formally postulated the scientific method. The work of these intellectual thinkers was expanded in the early seventeenth century by European scientists, astronomers, and mathematicians, including Sir Isaac Newton (1642–1727) and Galileo Galilei (1564–1642).

Something else forced the creation of the scientific method—the exploration of the concept of cause and effect. Referring back to the example of gravity, you can clearly observe that objects always fall toward the ground. Many observed this, including great thinkers, and formed a simple question—*why*? Answering this question caused the creation of physics. Physics provide and demonstrate proof. Use of the scientific method helps establish the relative laws. Laws and rules govern both physics and the evaluation of proofs.

By the seventeenth century, the following three general conditions had been observed and formulated:

1. An experiment could be designed and, when conducted in precisely the same manner, provide the same results each time. Identical results are considered *proof of fact*.

    For example, Galileo proposed that all objects, regardless of size or mass, fall at the same rate. Galileo created the famous Leaning Tower of

Pisa experiment that proved this observation. The experiment resulted in the development of the rate of the terminal velocity formula. This is now a basic component of physics.

2. An experiment could be designed and each time that experiment is conducted, the results may not be predictable. In this case, all that can be observed is that some type of result occurs. This is a trait of civics and politics. This type of experiment is *proof of the probable*. The overriding motivator in the variation of the results is founded in the culture of the population and that may change relative to living conditions.

    For example, a lawyer can present an argument in a court of law to a jury. The lawyer cannot try other approaches by repeating the trial over and over again to the same jury. Jury composition would be different in a new trial, and even the same jury hearing a new set of arguments cannot be expected to forget what they have already heard.

3. It is possible to create a condition where neither the experiment nor the results can be demonstrated. An example of this is religion. The resultant belief becomes an *article of faith*. Like the condition of civics and government, thinkers could not predict what could happen or how deeply a population felt about its faith.

    For example, many practiced religions in the world are based on the concept of a Supreme Being or Power. What distinguishes each religion is how that Supreme Being is conceived and what is required to satisfy that Supreme Being. The faith both guides and is guided by the belief systems, rites, and rituals practiced.

To the intellects that established these three conditions, the important dynamic was that each condition could in fact exist. One additional observation has been made—the second and third conditions could stir a population to war.

In every corporation, the executives and employees are affected by the conditions and the rules of the conditions. This is true even if they ignore or fail to notice the conditions. Similar to the governance of criminal law, you can be found guilty of a crime even if you did not know you participated in a crime. Ignorance of the law is no excuse for not abiding by the law. Therefore, each executive and employee is a recipient of any benefits or liabilities that are the outcome of any result.

By evaluating a proof and discussing a problem logically, a belief can become supported by proof and not remain an issue of faith. Therefore, the concepts illustrated in this book that support the ubiquity of the Framework should become proofs.

Proof is provided using several mechanisms. Methods include storytelling, analogy, metaphor, references to other material, quotations, and our own personal and professional experiences. In each case, a concept is made explicit. Each proof can be compared and evaluated against the three conditions set forth by great thinkers centuries ago.

The Framework can be applied directly to an enterprise's business operations. This is true even when a business operation is not focused on automation. This book expands the definitions for the perspectives and aspects of the Framework for new Framework uses. The sidebar provides definitions for each perspective and aspect from the viewpoint of business operations.

PERSPECTIVES REVISITED FOR BUSINESS OPERATIONS

Planner—one who establishes the universe of discourse; the background, scope, and purpose of the endeavor

Owner—a person or group that has the authority and responsibility to make a profit and keep the enterprise in business

Designer—one who receives mandates from the owner and transforms the mandates into the design of the business operations

Builder—a general contractor who has the responsibility and authority to oversee the production of the end product or service and to spend money to make it happen

Subcontractor—one responsible for building and assembling the parts for the end product or service

Functioning enterprise—the automated or manual physical manifestation of the end product or service

ASPECTS REVISITED FOR BUSINESS OPERATIONS

Things—the important items of the business that represent either a cost to do business or an income opportunity to stay in business; associated with the interrogative *what*

Processes—physical acts required to operate the business; associated with the interrogative *how*

Connectivity—locations and communications required to support the operation of the business; associated with the interrogative *where*

People—the organizations and individuals who make the business operate; associated with the interrogative *who*

Timing—defines the business event life cycles, their order and priority, and their scheduling requirements and time frames; associated with the interrogative *when*

Motivation—defines the reality-based impetus and raison d'etre for the enterprise; associated with the interrogative *why*

Management methods are grounded in physics, science, and engineering. So are all the rules of communications. Management methods and communications are subject to observable conditions. The following list describes how rules apply to a corporation:

1. If you are told to do something a certain way, you can probably track that rule back to a legislative mandate or a discipline based on either an engineering requirement or conformity to the laws of science and physics.

2. If you are instructed to do something and you cannot track it back to any scientific law, then you are probably dealing with something unique to the corporate culture.

For example, appropriate business attire may be defined as the requirement for men to wear a jacket, dress shirt, tie, pants, socks, and close-toed shoes. This is an issue of corporate culture, and demonstrates the probable because requiring proper dress is subject solely to the whims of corporate management.

3. If you are dealing with something that you cannot track back to anything, then you are being subjected to a corporate article of faith.

For example, the statement "We are the greatest company to work for in the whole wide world," is a corporate article of faith. The statement cannot be either proved on the basis of fact, nor can any experiment be constructed to demonstrate its truth.

When working for a company, it is helpful to analyze why things are done the way they are. It is useful to know the reason why something is done, especially if you neither like nor agree with what is being demanded. When you possess the knowledge of *why*, you are closer to being in a position to effect positive change. Enterprise architecture serves as a true compass. The Framework helps you determine what to ask and what forms of proof are required.

1.3.3 Key Terms

enterprise architect

Fortune 1000

Information Age

mandate

supply chain

systems thinker

thought leader

vision

1.3.4 Review Questions

The following questions relate to Section 1.3:

1. How can enterprise architecture and the Zachman Framework for Enterprise Architecture help keep a business healthy?
2. If thought processes are started in an abstract manner, what could be a positive result for the organization?
3. Statistically, many projects fail to be completed on time and within budget. What three things are missing in companies today that contribute to this problem?

The following questions relate to Sections 1.3.1 and 1.3.2:

1. Why is the Framework considered to be ubiquitous?
2. Explain the need for an enterprise to ask the question *why*.
3. Define the six different perspectives of the Framework.
4. Define the six different aspects of the Framework.

Because today's marketplace is evolving quickly, enterprise architecture should be used to lend order to the process of investing resources as the enterprise itself changes. This book provides a tool for managing and communicating the information needed to make broad decisions in order for the enterprise to successfully compete in the changing economy. You will learn how enterprise architecture considers the design and operation of a business from many perspectives, aspects, and disciplines.

The rest of this chapter focuses on what you can expect as you complete this book. You are about to embark on the journey of a lifetime. This journey has 36 key stops, and at each stop, you will be allowed to tour all the places of interest and learn all there is to know about that stop. Each stop is analogous to each cell in the two-dimensional schema of the Framework and is indicated by the Framework graphic. Consider this chapter an itinerary. Here is a list of questions you might have about this trip:

- What do I need?
- How am I going?
- Where am I going?
- Who am I going with?
- When am I going?
- Why am I going?

If you have any other questions about this trip, take a minute and write them down, now. Your list might look like this:

- What am I going to learn?
- Where am I going to learn it?
- How am I going to learn it?
- Who is going to teach me?
- When will I have to learn it by?
- Why is it important for me to learn it?
- What do I need to do to pass?

If this were not a classroom, but rather a real business environment, in the time you were thinking about other questions, your competition would have thought about the same set of questions. Your competitors are driven to succeed. You must out-think, out-plan, and out-execute all of them.

Who are your competitors? They are everyone who wants to get ahead of you in the business environment. This includes job candidates, peers, managers, and other corporations. We live in an extremely cutthroat world, and the victory usually goes to the smartest and the fastest.

The Framework will change your mindset about how you think about a problem. The concepts taught in this book allow you to cut out background noise and focus on real issues. The most complex problems in the world can be reduced to a total of 36 abstract issues. You will learn the rules of all of those issues.

Enterprise architecture can be expressed in a picture that is essentially a six-by-six matrix. To use the Framework, you must complete the following tasks:

- You must first learn the disciplines of the science.
- You must first learn the rules of the business physics.

- You must first learn the principles of the engineering.
- When you finally see the matrix in more detail, it will be entirely intuitive, and you will have probably figured it out long before we show it to you. That is the point of the book's approach.

1.4.1 Approach

Due to the complexity of an enterprise, the subject of enterprise architecture is also complex. The book addresses the topic of enterprise architecture from the approaches of science, business, psychology, and information technology. The book has two additional parts and appendices. The text introduces you to both the theory and practice of enterprise architecture. It illustrates how businesses work and why knowledge workers must understand both the theory of the business *and* information technology. You will learn how to ask questions to create a shared understanding of the organization.

Zachman's Framework for Enterprise Architecture, also called the Framework, is a classification schema made up of rows and columns. Each intersecting row and column identifies a primitive topic. When combined, these topics include every detail a business needs in order to make decisions that create wealth and value for the organization while conducting business.

The Framework is a structure for classifying and organizing the topics that are significant to the management of the enterprise, as well as to the development of the enterprise's systems. This tool is intended to simplify understanding and communication throughout the enterprise, while at the same time, it allows focus on independent variables without losing the importance of the holistic view.

Part II, Framing the Framework begins with a discussion of the scientific proof of the existence of the Framework. Through story, metaphor, analogy, and example, its first five chapters develop the logic and reasoning of why the Framework exists. This technique is used as a mechanism to set the stage for learning the fundamentals and principles of the Framework in Chapter 7 and Part III of the book.

Chapter 2 illustrates the importance of planning in the enterprise. Chapter 3 discusses the conceptualization of how the business operates in the marketplace. You learn how to apply systems thinking in order to view the organization holistically and create a shared knowledge. Chapter 4 focuses on why effective communication is required to develop a common language in order to logically design how the business operates. Chapter 5 illustrates how to work within the constraints of the current technology of the enterprise to build a new design, which is financially feasible and workable.

Chapter 6 shows you that change in business is inevitable, and people need to adopt change as a regular part of their activities. You learn how the Framework fits into writing business software applications. You also examine information about constructing designs using the tools and materials used by the information technology staff. The tool for managing and communicating all this information is Zachman's Framework for Enterprise Architecture, which is explained in detail in Chapter 7. This chapter examines the structure and rules of the Framework, and shows you how various construction techniques can be applied and supported by the Framework. You learn that enterprise architecture is about modeling every aspect of the business.

In **Part III, Implementing the Framework**, you are guided through the fundamentals of the Framework in order to apply it in real-world situations. Chapter 8 introduces a third dimension of the Framework, which provides for the disciplines and infrastructure to construct the Framework's models and products. This chapter also focuses on modeling to a specific audience's needs with a common language and understanding.

The appendices include a biography of the Framework's discoverer, John A. Zachman; examples of using the Framework outside of information technology; careers in information technology mapped to the Framework; and Zachman's original paper discussing the concepts of the Framework.

1.4.2 Fastpath

Time is a precious commodity. Many learning institutions may choose to use this book as part of an existing program. To facilitate shorter courses, a fastpath has been created through this book. Each section or critical element included in the fastpath is bound with the special icons shown in Figure 1-19.

Figure 1-19   Fastpath icons

1.5 SYNTHESIS AND CHAPTER SUMMARY

In this book, you will learn the laws of the Framework and the practical application of those laws. You will learn how to use this Framework for thinking through complex problems, reasoning, decision-making, communicating, succeeding, and making a difference in the corporate enterprise.

The Framework is a classification schema for descriptive representations of an enterprise. By observing design artifacts of various physical objects like airplanes, buildings, ships, and computers, John Zachman derived the Framework.

He further observed that the design artifacts (including the descriptive representations, product descriptions, and engineering documentation) for these complex products could be classified in two ways. The first classification is by the audience for whom the artifact was constructed—a perspective. A second classification is based on the content or subject focus of the artifact—an aspect.

Architecture should be viewed as an asset to the enterprise. The collective set of descriptive representations constitutes the knowledge base of the enterprise. Enterprise architecture enables alignment, integration, and change, and reduces time to market. This will be true whether the company uses any type of automation, develops custom software solutions, or runs software packages such as SAP, Baan, and Peoplesoft.

Alignment is the enterprise equivalent of total quality management. Aligning the enterprise ensures that the *owner's* desires and the enterprise's implementations are one in the same. Integration minimizes or eliminates redundancy, discontinuity, and disparity within the enterprise. Integration also seeks to make sure that everyone has a consistent interpretation of every aspect. Change means flexibility and adaptability.

An enterprise must facilitate change and also minimize the impact of change on all resources. Reducing the time to market is obviously critical for surviving in business. Using an architectural approach with an assemble-to-order philosophy provides a potential winning combination.

In a real-world scenario, you may be managing the holistic big picture—overseeing all activities across the Framework, or you may be a specialist operating in just one cell. Understanding how you fit into the big picture and how the big picture works can only help you perform your job or task better.

Important concepts covered in this chapter include:

- The purpose of the Framework
- The universal nature of the Framework to set and define items of importance
- The introduction of John Zachman
- The definition of enterprise architecture and what it includes
- The importance of the Framework to manage change
- The concept of a schema and its definition relative to the Framework
- The Framework as a key to understanding corporate dynamics
- The concepts of perspectives and aspects and their definitions
- The concept and definition of abstraction
- The present-day relevance of the Framework
- The concepts of theory and practice
- The significance of the Clinger-Cohen Act
- The importance of writing systems
- The concept of information persistence
- The evolution of arbitrary to formal
- The difference between implicit and explicit
- The creation and evolution of pedagogy
- The Framework as an effective and efficient communications tool
- How the prefix meta affects words
- The success rate of new projects
- The purpose of the management imperative
- The importance of learning the principles of physics, science, and engineering

The Framework may not be the mythical silver bullet, but if this schema enables you to be better, faster, and cheaper than your competitors...you will not get fired.

1.6.1 Discussion Topics

1. Describe what you believe to be the essence of enterprise architecture, as described in this chapter.
2. Describe the physical layout of Zachman's Framework.
3. Discuss how understanding is affected when individuals use different primitives and composites while communicating.
4. Discuss how using the six perspectives gives business participants a more complete view of the organization.
5. As previously mentioned, the ability to think and reason about things in an abstract manner is helpful when learning enterprise architecture. In a small group of two or three, practice thinking in terms of abstraction about the following:
   a. How would a company develop software that draws a shape?
   b. What would help make a VCR more user friendly?
   c. How might a grocery store use its courtesy cards to serve customers better?
   d. When entering a toll road, drivers frequently receive a punch card. In what ways could the information on this punch card be used?
6. Why is the Zachman Framework for Enterprise Architecture so important in helping a company achieve alignment and integration?
7. Explain why understanding how you fit into the enterprise and how the enterprise works could enable you to be a more effective employee.
8. In your opinion, what situations could have led to the creation of the Clinger-Cohen Act in 1996?
9. Explain the meaning of the aspects depicted by the columns in the Framework.
10. What are the three ways from which enterprise architecture considers the design and operation of a business?
11. Explain how an architecture can be described with words, pictures, models, and diagrams.
12. Explain what is meant by the proof when thinking scientifically.
13. Explain the difference between implicit and explicit. How do models help change something that is implicit into something that is explicit?

1.6.2 Critical Thinking

1. Using the analogy of the IT professional as the *doctor of the future*, write a one-page paper stating why you agree or disagree with the ideas presented.
2. Research the Zachman Framework on the Internet. Write a one-page summary of what you learn and be prepared to share your information with the class.
3. Using the Internet, research The Standish Group, Forrester Research, Gartner, or Giga. Write a two to three page summary that describes what you learn and how an organization could use this information.
4. Choose an organization in your community and interview a business participant of your choice. Through the use of carefully chosen questions, discover the job title and job description of individuals who represent all six perspectives from which to view an organization. Be prepared to share this information through a visual presentation to the class.
5. Using the *Wall Street Journal*, *CIO Magazine*, *Forbes*, or *Fortune*, choose an article that discusses how changes in management can affect an organization's vision or strategy. Be prepared to share your article with the class and to lead a discussion about how information technology would respond to the situation.

6. Write a two to three paragraph summary of your thoughts, describing how the extension Zachman DNA could transform and magnify the power of the Framework.

7. Survey a minimum of six individuals from the information technology community, as well as members of the business or management department of your university. Ask these individuals to define the term *enterprise architecture*. Write a short paper, which includes these definitions, as well as your interpretations of the data you collected.

8. Write a short essay describing a personal experience in which a writing system helped change something implicit to something explicit.

Endnotes

[1] In the context of the Framework, an artifact is a detailed representation of a product deliverable. The deliverable may include a list, a model, a picture, or a computer program. The deliverable is normally stored on paper or in an electronic format.

[2] In the far reaches of outer space, scientists have detected black holes. The gravitational pull is so strong that not even light escapes, hence the name. However, scientists are not really sure what they are. They use the laws of physics to help explain many of the observed phenomena. John Zachman also used the power of observation to explain the phenomena associated with building complex structures such as airplanes, skyscrapers, and software. He discovered the ubiquitous nature of the Framework. Zachman theorized the existence of the Framework without knowing its exact nature. In the same way that black holes existed before they were discovered, the Framework existed before it was discovered too.

[3] *Systems Journal*, Turning Points in Computing 1962–1999, Volume 38, Numbers 2 & 3, 1999.

[4] To conduct additional research on this topic on the Internet, use the following keywords: Zachman, Zachman Framework, Zachman Framework for Information Systems, and Zachman Framework for Enterprise Architecture.

[5] The American Heritage Dictionary of the English Language, Fourth Edition.

[6] DNA is an acronym normally associated with deoxyribonucleic acid—the double helix, the building block of life. See Chapter 8 for more information.

[7] The number of primitive cells will always equal c.

[8] After all, Da Vinci was Italian. The English translation is: "Those who are enamored of practice without theory are like a pilot who goes into a ship without rudder or compass and never has any certainty where he is going. Practice should always be based upon a sound knowledge of theory."

[9] Glaxo Wellcome, Boeing, Canadian Tire, Metadata Management Corporation, USAA, U.S. Government, Canadian Government, Australian Government, Ohio Bureau of Workers Compensation, City of Oakland, General Motors, and Intuit are examples of the many public, private, and government organizations that have successfully used the Zachman Framework for Enterprise Architecture to their benefit.

[10] The Standish Group International, Inc., is a recognized market research and advisory firm specializing in mission-critical software and electronic commerce.

What WHERE WHO HOW WHEN Why

PART 2

FRAMING THE FRAMEWORK

"You can know the name of a bird in all the languages of the world, but when you are finished, you will know absolutely nothing whatever about the bird. So let us look at the bird and see what it is doing—that's what counts. I learned very early the difference between knowing the name of something and knowing something."

— *Professor Richard Feynman (1918–1988), Physicist*

INTRODUCTION

An enterprise can be many things. The enterprise can be a production facility with production systems, product development, marketing, sales, economic planning and guidance, and personnel policies. The enterprise could also be a public school system with students, faculty, administration, school board, budgets, community, curriculum mandates, and graduation requirements.

An enterprise is a place or organization[1] that typically requires interaction between individuals. Every person has a set of attitudes and beliefs. An enterprise also has its own collection of attitudes and beliefs.

Poor cooperation due to conflicting attitudes and beliefs can destroy systems in an enterprise (IT systems, non-IT systems, automated, and manual, for example). The quality and extent of cooperation have a decisive influence on all the systems of the enterprise. Having the best technological equipment and the greatest pool of technical knowledge offers only a small advantage if the employees do not believe the climate of the enterprise supports individual beliefs, identities, and values.

The climate can affect employee concentration and productivity, as well as the following attitudes:

- An employee's willingness to use personal competencies
- An employee's willingness to stay with the organization during difficult times
- An employee's capacity to tolerate temporary difficulties, such as possible reduction of pay and client relationships

If individuals feel no unity within the enterprise, images of justice, community, and responsibility may be called into question. A slight improvement in the climate of the enterprise can sometimes lead to increased productivity and profitability.

The leadership of an enterprise is the leadership of a community. Leadership means encouraging and developing interactions between individuals. Leadership involves engaging people in facing a challenge, understanding and adjusting their attitudes and beliefs, changing perspectives, and developing new behaviors. Leadership is the creation of unity from diversity. Without unity, a productive enterprise culture may not exist. An enterprise benefits from having productive interplay among individuals.

Over time, every part of the enterprise can change. Individuals come and go. Old systems are retired and new systems are built. How can an enterprise retain its memory? Individuals can learn and cultures can change, but how much and how fast? How can an enterprise encourage thought leaders and system thinkers who believe that the chaos is the beginning rather than the end? How can an enterprise facilitate this communication? How can an enterprise pass on its culture?

Ancient Egyptians found an answer. Although they developed papyrus, for permanence, their communication tool was *carved in stone*.[2] See Figure Part II.

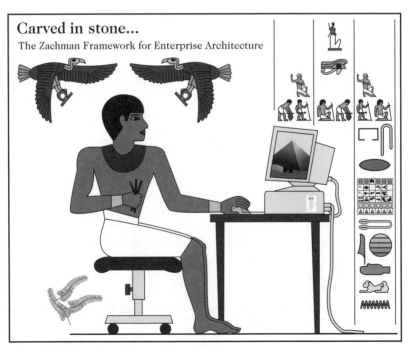

Carved in stone...
The Zachman Framework for Enterprise Architecture

Endnotes

[1] The amount of people involved in an organization can vary between one and infinity. An organization does not have to include only people who are alive and well.

[2] Carved in Stone was the working title of this textbook.

CHAPTER

SCIENCE

What WHERE WHO HOW WHEN Why

 "To master the discipline of innovation we must do three things: focus on mission; define the results we are after; and assess what we are doing and how we are doing it."
— *Peter Drucker (b. 1909), Writer, management consultant*

LEARNING OBJECTIVES

After completing Chapter 2, you will be able to:

1. Understand the importance of project management.
2. List six different aspects from which to examine a project.
3. Understand two big issues about which *planners* must think.
4. Explain how a list becomes a very useful and necessary tool for *planners*.
5. Explain the need for priorities.
6. Distinguish between rules and laws.
7. Discuss the processes involved in getting from the current state to the end state.
8. Discuss the importance of science to business.
9. Explain how a project can be affected by cultural buy-in.
10. Understand the effect assumption and misassumption can have on a project.
11. Compare and contrast the importance of intellectual capital during World War II and in today's enterprise.
12. Discuss the role of communication when many different teams are involved.
13. Understand why the concept of time is important to a project and the enterprise.

 ## 2.1 INTRODUCTION

Disciplines in both management and computer sciences help make people confident that they can compete in the marketplace. When solving problems, the disciplines also allow you to place a problem into the appropriate context. Every discipline is associated with a science. The science is based on physics and grounded in reality. This chapter presents six stories to illustrate disciplines and associated sciences. Each story provides a holistic view needed to solve a set of problems and lays out the basic physics, science, and disciplines that the enterprise must support.

Not all sciences are natural sciences. Often people limit their thinking of science to biology, chemistry, and physics. In addition to the natural sciences, a science can be viewed as a "methodological activity, discipline, or study."[1] Another definition describes science as an "accumulated and established knowledge, which has been systematized and formulated with reference to the discovery of general truths or the operation of general laws; knowledge classified and made available in work, life, or the search for truth; comprehensive, profound, or philosophical knowledge."[2] These are the contexts for the term science in this book.

Some disciplines in the stories involve lists and charts. A list is a useful and necessary tool. While making a list, the *planner* accomplishes a great deal. The following list identifies truths about a list:

- A list is a set of things that either need to be done or need to be acquired.
- One list may require or cause the creation of other lists.
- A list helps the *planner* prioritize and schedule.
- A list contains all the things about which the *planner* is concerned.
- Items may be modified, added, or subtracted as required.

Further, the list helps the *planner* think about the scope of the problem area in abstract terms. Making the list helps define boundaries, or more precisely, limits the area of concern. This is an important concept. The list confines the problem. Put another way, the list creates a box, which encompasses the entire problem area.

In the early part of World War I, Henry Gantt (1861–1919), a *planner* at the Frankford Arsenal in Philadelphia, was given the task of moving men and materials to Europe. The United States had never fought a war of this magnitude on foreign soil, so all the issues of logistics were unknown or unused. Gantt set about listing the things he had to do. As he made that list, he discovered and recorded the five truths about a list. The result was the **Gantt chart**, which is still the basis for many project management tools. The Gantt chart is a visual display used for scheduling that is based on time, rather than quantity, volume, or weight.

In the late 1940s and early 1950s, *planners* working on increasingly more complex projects noticed the Gantt chart did not address the concept of dependency. *Planners* recognized some tasks had to be completely finished before others could be started. A new model emerged, called the **critical path method (CPM)**. This was an ideal model for the *planner* because it clearly illustrated the order tasks had to be performed, and showed why. CPM also demonstrated the dependency of one **event** upon another. Figure 2-1 shows a list, Gantt chart, and CPM chart.

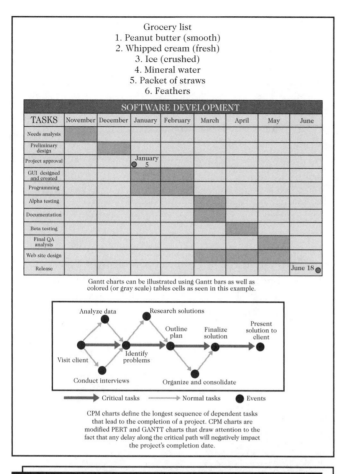

Gantt charts can be illustrated using Gantt bars as well as colored (or gray scale) tables cells as seen in this example.

CPM charts define the longest sequence of dependent tasks that lead to the completion of a project. CPM charts are modified PERT and GANTT charts that draw attention to the fact that any delay along the critical path will negatively impact the project's completion date.

Figure 2-1   *List, Gantt chart, and CPM chart*

CPM was supported by Gantt charts, and the Gantt charts were supported by detailed lists. The *planner* could now use three extraordinary tools. Together the tools allowed the *planner* to create and repeat a **methodology** for planning, which raised a project's overall success rate. Each person associated with a project could understand the set of **deliverables**. The methodology established planning as a science. These techniques can be traced back to the ancient Egyptian *planners* building the Great Pyramid of Giza.

SECTION 2.2 WHY THE SUN GOD LIKED HIS TRIANGLE—THE GREAT PYRAMID OF GIZA

> ## QUESTIONS TO CONTEMPLATE
>
> 1. What does building a pyramid have to do with project management, business management, and enterprise architecture?
> 2. What lists and questions used by the Egyptians can be used to improve communication in the enterprise today?

2.2.1 Introduction

Standing in the desert at Giza, Egypt are three huge piles of stones. See Figure 2-2. The tombs of the ancient rulers of that land, the Pharaohs, are 4,500 years old and still shrouded in mystery and controversy. How were these tombs built given the lack of any real architectural science at that time?

Figure 2-2   *Giza*

To understand the significance of their creation and construction, you must examine the task of building the tombs from six different **aspects: motivation, organization, locations, materials, building processes,** and **timing coordination**.

2.2.2 Motivation *(why)*

One morning, the Pharaoh woke up, stared out at the unrelenting ocean of sand, and thought to himself, you know what would look good out there? Then he turned to his subjects and said, "Build me a tomb. Not just any old tomb. It should be something really spectacular."

Because government and religion were unified, the **culture** supported such a bold idea. To the Egyptians, the Pharaoh was not merely a mortal. The Pharaoh was a God, and the most powerful of the Gods. The Pharaoh was Amen-Ra, the Sun God.

Figure 2-3 illustrates the questions the Egyptians needed to answer to build the pyramids.

Build me a pyramid.

How are we going to pay for it?

Where are we going to put it?

Who is going to build it?

When do you want it?

Why do you want it?

What is a pyramid?

Figure 2-3	*What is a pyramid?*

The Ancient Egyptian culture was based on a theocracy taken to the extreme. In addition to the ruler being leader of both the government and the religion, the ruler was God. The ruler was worshipped, adored, and obeyed. He had all the money, the power, and the army.

The need to build a tomb was founded on the Egyptian belief in an afterlife. The afterlife had both a spiritual and physical manifestation. Preparation for death was believed to be preparation for the afterlife. Therefore, the tomb had to accommodate all of the accoutrements from the life of its occupant. In the Pharaoh's case, this was no small task. The Pharaoh lived on a grand scale and would need to be maintained in that style after death.

Besides needing to build a tomb, the Pharaoh could afford to pay for a large one. Many tombs date from the same period as the Great Pyramids. Their size and opulence speak volumes about both the status and wealth of the occupants. The Pharaoh had the biggest and best.

The Pharaoh had all the power and made the laws of the land. The Pharaoh would and could rule on any matter worthy of attention. Matters unbecoming to a Pharaoh were delegated to another official to handle. When the word of the Pharaoh was not quite enough, the Pharaoh had a large, well-trained army. Force of arms can be a powerful incentive to comply. The ruler's orders could not be questioned; if for no other reason, the orders were the word of God. Failure to comply usually resulted in a quick and painful death.

However, the Pharaoh's money and power alone did not build the pyramids. The question had to be answered, "Can this huge structure be built?" The best priests, astrologers, *planners*, *designers*, *builders*, scientists, and craftsmen of the day were consulted, and all agreed that the structure could be built. They stated that adequate resources and technology were available, and what they did not know would be figured out. All became convinced the project would be successful.

The Egyptians were motivated to complete the pyramids for the following reasons:

- The Pharaoh was determined and dedicated to have his tomb.
- The culture of the populace embraced, accepted, or tolerated grand projects. They embraced the idea of the pyramids.
- Resources and technology were adequate for the undertaking. Experts believed they could figure out the unknown.
- All involved shared confidence for success in a reasonable amount of time. Failure was not an option.
- The Pharaoh had the money to finance the undertaking.
- The Pharaoh had the force of arms to ensure compliance with his wishes.

This list is very important. Take away any one item and the total project is put at risk. Eliminate any two items and the chance of failure increases exponentially.

The next area of concern was organization, and addressed a basic question: *Why a pyramid?* The answer to this question is a matter of physics, not a question of style. The Egyptians had years of experience building smaller pyramids, obelisks, roads, palaces, boats, weapons, tools, and statuary, but no experience building something on the scale of the Great Pyramid. Therefore, the question of *why* a pyramid became, *what* form will support such mass and weight, and *what* materials are available to use?

The pyramid was the only answer to this question. Each level is smaller than the one below, and the lower level distributes the weight evenly. The dimensions on all sides are the same. Theoretically, the only restrictions on building would be the amount of space available at the base and the strength of the building materials.

Egypt had a lot of hard stone. When the stone was quarried into large blocks, each stone could bear a lot of weight. The Egyptians solved the problems of weight distribution, mass, shape, and building materials. All other design issues, such as the size and shape of the internal chambers, halls, and passages, were limited by the shape of the building and the nature of the building materials.

Once the Egyptians understood all these principles, they designed the pyramids from the inside out because the architects had to consider all the factors of what to store and where. These factors included the size of the chambers, the size and slope of the passageways, and the size and shape of what had to be moved into the pyramid.

The Egyptians could solve these problems because they had the science and the arithmetic to model the Great Pyramid before they quarried the first block of stone.

2.2.3 Organization *(who)*

"Okay. Right over there, on that spot, we are going to build a pyramid. Who wants to help?" Starting the pyramid project might have happened that way. The Egyptians were about to embark on the largest building project in the history of the world. The project required people, and lots of them.

In the past, some Egyptologists believed the pyramids were built using slave labor. Others proposed the ludicrous notion that aliens landed, helped the Egyptians by levitating the blocks into place, and then when finished, they departed.

Modern Egyptologists have reached startling conclusions based on years of scientific archaeology, paleontology, and deciphering of ancient hieroglyphics. Construction took under twenty-five years and 25,000 workers at most, but not all of them worked at the same time. Relatively few slaves were used considering the total size of the project. Instead, people went to work willingly on this project. The building of the pyramid was a great national endeavor, dedicated to the glory of God and King. Citizens were honored to be included in the undertaking. They left their homes and went to the place where their skills were required and did their very best work. By the standards of the day, the workers were treated well and compensated with food, money, and entertainment.

The workers had a diet rich in meat protein, vegetables, and grain. Good housing with safe streets and the best medical attention was provided. The work was dangerous, so supervisors were concerned about on-the-job safety.

The use of slave labor in building the pyramids was unlikely because slaves could not be counted on to do good work. They could not be trusted with such important tasks as cutting and shaping stone. Slaves would have to be watched. Guards would need to carry arms and whips, and a rebellious slave with a sword would be a dangerous thing.

Because the project would require nearly as many guards as slaves to accomplish the work, using slaves would not be efficient. Additionally, a large army dedicated to maintaining the slaves would put the country in jeopardy because the army could not do the more important job of national defense.

The voluntary workers did the best work they could, leaving their villages and traveling to the cities built for them, but this created an **infrastructure** problem.

Consider the *planners'* responsibilities. They were faced with two sets of issues: one concerning the actual work, and another concerning the infrastructure of the country. The Egyptians created a group of *planners* whose sole purpose was to deal with the issue of personnel required to do the labor. In today's parlance, these individuals were **human resource managers**. The list the human resource managers might have created for the project's job openings would include:

- 1,000 road builders
- 6,000 masons
- 2,000 boatmen
- 1,500 sculptors
- 2,000 earthmovers
- Three guys with fans to keep the *planners* cool

This list became a list of questions that address issues of cultural infrastructure:

- Where are we going to find them?
- How do we get them where we need them?
- How much will we pay them?
- Where will they live?
- How will we feed them?
- How will we keep them happy?

The question was: Which list is more important? The lists went hand in hand and for each job category, the same set of questions had to be answered. The science of **logistics** was born.

The *planners* were faced with another thorny problem. Even a casual observer would note this was quite a *gang* of people. How will we organize them all? The Egyptians figured it out and coined the word gang, which consisted of about 100 workers. The gangs were organized into *houses*. The houses were part of an ankh or symbol, which represented a god. Gods, houses, gangs, and workers—the structure looked like a modern organizational chart. See Figure 2-4.

Figure 2-4   *Organization chart carved in stone*

The list of benefits derived from this organization includes:

- A common method of organization across the entire project
- The clear establishment of responsibilities and authority
- A common terminology to describe the organization

- Uniform rules of behavior and expectations
- Methods for giving directions and reporting progress
- The creation of a chain of command

The Egyptians also allowed each gang to select its leader by electing the *head-man*. The headman was expected to ensure the best working conditions for the gang. Failure to do so would cause a recall and a new headman would be elected.

This representation had far-reaching effects. Egypt would reorganize its entire political, religious, and cultural infrastructure around this structure. The representation would also serve as a model for many future generations and cultures. The first glimmers of a republic and a democracy were born with the idea of electing a headman.

The Egyptians created the whole concept of organization and placed its rules, literally, *in stone*.

2.2.4 Locations *(where)*

The location of Giza was convenient for the Pharaoh. Giza was just a stone's throw from the capital city of Inebhedj, later renamed Memphis. (*It seems kings always live just outside Memphis.*) In those days, a stone's throw was thirty-forty miles. That would be about a half-day's travel by horse or chariot from Memphis. Two days would be required if travel was by foot.

Giza was located outside the flood plain. The Egyptians had experience building outside the flood plain and were already familiar with the physical conditions of the area. In a previous dynasty, the Step Pyramid had been built for King Djoser (c. 2650 B.C.E.–2631 B.C.E.), the first King of the Third Dynasty. The Step Pyramid was completed at least 100 years before Khufu, Pharoah of the Great Pyramid, was born and is the world's oldest stone building of its size.

What was convenient for the Pharaoh was inconvenient for everyone else. The proposed site of the pyramid was not the only site with which *planners* had to contend. Each site involved created its own set of problems. The list of site locations probably looked like this:

- Giza
- Support cities
- Stone quarries
- Ports
- Roads
- Shipbuilding sites

Giza

The Great Pyramid is 481 feet high and, until the construction of the Eiffel Tower, was the tallest building in the world. It covers over thirteen square acres and its base has a length of approximately 750 feet (two-and-one-half American football fields). It contains over 2.4 million stone blocks, weighing an average of 5,000 pounds each. Until about 300 B.C.E., Giza was covered in limestone and alabaster, making the sides perfectly smooth.

Preparing a site for a building of this size and magnitude was difficult. Tasks included the following:

- Grade to horizon. See Figure 2-5. To do this, one should stand in the center of the lot; draw a circle with a radius 1.25 to 1.5 times longer than the size of the base.
- Go to the perimeter of that circle and drive a stake into the ground.
- Tie a long piece of string onto the stake about 1 inch above the ground.
- Walk to the other side of the circle, exactly opposite the first stake. Repeat the process to make the string taut. Very long stakes are needed to handle the pressure of the taut string.
- Start removing all the dirt that prevents the string from becoming taut. With the stakes 1,000 feet apart, the string will be resting on the ground in the middle.
- Remove the dirt and tighten the string until it is completely taut and level. The result will be a huge pit that is flat across the bottom. Without this step, the building will be incapable of standing.

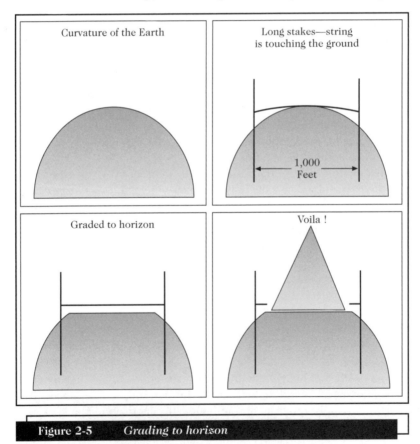

Figure 2-5   *Grading to horizon*

The Egyptians discovered and compensated for the curvature of the earth using this process of grading to horizon. They did not have the benefit of protractors, slide rules, multiplication, long division, the number zero, or the number *pi*. The Greeks would not invent geometry for another 1,200 years. Sir Issac Newton (1642–1727) would not invent physics for another 4,000 years or so.

The size of the building blocks had to be uniform. The base blocks measured approximately $5 \times 5 \times 6$ feet. However, the Egyptians did not deal in feet and inches, which were an English invention created under King Henry VIII (1491–1547). The Egyptians had to create a set of standard measures to construct the blocks. Those measures had to deal with everything from units of length, height, and weight to increments of time.

The Egyptians created the idea of metrics. When the Pharaoh asked, "How's it going?" he wanted and received a precise answer, such as "We have completed laying 2 million of the estimated 2.4 million stone blocks."

Without establishing this system of metrics, the *planners* and managers could not know what was happening. They needed answers to the questions of how much, how many, and how long. Today's management dictum, "You can't manage what you can't measure," was discovered more than 4,000 years ago and put into practice on a grand scale.

AN INTERESTING COINCIDENCE...

The Great Pyramid at the base is 36,524 inches long. The solar year is 365.24 days. Is this size a coincidence? This is just another mystery of the pyramids.

The *planners* of the Great Pyramid needed to deal with capacity planning. Before work could start on the pyramids, they needed to answer questions, such as: What was to be done with all the sand, dirt, and gravel taken out of the pit? How many workers were required to move all that dirt? How many tools, animals, gallons of water, loaves of bread, and latrines were required? How did the workforce get to and from the work sites?

They also had to prepare the site, understanding that they needed to grade to horizon. The Egyptians realized that no matter what needs to be done first, something else needs to be done beforehand. In fact, the site preparation task demonstrated to the *planners* the basic concept of an **event**, which would have to be planned, prioritized, scheduled, and managed. Thinking about the requirements of site location opened a Pandora's box of other concerns (though the Greeks would not create the story of Pandora for another 2,000 years). One of the thorniest problems was what to do with all those workers when they were not working.

The Egyptians did not have four tools that would have helped them build the pyramids: iron tools, the industrial wheel, the fulcrum, and an alphabet-based language.

IRON TOOLS

The tools used in the construction of the pyramids were fashioned from stone, wood, sand, and copper. These materials had short life spans and were in need of constant replacement. The copper tools (with an edge) were especially short lived. This created the need for a new industry—tool manufacturing.

This industry was created and placed into the supply chain for the project, with the entire infrastructure required to support, encourage, and monitor its growth. The problem of no iron tools was not caused by the unavailability of raw material, but rather the inability to create enough heat to melt iron ore and the inability to handle anything that hot.

THE INDUSTRIAL WHEEL

The myth that the Egyptians did not have the wheel during the building of the pyramids may be incorrect. Early hieroglyphics show chariots and two-wheeled carts. However, they did not have the heavy-duty, four-wheeled cart capable of transporting a massive stone block weighing several tons, and they did not have the axle. This is significant given the other problems they over-came. The secret of the axle baffled them and caused them to create a workaround, the sled.

THE FULCRUM

The early hieroglyphics depict workers using levers as pries to help move the massive blocks. This is very inefficient, as Archimedes (287 B.C.E.–212 B.C.E.) would calculate and demonstrate 1,000 years later. As Archimedes would state, "Give me a long enough lever and a fulcrum and I can move the world." Again, it is quite interesting that given all the other problems the Egyptians solved, this one remained beyond their grasp.

AN ALPHABET-BASED LANGUAGE

The Egyptians did not have a writing system based on an alphabet. They used pictures. This is surprising given that nearly 1,000 years before the Egyptians, the Sumerians invented an alphabet called cuneiform. The alphabet was so named because of the sharp tool used to impress the letters into clay tablets.

The Sumerians invented a standard symbol set, syntax, and a vocabulary. The Sumerians are also credited with the oldest known literature, The Epic of Gilgamesh, which was written circa 1200 B.C.E. The epic is a collection of myths about Gilgamesh, a king who lived 7,000 years ago and did not want to die.

The Egyptians discovered that building the pyramids caused new words and ideas to be created. Lack of an alphabet meant they had to create a new picture, which caused a communication problem. They had no dictionary. They did not

(continued)

create an enduring literature. Over time, people forgot what the pictures meant. The pictures could be so abstract; they defied translation.

Pictures make it difficult, if not impossible, to express a tense. Lastly, while an alphabet-based language requires little skill other than knowing how to form the letters and words, pictures require artists. Those artists had to commit to memory the thousands of pictures that made up the language.

The Egyptian hieroglyphic system consisted of 6,000 basic symbols representing either things or sounds. The system was difficult to remember and teach to others. Hieroglyphics were also inflexible. The hieroglyphics remained undecipherable until 1822, when a French linguistics expert cracked the code after working on the Rosetta Stone for eighteen years. The mastery, intelligence, ingenuity, and brilliance of the ancients remained a mystery for years.

Support Cities

At Giza, the Egyptians erected a temporary city to house 25,000 people. What do you do with the trash, waste, and sewage produced by 25,000 people every day? Here is a list of other concerns the *planners* had to address before they could build the city, grade to horizon, and build the pyramid:

- Where should the city be located?
- How many people would the city support?
- How would they supply food and water?
- How could they keep the populace safe?
- How could they keep the populace entertained?
- How long would it take to build?

Other concerns included how big to make each dwelling, how to divide the town around the organizational concepts, how many shops to build, and how many services to provide. The list is almost endless. These problems were not confined to Giza, but were common to all pyramid-building sites. The Egyptians applied their intelligence and ingenuity to the problems and created a new science: civil engineering. As the Egyptians created this new science, they again *carved its rules in stone*.

Even a casual review of the list of concerns or questions reveals that each question creates more questions. This is the point of the list. A *planner* is charged with figuring out all that *stuff*. What a *planner* cannot answer forces an assumption. A misassumption can have devastating consequences.

A *planner* should not make assumptions. Assumptions are an art. Planning, the way the Egyptians did, is a science. When the *planners* did not have an answer, they found someone who did. This meant the *planners* had to work with many others, including the architects, *designers*, and *builders*, as well as the other *planners*. Involving so many people in the endeavor created a huge communication problem. Information could be shared only by writing hieroglyphics on papyrus.

COMMUNICATION

We know the Egyptians did not use an alphabet-based writing system. As it turns out, a picture-writing system is not all bad. Consider the example of the block. In a hieroglyphic system, a block represents a *block*. By simply putting the standard unit of measure on each face of the block, they created a blueprint. When they added a number at the top that signified the total quantity required, they created an order to build.

Give the hieroglyphic to stonecutters and they have no further questions about how many or what size and shape. Manufacturing stones becomes an issue of keeping score. On the same hieroglyphic, place a symbol for an amount and a symbol for a time frame, like the statement *100 a day*, and a work schedule is produced. From this information, the stonecutter *planner* can determine how long it will take to quarry and shape each stone and how many stonecutters will be required to produce 100 blocks a day. All of this information can be derived from a single hieroglyphic.

To extend this metaphor, make a picture showing six men with levers and six men pushing a stone block on one side, and a sled and twenty men catching and lowering the stone onto the sled on the other side. This hieroglyphic now explains how the stone will be transported. The hieroglyphic also shows the size of the work crew and the tools required to get the stone positioned. This method of communication allowed anyone to get on with the job at hand.

Of course, as the concepts get more elaborate, the hieroglyphics grow in complexity and number to express more profound ideas. However, at many levels, a hieroglyphic is a powerful tool for communication. When a basic hieroglyphic system is tied to an alphabet-based writing system, the most powerful communication system is created. This concept is intrinsic to the Zachman Framework.

2.2.5 Materials *(what)*

Here is a list of materials required for the pyramid enterprise:

- 2,400,000 granite blocks
- 100,000 limestone blocks
- 25,000 alabaster blocks
- 5,000 chisels
- 5,000 hammers
- Another three large feather fans

Think about the complexity of locating, producing, and delivering these materials to Giza. This list does not begin to include all the items that were probably required. As previously discussed, each item creates its own set of infrastructure problems. Not only did the materials *planners* have to figure out where to get everything, they had to solve the problems of storage and management. These *planners* also had to address the issues of who is paying and how.

Once again, the Egyptians figured out the real problems and reduced the subject to one of accountability. **Materials management** included and required input from all the *planners*. The *planners* needed to assign responsibility and accountability for the expenditure and use of the resources.

The materials *planners* determined they could not actually do any of the work, scheduling, or design themselves. They may not have been strong, but they were smart. They could keep count and figure out how much everything cost. They figured out how to keep track of all the things that were essential and part and parcel of this enterprise. Although the Pharaoh had all the money, he still wanted to know "How much?"

To the Egyptians, materials management was essentially keeping track of all the **assets**. To do this, they invented accounting. They accounted for everything from the number of bushels of wheat required to feed any given village, to the number of blocks quarried every day from every site. Literally nothing got past their scope. They counted, calculated, and reported to the Pharaoh on a regular basis exactly *how much*.

From this information, the Pharaoh knew how much was needed in taxes and tribute and how much would have to be garnered from conquering neighboring territories. Egyptians also invented another concept to help reduce the expense of the enterprise: the state-owned monopoly.

The first and most important of the state-owned monopolies were the quarries. The Pharaoh owned all the quarries, as he did the shipbuilding industry, the mines, the tool manufacturing, and the roads. As a result, theft was considered to be an extremely serious offense. The materials managers counted everything to make sure nothing was missing, and woe to the manager who let something walk away.

The need to manage created the concept of standard laws. The Pharaoh delegated authority and responsibility, and recorded those laws, setting a standard for how people were to be punished. Stealing a hammer was equally punishable everywhere in Egypt.

A law is based on a science and is irrefutable because it is based on what is currently known or believed to be true—both of which can change. A law cannot be broken until the basic underlying science is changed. For instance, gravity predicts that things fall down. This is a law. The only way this law will change is if gravity behaves differently, or the language is changed, and another word is substituted for *down*.

Section 2.2.2 presented a list of six ideas for motivation. This was a list of laws. By restating that list and changing just a few words, the implication of a mandate becomes clear:

- Some person or organization was determined and dedicated.
- The culture of the populace embraced, accepted, or tolerated the undertaking.
- Resources and technology were adequate for the project, and the experts believed they could figure out the unknown.
- There was a high degree of confidence for success in a reasonable amount of time.
- Money was available to finance the effort.
- Leadership had the authorization to discipline, reward, or punish to ensure compliance.

These six laws are irrefutable for the science of doing a project. Take away or violate even one of these laws and the entire project may collapse. The six laws are the basic physics of the concept of enterprise architecture, and all succeeding concepts and uses can be easily tracked back to these laws.

Laws are not adequate to ensure compliance. To ensure action, you need rules of compliance, which articulate exactly how the law will be obeyed. An example is the U.S. law requiring payment of income taxes. That is the law. To ensure compliance with that law, the Congress had to prepare a list of rules called the U.S. Tax Code. This list is so long and so complex, no one person knows it all. Instead, the tax code demands specialists, each of whom is an expert in particular areas of the rules.

Rules are not irrefutable. They may be challenged and changed as circumstances warrant. However, any challenges or changes must comply with the present-day laws of motivation. Another set of rules is far subtler. These are rules of behavior, which do not demand compliance. They speak instead to how people think and act and they are rooted in culture and education. Rules of behavior address the issues associated with a discipline.

The concept of law is rooted in science. For example, a prescribed punishment would be a rule of compliance to enforce the idea that stealing is bad. This example could be a law because it is rooted in the science of civics.

2.2.6 Building Processes *(how)*

The Egyptians used hieroglyphics on a stone block to create three things: a blueprint, a production order, and a production schedule. The hieroglyphics do not convey exactly how that stone block was to be produced. To convey this concept, the Egyptians realized the pyramid was essentially an **end state**, and to achieve the end, many steps were required. Each step had a life of its own with a logical start and end, and each step had smaller steps until, at some point, no smaller steps were needed. At the lowest step, a term was required to describe it, as well as a hieroglyphic to accurately express it.

Next, the smallest steps had to be assembled in order to give a pictorial context and content to the overall process. This was made much more difficult by the hieroglyphic system because the hieroglyphics could be assembled from three directions: left to right, right to left, and top to bottom. Once again, the Egyptians solved these problems.

The smallest step was essentially called a basic or primitive process. This term held great power for the Egyptians. At this low level, a single hieroglyphic conveyed the exact nature of the work. For instance, if the sides of a block had to be made smooth, a hieroglyphic was created showing the workers grinding the block using sand and a pestle.

The hieroglyphic also showed two states and a process of transformation—the rough state, the grinding process that was the transformation, and the final smooth state. In addition, the other exposed sides of the block were all pictured smooth.

The next problem to overcome was how to give the sense of order of all the primitive processes to the total process. For example, if the total number of primitive processes needed to make a single block was seven, what should be the order of those primitive processes? The order was not always intuitively obvious. The Egyptians created a literary device. They positioned the central character facing the direction from which the hieroglyphics were to be read and the number of the sequence order in the same position on every hieroglyphic in that set. See Figure 2-6.

Figure 2-6   *Hieroglyphics are interpreted in the direction the characters face*

In a masterstroke, the Egyptians created what today are called the **task model** and the **process model**. These two basic concepts are today part of **industrial engineering**. They also placed the rules for this new science *in stone*.

THE TOMB'S SHAPE

Does any other naturally occurring structure look like a pyramid? You can see the answer in any sandbox or on any beach in the world. Pour sand and it naturally forms a cone. The size and shape of that cone depend on the amount of sand poured. The texture, shape, hardness, and density of the sand determine the base and slope of the cone. The slope and the base stay in that exact ratio forever.

As you pour more sand on the top, the sand slides down the slope to the base until the laws of physics governing that motion are satisfied. The size of the cone is theoretically infinite, constrained only by the amount of room available at the base and the amount of material available to heap onto the pile.

Think of the intellectual leap necessary to get from a cone to a pyramid. The same laws of physics apply to both shapes. By changing the nature of the material going onto the pile, the shape is changed and a cone with square sides is realized.

By the time the Egyptians got around to building the Great Pyramid, they had over 100 years of experience in construction, all in the great plain of Giza. The very first pyramid was the Step Pyramid. The successful construction of this pyramid demonstrated the basic physics of the shape and its practicality.

The next pyramid was the Red Pyramid. This pyramid had a basic design flaw. The architect did not understand the geometry of the pyramid and halfway up, the architect had to correct the angle of the slope. The correction was to accommodate the imposed laws of geometry relative to the physics.

If the slope had not been altered, the pyramid would not have been stable and would have crumbled, regardless of the building materials. The architects did

(continued)

not understand the issue of grading to horizon, which further worsened the problem. The corrected slope had to account for the fan effect caused by going higher.

By the time of the Great Pyramid, the architects had learned all these lessons, and recorded them in stone. They understood the geometry based in physics and why the shape had to be that shape. They did not have other options.

Thinking about the pyramids in this manner tends to demystify them, even though popular culture wants to apply a mystical shroud on them and the people who created and built them. This is most unfortunate and diminishes the value of the real accomplishment. Forty-five hundred years ago, a creative civilization looked at the challenge and collectively said, "We can do this." And they did.

 ### 2.2.7 My Cousin, the Pharaoh *(when)*

By happenstance, the chief architect, Imhotep, was the Pharaoh's cousin. He was responsible for making sure whatever Khufu wanted, Khufu got, at least as far as buildings were concerned.

Imhotep probably never saw the request coming the day Khufu invited him to lunch. After all, they were cousins and saw each other often. He was probably looking forward to the feast of fatted camel haunch roasted with salt and honey, flat bread, mashed beans and greens, prepared as only the Pharaoh's cooks knew how. And then the request was laid on him. "Cousin, build me a pyramid for my tomb."

Khufu was still a young man and yet he was ordering a tomb over lunch. A dizzying amount of questions probably flooded Imhotep's mind. Perhaps the most important question was, "When does it have to be finished?" Imhotep was really asking about the health of his cousin. Khufu's response must have been, "The tomb has to be ready for me by the time I die." Khufu wanted to be assured he would get the tomb and that the structure would be completed before his death.

Therefore, the tomb had to be built in twenty-five years. This was a drop-dead date taken to its logical extreme. The Pharaoh was in a race against the clock, meaning the architect was in that exact same race. The Pharaoh had the power to command and he made his cousin personally responsible for the success of the tomb.

Both were intelligent men, but only one of them was a god. Imhotep knew what he had to do and how he had to do it. Nothing less than the world's largest pyramid would be adequate. Money was not the issue. Location was not the issue. Time was the only issue. Everything else would be forced to comply with the drop-dead date.

Imhotep's first list may have looked like this:

- What is the last task to do?
- What is the first task to do?
- What are the tasks that have to be done between the first and last tasks?
- Who can I get to help me?
- How do I keep my cousin happy?
- How many fan bearers do I need to keep me cool while I do this?

This tomb was an immense undertaking. Not only did Imhotep have to resolve what came first and last, he had to come to grips with how each was dependent on the other, and how much time each thing would take. Additionally, he still had to design the tomb. He realized if he did not resolve all the other matters, the design would quickly become a moot point. Imhotep's life depended on his own success.

Imhotep may have started his thought process with sealing the tomb and the final clean-up. In other words, he could have focused on the final series of events required for the *undertaking*.[3] Alternatively, his thinking may have focused on the first event—site selection for the pyramid.

He might have tried to tackle the problem from both ends at the same time. In any event, he had to keep his cousin, Khufu, informed of what he was doing. Khufu and Imhotep may have started to schedule regular power lunches to discuss progress. *McCamel and fries anyone?*

Whatever Imhotep ultimately decided to do, he discovered a new science if for no other reason than to save his life. That science was logistics, and that science answers all questions about the scheduling and timing of events.

As chief architect, Imhotep probably visited Giza and spent a long time studying the area. He had to have a complete understanding of the site. Nothing could be overlooked. Once he was familiar with the site he could begin the design of the Great Pyramid. This is exactly the way architects work today.

After studying the site and the basic design and building issues, he had to figure out what came next. A serious amount of infrastructure would be required. Each aspect of the total enterprise would have to work with and understand each other aspect. The timing of each event became crucial. Because he had an absolute drop-dead date, he must have worked backwards.

Imhotep was faced with a serious time problem. He had to figure out all the major steps of the total project, how each step depended on every other step, the maximum amount of time each step could take, the general processes required, and the number of people required for each step. One person could not handle all of these responsibilities. He first figured out the general things that needed to be done and in what order. Then he enlisted others to help review all the other relevant matters.

Imhotep discovered the concept of an event. An event, for our purposes, is a step or action that must be accomplished. The first event in the construction of the Great Pyramid was planning. Therefore, Imhotep discovered that the construction would require events. Events were dependent on other events. Each event spawned subordinate events. Each subordinate event would create its own time requirements.

Many different events could go on at the same time, and each of these events was part of a much larger set of events. Each event had to be performed and accomplished in the allotted amount of time. Timing was everything, especially with a drop-dead date. The concept of timing drives all the current business challenges of time-to-market.

Logistics made getting the right people in the right place and doing the right work with the right things, at the right time, for the right reasons, at the right cost a little easier to manage. Imhotep extended the science of logistics to include the concept of critical path method (CPM).

Not one block of stone was quarried before the tomb was designed. Getting the men, materials, and equipment to show up at the same time was no easy task. Both CPM and the Gantt chart are two essential techniques used to support the science of logistics. The Egyptians put all these concepts and sciences into practice 4,500 years ago. See Figure 2-7.

Figure 2-7 *They're fine, but there's just something about this one that bothers me*

2.2.8 Key Terms

aspect

asset

building process

critical path method (CPM)

culture

deliverable

end state

event

Gantt chart

human resource manager

industrial engineering

infrastructure

location

logistics

material

materials management

methodology

motivation

organization

process model

task model

timing coordination

2.2.9 Review Questions

1. In what part of their planning did the Egyptians discover the concept of an event? What did they realize would need to be done in relation to that event? How does the concept of an event affect the enterprise today?

2. When considering the issue of cultural infrastructure during the building of the pyramid, what would be a similar example of this issue in today's enterprise?

3. Suppose that in addition to a hieroglyphic system of communication, the Egyptians had had an alphabet-based writing system. What effect, if any, might that have had on the project?

4. What three tools allow the *planner* to create a repeatable methodology?

5. The list of six ideas (laws) included as motivation for the pyramid project became the basic physics of enterprise architecture. What would happen to a project today if one of these laws was taken away? Why?

6. From what aspects is it important to examine the creation and construction of the pyramids? How could these same six aspects be used in project management today?

SECTION 2.3 WHERE THEY CAME TO PRAY — THE CATHEDRAL OF CHARTRES

QUESTIONS TO CONTEMPLATE

1. What assumptions have you created about taking this class?
2. How can the lists for the Cathedral and the pyramids be applied to today's enterprise?
3. What happens when the culture does not embrace an idea?

2.3.1 Introduction

When undertaking any project, you typically make assumptions, possibly because you are not willing to invest the time and energy to thoroughly work through an issue, or because you assume all related issues are well understood.

In the early stages of any project, if an **assumption** turns out to be incorrect, or the number of assumptions made is too numerous, there is an increased chance that a serious problem will affect the later phases of the effort. Sometimes these mistakes have dire consequences. Assumptions are **implicit** in nature because you do not examine the issue, nor do you present any form of proof to support your assumption. Lastly, a **misassumption** of one aspect may cause a misassumption of another aspect.

The antonym of implicit is **explicit**. When something is made explicit, the possibility of misunderstanding is reduced. Explicitness also decreases risk. Explicitness helps to examine and understand an issue. Explicitness helps create supporting proof and **documentation** that can be saved and shared.

The greater the number of things explicitly understood and documented in the early phases of a project, the greater the potential for success. The general nature of the discipline of being explicit sets a tone for the entire project. If every phase of a project and every step within a phase are made explicit, upon completion of the project, a thorough historical record is available. This record may be used as both a benchmark and a guide for future efforts.

Abbot Suger (pronounced "sue-jay") is believed to have been born at or near Saint-Denis in France in 1081, and he died some seventy years later close to where he was born. The Abbot lived during the Dark Ages, a period in Europe's history that began in the eighth century and lasted until the early fifteenth century.

Times were hard, and being born a peasant offered little chance of living the good life. In the twelfth century, Abbot Suger helped establish the Gothic era of architecture and was responsible for building the Cathedral of Chartres. His accomplishments were significant, especially at a time when the predominate way of life was either to farm or go off to war.

Europe was suffering under a feudal system of government. The basic premise of a feudal system is the ongoing ignorance of the population. An ignorant population is easy to control and keep tied to the land. Other premises include rule by force of arms and the edict to make nearly every crime punishable by death. Every peasant was also penalized with a heavy tax burden. These premises worked for a long time and allowed the nobility to indulge themselves. The peasants had no way to improve their lives and none would be offered.

During this period, advancing science was not encouraged, especially if the science in any way challenged the beliefs of the church. To propose anything that challenged the correctness or authority of the church was heresy and had only one punishment—death.

There was no literature. Why would there be when so few people could read or write? Even if someone could write and dared to write a book, how would that book be produced and distributed? There was no moveable type printing press. That would not come along until 1450. If someone did write a book that challenged the government or church, well just refer to the previous paragraph.

Life for most was bleak during the Dark Ages. As bad as the twelfth century was, the thirteenth would be worse. The thirteenth was the century of the plague. Government brutality bordered on the barbaric. Most of Europe was ruled by greed, ignorance, and stupidity. Life for the average person was quite dismal and oppressive. Oppressive rulers and disease were the order of the day.

The story of the Cathedral of Chartres demonstrates the devastating effects of misassumption. Fortunately, in this case, the outcome became a positive milestone in a dark age. Chartres was the first of the great Gothic cathedrals. The project ushered in new art and music forms, building processes, architecture, uses of technology, and science and engineering principles. The cathedral established a style and tone that would endure for several centuries. The efforts to build the Cathedral of Chartres opened new doors of exploration and thought.

Historians point to the building of Chartres as the single event that began to pull Europe out of the Dark Ages. Approximately 200 years later, the Renaissance began. Chartres was the event that started the intellectual reawakening of Europe. See Figure 2-8.

| Figure 2-8 | *Cathedral of Chartres* |

2.3.2 A Main Thoroughfare *(where)*

The town of Chartres was a crossroads town, ninety kilometers from Paris. The village was the intersection for those traveling to and from Paris and to and from Tours and Le Mans. East or west, north or south, travelers passed through Chartres. As such, the town of Chartres flourished.

The old church burned to the ground in 1134, a grim year. It was a large Romanesque church built of wood and stone. Once the blaze started, no one could do anything to stop it. Enter Abbot Suger.

A leading cleric, Abbot Suger established the Gothic movement that was the precursor of the Renaissance. He had just completed building the church at Saint-Denis when the Chartres church burned to the ground. Where everyone else saw tragedy, the Abbot saw **opportunity**.

The Abbot went to Chartres and surveyed the destruction and the site. Other than the fact that the site was situated on a hill, he believed the site was perfect. Moreover, the land had already been prepared and graded. Abbot Suger believed the area was easily accessible and could hold a substantial structure. These factors made the site perfect for his new church.

There are three major reasons why Abbot Suger wanted to build a new church at Chartres:

- Chartres was a major crossroads.
- The site was prepared.
- Craftsmen could get there.

In the eyes of Abbot Suger, this opportunity was heaven sent. All he had to do was convince the Holy See and the King to support and fund the building of the new church. Abbot Suger was an articulate man and had no problem getting the approving nod from both men.

When deciding to build a great cathedral, Abbot Suger made the following assumptions:

- The church and royalty would provide adequate funding for the entire project, provided as needed.
- The building processes were understood and had been mastered.
- The building site was perfect and prepared.
- The French craftsmen could provide an adequate supply of workers with the correct skills required to do the tasks at hand.
- A complete understanding of the order and duration of each step of the building process existed.
- Everyone wanted this great cathedral, so support would be ongoing until completion.

Abbot Suger's list of assumptions represents the complete spectrum of information that should be made explicit in any project. Each assumption played a role in the completion of the cathedral. However, not all of his assumptions were correct.

Figure 2-9 shows where Chartres is located in France. The building site was not as perfect as he believed. It sat on a hill. This is a good thing if you are interested in a view. This is a terrible thing if you have to move very heavy materials up that hill. Seasons make matters even worse. Winter brought freezing temperatures and snow, often making the roads impassable. As winter turned into spring, heavy rains and warmer temperatures caused any remaining snow to rapidly melt, turning the dirt roads of Chartres into quagmires. Getting up that hill was no easy task. The horse collar was not yet invented, so using draft animals was not an option.

The site problems would be one of the contributing factors that caused the building process to last thirty-three years. To help alleviate the transportation problem, the local royalty, the lords and ladies, pitched in by helping to haul the wagons up that hill, but not in the early spring or winter. The nobility did this as an act of contrition and faith. This cathedral was being raised in glory to God, a most noble cause, so the nobility had to do their share. They also helped pay for the church.

Most of the work was done by peasants for a day's meager wages. The average peasant was every bit as illiterate as the average Egyptian worker who preceded them by 4,000 years. The location of the site was handy. It was easy to get to and therefore workers could find their way despite their inability to read the few posted road signs.

Figure 2-9 *Location of Chartres*

The Abbot assumed the new church would be built on the existing footpad of the old church. Site preparation became a rather simple matter of clearing away debris and performing a final leveling. Or so the *planners* thought. Eventually, this misassumption would have a devastating impact and add two years to the building process.

As masons built the west portal, the higher they built, fitting and leveling the great stones became more difficult. They could not make the windows fit. The building was settling. The foundation was not adequate to support the great weight.

There was only one thing to do—tear it down, stone by stone, and rebuild it. This is exactly what they did. The foundation site was reworked about seven meters forward and the west portal was rebuilt. The masons used cement in the construction. Imagine the problems they had in separating those heavy stones. Once separated, the masons had to chip off every trace of cement before they could reuse the stones. It was much more difficult to take the stones apart than it was to put them together. Generally, undoing something is more difficult than doing something right the first time.

In the long run, this weighty error would turn out to be a blessing. Late in the century, a fire rampaged the church. The 7-meter difference created by the mistake resulted in a large foyer between the entrance and the actual church. The fire did not destroy the west portal, the walls, or the roof. As serious as the fire was, the building was not totally devastated and could be rebuilt.

2.3.3 Glory to God *(why)*

To begin this discussion, review the motivation list from the previous section on the Great Pyramid:

- The Pharaoh was determined and dedicated to have his tomb.
- The culture of the populace embraced, accepted, or tolerated an undertaking. This particular idea was embraced.
- Resources and technology were adequate for the undertaking. Experts believed they could figure out the unknown.
- There was a high degree of confidence for success in a reasonable amount of time. Failure was not an option.
- The Pharaoh had the money to finance the undertaking.
- The Pharaoh had the force of arms to ensure compliance with his wishes.

At the heart of the list, six issues are addressed:

- Someone with authority and responsibility wants something done and has the strength of purpose, power, and dedication to see it through.
- The culture will cooperate with that person and work to ensure the completion of the task.
- The basic processes, are known and understood; technology exists to facilitate those processes, and what is not known can be figured out along the way.
- The undertaking can be completed in a reasonable amount of time.
- The money exists to finance the undertaking.
- A location exists that is appropriate for the undertaking.

After completing the church at Saint-Denis, Abbot Suger was looking around for something new to do when the opportunity at Chartres presented itself. Abbot Suger invented Gothic architecture. His first attempt to develop this radical new style was at Saint-Denis and although the project was very successful, the structure did not fulfill his vision.

What he saw was a church with great open spaces, full of light, and decorated with great art that would truly express the glory to God. The glory to God would be his ultimate reason and motivation for moving forward with the project. He indeed had a divine inspiration.

At Saint-Denis, the architect employed by Abbot Suger proved the practicality of the arch. What Abbot Suger now wanted was something much bigger than Saint-Denis. To build something much larger, Abbot Suger's architect invented the flying buttress—a breakthrough in design. See Figure 2-10. The flying buttress embodied the early discoveries of the Egyptians regarding distribution of weight.

Figure 2-10   *Flying buttress*

The arch and flying buttress could support the great weight of a very large roof. Creating a larger roof allowed the architect to design a larger open space. The higher a roof is built, the larger that roof can be. The arch eliminated the need for internal columns. The flying buttress eliminated the need for massive external walls. These two elements created a building that had a very large, open space with large windows to let in light. The laws of physics determined the mathematics and engineering requirements of the cathedral.

Abbot Suger had other inspirations. He wanted this church to be adorned, inside and out, with great art. He commissioned the construction of great sculpted columns, marvelous painted windows, and spires rising up to touch heaven. The Abbot believed God was the great geometer and geometry made the cathedral possible. Therefore, he paid tribute to God by placing a painted glass window in His honor on the east wall.

Abbot Suger was a man of vision and insight, an anomaly at that time in history, and he wanted Chartres to be a center of intellectual thought. Chartres was dedicated to the study of the Greeks: Plato, Aristotle, Euripides, Archimedes, and Euclid, to name a few. The Abbot had lofty intentions at a time when neither great art nor great thought was encouraged.

The following list summarizes the motivation model Abbot Suger used:

- The king, the nobility, the church, and Abbot Suger were dedicated to this project and willing to see it through.
- A large pool of craftsmen and laborers were willing to work on this project for pay, and the nobility were willing to contribute labor for free.

- The arithmetic and geometry needed for this project were well understood and all the building procedures were well established. In addition, the technology existed to facilitate the construction.
- The time frame for completion was appropriate. The original estimate for the building construction was twenty years.
- The king, the nobility, and the church would provide the funding through tithing and taxing.
- Chartres was considered a perfect place for the new cathedral.

2.3.4 Building the Cathedral *(how)*

The breakthrough of the arch and flying buttress precipitated a new approach to how the cathedral would be built. While the weight distribution principles of the pyramid caused the design and construction to be from the inside out, the weight distribution of the arch and flying buttress required design and construction to be from the outside in. These were radical concepts in 1130. See Figure 2-11.

Figure 2-11   *Flying buttresses at Chartres*

No wall could be constructed until the flying buttresses were in place. Although the area size and pitch of the roof were calculated, no real work could be started until both the walls and flying buttresses were complete. The flying buttresses could not be started until the site had been properly prepared for them.

All known technology had to be employed. The basic design and use of scaffolding would be forced to evolve. Scaffolding would have to provide temporary support until the concrete hardened and the stones would stay in place. The supporting scaffolding used the same principles of weight distribution as the flying buttress. The nature of the use of the hoist was altered, and the block and tackle were added.

2.3.5 Raw Materials and Tools *(what)*

Abbot Suger had everything going for him. He had the location. He had the vision. He knew what he wanted to build and he had agreement from the prevailing powers.

What he needed next was money. The Abbot was a frugal and wealthy man, but he was not planning on spending his own money. He needed other people's money. He identified several sources of supply:

- The church
- The king
- The nobility
- The peasants

The church was positive it could provide adequate funding from donations and tithing. The king knew he could contribute through taxation, extortion, and coercion. The nobility knew they could help finance the project by raising the rents on their land holdings. The peasants knew they had to contribute because they had no choice.

In the end, the peasants paid for everything. Nobody asked the peasants if they wanted or needed this church. The decision was not theirs to make. This is another basic tenet of a feudal government. The people have no choice. In today's society, public ventures are financed the same way—through taxing and contribution. However, the contemporary populace has some choice, though the government still taxes us whether we want it or not.

In the mind of the Abbot, there was no risk, only reward. This undertaking was for the glory to God, which was the same basic motivation as the Great Pyramid. Even better, Abbot Suger could build the cathedral with other people's money.

Here is a list he might have made of needed resources:

- Money
- Materials
- People
- Technology
- Know-how
- Support

Abbot Suger had a plan to get them all, and get them all he did. The existing technology of the day provided Abbot Suger with the following:

- Heavy metal tools made of iron and steel
- An industrial axle capable of supporting heavy weights
- An industrial wheel that was iron rimmed
- Greek arithmetic
- The lever and fulcrum
- The block and tackle
- The hoist
- Scaffolding
- Glass-making capabilities
- Cement

With money, the Abbot would need to pay skilled artisans who could understand the technology and employ it. Here is a list of artisans Abbot Suger needed:

- Masons
- Artists
- Laborers

- Architects
- Designers
- Managers
- Guards

One reason Chartres was an ideal site was that the village lay at a crossroads. Abbot Suger knew the people he would need could get there. He did not have to worry about their transportation. In those days, the workers were responsible for their own transportation, housing, tools, and basic equipment. See Figure 2-12.

Figure 2-12 *Handyman wanted*

He also knew people needed work and what better way to employ their skills than a project committed to the glory to God. The fact that he was paying the workers was almost of secondary concern to Abbot Suger. Moreover, for what he needed, only the best would do. Wanting the best created competition for the work, and the competition drove down the cost of the labor. There were no unions and the existing early guilds had little or no influence on either the contractors or the workers. This was good for the nobles and lousy for the workers.

Abbot Suger's master designer-mason was well paid. The Abbot recognized genius when he saw it and he wanted this mason to complete the whole job. Unlike the mason, the Abbot would not live to see the completion of the church.

The genius that figured out the flying buttress also created the basic building process and carved almost all of the columns on the west portal. At the time of its construction, the west portal was unique. It was the first time the supporting columns were made into works of art and great sculpture. Even the sculpture of the statues was new. It was the first time the human figure would be presented in an elongated view, distorting the perspective. This was a radical concept and would set the tone for all following Gothic art.

The architect went without historical notice and his name has been lost. Could it be his last name was Gothic? We will never know. It was he who created the style and tone of all that would follow. Abbot Suger provided the inspiration; the mason provided the perspiration.

No more than 200 hundred men worked on the cathedral site at one time, not including the nobles who lugged the stones up the hill. But then, they were not there for the work, but for the glory. The stonecutters and the masons were the most important men on the job. Next were the scaffold builders. The framers (carpenters) were next on the hierarchy of skills and the glazers followed them. One skilled worker the Abbot lacked was an expert foundation layer. It was not until the west portal had to be taken down and reconstructed that the rest of the foundation was retrofitted.

2.3.6 The Artisans *(who)*

As previously discussed, Chartres was an ideal location because the craftsmen could get there. Who were these craftsmen?

In twelfth-century Chartres, craftsmen were special people. Each possessed a unique knowledge that had been handed down from father to son, or learned as an apprentice to a skilled worker. Their skills were not documented. In other words, they had no manuals. A boy was apprenticed at a young age and lived and worked with his mentor.

Once trained, a craftsman found himself in demand. People needed the skills he possessed. Masons and carpenters, in particular, were in great demand. *There were no plumbers or electricians*. Craftsmen with highly demanded skills were still looked down upon by the royalty who refused to pay for the value of those skills. Although the skilled craftsman always had work and could make a living, none of them got rich. They did not enjoy a free market; services and skills rendered were not bid upon. A craftsman could always work, but not set the price for his skills.

The historical record indicates no more than 400 men participated in the design and building of the cathedral. That record also says no more than 200 men were on the site at any one time. The physical location, size of the building, and scheduling of work would not support any more than 200 men at any one time. Managing 200 people was a nightmare for Abbot Suger.

Abbot Suger had a problem getting skilled workers. He had to advertise for them. This was not done with Help Wanted advertisements in the newspaper. Word was sent out by way of mouth throughout the land, saying what and when specific skills would be needed. Once done, Abbot Suger had to wait for the craftsmen to show up. Travel was hard and dangerous. Craftsmen could find work almost every-where. Eventually, Abbot Suger got all the help he needed.

Just because a man was skilled in masonry did not mean he could perform the tasks required to build something as radically new as this cathedral. A skilled mason would still need on-the-job training to complete this type of work. The training would provide a competitive advantage for those trained, and they would have a life-time of work building other structures in the Gothic style.

In addition to the craftsmen, the project required many laborers. Abbot Suger had little or no problem getting laborers. Many of them were local farmers who had relatively little to do once the crops were planted. The problem was that this labor force was always changing. As menial as the work might be, it was difficult and required some training.

2.3.7 Scheduling the Effort *(when)*

Abbot Suger understood the schedule required to build the cathedral. From past experience building the church at Saint-Denis, he knew what had to be done in what order, and he had a firm handle on all the issues. Based on his initial planning, it would take twenty years to build the cathedral, or so he thought. Things did not go exactly as he planned.

Everything else was based on his original plan. This included the scheduling requirements for the craftsmen, the schedule for the spending of money, the order and timing of the building processes, and the scheduling of all the materials to arrive at the site, as needed.

Unlike the pyramids that were built on a **finite** definition of time, the cathedral was built on the concept of an infinite amount of time. However long the project would take is how long it would take. The initial plan predicted a time frame of twenty years to complete the church, and that was acceptable to all. This calculated and predicted time frame would eventually create a condition that put the successful conclusion of the project in jeopardy.

Abbot Suger had not anticipated the problems caused by the building site. The hill and the roads delayed the shipment and arrival of materials. The delay in materials changed the construction schedule. The changed construction schedule caused the wrong craftsmen to show up at the wrong times. The delays caused the plans for acquisition and spending of the funds to change.

The rebuilding of the west portal caused both a redesign of the structure, and a retrofitting of the existing foundation for the rest of the structure. The ongoing delays caused a flagging of dedication and interest in the project, and funding became more difficult to acquire. The domino effect of one misassumption created havoc with the total project.

One other factor contributed to the delays—theft. Any object of value would walk away from the site. Building lumber could not be left unattended. A worker could not afford to turn his back on his tools. Money was misappropriated and stolen. Bribes and kickbacks were routine and a part of the business. Everybody had his hand out, including the church officials and the royalty.

The delays and theft meant the Abbot had to allocate and raise more money. The need for more money caused additional taxation. Additional taxation caused more civil unrest. The civil unrest caused those in power to use additional force to get the money. The additional force had to be paid for and the taxation had to be further increased. The ripple effect of any misassumption is wide ranging and can even have an impact on those who are not part of the project.

This ripple effect must be prevented. The only way to prevent this negative effect is to make sure nothing is left to chance and to be certain all matters are resolved explicitly. The very nature of implicit assumption is an indication for failure. Every assumption Abbot Suger made was incorrect. The total effect of the misassumptions added thirteen years to the building process and more than doubled the original estimated building costs.

Making something explicit does not mean an error or a misunderstanding cannot arise. Making something explicit is how you can mitigate an implicit assumption—this is therefore a proactive step used to minimize errors and misunderstandings. If after making something explicit, an error or misunderstanding is discovered, it should be easier to correct and then move forward. In both the short term and long term, making something explicit can improve communication, minimize rework, establish traceability, and promote quality improvement initiatives.

2.3.8 Key Terms

assumption
documentation
explicit
finite

implicit
misassumption
opportunity

2.3.9 Review Questions

1. By making every phase of a project and every step of that project explicit, what is made available? Why is this valuable?
2. Which of Abbot Suger's assumptions proved to be inaccurate and why? What effect can an incorrect assumption have on projects today?
3. In reality, who actually paid for the building of the cathedral and why? Keep in mind that many employees in today's enterprises work evenings and weekends unpaid.
4. What problems did Abbot Suger encounter in employing skilled workers? What problems are

organizations facing today regarding hiring and retaining good workers?
5. Was the building of the cathedral based on a finite or an infinite definition of time? What effect did this have on the successful completion of the project? Give examples of how time can effect project success or failure today.
6. Why was it important that Chartres was a crossroads town? What factors should be considered when the *planner* thinks about location?

SECTION 2.4 HOW THE MANHATTAN PROJECT BECAME A REALITY—THE FIRST ATOMIC BOMB

QUESTIONS TO CONTEMPLATE

1. How does a company hire a labor force that will create a product for a top secret project?
2. How can effective communication occur when a project is top secret?

2.4.1 Introduction

Slowly the Boeing-built military bomber, serial number B-29-45-MO 44-86292, moved over a pit in the runway and came to a halt. It was August 5, 1945. *Little Boy*, the nickname given to the uranium-filled bomb weighing in at 4.5 tons, was carefully loaded into the bomb bay. The ground crew painted the name Enola Gay on the aircraft's nose. See Figure 2-13.

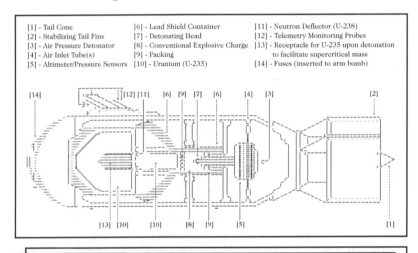

[1] - Tail Cone	[6] - Lead Shield Container	[11] - Neutron Deflector (U-238)
[2] - Stabilizing Tail Fins	[7] - Detonating Head	[12] - Telemetry Monitoring Probes
[3] - Air Pressure Detonator	[8] - Conventional Explosive Charge	[13] - Receptacle for U-235 upon detonation
[4] - Air Inlet Tube(s)	[9] - Packing	to facilitate supercritical mass
[5] - Altimeter/Pressure Sensors	[10] - Uranium (U-235)	[14] - Fuses (inserted to arm bomb)

Figure 2-13   *Anatomy of Little Boy*

At approximately 02:00 the following morning, the Enola Gay started its 1,500-mile flight from Tinian in the Pacific Ocean. Two observation planes carrying cameras and scientific instruments followed behind. Shortly after 06:00, Pilot Paul Tibbets, Jr. (b. 1915), known to his men as Colonel Tibbets, announced to the crew the secret he had been keeping. The plane was carrying the world's first atomic bomb. At 08:16, after free falling 31,600 feet, a 10-kiloton atomic bomb detonated on Hiroshima. This significant event would change the world forever.

Three days later, a 22-kiloton plutonium bomb nicknamed *Fat Man* fell on Nagasaki. The following day, after four years of all-out unrelenting war, Japan unconditionally capitulated.

In 1934, Dr. Leo Szilard (1898–1964), a physicist and professor at the University of Chicago, lay soaking in his bathtub when *eureka*, the idea of how to create a sustained chain reaction occurred to him. He had been working on this problem for many years. There is no substitute for genius.

Dr. Szilard and Dr. Harold Urey (1893–1981), a Noble Prize winner, went to work on making the solution practical and possible. Creating a solution would take many years, from 1934 to 1942. The resulting breakthroughs in physics were an extremely important advance in science and technology. The work was performed under the utmost secrecy and was precipitated by a single event—the bombing of Pearl Harbor.

Upon watching what was going on in Europe, Dr. Szilard convinced his friend Albert Einstein (1879–1955) to write a letter to the 32nd President of the U.S. In his two-page letter, dated August 2, 1939, Einstein urged President Franklin Roosevelt

(FDR) (1882–1945) to financially support and expedite the creation of an atomic bomb. Incidentally, FDR was elected on his promise to keep America out of the war.

President Roosevelt understood the need for such a weapon and got the support of the United States Congress and the required funding. All of this was accomplished under tight security restrictions. The supporters in Congress, who assured the funding, were not aware of why the funding was required or what would be produced, but they did understand the threat of war. It would be Commander-in-Chief Harry Truman (1884–1972) who would give the final order to use the weapon.

The Manhattan Project was created to develop the atomic bomb. The project was given top-secret status. All assigned personnel were on a need-to-know basis. Control of the project was given to General Leslie Groves (1896–1970), one of the few people given clearance for a *need-to-know…everything*.

The Manhattan Project taught America and the world important lessons. Like the pyramids and the Cathedral of Chartres, the atomic bomb represented a major turning point in the advancement of mankind. Here are some of the more important lessons:

- If you are dedicated and determined enough and have enough money, you can do anything.
- The use of advanced technologies has strategic and imperative advantages.
- Information is worth more than the thing it represents.
- The more important the thing, the more secrecy must be maintained.
- A friend today may be an enemy tomorrow.
- An enemy today may be a friend tomorrow.
- There is strength in strategic alliance.
- To get the best results, get the best people.
- There is no substitute for good engineering and good science.
- There is no substitute for genius.
- Anything you do today may have serious repercussions in the future.

The Manhattan Project created new sciences and technologies. It created new management techniques and project development methods. It extended the nature of communication and the value of information. The *big boom* these weapons created was more than just an explosion.

2.4.2 One Step at a Time *(how)*

General Groves was faced with a daunting challenge. He was smart. He realized the first thing he had to do was determine all the tasks that needed to be done. Much of the record is either still classified or just plain forgotten, but his initial list may have looked like this:

- Drop the bomb.
- Move the bomb.
- Test the bomb.
- Build the bomb.
- Design the bomb.
- Design the firing mechanisms.
- Produce the explosive materials.
- Create the physical mathematics.
- Create the theoretical mathematics.

- Get all the right people.
- Determine where the work will be done.
- Keep everything top secret.
- Get this done as soon as possible (ASAP).
- Get money.
- Make sure FDR really supports the project.

It does not take a rocket scientist (or in this case a nuclear scientist) to see that the list is in reverse order. This is exactly the point. General Groves had to start his thinking with what needed to be accomplished. The desired result is known as an end state. The list represents all processes required to get from the **current state**— no bomb—to the end state—a really big bang. It is easy to see that each process requires other processes and more. Each process relies on other things to happen— **resources**, locations, people, and scheduling.

The issues facing General Groves were no different from those facing Imhotep, the architect of the Great Pyramid at Giza, four millennia earlier. The ends were far different and the actual problems much more complex for General Groves; but the fact remains, he had to go through the same thought processes. Take any one of the processes listed previously and try to imagine all the complexities associated with it. Then try to figure out how to keep everything top secret.

Here is a partial list of the processes required to ensure secrecy:

- Perform an in-depth background check on everyone involved in, associated with, or who in any way comes into contact with any person, place, or thing that is part of the Manhattan Project.
- Create a secure telephone line communication network.
- Isolate workplaces to avoid contact with the general public.
- Create a special military police force to guard workplaces.
- Limit the number of people who have knowledge of the project.
- Ensure that no one group knows exactly what any other group is working on.
- Constantly monitor the media to prevent any possible leak.

Each process can be further refined. The Manhattan Project directly employed over 200,000 people. These people came from every walk of life, all united in a common cause. Whatever the rationale for each individual, they still had to be vetted. This required a huge number of agents from the Federal Bureau of Investigations (FBI). The FBI more than doubled in size during this period. Each FBI agent had to be examined thoroughly. The mood of the day was *trust no one*.

Work for the project was conducted at four principal locations in Tennessee, Illinois, Washington, and New Mexico. Each location required an infrastructure. This meant contractors had to be hired to build buildings, cables had to be laid for electricity, and pipes had to be laid for both water and sewage. Daily catering services and clothing had to be provided. Nothing could be arbitrarily delegated, and details could not be deferred because they were too numerous.

In Washington and New Mexico, small towns would be constructed to support this effort, while everyone involved maintained secrecy. What kind of cover stories had to be created? All the people who provided services and goods had to be thoroughly examined, albeit, secretly.

This list of processes required to ensure secrecy is important because the United States had identified an enemy, the Axis powers.[4] This enemy was dedicated to the destruction of the United States, and every other country for that matter. Having identified the enemy, the U.S. had to gain a strategic advantage and commit itself to self-preservation. The *planners* had to figure out how to get everything accomplished. This is no different from how today's modern corporations operate.

For the Manhattan Project, new processes were invented. When the project started, no one could imagine what those new processes might be. Many of the new processes were dictated by the nature of the science and physics being discovered.

For example, the scientists had to create a process to handle and move fissionable material. Exposure to even small amounts of uranium or plutonium causes painful death. As a rhetorical question, how were they able to create the needed quantities of those materials when the basic technology was not known?

For General Groves, this list of processes gave him a starting point. Other lists would be required that addressed other problems. But this first list, this list of processes, was the first of the military-required **strategic imperatives**. A strategic imperative is a goal that is highly desirable, but presently out of reach, and when accomplished, provides a significant advantage.

2.4.3 Logistics *(when)*

The four locations where work was carried out on the Manhattan Project were Oak Ridge, Tennessee; Chicago, Illinois; Hanford, Washington; and Los Alamos, New Mexico. Three locations had to develop huge amounts of infrastructure. All three required the same civil engineering developed for the construction of the Great Pyramid at Giza. A major difference between the two projects was that Giza was an open project and the Manhattan Project was top secret.

General Groves had to create the **critical path** for each of the processes and set deadlines for each phase. Many of these deadlines were estimated and imposed because of the need to produce the weapon. These deadlines were an onerous responsibility for the men who had to lead each of the efforts.

What made these efforts even more difficult was that each leader did not know how his team's work affected the other teams. Only the general could see the whole picture. Robert Oppenheimer (1904–1967) was the scientific director at the Los Alamos laboratory and was known as the *Father of the Bomb*. Dr. Oppenheimer knew most of what went on in the other locations, but was not privy to the complete details.

At Los Alamos, the group of mathematicians had no idea what was going on in the hut next door where the engineers were working. Neither group knew what was going on in the hut where the weapons designers were working. Of course, nobody at Los Alamos knew what was going on in Hanford or Oak Ridge.

Think of the logistical nightmare this caused. Each group had to have the appropriate supply of information to further their work, and then had to create a feedback loop to report the results of the information for correctness and practicality. Of all the specialized problems of moving material, the moving of information was one of the most complex. The accuracy, maintenance, and communication of information are problems that plague us to this day.

Each location needed specialized equipment and buildings. The designs had to be kept secret so no one could guess about the use of either the buildings or equipment.

Top-secret materials had to be moved under cover of darkness. Each morning, scientists would arrive to find new materials and gadgets. They had no idea when or how these things got there. Dr. Richard Feynman (1918–1988), a future Nobel Prize winner, observed there must be a Santa Claus (b. 0357).

The facility at Hanford covered several square miles. Almost every kind of dangerous or hazardous material developed by mankind made its way to Hanford. The staff at Hanford had to produce the nuclear weapons payloads. Once produced, these materials had to be transported to the appropriate location.

The truck that carried the initial bomb cores was part of a special convoy that could not be stopped. The cores had to be placed on a special suspension system that did not allow contact with any part of the truck and isolated the vibrations caused by the road. Three armed military police personnel rode in the back of the vehicle with the bomb. Who sweated the most during the trip from Hanford to Los Alamos—the drivers, the armed escort, or the other vehicles in the convoy?

During the war, the U.S. would identify and capture only one spy, Klaus Fuchs (1911–1988), an agent of the Soviet Union. He worked at the Los Alamos facility. This was the first time in recorded history an ally sent spies to learn about ally activity. No matter how secure you try to make something, a determined friend or enemy will often try to find a way to learn your secrets. Figure 2-14 shows where the atomic bomb was developed.

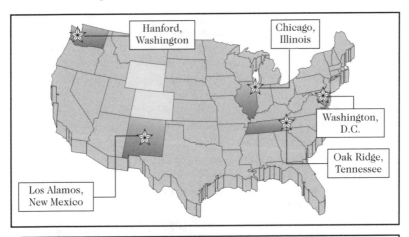

Figure 2-14 *Atomic bomb development locations*

The bomb itself was not important to Joseph Stalin (1879–1953) who sent the spy, but rather the **intellectual capital** that made the bomb possible. Information continues to be an important asset.

In today's world, the actual thing is not necessarily what is important. The intellectual capital is what is important. For example, when Intel introduces a new computer chip, competitors like AMD find little value in the chip itself, but great value in the intellectual capital required to create a competing chip. Hiring an Intel engineer is more advantageous for AMD than purchasing an Intel computer chip to **reverse engineer** its design.

The Second World War demonstrated the need for intelligence (intellectual capital) and how that intelligence could create a **strategic advantage**.

2.4.4 Survival *(why)*

The motivation for building the atomic bomb is simple; the first item on the following list explains the motivation: The United States was dedicated and determined to ensure its own survival at any price.

This simple statement of motivation would force all the other issues of materials and resources, processes, locations, people, and schedules into alignment.

Not only did the United States have to win, the enemy had to be conquered and destroyed. All of our allies were committed to the same goal. The goal was predicated on the U.S. policy of not conquering for possession. It was U.S. policy that once a war was over, the Americans go home. In this case, however, the basic root of the cause of the war had to be eradicated. The allies did not want to take the chance that the root would ever grow again.

2.4.5 No Clear Path *(where)*

The work on the bomb was done in the four sites previously mentioned, while all the coordination was done in Washington, D.C. Much of the dangerous work was done in Oak Ridge, Hanford, and Los Alamos. These sites share the following:

- They are remote.
- The nearest centers of population are small towns.
- Access into and out of the facilities could be closely monitored.
- Any approach other than the only road leading to the facility could be easily detected.
- The work teams could be isolated from the general population.
- The same cover story would work for all—it was war work. The American culture now supported such an answer and would not ask any further questions. This was especially true in small towns where regular prayer vigils were held in honor of the young men and women who went off to fight the war.

Other problems had to be overcome:

- Limited access meant paved roads had to be built.
- Tracks needed to be laid to provide railroad transportation.
- Houses and support buildings had to be constructed.
- Primary infrastructure facilities for sewage, water, and electricity needed to be established.
- Facilities for the supply of basic necessities like food, clothing, and medicine had to be established.
- Means of entertainment and other diversion facilities needed to be created.

General Groves discovered what Imhotep discovered: no matter what one thinks has to be done first, something else has to be done before it. In every location,

General Groves was faced with building another Giza. In addition to selecting and developing each location, it all had to be done secretly.

Large numbers of support people were required to build and maintain these facilities. They could not know what or why they were building; they were given plans and told to go build. The architects from the Army Corps of Engineers did not know what they were designing. These people were given descriptions only of the type and number of buildings required. All facilities had to be built and working by the end of 1942 when the mobilization of America was complete.

2.4.6 Blank Checks *(what)*

Two billion dollars was the sum of money needed for the work. The Manhattan Project used a virtual blank check to fund it. Everything that had to be acquired was paid for from this inexhaustible fund, all in secret. One of the motives leading to the eventual use of the bombs was the concern that the U.S. had spent all this money and it had to see something for the investment. If the American public learned about this weapon at the end of the war and discovered it was not used to defeat Japan, a political firestorm could have ensued.

2.4.7 Shhh, It's a Secret *(who)*

In addition to those already mentioned, here is a small sampling of the people who worked on the Manhattan Project: Enrico Fermi (1901–1954), Edward Teller (b. 1908), Hans Albrecht Bethe (b. 1906), Joseph Rotblat (b. 1908), and Louis Slotkin (d. 1946). The basic requirement for the people placed on this project was sheer intellectual brilliance. Nothing less would do. The crème de la crème of the best chemists, mathematicians, physicists, engineers, materials experts, weapons builders, and more were asked to participate. However, before the invitation was extended, the participant was vetted.

This need for intellect extended to much of the support staff. Even the guards were selected for their intelligence. Military police had to be specially trained, especially to recognize the staff. An unfamiliar face had to be challenged immediately. The guards knew everyone on sight and knew where they were working. When and if they noticed someone not going to their usual work location, that person would be reported. Sentries were instructed that if they did not know someone, they were to challenge and detain them.

The scientists mentioned represent the core team. Consider how many laborers, masons, carpenters, plumbers, road builders, glazers, roofers, and other tradesmen and craftsmen were required to complete this work. The number of cooks, dishwashers, suppliers, delivery personnel, messengers, fence builders, and maintenance workers required was not recorded.

Imhotep had to be concerned with 25,000 people when building the Great Pyramid. Abbot Suger had several hundred people to manage in building the Cathedral of Chartres. General Groves managed 200,000 people, and each individual had to have security clearance. Figure 2-15 shows the art of keeping secrets.

"These are great for keeping secrets!"
"Yes, the sky is very blue today."

Figure 2-15   *The art of keeping secrets*

81

2.4.8 Key Terms

critical path
current state
intellectual capital
resources

reverse engineer
strategic advantage
strategic imperative

2.4.9 Review Questions

1. What led to the funding for the creation of an atomic bomb? What kinds of projects might have access to a virtual blank check for funding?
2. Explain what is meant by a strategic imperative. Give an example of a strategic imperative that an enterprise might have today.
3. What was the biggest logistical problem facing General Groves and why? What kind of logistical problems might a manufacturing facility face?

4. What is meant by the term intellectual capital? Why is intellectual capital important to today's enterprise?

5. What was the motivation for the Manhattan Project? Give an example of a situation in today's economy where the motivation for a company is the same.
6. What important discovery in regard to planning for location was made by both Imhotep and General Groves? Would this discovery apply to CEOs in the current business environment? Why or why not?

Science

SECTION 2.5 WHEN THEY MOVED—THE STORY OF LEVITTOWN

2.5.1 Introduction

World War II ended in August of 1945. By mid-1946, the U.S. had essentially demobilized. Historically, demobilization had caused a period of inflation and economic uncertainty. The problem had been what to do with all those returning soldiers. In 1946, this was not a problem. The U.S. economy had broken out of its lethargy from the Great Depression.

The emphasis of the great manufacturing engine that had been created to serve the war effort now turned to producing consumer products. Americans wanted everything and they wanted those things now. Average Americans had barely been able to provide themselves with the basic essentials of life since 1930. Sixteen years later, many consumer products were wearing thin and needed to be replaced.

In 1944, the General Inscription (GI) Bill was passed. President Franklin Roosevelt and Congress agreed that the American soldiers should be rewarded for their heroic efforts and passed the GI Bill. This bill guaranteed returning and future veterans a college education.

During the depression, the Federal Housing Authority (FHA) was created. The FHA guaranteed mortgages and pumped money into the housing trades in an effort to help people build new homes. This effort failed. During the depression, high housing prices and the rules of obtaining a mortgage were too onerous. In 1947, the GI Bill was tied to the FHA. A new set of rules allowed Americans to buy new homes and provided special entitlements to veterans.

The three key elements that define any market were now in place:

- Need
- Opportunity
- Money

Abraham Levitt (1880–1962), a lawyer, had two sons: William (1907–1994), a salesman and financier, and Alfred (1912–1966), an architect. These three men started a social revolution. They did it without guns and explosives, and instead used hammers and saws.

2.5.2 Homecoming *(when)*

Timing is everything; this is an axiom in business. An innovator only has a brief opportunity to introduce something new. The year 1947 presented a window of opportunity for the Levitts, and they took advantage of that opportunity.

On May 7, 1947, Levitt and Sons publicly announced their plan to build 2,000 mass-produced rental homes for veterans. They masterminded and built Levittown, a place that started out as an experiment in low-cost, mass-produced housing and became, perhaps, the most famous suburban development in the world.[5] Levittown did not happen just by chance. A lot of factors had to come together to make the development a reality. Eventually, the Levitts would build 140,000 houses in twenty years.

The returning veterans were living in attics, spare bedrooms, rented rooms, and with family. These places had old appliances and years of accumulated living debris, and they were in various states of dilapidation. None of these things is conducive to starting and raising a family.

The Levitts' initial idea was to build houses that would rent for $60 a month. The idea of actually selling the houses was adopted after the need for money to fund the next housing effort grew greater than the rental cash flow. Demand for the $60-a-month houses was immediate and almost overwhelming.

Not a single house had been built when the Levitts accepted the initial rental applications. Almost 4,000 people applied for 2,000 houses. Levitt and Sons immediately announced plans for another 2,000 houses.

The veterans had wives, jobs, and money. What they lacked was decent, clean, and affordable housing. The Levitt houses were neat, new, and affordable. The new communities were well planned. Veterans and their families would realize an improved standard of living.

Once committed to this project, the Levitts could not turn back. Their program worked because their housing was affordable. To produce lower-priced housing and still make a profit, the Levitts had to solve many business problems including logistics. Building materials had to show up on time, exactly when they were required. A day early was manageable, but a day late was catastrophic.

The Levitts had to master the entire supply chain, including the forests from which the lumber came, the quality and types of wood, and the milling processes that produced the lumber. At the other end of the supply chain was the delivery and receipt of materials at each building site. They had to manage and understand everything.

Scheduling was difficult because each house could have a different layout. Veterans could select from two- or three-bedroom Cape Cod style homes, or one to four-bedroom ranch homes. The Levitts figured out how to manage the supply chain and other industries copied their solutions.

To solve the scheduling problems, the Levitts refined the practice of building to order from standard parts. For example, when you buy a can of Coke, the beverage typically comes in a 12-ounce can (or 330 milliliters in Europe). Coca-Cola is able to purchase standard materials to hold its beverages. Using the practice of building to order from standard parts allows Coca-Cola to create standard shipping packages and standard wholesale prices for retailers. So, using this practice, the Levitts were able to apply all the principles of mass production to the housing market. In doing so, they changed forever how Americans, and eventually people the world over, viewed buying a house.

In the process of determining how to go about building a large town, the Levitts mastered all the principles and techniques of critical path method and Gantt charting. This mastery was key to their success. Tight and controlled schedules also drove down costs, and kept them down.

2.5.3 Overcoming Obstacles *(what)*

In order for the Levitts to be successful, they required:

- Money
- A reliable basic design for the structures
- Salesmanship
- Political clout

By resolving how to acquire and develop the items on the list, the Levitts overcame every obstacle.

Abraham Levitt provided the initial money from options he bought on the vast tracts of land on Long Island just prior to World War II. Almost all the rest of the money came from the government in the form of subsidies and mortgages.

Alfred, the architect, developed the basic designs for the houses. They were unremarkable, in and of themselves, but basic design allowed the Levitts to create standards, which minimized waste materials. Standards included making all building elements multiples of four and eight. Even today, 2-by-4 lumber comes in 8-foot lengths, and plywood and sheetrock come in 4-by-8-foot sheets. Using a standard design meant that many parts of the house could be **prefabricated**, including all the doors and the white metal Tracy cabinets in the kitchen.[6]

Someone once said that William Levitt could sell ice to Eskimos. He was also an expert at numbers and in his head could figure out the return on investment of 100 houses. Who now knows what is truth from the legend? The fact is that William Levitt sold the idea of Levittown to bankers, congressmen, and President Truman.

William Levitt understood the value of political clout. He was a master at acquiring and maintaining support from politicians of every stripe. He did not care what political party someone represented; he understood how to *play* politics on Capitol Hill. During frequent trips to the Hill, Levitt adopted the rhetoric of anticommunism to further his cause. Levitt repeated slogans like, *No man who owns his own house can be a communist because he has too much to do*. Levitt was personable and persuasive. He was shrewd. He was intelligent. He was a man of business and he was successful.

2.5.4 Another Day, Another Dollar *(who)*

The basic governance for hiring a worker on a Levittown project was simple. If the applicant could stand up, use a hammer, and handle a saw, he was hired. The idea of using untrained labor was an anathema to the unions' view of using only skilled and trained craftsmen. The unions set up pickets and threatened lawsuits, all to no avail. The Levitts broke the back of the unions through coercion, manipulation of the judiciary process, and public relations.

Hiring skilled labor was not a problem. Even if a worker knew nothing about roofing, by the fifth house, he was an expert. In the end, on-the-job training proved to be advantageous for America. The unskilled laborer became a highly marketable skilled craftsman after working for the Levitts a few years. In the future, these workers would have to join the union to ply their trades, but for now, they learned and earned.

The Levitts employed thousands of individuals who worked hard to meet predetermined standards dictated by the requirements of scheduling and the principles of mass production. Each worker was paid by piecework, which provided ample incentive to work long hard days, providing the motivation for making sure materials arrived when they were required. When the men came to work, they expected all materials to be on the job site and the Levitts had to make sure this happened.

The Levitts relieved themselves of all liabilities usually associated with **human resources**. They offered no pension plans or any real benefits, and they offered no salaries for the line workers. The worker would show up at the time and place designated, do the work assigned, and get paid for what was finished. This is piecework. Managing human resources was reduced to an accounting task of counting and multiplying.

2.5.5 Move It on Down the Line *(how)*

The Levitts employed many of the tactics first developed by Henry Ford (1863–1947) for mass production. Ford was the first industrialist to put the principles of mass production into play. His company was able to literally roll out thousands of automobiles each day thanks to mass production and the assembly line. The assembly line works on the idea of delivering a part to a predetermined spot and having one person place that part on the car as it goes by.

What starts out as a collection of pieces ends up as a machine that functions and can be driven away at the end of the line. With the exception of the inhumane working conditions, the repetition of the work, and the constant pressure to do more in less time, the main disadvantage of the assembly line Ford created was the inflexibility of the end product.

Of course, the major advantage of mass production and the assembly line was the reduction of cost to manufacture. Because the Model T was so successful, it created a ripple effect backward on the supply chain. Ford purchased in large quantities. The promise of large orders provided Ford with leverage to force suppliers to offer lower prices on materials and sub-assemblies. This combination of factors allowed Ford to produce a vehicle that was affordable to the common man.

The design of the Model T was basic and simple with no unnecessary enhancements. The automobile's basic and simple design reduced the number of assembled parts required to build the car. Fewer parts meant fewer things could break. The net result of the design was that it guaranteed a certain degree of quality.

The manageable and controllable steps of production provided even more quality. The car was dependable and nearly impossible to break. The car could handle all but the toughest of roads, and its high ground clearance allowed the car to get through mud and snow. Lastly, the production line meant a relatively unskilled worker could be taught how to do a single task repeatedly and often—driving down the cost of labor.

The advantages of the production line are:

- Low cost per unit
- High levels of production
- Cheap unskilled labor

The disadvantages of the production line are:

- Inhumane working conditions
- Inflexibility of the end product
- High turnover rate of employees

The Levitts considered all these factors and made an intellectual leap. Instead of delivering the materials and the work to a person at a worksite, they would deliver the materials and the person to a worksite. This twist would have far-reaching influences. From laying the slab to the presentation of the house key to the new owner, every phase of production was planned and scheduled.

Each worker did the same work at each worksite and, as in a production line, completed his tasks and moved on to the next worksite. Instead of a product moving down a production line, the workers moved down the production line. Each crew arrived at the worksite at the appropriate time. The blueprints and materials were waiting for them. All that remained was for workers to complete their tasks in the allotted amount of time and then move on down the line.

The backward ripple effect was astounding. Upon receipt of an order, the Levitt mill, where all the prefabrication was done, knew exactly how much of what to produce. In a short time, the orders indicated buying preferences, and the mill could predict how much of what would be needed.

Armed with this information, the Levitts could meet with their suppliers and demand lower prices based on predicted and promised volumes. This would be true regardless of the supplier's point in the supply chain. Providing supplies, materials, and products on the forecasted need of 140,000 houses served to be a powerful incentive to reduce prices. Each lower price resulted in incremental reductions in the cost of the finished product.

Using the advantages of this method of mass production, the Levitts realized they could offer something that had never been offered before—options.

The Cape Cod model could now be offered with an optional garage. If consumers wanted a garage, they could select a one- or two-stall model, and choose whether they wanted the garage attached to the house. They could choose a house with or without air-conditioning and with different quality appliances, furnishings, and carpets.

To a new buyer, the list of options seemed endless. Purchasers were generally content, knowing they could afford what they were buying and that they were buying what suited their needs and desires. The Levitts used a standard pricing list to offer each buyer the same options and prices.

The standard units of measure, design, and building techniques created by the Levitts have affected all building trades, including heating, ventilation, and air-conditioning (HVAC) designs, as well as plumbing and electrical supplies. These standards became mandatory for all the building trades. They were incorporated into zoning codes, which further increased the requirement for standards. Municipalities took these standards and turned them into laws.

Options created a new way of thinking about production. Offering a list of fixed options produced the concepts of custom building from standard parts and from reuse. These two concepts produced the idea that almost any size house in almost any style could be mass produced. Standard sizes led to standard building techniques. Reuse meant builders could reapply designs, techniques, and material fabrication methods in a variety of ways, which required no new inventions.

The automobile industry caught onto the idea almost immediately. The industry had to rethink its supply chain and how different optional parts arrived at the necessary point of the assembly line. Soon the automakers began offering what appeared to be a dazzling array of options.

The Levitts anticipated and addressed all the manufacturing issues at the outset. What they really did was take all the principles of industrial engineering and refined them. This had never been done before in the housing market. Other builders looked at the example the Levitts created and said to themselves, *I can do that.* The techniques were repeatable, defined, and controlled.

CAPABILITY MATURITY MODEL

In the 1990s, the Software Engineering Institute (SEI) of Carnegie Mellon University recognized these traits (techniques that were repeatable, defined, and controlled) as being highly important in a corporation's ability to produce software.

SEI created the **Capability Maturity Model (CMM)**. See Figure 2-16. CMM contains five levels. Each level identifies the aptitude a company demonstrates in building and implementing a software project. Corporations regularly submit project achievements to the SEI in hope of obtaining certification at one of the model's levels.

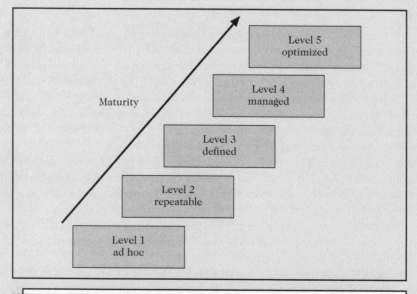

Figure 2-16   *Capability Maturity Model*

(continued)

Starting with Level 1, the model classifies organizations whose software development or maintenance processes are ad hoc and unstable. Planning is ineffective and not managed. Management commitment is driven by reaction, often creating a crisis and resulting in an abandoned project.

Level 2 introduces basic management control, where software processes are repeatable. Project planning and tracking are seen as necessities, not necessary evils. This is the first stage of quality.

Level 3 suggests that an organization's process is adequately defined, and the pain of change management has eased. Unfortunately, this is where some organizations plateau and stop growing. Level 3 is also seen as the most cost-effective level of quality achievement.

Level 4 dictates that the software process is well managed.

Level 5 is the optimized state of process control.

The Levitts' processes and techniques were certainly repeatable. Therefore, they would have easily reached certification at Level 2. Furthermore, the processes and techniques were well defined, so they should have been able to reach Level 3. Finally, the Levitts tightly controlled all the management activities and would have been able to demonstrate why they were candidates to receive CMM Level 4 certification.

2.5.6 Realtors Will Always Tell You It's Location, Location, Location *(where)*

The Levitts purchased forests and sawmills in Oregon, but required their fabrication mills to be local. Therefore, the Levitts selected sites for their houses based on two factors: the size of the continuous tracts of land and distance from the fabrication mill.

The requirements of easy travel and short distance from the fabrication mill limited the Levitts to three areas for development: lower New York, New Jersey, and eastern Pennsylvania. The tracts also had to be relatively flat. The Levitts were not just building houses; they were building communities. The size and scope of the new communities required civil engineering on a massive scale.

The new community plans included swimming pools, playgrounds, schools, fire departments, police departments, civic buildings, and retail services. The Levitts did not build many of the public facilities, but they allocated space for them. This was a novel concept. William Levitt said, "We will build the houses and provide basic services like water, sewer, and electricity. We will even build some swimming pools and playgrounds. Everything else is up to you." In this context, *you* would be a potential entrepreneur or municipality.

Abraham Levitt was personally responsible for the shrubbery and trees that were planted in the Levitt developments. He loved green and would even go from town to town giving presentations on how to care for the trees and bushes. Today, visitors to any of the Levitt developments note the beauty, variety, and quantity of green. They are all there because Abraham loved trees.

Creating new, total communities put the principles of democracy into action. The Levitts were unaware they were doing this, but new governments had to be formed in these new communities. The new communities were large and they were incorporated. Local governing bodies had to be created, which meant elections.

The form of the new government had to be decided upon by the new community inhabitants, requiring more elections. Schools had to be built. This required school boards and school administrations. Even more elections had to be organized.

Retail space had to be allocated, requiring zoning laws and a zoning board—more elections. Police officers, firefighters, hospitals, maintenance workers, parks, and more had to be created, managed, and financed. The local government had to be given taxing authority. That approval came from gaining enough votes at an election.

The new communities desired their own newspapers and other support businesses. The new communities changed the density and wealth of the population centers. This new dense population caused redistricting, which affected both the state and federal governments. Each new community needed to write a charter of incorporation. Each provision had to be agreed upon by the citizens of the community, establishing the need for another election.

The Levitts created three new population centers of over 150,000 people each. The size of these towns affected everything from the environment to the government. The new citizens had to come to grips with every issue and deal with it. The communities were organized as democratic societies, and all the new communities built across the nation would copy the model the Levitts created.

While the Levitts built these centers, other builders used the Levitt model to build adjoining developments. All these new housing developments stimulated growth across the nation. The need for new highways highlighted the need for an organized infrastructure. The National Highway System was created. County governments overhauled their operations to accommodate the growing needs of their citizens. The effects of Levittown continued to propagate.

2.5.7 Just Greed *(why)*

By the late sixties, sociologists had their say about the Levittowns and William Levitt. Some sociologists damned him, while others praised him. William Levitt was asked why he had wrought such change and what plans he had for the changes he had made. William Levitt never set out to be a social engineer. Like most entrepreneurs, he was just trying to make a living. He made millions.

Levitt and Sons created the standard model for building housing developments. The company was sold in 1968 for $92 million to ITT Industries. After selling the company, William Levitt was forbidden to develop new communities in the U.S. for ten years. Levitt took his techniques to Iran, Venezuela, and Nigeria, but lost millions of dollars when his ITT stock lost 90 percent of its value.

In 1994, Bill Levitt lay dying. He had lost most of the money he made and was unable to pay for treatment at the hospital he had given millions of dollars to build. Sometimes you need to plan for the unexpected. See Figure 2-17.

One morning, the Levitts woke up, stared out at the unrelenting ocean of green fields, and thought to themselves:

"You know what would look good out there?"

Figure 2-17   *History repeats itself*

2.5.8 Key Terms

Capability Maturity Model (CMM)
human resources

prefabricated

2.5.9 Review Questions

1. What are three needs that help define any market?
2. Explain how the Levitts used a *just-in-time* approach to build their houses. Give an example of how the just-in-time approach is used in manufacturing facilities today.
3. What four things enabled the Levitts to be successful? Would these same four things be requirements for success in the twenty-first century?
4. How was the concept of the production line applied to each Levittown?
5. What location requirement limited the scope of this housing project? Give another example of how scope can be limited by location.
6. What are the advantages of having a technique be repeatable, defined, and controlled?

SECTION 2.6 WHO TOOK ONE SMALL STEP FOR MANKIND—LANDING ON THE MOON

> ## QUESTIONS TO CONTEMPLATE
>
> 1. How do the risks of landing on the moon compare to the risks of building a pyramid?
> 2. What effect can feelings of fear and determination have on the success of a project?

2.6.1 Introduction

On July 20, 1969, the population of the whole world was glued to a radio or television set to see and hear the following, "That's one small step for man, one giant leap for mankind." The speaker of those words was Neil Armstrong (b. 1930). He said them from Tranquility Base, 234,000 miles from the Earth. The Eagle had landed; he was on the moon.

When Neil Armstrong and Buzz Aldrin (b. 1930) landed on the moon, the journey represented an unprecedented accomplishment. Landing on the moon was the culmination of eight years of grueling work by over 400,000 people. As astronomer Dr. Carl Sagan (1934–1996) could have said, "landing on the moon cost 'billions and billions' of dollars." Even by today's standards, this was a remarkable achievement.

On October 4, 1957, Americans woke up to a shock. The Soviet Union had successfully launched the first man-made satellite called Sputnik into outer space. The arms race was immediately raised to a new level as the United States and the Soviet Union would vie to be the first to control the skies from outer space. To say that America was frightened by that *beep, beep, beep* sound emitted by Sputnik would be an understatement.

The world's first artificial satellite was about the size of a basketball. It weighed 183 pounds, and took about 98 minutes to orbit the Earth on its elliptical path. That launch ushered in new political, military, technological, and scientific developments. Although the Sputnik launch was a single event, that event marked the start of the space age. It also marked the start of the space race between the United States and the Soviet Union, putting the arms race into high gear.

2.6.2 Can Someone Think of a Job Title? *(who)*

In 1961, John Kennedy (1917–1963), the thirty-fifth president of the U.S., gave a rousing speech urging the nation to place a man on the moon by the end of the decade. The following year, he gave another speech, this time at Rice University in Texas, where he said,

> *We choose to go to the moon. We choose to go to the moon in this decade and do the other things, not because they are easy, but because they are hard, because that goal will serve to organize and measure the best of our energies*

and skills, because that challenge is one that we are willing to accept, one we are unwilling to postpone, and one which we intend to win, and the others, too.[7]

The American public responded to the President's words with support and money. In the previous year, the President had appointed his Vice President, Lyndon Johnson (LBJ) (1908–1973), as the presiding officer of the National Aeronautics and Space Council and had appointed James Webb (1906–1992) as head of the National Aeronautical Space Administration (NASA). The two men made a formidable team.

The first question Johnson asked of Webb was, "*Who* do you need?" This is interesting given that the first question often asked is, "*What* do you need?" Johnson had already figured out he had to get the best people for this project. These people would figure out what was needed.

Here is part of the list that Webb probably made:

- Space scientists
- Aeronautical engineers
- Civil engineers
- Industrial engineers
- Planning engineers
- Materials managers
- Architects
- Pilots

The list probably went on for several pages. The first question would have been, "*Where* are we going to get all those engineers?" The section on Levittown discussed the GI Bill and how that piece of legislation afforded an education to all the returning veterans. Many of those veterans became engineers, and those people formed the bulk of engineers hired.

President Roosevelt, when he was pushing the GI Bill through the U.S. Congress in 1944, said that the bill would be beneficial immediately for veterans, and that the country would benefit greatly in the long term. Sixteen years after he made this prophecy, it all came true.

At hand was a pool of great engineers and scientists. Each of them was ready and willing to accept the challenge of getting a man on the moon. In 1961, going to the moon was still science fiction. No one had a vague idea of exactly what would be required. Johnson was right; the best people would determine what was needed. These people invented thousands of new gadgets, widgets, and thingamabobs that were required to successfully complete the project over the next eight years.

The astronauts came from another unique pool. The United States had lived through two armed conflicts in the past twenty years: World War II and Korea. The wars required great advancements in avionics. New airplanes had to be tested, and a new breed of pilot was created—the test pilot. Test pilots had to be good flyers and engineers. The first astronauts were career military officers with engineering degrees.

Because so much of the project was new and required so many people, Webb was forced to create an organizational structure that would support the effort. NASA would be forced to advance human resource sciences in terms of accountability, functionality, and responsibility. NASA took the concept of the military chain of command and adapted it to extend to civilians and civilian contractors.

Thousands of contractors and subcontractors were involved. The business enterprises affected ranged from a small company in Pennsauken, New Jersey that invented and manufactured the clamps and seals for the space suits, to large corporations such as Boeing and Thiokol for airframes and engines. The United States prepared itself for a moon landing, and the right people made *the right stuff* in the right place.

2.6.3 The Power Game *(where)*

NASA had to deal with many *where* questions, including *where* to place operation and construction centers and *where* to hire the contractors. The work of flying to the moon was managed and performed in three principal locations: Houston, Texas; Huntsville, Alabama; and Cape Canaveral (currently Kennedy Space Center), Florida.

The Manned Spacecraft Center (currently Johnson Space Center) in Houston focused on spacecraft development and astronaut training. Marshall Space Flight Center in Huntsville focused on rocket development. Cape Canaveral became responsible for the actual launches. These locations were chosen as a result of one thing—politics.

The political choice of location helped build a coalition of support for NASA in various regions throughout the country and among the legislators who represented them. Each location had powerful and influential U.S. senators. One of the most noteworthy decisions was the choice to locate the Manned Spacecraft Center in Houston. At the time, Houston was the home of the Chairman of the House Appropriations Subcommittee. This committee was responsible for NASA's budget. Each location could be justified for technical reasons in order to hide the political rationale.

NASA's principal locations became the in-house laboratories and housed the technical managers for most of the contracts. The most important contracts were awarded to Boeing Corporation, North American Aviation, Douglas Aircraft Company, and the Massachusetts Institute of Technology. NASA found itself heading a coalition of diverse and competitive enterprises from within government, industry, and universities. Strong communication among these political and administrative alliances was key to Apollo's technological success.

As with the Manhattan Project, every location required large amounts of infrastructure, all of which had to be designed and built. The expenditures used to build the infrastructure and for ongoing payroll and supply would benefit the local and state economies with a continuous money supply.

The new infrastructures allowed project managers to install and use new tools. The project forced the advancement of telecommunication techniques. The buildings were designed around computers, display stations, and monitoring technology. Also included were large design rooms, meeting rooms, and press facilities. The media was given unprecedented access to the progress of the project.

Unlike the atomic bomb, where everything was top secret, NASA's coalition selected what they wanted to keep secret.

2.6.4 Yes, We Want It Yesterday *(when)*

Although project managers did not know what had to be accomplished, they did know by when it had to be accomplished—in eight years. Accurately predicting the future is usually impossible. Managing a project that requires dealing with unknown situations within a predetermined time frame offers considerable challenges. The project managers addressed their scheduling problems by using four different methods—**Program Evaluation and Review Technique (PERT)**, critical path method (CPM), Gantt charts, and **concurrent development**.

PERT was developed to assist the military. See Figure 2-18. The technique established a feedback loop for every phase of a large project. This kind of project required simultaneous work in multiple locations. Every location needed to know the progress of every other location on a continual basis. PERT helped enforce quality control on the entire effort.

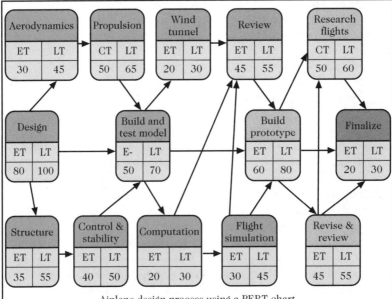

Aiplane design process using a PERT chart

PERT charts are typically used for projects involving numerous contractors, departments, and organizations where the duration times are difficult to define and the relationships between the tasks are complex. Each PERT chart starts with an initial point from which all tasks originate. Each subsequent task is connected to other tasks and is either coded or annotated with its name, the people assigned to it, and its best, worst, and average duration time. The chart is completed when all networked tasks come together to a completion.

Figure 2-18   PERT chart

In efforts of this magnitude, people can unknowingly make design errors that affect small areas of construction. Unfortunately, even small design errors can culminate in a catastrophic circumstance. In the early days of the space program, small design errors resulted in failing to successfully get a rocket off the launch pad. Rocket after rocket exploded on launch. All the failures were broadcast live on television. These failures were an embarrassment to the United States and gave succor to the Soviet Union.

When NASA started to use concurrent development and PERT together, the success rate began to improve. The combined techniques acknowledged that multiple efforts went on at the same time, and many of the efforts advanced the state of the art. This is a rather strange idea. The idea says that it is possible to begin building a second generation of technology before the first generation has been proved entirely. This concept allowed relatively rapid advancement in technology for rockets and spacecraft.

A project deals with finite and infinite resources. The more time you have, the less of everything else you need or have available at any given time in the **life cycle** of the project. The less time available, the more of everything is required in the limited life cycle of the project. The completion date to get to the moon required a backward loading of the schedule. Finite scheduling implied that in order to accomplish a task, a specific resource amount was required.

Kennedy's desire to put a man on the moon by the end of the 1960s meant the Apollo project had a finite time frame. The finite time frame meant that the government would need to provide a huge budget. Such an expense required the government to rally the American public—politics helped accomplish this objective.

2.6.5 Uniting the Country *(why)*

The United States perceived itself to be in clear and present danger following Yuri Gagarin's (b. 1934) orbit of the Earth from outer space and the standoff at the Bay of Pigs in Cuba. The American government placed the Soviet Union at the top of its motivation list in the category of concerns. The Soviet Union seemed to be far ahead of America in rocket technology. The Soviets possessed comparable or superior nuclear technology, and most importantly, boasted the intention of putting the entire world under communistic governments. At least that is what American intelligence agencies reported.

The United States took this threat seriously and believed the country's existence was at stake. The motivation of fear and survival demanded the nation take immediate action. All the other issues of assets, process, locations, people, and scheduling were hammered into compliance to support this motivation.

The only difference between the atomic bomb and the space program was that the government needed to reassure the American public that they were taking steps to win the space race. Media was forced to participate in an open nature. The publicity was always favorable, regardless of what the nation saw on television. The need to provide the television audience with positive publicity created a new breed of communicators—the spin doctors.

With Kennedy's popularity and the media's positive spin on the space program, government poured the American taxpayers' money into NASA.

2.6.6 Thank Goodness for Taxes *(what)*

Money, money, money, and more money. The space program spent money openly with public support. If a project's schedule is finite, all other resources should be unlimited. This was true with the building of the pyramids, where the Pharaohs owned everything, and it is true today. The U.S. Congress told NASA it could have practically whatever it needed and started the project's annual budget with $1.7 billion.

At the same time the United States was funding the space program, the government was also funding the Vietnam War and LBJ's War on Poverty Program. LBJ's program was limited to a defined underclass of American society. The Vietnam War and the space program were both directed toward the vast military industrial complex warned against by President Dwight Eisenhower (1890–1969) in his last speech to Congress. The political tradeoffs for funding would, in time, become obvious.

During these high government-spending years, the economy appeared to be strong. In reality, the U.S. was spending itself into a coming period of economic recession and inflation. An economic enterprise must consider the value of any investment to analyze the risk and reward of the endeavor.

 ### 2.6.7 One Small Step at a Time *(how)*

Vice President Johnson and Webb, the project manager, confronted a dilemma when they had to determine what needed to be done and how those activities, once identified, would be accomplished. When Johnson asked the first question, "Who do you need," he showed great foresight. Johnson was counting on the best people to create the mechanics of *how* to accomplish the project. He did not care *how* it got done, only that it got done. A finite schedule helps impose this line of thought.

Creating a list of concern is always helpful. If Webb made a list, that list probably would have looked like this:

- Determine who is needed.
- Understand the skill levels required.
- Plan the work schedule.
- Establish where the work will be accomplished.
- Anticipate the cost of the project.
- Make sure the project commitment is solid and steadfast.

You do not need to be a rocket scientist (forgive us, we could not resist) to see that each process is dictated at the highest level of action for every other issue associated with the project. However, the list does not really address the known and unique processes required for this particular project.

Another list might look like this:

- Get the astronauts back home safely.
- Put a man on the moon.
- Determine intermediate steps to prove feasibility of the next phase.
- Prototype and build all the systems and equipment required.
- Design the equipment and systems required.
- Do the math to set the requirements for the design of the equipment and systems.

Again, this list has been presented in reverse order. It is a helpful technique to work backward from the end step. Earlier sections discussed this backward concept relative to scheduling. Since scheduling is of paramount importance for large projects, the same rules naturally apply to all other problems.

Among other things, activities and tasks found on a schedule help determine *who* is needed and *what* resources are required. Activities and tasks also help the schedulers dictate the nature of the facilities required. Knowledge of the location helps determine the nature of the infrastructure and communication.

Once this highest level of abstraction for the activities and tasks is determined, the project *planners* must determine the nature of engineering, design, manufacturing and production, and quality control. These activities and tasks are then subjected to and validated in relation to the requirements of the schedule, and the dependency for all other project resources is determined. Communication is fundamental to the creation of a schedule; scheduling or project assessment is impossible to do in a vacuum.

The schedule constrains the processes required to carry out an activity or task, and the processes create a feedback loop to the schedule. The schedule and the processes work in tandem to help determine the acquisition of people and locations. The acquisition of people and locations helps determine the financial resource requirements. To overlook any of these constraints and not make them explicit forces implicit assumptions to be made. As you learned with the Cathedral of Chartres, implicit assumptions can have devastating effects.

As a project proceeds, each task helps move the effort from a current state to an end state. The task becomes the transition from one state to another. Steam is the end state of water being boiled. The task is heating water. A dark room is the current state before a light switch is turned on. See Figure 2-19.

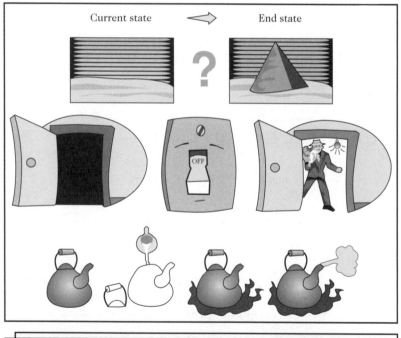

Figure 2-19   *From the current state to an end state*

In order for a schedule to be worthwhile, the *planner* must understand both the current state and the desired end state, as well as the transition required to get from one state to the other. The Apollo mission *planners* were successful in predetermining every state change required to put a man on the moon—per President Kennedy's desire.

2.6.8 Key Terms

concurrent development

life cycle

Program Evaluation and Review Technique (PERT)

2.6.9 Review Questions

1. Why did Vice President Johnson ask the question, *Who do you need*? Be specific. Why is getting the right people for the job helpful in moving a project forward?
2. What helped determine where the space race work would be managed and performed?
3. How and why was a PERT diagram used for this project?

4. Explain the difference between finite and infinite, pertaining to schedules.
5. What process is best done from the end state backward and why?
6. From where did Webb obtain the bulk of the engineers hired for this project?

SECTION 2.7 WHAT WAS SPECIAL ABOUT THE 777—BOEING'S FIRST ALL DIGITALLY DESIGNED AIRPLANE

QUESTIONS TO CONTEMPLATE

1. How do strategic partnerships enable companies to achieve goals?
2. How can adopting new technologies help drive down the cost of developing new products?

2.7.1 Introduction

Man has always been fascinated by flight. In Greek mythology, Icarus flew like a bird, but got too close to the sun, and his wings melted. During the Italian Renaissance, Leonardo da Vinci created a blueprint of what today looks nearly like a hang glider.

Bicycle builders Orville and Wilbur Wright (1871–1948, 1867–1912) took their hand-built flying machine from Dayton, Ohio to Kitty Hawk in the Outer Banks of North Carolina because of the continuous favorable winds. On December 17, 1903, after numerous attempts, they succeeded in flying the first machine-powered airplane.

Commercial airplanes stay viable for many years. The **Federal Aviation Administration (FAA)** forces the retirement of aircraft long before they physically need to be retired. When a commercial airplane is retired, many of its key components are still state of the art. This is because airplanes are upgraded continuously. Airplanes are designed with the idea that changing and upgrading parts will be simple.

These parts include not only the engines, structural components, and wiring components, but also the flight instruments in the cockpit.

In the mid-1980s, the Boeing Corporation, then headquartered in Seattle, Washington (currently headquartered in Chicago, Illinois), developed a new type of facility for the designing, building, and testing of commercial aircraft. This new facility was digital; it was virtual. It was the land of Lara Croft; it was cyberspace. Every detail of this plane was known before one piece of sheet metal was cut, one rivet was sunk, or one sick bag was used.

Everything that had to be known was made explicit. Every assumption had to be proved at an excruciating level of detail, or else rejected. New materials had to be invented and new technologies needed to be built. The sky was the limit, but that was not the only **constraint**. Born and proven in cyberspace, this is the story of a technological triumph, the Boeing 777 (pronounced seven-seven-seven).

2.7.2 To Get It off the Ground *(what)*

In addition to the intellectual capital, mental labor, and physical labor, approximately four billion dollars was needed to get the Boeing 777 airborne. The exact monetary figure is unknown. Boeing and its **strategic partners** never revealed the total cost of their financial investment. The amount of $4 billion is the sum estimated by industry experts.

In addition to the required capital, the project was governed by two primary factors. The aircraft had to meet customer specifications and be completed within a finite time frame. For the Boeing 777 project, meeting the customers' specifications and the time frame established the total scope of the endeavor and imposed constraints at every level of design, manufacture, and production.

The Boeing 777 is the largest privately financed project in history. Not one penny came out of taxpayers' pockets. The Boeing 777 project is an example of the free enterprise system working at its best. Every dollar invested had to be justified to the stockholders and board of directors. At each level of management and authority, the risks and rewards had to be analyzed, understood, and approved.

Initially, Boeing was approached by several airline companies that expressed the desire for an airplane larger than the Boeing 767, but smaller than Boeing's Jumbo Jet, the 747. During the next few years, Boeing listened to these requests and put together a group of the most interested airlines to create the design specifications. Those airlines were United Airlines, All Nippon Airways, Japan Airlines, Cathay Pacific, and British Airways.

What separated the most interested airline companies from the others was the basis of their upfront commitments. These five airlines committed to the project in a big way. Each contributed money and provided Boeing with commitments to purchase the finished product. These companies provided their own full-time engineering teams that worked closely with Boeing engineers. Private vested interests are a powerful driving force.

Prior to 1990, these teams created all the basic design criteria. Here are some of the items specified:

- Range, cruising speed, and operating altitudes
- Customer capacities and seating configurations
- Maximum empty weight
- Cabin amenities

- Flight control systems
- Airport facility adaptations
- Optional engine specification

This list contains some of the items that would establish the constraints on the project. This particular list highlights customers' concerns. In addition to these constraints, the FAA and the Joint Aviation Authorities would impose regulatory requirements.

One of the mandated regulatory requirements was the ability for the airplane to fly three hours on a single engine. From the beginning, the project had to comply with some very stringent constraints. At the outset, the total cost of investment was unknown to Boeing and its partners.

In the case of the Manhattan Project, which produced the atomic bomb, and NASA's Apollo XI moonwalk, funding for work was provided via the traditional government bidding process. In this process, a **supplier** is allowed to quote costs and add an additional percentage for profit.

The drawbacks to this basic funding concept are numerous. For example, the bidding process often encourages out-of-scope work and the establishment of unrealistic completion schedules. This process may necessitate the need for one or more Congressional oversight committees—introducing bureaucracy and seemingly endless red tape. Finally, the bidding process encouraged extensive cost overruns.

The bidding removes much of the sense of urgency and relieves many individuals from being accountable. This effect is sometimes known as *passing the buck*. Ultimately, the taxpayer is held hostage in this type of environment.

In the case of the Boeing 777, it was different. As the project started to unfold, the members of the initial strategic alliance began to lay out further constraints. Included in this list of constraints was the total investment each was willing and capable of making. The Boeing Corporation had to pick up any monetary slack not covered.

A **classification system** had to be developed immediately. At this highest level of enterprise abstraction, here is a list of items of concern for the classification system:

- Environmental physics
- Technology
- Culture
- Vendor
- Customer
- Legislature
- Competition
- Opportunity
- Risk
- Money
- The corporation

Every item on this list had to be understood in great detail. The list is complete and represents a total system or schema of classification. This schema is particularly powerful and represents the total domain from which constraints are placed on any project.

Here is a list of the important items needed to start and complete this project:

- Strategic alliances
- Funding
- Technology understanding and advancement
- Smart people
- Work locations
- Acceptable time frames
- Dedication to get this project accomplished

This list bears a similarity to the motivation list presented in the section on the Pyramid of Giza.

- The Pharaoh was determined and dedicated to have his tomb.
- The culture of the populace embraced, accepted, or tolerated an undertaking. This particular idea was embraced.
- Resources and technology were adequate for the undertaking. Experts believed they could figure out the unknown.
- There was a high degree of confidence for success in a reasonable amount of time. Failure was not an option.
- The Pharaoh had the money to finance the undertaking.
- The Pharaoh had the force of arms to ensure compliance with his wishes.

The motivation list explains what is required for the successful completion of a project. The list represents *why* the project is being undertaken. From an abstract point of view, this list represents the justification and rationale for the *what, how, where, who,* and *when.* All planning activities attempt to resolve these questions for any project or endeavor.

The list of important items needed to start and complete the project focuses on assets. Specifically, the list helps spotlight the type of funding required and the items to be purchased. Determining answers for the items on the list establishes limits for the project and starts to set the terms of finite constraints.

For example, if a management team establishes a ceiling for the budgetary amount and a due date for completion of the work in the motivation list, resolving the list of *what* is needed to start and complete the project helps force those working on the list to understand the process of monetary allocation. At this point in the planning process, the intention is not to actually resolve the allocation problems, but rather to set up the criteria required to assist in the resolution.

Understanding the issues regarding the total assets required helped build the Great Pyramid of Giza, and answered the Pharaoh's question, *How much is this going to cost me.* In the case of Boeing, the alliance partners were able to understand all the constraints imposed by time and money. This understanding helped drive the effort to resolve all assumptions and make everything clear and explicit. Had this not been done, the project would have failed.

2.7.3 From Cyberspace to Reality *(how)*

When creating anything completely new, one of the first lessons learned is the old way of doing things does not apply. The more radically new the creation, the truer this lesson becomes. In every example we have used, new processes had to be created and existing ones expanded or changed.

Many new processes resulted in new application of technologies. These technologies either existed at the time the project started, or were invented to satisfy the needs of the process. Technology and process become entwined. Many times, we can observe that the more advanced a process, the more advanced the technology. At some point, the technology becomes the process, or vice versa, depending on your point of view.

Here are some of the processes the Boeing engineers had to understand:

- Prototyping
- Design
- Manufacturing
- Production
- Materials supply

This list represents a small sample of what Boeing engineers had to fully understand. They had to remove or resolve every assumption and define explicitly how each process would be accomplished.

The Boeing 777 was the first jetliner to be 100 percent digitally designed using three-dimensional solids technology. The technology allowed the designers to form the 3D geometry of a part and provided the means to make sure that part would integrate perfectly. Throughout the design process, the airplane was pre-assembled on the computer, eliminating the need for a costly, full-scale mock-up.

In Seattle's Puget Sound area, approximately 1,700 individual computer workstations were linked to the largest mainframe installation of its kind in the world. The mainframe was also linked to mainframes and workstation installations in a number of different locations, including Philadelphia, Pennsylvania; Wichita, Kansas; and Japan.

These locations added over 500 additional workstations, bringing the count to over 2,200. The software required to accomplish this task came from multiple vendors and needed to be integrated, and then either modified or enhanced to accomplish the project's aims. The benefit of this newly created environment improved the overall quality and reduced changes, errors, and rework. All of these factors helped minimize the partners' investment costs.

The Boeing 777 flew for the first time without the benefit of physical **prototypes**. All design criteria were modeled on the computer and the airplane was entirely pre-assembled. The airplane was assembled from 3 million parts, of which 130,000 had to be custom designed.

The digitally created aircraft was test flown in all flying conditions, and all in cyberspace. The results of the test flights dictated design changes and new engineering requirements. The airplane was changed to reflect the new demands and test flown again. This process was repeated many times until the new design could fly at 35,000 feet above sea level, while maintaining a cruising speed of 600 miles per hour, carrying 440 passengers for a distance of 6,000 miles at a fully laden weight of 545,000 pounds.

The maximum allowable weight for the aircraft in a dry state was 298,900 pounds. A dry state means the airplane is completely empty of all fluids and propellants, passengers, baggage, and cargo. If the airplane was over this weight, Boeing would have to pay penalties imposed by its partners.

Penalties were based on increased operating expenses that would be incurred as a result of the additional weight. Paying penalties was not an option for Boeing. The finished airplane was 3 pounds under the weight constraint. This represents a success by .00001 percent, or the equivalent of six Big Macs with the sesame seed bun, lettuce, cheese, pickles, onions, and sauce. This was obviously not a government contract. Figure 2-20 shows a cartoon representing this concept.

Figure 2-20 *Weighing the Boeing 777*

The weight requirement forced engineers to develop new materials. Other engineers applied the new materials to other areas, including tennis racquets. The new materials set new standards for strength to weight. The manufacturing process had to evolve and change. New rules for assembly were created—all predicted and modeled. All were developed in cyberspace, before the very first screw was produced.

The Boeing engineers had to physically prototype the landing gear because maneuvering around an airport is so important. This one part was so critical and its resolution so important that the landing gear was one of the design considerations to be kept secret. The overall design of the aircraft was not secret, just the technology employed. The lessons studied and learned from the atomic bomb, regarding classification and sharing of information, were of great importance.

In the late 1950s, the early results of the space race were a disaster. As each countdown reached zero and someone pushed the liftoff button, rocket after rocket blew up, on or just over the launch pad. The explosions were traced back to small, but significant, quality control mistakes. The 777 project could not afford any mistakes. Quality was built right into the processes. The computer support was very helpful, but the engineers were responsible for ensuring that nothing was overlooked.

2.7.4 A Global Effort *(where)*

Each work location shared a common concern. They were in different time zones on a global basis. This made coordination a tremendous challenge. Differences in time zones made teleconferencing impossible. Since the facilities at each location were already built, they were adapted to meet the project's needs. The tricky part was putting in the infrastructure of computers and communication networks. The need for sharing of information in a secure manner placed constraints on the facility adaptation.

In addition to the Boeing facilities, **vendors** and suppliers had to be included in this network. For instance, the engine suppliers of Pratt-Whitney, Rolls-Royce, and General Electric had to be included in all design phases. Weight constraints, distance, altitude operation, and speed all had to be considered in the design of the power plants. The engines for the Boeing 777 are as big as the circumference of the Boeing 737 fuselage.

Transporting the parts from one location to another became a big problem. The new engine was so large; there were no airplanes that could accommodate the girth of the new engine. The inability to physically transport parts forced transportation problems to the foreground.

The housing support for the Boeing 777 engine had to be made to exacting precision. The part had to be cut from a solid, thick sheet of titanium. Engine producers did not have the technology or facilities to accurately cut large blocks of titanium. Therefore, they subcontracted the work. Subcontracting placed backward constraints on the overall project. Disparate locations placed additional constraints on the project.

The *planners* had to consider all location issues and make them explicit. Any misassumption could be devastating.

2.7.5 Turned on, Tuned in, and Pumped *(who)*

Here are the types of people the *planners* required:

- Vendors
- Engineers
- Computer experts
- Industrial design specialists
- Mathematicians
- Purchasing and acquisition specialists
- Manufacturing experts
- Skilled aircraft assemblers

Once again, this list is not inclusive or complete. The processes dictated the skills required to accomplish the mission. The *planners* might have gone to the trouble of creating an organization chart. However, that chart is not required for the plan at this level of abstraction.

At the peak of the design effort, 238 teams existed. Design engineers and manufacturing engineers worked concurrently on the design of parts to decrease change orders and increase efficiency. Outside suppliers and airline customers also had to be represented on the teams. Thousands of people working for hundreds of companies played roles in the design, manufacture, production, and ongoing maintenance of the Boeing 777. All were tied together by the Boeing computer network and shared the same appropriate information in or near real time.

2.7.6 Better, Faster, Cheaper *(when)*

Nearly every aspect of the Boeing 777 project was complex. Scheduling was another component of the project. This, too, was a complex issue with which managers and engineers had to deal. Important business events for this project included:

- Deliver the 777 to customers
- Get the plane certified
- Prototype
- Build the plane
- Manufacture or buy all the parts for the plane
- Test the engines
- Prove the flying capability of the plane
- Hire the people
- Get the facilities

As you have learned, each of the items will create more lists. At times, you might think the list of lists is endless. It is not. Every project list eventually reaches the appropriate level of detail and does not need to make any more items explicit. Determining the appropriate level of detail is a most important point. The practitioner knows when this level is reached because there is nothing else about which to worry. In addition, all that needs to be communicated has been listed. At this moment, everything of importance has been made explicit.

The Boeing Corporation cultivated the expertise of making all items explicit in all planning phases. As prime contractors on many government projects, they had to master all the concepts of PERT, concurrent development, and CPM. Boeing has applied these concepts to the management of its commercial business for a long time. These concepts became part and parcel of the development life cycle of the 777.

Working with their strategic partners, Boeing took several years to collect the basic design requirements. The real physical design process began in 1990 and the plane debuted in 1994. The 777 went from a specification sheet to a flying airplane in only four years. This four-year time frame is approximately the same duration required for many automobile manufacturers to develop a new model car. In that time period, Boeing designed, manufactured, and built the 777 and also created the production facilities for the plane.

When the plane debuted, Boeing had to plan on 100,000 people touring the facilities and looking at the accomplishment. The debut was scheduled to last two days. To control crowds, Boeing had to use another facet of its expertise. Flow control established the number of people allowed to tour the facilities at any one time and determined the length of the tour.

2.7.7 Controlling Costs *(why)*

The Boeing Corporation and its strategic partners were determined and dedicated to the success of the 777. They were motivated. They carefully analyzed the potential risks and rewards for the project and sought to resolve each issue by making each known and traceable. In other words, each issue was made explicit. Management expressed confidence in the project and made major commitments to guarantee success. Nothing was overlooked and nothing was left to chance. They did not waver in commitment and support.

Boeing had many years of experience in cost accounting, and knew explicitly how to budget and control all expenses. It researched all the legislation that might affect the project in any way and made provisions for compliance with those laws. It made sure the assets aligned with the motivation.

The underlying technologies required had already been mastered. Boeing's project and manufacturing experience helped the company invent and master the new technologies required for the 777. From years of practice, Boeing has explicitly stated all the issues of process and has taken advantage of this well-learned behavior. It made sure processes were aligned with the assets and motivation.

Boeing knew all about the locations involved in the undertaking and could handle any of the required civil engineering upgrades to the facilities. It understood the nature of the technical communication infrastructure that would have to be in place. It made sure the connectivity was aligned with the processes, the assets, and the motivation.

The internal corporate culture embraced the ambitious 777 project. Employees clamored for the opportunity to be a part of the effort. Boeing applied its expertise in organizational science to the thousands of people who were required to complete the project. Boeing made sure the organization was aligned with the connectivity, processes, assets, and the motivation.

As a prime contractor on large government projects and developer of commercial airliners, Boeing is a master of logistical science. It knows how to identify every phase explicitly, including business processes, prioritizing, scheduling, and reporting. In its overall methodology of managing and controlling every event, nothing was left to chance.

Everything was made explicit at an **excruciating level of detail**. This commitment to detail cannot be overemphasized. The overall time frame to completion was acceptable. The alliance made sure every benchmark was hit. It made sure the business events were aligned with the organization, the connectivity, the processes, the assets, and the motivation.

Achieving integrated alignment between assets, processes, connectivity, organization, events, and motivation ensured that every partner, every team, and every individual could focus on a common cause and a common goal.

2.7.8 Key Terms

classification system	prototype
constraint	strategic partner
excruciating level of detail	supplier
Federal Aviation Administration (FAA)	vendor

2.7.9 Review Questions

1. How did the funding process for the Boeing 777 differ from that of the Manhattan Project?
2. What different types of constraints were placed on building the 777? Give some examples of constraints placed on other types of projects.
3. How did integrated alignment benefit Boeing?
4. What significance could the global location of networks, vendors, suppliers, and facilities have on the success or failure of the project?
5. The development life cycle of the 777 involved what planning techniques that are currently used by many project teams?
6. Explain the importance of making everything explicit at an excruciating level of detail for successful completion of this project?
7. Explain how the classification system applies to projects in today's enterprise.

2.8 SYNTHESIS AND CHAPTER SUMMARY

In the six sections, discussions were based around the six interrogatives (*what, how, where, who, when,* and *why*). Examples within each interrogative were tied to specific sciences or disciplines.

The chapter has six sections because there are six interrogatives. You will see this pattern repeated throughout Part II of the textbook. Each story starts with a different interrogative. The story of the pyramid started with *why*. The Cathedral of Chartres started with *where*. The atomic bomb story began with *how*. Levittown entered with *when*. The landing on the moon vignette began with *who*, and finally the Boeing 777 began with *what*.

The interrogatives were presented in different sequences to demonstrate that there is not necessarily a given sequence to solving a problem. Regardless of the starting point, each aspect must be understood and aligned with the others to solve the problem successfully.

Much of the chapter focused on the importance of lists. Therefore, it seems appropriate to present the summary of each section in list form.

The Great Pyramid of Giza—major themes:

- Entry point is *why*
- The creation of science and engineering based on laws of physics
- Issues of communication and advantages and disadvantages of a symbolic alphabet
- Importance of lists
- What constitutes motivation
- Role of the *planner*
- Concerns of the *planner*
- Importance of laws and rules
- Impact of technology
- Concepts of getting from a current state to an end state

The Cathedral of Chartres—major themes:

- Entry point is *where*
- Misassumption and assumption

- Implicit versus explicit
- The ripple effect of one misassumption on other aspects of a project
- Need for project security
- The importance of creating, saving, and sharing to support a proof
- The difficulty of undoing
- Six issues at the heart of motivation
- The idea of finite versus infinite
- Expansion, creation, and use of technology

The first atomic bomb—major themes:

- Entry point is *how*
- Importance for advancement of technology
- Importance of security and secrecy
- Importance and value of information
- Importance of knowing where you need to be and where you are
- The need for strategic advantage
- Importance of deadlines
- Importance of intellectual property

The story of Levittown—major themes:

- Entry point is *when*
- Key elements of the marketplace
- Mastering the logistics of a project
- Understanding the entire supply chain
- Importance of scheduling
- Building to order from standard parts
- The need for standards
- Advantages and disadvantages of mass production
- How projects cause changes in laws
- The impact of ripple effect
- How culture is established, changed, and supported

Landing on the moon—major themes:

- Entry point is *who*
- The importance of getting the right people
- How to think about a very large project
- Enabling the people to do their jobs
- The pressure a finite schedule places on a project
- The impact of small errors
- Differences between finite and infinite
- Importance of analyzing risk and reward

Boeing's first all digitally designed airplane—major themes:

- Entry point is *what*
- The concept of putting the need for continuous upgrades in the initial design of a product
- Establishing total scope and constraints of an endeavor
- The power of private investment
- Establishment of constraints
- The generation of a classification system
- Asset determination
- The need for explicit understanding
- Evolution of technology and process
- Importance of information sharing
- The need for supply chain coordination and control
- Importance of support
- Importance of getting every aspect in synchronization

These lists illustrate the principles of physics, science, and engineering that were used in the stories. Starting with a basic list, the lists were continually expanded and enforced at each level of abstraction and understanding. For any science or discipline, there must be a common sharing of ideas, vocabulary, principles, communication, and presentation. The expansion of each list to an excruciating level of detail ultimately enabled the success of each project.

A *summary list* of the summary would be:

1. The nature of asset—*what*
2. The mechanics of process—*how*
3. The fundamentals of location—*where*
4. The basis of organizational management—*who*
5. The importance of scheduling—*when*
6. The understanding of motivation—*why*

To place these concepts in the initial terms of the pyramids, we have graded to horizon and *carved them in stone*.

2.9 CHAPTER ACTIVITIES

2.9.1 Discussion Topics

1. Which one of the six items included on the motivation list for the pyramid contains an assumption? Why?

2. Sometimes the physics involved forces people and companies to make certain decisions. For example, the Egyptians needed to build a structure that would support a huge mass and weight with the available materials. The pyramid was the answer to the problem—style had nothing to do with it. What characteristics of physics might sway decisions made by companies today?

3. How does Abbott Suger characterize a business leader who always strives to better the goods or services his company produces?

4. During the building of the Cathedral of Chartres, the design and use of scaffolding was forced to evolve in order to support the structure. Give an example in today's enterprise that exhibits a similar need for technology to evolve to solve a problem.

5. Explain the advantages and disadvantages of funding methods described for the Boeing 777 and the Manhattan Project.

6. When President Roosevelt pushed the GI Bill through Congress, he said the bill would benefit veterans immediately and the country in the long term. How does a company make a choice between short-term and long-term decisions?

7. Explain how a model becomes the basis for how to think about any project.

8. Give an example in today's economy where it has been shown that there is only a small window of time for the execution of something new and different.

9. The peasants had no choice in financing the building of the Cathedral of Chartres. In regard to America's War on Terrorism which began in September 2001, who actually pays for this effort and why?

10. The artisans who came to Chartres were not necessarily trained to build something as radically new as a Gothic cathedral. Give an example of a situation in the enterprise today that parallels the problem of obtaining skilled workers.

11. Discuss how a motivation list describes what is needed for the successful completion of a project.

12. How was quality assured in the creation of the Boeing 777?

13. Why does a requirement or constraint restrict what you do? How does it help establish the scope of the project?

14. Discuss how a list can become a very useful and necessary tool for planners.

15. What is the difference between a rule and a law?

16. Discuss the kind of processes that could be involved in getting from a current state to an end state.

17. Explain the need for priorities.

18. Discuss how a project can be affected by cultural buy-in.

19. What effect can assumption and misassumption have on a project?

20. Compare and contrast the importance of intellectual capital during World War II and in today's enterprise.

2.9.2 Critical Thinking

1. Choose four of the more important lessons learned from the Manhattan Project and write a two-page paper explaining what the lessons mean to you and why you feel they are important.

2. Using the Internet, research CMM, and be ready to share the information you learn regarding why companies seek certification.

3. What causes a CEO to continue improving a successful company today? Using the Internet, choose a business leader and explain in a one- to two-page paper what that individual has done to continuously improve his or her company.

4. Levitt sold his company because he believed he could take his idea abroad and make lots of money. William Levitt was told by ITT Industries that he could not develop new housing communities in the U.S. for ten years. After deciding to develop his techniques internationally, Levitt took his ideas to places like France, Iran, Venezuela, and Nigeria. Using the Internet, see if you can discover other entrepreneurs who have made the decision to do business internationally in hope of duplicating a business plan that was previously successful in the U.S. Were these companies successful? Were Levitt's international efforts successful? Why or why not? Be prepared to share your findings with the class.

Endnotes

[1] The American Heritage Dictionary of the English Language, Fourth Edition.

[2] Webster's Revised Unabridged Dictionary, 1996, 1998.

[3] Undertaking is used for its double meaning: A task or assignment undertaken; a venture. The profession or duties of a funeral director.

[4] Axis powers was a coalition of countries that opposed the Allied powers in World War II. The coalition originated as the Rome-Berlin axis with the 1936 Hitler-Mussolini accord and their military alliance of May 1939. It was extended to include Japan in September 1940. Although other countries joined the pact, by 1944, only Germany and Japan remained.

[5] Few community names in America are as well known as Levittown, New York. In addition to its distinction as the childhood home of world-famous singer and songwriter, Billy Joel, Levittown is the model on which scores of post-World War II suburban communities were based.

[6] The pre-assembled white metal Tracy cabinets were not just trendy, even the White House kitchen used them. The Tracy cabinets were faster and cheaper to install than wood kitchen cabinets, which had to be measured, painted, sanded, and painted again.

[7] Kennedy, President John. Taken from the address on the Nation's Space Effort, given at Rice University, Houston, Texas, September 12, 1962.

COMMERCE

"We live in an age of acceleration. Whatever the formula was for business success a few years ago, it won't work today. Today there needs to be more and more work crammed into less and less time. There are fewer people doing more and doing it faster in less space with less support and with tighter tolerances and higher quality requirements than ever before. The average manager or knowledge worker is so busy today that there is simply not a spare moment for anything. There isn't time to plan, only to do. There is no time for analysis, invention, training, strategic thinking, contemplation, or lunch."

— *Tom De Marco (b. 1946), IT consultant, methodologist, author*

LEARNING OBJECTIVES

After completing Chapter 3, you will be able to:

1. List the six interrogatives needed to facilitate communication in the enterprise.
2. Understand the importance of creating a shared knowledge for the business enterprise.
3. Understand how systems thinking is used to view an organization holistically.
4. Describe the difference between systems thinking and traditional analysis.
5. Discuss how the vision, mission, and objectives help an organization focus on creating value and wealth.
6. Recognize the ramifications and trade-offs of the actions individuals and enterprises choose.
7. Distinguish between relief and recovery for an enterprise.
8. Discuss the advantages and disadvantages of different types of businesses.
9. Explain the meaning of the phrase *the system is the enterprise*.
10. Discuss how conceptually thinking about a business plan or business issue can benefit the enterprise.
11. List and explain the three principal responsibilities of the *owner*.
12. Discuss the choices an enterprise has when the marketplace changes.
13. Understand how laws and regulations can affect operations.
14. Explain why solid relationships are important to the enterprise.
15. Understand how standards certification can benefit an organization.
16. Explain how the enterprise benefits from having employees with strong leadership skills at all levels of the organization.

3.1 INTRODUCTION

In the 1960s, scientists started to realize how the single flap of a butterfly's wing in China has the potential to start a ripple effect in the atmosphere that could result in torrential rain in the United States. The **Butterfly Effect**, often ascribed to Edward Lorenz (b. 1917), was given a technical name, *sensitive dependence on initial conditions*.

Lorenz originally assumed that a small event such as the flap of a butterfly's wing could have no significant effect on its surroundings. But in fact, a small difference extended over a long period of time can produce a large effect. The way the difference affects the outcome can be sensitive to small changes.

The nursery rhyme, *For Want of a Nail*, points out that for centuries, some people have been aware of how seemingly small situations can escalate into big problems.

> *For want of a nail, the shoe was lost;*
> *For want of a shoe, the horse was lost;*
> *For want of a horse, the rider was lost;*
> *For want of a rider, the battle was lost;*
> *For want of a battle, the kingdom was lost!*

The nursery rhyme illustrates a simple **chain of events**. This **cause and effect** chain is what Lorenz identified as a sensitive dependence on initial conditions. The structure of this nursery rhyme makes it easy to see why the kingdom was lost—for want of a nail. When a problem occurs in a business environment, working backward through the problem may help uncover the **root cause**. A technique for doing this is known as the **five whys**. Using the example of the nursery rhyme, you can pose the following questions:

Q. Why was the kingdom lost?
A. Because the battle was not won
Q. Why was the battle not won?
A. Because one more rider was needed
Q. Why was one more rider not available?
A. Because there was no horse
Q. Why was there no horse?
A. Because the horse needed a horseshoe
Q. Why did the horse not have a horseshoe?
A. Because the supply of horseshoe nails had run out

Sometimes more than five whys are needed—but calling something *n*-whys does not have the same ring to it.

Q. Why did the supply of horseshoe nails run out?

Because the nursery rhyme did not provide the answer to this question, one of the following answers might be suitable:

- Nobody realized a horseshoe nail was an asset of the kingdom. Therefore, no one knew that the number of inventoried horseshoe nails should be proportional to the number of horseshoes and horses. This answer illustrates the need to understand and value all organizational assets.

- The kingdom had an adequate supply of horseshoe nails, but the quality was poor—either too soft or the wrong size for the shoes. The blacksmith's shop lacked **quality control**. Perhaps the **process** the blacksmith used to manufacture the nails was not quite right.

- The blacksmith got his iron ore for horseshoe nails from another kingdom, possibly the enemy's kingdom. Having your supply chain contingent on the enemy is one way to run out of **raw materials**. The connections in the supply chain—the location and methods of transporting raw materials—must be considered when times are good as well as bad.

- Basking on the French Riviera, the blacksmith had not checked his e-mail before leaving his workshop. He failed to discover that the king had cancelled all vacations due to an upcoming battle. Possibly, the blacksmith only read and spoke French and ignored the e-mail because he could not understand English. These problems point out how the king mismanaged the communication within the organization.

- The blacksmith focused on making victory rings and medals before starting to make the required quantity of horseshoes and horseshoe nails. Perhaps the blacksmith did not understand how to use the critical path method, or recognize the association between the dependent parts—when shoeing a horse, the horseshoe and horseshoe nails are required at the same time.

- The king had not shared his **vision** (an **end**) of a happy and stable kingdom with the blacksmith. Possibly, the blacksmith did not understand the king's motivation to always be ready for battle (a **means**). The *means* explains how an *end* can be accomplished.

These are six possible answers to the question of why the supply of horseshoe nails ran out, and they involve organization, process, assets, connectivity, critical path method, and motivation. In other words: *what, how, where, who, when,* and *why*.

No matter what you determine to be the root cause of this problem, the king did not adequately perform his kingly duties. In the end, the final result could not have been worse.

3.1.1 Relief and Recovery

If an organization has a problem and discovers a root cause, it may not deal with the cause directly. Sometimes it employs solutions to mask the problem in the hope that it goes away. Or, the organization might believe that the real problem can be solved by faith. Several examples illustrate these points.

Do you remember the last time you had a cough? You probably went to your medicine cabinet and reached for a bottle of cough medicine. If your mother was not watching, you probably drank an estimated level teaspoon directly from the bottle. As the thick syrup began to slide down your throat, you experienced a sensation of relief. It felt good. The medicine was coating your irritated throat, making it feel better for a while. You had not yet recovered from the cough, but at least your throat would not hurt for the next hour or two.

Relief is fundamentally different from *recovery*. Relief is the short-term ease or lessening of pain or discomfort, while recovery is a more permanent return to an original state of being. In business, relief is generally perceived to be quicker and cheaper than recovery. Management often prefers to keep applying quick fixes (*relief*) rather than tackle issues head on (*recovery*).

In the early 1970s, Ford offered the Mach One (a true muscle car), a Mustang with hundreds of horsepower (presumably whose horseshoes had enough nails!) and little else. The Mustang ran on the highest-octane fuel (100 octane), and could leave most cars coughing in the bowl of dust it left behind. The people who bought the Mach One had only one objective—to keep competitors in their rearview mirrors.

In 1999, the Ford Motor Company distributed the 1999 Cobra, a special edition of the Mustang automobile, to its North American dealerships. The Mustang was originally released to the general public in 1964 by a design team headed by Lee Iacocca (b. 1924), the person responsible for saving Chrysler in the 1980s.

The 1999 Mustang Cobra had a rating of 320 horsepower. Ford's engineers knew the Cobra would live and die by its horsepower numbers. The targeted **consumer** for this vehicle was a person who cared about these numbers. By the time the winter snow melted and the trees began to bloom in the spring of 2000, many Cobra owners started to think their cars did not have all of the advertised 320 horsepower. They were appearing in the rearview mirrors of Chevy Camaros instead of the other way around. In droves, Cobra owners tested their cars on dynamometers and found that their vehicles' big-block V-8 engine contained 15 to 20 less horsepower than Ford had promised.

Ford scrambled to fix the 8,100 cars that had been sold and needed to determine what happened to the missing horses. The engineers discovered the cause of the problem in the Cobra's exhaust system that passes under the control arms of the rear suspension. During design, engineers lowered the mounting points on the lower control arms by 20 millimeters. This change put the 2.5-inch exhaust pipe too close to the ground.

To address the problem of the exhaust pipe being too close to the ground, Ford's construction people simply flattened the pipe to create the needed clearance. Ultimately, this was not a good idea. This small quick fix increased backpressure and reduced the Cobra's horsepower. In addition, the lower intake manifold was found to have a lip of extra material in the intake port, which also restricted the exhaust flow and took away even more horsepower.

Ford discovered that targeted consumers could tell the difference between 305 horsepower and 320 horsepower. Ford also found out that fixing a problem (in this case, flattening the exhaust pipe) without first reviewing the original design could cause more problems. Ford learned that consumer satisfaction is part of a cause and effect chain that starts with how the car is engineered—one of its *sensitive dependencies on initial conditions*. Ford also learned that *relief* is not the same as *recovery*.

A number of archetypes illustrate how a company seeks relief at the expense of recovery. Often people do not understand the essential differences between relief and recovery, and the need for maintaining strategic views instead of taking operational or tactical measures, as shown in the following generalizations:

- Employees pursue immediate gratification versus determine the correct thing to do.

- Employees generally pursue short-term rather than long-term options.
- Solutions are rushed into production without considering an **integrated enterprise solution**.
- Management opts for a point-in-time solution rather than confronting the corporate infrastructure.
- Management views costs as an expense rather than an asset.
- Employees seek quick-and-dirty solutions versus doing it right.
- Employees solve a problem at the expense of the enterprise, instead of solving the problem to benefit the enterprise.
- Employees stay with a known method versus try an innovative method.
- Management takes a pay-me-now approach because everything else takes too long and costs too much.

Have you ever heard the phrase *the system is the enterprise*? Many corporations can no longer conduct business when their IT systems are down. As a result, the business may not be able to take and fill customer orders, or provide customers with service.

When a company reaches the point where the system is the enterprise, the company is at the mercy of the **computer programmer**. The programmer is keeper of the system and, in many instances, throws away the keys by taking the path of least resistance—choosing *relief* over *recovery*. Sometimes programmers do not understand the essential difference between relief and recovery, or that strategic views should be in concert with operational and tactical measures.

3.1.2 The System Is the Enterprise

When the system is the enterprise, the enterprise is constrained by the capability and availability of its systems, and by how quickly the system can be modified and made available to its users. As a case in point, on June 8, 2001, a software upgrade failed at the New York Stock Exchange (NYSE). Trading ceased on stocks and bonds for nearly two hours.

The NYSE, sometimes referred to as the Big Board, is one of the world's largest financial centers for trading stocks and bonds. On an average trading day, over 1 billion shares with a monetary value exceeding $43 billion exchange hands. The software glitch on June 8, 2001 affected trading in half of the exchange's 3,000 stocks, prompting the Big Board to stop all trading.

Richard Grasso, chairman of the NYSE, stated, "The fair thing to do is bring the entire market down." Not only did the glitch affect the calculation of major market indexes, the problem affected trading at the American Stock Exchange (AMEX) and the Chicago Board of Trade (CBOT), which trades futures and options. Although the National Association of Securities Dealers Automated Quotations (NASDAQ) computer systems were not affected, the problem made traders leery of conducting business on the NASDAQ.

Several weeks later, the NASDAQ had its turn. Two systems crashed while a WorldCom employee conducted a diagnostic test. Not only did the test interrupt the systems, but it prevented anyone from using the systems' password to bring the systems back into operation.

A year earlier, the Toronto Stock Exchange (TSX) had to stop trading on a single stock because of a software problem, the tenth serious bug in two years. That stock was Nortel, which represented about 30 percent of the TSX 300 Index (currently known as the S&P/TSX Composite Index).

Although shutdowns and slowdowns are rare on the electronic markets, they highlight that the system *is* the enterprise. See Figure 3-1.

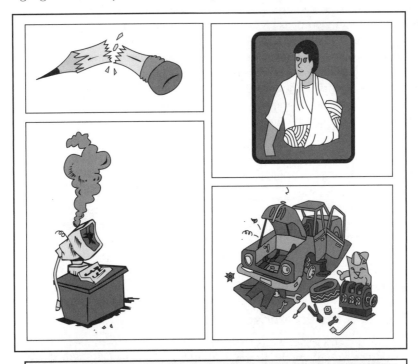

Figure 3-1   *The system* **is** *the enterprise for more than just computers*

To be fair, some organizations replace an automated system with a manual standby. In 1998, the Arizona Lottery suspended its nightly Pick 3 game after uncovering a programming error. Anyone who chose the number nine had no chance of winning. Pick 3 players select three numbers from zero to nine, and a computer generates the winning numbers. Lottery officials said computer testing of the game had only been done on numbers zero to eight.

Governor Jane Hull (b. 1935) ordered the game suspended until a traditional mechanical-ball system could be installed to replace the computer system. Players who held tickets with the number nine were eligible for a refund of the $1 cost of the ticket.

Number problems can interrupt systems because there is no fixed way to count. That sounds strange, but some programmers count from zero to nine, while other programmers count from one to ten. The counting range and the programmer's number ceiling caused the Arizona Lottery system to break. Consistency is essential in business, as is indicated by this example.

Sometimes you cannot find a quick mechanical fix. For example, in September of 1997, a software snafu left the USS Yorktown, an Aegis missile cruiser, dead in the water.

Top Navy officials declared the Yorktown Smart Ship pilot a success in reducing manpower, maintenance, and costs. The Navy began running shipboard software applications in the Microsoft Windows NT operating system so that fewer sailors would be needed to control key ship functions. The Navy learned a difficult lesson about automation: The information technology upon which the ship depended also made the ship vulnerable.

The Yorktown suffered a systems failure when a petty officer entered a zero in a database while calibrating a fuel valve during maneuvers off the coast of Cape Charles, Virginia. A computer program used the zero entered by the petty officer to perform a mathematical division. Bam!!

The divide-by-zero error caused buffers in the computer to overflow, which, in turn, caused the battleship's propulsion system to fail. In other words, every engine that moved the battleship through the water stopped working. The Yorktown was crippled. The battleship had to be towed into the naval base at Norfolk, Virginia, where it took two days to repair the problem.

If you pull out your $2.95 calculator and divide any number by zero, you will probably get zero (not the correct answer, infinity). The calculator doesn't stop working because of a divide-by-zero error—it still executes the next set of instructions. For the systems on board the Yorktown, a divide-by-zero problem crippled the enterprise. Behold the power of the programmer.

3.1.3 A Supply of Money

Recall the nursery rhyme and the 1999 Cobra. Both represent a failure to execute a plan. Many of the early dot-com corporations never had a plan. They went straight to execution—they did not consider creating a business plan.

They did not take the time to think about how their businesses should be operated. They did not consider how to design the processes needed to conduct business, let alone how the businesses would be built. They often started with a published Web page and hoped the business would become a viable buy-out candidate.

Most dot-com entrepreneurs never truly explored the questions, *What business are we in?* and *Why are we in it?* beyond the obvious desire to make a quick profit. In fact, many entrepreneurs never asked whether their businesses were viable for online operations, or if partners, suppliers, and customers were available to them.

Instead, they built Web sites and expected to receive massive profits from unseen millions of shoppers. To the chagrin of these entrepreneurs, they ended up waiting and watching. They watched hundreds of millions of dollars disappear from their bank accounts and the bank accounts of the venture capitalists that blindly funded them. Once the money was gone, with no other option, the companies vanished. A few dot-com companies have sustained longevity, but they have had problems.

For example, Amazon.com had problems with its supply chain. The company was concerned about the availability of merchandise from its primary vendors. Amazon also had problems in its accounting department. Since its inception, Amazon.com classified shipping charges as revenue. This means that the company was earning less money than it was reporting to its investors. See Figure 3-2. The following excerpts are taken from Amazon.com's SEC 10K filing for December 31, 2000.

Veni, Vidi, Vici.
I came, I saw, I conquered.

Veni, Vidi, Napi.
I came, I saw, I napped.

Figure 3-2   *Dot-com entrepreneurs*

Inventory Vendors

During 2000, approximately 27 percent of all inventory purchases were made from three major vendors. The company does not have long-term contracts or arrangements with most of its vendors to guarantee the availability of merchandise, particular payment terms, or the extension of credit limits.

New Accounting Pronouncements

In September 2000, the Emerging Issues Task Force (EITF) reached a final consensus on EITF Issue 00-10, "Accounting for Shipping and Handling Fees and Costs." This consensus requires that all amounts billed to a customer in a sale transaction related to shipping and handling, if any, represent revenue and should be classified as revenue. The company historically has classified shipping charges to customers as revenue. With respect to the classification of costs related to shipping and handling incurred by the seller, the EITF determined that the classification of such costs is an accounting policy decision that should be disclosed. Adoption of this consensus did not change the company's existing accounting policies or disclosures.

eBay, Inc., the online auctioneer, has problems with security. Anyone in charge of technology should understand the need for a sophisticated firewall. A firewall is hardware and/or software that controls traffic on a computer network. The following excerpt is taken from eBay's SEC 10K filing for December 31, 2000.

Unauthorized Break-Ins or Other Assaults on Our Service Could Harm Our Business

Our servers are vulnerable to computer viruses, physical or electronic break-ins, and similar disruptions, which could lead to interruptions, delays, loss of data, public release of confidential data, or the inability to complete customer transactions. In addition, unauthorized persons may improperly access our data. We have experienced an unauthorized break-in by a "hacker" who has stated that he can in the future damage or change our system or take confidential information. We have also experienced "denial of service" type attacks on our system that have made all or portions of our website unavailable for periods of time. These and other types of attacks could harm us. Actions of this sort may be very expensive to remedy and could damage our reputation and discourage new and existing users from using our service.

Money is something every business needs. Essentially, everything a company does or aspires to be is secondary to its ability to raise capital. Without capital, a company has a limited life span. A company can raise money by borrowing from a bank, receiving donations, issuing and selling stock, or by using the preferred method of continuously selling its products or services. See Figure 3-3.

| Figure 3-3 | *Contrary to popular belief,* *this is a profit making organization* |

Organizations with a continuous supply of money can achieve great things for their society, employees, and shareholders. These organizations can be for profit, nonprofit, sole proprietorships, huge conglomerates, civic centers, or religious organizations, but each still needs money to survive.

3.1.4 Types of Enterprises

You can engage in a business venture alone or with others. You can elect to incorporate and issue shares, establish a sole proprietorship, create a partnership, or set up a nonprofit corporation, for example, whether your endeavor is religious, civil, nonprofit, charitable, or criminal.

You do not have to be a business giant to have the financial and other benefits (including tax benefits) of operating a corporation.

General Corporation

A common business structure is a general corporation. The corporation is a separate legal entity owned by stockholders. A general corporation may have an unlimited number of stockholders that, due to the separate legal nature of the corporation, are protected from the creditors and actions of the business. A stockholder's personal liability is usually limited to the amount of investment in the corporation and no more.

Closed Corporation

There are a few small, but significant, differences between general corporations and closed corporations. In most states where they are recognized, closed corporations are limited to 30 to 50 stockholders.

This type of corporation is particularly well suited for a group of people who own the corporation, with some members actively involved in the management while other members are involved only on a limited or indirect level.

S Corporation

With the Tax Reform Act of 1986, the S Corporation became a highly desirable entity for corporate tax purposes. An S Corporation is not really a different type of corporation. It is a special tax designation granted by the Internal Revenue Service (IRS). Many entrepreneurs and small business owners are partial to the S Corporation because it combines many of the advantages of a sole proprietorship, partnership, and the corporate forms of business structure.

S Corporations eliminate the problems faced by standard corporations whose shareholder-employees might be subject to IRS claims of excessive compensation. *CHA-CHING*!!

Not all domestic general business corporations are eligible for S Corporation status. These exclusions include:

- A financial institution that is a bank
- An insurance company taxed under Subchapter L
- A Domestic International Sales Corporation (DISC)
- Certain affiliated groups of corporations

Limited Liability Company (LLC)

LLCs have long been a traditional form of business structure in Europe and Latin America. LLCs were first introduced in the United States by the state of Wyoming in 1977 and authorized for pass-through taxation (similar to partnerships and S Corporations) by the IRS in 1988. Many business professionals believe LLCs present a superior alternative to corporations and partnerships because LLCs combine many of the advantages of both.

Sole Proprietorship

A sole proprietorship is an unincorporated business owned by one person. The most important feature of a sole proprietorship is that the law makes no distinction between you, the sole proprietor, and your business. Virtually all the legal and tax consequences associated with sole proprietorships flow from this essential element. A sole proprietorship can hire any number of employees.

A sole proprietor can conduct business under an individual's name or under a trade name. For example, a plumber could conduct business under her own name, Leigh Key, or under a trade name, such as Contin-u-Drip. In either case, the business is a sole proprietorship.

Nonprofit Corporations

The IRS grants nonprofit tax status. The corporation's charter must indicate that it is organized for charitable or other acceptable purposes to qualify under the IRS rules. Documentation must be provided to the IRS that designates how the corporation's assets will be distributed should it dissolve.

Offshore Corporations

Simply put, people and companies use offshore trusts, corporations, and limited liability companies to keep money from the U.S. government. Companies justify this practice with use of the following phrases:

- Financial privacy
- Legal income, capital gain, estate, and gift tax reduction
- Tax reduction
- Asset protection
- Protection from inflation
- Asset and currency diversification
- Immunity to domestic law
- Higher returns on investment
- Estate planning
- More favorable foreign laws

An especially attractive offshore jurisdiction is the Caribbean island of Nevis. Because its corporation laws are derived from the British common law and Delaware corporation law, and because Nevis has a stable government and modern infrastructure, this island is the premier offshore center in the world.

General Partnership

In a general partnership, two or more co-owners engage in business for profit. Typically, the partners own the business assets together and are personally liable for business debts. In the absence of a partnership agreement, profits are shared equally among the partners. A partnership agreement usually describes how profits and losses are shared. Jointly and separately, each partner is personally liable for debts and taxes of the partnership.

Organized Crime Family

Most people are honest and attempt to live within the law of the land; however, some corporations or business people attempt to bend or subtly break the law, knowing that the penalties can involve the loss of a license, payment of fines, or time in prison. Some business entities are created with the explicit intent not to conform to government laws and regulations. Organized crime families are one example. They are unique because their members are willing to pay with their lives if caught. This choice is obviously extreme, but indicates how far people are willing to go when they perceive the rewards outweigh the risks.

La Cosa Nostra, also known as the Mafia, is a group organized into *families*, operating primarily in North America. Originally, there were 26 *families* in the United States—roughly one for each major city. The Mafia commission, composed of bosses of numerous families, mostly from New York, was the overseeing authority for all of the other La Cosa Nostra families.

With Prohibition came the birth and growth of nationally organized crime. Newly conceived Mafia families jockeying for power were waging battles that killed scores, frightened citizens, and gave way to screaming headlines and grand funeral processions never before experienced in the New World. But it all began years ago and miles away.

The Mafia has its roots in Sicily, where the larger and more powerful Sicilian Mafia operates. Over the years, Greeks, Romans, Byzantines, Normans, French, Spanish, and Austrians have all conquered the island of Sicily. Sicilian peasants were little more than slave labor to their foreign overlords. Thus the Mafia was born, a secret society that provided the poor, oppressed Sicilians with protection, stability, and pride. The Mafia vendetta was the Sicilian form of justice. The victimized were quiet and patient. Vengeance was saved for a future time.

Consequently, the Mafia golden rule of *omerta* (translated as honor) was established. Because of the inherent instability of being conquered by so many different peoples, the Sicilians came to distrust all forms of government. It became an unwritten rule to leave the government out of private affairs. Crimes were considered to be personal, with justice served by the vendetta.

Criminal organizations typically need sophisticated accounting techniques to manage money and other assets the organization controls and uses. Information systems in this type of organization are usually not computerized and are under the tight control of a select few individuals. Keep in mind with criminal organizations, it may be harder to set up vacation schedules and paid holidays for employees.

3.1.5 Separate the What from the How

Technology is an enabler of the business, and in and of itself does not fix things magically, but it can help in understanding, identifying, and solving many different problems. Often problems can be traced back to executive management. Others can be directly attributed to **knowledge workers**. Of course, everybody in between can initiate a problem too.

Members of an organization need a way to share information about every aspect of the business so that everyone can make decisions based on explicit information. Business participants should not have to make assumptions and guess what to do. Shared information must include: information of interest to the business, processes, location and **connectivity**, organization, business cycles, and business plans that include the vision and **mission**.

Peter Drucker in Forbes ASAP wrote,

The next information revolution is well underway. But it is not happening where information scientists, information executives, and the information industry in general are looking for it. It is not a revolution in technology, machinery, techniques, software, or speed. It is a revolution in concepts.

He then went on to say,

...business success is based on something totally different, the creation of value and wealth. This requires risk-taking decisions: on the theory of the

business, on business strategy, on abandoning the old and innovating the new, on the balance between the short term and the long term, on the balance between immediate profitability and market share. These decisions are the true top management tasks.[1]

Chapter 2 outlined the importance of a business having a plan and identified the effectiveness of a list. The next natural step is to start thinking about how to put these plans to work. Thinking about *what* you need independent of *how* it is going to work can provide several benefits, including seeing multiple ways to resolve a problem and revising an existing mode of execution. Both of these are evident in **systems thinking** and thought leadership.

Systems thinking has its foundation in the field of system dynamics. Jay Forrester (b. 1918), professor at Massachusetts Institute of Technology (MIT), founded system dynamics in 1956. Professor Forrester recognized the need for a better way to test ideas about social systems, in the same way that ideas can be tested in engineering or computing. Systems thinking allows people to make their understanding of social systems explicit and improve them in the same way people can use engineering principles to make explicit and improve their understanding of mechanical systems.

In systems thinking, a **system** is an entity that maintains its existence through the interaction of its individual parts. A complex system may behave in ways that cannot be predicted from looking at the individual parts. Many forms of analysis are quite different from the systems thinking approach, which focuses on a **holistic view** of the system. In fact, the word *analysis* comes from the root meaning *to break into constituent parts*. In the past, analysis methods often only included breaking things down to study the individual separate pieces.

However, in today's environment, enterprises need to be increasingly aware of both singularities and connections. This means understanding the primitive models and thoughts (a single part) and the **composite** models and thoughts (interactions of the parts). Primitive models can be summarized as *things, processes, connectivity, people, timing,* and *motivation.* See Figure 3-4.

```
Primitive Models
 — Things
 — Processes
 — Connectivity
 — People
 — Timing
 — Motivation
```

Figure 3-4   *High-level terms for the six primitive models*

The holistic view of the primitives provides the information needed to make knowledgeable business decisions and create value for the enterprise. The composite models can be summarized as all the possible combinations of primitives. See Figure 3-5.

```
Composite Models
— Things + Processes
— Things + Connectivity
. . .
— Things + Processes + Connectivity
— Things + Processes + People
. . .
— Things + Processes + Connectivity + People
— Things + Processes + People + Timing
. . .
```

Figure 3-5   *Examples of composite models built on primitive models*

Using systems thinking, one learns how the element being studied interacts with other parts of the system. Therefore, rather than breaking things down into tiny parts, systems thinking works by expanding the view and seeing the larger picture of interactions going on within the system. See Figure 3-6.

```
How to calculate the possible number of model interactions:

2⁶ — 1

The power is determined by the number of primitive models
being considered. In this example, there are six (See
Figure 3-2).

∴ (2 * 2 * 2 * 2 * 2 * 2) — 1 = 63

63 — number of primitive models = number of composite models

6 Primitive Models
57 Composite Models
```

Figure 3-6   *Calculating the possible number of model interactions*

When studying a dynamically complex organization, systems thinking can generate conclusions that are different from those in other forms of analysis. Since many corporate enterprises are complex and dynamic, involving many participants and numerous levels of problems, systems thinking can help broaden the perspective of participants so that better long-term solutions can be created.

3.1.6 Authority and Responsibility

The authority and responsibility for the performance and behavior of an enterprise rest on the shoulders of the *owner*. The role of the owner is frequently observed to be one of leadership. However, the role of the *owner* is not limited to the chief executive officer or the president. All employees may find themselves in the *owner's* role—someone with authority and responsibility over a specific domain.

The *owner* in an enterprise has three principal responsibilities:

- Provide a product or service
- Control costs of a product or service
- Ensure the continuing existence of the enterprise

Boeing, a general corporation, works to determine how to sell the 777. The work started prior to the airplane's production and is continually reviewed and revised during the product's life span. The American Red Cross, a nonprofit organization, gives away its services to those in need. The Apollo space mission was a government service that was supported by taxpayers.

All types of organizations and government agencies attempt to control the costs of providing their products or services. The desire to control costs is always present. The single exception may be during times of war because priorities shift.

The desire to preserve liberty allowed the federal government to provide an open checkbook for the Manhattan Project. The Levitt family went to extraordinary lengths to control costs in order to maintain a profit for their low-cost housing. Boeing and its strategic partners needed to control costs for the 777 from the onset. Educational authorities and families also need to control costs and maximize the return on assets.

To ensure the continuing existence of an organization, a for-profit company needs to make a profit, or at best minimize losses. A nonprofit organization tries to break even—not show a profit nor incur a loss. Governments are not directly motivated by profit. However, governmental programs, administrative costs, and hidden political agendas necessitate the acquisition of funds. Many politicians attempt to limit spending to match anticipated revenue, thereby illustrating the need to control costs.

The *owner's* desire for the enterprise to stay in existence creates the impetus to establish rules for selling and controlling costs. In addition, the need for the enterprise to stay in existence drives the motivation for the entire organization. Existence itself may sometimes supersede the need or ability to control costs.

One of the challenges facing an *owner* is to understand the classification system introduced in Chapter 2. The list illustrates the items of interest to the *owner*, as stated by the *planner* at the highest level of abstraction. The *owner's* challenge then becomes one of identifying all the nuances of the classification system, as in the following list:

- Environmental physics—Topography, location idiosyncrasies, and weather are some of the concerns affecting an enterprise's ability to conduct business. For instance, if you are doing business in the Canadian province of Saskatchewan, you must understand the problems caused by inclement weather.
- Technology—Limitations or opportunities derived from current technology need to be known. Enterprises may also need to determine what technologies should be enhanced, invented, or **sunsetted**. Sunsetting implies a plan to phase out or retire a technology, and to cease finding new ways to use that technology.
- Culture—Every location has a unique set of beliefs, ethics, and values. Over time, the enterprise develops its own corporate culture and needs to understand and honor the cultures of its surroundings.
- Vendors—Companies and people from which the enterprise buys products or services are part of an enterprise **value chain**.

- Customers—Companies and people that can and will buy the corporation's products or services are part of an enterprise's value chain.
- Legislatures—A governing body that creates laws and rulings at the national, state, county, and municipal levels, legislation establishes an imposition on an enterprise, including collecting taxes and restricting how products or services are produced or sold.
- Competition—Companies and people capable of competing for **market share** in any **marketplace** are your competition.
- Opportunity—Anything that causes the enterprise to take action, such as the introduction of a new product or service, the ability to optimize costs, or the ability to improve revenue, market share, or profitability.
- Risk—Anything with the potential to cause harm or have a negative effect on the enterprise is a risk. In an extreme case, the resulting effect may threaten the enterprise's existence.
- Money—This is an expression of investments, sales, expenses, and profits.
- Corporation—Any legal entity that represents a business enterprise is a corporation.

Once the *owner* understands the challenges and assumes the authority and responsibility of the domain, the *owner* must exhibit characteristics of an effective communicator and thought leader. **Thought leaders** respect and listen to the opinions of others. They value the voice of experience. They free their imaginations to consider the questions beneath the answers and the questions beneath the questions. Thought leaders are willing and able to share with others. They believe in being part of a learning community. They are cautious of being judgmental. They let go of assumptions and harvest **wisdom**.

Next, the *owner* must consider the legal and ethical implications of any and all actions. The CEO of a Fortune 500 company once said that leaders should always take the ethical high ground on any issue. Leaders who do this will not have to worry about the law. When leaders think through any issue and find themselves asking, *Is this legal*, astute leaders know they are on thin ice. If they start asking, *How do I make this legal*, they know they are in deep water. Business people find themselves in this quandary on a regular basis.

As an example of a legal and ethical issue, imagine the following scenario: You are the CEO of a company that transports crude oil from producers to users. To satisfy this need, you have a large fleet of oil tankers. Some of the oil tankers are capable of carrying 50 million barrels of crude oil. An oil tanker of this size cannot be considered a pleasure boat.

Pumping out the bilges on a regular basis is routine maintenance for the tankers. Each government, from every nation with which you do business, has decreed and enacted laws that state bilges must be pumped out in port. The cost for pumping the bilge in port is $75,000. The charge, a rather hefty sum, reflects the cost of handling the toxic bilge to prevent pollution of the oceans. An alternative would be to pump the bilge at sea. Other than the cost of turning on the bilge pumps, there are no expenses.

As CEO, you are faced with a choice. You can pump the bilge in port for $75,000, or perform the same function at sea for $0. By the way, the fine for violating this law and pumping the bilge at sea is $100,000. Statistically, the chances of getting caught pumping the bilge at sea are about 1 in 1,000—if the ship steers out of the shipping lanes, who would know?

If you were the CEO, what would you decide to do?

Based on the high level of oil pollutants in the world's oceans, you issue an order to all of your captains to pump at a port. Would your ethics allow you to add the following dictum to your captains:

If you have a mishap at sea that requires you to pump out the bilges at sea, we will not make a big deal of it, and, of course, you do realize that your bonus is figured on the net profit of the operation of this vessel, don't you?

As the CEO, depending on your mettle, the law has set up a potentially serious conflict of interest for you. You must resolve what to do, assess the risks, and understand the inherent punishments. If you are unsure what choice you would make, consider this—unethical behavior goes on all the time. Sometimes flouting of the law is so gross, it causes the law to change. For example, consider the Blue Laws.

The Blue Laws are legislation regulating public and private conduct. The laws are primarily related to the observance of the Sabbath. The term was originally applied to the seventeenth-century laws of the theocratic New Haven colony; they were called Blue Laws after the blue paper on which they were printed. At one time, almost every state had a set of Blue Laws.

The laws made conducting commerce on Sunday a crime punishable by a fine. However, many retailers forecasted profits from being open on a Sunday and concluded it was better to be open and pay the fine. In no time at all, the issuers of the fines could not keep up with all the fines that had to be served. In addition, the retailers stopped paying the fines and demanded court trials. This immediately placed a huge burden on the entire judiciary system. The state legislatures took one look at the growing problems and repealed the Blue Laws.

Owners look at issues of risk and possible consequences of taking risk based on the law, their beliefs, and ethics. *Owners* may conclude that an opportunity or reward outweighs the consequence of taking a risk, even if the risk means losing your life. This extreme appears not to be a problem for organized crime families and drug cartels.

OWNERSHIP IN PUBLIC EDUCATION

The organizational structure of a public school district in the United States illustrates how an enterprise can have many *owners*. This list provides an indication of the types of authority, responsibility, and leadership traits required by the *owners* of

(continued)

public education for a given domain. The *owners* are presented in a hierarchical form, where each *owner* may mandate policies or initiatives to the *owners* below.

Federal Government
- Domain:
  - The nation
- Authority:
  - Establishes the rules for fund requests
  - Budgets the allocation of money to federal agencies
  - Mandates national policies
- Responsibility:
  - Includes the well-being and survival of the nation
  - Determines how to invest money
  - Enforces national education policies
- Leadership Traits:
  - Communicates effectively
  - Sets goals

Department of Health, Education, and Welfare
- Domain:
  - All state departments of health, education, and welfare
- Authority:
  - Establishes the rules for fund requests
  - Budgets the allocation of money to state departments of education
  - Performs due diligence to maintain fairness in budgeting funds
- Responsibility:
  - Effectively lobbies for educational funding
  - Determines how to invest money to state departments of education
- Leadership Traits:
  - Communicates effectively

State Department of Education
- Domain:
  - All local school districts within the state
- Authority:
  - Budgets the allocation of money to local districts
  - Sets state graduation requirements
  - Mandates state education policies
- Responsibility:
  - Determines how to invest money
  - Withholds financial resources from local districts if necessary
- Leadership Traits:
  - Communicates effectively

(continued)

Community
Domain:
- Local school district

Authority:
- Members can choose to vote or not to vote
- Permission to vote

Responsibility:
- Determines how to invest money
- Elects school board members

Leadership Traits:
- Communicates effectively
- Provides public service

School Board
Domain:
- School community

Authority:
- Disciplines students
- Approves textbooks
- Employs or terminates staff
- Establishes funds to support individual initiatives
- Aligns state and local graduation requirements

Responsibility:
- Determines how to invest money
- Sets vision, mission, and goals
- Formal discipline of employees
- Determines funding for various initiatives
- Establishes district calendar

Leadership Traits:
- Communicates effectively
- Provides public service
- Possesses vested interest in education

Superintendent
Domain:
- Entire local school district organization

Authority:
- Approves funds for various district efforts
- Recommends hiring and firing of district personnel
- Influences culture of school community
- Manages staff
- Sets vision, mission, and goals

Responsibility:
- Prepares budget and determines how to invest money
- Tours buildings and observes staff and students

(continued)

- Arbitrates district disputes regarding staff and students
- Keeps up to date on laws and regulations affecting the school district

Leadership Traits:

- Good communicator
- People skills
- Political skills

Principal

Domain:

- The school building

Authority:

- Approves funds for building initiatives
- Recommends hiring and firing of employees

Responsibility:

- Creates the culture of the building
- Makes decisions regarding hiring and firing
- Manages staff and students
- Manages conflict
- Budgets allocations

Leadership Traits:

- Good communicator
- Good people skills

Department Chairperson

Domain:

- Individual department

Authority:

- Approves funding for department efforts
- Recommends textbooks

Responsibility:

- Determines how to spend money
- Dispenses information
- Curriculum decisions

Leadership Traits:

- Good communicator
- Results oriented

Teacher

Domain:

- Classroom

Authority:

- Sets discipline standards
- Assigns homework
- Assigns grades

(continued)

Responsibility:
- Establishes a safe environment for students
- Grades homework
- Educates
- Assesses student performance
- Follows state benchmarks for curriculum standards

Leadership Traits:
- Goal oriented
- Vested interest in public education

The *owner* of a corporation has to accept authority and responsibility. The *owner* has to address the challenges of the enterprise and effectively communicate and lead. The *owner* must understand the issues of cause and effect, determine short-term and long-term directions, budget the allocation of money, and be governed by laws, beliefs, and ethics. The following six stories illustrate the issues of the leader.

SECTION 3.2 WHERE IT'S THE REAL THING— COCA-COLA ENTERPRISES

QUESTIONS TO CONTEMPLATE

1. What do butterflies, horseshoes, and a nursery rhyme have to do with enterprise architecture?
2. What would happen if Coca-Cola published its secret recipe?

3.2.1 Introduction

Coca-Cola is the world's leading manufacturer and distributor of nonalcoholic beverage concentrates and syrups. It currently produces more than 230 beverages. Company products are sold through bottlers, fountain wholesalers, and distributors in approximately 200 countries. Physical presence throughout the world is the basis of this brand's success story. The enterprise has operations in Asia, North and South America, Europe, and Africa. The geographic locations are key to the success of the enterprise.

Coca-Cola was invented in 1886 by Dr. John Pemberton (1831–1888) in Atlanta, Georgia. The secret syrup was named by Dr. Pemberton's bookkeeper, who wrote its name in the now famous flowing script. During the company's first year of sales, soda jerks poured and served an average of six 8-ounce glasses of Coca-Cola per day. In 2001, Coca-Cola products were consumed at the rate of over 720 million servings per day worldwide.[2] This includes Coke from soda fountains, cans, and plastic and glass bottles.

3.2.2 Franchising the Bottlers *(where)*

The founders' **strategy** included putting their products in every home, store, and fountain shop. They succeeded in doing this by enlisting hundreds of bottlers throughout the world in a franchise system. See Figure 3-7. The agreement between these energetic entrepreneurs and Coca-Cola was that the price of the syrup would be fixed and the bottler was granted an exclusive territory. The company marketed its brand through national advertising to consumers. The advertising campaign led to huge brand awareness.

During the 50-year period between 1920 and 1970, consumer sales soared, the entrepreneurs made lots of money, and the Coca-Cola Company became the number one worldwide soft drink seller. Everyone was happy—at least for a while!

```
The Coca-Cola Company began bottling operations in...
1907 Hawaii
1912 The Philippines
1920 France
1927 Belgium, Bermuda, Colombia, Honduras, Italy,
     Mexico, Haiti, and Burma
1928 Antigua, China, Guatemala, Holland, Spain,
     Venezuela, and the Dominican Republic
1929 Germany and Spanish Morocco
1938 Australia, Austria, Gutana, Surinam, Jamaica,
     Curacao, Luxembourg, Norway, Scotland,
     South Africa, The Virgin Islands, and Trinidad
1940 Ecuador and El Salvador
1942 Nicaragua, Argentina, Brazil, Costa Rica,
     Iceland, and Uruguay
1945 Egypt and Martinique
1946 Barbados, Japan, and Okinawa
1947 Morocco and Tangier
1948 Liberia, Rhodesia, and Guadeloupe
```

Figure 3-7   *Bottlers' timeline*

3.2.3 Triggering Demand *(when)*

The initial advertising campaigns for Coca-Cola triggered demand by consumers for the end product, resulting in a greater demand by bottlers for the syrup used to make the end product. This line of supply and demand worked well, but was dependent upon the existence of growth opportunities for the bottlers.

During the Vietnam War era came the propagation of the large supermarket chain. These stores crossed the territories of the bottlers, who were accustomed to dealing with small, privately owned shops and were not ready to meet the needs of the large chain stores. This network of bottlers, which had been so crucial to Coke's success earlier in the twentieth century, now was unable to compete as the new chain stores emerged.

The independent bottler franchises could not agree on a common price, and the chains refused to do business with them. Because the bottlers could not unite in order to accommodate the needs of these new customers, Coca-Cola's distribution system lost business to its rival, Pepsi, which, in 1980, was only nine percentage points behind Coke in market share.[3]

The company's leadership responded by changing the contract agreement with the bottlers. By using the development of a substitute for sugar in Coke as a way to save costs, the company was able to help bottlers reduce their own costs if they agreed to eliminate the fixed price in the original contract.

Most bottlers agreed to the amendment to the contract. Coca-Cola then began buying bottling franchises and purchasing stakes in these bottling companies to create an overall strategy for growth, which was in alignment with the corporate strategy of Coca-Cola. With corporate leadership backing, the acquired bottlers were able to update equipment, advertise effectively, and increase marketing to important customers. Through this consolidation of bottlers, Coca-Cola eventually gained control of the U.S. market with a well-known brand. See Figure 3-8.

```
In August, 2001 Business Week ranked 100 global brands that
have a value greater than $1 billion on two criteria. They
had to derive 20 percent or more of sales from outside their
home country, and there had to be publicly available marketing
and financial data. The top 10 brands were:
     1.  Coca-Cola
     2.  Microsoft
     3.  IBM
     4.  GE
     5.  Nokia
     6.  Intel
     7.  Disney
     8.  Ford
     9.  McDonald's
     10. AT&T
```

Figure 3-8   *Branded...the value of a symbol*

3.2.4 Trademarks *(what)*

During the 1950s, Coca-Cola's **business model** included both the soft drink *drinkers* and the bottlers as its customers. When executives discovered the marketplace had changed, Coca-Cola changed its business paradigm and focused on the bottler as its primary customer.

Today, Coca-Cola's prime assets include its trademarks, the secret recipe, each of its marketed products, every retired product, the brand, the bottlers, administration, manufacturing and distribution facilities, and customers. The enterprise has also built up a large knowledge base on the marketplace, consumer preferences, and the competition.

TRADEMARKS

Sellers use trademarks to distinguish and identify their products. A trademark is a distinctive symbol, picture, or phrase. Trademark status may also be granted to building designs, product styles, color combinations, distinctive and unique packaging, and overall presentations.

Trademark status can also be received for identification that may not seem distinct or unique, but which has developed a secondary meaning over time that identifies it with the product or seller.

The owner of a trademark has exclusive rights to use it on the product it was intended to identify and often on related products. Service-marks receive the same legal protection as trademarks, but are meant to distinguish services rather than products.

3.2.5 Secret Recipe *(how)*

Coca-Cola Company obtains the ingredients for its secret syrup recipe and mixes them together into a beverage base. It sells the syrup to the bottlers for use in the preparation of finished beverages through the addition of both a sweetener and water. The bottlers convert the concentrates or syrups into products. The bottlers then package them and sell the finished products to their customers, which are retailers of many sizes. See Figure 3-9.

```
What is in a can of Coke?
    1.  Carbonated water
    2.  High fructose corn syrup
    3.  Caramel color
    4.  Phosphoric acid
    5.  Natural flavors
    6.  Caffeine
```

Figure 3-9   *Yum yum*

3.2.6 The Pepsi Challenge *(why)*

Coca-Cola had to change its strategy due to external influences. Its number one archrival, Pepsi, was causing the company to lose market share. Pepsi's gain in market share was spurred on when large supermarkets became popular in North America. Pepsi was better able to capitalize on supplying and displaying its product prominently on store shelves. Corporate leadership was taking a big risk by making the decision to consolidate the bottlers, but believed it could align its bottlers, create a low-cost distribution network, and create value for both the shareholders and the bottlers.

3.2.7 Global Domination *(who)*

During the 1990s, Coca-Cola focused on international business and a strong network of bottlers that would serve entire regions or countries. In order to streamline the workflow, Coca-Cola chose to organize operations geographically. The structure includes the Africa and Middle East Group, the Asia Pacific Group, West Europe Group, Central Europe and Eurasia Group, Latin America Group, and North America Group, thus meeting the Pepsi Challenge and remaining the number one soft drink maker.

This organization means that the flow of information throughout Coca-Cola is based on geography, rather than the product line, with the exception of one product, which Coca-Cola elected to manage globally—Minute Maid. Coca-Cola's senior management realized not all products within a vertical industry need to be treated in the same manner.

3.2.8 Key Terms

business model	market share
Butterfly Effect	marketplace
cause and effect	means
chain of events	mission
composite	process
computer programmer	quality control
connectivity	raw materials
consumer	root cause
corporation	strategy
data	sunsetted
end	system
enterprise	systems thinking
five whys	thought leader
holistic view	value chain
integrated enterprise solution	vision
knowledge workers	wisdom

3.2.9 Review Questions

1. How did the relationships among the bottlers affect Coca-Cola's ability to respond to its customers?
2. Why are priorities important to the *owner*?
3. How does Coca-Cola's trademark benefit the organization?
4. What did Coca-Cola do when the enterprise discovered the marketplace had changed?
5. Through the consolidation of bottlers, what was Coca-Cola able to accomplish?
6. What external influences caused Coca-Cola to change its strategy?

SECTION 3.3 WHAT IS SPECIAL ABOUT THIS RELATIONSHIP—THE WALT DISNEY COMPANY

> **QUESTIONS TO CONTEMPLATE**
>
> 1. When you think about Disney, do you think about the environment or Mickey Mouse?
> 2. As the world becomes more environmentally conscientious, why would people want to do business with Disney?

3.3.1 Introduction

Walt Disney (1901–1966) first opened his Magic Kingdom in 1955. Anyone who has been a child or had a child since then knows that in the Magic Kingdom, every story has a happy ending. Every performer on the Disney stage—from Mickey Mouse and Donald Duck to the latest batch of audio-animatronic creations—smiles and waves. Open, friendly gestures are a matter of company policy. Disney wants you to believe that the Magic Kingdom is the happiest place on earth. It is the corporate mission to make you, the guest, as happy as possible.

The Walt Disney Company focuses business activities on five areas: media networks, parks and resorts, consumer products, studio entertainment, and its Internet group.

3.3.2 The Guest *(what)*

The Walt Disney Company is a recognized world leader in providing the highest-quality entertainment. Because the company has held a unique position of public confidence and trust for more than 50 years, Disney has become aware of its inherent ability to influence public opinion and inspire action.

The company's leadership strives to make caring for the environment an explicit and integral part of its corporate **business objectives** and operating philosophy. Disney has realized that its corporate business objectives and the philosophy of being responsible to the environment can have both a **tangible** and **intangible** effect on customer satisfaction.

When appropriate, Disney integrates environmentally sensitive themes into the attractions of the park. The integration is carried over into publications, film and television programming...and your subconscious.

3.3.3 Garbage, Water, and Energy *(where)*

Theme parks generate a lot of waste. Disney seeks to minimize the creation of waste in its operations. This includes minimizing the packaging needed for selling its products. Senior leadership encourages its employees to reduce, reuse, and recycle garbage before any of it is disposed of as waste. The organization has gone a long way in developing programs and facilities that promote and facilitate this attitude.

In all its existing operations and locations worldwide, Disney invests in technologies and systems that enhance water and energy conservation. Energy and water management are included as an integral part of all planning for future projects.

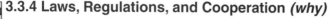 3.3.4 Laws, Regulations, and Cooperation *(why)*

Disney makes every effort to understand and adhere to both the spirit and the letter of environmental laws and regulations. In fact, Disney strives to exceed required levels of compliance. Employees are encouraged to discover issues that may not yet be identified in the law, but could result in adverse environmental effects. Whether or not the motivation for being environmentally conscious is altruistic—it should enhance guest loyalty. People may be more likely to give their business to environmentally friendly organizations.

Executives seek out business relationships with companies that demonstrate superior **environmental ethics**. The executive leadership encourages licensees, vendors, suppliers, and participating companies to conduct business in an environmentally responsible manner. Disney reevaluates these relationships regularly to assure the conscientious adherence to environmentally sound business practices.

3.3.5 Evaluation and Impact *(how)*

Disney conducts **internal audits** regularly to measure the environmental performance of its individual business units, as well as the company as a whole. The company has established a series of standards from which it measures performance on a continual basis.

3.3.6 Education and Research *(who)*

Disney employees are educated on the particulars and the significance of the company's environmental philosophy. Employees are encouraged to demonstrate leadership by making suggestions, acting, and getting involved through community participation. Disney encourages environmental conscientiousness and actions, both on and off the job, for the employee.

Disney supports, encourages, and enables operating entities, subsidiaries, and unit managers to implement green environmental policies. The leadership holds business units accountable for performance and measurement of results, including corrective action when necessary.

3.3.7 Accountability *(when)*

Each Disney facility, operation, business practice, product, and service may directly or indirectly have negative consequences on the guests, the general public, the employees, and the environment. Disney is concerned about the health and safety of all of these people and things. When a negative environmental consequence is found, Disney assigns a team to assess and control the problem by developing an emergency response guideline.

Disney supports, performs, and participates in research that seeks to find realistic solutions to environmental problems. The company advocates and applies promising and cost-effective technologies to demonstrate environmental efficacy.

3.3.8 Key Terms

business objective
environmental ethics
intangible

internal audit
tangible

3.3.9 Review Questions

1. The Walt Disney Company focuses business activities on what five areas?
2. Describe how Disney's executive leadership commitment to caring for the environment could have a positive, intangible effect on customer loyalty.
3. In what ways does Disney seek to minimize waste in its theme park operations?
4. How does Disney build a shared knowledge regarding its philosophy of environmental responsibility?
5. Describe how leadership responds to environmental laws and regulations during business activities.
6. What process does the company follow when an environmental problem is discovered in relation to one of its facilities, services, or products?

SECTION 3.4 WHEN THE WEEKEND COMES— MOVIE OUTPOST

QUESTIONS TO CONTEMPLATE

1. How can a rural video store compete against satellite television?
2. Do smaller enterprises have smaller issues than their larger counterparts?

3.4.1 Introduction

Movie Outpost is a small, privately owned video rental company in southwestern Michigan. See Figure 3-10. The company has been operating since 1980 and has changed and improved many operations based on experiences and a changing marketplace. The corporation's mission is to provide customers with a wide selection of home entertainment products in an attractive setting served by friendly and knowledgeable people. Originally started in the basement of a little farmhouse at the end of a long dirt road, Movie Outpost derived its name from that remote location.

MOVIE OUTPOST

Figure 3-10 *Movie Outpost corporate logo*

Movie Outpost provides a wide selection of video and game titles for rental and sale to rural customers who are looking for home entertainment at a reasonable cost. **Inventory** is displayed in bright, clean, attractive stores staffed by knowledgeable and helpful staff. In addition to selling and renting videos and games, the company sells movie concessions, such as soft drinks, snacks, and candy. The company rents or sells all major formats for video (VHS and DVD) and games (Playstation 2, Gameboy, Nintendo 64, X-Box, Game Cube, and Dreamcast), as well as player hardware.

3.4.2 The Ring of the Cash Register *(when)*

The corporation operates on three business cycles of different lengths:

- An **annual cycle** that is based on Michigan's seasonal weather patterns. Movie Outpost exhibits strong rentals from November through April, when staying at home and watching a movie is often more attractive than braving the elements, and likewise weaker rentals from May through October, when the warmer weather invites outdoor activities.
- Movie Outpost also has a notable **weekly cycle**. Sales and rentals are stronger on weekends, particularly Friday night and Saturday. This is attributed to people having more leisure time on the weekend. Rentals are weaker during weekdays, when most people are occupied with work and other scheduled activities.
- The last cycle is a **holiday cycle** based on state and federal holidays. Movie Outpost experiences higher demand just before and after these periods.

The company responds to these cycles by scheduling more employees in its stores to service heavier customer demand during the peak periods of the three cycles and fewer employees during the lower points.

Inventory is adjusted slightly based on the annual cycle, but not for the weekly and holiday cycles. The **shelf life**, or the longevity of the audio and video quality of the rental videotape, is only six months, and the shelf life of a rental game is slightly longer. For example, if the company purchases 20 copies of one movie, after six months, five copies might remain. If the company purchases 20 copies of one video game, after six months, 15 copies might remain. Therefore, little adjustment is needed in inventory due to the three business cycles.

3.4.3 A Rural Niche *(where)*

Movie Outpost has six stores in small towns in rural southwestern Michigan and one corporate office located in Bangor, a small town located midway between Kalamazoo and South Haven. The stores range in size from 5,000 to 9,000 square feet, all relatively large by national video store standards.

There is a reason the company provides physical facilities of this size to customers. One of the company's innovative strategies is to bring big-city video selection to rural customers. The larger facilities mean they can display a greater variety of products in a convenient manner for customers to make selections. This company has learned to think outside the box. See Figure 3-11.

Figure 3-11   *Think outside the box*

3.4.4 Structure *(who)*

The company has approximately 70 local employees. The organizational structure includes the owner, regional managers, accountants, store managers, assistant store managers, technicians, shift supervisors, and sales associates.

Weekly staff meetings allow the managers to communicate the company's ideals to the sales associates. During the meeting, managers discuss and review new inventory items so that the sales associates are always able to provide customers with appropriate and helpful information.

3.4.5 Demographics *(what)*

Although all of the stores are within a 50-mile radius, there are major demographic differences between some of the stores. For Movie Outpost, useful **demographic information** includes average household income, proportion of blue-collar and white-collar consumers, and ethnic background interests.

When purchasing inventory for its stores, Movie Outpost uses demographic differences to determine what types of product to place in each store. The demographic knowledge base also includes information about competition.

The company's leadership uses national companies to supply its major videos, games, and equipment. Most services are purchased from local or regional companies. Good relationships with all suppliers and service providers are a high priority. Other assets include company vehicles, customers, employees, physical facilities, inventory, store and office equipment, and community goodwill. See Figure 3-12.

Figure 3-12   *Bringing home theater to the home theater*

3.4.6 National Suppliers *(how)*

The owner purchases movies and games that appeal to its customers from national suppliers and displays them for rental in an attractive setting. The company then rents this inventory to an established customer base and eventually sells most videos and games to make room for new merchandise.

Movie Outpost purchases the equipment that plays the movies and games, as well as the movies and games to play on that equipment. The company runs seasonal advertising and promotions, as well as daily specials (e.g., customers can rent a new release on any day between Monday and Thursday and get an older title free), to help smooth out the curve of normal **business cycles**.

3.4.7 Service Locally *(why)*

The vision of Movie Outpost pushes the company to continue to give customers the products they want at a reasonable price in order to maintain profitability. The company's philosophy is to develop long-term relationships with its customers and provide local access to products and services so that residents will not have to drive the distance to a larger metropolitan area.

The corporation values the relationships with its customers and communities and demonstrates this belief by making itself a useful, contributing member of the communities it serves. Movie Outpost's owner, managers, and employees accomplish this by contributing time, manpower, and money to these communities.

3.4.8 Key Terms

annual cycle
business cycle
demographic information
holiday cycle

inventory
shelf life
weekly cycle

3.4.9 Review Questions

1. In what types of business cycles does Movie Outpost operate?
2. Why is this corporation's mission statement important to the success of the business?
3. What kind of questions does the corporation need to ask to know how to respond to its business cycles?

4. How does the company address the differences in demographics of the communities it serves?
5. Why is this corporation's philosophy important to the types of communities it serves?
6. What other products might Movie Outpost introduce for its customers?

SECTION 3.5 WHO LOVES YA, BABY— KEANE, INC.

QUESTIONS TO CONTEMPLATE

1. What is an 80-hour rule?
2. Why are relationships so important to this consulting firm?

3.5.1 Introduction

Keane, Inc. has provided information technology and business consulting services since its foundation. When the company started in 1965, the owner established its corporate headquarters above a doughnut shop in Hingham, Massachusetts. It has since moved its headquarters to Charlestown, a suburb of Boston. It expanded its presence across the U.S. and around the globe with offices and operations in many U.S. cities, Canada, and the United Kingdom. See Figure 3-13.

Keane is primarily a service company, although it does sell some of its methodologies as products. Keane's mission is to help its customers optimize their business performance through the innovative use and management of information technology. Many of Keane's customers are **Global 2000 companies** and government agencies. Keane adopted a *plan, build, and manage* **paradigm** to framework its services. These services include consulting, software development, and **IT outsourcing**.

Figure 3-13   *Keane corporate logo*

3.5.1.1 Plan, Build, and Manage

Plan

Financially, businesses usually try to show revenue growth in operations every year. Accomplishing this growth may involve streamlining operations, optimizing supply chains, enhancing customer relationships, implementing new e-business initiatives, or aligning IT and business strategies. Growth may also entail mergers and acquisitions.

Keane's *plan* strategy is to take a holistic view of business processes, organizational design, and technology architecture. Keane offers business alternatives for maximizing productivity, increasing revenue, reducing costs, and creating capacity for future growth. The company does this by identifying high-value, high **return on investment (ROI)** business opportunities and by providing clients with both strategy and implementation services.

Build

In an increasingly global, networked, and information-based economy, next-generation e-business initiatives are becoming more complex, requiring tighter and more sophisticated integration between **front-end** and **back-end** applications.

Most corporations find that they need to enhance access to critical data, perform high-value process improvements, and offer improved customer service. Keane's *build* strategy helps its customers use new technology to meet their business objectives.

Manage

Writing business software applications is complex. This complexity is compounded by the need of businesses to continually add more and more software systems to their operations. The ability of a business to manage its IT function internally can often become a thorn in the side of the senior executives. After all, IT is not usually a business's core competency. For many corporations, the solution is to turn to companies like Keane to provide everything from a single system to an entire IT portfolio for development, ongoing maintenance, and **keep the lights on (KTLO)** support.

Keane's outsourcing service and methodologies help clients manage business systems more effectively. Keane's *manage* strategy hopes to provide its customers with satisfaction and cost savings by improving operational efficiencies, finding quicker ways to adapt software to changing business needs, and optimizing resource consumption.

3.5.1.2 Establishing a Discipline

Keane's philosophy is to develop long-term relationships and recurring revenues with its customers based on outsourcing contracts. To achieve these aims, Keane consistently delivers high-quality, cost-effective, and responsive services. Keane's foundation for success is its ability to develop and adhere to repeatable and proven processes and management disciplines.

Keane realizes that people are fundamental to the success of each project. Since the early 1970s, Keane has also understood that people are the key reason projects fail. The organization created a set of principles and procedures and adopted an organizational structure to support its mantra of Productivity Management™.

Productivity Management

Implementing systems on time, on budget, and on target has become increasingly difficult. As pointed out in the Standish Group's *The CHAOS Report*,[4] meeting the exact needs of the user is something most corporations are unable to achieve.

Keane's solution gets everyone involved in the project, from the most inexperienced junior programmer to senior leaders and executives, as well as the customer. Based on extensive research and Keane's collective experience, the six principles of Productivity Management promote success. The six principles are:

1. Define the job in detail.
2. Get the right people involved.
3. Estimate the time and costs.
4. Use the **80-hour rule**.
5. Establish a **change procedure**.
6. Agree on **acceptance criteria**.

DEFINE THE JOB IN DETAIL

Create a document that explicitly identifies the work that needs to be done. The document includes the major deliverables that will be produced during the project. The non-technical environment is described and the customer's expectations are noted. All areas of concern or interest are written down.

(continued)

GET THE RIGHT PEOPLE INVOLVED

Use people in their most effective and appropriate capacities based on the needs of the project. The entire project team needs to be involved during the lifetime of the project, including the customers, especially during any planning and assessment stages. Each member of the project team is required to define his or her own goals for participation.

ESTIMATE THE TIME AND COSTS

Prior to each phase or stage of a project, develop a detailed estimate of the effort required for the undertaking. Estimate each component of the job separately to increase accuracy. An important creed in this principle is: *Do not estimate what you do not know*.

BREAK DOWN THE JOB USING THE 80-HOUR RULE

Break down a job into tasks that can be completed within 80 contiguous business hours to keep track of a project's progress. The work produced for each task must result in a tangible product. The 80-hour rule helps you set schedules, assign tasks, identify problems early, confirm time and cost estimates, and evaluate project progress and individual performance.

You typically produce a detailed schedule based on the 80-hour rule for the upcoming 60 to 90-day work period. At the beginning of each month, add another month's worth of detail.

ESTABLISH A CHANGE PROCEDURE

Handling change is an inherent part of application development. You must have a formal procedure for dealing with change to ensure that all parties agree to help manage expectations. Everyone involved should agree to the change procedure before the project starts.

AGREE ON ACCEPTANCE CRITERIA

Determine, in advance, what constitutes an acceptable model, solution, or application. Obtain written acceptances of deliverables throughout the project so that acceptance is a gradual process, rather than a one-time event at the end. Understanding the project's goals and challenges is essential to determining what constitutes an acceptable deliverable.

3.5.2 Strong Organizational Structure *(who)*

The basic structure of Keane's internal project organization is shown in Figure 3-14:

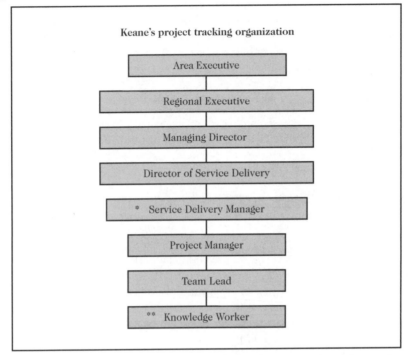

Keane's project tracking organization

Area Executive

Regional Executive

Managing Director

Director of Service Delivery

* Service Delivery Manager

Project Manager

Team Lead

** Knowledge Worker

* Based on the size of a project, the team lead and project manager roles may be assumed by the service delivery manager, who is the person responsible for managing and communicating the project's progress with the client and the Keane branch.

** The knowledge worker may be an analyst, developer, architect, or project administrator.

Figure 3-14 *Organization structure*

This structure and Keane's use of productivity management allow senior executives to know almost immediately when a project is starting to veer off course, enabling Keane to correct problems and avoid customer conflicts.

3.5.3 Keeping Track *(how)*

Integral to Keane's success are the processes it chooses to follow. Leadership developed a type of methodology similar to a **Balanced Scorecard** to keep track of projects, using green for completed work, yellow for candidate trouble spots, and red for areas at risk. Keane has developed a set of reusable methodologies for its client engagements. The methods detail step-by-step instructions for governing the software development process.

Another method Keane uses is the 80-hour rule. The rule means that no matter what is included in the task, no more than two weeks should elapse before the task is completed and a deliverable is produced. The deliverable must be something that is both tangible and measurable.

3.5.4 Critical Mass *(where)*

In order to support long-term relationships with customers and communities, Keane seeks to reach **critical mass** in a market and establish a full-time office with a complete infrastructure of administrative and employee support staff. Critical mass is a predetermined number of clients and projects, revenue base, and group of Keane consultants assigned in a given geography to support the infrastructure for a local branch. To support the location, Keane once again draws upon the strengths of its organizational structure.

Critical mass in the IT services industry is a key driver of profitability. Reaching critical mass allows a company to reduce sales, general, and administrative (SG&A) costs as a percentage of revenue. Keane's leadership seeks critical mass at all levels of the organization, including: the company, business unit, account, and project.

3.5.5 People Assets *(what)*

As already mentioned, Keane realizes that it owes a great deal of its success to its employees. Because Keane recognizes that each employee represents a key asset, the company provides a complete benefits package that includes ongoing training in the latest technology advances.

Keane also provides managers whose only responsibility is the care of the employee.

3.5.6 Quality and Effectiveness *(why)*

Keane's vision is to be recognized as one of the world's great IT services firms by its:

- Customers—due to the quality and effectiveness of Keane's business and IT solutions
- Employees—because Keane is a great place to work and build a career
- Shareholders—because of Keane's ability to consistently generate long-term shareholder value

These tenets of Keane's vision statement provide the hook that links everything together and the drive to excel.

3.5.7 Sell, Sell, Sell *(when)*

With every success comes the need to have another success. To continue to find opportunities, Keane has a full-time sales team. The sales team can sell work anywhere in the world. In fact, Keane has written software in over 30 countries and deployed software in over 50 countries. Keane supports its sales team with the resources (employees) needed to start most projects immediately after a contract is signed.

3.5.8 Key Terms

80-hour rule
acceptance criteria
back-end
Balanced Scorecard
business objectives
change procedure
critical mass

front-end
Global 2000 companies
IT outsourcing
keep the lights on (KTLO)
paradigm
return on investment (ROI)

3.5.9 Review Questions

1. According to Keane's management, what is the primary reason for the failure of projects?
2. What steps would you take to motivate Keane's employees?
3. What does Keane's leadership do to support long-term relationships with customers and communities?

4. What enables Keane's executives to take corrective action immediately when a project is starting to veer off course?
5. Give examples of some of the processes this company follows that make it successful.
6. Why is Keane's vision to be recognized as one of the world's great IT services firms so important to the success of this consulting company?

SECTION 3.6 HOW TO WIN WITH PLASTICS— CASCADE ENGINEERING

QUESTIONS TO CONTEMPLATE

1. What do you do with a 9,000-ton injection molding press?
2. Why would a company like Cascade Engineering want to do value-added work?

3.6.1 Introduction

A young man graduated from Cornell University with a degree in engineering and left his hometown to work for a large aerospace company in Connecticut. He always enjoyed tackling tough problems. After six years, he was ready for another challenge and returned to Grand Rapids, Michigan, where he started his own plastics firm next door to his father's tool and die shop.

Fred Keller (b. 1944), the chairman and CEO of Cascade Engineering, believes the vision that drove his company nearly 30 years ago remains an accurate reflection of the philosophy of the organization today—*Cascade Engineering thrives on tough challenges.*

Cascade Engineering has grown into a world leader in the development and manufacturing of injection molding systems and components. Cascade Engineering supplies the automotive, container, furniture, and consumer products industries with plastics products. Cascade Engineering is actually a family of companies, founded in 1973. The family of companies is located not only in Michigan, but throughout other parts of the world. See Figure 3-15.

Figure 3-15   *Cascade corporate logo*

These organizations share information and learn and profit from each other. Cascade Engineering draws from a worldwide network of resources to ensure that each project meets or exceeds customer expectations. Ideas and manufacturing processes are exchanged with international firms and corporate partners located in North America, Europe, and Asia. The Cascade Engineering Family of Companies, which employs more than 1,200 people, reported year 2000 revenues of $215 million.

The company is known globally for having a 9,000-ton injection molding press—the largest in North America. This press is used to produce high-tech waste containers for Waste Management Corporation, the nation's largest waste hauler. In 1997, Cascade Engineering made international headlines by using that same press to develop the world's first all-plastic automobile body, the Composite Concept Vehicle, for Chrysler Corporation. See Figure 3-16.

Figure 3-16   *Cascade's composite concept vehicle for DaimlerChrysler*

The company became a global competitor through strategic alliances, the first of which was established in 1988 with Japan's Starlite Company in a **joint venture** known as StarCade, Incorporated, now Automotive Trim Solutions. Present-day affiliations and wholly owned subsidiaries such as Systex Products Corporation, Dow Automotive, Noble Polymers, Pyper Products, and 21st Century Plastics Corporation enable Cascade Engineering to create solutions to challenges of every size, shape, and color for customers throughout the world.[5]

3.6.2 Pellets to Dashmats *(how)*

Cascade Engineering has an exclusive contract with DaimlerChrysler for one of its automobiles, the compact Dodge Neon. The Dodge Neon **dashmat** is produced solely by Cascade Engineering in one of its Grand Rapids, Michigan plants. Approximately 250,000 dashmats roll off the production line in the Automotive Acoustics division each year and are shipped directly to DaimlerChrysler. See Figure 3-17.

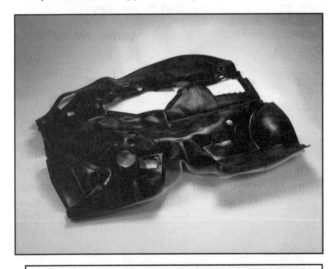

Figure 3-17   *Cascade's dashmat*

Dashmats are made from plastic pellets that are vacuum fed from storage silos. The silos are attached directly to the machines that make the components. See Figure 3-18. The pellets are heated to the melting point in a long barrel and then injected into the mold under very high pressure. The finished parts are often robotically removed.

Plant employees then add pads to the dashmat. This value-added work creates wealth for the corporation. The corporation is trying to do high-volume value-added work. In other words, very few of the jobs involve just taking parts off the press and putting them in a box. Instead, parts come off the press and are transferred to a contiguous operation area where activities such as adding pads occur.

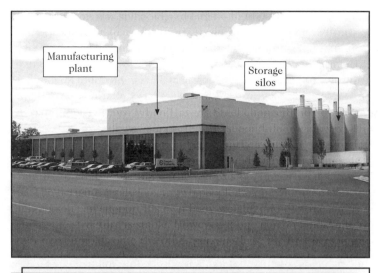

Manufacturing plant

Storage silos

Figure 3-18   *One of Cascade Engineering's*
                    manufacturing plants

Employees check for quality and the finished products are packaged for shipment. Boxes to be shipped are moved and stacked in an area adjacent to the loading docks. Generally, DaimlerChrysler's trucks are staged and waiting for product releases. Within 30 minutes of leaving the dock at Cascade Engineering, DaimlerChrysler knows what is in transit. DaimlerChrysler sometimes houses a small inventory of the dashmats in its warehouse as well. The inventory is used as a backup in case of manufacturing delays.

When Cascade Engineering receives a contract, such as the one to manufacture dashmats for the Dodge Neon, the company's engineering team must first envision how to produce the product. They do this by studying the product specifications. Cascade needs to understand and determine what raw materials are required and available. Then, Cascade thinks about how the transformation processes will work to create the product.

Quality Certification

Approximately 50 percent of Cascade Engineering's plastics are obtained from Noble Polymers, also located in Grand Rapids. Additional raw materials are supplied by outside vendors. Noble Polymers produces custom compounds using a **QS-9000** certified quality system.

ISO-9000 alone no longer meets the international quality system requirements for automotive parts manufacturers. Organizations should implement QS-9000 in order to remain competitive in the global market. Both ISO-9000 and QS-9000 are examples of why making knowledge explicit is fundamental to achieving a quality product. Each year, the major automobile makers introduce new or modified vehicles. Maintaining explicit knowledge promotes speed to market for products.

QS-9000 quality system requirements have been developed by US-based DaimlerChrysler, Ford, and General Motors to define fundamental quality system expectations. Revisions from European affiliates have been included in order to facilitate the implementation of QS-9000 in Europe. QS-9000 requirements apply to suppliers of production materials, production or service parts, as well as heat-treating, painting, plating, and other finishing services.

QS-9000 quality system requirements are increasingly accepted and demanded internationally by automobile manufacturers. QS-9000 is based on the international standard ISO-9000:1994 and includes all ISO-9000 requirements, plus additional requirements specific to the automotive industry.

The ISO-9000 standard is made up of four parts: 9001 is for service industries, 9002 is for manufacturing industries, 9003 is for computer hardware and software, and 9004 is for quality management.

ISO-9002 is international certification that a company conforms to certain standards. There are various certifications bodies that approve a company to the ISO-9002 level of quality and service. In order for Cascade Engineering to achieve ISO-9002 certification, the company must have:

- An established policy on quality and a quality procedure manual
- An officer designated for ensuring and maintaining quality standards
- Regular reviews of quality. Audits must be performed in-house and by an external independent body
- Policies on various other issues including staff training and development
- A list of approved suppliers
- All written procedures stated simply, unambiguously, and understandably

When you are certified to ISO-9002, you must:

- Say what you do
- Do what you say
- Prove that you do it

3.6.3 Business-to-Business—B2B *(when)*

Daily orders are received electronically from DaimlerChrysler, which outline a 15-day forecast that specifies how many parts Cascade Engineering should ship, when they should be shipped, and where they should be shipped. When an order is received in the Automotive Acoustics division, the line manager checks to see what materials are needed to fulfill the request.

The line manager then checks with inventory control to see how much is on hand. Next, if more raw materials are needed, the inventory manager places an order with either Noble Polymer or another outside vendor. Inventory has a lead time of 10 days. If additional inventory is needed, trucks are scheduled for pickup at Noble Polymers, where plastic pellets are blown into trucks. The trucks then return to Cascade Engineering's plant and unload the materials into silos attached to the manufacturing building.

Analyzing the cycle times are established permits Cascade Engineering to think about everything that needs to be scheduled. The critical path of all tasks to perform is discovered, and appropriate lead times are established to schedule labor, materials, and transportation. See Figure 3-19. Imhotep was concerned with similar issues during the building of the Great Pyramid. As the saying goes: *The more things change, the more they stay the same.*

Figure 3-19   *Critical path method*

3.6.4 Avoid a Disaster *(what)*

The molds can be removed from machines by crane and then transported by trucks to another plant in the event a backup site is needed. The molds are made of by Paragon Die and Engineering. Other important assets and things for the company to keep track of include: manufacturing facilities, employees, customers, products, the molds, inventoried products, raw materials in stock, and accounts receivable.

Cascade Engineering considers everything needed for manufacturing a product. This is done not only for **total quality management (TQM)** purposes, but so management can understand all the relationships between its items of interest.

Failure to deliver dashmats can stop the entire Dodge Neon production line at DaimlerChrysler. One of the items that the leadership must consider for its manufacturing process is a **disaster recovery plan**. Leadership considers every aspect of the disaster recovery plan so that it knows exactly what is needed to resume business. Therefore, Cascade's leadership team is able to proactively answer such questions as: *Where will Cascade produce dashmats in the event production cannot continue? Where will inventory be housed?*

3.6.5 Come and Get It *(where)*

Cascade Engineering is located strategically in North America, Asia, and Europe. The company's corporate offices are located in Michigan. See Figure 3-20.

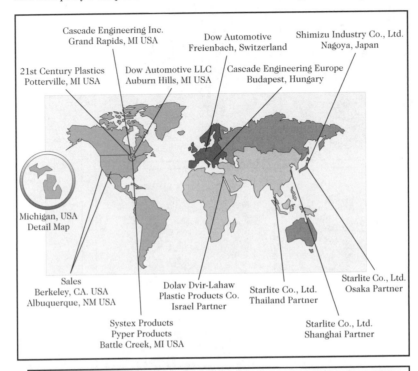

Cascade Engineering Inc.
Grand Rapids, MI USA

Dow Automotive
Freienbach, Switzerland

Shimizu Industry Co., Ltd.
Nagoya, Japan

21st Century Plastics
Potterville, MI USA

Dow Automotive LLC
Auburn Hills, MI USA

Cascade Engineering Europe
Budapest, Hungary

Michigan, USA
Detail Map

Sales
Berkeley, CA. USA
Albuquerque, NM USA

Dolav Dvir-Lahaw
Plastic Products Co.
Israel Partner

Starlite Co., Ltd.
Thailand Partner

Starlite Co., Ltd.
Osaka Partner

Systex Products
Pyper Products
Battle Creek, MI USA

Starlite Co., Ltd.
Shanghai Partner

Figure 3-20 *Cascade Engineering family of companies*

Each operation is formed around the concepts of **just in time (JIT)** delivery and **lean manufacturing**. JIT ensures that Cascade Engineering's customers receive products on time and to their exact specification. Benefits from JIT for both Cascade Engineering and its customers include:

- Reduced inventory expense
- Reduced administrative expense
- Reduced storage space needs
- Reduced handling expense
- Reduced insurance expense
- Expanded production capabilities
- Reallocation of valuable capital

Lean manufacturing strives to reduce waste from the customer's order to the customer's receipt of that order by eliminating unnecessary steps in the production stream. The seven types of waste addressed with lean manufacturing include convenience, correction, overproduction, motion, waiting, inventory, and processing. The ideal of a lean system is a one-piece flow. A lean manufacturer, such as Cascade Engineering, strives to improve continuously in the direction of that goal.

3.6.6 Customer Focus *(why)*

Keller, the company owner, has always believed that trust and teamwork are the basis upon which worthy goals are achieved. His company spends a lot of time building strong foundations with its customers. One of the elements of Cascade Engineering's ascent has been the solid relationships the company has with customers, vendors, employees, and the community. According to Keller, the company was created with the vision that Cascade Engineering would "not say no when asked to tackle big challenges."[6]

Today's vision is "to become a valuable partner to our customer through technology leadership, innovative applications, global participation, and by being the lowest total cost developer and producer."[7] The spirit of innovation is a motivating force for this company, and this philosophy meets the needs of its customers who come with challenges and problems.

3.6.7 Organizationally *(who)*

Vision-oriented managers lead the product groups, teams, and individuals in an effort to meet Cascade's enterprise goals. The Family of Companies has expanded, as did the range of products and processes being used. Every partnership has its own organizational structure. See Figure 3-21 for clarification.

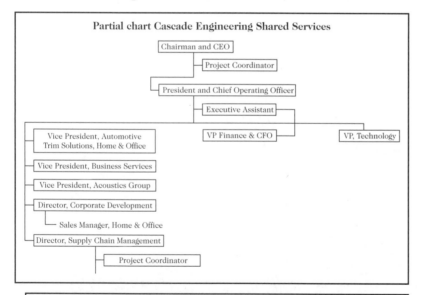

Figure 3-21   *Cascade Engineering shared services*

3.6.8 Key Terms

dashmat

disaster recovery plan

ISO-9000

joint venture

just in time (JIT)

lean manufacturing

QS-9000

total quality management (TQM)

3.6.9 Review Questions

1. How does Cascade Engineering maintain quality standards in the corporation? How does standards certification benefit this organization?
2. What is meant by the Cascade Engineering Family of Companies?
3. What things must management think about when it receives a contract, such as the one for the Dodge Neon dashmat?
4. Why is the critical path of all tasks to be performed so important to a company like Cascade Engineering?
5. What could happen if Cascade Engineering failed to deliver the dashmat to DaimlerChrysler?
6. Why is it advantageous for this company to have affiliates around the globe?

SECTION 3.7 WHY IT'S A RISKY BUSINESS— EQUIFAX, INC.

QUESTIONS TO CONTEMPLATE

1. Who regulates the amount of credit information that is kept and reported about you?
2. Why is a consumer's credit information important to a business?

3.7.1 Introduction

Equifax, Incorporated is a leading international financial risk and marketing information company specializing in commercial and consumer credit data. Cator and Guy Woolford (1869–1944, 1873–1946) founded the company on March 22, 1899, under the name of Retail Credit Company. Equifax helps its U.S. customers reduce their **risk** by providing information on a consumer's credit worthiness. Equifax not only helps consumers identify credit fraud, but also works with the federal government to improve homeland security. See Figure 3-22.

Figure 3-22 *Equifax corporate logo*

The U.S. Government, through legislation, helps control the way credit information is kept and reported. In the 1970s, the federal government passed the Fair Credit Reporting Act (FCRA). This act has been amended several times. The legislation regulates the types of data stored, with an eye toward protecting the consumer. Since becoming law, many interpretations and legal decisions have shaped the way this industry is regulated.

The World of Credit Information

Credit is the confidence in a buyer's *ability* and *intention* to fulfill financial obligations. If someone asks about your credit, the underling question is, *What is your reputation for paying your debts?*

The attraction of credit to a buyer is that it allows future income to be used for current purchases. The attraction of credit to the seller is that it can increase the volume of sales and, hence, gross profits.

When a business is extending credit, it assumes a risk. To reduce this risk, the credit extender may want to know:

- If the customer has the *ability* to pay the bill
- If the customer has the *intention* to pay the bill

The information traditionally used to make decisions about the ability and intention to pay is the consumer's historical record of previous credit performance and current financial situation (savings and income). This type of information is gathered and sold by Equifax, as well as other companies in the credit information industry.

A credit extender, like most companies, needs to maximize profits and minimize risk. Therefore, credit extenders use consumers' credit information along with other variables to make an intelligent decision regarding the lending of money.

Essentially, risk can be viewed as an expense to a credit extender. All businesses have expenses. Most have revenue too. Consider a typical store. The expenses for the store owner include: inventory (such as VHS videos, DVDs, players, popcorn, and magazines for a video rental store like Movie Outpost), payroll, rent, and utilities.

From an accounting standpoint, inventory is not recorded as an expense on the general ledger because it is considered a cost of goods sold (COGS). The shop's revenue comes from money the *owner* receives when a sale is made. The **profit** is the difference between the **revenue** and **expenses**.

When someone buys a product on credit, the revenue is uncertain. If the customer defaults on the debt, the *owner* is forced to absorb that debt as an expense. If the *owner* can reduce the amount of **bad debt** expense, profits will increase. The *owner* can reduce risk of incurring bad debt expense by using information about the consumer. This model is true for every business.

In the Beginning

Imagine it is 1890, and you are observing a small rural town in Montana with a population of two. One of the townspeople owns a store. In all likelihood, the store owner knows the other consumer personally.

Once again, it is time for the consumer to make her yearly purchase of a gown from the store. The *owner* knows the consumer's purchasing history because she bought a gown on credit last year and paid the debt according to the terms of the agreement. The *owner* believes she still has the ability and the intention to pay. Using this first-hand information, the *owner* decides to extend additional credit because the perceived risk is minimal.

As you watch the years roll by, the community prospers and grows. More and more merchants set up shop to serve the town's growing population. Not every merchant has first-hand knowledge of every consumer in the community.

The local merchants find it necessary to gather their first-hand information regarding consumer credit histories and share it with one another. This sharing allows the local merchants to create a list detailing who in town has the ability and intention to pay, and who does not. Merchants armed with this information can now make smarter decisions regarding to whom they extend credit, thus lowering risk and improving profitability.

The first credit reporting bureaus emerged as mutual protection associations for local merchants to share information regarding consumers. The member merchants were the first customers of these new credit bureaus, which evolved into independent businesses operating for a profit. They functioned by gathering and organizing consumer information contributed by member merchants into files representing the credit history of the consumers of the community. The revenue stream of the bureaus came from selling access to the consolidated information in these files.

In the 1960s, the population became transient due to social changes, the Vietnam War, shifts in job availability, and the establishment of suburbs like Levittown. When people moved, they wanted their credit histories to move with them. Therefore, independent credit bureaus banded together to form the Associated Credit Bureaus of America. The affiliation allowed member bureaus to share consumer information, enabling them to better handle risk.

3.7.2 The Credit-Based Economy *(why)*

Credit has become vital to the American economy. See Figure 3-23. So vital, in fact, that if Equifax's computer systems go down, the enterprise is obligated by law to route the requests for credit information to one of its competitors. The customer is not obligated to go back to Equifax when its systems are back up and running. For Equifax, *the system is the enterprise.*

Figure 3-23 *It's not just a card. It's the basis of the modern economy.*

3.7.3 Profiles *(what)*

Equifax builds its knowledge base around the consumer, keeping track of consumer names, including aliases, dates of birth (in some cases multiple dates of birth), social security numbers, addresses, student loans, mortgages, credit card companies, and personal installment loans.

Based on the FCRA, credit bureaus cannot share all the information they gather. In the United States, Equifax keeps track of positive and negative (derogative) data. In countries such as Australia, the law allows only derogative data to be kept about a consumer. The use of positive data can cause you to receive multiple credit card applications every week! Remember, under the FCRA, you can opt out if you do not want to receive these offers.

3.7.4 The More You Buy, the More They Know *(when)*

Equifax is a global organization. In our $24 \times 7 \times 365$ global economy, information on a consumer can be requested at any time. Equifax needs to make sure all of its files and processes are able to respond when a request comes in.

Many people now apply for credit over the Internet. Because the credit extender does not see the applicant physically, many financial institutions use Equifax's Internet capability to access credit information immediately and make the consumer prove identity. This technology is known as authentication of a networked user and is protected by U.S. patents 6,263,447 and 6,282,658. Patents are pending in other countries.

3.7.5 Guarantees *(how)*

Equifax can offer guarantees to credit extenders on some product offerings. This guarantee encourages customers to use Equifax's products. Equifax, through the extensive collection of consumer information, can paint a reliable picture of a consumer's intention and ability to pay debt.

3.7.6 Statistically Speaking *(who)*

Equifax employs many statisticians who prepare models to analyze consumer data. The information these statisticians process allows Equifax to constantly update its credit worthiness assessment of a consumer.

3.7.7 From the Corner Store to Sears *(where)*

The amount of information Equifax gathers each month is staggering. In the U.S. alone, over 10,000 companies provide Equifax with information on customers. For our credit-based economy, this translates into Equifax receiving nearly 3 billion consumer records each month.

3.7.8 Key Terms

bad debt	profit
credit	revenue
expense	risk

3.7.9 Review Questions

1. How does the fact that Equifax is a global organization affect the time requirement for responding to customer requests?
2. Explain the phrase—Equifax builds its knowledge base around the consumer.
3. Why are both parts of the definition of credit important to a business? How does Equifax help its customers reduce their risks?
4. In the credit information industry, what type of information is gathered and sold by companies like Equifax? Equifax currently receives credit information from approximately how many United States companies?
5. What happens if Equifax's computer systems go down? What could be the long-term impact of this event on the enterprise?
6. Why is it important for most companies to maximize profits and minimize risk?

3.8 SYNTHESIS AND CHAPTER SUMMARY

Have you ever put new strings on a guitar? Six-string guitars come in many styles (classical, Spanish, solid body, hollow body, arch top, flat top, etc.) and generally in one of three varieties: acoustic, electric, or a combination of acoustic and electric. A guitar may be strung with strings made of steel, nylon, or catgut. Strings are available in a variety of gauges (or thicknesses). Each of the six strings has a name: lower E (the thickest), A, D, G, B, and upper E (the thinnest). Most guitarists tune each string to the tone associated with the string's given name.

When putting a new set of strings on a guitar, or tuning a guitar that is way out of tune, the musician generally starts with a rough tuning. Each string should sound approximately like the note. This procedure needs to be followed for all six strings. It is not important with which string you start or end. However, most guitarists will pick an order and generally stick with it.

After the rough tuning is complete, the guitarist then fine-tunes each string. After each string has been fine-tuned, the guitarist once again returns to each string, making sure it is still in tune. If a string has moved out of tune, the tuning keys are adjusted until that perfect note is reached once again. This process is repeated until each string is perfect to the ear of the guitarist.

The tension the string places on the guitar's neck causes a tuned string to go out of tune while another string is being tuned. Similarly, you can refer to the six strings as the six interrogatives: *what, how, where, who, when,* and *why*. As you have seen in the stories about Coca-Cola, Walt Disney, Keane, Equifax, The Movie Outpost, and Cascade Engineering, each company has to reason conceptually about topics associated with the six interrogatives.

When the company implements what it has envisioned conceptually, fine-tuning may be needed. Each primitive thought (a concept associated with a single interrogative) is going to form a composite with one of (and eventually all) the other primitive thoughts.

To fine-tune the company, each primitive concept is fine-tuned repetitively as the effects of the composite are discovered. As with guitar strings, the sequence does not really matter. Like a guitarist, you will find a sequence that suits your needs, and you will probably stick with it. This forms the basis of a methodology.

The key about tuning the strings on a guitar is that you tune them one at a time. Each string has to be in tune with the others. If the guitar is out of tune, you fix it by finding the specific string or strings that are out of tune. Many business operations or software systems that run a business are so complex that the business is unable find the single *string* that is out of tune in order to retune the business. All too often, these companies find it easier to throw away the guitar and buy or build a new one. Every few years this practice is repeated.

Tuning a single string can also place the other strings out of tune or *in jeopardy*. Focusing on one department or one product line can place a business in jeopardy too. Tuning becomes a fine balancing act where the end-result is to have all the strings tuned, and all the strings have to be in tune for the instrument *or business* to be in tune. Tuning an instrument or business takes on a holistic view—this is systems thinking. Understanding that the business as a whole needs to be in tune is imperative to long-term success.

3.8.1 Leadership: The Differentiator

An orchestra is a group of musicians who play music together. The term describes a symphony orchestra typically composed of people who play string, woodwind, brass, and percussion instruments. Other types of orchestras, such as jazz orchestras, are composed of different collections of instruments. The word "orchestra" comes from the Greek language and refers to the front part of an ancient theater where the performers stood.

The orchestra is a team with a leader. As on any team, certain players have specific duties. The conductor selects the music the orchestra plays and leads rehearsals and performances. Musicians sit in sections based on the kind of instrument they play. In a business, the leader is the CEO, and what an orchestra calls a "section," a business calls a "department." An orchestra section has a principal; so does a business department.

It is the conductor or leader who sets the tempo and alerts the musicians about practical matters, such as whether a section of a work is or is not repeated. The conductor is responsible for determining the dynamics, or volume, of each part of the music, as well as the overall interpretation. Conductors also maintain balance between the orchestra sections.

The *musicians* of a business play all along the company's supply and value chains. The dynamics of the supply chain may change as the company gets involved with mergers, acquisitions, spin-offs, corporate partnerships, and alliances. Corporate leadership needs to make sure each department and each employee understands its role and stays in tune with the rest of the organization. See Figure 3-24.

Figure 3-24   *Working together...recognizing leadership*

3.8.2 Leadership: Tuning to Success

If you have ever heard an out-of-tune piano, you know that a familiar melody played on it can sound quite odd. Orchestras must solve this problem as well. A note played on one instrument must be played at the same pitch as the corresponding note played on another instrument.

Orchestras solve this problem in several ways. Before a conductor comes to the podium, the principal violinist rises and asks the principal oboe player to sound a tuning A. The other musicians tune their own instruments, adjusting the pitch up or down until they hear that their notes are the same as the oboe's. At sea level and at 72°F, the frequency of the tuning A is 440 hertz or A-440.

As part of their long training, professional musicians become sensitive to pitch and tuning. They become very skilled at making any necessary adjustments during a performance. Sometimes the music moves too quickly, or the pitch changes too drastically, for the players to adjust their instruments in time. For the most part, however, musicians make sure their tuning is correct at the beginning, and then they listen closely as they play.

If an orchestra plays out of tune, you will not buy its CD. If a business is out of tune, you will not buy its product. Both the orchestra and the company need satisfied and delighted customers.

In ancient Greece, the great mathematician Pythagoras (569 B.C.E.–475 B.C.E.) thought about the peculiar behavior of waves that traveled up and down a plucked string. Pythagoras noticed that some notes were allowed while other notes were forbidden.

When Pythagoras plucked or strummed an open string, it sounded a nice, clear note. The tone was called the fundamental. When he placed a finger gently in the middle of the string and plucked again, he noticed he got another nice, clear note. This time, the tone was one octave above the fundamental. When Pythagoras tried placing his finger one-third of the way down the string, he noticed once again that he got another clear sounding note. Then he started placing his finger randomly up and down the string. Pythagoras noticed that he seldom got a clear note. He was able to determine that only certain notes can be played on the string. Many of the notes were excluded.

The Orchestra and Leadership Skills

In order for you to begin understanding the orchestra's enterprise architecture, the skillful conductor demonstrates and shares how the activities of the musicians are aligned with the orchestra's objectives (to give a concert), and how the conductor is able to manage the supply and value chains (through hiring the right musicians, purchasing quality instruments, having the musicians learn the appropriate techniques and music, and demanding punctuality).

The Corporation and Leadership Skills

In order for you to begin understanding the corporation's enterprise architecture, the skillful leader or business *owner* demonstrates and shares how the activities of the employees are aligned with the corporate objectives (to provide a product or service), and how the business leader is able to manage the supply and value chains (through hiring the right employees, purchasing quality materials, having the employees learn the appropriate techniques or tools, and demanding punctuality).

Like the notes on a guitar's string, a company cannot *pluck* anywhere it wants to achieve success. The company is restricted by technology, physics, competition, suppliers, regulations, vendors, customers, scope, and background. It is the panache of the company's employees that finds the sweet spots to create harmony and excellence for the organization in order to conduct commerce.

Whether establishing an enterprise for commerce or some other purpose, the *owner* creates a mandate. The *owner's* mandate consists of what is actually required for the enterprise to survive (in the marketplace), the resources that are needed or should be available, a budget to limit expenses, and a target date for time-to-market. These things comprise the *owner's* mandate.

3.9 CHAPTER ACTIVITIES

3.9.1 Discussion Topics

1. Explain the differences between the terms *relief* and *recovery* when talking about how business responds to problems.
2. How was the Ford Motor Company affected when its engineers decided to *redo* the design of the Mustang Cobra without referring back to the vehicle's original design?
3. What is the meaning of the phrase *the system is the enterprise*?
4. Give some examples of why or how companies choose relief rather than recovery.
5. Explain why you believe many of the dot-com companies failed during the year 2000.
6. Compare and contrast the advantages and disadvantages of a limited liability corporation and a general corporation.
7. Do you believe there is one thing every business needs? If so, what is that one particular thing, and how does it enable organizations to achieve great things for their communities and shareholders?
8. How does the enterprise benefit when the business *owner* works toward building a shared knowledge for the business participants?
9. Describe how the company benefits when a business participant has the ability to think conceptually about what he needs, independent (for consistency) of how it is going to work?
10. Give examples of at least four *systems* that exist in your community. Compare and contrast the ways these *systems* operate, in terms of primitive models and composite models.
11. Describe the differences between traditional analysis and the systems thinking approach.
12. Using the analogy of the six strings of the guitar being the six interrogatives, describe how the method of tuning a guitar parallels the method of *fine-tuning* a company. Use each primitive concept and the composite effects that occur as a result of each tuning.
13. Discuss how clear understanding and communication of an organization's vision and mission can create value and wealth for the enterprise.
14. Discuss your understanding of the *owner's* principal responsibilities.
15. Why does thinking conceptually about a product benefit Cascade Engineering?
16. Do you believe it is possible for any employee to take on an *owner's* role in the enterprise? Why or why not?

3.9.2 Critical Thinking

1. Look at the *Wall Street Journal*, or an equivalent business newspaper, and read an article that describes a company that chooses relief or recovery. Summarize your findings in a one-page paper.
2. Research QS-9000 standards on the Internet and write a one-page summary of what you learn.
3. Research one of the dot-com companies that failed in the year 2000. Be prepared to share your findings with the class.
4. Find examples of a limited liability corporation and general corporation in your own community. Compare and contrast these two organizations in a one to two-page paper.
5. Research a nonprofit organization in your own or nearby community. How does that organization generate income? Using the six interrogatives, find out as much as you can about this organization and summarize your findings in a one to two-page paper.

6. All of the companies highlighted in this chapter refer to the importance of solid relationships for success. Interview a business *owner* in your area and ask questions to learn about what relationships are important for the company. Find out what specific actions this business takes to build a shared knowledge for the organization. Write a two-page paper that explains what you learned.

7. Keep a log of all the trade-offs you observe or experience in one week. List the ramifications of the tradeoffs.

8. In a short one to two-page paper, explain how two of the enterprises in this chapter illustrated the need for strong leadership skills in the organization. Be prepared to share your thoughts regarding the need for strong leadership skills at all levels of an organization.

Endnotes

[1]Drucker, Peter. *The Next Information Revolution.* Forbes ASAP August 24, 1998.

[2]The Coca-Cola Company 2001 Annual Report.

[3]Pendergrast, Mark. *For God, Country, and Coca-Cola.* New York, NY: Macmillan, 1993.

[4]The Standish Group International, Inc. *The CHAOS Report (1994).* 1995.

[5]Keller, Fred. Personal interview. November 2002.

[6]Ibid.

[7]Ibid.

"The key is to keep company only with people who uplift you, whose presence calls forth your best."

— *Epictetus (0055–0135), Philosopher*

LEARNING OBJECTIVES

After completing Chapter 4, you will be able to:

1. Discuss why the design process involves many compromises.
2. Explain why it may not be possible to build everything you design.
3. List Covey's Seven Habits and explain how using them can assist the *designer* in establishing healthy relationships in the workplace.
4. Explain why good communication skills assist the *designer* in fulfilling his function.
5. Discuss the principal forces that constrain a design.
6. Explain why the *designer* must understand the anatomy of the domain.
7. Explain how measuring sticks can impose standards and constrain a project.
8. Compare and contrast the different roles individuals play in a meeting.
9. Describe why design is a complicated and complex undertaking that demands attention to detail.
10. Describe how metrics affect a project in relation to assets, process, location, people, events, and motivation.
11. Explain what is meant by the design mandate.
12. Identify ways *designers* use psychology to get desired results.
13. Explain why a *designer* needs to allocate resources.
14. Explain why detailed documentation must replace retained mental models in order for the enterprise to survive.
15. Identify the *designer's* most important function.
16. Explain how compromise, trade-offs, and established rules can help the *designer* get results.
17. Describe how an awareness and understanding of the organization's cultural and religious aspects can benefit the *designer*.

(continued)

18. Discuss why the *designer* must have a practical knowledge of individuals, teams, and the organization.

19. Discuss the importance of *designers* understanding the short- and long-term ramifications of their decisions.

20. Name the three distinct roles the *designer* plays when interacting with the *owner*.

21. Discuss what the *designer* can learn from SWOT analysis.

22. Explain how using the four organizational frames can assist the *designer* in finding simplicity and order within the chaos of an organization.

4.1 INTRODUCTION

When Captains James Kirk and Jean-Luc Picard summoned their respective flight commanders to increase the Enterprise's speed to warp factor four, the dilithium crystals, a matter-antimatter reactor core, and an antimatter containment field provided the burst of energy needed to send the starship on its way. Without antimatter, Kirk would not have cavorted to distant galaxies, and Picard would not have been able to *make it so.*

The Enterprise was able to travel to distant quadrants of the universe because of the energy produced by the matter coming into contact with antimatter. Antimatter is simply matter made up of the antiparticles of ordinary matter. Antimatter particles have the same mass as their counterparts and are essentially mirror images of the corresponding particles.

Gene Roddenberry (1921–1999), creator of Star Trek, could have used an alternative approach to traversing the universe—the wormhole. See Figure 4-1. In addition to traveling across large voids, the wormhole has the advantage of allowing the traveler to move forward and backward through time. Travel through outer space by means of a wormhole, or the power of antimatter, is confined to the lore of science fiction. However, NASA currently spends lots of money investigating both concepts.

In general relativity, one is free to specify whatever geometry one cares to imagine for spacetime; but then Einstein's equations specify what the energy-momentum content of matter in that spacetime must be in order to produce that geometry.

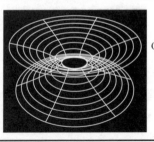

Generically, wormholes require negative mass exotic matter at their throats, in order to be traversible.

Figure 4-1   *The wormhole*

Not everything that can be designed can be built. In 1840, Charles Babbage (1791–1871) designed the analytical engine. See Figure 4-2. Babbage's analytical engine is often regarded as the first computer. Unfortunately, the engine was nineteenth century science fiction. The machine could not be built and stayed literally on the drawing table.

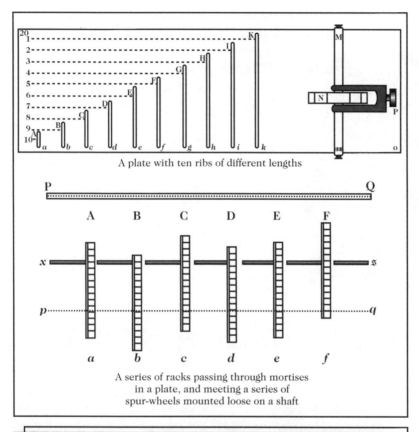

A plate with ten ribs of different lengths

A series of racks passing through mortises
in a plate, and meeting a series of
spur-wheels mounted loose on a shaft

Figure 4-2   *Babbage's analytical engine*

The analytical engine had four components: the store (memory), the mill (computational unit), the input section (punched card reader), and the output section (punched and printed output). The engine was completely mechanical and needed thousands of cogs, gears, and wheels to function. Babbage could not produce most of these parts to the degree of precision or tolerance needed, due to the technology available at the time.

Every design is constrained by physics, science, and engineering principles. Often the seemingly impossible is made possible by ingenuity, discovery, and resourcefulness. For example, in 1959, Lockheed, currently known as Lockheed Martin, began work on a project code named Oxcart. This project was funded by a development contract awarded by the Central Intelligence Agency (CIA). Project personnel had to overcome significant technical and psychological challenges before the project could be considered successful.

4.1.1 Technical and Psychological Challenges

Lockheed won a contract over its rivals—Boeing, General Dynamics, and North American—to design and build an aircraft capable of flying at a sustained airspeed of Mach 3, at an altitude exceeding 32,000 meters. See Figure 4-3.

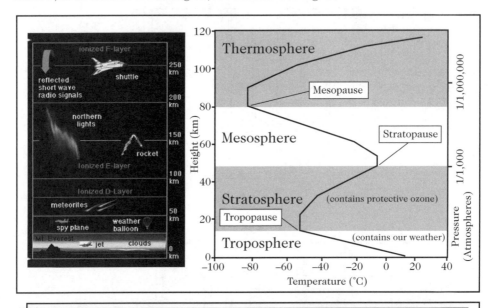

Figure 4-3 *Up, up, and away...*

Participation by the *designers* in the Oxcart project was an imposing ordeal. Parts of the project were deemed *Q Sensitive*, which is a designation two levels higher than top secret. The *designers* and engineers were not allowed to bring their briefcases or lunch to work. Notepapers could not be transported to or from the work environment. Everyone had to wear uniforms with no pockets. With no place to carry a pen, the *designers* could not use the pocket protectors they received for the holidays from their families.

At the time, revealing any information about the project was considered an act of treason against the United States. Many workers found their marriages ending in divorce due to psychological stress associated with the project and to never being allowed to answer the question, "How was your day, dear?"

In 1959, Lockheed's state-of-the-art plane was the F-104A, which had entered military service the previous year. The plane could only reach an altitude of 60,000 feet and briefly sustain a top speed of Mach 2. By April 1962, the first of the Blackbird aircraft series, the A-12, began taxiing trials at Groom Dry Lake, Nevada. The center of the lake bed is located at 115°47'30"W and 37°16'30"N and is within Area 51.[1]

Engineers at Lockheed needed to design a jet aircraft that could fly for long periods in a domain entered previously and only briefly by rocket planes. In addition to the prolonged exposure to high altitudes, the design had to allow for extremely cold air temperatures and extremely high surface temperatures on the plane.

Starting with a blank sheet of paper, the *designers* for the Oxcart project created a small supersonic airliner. To achieve long-range distance, the engineers emphasized the aircraft's streamlined shape at the expense of other flying characteristics, such as the plane's turn rate and ground performance.

The delta shape of the wing handled the low drag at Mach 3. See Figure 4-4. The fuselage was projected well ahead of the wing to provide ample space for fuel. The design helped keep the center of gravity forward. The engines and fuselage were given chines, which are aerodynamic projecting vanes that merge with the wing to improve directional stability. The fuselage was canted up so its chines would serve as a lifting canard. A canard is a horizontal stabilizing surface situated in front of the main wing.

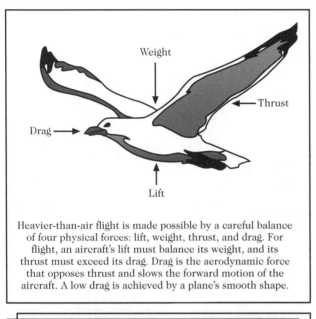

Heavier-than-air flight is made possible by a careful balance of four physical forces: lift, weight, thrust, and drag. For flight, an aircraft's lift must balance its weight, and its thrust must exceed its drag. Drag is the aerodynamic force that opposes thrust and slows the forward motion of the aircraft. A low drag is achieved by a plane's smooth shape.

Figure 4-4   *Low drag makes it easier to fly*

The long fuselage, delta wing, and conventional vertical tail surface were not conducive to take-offs and landings. To compensate, a pair of vertical surfaces was mounted on the large engine nacelles, which are streamlined enclosures for housing an engine. See Figure 4-5.

Designers predicted accurately how the A-12 would heat while cruising. The aircraft's leading edges and intakes reached temperatures of 800°F due to the kinetic heat produced by surrounding air. The wings and fuselage heated to 500°F. Outer skin temperatures around the rear of the engine nacelles reached 1,100°F, and the jet pipes glowed white-hot, even on minimal afterburner settings while cruising.

To cope with these temperatures, more than 90 percent of the fuselage was designed to be built of titanium alloy. In the late 1950s, the United States was in the middle of the Cold War with the Soviet Union. In an attempt to keep the Oxcart project a secret from the Soviets, the U.S. Government violated federal law by conspiring to purchase large amounts of titanium on the black market.

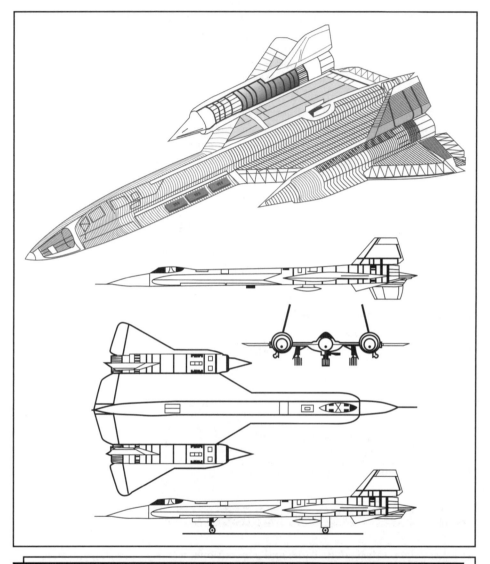

Figure 4-5   *Blueprints of the Blackbird A-12*

Anticipating high temperatures, *designers* knew conventional fuels and lubricants could not be used for the A-12. Instead, Pennsylvania State University's Petroleum Research Department helped develop a highly toxic, gel-like fuel known as JP-7. The fuel was so stable it could not be ignited by a match.

JP-7, capable of withstanding high temperatures, was stored in tanks in the wings and fuselage, with no insulation. As the plane consumed the fuel, liquid nitrogen was pumped into the tanks to fill the void in the fuel tanks. The liquid nitrogen prevented the tanks from crushing under the weight of the atmosphere as the plane descended back to Earth.

A cold Blackbird fuselage had many leaks, leading to fuel spillage. Ground crews had to be protected from exposure to spilled toxic JP-7 fuel. The Blackbird's leaks closed as the plane's skin temperature rose after the plane was airborne. Once the plane's heated skin had sealed, the plane had to be refueled in midair to compensate for the fuel leaked on the runway prior to take-off. The specially designed lubricants used for the aircraft were preheated before takeoff. All parts susceptible to failure due to extreme heat were addressed during the design process.[2]

Imagine designing a plane that would dump more than 12,000 gallons of fuel on the runway if delayed in takeoff. Then imagine designing a plane that, under normal circumstances, leaked so much that it would need refueling within minutes of take-off. Then imagine going to your boss and saying, "Is it okay if it leaks a bit...or a lot?" These were some of the engineering compromises *designers* had to make to accommodate the physical properties of titanium.

LOCKHEED'S BLACKBIRD

JP-7 contains a kerosene base and has to be ignited by a catalyst, tetraethyl borane.

Paint used for the plane consists of a pigmentation containing minute iron balls. The iron balls dissipate electromagnetically generated energy and effectively lower the chances of the plane being picked up by radar.

The operational turning radius of the plane is nearly 100 miles. In other words, it takes almost the width of the entire state of Utah to turn around.

The cost of flying a Blackbird is around $40,000 per hour.

The last A-12 flight took place in June 1968. The A-12 fleet (approximately eight aircraft) was moved to Palmdale, California for storage. All flights requiring A-12 capability were taken over by the newer Blackbird series, SR-71.

The A-12's successor, the SR-71, holds the world record for speed over a recognized course. Flown by Major James Sullivan (b. 1937) and Major Noel Widdifield (b. 1941) on September 1, 1974, the aircraft flew from New York to London in 1 hour, 56 minutes, and 4 seconds.

At Mach 3, you are flying over 30 miles per minute.

The Mach number is named for the Austrian physicist, Ernst Mach (1838–1916). Mach's inertial theories were cited by Einstein as one of the inspirations for his theories of relativity. The Mach number is a speed ratio. Mach is calculated by dividing the object speed by the speed of sound. The speed of sound varies based on the temperature and the density of the Earth's atmosphere. If the temperature was 20°C at sea level, the speed of sound would be approximately 770 mph.

Area 51 is best known for the U.S. Air Force's testing of exotic aircraft and weapons. Over the years, the government has closed many areas from which the base can be seen. The lights in the night sky over Area 51 are thought to be the

(continued)

> result of testing that captured UFOs. In 1989, a physicist named Robert Lazar (b. 1959) claims to have worked on the base, and he has stated that UFOs acquired from trading with aliens are being tested there.
>
> Lockheed Martin's current state-of-the-art aircraft is the undisclosed Aurora. The aircraft is rumored to go from speeds of Mach 6 to Mach 20. It is also rumored that Lockheed is working with the Air Force on a version that can travel at Mach 50. At Mach 50, you can travel around the world three times in two hours. To travel this fast is to travel at hypersonic speeds.

By building corrugations into the wings that accommodated expansion and increased the area available for heat dissipation, *designers* could generally reduce heat. The aircraft was painted a dark blue, which enabled heat emissions to occur 2.5 times faster than unpainted titanium.

To make the Oxcart project feasible, the *designers* and engineers needed to understand the physics associated with materials selection, kinetics, and aerodynamics. One problem they could not solve was how to have the plane fire a missile without shooting itself down.

Mathematics demonstrated how firing a missile that could not fly faster than the plane would result in that missile reconnecting with the plane within moments. The tactic of slowing the A-12 to fire a missile was not practical because the aircraft would then become a target for enemy-launched surface missiles. As a result, the Blackbird was limited primarily to the reconnaissance role of taking spy photographs.

In the end, Lockheed *designers* succeeded in overcoming many of the arduous technical challenges they encountered.

4.1.2 People and Design Challenges

Another significant challenge with which the Lockheed team battled, and one that still challenges many of today's enterprises, is the science of **industrial psychology**. Consider the Social Security Act of 1935. The Social Security Act, signed into law by President Franklin Roosevelt on August 14, 1935, included several provisions for general welfare. The new Act created a social insurance program that was designed to pay a continuing income to retired workers age 65 or older.

Upon signing the Act into law, President Roosevelt said:

> *We can never insure 100 percent of the population against 100 percent of the hazards and vicissitudes of life, but we have tried to frame a law, which will give some measure of protection to the average citizen and to his family against the loss of a job and against poverty-ridden old age.*[3]

The House Ways and Means Committee and the Senate Finance Committee held hearings during January and February of 1935. The actuaries working with Congress decided upon 65 as the retirement age. The actuaries and politicians believed that few Americans would ever reach that age, and if they did, statistically they would collect a government pension only for two, or possibly three, years. In the mid-1930s, 65 seemed to be a safe, minimal-cost age based on the life expectancy of the U.S. adult male.

The *designers* failed to account for how rapidly life expectancy had climbed for both men and women during the preceding 20 years. Despite the recent economic depression, living conditions, medicines, and food quality had improved. Since the enactment of the Social Security Act, life expectancy for U.S. males has increased about three years every decade and has doubled in the last 150 years. See Figure 4-6.

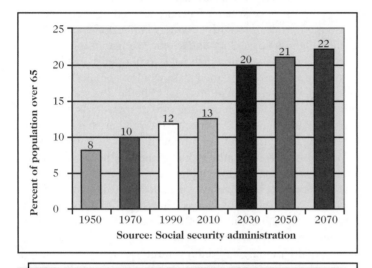

Figure 4-6   *The aging population*

When the government specified the retirement age in the Act, it assumed the population did not know the government was hoping to minimize payments. The longevity and the growing number of retired persons in the U.S. have strained the entire social security system.

A design process includes establishing policies and rules. *Designers* must understand the importance of short- and long-term ramifications of their decisions, which usually involve trade-offs. To fully understand the trade-offs involved, a *designer* must understand how and if he can change the product. Using the Social Security Act as an example, the actuaries and politicians should have taken into account *how* and *when* they could raise or lower the retirement age. They also should have considered *what* effect this action would have on the attitude of the American people, and how much money they could collect or pay out.

This chapter explores the role of the *designer* in an organization. When you design, you seek advice and opinion, and you *always* seek approval. Because designing involves working with others, this chapter emphasizes the psychology of working with people to make compromises and trade-offs, and to establish rules to get results. Establishing proper, healthy working relationships with your boss, peers, and customers can only help you succeed.

Certain behaviors and norms are expected in the work environment. For example, throwing pencils across the table at someone is not considered professional behavior. Insulting coworkers is not advisable, although the instant gratification might seem worth the action at times. However, tolerated behavior and accepted values vary based on **culture**, **corporate culture**, and **ethics**.

In 1935, the Social Security Act was passed. Those involved had **hidden agendas** and political ambitions, and they played upon the human psyche.

4.1.3 The Art of Compromise

In 1932, Ash Wednesday fell on February 10th. Marguerite Brunswig Staude (1899–1988) attended the Lenten service at Saint Patrick's Cathedral in Manhattan. Heading out of the great Gothic portals onto Fifth Avenue, Marguerite wondered why church design continued to cling to its past glory and seemed to ignore the present.

Marguerite, an art student, began the walk north back to her penthouse apartment on 85th Street. Walking away from the stained glass windows created by artisans from Chartres, France, she wondered if a church could be built to speak in today's contemporary language and provide an opening into liturgical arts.

Still thinking about church architecture, Marguerite entered her apartment and peered out the window. Looking down the avenues, under the cloudy New York sky, past Rockefeller Center and Saint Patrick's Cathedral, she noticed the construction of a skyscraper that, in the movies, King Kong would have the honor of climbing.

In February 1932, the Empire State Building was shrouded in scaffolding and naked steel girders. Marguerite saw the shape of a cross emerging from the scaffolding where major vertical and horizontal beams came together. Awestruck, she entertained thoughts of how she could build a modern Gothic structure.

Marguerite came from a wealthy family and did not want for money. In addition to her Manhattan penthouse, the art student had another apartment in California, where she transformed her plans into a sketch. Marguerite's friend, Frank Lloyd Wright, Jr. (1890–1978), son of the famed architect, was renowned and respected in his own right. Lloyd, as he was known, was impressed by her drawings and agreed to help create the necessary architectural designs.

For 12 months, the two spent time researching Gothic cathedrals and searched for ways to balance modern and classical architectural themes. The pair created a cruciform church. The structure involved a perforated double wall in tiny cement crosses. The whole structure would be lined with glass and the building would be built to a 500-foot scale.

Marguerite hoped to build her new cathedral of the future around a square block owned by the Catholic Church in Los Angeles, California. Because the Archbishop could not understand the architecture, he rejected Marguerite's ideas and designs. He thought they were too futuristic.

In 1937, Marguerite found a new location for the cathedral. An order of nuns in Budapest, Hungary was eager to build the church on Mount Gelert, overlooking the Danube River. Unfortunately, the plans were abandoned permanently when Europe entered the Second World War in 1939.

In 1941, Marguerite and her new husband purchased a ranch in Sedona, Arizona. They selected the site as a refuge from Los Angeles in case the Japanese attacked the west coast of America. At that time, Sedona did not have a church, though religious services were held in a one-room schoolhouse.

Within five years of moving to Sedona, Marguerite's parents died, and a patrimony was established for a memorial in their name. Marguerite was determined to build a chapel to honor the memory of her parents in the name and form of the Holy Cross.

Marguerite once again contacted Lloyd and described how she wanted to scale down the project in accordance with her current financial means. This time, Lloyd refused to work with Marguerite. He was only interested in building the cathedral according to their original plans.

However, in April 1955, she broke ground on the site of the Chapel of the Holy Cross, just south of Sedona. Marguerite had found two new architects from San Francisco, Robert Anshen and Steven Allen. Together they designed a new chapel and scoured Sedona and the surrounding terrain by foot, jeep, and air to find a suitable site. See Figure 4-7.

| Figure 4-7 | *Chapel of the Holy Cross* |

The U.S. Forest Service owned the land Marguerite found, though the local forestry service did not have the authority to grant approval to build. The local forestry service sent her to the area's main office in Flagstaff; they referred her to the regional office in Albuquerque, New Mexico. The regional office referred her to the national headquarters in Washington, D.C. In fact, it practically took an act of Congress to receive a deed and building permit. Much help and influence was received from Arizona Senator Barry Goldwater (1909–1998).

In addition, Marguerite needed permission from the diocese of Arizona in Gallup, New Mexico. Gallup is located along the famed Route 66 and is mentioned in the song of the same name. Bishop Bernard Espelage was reluctant to approve the plans. He could not understand why anybody would want to build a strange-looking church, and he felt the project's $300,000 cost could be better spent doing missionary work for local Native Americans.

Marguerite persevered and was soon able to hire the William-Simpson Construction Company of California, which built the church over 18 months. In the spring of 1957, the dedication ceremony took place. Twenty-five years after her initial plan, Marguerite had her church. However, its final design was much different from her original sketch. The location was not her first or second choice. She had to enlist help from different architects, and the initial purpose for wanting to build the structure evolved from artistic to personal.

The compromise did not end there. Marguerite had commissioned San Francisco artist Keith Monroe to create a sculpture of Christ to hang on the cross above the altar. The sculpture became known as the Atomic Christ and startled many visitors and the clergy. Finally, the criticisms proved too much for Marguerite. The sculpture was taken down and destroyed.

With the Atomic Christ removed, the chapel that had been dedicated to *finding God through art* saw attendance fade at its worship services. In the end, a decision was made to stop regularly scheduled sacramental services. This policy remains in effect today. However, the doors remain open for people of all religions to partake in personal solace and worship. The church continues to be visited by tourists and local residents who admire the architecture, artwork, and surrounding landscape.

Marguerite died in 1988, but the modern Gothic chapel on a 200-foot spur of red rock, seven miles south of Sedona, remains a monument to the compromise of design for visitors the world over to enjoy. As you walk inside the chapel and look to your right, there on a pedestal sits a granite bust of Christ—from the Cathedral of Chartres. See Figure 4-8.

Figure 4-8   *Bust of Christ originally from the Cathedral of Chartres*

SECTION 4.2 WHY PEOPLE SKILLS ARE IMPORTANT

> ## QUESTIONS TO CONTEMPLATE
>
> 1. How does the *designer* benefit from labeling or classifying people?
> 2. What are the areas of business contention with which the *designer* has to deal?

4.2.1 Introduction

Many books have been written about how to evaluate yourself, gain acceptance into society, and communicate in the corporation. Authors and pundits offer training courses on everything from teamwork and stress relief to how to write an interoffice memo and letter. Many of these books don't address the one reason that people skills are necessary—survival.

An old African proverb states, "Sticks and stones may break my bones, but words will never harm me." However, industrial psychology indicates that behaviors such as name-calling, verbal intimidation, and inappropriate physical gestures, might hurt. Survival involves protecting yourself and others in the workplace by using the necessary people skills. These skills are useful whether the *designer* is involved with office politics, allocating accounting resources, selling ideas, compromising, or dealing with any other aspect of the design process.

Imagine a group of office workers inside a glass building. Each worker seems to be working diligently. In a glass building, you may think you can see everything about every worker. However, even in a glass house, some things remain hidden.

A worker's reputation, image, and sense of self-worth might be on display, yet all viewers see only what they want to see. Those inside and outside the glass house communicate through **emotional filters** learned and formed at early ages of development. Emotional filters protect us from emotional harm and provide a barrier for self-protection. They help establish our individual constraints of understanding and communication.

A commonly heard grouse is, "If only he would just tell me what he is really thinking, everything would be so much easier." Within our population, a small group of people can easily articulate their wants, though only on national television talk shows, such as Oprah, Maury, and Jerry Springer.

In general, people like to be heard and respected. Many employees view the corporate environment as a large impersonal structure where listening and respect pose a significant challenge. Normally, everyone wants to be liked and considered part of the team or family. To receive the respect they want, people rely on the strength of their personalities and communication skills.

Work teams typically tolerate wide ranges of behavior, from bad hair days to depression or wild exuberance. Teams tolerate erratic behavior because individuals are viewed as part of the family. Team members understand how it feels to have *one of those days*. Only certain behaviors are not tolerated, particularly when someone who has not earned a place in the family misbehaves. For example, a team might freeze out someone who condemns an idea using a statement of fact, instead of offering an opinion that something is wrong. The team might label such people the *black sheep* of the family.

The basic premise that all employees work together does not hold true for all corporations. Every organizational unit forms a culture based on the personalities and values of the family members. A basic tenet of many corporate cultures is to beware of outsiders. See Figure 4-9.

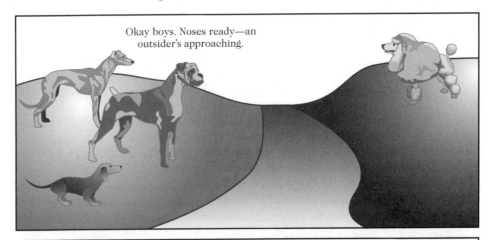

Okay boys. Noses ready—an outsider's approaching.

| Figure 4-9 | *A basic tenet of dog culture is beware of outsiders until sniffed* |

Proficient *designers* recognize these facts: No one wants to change anything for any reason at any time, and everyone wants everything done by the deadline, the way it has always been done. To compound the problem, *designers* have to contend with managing compromise. After all, nobody will get everything she wants.

For many teams, not getting what they want sets the stage for war.

 ## 4.2.2 To Have Lots of Fans *(why)*

People in an organization often are drawn to and follow certain other people who are recognized immediately as leaders. Leaders stand out. Leaders hold most of the political power in a corporation, without having to strive for that power. Members of the organization cede power to the leader. Even a leader's manager cedes power. The leader's advice is sought and usually followed.

A leader's forté involves people skills associated with bringing out the best in individuals and rallying teams to a common goal. Several key indicators make the leader recognizable. The leader:

- Exudes charisma, which is a combination of confidence, desire, ability, charm, and presence
- Presents a forceful front, including confidence that a problem can and will be solved
- Is intelligent and can consider options
- Makes decisions

- Has good ideas, but not necessarily the best
- Seeks and accepts opinions and ideas
- Is truthful and earns trust
- Creates an environment of cooperation
- Is thoughtful
- Fosters a sense of enthusiasm in the group

Everyone wants to be like the leader.

4.2.3 Types of Skills *(what)*

To handle a potential hostile work environment, the *designer* must exhibit the following set of skills, traits, and attributes:

- Leadership
- Management
- A sense of urgency
- An understanding of human psychology

Every new project forces the *designer* to demonstrate mastery of the corporate functions and requirements and tests the *designer's* mettle in keeping everyone heading in the same direction for the same reason. The *designer's* most important function is balancing the disparate needs of people, management, and **business requirements**.

The *designer*, whether a person or team, has the onerous responsibility of continuous compromise. The *designer* must balance the requirements or mandate with the resources that the *owner* makes available. This balance is difficult to reach. Improper design may result in failed business operations and the misuse of technology. Consequences of poor design include aggravated customers, alienated internal staff, and money spent without delivering a benefit.

THE MANDATE

Little League Baseball may be for children, but it is also big business. Started in 1939, the league lets children show they have the right stuff for baseball. As an organization, the league does not limit participation in its activities on the basis of disability, race, creed, color, national origin, gender, sexual preference, or religious preference. The organization does put down a heavy foot, however, regarding the age of a player.

The distinction between a 12-year old and a 14-year old may not seem significant, but for Little League Baseball, the age gap means everything. Twelve-year old children play on smaller baseball fields, where the pitcher's mound is 46 feet from home plate. Older children play on regulation diamonds, where the mound is more than 60 feet from home plate.

(continued)

Little League pitchers throw the ball at an average rate of 52 mph. In the summer of 2001, 12-year old Danny Almonte was clocking speeds of 78 mph. Danny played for the Paulino All Stars in The Bronx, New York. Danny had a great season and led his team to a third place finish in the Little League World Series. During the World Series, he pitched the first perfect game since 1957. He struck out an amazing 46 hitters in three games. During his turn to bat, Danny hit nearly 50 percent of the balls thrown to him.

A number of the teams that played against the All Stars expressed concern about whether some All Star players were over the age limit. A Staten Island, New York, coach hired a private detective to investigate the team. Although the detective received $10,000, he could not find any evidence to incriminate the All Stars.

A journalist for *Sports Illustrated* magazine visited Danny's native country and made a startling announcement. The journalist found Danny's Dominican Republic birth certificate, showing Danny's birth date as April 7, 1987. Overnight, Danny went from being twelve years old to fourteen. Danny was too old to play Little League ball. Oops.

The news about Danny led league officials to rule that the Paulino All Stars forfeit all their games for 2001, including the title for third place finish in the World Series. Danny's father and Rolando Paulino, the team founder, were banned from the Little League for life.

Little League is serious about its rules. The rules are mandates, not idle guidelines. If you walk away from breaking a mandate with a slap on the wrist, consider yourself lucky. Danny was not.

The *designer's* position is similar to a general practitioner of medicine. While the *designer* is responsible for the success of the work as a whole, she must also know when to consult a specialist. The range of consulting skills required can include business knowledge, distributed computing architectures, protocols, and application program interfaces (APIs).

The *designer* must understand the anatomy of the **domain**, or else become a mere decorator. In other words, the *designer* must fully understand all the intricacies of the given subject area. The *designer* is intrinsic to the success of a complex project. Remember that the final construction is the true deliverable.

4.2.4 The Balance (how)

In practice, the *designer's* function is twofold. In a project or organization, the *designer's* first function is to design a product or service. The second deals with egos and politics involved in creating the design. The *designer* may consume more time dealing with politics than designing.

The division of effort may follow Pareto's Law,[4] the **80/20 rule**, which suggests that 20 percent of a project is spent designing. The other 80 percent is spent dealing with background noise, which might have nothing to do with the end product, but everything to do with the transition to the end product.

The *designer* has a staid accounting responsibility. By the time the *designer* gets involved, the *owner* has established a budget, which is usually an estimate based on experience, facts, intuition, and hope. The *owner* does not usually define how resources are to be used. Instead, the *designer* typically uses the *owner's* budget to allocate resources to key areas of the organization, such as people, process, technology, and location.

The *designer* then creates a budget for each area and reports to management how and when resources will be used. Management constrains the project; it is likely to generate many questions regarding progress, which involve elapsed time and committed resources.

Starts

The *designer* can start a project by listing everything of interest to the project, as the architect Imhotep did when he built the Great Pyramid of Giza. The *designer* should categorize the lists by the six interrogatives and avoid assumptions and implications by making everything explicit.

Making something explicit does not avoid all errors and misunderstandings, but it lets you lessen implicit assumptions, thereby minimizing errors and misunderstandings. If you make something explicit, but an error or misunderstanding is discovered later, it should be easier to correct the problem and move forward. In both the short term and long term, making something explicit can improve communication, minimize rework, establish traceability, and promote quality improvement initiatives.

If you do not address assumptions and implications, you usually end up making a compromise, which can place the project immediately at risk. Depending on the context, **compromise** can mean *to place the project at risk if certain practices are not followed in a diligent manner*. For example, because a manager did not approve the purchase of a software license, the project now risks being late. Another definition of compromise is *when two or more parties reach a settlement with nobody getting exactly what was wanted at the onset*. For example, one person wants a purple background on the Web page, not a pink background. The other person wants a pink background, not a purple one. They can settle on a color they both like—lime green.

A third definition of compromise is to *accept something even though you do not really like it or are not in favor of it*. For example, two Web page *designers* are arguing about whether to use a drop-down list box or a set of radio buttons on the Web page. Finally, one *designer* gives in to the other's preference to keep the project moving in the right direction.

A **trade-off** is similar to a compromise, but involves an exchange of one thing in return for another. The trade-off is probably relinquishing one benefit or advantage for another that is regarded as more desirable. A compromise does not always include an exchange.

A person with a vested interest in the project is a **stakeholder**. All stakeholders in a design project should assemble to ensure they have a clear understanding of *what* is required and *why*. The *designer* must make sure all stakeholders understand the *what* and *why* of their own areas and the areas of others. **Inter-organizational communication** guarantees the eventual alignment and integration of business operations. If the *designer* does not meet with the stakeholders, she is forced to meet with each stakeholder individually. Communicating with one person at a time prolongs communication and often leads to misunderstanding project expectations.

Overall, the *designer* is responsible for the following activities:

- Creating high-level or general designs
- Managing team members who design the individual parts of the endeavor
- Coordinating with stakeholders
- Allocating budget to all functions required for the design
- Placing the appropriate infrastructure to support the design effort
- Communicating the *as is* or current state
- Designing the *to be* or end state
- Designing the transition process from the current to the end state
- Communicating and reporting the team's progress
- Keeping everybody happy

As the project progresses, the *designer* must be sure all business needs are being met. Failing to do so adds another layer of risk to the project. The *designer* must also communicate regularly with the boss and every stakeholder. The list of responsibilities for the *designer* relates to all areas of **business contention**.

4.2.5 Advisor, Agent, and Arbitrator *(who)*

The *designer* is a professional advisor to the *owner*. The *designer* advises the *owner* on how best to solve a business problem, or address a business opportunity, and provides information about using the project's budget. As an agent of the *owner*, the *designer* deals with others on behalf of the *owner* when selecting the methods, languages, and tools of construction. As arbitrator, the *designer* sides neither with the *owner* nor the *builder*, discussed in Chapter 5, but uses her skills to enforce the requirements and needs of both parties.

A *designer* is a master of the art of design and associated arts and sciences. If the *designer* violates a principle of a related science, she jeopardizes the success of the project. Just as a physician should refuse to treat a case in a manner medically unsound, even at a patient's request, the *designer* should refuse to build an unsound software application, which is not manageable, cannot accommodate ongoing stakeholder needs, or violates regulatory laws. Under extreme conditions, this obligation may require the *designer* to relinquish her employment.

The *designer* therefore plays three distinct roles when interacting with the *owner*—advisor, agent, and arbitrator. To understand the venerable position of the *designer*, you must first understand the *owner's* mandate.

4.2.6 Informed *(where)*

Planning is an important part of creating a mandate or management imperative. A CEO can do all the planning and still satisfy all the requirements of an *owner*, who must accept the *planner's* definition of scope. The mandate consists of what is actually required for the enterprise to survive (in the marketplace), what resources are needed or should be available, a budget to limit expenses, and a target date for introducing the product to market.

The *owner's* mandate has inherent weaknesses. Because the mandate is issued at a specific time, it is influenced by the prevailing market and legislative conditions. The mandate probably changes over time. The longer the project takes, the more the mandate is likely to change. The mandate reflects a specific set of learned experiences and is made with a specific set of objectives in mind.

The statistics against the success of a high-cost, long-term project are appalling. The failure is due primarily to the impact of time on the life cycle of the project. Typical conditions that may hamper the project's progress include:

- Frequent scope changes (e.g., every three months)
- Important new requirements discovered frequently (e.g., every month)
- Beneficiaries of the system fail to state important parts of the operation
- Significant requirement changes occur with frequency and regularity
- Every day a *gotcha* is revealed

The *designer* must meet budget and keep the *owner* informed of progress. The Manhattan Project, discussed in Section 2.4 of Chapter 2, illustrated the concept of the feedback loop and the problem of communication. The *designer* must communicate not only upward to management, but also outward to all the organizational units affected by the design. A vehicle often used for communicating is the meeting.

4.2.7 The Meeting *(when)*

The business meeting is sometimes one of the horrors of the modern corporation. When the business meeting fails to be productive, attendees frequently share the following beliefs:

- It lasted too long.
- The proper subjects were not covered.
- There were more issues generated than resolved.
- Nothing was accomplished.
- A follow-up meeting is required.
- Some of the more important players were not present.
- Many of the attendees had little to do with the subject.
- The breaks were too long.
- The breaks were not frequent enough.
- The meeting chair was inefficient.
- The agenda was incorrect.
- Nobody had any dry erase markers that worked.
- We ran out of decaf and there were no cookies.

When all this is considered, the only likely conclusion is that the attendees are a *bunch of morons*. They are not. Each attendee brings a unique set of requirements and has a different role to play.

Meeting Types

Effective business meetings are often successful because an agenda was prepared and distributed to attendees prior to the meeting. The agenda allows each participant to review the meeting topics and come prepared. In essence, the *designer* need only address six basic questions at each meeting:

- *What* is required?
- *How* is it to be done?
- *Where* is it to be done?
- *Who* is required?
- *When* is it to be done?
- *Why* is it to be done?

In the previous list, the word *it* represents appropriate topics for the meeting. If the *designer* attempts to discuss any topic outside of these questions, the topic is likely to be background noise and may potentially lack purpose. The designer should try to conduct an orderly meeting.

A typical meeting agenda includes:

- Call meeting to order
- Take roll call
- State purpose of meeting
- State length of meeting
- Discuss housekeeping details, such as schedules for breaks, refreshments, etc.
- State agenda
- Discuss topics that still remain open
- Address topics on agenda
- State time and place of next meeting, if required
- Adjourn meeting

Starting meetings on time shows you are prepared and expect the same from attendees. If you are the facilitator, you must make sure all visual aids, required equipment, and supplies are in the meeting room by the time the meeting starts. Two examples of meeting types include the status meeting and the brainstorming session.

Status Meeting

Managers are very fond of the status meeting. During this meeting, participants are required to justify their existence. Justification is offered by explaining what has been accomplished, what is being worked on, and what is being planned. A manager reports the status of his department to his management, and so on up the line. In addition to attending these meetings, participants are typically required to bring a written report.

Brainstorming Session

Many meetings are labeled as brainstorming sessions. Participants are expected to think of ideas to move the project forward. The sessions are supposed to be no holds barred and active participation is expected. During this meeting, the first of the **political agendas** begins to emerge. Every participant comes prepared with some vested interest to protect. As the session progresses, the positions are presented subtly as objectives of the project. The *designer* must be observant of the underlying politics revealed by different personalities.

Personality Roles

Many people in an organization are team players. A team player directs energy and knowledge toward making the project or enterprise successful and is capable of setting aside any personal agenda. If everything in the enterprise worked smoothly, there would be no need to address pitfalls, such as the meeting and its participants, in a textbook.

Some roles impede progress. Recognizing negative roles can help the *designer* and team players respond and act appropriately to counteract the inhibitors. Roles that may inhibit progress include the following:

- Passive aggressive resistor
- Facilitator
- Dominator
- Hermit
- Obstructionist
- Malcontent
- Essene
- Unopinionated

The Passive Aggressive Resistor

Organizational psychologists have given a name to the behavior of individuals in an organization who have either ignored or overlooked any of the basic business and personal needs. The behavior is called passive aggressive resistance. The pattern of behavior includes:

- Missed deadlines
- Failure to attend important meetings
- Always too busy to really discuss the project
- Promised performance not delivered
- Misstatement of requirements
- Responsibility shunted off to lowest level of organizational unit

During meetings, the passive aggressor brings up many issues that have nothing to do with the project and diverts attention from the real issues. The behavior is done for two reasons:

- To divert attention from the aggressor's lack of preparation
- To create background noise that makes it appear the aggressor is participating

The aggressor has one other unique behavior pattern. He is always off to another meeting that is more important than the one you have scheduled. Here is a list of other meeting behavior patterns:

- Last one to arrive
- First one to leave
- Causes delays during meeting by asking for frequent breaks
- Does not return from a break until after the allotted time
- Takes telephone calls during the meeting and steps outside to talk
- Requires many beverages
- Requires much review to ensure understanding of status and progress

- Forces the team back over established ground
- Tells too many jokes
- Has a story about everything—except the work at hand
- Likes to participate in corporate gossip

The Facilitator

Facilitators want everyone to play nice and agree on everything. Facilitators make sure that everyone has a notepad and pen, the visual aid equipment is ready, and refreshments are in place. The facilitator is there to resolve personality clashes or major disagreements. The facilitator strives for compromise in all things, but is most likely to support people needs over task needs. Many of the facilitator's comments and suggestions begin with the words, "I feel," "In my opinion," or "It sounds to me."

The Dominator

The dominator is always right, and if you do not believe so, just ask. The dominator has little empathy for the needs of others and is focused on the task at hand. The dominator runs over those disagreeing, trying to take control of meetings by sheer force of will. Dominators, when in management positions, believe in management by fear. There is little or no room for compromise, and the gist of the conversations are, "I say," and "You do."

The Hermit

The hermit has little to say and takes many notes. The hermit is usually analytical and requires many forms of proof before agreeing with any notion. Hermits never accept accountability or take responsibility. Hermits feel no need to provide any leadership. The hermit's conversation usually begins with, "Based on what I have learned, I do not have enough information to reach a conclusion."

The Obstructionist

The obstructionist believes in preventing progress and does just about anything to either attract attention or sideline the discussion.

The Malcontent

The malcontent is a person who can clear out a room faster than a broken rotten egg. The malcontent complains about everything. The malcontent's complaining is made even worse if the malcontent is a whiner. The malcontent can find bad in everything and good in nothing.

The Essene

In every large group, someone is always compelled to make notes about everything. This individual prints the notes and files them in a cave or in a hidden file somewhere on the computer. Whatever the storage device, one thing remains—neither the knowledge nor the notes are shared. The organization has to wait until a shepherd boy stumbles upon them.

Essenes are a secretive group and rarely propose new ideas or share any thinking. These individuals appear to be analytical, but are not. The Essene's favorite answer to almost any question is, "It is not for me to say."

The Unopinionated

The unopinionated are difficult. They neither make decisions, nor reveal what they think.

The Team Player

A successful team player works cooperatively with others in both formal and informal settings for the greater good and success of the team and project. The team player creates and supports consensus through an open, candid, and collaborative environment. Scottish soccer legend Billy Bremner (1942–1997) held a philosophy about the game, "Side [team] before self every time."[5] A good team player can live by this statement in the workplace.

A valuable trait of the team player is offering criticism about an idea or piece of work, without directing the criticism toward the people who presented the work.

These behavior patterns pervade corporate America today. The fundamental reason for the negative behaviors is that change is difficult. People respond to change in different ways; typically, those who tolerate or welcome change exhibit positive behaviors.

Dealing with the psychology of the corporation and its employees allows the *designer* to use all resources to their full advantage. The *designer* must understand the corporate psyche. To satisfy both personal and business needs, the *designer* must be an advisor, agent, arbitrator, facilitator, and psychologist. Some call this *going with the flow*. To go with the flow, the *designer* must know where the rocks are and how to avoid or remove them.

4.2.8 Key Terms

80/20 rule	ethics
business contention	hidden agenda
business requirement	industrial psychology
compromise	inter-organizational communication
corporate culture	political agenda
culture	stakeholder
domain	trade-off
emotional filter	

4.2.9 Review Questions

1. How do emotional filters color our worlds? How might these filters affect a team at work?
2. Why is it critical for the *designer* to balance the needs of people, management, and business requirements?
3. What would you recommend the *designer* do to understand the anatomy of a domain?
4. How can the stakeholders meeting help the *designer* communicate outward to all organizational units affected by the design?
5. Explain how Pareto's Law applies to the *designer*. How does knowledge of human psychology help the designer comply with the *owner's* mandate?
6. When interacting with the *owner*, what three roles does the *designer* have to play and why?

SECTION 4.3 HOW MYERS-BRIGGS KNLP

QUESTIONS TO CONTEMPLATE

1. Why would it be advantageous for the *designer* to determine what motivates others?
2. Which personality type best identifies you?
3. Which personality type best identifies your manager or your instructor?

4.3.1 Introduction

Seth and Emily are systems analysts for competing software consulting organizations. At a local e-commerce users' group meeting, they both met Shannon, the vice president of Internet development for a large cosmetics and candle wax company.

Eager about the prospect of signing Shannon as a client, both Seth and Emily talked with Shannon during the meeting and offered her their business cards. An important trait of a software consultant is to be first and foremost a salesperson, regardless of technical skills.

Seth and Emily have other things in common besides their jobs. Both are outgoing, friendly, resourceful, and spontaneous people who pride themselves for their natural warmth and ability to establish personal relationships with their clients.

Seth followed up with an immediate personal contact to Shannon, the way he pursues all of his leads. The day after the users' group meeting, Seth stopped by Shannon's office, hoping Shannon would have time to talk with him. With a full schedule of appointments, Shannon was mildly annoyed by the intrusion, but managed to spare a few minutes for him. Seth tried his best to quickly sell Shannon on using his company to develop the next wave of B2B software for the cosmetics and candle wax company.

Unlike Seth, Emily had quickly pegged Shannon as a thoughtful, methodical, organized, practical, and logical person. Shannon is someone who is impressed by data, facts, and demonstrable past experiences. Emily realized that Shannon's natural personality style was different from her own.

Understanding Shannon's personality type and preferred way of communicating, Emily realized Shannon's natural tendency would be to think about something before discussing it. Emily knew Shannon would want to know all relevant facts and details, as well as specific advantages, and then, if convinced, would be most heavily influenced by the bottom line.

Emily also knew by Shannon's personality type that she scheduled her time judiciously and would not appreciate an unannounced visit. Emily took a different approach from Seth and drafted a short e-mail message to Shannon, which highlighted the practical benefits of outsourcing new e-commerce development to Emily's company. She included information about the company's track record of successful Internet solutions. Emily followed up the e-mail with a telephone call to schedule a meeting to answer any of Shannon's questions and address any possible concerns.

Emily's approach paid off and won her the new account—a major coup for her and her company. Although Emily's and Seth's solutions were similar, Emily was a more effective salesperson because she had determined Shannon's personality type. Therefore, Emily knew how Shannon liked to make decisions and preferred to communicate.

Emily knew how to gain insights into understanding others by observing clues about their appearance, vocabulary, body language, occupation, education, and interests. When Emily first met Shannon, she spent time trying to understand what motivated her and influenced her behavior.

These skills are valuable, whether you are bargaining for the raise you think you deserve, negotiating a peace treaty, or trying to understand how to facilitate a **joint application development (JAD) session** to gather design features necessary for a software solution.

While each person is unique, personality differences are not usually random. Human characteristics are identifiable and often predictable. A powerful and well-respected model of psychology is called **personality typing**.

Personality typing originated with the Swiss-born psychologist, Carl Gustav Jung (1875–1961). In the early 1920s, he published a paper on psychological types. In 1923, when Jung's work was published in English, Katharine Briggs (1875–1968) set aside her own research and became an exhaustive student of Jung. With her daughter, Isabel Briggs Myers (1897–1996), Katharine spent the 1930s observing and developing better ways to measure differences among people.

During World War II, the mother-and-daughter team observed that many people involved in the war effort were working on tasks unsuited to their abilities. The two women set out to design a psychological instrument that would explain personality differences in scientific and reliable terms, according to Jung's theory of personality preferences. The result was the **Myers-Briggs Type Indicator**.

4.3.2 The Evaluation Process *(how)*

Personality typing holds many benefits for a *designer*. Many people place the focus of the *designer's* role on the produced output or deliverables. For **software architects**, the deliverable may include a logical data model or a class model. However, the model is the result of many hours of analysis and communicating with people.

In most cases, analysis is achieved by communicating with numerous people inside and outside the organization, including stakeholders, managers, executives, customers, knowledge workers, and peers.

Harnessing the power of **intellectual capital** during the design process keeps people motivated and cultivates their natural strengths. Intellectual capital includes a person's brainpower, mental skills, and knowledge that are critical to a company's success. The *designer* may also need to handle interpersonal interactions, including dealing with difficult colleagues, keeping clients happy, assessing adversaries' strengths and weaknesses, and communicating better with all levels of people in the organization.

Personality typing can be insightful and useful because it accurately identifies key characteristics of personalities and describes behavior in positive, nonjudgmental terms. One personality type is not preferable to another; each simply identifies natural strengths and potential weaknesses.

Some people resist the notion they can be typed, insisting that they exhibit different characteristics depending on the situation. While this may be true, people do not exhibit different characteristics with equal frequency, energy, or success.

For example, suppose you use a pen to write your signature on a piece of paper. The physical act of writing probably feels easy. Using the opposite hand, most people would describe the experience as awkward, difficult, or unnatural. Writing with your unpreferred hand probably took more time and energy, and the final signature was almost certainly not as good.

Like using a preferred hand, when someone exhibits the preferred side of her type characteristic, she is doing what comes naturally. People may act differently during a job interview than they do when attending a rock concert. People behave differently around family than they do when they are with their closest friends. However, the differences in behavior do not mean their personalities change in each situation.

Verifying a personality type is a process of elimination. Each personality type consists of traits. By observing the traits that someone exhibits or does not exhibit, you can type that person.

4.3.3 Classification Scheme *(what)*

Four components or dimensions make up a personality type, and they can be determined by answering the following questions:

- What energizes people?
- What kinds of information do people naturally notice and remember?
- How do people make decisions?
- How do people like to organize the world around them?

Each dimension has two opposite extremes. See Figure 4-10.

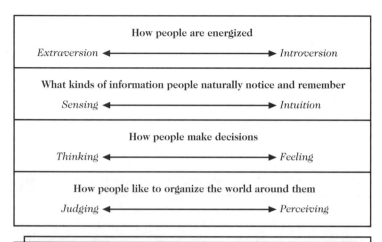

How people are energized	
Extraversion ◄─────────────► *Introversion*	

What kinds of information people naturally notice and remember	
Sensing ◄─────────────► *Intuition*	

How people make decisions	
Thinking ◄─────────────► *Feeling*	

How people like to organize the world around them	
Judging ◄─────────────► *Perceiving*	

Figure 4-10   *Components making up a personality type*

JUST BECAUSE...

When writing about personality typing, the word extrovert is often spelled extravert because Carl Jung preferred that spelling.

When interacting with people, notice how they primarily direct their energy. Is the energy directed to the outer world of activity and through spoken words (an extraverted person), or is the energy directed toward the inner world of thoughts and emotions (an introverted person)?

Table 4-1 provides words that characterize extraverted and introverted traits.

Extraverted	Introverted
Social	Private
Expressive	Quiet
Many	Few
Broad	Deep
Interaction	Concentration
Outward	Inward
Action before thought	Thought before action

Table 4-1   *Extraverted and introverted traits*

Also notice how people prefer to process information. Do they prefer known facts and familiar terms (a sensing person), or possibilities and new potential (an intuitive person)?

Table 4-2 provides words that characterize sensing and intuitive traits.

Sensing	Intuitive
Facts	Possibilities
Experience	Novelty
Present	Future
Practicality	Aspiration
Enjoyment	Development
Realism	Idealism
Using	Changing

Table 4-2   *Sensing and intuitive traits*

Pay attention to how people prefer to make decisions. Is the preference based on logical and objective considerations (a thinking type of person), or on personal values (a feeling type of person)?

Table 4-3 provides words that characterize thinking and feeling traits.

Thinking	Feeling
Analyzing	Sympathizing
Objective	Subjective
Logical	Personal
Criticism	Appreciation
Onlooker	Participant
Decides on principle	Decides using values
Long-term view	Immediate view

Table 4-3   *Thinking and feeling traits*

Notice how people prefer to organize things around them. Is the organization structured, making decisions and knowing where it stands on issues (a judgmental person), or is it flexible, discovering life as it goes along (a perceptive person)?

Table 4-4 provides words that characterize judgmental and perceptive traits:

Judgmental	Perceptive
Closed	Open
Decide	Explore
Structure	Meander
Organize	Inquire
Firmness	Flexibility
Control	Spontaneity

Table 4-4   *Judgmental and perceptive traits*

Each characteristic trait identified by Myers-Briggs is designated with a letter. The associated letters are:

- E—Extraversion
- I—Introversion

- S—Sensing
- N—iNtuition
- T—Thinking
- F—Feeling
- J—Judgment
- P—Perception

The letters are combined to create 16 unique personality types.

 ### 4.3.4 Preferences *(who)*

Although every person is unique, Myers-Briggs highlights general themes and similarities shared by people. There are 16 personality types resulting from the Myers-Briggs Type Indicator model.

ESTJ—Life's Natural Administrators

ESTJ (Extraversion, Sensing, Thinking, Judgment) types take energy from the outside world of actions and spoken words. They prefer to deal with facts and the present, and they make decisions using logic. Their lives are organized logically. They are practical and likely to implement tried and trusted solutions to practical problems in a businesslike and impersonal manner. They prefer to ensure details have been handled, rather than spend time considering concepts and strategies.

INFP—Making Life Kinder and Gentler

INFP (Introversion, iNtuition, Feeling, Perception) types take energy from the inner world of thoughts and emotions. Preferences include dealing with patterns and possibilities and making decisions on the basis of personal values. Their lives are flexible, following new insights and possibilities that arise. Normally, they are quiet and adaptable. Often they seem to be interested in ideas and can sometimes make creative contributions. They do not always show how much they care for people, but like to see themselves and others grow and develop. They prefer to undertake meaningful work.

ESFP—Trying to Make Work Fun

ESFP (Extraversion, Sensing, Feeling, Perception) types take energy from the outside world of actions and spoken words. They prefer dealing with facts, which are usually taken at face value. They also prefer dealing with the present and with people, usually deriving considerable enjoyment out of friendships. Their lives are flexible, living in the present and responding to events as they arise. They are impulsive and friendly, seeking enjoyment out of life and making new friends easily. They like taking part in solving urgent problems, such as firefighting or troubleshooting. They operate best in practical situations involving people.

INTJ—Life's Independent Thinkers

INTJ (Introversion, iNtuition, Thinking, Judgment) types take energy from the inner world of thoughts and, perhaps, emotions. They prefer dealing with patterns and possibilities for the future, making decisions using impersonal analysis. Their lives are organized on a logical basis. They are strategists, identifying long-term goals and organizing life to meet them. They tend to be skeptical and critical of themselves and others, with a keen sense of deficiencies in quality and competence. They often have a strong intellect, yet are able to attend to details relevant to the strategy.

ESFJ—Everyone's Trusted Friend

ESFJ (Extraversion, Sensing, Feeling, Judgment) types take energy from the outer world of actions and spoken words. They prefer dealing with facts and making decisions based on personal values. They like dealing with people, organizing life on a personal basis. They are warm and seek to maintain harmonious relationships with colleagues and friends. They may find conflict and criticism difficult to handle. They have a strong sense of duty and loyalty and are driven by a need to belong and be of service to people.

INTP—Life's Problem Solvers

INTP (Introversion, iNtuition, Thinking, Perception) types take energy from the inner world of thoughts and, perhaps, emotions. They prefer dealing with patterns and possibilities and making decisions on a logical basis. Their lives are flexible, following new insights and possibilities as they arise. They are quiet, detached, and adaptable. Sometimes they may stop adapting, insisting a clear principle is at stake. They are not interested in routine and often experiment or change habits or surroundings to see if the situation can be improved. They operate best when solving complex problems requiring the application of intellect.

ENFP—People Are the Product

ENFP (Extraversion, iNtuition, Feeling, Perception) types take energy from the outer world of actions and spoken words. They prefer dealing with patterns and possibilities and make decisions on the basis of personal values. Their lives are flexible, following new insights and possibilities as they arise. They are creative and insightful, often trying new ideas that can be beneficial to others. They may sometimes neglect details and planning, but enjoy work involving experimentation and variety.

ISTJ—Life's Natural Organizers

ISTJ (Introversion, Sensing, Thinking, Judgment) types take energy from the inner world of thoughts and, perhaps, emotions. They prefer dealing with facts and making decisions after considering various options. Their lives are organized logically. They are quiet, serious, and well prepared for most eventualities. They are keen observers of life, developing a good understanding of situations, which is often not expressed. They have a strong sense of practical objectives and work efficiently to meet them.

ESTP—Making the Most of the Moment

ESTP (Extraversion, Sensing, Thinking, Perception) types take energy from the outer world of actions and spoken words. They prefer dealing with facts objectively and make decisions based on logic. Their lives are flexible, consisting of a series of activities that interest them. They are action-oriented problem solvers and prefer to work with practical organizational issues. They can be impulsive and like taking part in troubleshooting-type work. They often neglect follow-through, but work best when there is a lot going on that needs organizing and solving.

INFJ—An Inspiring Leader and Follower

INFJ (Introversion, iNtuition, Feeling, Judgment) types take energy from the inner world of thoughts and emotions. They prefer dealing with patterns and possibilities and make decisions using personal values. Their lives are organized on a personal basis. They often have a private sense of purpose in life and work steadily to fulfill that goal. They demonstrate a quiet concern for people, helping them to develop and grow. They are insightful when dealing with people, although many times do not express their thoughts.

ENFJ—Smooth-Talking Persuaders

ENFJ (Extraversion, iNtuition, Feeling, Judgment) types take energy from the outer world of actions and spoken words. They prefer dealing with patterns and possibilities and make decisions using personal values. Their lives are organized on a personal basis, seeking to develop and maintain stable relationships with people they like. They are actively concerned with promoting personal growth in others. They are also sociable and expressive of feelings toward others, but can find conflict and criticism difficult, particularly if it might damage long-term relationships. They work best in situations involving people.

ISTP—Just Do It!

ISTP (Introversion, Sensing, Thinking, Perception) types take energy from the inner world of thoughts and, perhaps, emotions. They prefer dealing with facts and making decisions on a logical basis. Their lives are flexible, demonstrating an interest in acquiring new information that leads to practical understanding of the way the world works. They are quiet, detached, and adaptable. They are often good at solving organizational problems that need attention. They are curious about how and why things work and can seem impulsive, sometimes producing surprising ideas or doing something unpredictable.

ENTJ—Life's Natural Leaders

ENTJ (Extraversion, iNtuition, Thinking, Judgment) types take energy from the outer world of actions and spoken words. They prefer dealing with patterns and possibilities and making decisions after considering the consequences of the various courses of action. Their lives are organized logically. They tend to control life, organizing systems and people to meet task-oriented goals. They often take the role of executive or manager, using a businesslike and impersonal approach. They may appear intolerant of people who do not set high standards for themselves, or do not seem good at what they do.

ISFP—Action Speaks Louder than Words

ISFP (Introversion, Sensing, Feeling, Perception) types take energy from the inner world of thoughts and emotions. They prefer dealing with facts and people and making decisions on the basis of personal values. They are adaptable, quiet, and friendly.

They are interested in people, enjoying their company preferably on an individual basis or in small groups. They take a caring and sensitive approach to helping others. They enjoy the present and tend to dislike confrontation and conflict. They usually act as supportive members of a team.

ENTP—Progress Is the Product

ENTP (Extraversion, iNtuition, Thinking, Perception) types take energy from the outer world of actions and spoken words. They prefer dealing with patterns and possibilities and make decisions based on logic. They are adaptable, focusing on new ideas and interests, particularly those involving increased competence or skill. They are ingenious problem solvers, constantly trying out new ideas, and they enjoy a good argument every now and then. When a solution requires creativity, they are interested in instigating change and work well overcoming difficulties.

ISFJ—Committed to Getting the Job Done

ISFJ (Introversion, Sensing, Feeling, Judgment) types take energy from the inner world of thoughts and emotions. They prefer dealing with facts and people and making decisions on the basis of personal values. Their lives are organized on a personal basis, seeking to enjoy relationships with people they like. They are quiet, serious observers of people and are both conscientious and loyal. They prefer work involving practical service to people. They are concerned about how others feel and dislike confrontation and conflict.

Understanding each of these types can fundamentally help with communication. Whether communicating in person, on the telephone, or through e-mail, understanding the Myers-Briggs Type Indicator can help one achieve a desired end.

4.3.5 In Person, over the Phone, and E-mail *(where)*

Communication may be defined as any process whereby decisional premises are transmitted from one member of an organization to another. Obviously, without communication, there can be no organization. An individual's behavior can influence others; communication allows one to wield influence.

Not only is communication essential to the enterprise, but also the application of techniques to facilitate this communication. These techniques can involve communicating in person, over the telephone, or via e-mail. These techniques determine ways design elements should be distributed throughout the organization to facilitate communication and understanding. Positive communication can be affected by the stress people experience in their personal lives.

4.3.6 Biorhythms, PMS, and the Mid-Life Crisis *(when)*

People are often confronted with different forms of stress, such as premenstrual syndrome (PMS) and mid-life crisis. Reactions to stress may last several minutes, days, weeks, or longer. Often stress tempts people to defer tough decisions. When people have to choose between the lesser of two evils, they do not behave like Bayesian statisticians, weighing the bad against the worse. Instead, they postpone the decision, searching for new alternatives that do not have negative outcomes.

Stress is a powerful emotional force that can divert behavior from the urgings of reason. Someone a *designer* had previously typed according to the Myers-Briggs Type Indicator may exhibit uncharacteristic behavior under stress. Recognizing uncharacteristic behavior allows the *designer* to defer any sensitive decisions. Delaying the decision may reduce future rework and help the person forego feelings of guilt, further anxiety, and embarrassment.

Designers need to analyze people problems systematically so they can respond quickly to problems. A *designer's* skills should include intuition and judgment. A *designer* must behave like a manager, having command of the whole range of people management skills and applying them whenever appropriate.

4.3.7 Winning *(why)*

Effective communication in organizations promotes teaching and learning, which ultimately allow for improved decision-making in design. An organization's knowledge is comprised of the relevant knowledge stored in the memories of its people and in paper and electronic form. Systems thinking allows you to discern coherent information out of seemingly random shared information.

The boundary between one biological organism and others is defined by identity of the shared DNA of all the organism's cells. In a similar way, the shared information determines the boundary of the organization, although the sharing is not nearly as complete as it is among an organism's cells.

You must understand the processes of organizational decision-making and learning to also understand the roles of organizations and markets in the economy. Shared knowledge makes it possible for organizations to leverage coordinated design decisions in ways that are not as easily available to coteries of independent departments.

Organizations take on personalities just as individuals do. The following core values and traits characterize an ENTJ organization: Extraverted, iNtuition, Thinking, and Judging. This type of organization promotes a non-threatening environment that rewards success.

Core value: uncompromised value

- Everyone should pay attention to detail.
- Stop the job, process, or design if quality is unacceptable.
- Select quality over price when choosing a vendor.
- Hire people with high standards, including both staff members and vendors.
- Do whatever it takes to deliver quality work—do not cut corners.
- Quality needs to be everyone's job.

Core value: relationships—mutual respect

- Listen, understand, and then take appropriate actions.
- Exceed expectations.
- Openly communicate costs and services.
- Take ownership of each project and be partners in the results.
- Be honest.
- Do not ask someone to do something you would not do.
- Clearly define expectations.

Core value: strategies that work

- Give people what they need versus what they think they want.
- Deliver high value-to-price ratio.
- Collaborate internally to reach consensus on the strongest ideas to generate desired results.
- Observe, investigate, and consider every reasonable possibility and option.
- Put yourself in the end-users' shoes.
- Understand how the business runs so the designs and implementations work with the organization's resources.

Core value: accountability

- Take responsibility for your actions.
- Do what you say.
- Do your job to your full extent.

Core value: enjoy work

- Be supportive of each other.
- Use appropriate tools to facilitate success.
- Respect differences.
- Establish a creative environment.
- Remove internal politics.
- Encourage and allow personal and professional growth.
- Allow yourself to be self-directed and self-motivated.
- Feel free to talk with any manager.
- Share high expectations and standards.

Understanding the personality types of individuals and organizations can help each individual yield maximum results.

4.3.8 Key Terms

communication	Myers-Briggs Type Indicator
intellectual capital	personality typing
joint application development (JAD) session	software architect

4.3.9 Review Questions

1. Considering that a deliverable is usually the result of hours of analysis and communication, how does harnessing the power of intellectual capital benefit the enterprise?

2. Name the four components that make up a personality type. How can knowing these personality types benefit the individual? The enterprise?

3. Why should *designers* analyze people problems systematically?

4. Make a list of core values that characterize an ENTJ organization. Now list the core values of your workplace or school. Which personality type does it match?

5. How might stress affect the design process?
6. How can knowing one's strengths as well as one's potential weaknesses benefit an individual? A project team?

SECTION 4.4 WHAT SEVEN HABITS ARE GOOD FOR YOU

QUESTIONS TO CONTEMPLATE

1. How can the *designer* use the four organizational frames, Seven Habits, and systems thinking to allow more time for actual design activities?
2. Why is detail important to the *designer*?

4.4.1 Introduction

When creating solutions, such as software or other products, a *designer's* challenge becomes how to get everybody in the organization to support the ideas expressed in the solution. What types of knowledge and skills can the *designer* use to have ideas accepted? The answer to this question may depend on communicating those ideas. In addition to knowing the domain she is designing, the *designer* should know about all facets of the organization, including the stakeholders, to better communicate the solution. Two techniques that the *designer* can use to facilitate communication of ideas are reframing, using four organizational frames, and the Seven Habits.

Frames of the Organization

The four frames of an organization, identified by Lee Bolman (b. 1941) and Terrence Deal (b. 1943) in *Reframing Organizations*, help develop a better understanding of people within an organization and increase the level of communication. The term **frame** means a personal image or perspective from which to gather information, make judgments, and determine how best to get things done. Bolman's and Deal's work in organizational theory encompasses the public and private sectors and focuses on management and leadership.

Bolman and Deal believe that by looking through a particular frame, individuals operate more effectively because alternative approaches become easier to recognize and consider. "We need more people in managerial *designer*[6] roles who can find simplicity and order amid organizational confusion and chaos. We need versatile and flexible leaders who are artists as well as analysts, who can reframe experience to discover new issues and possibilities."[7] Reframing helps individuals better understand the perspectives of others.

According to Bolman and Deal, organizations operate primarily in one of four frames, and individuals generally are more comfortable operating in one frame than they are in the others. The four frames are:

- Structural
- Political
- Human resources
- Symbolic

Structural Frame

The structure of an organization constrains and enhances what can be accomplished. In many organizations, the structural frame is communicated by means of an organizational chart. The structure eventually lays out expectations and exchanges among internal and external stakeholders. Examples of internal stakeholders include executives, managers, and employees. External stakeholders may include customers and suppliers.

To work cooperatively, Bolman and Deal state, "Understanding the complexity of organizational contexts and the variety of structural possibilities can help create structures that work for, rather than against, both people and the purposes of organizations."[8] Restructuring a group of people is easier than restructuring an individual's personality.

Political Frame

The political frame focuses on both personal and organizational politics and involves competition and power. Departments and business units vie for headcount[9] and money. Managers often battle to be awarded these types of limited resources, thus creating competition and power struggles. Each manager maneuvers to improve the probability of obtaining resources.

Human Resources Frame

In the human resources frame, the needs of people and the organization are matched. Time commitment is a typical issue related to the human resources frame, and individuals need to choose how they spend their time. An existential psychologist, Abraham Maslow (1908–1970), described how virtually every person has a hierarchy of emotional needs—from basic safety, shelter, and sustenance to a desire for respect, satisfaction, and a sense of accomplishment.

In its guidebook for managers, Federal Express, the global shipping company, states that the needs expressed by Maslow and how an employee chooses to use his time may affect the company's results. Placing employee personal values as the centerpiece of company policy has always achieved remarkable results. For example, Federal Express recognizes that operating in the human resources frame is one sign of a progressive enterprise.

Symbolic Frame

The symbolic frame refers to the culture of an organization, which is the interwoven pattern of beliefs, values, practices, and artifacts. The culture defines who employees are and how they should do things.

According to Bolman and Deal, the symbolic frame is both a product and a process. As a product, culture is the accumulation of wisdom from people who have worked for the organization. As a process, culture evolves continuously. As new people join the organization, they learn the old ways and often teach new ways.

Understanding the four frames is helpful when attempting to gain **consensus** for an idea. As previously mentioned, organizations, departments, and individuals tend to operate in one of the four frames. The chances of meeting the needs and expectations of the stakeholders can be improved if the *designer* has a useful knowledge of individuals, teams, and the organization.

In Chapter 3, Section 3.1.5, systems thinking illustrates how to view the organization holistically and handle complex situations effectively. Systems thinking can be applied to understand individuals within the organization and their ability to interact. The systems thinking approach requires that practitioners view their work in the context of the larger organization. Systems thinkers recognize the need to identify, cultivate, and understand relationships among individuals and teams both inside and outside the organization.

By viewing the situation or problem through multiple frames, the *designer* has more tools to use in articulating and communicating the vision so that business participants can also learn to shift **perceptions**. In *Creating Corporate Culture: From Discord to Harmony*, Charles Hampden-Turner (b. 1938) states that one cannot begin to learn without a concept providing a set of expectations and hypotheses, which establish a **mental model**.

This mental model or perception may be right or wrong. It does not really matter because people experience paradigm shifts as more information becomes available. Stephen Covey (b. 1932), cofounder of the largest management and leadership development organization[10] in the world and one of America's most influential and effective people, discusses these paradigm shifts in his work that provides ideas on how to cultivate stronger relationships.

In *The 7 Habits of Highly Effective People*, Covey offers several specific steps individuals can choose to increase their ability to get along with others. These seven habits, like the Zachman Framework for Enterprise Architecture, are ubiquitous to all aspects of life. Because much of the *designer's* time is spent dealing with people issues, the following habits may assist the *designer* in creating a cooperative work environment.

Habit 1—Be Proactive

People choose how to respond to different situations. Having knowledge about oneself, colleagues, and the organization can assist business participants in anticipating problems and change. This enables the individual to respond proactively instead of reactively.

Habit 2—Begin with the End in Mind

In organizations, the *owner* communicates the enterprise's mission and vision. People also need to focus on their personal missions and decide what they want to accomplish. Covey's research has shown that although people working in large organizations feel they are working at their maximum level, less than 20 percent of human talent is being used.[11] He believes the problem many companies face is the lack of alignment between personal and organizational missions.

Habit 3—Put First Things First

This habit involves time management. Covey created a system that urges individuals to spend more time performing important tasks, rather than those things that are simply urgent. The message in this habit is to plan and do the important things first.

Habit 4—Think Win/Win

Most people find win/win is easier to say than to accomplish. During conflicts and competition, people cannot always work together and create acceptable solutions. However, Covey suggests that choosing this attitude increases an individual's ability to get along with others.

Habit 5—Seek First to Understand

Communication facilitates understanding others. Developing a rapport with others encourages them to talk to you. Once a rapport is established, communication opens and the *designer* can understand what motivates others. Covey states **empathic listening** is a skill many people do not practice. Good listeners focus on five key areas when another person is talking: purpose, main points, evaluation, application, and value.

Habit 6—Synergize

The idea behind this habit is that people can accomplish more collectively than individually. When people work together toward a common mission, the synergy can produce far greater results.

Habit 7—Sharpen the Saw

This habit refers to people taking time to renew mentally, physically, spiritually, socially, and emotionally. These activities are both independent of and dependent on each other and can have a positive effect on the organization. Organizations sometimes encourage sharpening the saw by providing additional rewards, which serve as motivators for employees.

People need to understand and honor each other's differences. The more individuals learn about themselves, each other, and their organization, the more effectively they can work as a group and produce desired results.

The techniques of the Myers-Briggs Type Indicator, Bolman's and Deal's frames, and Covey's observations of Seven Habits interweave. Each technique focuses on specific aspects or qualities of people within the enterprise. Viewing the techniques holistically provides the *designer* with an unparalleled insight into the enterprise's soul—the workforce of the organization.

4.4.2 Things and Relationships *(what)*

The *designer* can choose how to react or respond in different situations. Knowing people, the organization, and oneself helps the *designer* anticipate problems and take a proactive stance. Ben Nelson (b. 1941), a candidate for the governorship of Nebraska, chose to be **proactive** (Habit 1) rather than reactive when running for office.

After announcing his candidacy, Nelson hired a pollster to seek public opinion. The pollster solicited opinions from 899 people regarding his client. Compiling the results turned out to be a simple task. A grand total of two people supported Nelson. Like all good politicians, Nelson hit the campaign trail, making speeches, shaking hands, and issuing position papers. Slowly, his support grew. In a local newspaper, Nelson saw a letter that was critical of him. He sensed the writer did not understand his positions, so he gave the man a call.

Nelson began making several calls a day to voters. After the ballots were counted, Nelson won the primary and the Democratic Party nomination by 42 votes. Nelson believes the telephone calls helped him win the nomination. In November 1990, Nelson was elected Nebraska's governor.

Nelson practiced the secret many winners know: paying attention to details can make the difference between succeeding or settling for something less. In other words, Nelson took the time to develop the relationships with the right people to help him reach his goal.

4.4.3 Transformation *(how)*

Constrained by many forces, *designers* must make everything work together through ingenuity and resourcefulness. To accomplish the organization's mission and vision, the *designer* can begin a project with the end in mind (Habit 2).

Pat Riley (b. 1945), a National Basketball Association (NBA) coach, was challenged to figure out how he could best use game and player statistics to transform his team into a winning organization. His former boss, *owner* of the Los Angeles Lakers, made a simple mandate. You need to create a team capable of winning the *ring*.

Riley has commented that his talent lies in attention to detail. For example, every NBA team studies videotapes and compiles statistics to evaluate players' game performances. By using these tools more comprehensively than many of his rivals, Riley measures areas of performance that are often ignored. He examines how his players jump in pursuit of every rebound, even if they do not win the ball. He examines how players swat at every pass, dive for loose balls, and let someone smash into them to draw a foul.

At the end of each game, these effort statistics are recorded in a computer program. Riley explains that effort is what separates journeyman players[12] from impact players, and knowing how well a player executes every action in a game is the key to unlocking career-best performance.

When Riley became the head coach, he needed a game plan. He designed how to stimulate and educate his players. The often overlooked game statistics provided the clues—in them, he found the rules to play the game effectively. The coach found ways to help players focus on their personal missions and encouraged them to put forth their best efforts in order to align the players' personal missions with the team's mission. See Figure 4-11.

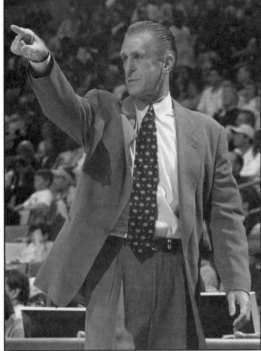

Copyright 2002 NBA Entertainment. Photo by
NBAE/Getty Images.

Figure 4-11   *Pat Riley — The designer*

4.4.4 Time and Cycles *(when)*

Meijer, a $4 billion-a-year grocery chain headquartered in Walker, Michigan, may
make as little as one cent on each product it sells. Meijer has over 160 stores located
in Michigan, Indiana, Ohio, Kentucky, and Illinois. Meijer makes a profit solely on
the Christmas selling season, when it sells the greatest volume of product. Time
management is key to this strategy. Essentially, this company designs a plan to survive for 11 months so that it can generate sufficient profits during the last month of
the year.

   To make a profit, Meijer has put first things first (Habit 3) since its inception. It
grew from an expanded barbershop called Meijer's Grocery in Greenville, Michigan
in 1934 to Meijer Thrifty Acres, which caused an uproar when stores opened for
Sunday sales during the 1960s. Today, Meijer's mega-stores sell everything from
tomatoes to tires. Meijer understands that business revolves around the Christmas
selling season.

   By concentrating and acting on things that are important to the company, rather
than those things that are simply urgent, companies and people can succeed.

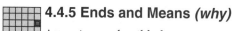

4.4.5 Ends and Means *(why)*

Attention to detail helps create a win/win (Habit 4) environment because you can never be sure that everyone involved in a project is producing a solution. In the case of IEFBR14, a computer program produced by IBM in the 1960s, the *designers* did not specify enough detail, nor did the company anticipate the level of inexperience among the programmers who would build the program. In fact, the program was deemed so simple to create, no specifications were written. In the end, IEFBR14, initially thought to be a one-line program, needed multiple programming iterations to get the desired result.

IEFBR14 was designed to be a null program to assist in allocating and deleting files. A null program does nothing. When executed, IEFBR14 starts and then stops without processing If-Then-Else logic or **business logic**. The program does not process, open, or close files, or use any internal or external data. The program simply starts and then stops.

Normally, the program is executed on a mainframe computer from a set of job control language (JCL) statements. These statements are like a *.bat* file on a personal computer, or a *shell script* on a UNIX computer. The JCL is controlled by IBM's job entry system (JES) environment.

JES can catalog or delete hard disk files before a program formally requests the files. Therefore, if a file needs to be created and cataloged in the computer, a programmer can specify IEFBR14 as a null program in the JCL, causing JES to allocate the file when the program is executed.

The first version of the assembler language null program resembled Figure 4-12, using a branch to register 14 to terminate the program.

```
IEFBR14 START
        BR 14 Return address in R14 — — branch at it
END
```

Figure 4-12   *IEFBR14 — 1st attempt*

First bug: An IBM assembler language program indicates a successful completion by moving zeroes to register 15 and then issuing a branch to register 14 for program termination. This version of the null program failed every time. The program was modified, as shown in Figure 4-13.

```
IEFBR14 START
        SR 15,15 Zero out register 15
        BR 14    Return address in R14 — — branch at it
END
```

Figure 4-13   *IEFBR14 — 2nd attempt*

Much better...or so the programmer thought. However, this version caused other problems with the linkage editor. The END statement did not specify the primary entry point of the routine. Version three was then attempted, shown in Figure 4-14.

```
IEFBR14 START
        SR 15,15 Zero out register 15
        BR 14    Return address in R14 -- branch at it
END     IEFBR14
```

Figure 4-14   *IEFBR14 — 3rd attempt*

By now, the null program was functioning correctly. However, dump analysis was impeded because the program did not include its own name in the source code as an eye catcher (a time-honored programming convention). Null program, mark four. See Figure 4-15.

```
IEFBR14 START
        USING IEFBR14,15  Establish addressability
        BR GO             Skip over our name
        DC AL1(L 'ID)     Length of name
ID      DC C'IEFBR14'     Name itself
        DS OH             Force alignment
        GO SR 15, 15      Zero out register 15
        BR 14             Return address in R14 -- branch at it
END IEFBR14
```

Figure 4-15   *IEFBR14 — 4th attempt*

The next change addressed an esoteric problem involving the save-area chaining conventions. More changes addressed standard conventions and dump analysis tools. The null program had grown in terms of the number of source statements and instructions executed.

Figure 4-16 shows how IEFBR14 is executed in a JCL stream. The first line, the EXEC statement, identifies the program to execute. Most JCL statements start with two forward slashes. The name STEP01 is a mnemonic or step name associated with the program for this JCL stream. Step names are usually unique in a JCL stream. If a program is executed more than once, the unique step names identify which iteration of the program was executed.

```
//STEP01   EXEC PGM=IEFBR14
//DD01     DD DSN=SYS1.EABOOK1.DATA,
//            DISP=(OLD,DELETE,DELETE)
//DD02     DD DSN=SYS1.EABOOK2.DATA,
//            DISP=(NEW,CATLG,DELETE),
//            UNIT=SYSDA,
//            SPACE=(CYL,(1,1),RLSE),
//            DCB=(RECFM=FB,LRECL=80,BLKSIZE=6240,DSORG=PS)
//
```

Figure 4-16   *Sample JCL to execute IEFBR14*

The DD, or data definition statements, identify the files a program can use. IEFBR14 is designed not to reference any files. Because the files are hard disk files (denoted by UNIT=SYSDA), JES directly handles the file allocations. The file associated with DD01 has a file disposition of OLD, meaning it already exists in the system. The first DELETE option instructs JES to delete the file if the program ends successfully, and the second DELETE instructs JES to delete the file if the program ends abnormally.

The file associated with DD02 is a new file, designated by the NEW option. If IEFBR14 ends successfully, the CATLG option instructs the operating system to catalog the file. If the program fails or crashes, the DELETE option instructs the operating system to remove the file from the system. A cataloged file has two characteristics:

- The file is known to exist by the operating system.
- The operating system knows on which hard drive it exists.

JCL also recognizes uncataloged files, but needs to include information directing the operating system to a hard disk so that the operating system can find the file.

The programmer, discussed earlier, had problems because he and others lacked attention to detail. You can never be sure what resources are available in the organization to actually accomplish the task at hand. Attention to detail becomes an imperative, no matter how simple the task.

4.4.6 Connecting *(where)*

Recall that *designers* should understand what motivates others by developing a rapport with them so that they are willing to open up and talk.

Designers must acquire and practice good listening skills to understand their cohorts. In other words, you should seek first to understand (Habit 5). Michele McCormick started MMC Communications in 1991 and discovered how she could seek first to understand and drive her company toward success.

When McCormick started her own public relations business, she found out what it took to prosper. One day, she was explaining her communication techniques to a prospective client. A company executive from the client company interrupted and asked if she could promise her work would not be marred by misspellings.

McCormick could not imagine why the executive asked this question. Subsequent client calls revealed similar patterns. Inattention to details, such as not returning telephone calls promptly, not itemizing bills, and acting before asking for approval, outraged prospective clients. McCormick believes the real key for succeeding in business is not brilliance, but competence in day-to-day details. McCormick discovered early on what is important to clients.

4.4.7 People and Work *(who)*

People can generally accomplish more together than individually. Walking down the hall of Cascade Engineering's Learning Community building in Grand Rapids, Michigan, visitors may see Dave Barrett, Senior Organizational Consultant for Learning and Development, conducting a class on Covey's *7 Habits of Highly Effective People*.

CEO Fred Keller has always emphasized trust and teamwork. Keller's company spends a lot of time building strong foundations with its employees and customers. Cascade Engineering takes pride in its solid relationships with customers, vendors, employees, and the community.

Cascade needed to design a way to communicate its belief in trust and team-work and chose to use Covey's seven habits to accomplish this goal. Keller needed to **synergize** (Habit 6) his team. Cascade discovered that people working together toward a common set of goals and objectives produces better results.

Keller also believes in sharpening the saw (Habit 7) by providing education, training, and comprehensive benefits packages to keep employees mentally and physically competent. Sharpening the saw helps employees stay energized.

Cascade's manufacturing facility lines many of its walls with posters of the seven habits. The posters remind everyone entering the plant of the importance of working together to accomplish a common goal.

4.4.8 Key Terms

business logic	mental model
consensus	perception
empathic listening	proactive
frame	synergize

4.4.9 Review Questions

1. Explain how practicing the seven habits introduced by Stephen Covey can assist the *designer* in developing healthy relationships with peers and stakeholders. How are Covey's seven habits and the Zachman Framework for Enterprise Architecture similar?

2. Name the four organizational frames suggested by Bolman and Deal. How can use of these four frames foster development of a better understanding of people within the organization and increase the level of communication?

3. Give some examples of how a *designer* might be constrained in her work duties.

4. How does the *designer's* skill of articulating the vision aid business participants in shifting perceptions and sharing mental models?

5. Describe why creating IEFBR14 became problematic.

6. Why should the *designer* develop a rapport with individuals?

SECTION 4.5 WHERE POLITICS RULE

QUESTIONS TO CONTEMPLATE

1. What are some of the ways *designers* handle office politics?
2. Why is it important to establish metrics?

4.5.1 Introduction

Barbra Streisand (b. 1942) advocates that "People who need people are the luckiest people in the world." In office politics, these people are probably also the smartest people in the office. The *designer* needs friends and allies within the company who she can count on as her workload increases.

One of the best ways to build allies is to help colleagues who are overwhelmed with work and anticipate how to be helpful, rather than wait to be asked. Of course, this means extra work for you, but it also means you have some credit in the *you-owe-me-one bank*.

Dealing with office politics involves handling different personalities, learning how to be accountable, providing the right kind of feedback, being a keen observer, and learning what does and does not work for the enterprise.

After you first earned your driver's license, driving on a parkway entrance ramp for the first time probably seemed like climbing Mount Everest. Chugging along at seven miles per hour, with the wind barely ruffling your hair, you had the illusion you were really cruising and fully observing the surroundings. When your passenger said, "Did you see that hawk perched on that tree," you realized you were not observing everything.

When driving your car, you have faith the vehicles approaching from the opposite direction, or driving beside you, will not purposely veer into you. In the office, you cannot afford to have this same type of faith. Regardless of the pace of the work environment, you need to look around and be aware of your surroundings. The *designer* needs to pay attention to many kinds of details to understand the corporate culture, recognize office politics, and assign accountability.

4.5.2 Look Around *(where)*

Many organizations maintain corporate cultures based on dusty traditional models. Some organizations have adapted their internal company cultures to keep up with the trends and multicultural makeup of the real world. A *designer* cannot assume everyone is enlightened about cultural change.

To better understand a company's culture, look around and answer the following questions:

- Who gets hired?
- Who gets fired?
- What is stated at employee orientation sessions?
- What are the rules and guidelines outlined in the employee handbook?
- What is the company teaching in its training programs?
- What is the organization's avowed mission?
- What is the company's marketing position?
- What forms of advertising does the company use?
- Do coworkers arrive early?
- Which coworkers consistently arrive late?
- Who stays late?
- What kind of information is conveyed via the office grapevine?
- Which unwritten rules can you learn by talking to people?
- Who are the office heroes?

- How formal or informal is the language used in the office?
- What type of clothes do people wear?
- Where do people eat lunch?
- What type of social events does the company sponsor?
- How does the company communicate with its employees and customers?
- What is the tone used in the corporate newsletter?
- How do people get ahead?
- Does the organization value diversity or homogeneity?

4.5.3 Stay off My Project *(who)*

Earlier, you examined several behavior types. Two additional behavior types are the eel and the backstabber. Into every life, a little indecision must fall, and the behavioral pattern of the eel makes sure this happens.

The eel cannot or will not make a decision, which makes working with an eel frustrating. When asked for an opinion, the eel takes one position and argues it from sun up to sundown. The next day, the eel takes an opposing position and the never-ending discussions begin again. The eel is a major impediment to any undertaking.

The eel does not fulfill obligations, so his work is often late and incomplete, and he misses or postpones appointments. The behavior of the eel is consistently inconsistent. The eel does not get headaches or heart attacks, but gives them. His behavior is always contradictory.

The eel's communication changes with the audience, but often starts with the following statements:

- Let's make sure everyone agrees on this.
- Tell me your ideas.
- When in Rome, do as the Romans.
- What is more important, the job or someone's feelings?
- What is more important, sales or controls?
- How do we get universal consensus?
- What is the latest rumor you have heard?
- Who is the one with the real power?
- What do you think we should do?
- I told you that would work.
- I tried to warn you.
- The reason we cannot do this is...
- The reason we can do this is...

The *designer* should not tolerate the eel's behavior. An eel adds hours to any meeting and leaves nothing agreed to or decided upon. Every design idea is either good or bad, depending on the tide and time of day. On any issue, an eel can give many reasons that an idea is good, and just as many reasons that the idea is bad. The eel is not mean-spirited and would never acknowledge that he cannot make a decision.

The *designer* should try to remove the eel from a project because the eel impedes accountability and measurement gathering to analyze performance.

"It would be best if you ran this through me before you showed it to anybody else." These are the words of the most cunning and cynical employees of any corporation—the backstabbers. The backstabber poses a serious threat to the *designer* and, if not abrogated, ensures the failure of any project.

The backstabber has interesting and observable communication characteristics. Unfortunately, the uninitiated never see what is happening and are left puzzled by how so much could go so wrong so fast.

The backstabber does not believe in excelling and demonstrating superior performance. In taking advantage of people, the backstabber counts on workers being naïve and gullible. The better natured and well-meaning an employee, the easier they are felled by the backstabber. The backstabber excels by making all those around look bad.

The backstabber uses the following vocabulary phrases:

- I know nothing about this.
- What do you think the boss will say?
- Is this the best we can do?
- Have someone else look at this after I review it.
- Leave it to me; I'll carry it forward.
- You will be rewarded for this on your next review.
- I promise I will do everything I can to get you a raise.
- We cannot promote you now because we need you too much right here.
- The time is not right to talk about this.
- I need more documentation.
- I need better cost benefit.
- Communicate to me orally on this and keep me informed as to your progress.

Once recognized, the unethical behavior of the backstabber must be used to remedy his effect. Turnabout is fair play and, in this case, necessary for survival. Actions to take include the following:

- Document every conversation with the backstabber. Provide the date and time and all subjects discussed, especially the instructions given.
- Send this information in an e-mail to yourself. A sent e-mail automatically documents the date and time of the transaction.
- Send the e-mail to a personal off-site account.
- When responding to an e-mail on which the backstabber is carbon copied, remove the backstabber from the reply list.
- Keep good records about the backstabber.
- Never argue with the backstabber.
- Always smile and agree with the backstabber.
- Never tell anyone in the organization about the backstabbing.
- Confide in no one; backstabbers always seem to have friends in the most unlikely places.
- Never complain about the backstabber.
- Give no indication of your mistrust.
- Keep as informed as possible.

Sooner or later, every backstabber falls on the sword of betrayal, so handling the backstabber is mostly a matter of waiting. Only the patient win. Some might conclude the recommended courses of action are devious and unethical.

The *designer* can only remove the backstabber from the project, which requires tact and agreement with senior management. A good approach could be to say the backstabber is an invaluable contributor and might be of better use to the corporation elsewhere.

4.5.4 Accountability *(what)*

When delegating authority and responsibility, you need **accountability** to measure an activity's effectiveness. Without accountability, you cannot answer the question, "How is it going?"

When you are accountable, it is more difficult to hide. The only group usually held 100 percent accountable for all its actions is the sales group. Sales people live on a quota and their paychecks are tied to performance. No one else in the corporation is linked so directly to actions. The sales group is accountable for income, profitability, and expense control. In most corporations, sales employees are the highest compensated.

The *designer* must decide how accountability is assigned and reported. By its nature, accountability causes **pushback** because people develop the sense that big brother[13] is watching, which makes them uncomfortable. Working with each personality type, the *designer* makes sure each member of the project team accepts accountability. Although some people do not like to be counted and accountable, the success of any project depends on participants who are both.

4.5.5 Impact of Metrics *(how)*

Albert Einstein once remarked, "Not everything that can be counted counts, and not everything that counts can be counted." To that end, people have added that *You cannot manage what you cannot measure*. Defining appropriate and essential metrics helps separate **objectives** from **goals** and **strategies** from **tactics**.

Metrics stipulate what needs to be measured. Defining a set of metrics helps to impose standards, and standards constrain any project. An example of a metric is how many 250-count bottles of ibuprofen capsules are sold each day. The discipline of management science uses the following common **measuring sticks**:

- Vision statement
- Mission statement
- Goals
- Objectives
- Strategies
- Tactics

MEASURING STICKS

Vision statements are future states to which the management wants the company to aspire. A vision statement sets out the general direction of the corporation. For example, a drug retailer might use the following vision statement: *To offer customers the best drugstore service with the lowest retail cost.*

The captured measurements associated with the vision statement may be either objective or subjective. The vision statement previously mentioned poses two important questions:

- What is the best drugstore service?
- What is the lowest retail cost?

The answer to the best drugstore service can only be derived subjectively, while the answer to the lowest retail cost can be obtained objectively by analyzing the retail prices of competitive drugstores.

Mission statements complement vision statements with actionable operational statements. A mission statement generally includes words that describe what the enterprise will be doing on a daily basis. For example, "Provide over-the-counter and prescription drugs in every major metropolitan area within the continental United States."

Goals relate to reputation and provide a pseudo benchmark of progress. A goal might be to hire the handicapped. A goal is typically qualitative in nature, whereas an objective tends to be quantitative. Therefore, objectives should support goals.

Objectives are designed to be measured quantitatively. A number is always attached to an objective. For instance, if the goal is to improve revenue, the objective may be to increase sales by 100 percent by the end of the next fiscal quarter. The direct link is clear and obvious. An objective must be clear in its purpose and have numbers that the organization believes are achievable. If the bar is raised too high, the corporation suffers loss of morale.

Strategies lay out the overall plan of how to accomplish some end. The strategy itself is not doable immediately. For instance, a strategy for a company wishing to increase sales may be to double the sales force, but that will take time. It is impossible to wave a wand and double the sales force, even if your name is Merlin (c. 400). Another strategy might be to open more locations. Each strategy is created to satisfy some goal, and each strategy requires tactics to make it possible.

Tactics are actions the corporation takes to execute the strategies. Tactics also help satisfy the objectives. Tactics are always actions and always measurable. Using the example of doubling sales, measurable tactics might be any of the following:

- Use five outside recruiters.
- Spend $25,000 a month on print media advertising.
- Place recruitment notice on the corporate home page.
- Place advertisement on Internet portal and search engine sites for three months.

All measurements address the issue of *what*, and in metrics, *what* is a **constraint** applied to assets, process, location, people, events, and motivation. Each constraint dictates the following ways to measure:

- *Units of measure* are usually expressed as weight, volume, length, currency, or time. Examples of weight are: tons, pounds, ounces, and grams. Examples of volume are: cubic yard, liter, and quart. Examples of length are: mile, meter, yard, and foot. Examples of currency are: U.S. dollar, Euro, Danish kronen, and Japanese yen. Examples of time are: light-years, months, hours, and nanoseconds.
- *Quantity* is a count of the unit of measure, usually an issue of whole or partial item counts. Examples are: 14.5 tons, 42 liters, 27 meters, 31 U.S. dollars, and four light-years.

Time constrains almost every project. Combine time with one of the other units of measure to establish a complete constraint. For example, *We need 100 metric tons of steel in four days* is a complete constraint.

Verb tense alters the meaning of a measurement. The *designer* of an **enterprise resource planning (ERP) system** establishes requirements for materials management, materials usage, and materials planning. You identify each requirement by its tense. For example, the past tense—*We used 100 metric tons of steel in the past four days*—is different from the present tense—*The production line capacity is 100 metric tons of steel*, which is different from the future tense—*We are forecasting a requirement for 1,000 metric tons of steel over the course of the next year.*

The past tense implies a reporting requirement, the present tense implies an immediate need, and the future tense implies an asset acquisition requirement. Each tense usually supports a different group in the organization.

A reporting requirement might be defined as sales analysis, materials management, and accounting. An immediate need is usually a requirement of the organizational groups on the frontline of the corporation. Frontline operational groups influence customer service. An asset requisition is usually the domain of those planning for the future. Teams involved in asset requisition include sales managers, materials managers, production managers, strategic planners, and tactical planners.

The group responsible for producing most units of measure reports is the accounting department. Accounting compiles the units of measure for the entire corporation. Units of measure are correlated to a monetary unit of measure and reported. The two most important reports the accountants create are the income statement and the balance sheet.

U.S. accounting practices mandate that companies produce these two reports and follow strict accounting standards. The overall method of accounting is called Generally Accepted Accounting Principles (GAAP). The Financial Accounting Standards Board (FASB) creates many of the standards used. The standards are generated to comply with laws passed by state representatives.

Account reporting is post-facto, meaning that all of it is past tense. However, this past tense reporting is completed by an inflexible due date based on the corporation's fiscal calendar. For example, the corporation's current month's accounting books must be closed by the tenth day of the following month. Knowledge of *when* corporate books are closed is an illustration of the important types of details the *designer* must uncover when undertaking a design. Without accurate establishment and reporting of units of measure, statistics cannot be developed.

Statistics allow for comparison to past performance and act as a measure of how the corporation is performing relative to its competitors. All are vital signs to the corporation's health. Statistics form the basis of reward and punishment and the essence of accurate risk and reward analysis. Statistics help influence what changes must be made to either continue growth or survive during economic slowdowns—*thrive or survive*.

A MANTRA

- Units of measure create standards.
- Standard units of measure create reporting requirements and standards.
- Reporting standards create vital statistics.
- Vital statistics create measurement standards.
- Standards place constraints on any project.

The *designer* of any major project must have a firm handle on the requirements of metrics. Metrics are imposed on the *designer* by mandated legislation at the national, state, county, and municipality levels, and may also be imposed by the *planner* or the *owner*.

You must comply with many laws, which can be just as onerous from an inside authority as an outside mandate. Reporting requirements and the metrics needed to satisfy the requirements place significant constraints on a project and the enterprise.

When metrics and reporting requirements are not completely understood, the *designer* is trapped by old methods of developing systems and going back later to create the reports. If this happens, the *designer* creates a generalized report, which attempts to take into account the requirements of many organizational units in order to supply the information each needs. A report designed to accommodate many people often proves to be less useful. Generally, in business, a one-size-fits-all is not sufficient.

Metrics are important to the *designer's* overall project strategy. Metrics set up another area of **contention**. Metrics, when explicit, assign accountability, but recall that some workers do not want to be accountable.

Satisfying everyone's business needs, capturing metrics, and assigning accountability causes serious areas of contention. Contention should be viewed as a corporate dynamic that is part of the corporate culture. The dynamic is essential to the survival of the enterprise. Without contention, the corporation may suffer the same fate as the Chinese Civil Service. The corporation becomes more and more inwardly focused, until the only thing the corporation worries about is how to maintain and keep its internal powers.

THE CHINESE CIVIL SERVICE

Around 200 B.C.E., the Chinese Civil Service, which had been set up to manage a widely spread empire and collect taxes, was changed to hire those that could pass a difficult three-day test. The testing was based on the philosophical core of Confucianism. The tests resembled those given today, such as the Bar or the Certified Public Accountant (CPA) exam.

Two principal reasons for establishment of the Chinese Civil Service were to prevent friends and family of the Emperor and royal court from being appointed and to eliminate graft and corruption. The Emperor also wanted to be sure that every possible tax collected ended up in the royal treasury. The service was very successful for several hundred years.

But, over time, corruption crept into the system. Administrators became more obsessed with maintaining their power and living the good life than looking out for the best interests of the Emperor. This self-obsession caused the Chinese government to become more and more xenophobic and to shun foreign ideas. The Chinese people became alienated and distrustful.

By the early twentieth century, the situation became so bad that the Empress Dowager was forced to eliminate the service. The administration of the country was left in the hands of the ruling monks, which was even worse. The government became so dysfunctional that the Chinese were unable defend themselves against the Japanese.

A large organization may eventually become inwardly focused to protect its turf or power. At this time, no attention is applied to external vigilance.

4.5.6 The Stupid Question *(when)*

At the beginning of many meetings, someone makes the following statement, "There is no such thing as a stupid question." Of course there is. These questions are asked often, and occur in almost every human transaction. If many people are involved in a conversation, someone usually asks the *I can't believe he's really asking this* question.

Here are the most common reasons for this type of question:

- An individual was not paying attention and perhaps thinking about something irrelevant to the conversation. If you find yourself in this position, keep quiet and try to pick up the thread of thought. If you feel the need to ask a question, try phrasing a statement this way: "I have lost the thread of thought and I am confused about the meaning of what you are saying."
- Being unprepared imposes on other attendees and demonstrates a lack of respect for peers. If you are not prepared, a better choice may be to not attend. If you find yourself attending a meeting for which you are unprepared, keep quiet.

- If an individual is not knowledgeable about a subject, the propensity to ask a silly question is heightened. There is neither shame nor harm in knowing you are unknowledgeable. However, informing other attendees that you are not familiar with the issues can be helpful to the meeting's progress. Generally, attendees are thankful for the honesty and take extra pains to be helpful. Most people have found themselves in this position, even Albert Einstein.

How the *designer* reacts and handles this question and the individual asking the question is important and helps influence the overall success of the meeting. Here are some guidelines to ease the embarrassment of almost all inappropriate questions:

- Act as if nothing has been said. Ignore it completely. Most people realize quickly that they have asked a poor question and wish they could take the words back. See Figure 4-17. Answering it only makes everyone more uncomfortable. If the question is believed to be valid, the individual will repeat the question.
- As a *designer*, you could be the person asking this type of question. Although you may wish you could take your words back, do not say another word. If the question is noticed, simply say, "Never mind, the question is not important." Everyone will thank you for it.
- The *designer* can ask the person to rephrase the question, giving the person sufficient time to think about what has been said. The individual then has the option to withdraw the question.
- In the event the question persists, the *designer* should not try to answer it. An inappropriate question can only be answered with an inappropriate answer. Simply say, "I do not know the answer to that question." Discuss the question no further and move on.

Figure 4-17   *Sometimes we wish we could eat our words*

4.5.7 Strengths, Weaknesses, Opportunities, and Threats *(why)*

Strengths, weaknesses, opportunities, and threats (SWOT) are four primary factors recognized by most enterprises when developing their designs to conduct business. **SWOT analysis** is a deliberate attempt to analyze **internal influences** (strengths and weaknesses) and **external influences** (opportunities and threats).

Examples of internal influences are infrastructure, human resources, management prerogative, and corporate culture and values. Examples of external influences are the laws of nature, the economy, technology, customers, competitors, partnerships, suppliers, and regulations and legislation. The design team must consider all of these items.

Looking at a company's strengths, the *designer* determines the corporate points of proficiency, such as core competencies and treatment of its employees to generate loyalty and motivation. When examining weaknesses, the *designer* examines potential liabilities. Liabilities may involve management's shortsightedness to upgrade and reinvest in its technology infrastructure.

When a *designer* thinks about the corporate opportunities, a possible opportunity could be how to exploit the current and potential customer base. Another opportunity could be deployment of a broad-based extranet to provide ability to shorten delivery cycles with vendors promoting just-in-time capabilities. When assessing threats, the *designer* is looking primarily at the competition. Threats might also include new or modified legislation limiting where business can be conducted, or mandates causing change in design specifications. Other challenges or threats for the company may include a volatile foreign stock market or changing government leaders.

When performing a SWOT analysis, brainstorm to list solutions and then prioritize the list. For strengths and weaknesses, look at the performance and importance of each item. See Figure 4-18. For opportunities and threats, look at the external conditions and the probability of occurrence or success for each item. See Figure 4-19. A graph can then be plotted to help analyze the data. See Figures 4-20 and 4-21.

Strengths/Weaknesses								
Item list	Performance					Importance		
	Major strength	Minor strength	Neutral	Minor weakness	Major weakness	High	Medium	Low

Figure 4-18 *Strengths and weaknesses*

Opportunities/Threats								
Item list	External condition					Probability of occurrence or success		
	Major strength	Minor strength	Neutral	Minor weakness	Major weakness	High	Medium	Low

Figure 4-19 *Opportunities and threats*

Performance		
	Low	High
Importance — High	Concentrate here	Keep up the good work
Importance — Low	Low priority	Possible overkill

Figure 4-20   *Plotting strengths and weaknesses*

Probability of occurrence/success		
	Low	High
Attractiveness/ Seriousness — Opportunity	Monitor for change	Major opportunity
Attractiveness/ Seriousness — Threat	Monitor for change	Major threat

Figure 4-21   *Plotting opportunities and threats*

4.5.8 Key Terms

accountability

constraint

contention

enterprise resource planning (ERP) system

external influence

goal

internal influence

measuring stick

metric

objective

pushback

strategy

SWOT analysis

tactic

vision statement

4.5.9 Review Questions

1. What are some ways a *designer* addresses office politics?
2. Why must the *designer* analyze internal and external influences? Give examples of each type of influence.
3. Why must the *designer* assign and report accountability?
4. How do appropriate measurements separate objectives and goals, and strategies and tactics?

5. How do statistics help organizations decide what changes must be made in the enterprise to stay competitive?
6. What are some of the things that constrain a design? List some of the most common measuring sticks and explain how a project can be constrained by their use.

SECTION 4.6 WHO NEEDS TO KNOW ABOUT RELIGION AND CULTURE

QUESTIONS TO CONTEMPLATE

1. When setting up a global image for a company, what must be considered?
2. Why is it important to understand the religious and cultural aspects of not only a country, but also an organization?

4.6.1 Introduction

You can categorize employees as gentiles, believers, disciples, and cynics:

- *Gentiles*—those who are there but not part of the action are the nonbelievers, whether benevolent or simply uninvolved.
- *Believers*—those who are infected with religion and imbued with some level of faith in what lies ahead.
- *Disciples*—those who want not only to belong and be a part of the system, but also take an active part in spreading the word; causing others to join the march.
- *Cynics*—those who just do not, or will not, get the corporate objectives. Those who insist on either staying put, or actively get in the way of your journey.

The gentiles, believers, disciples, and cynics not only hear different messages, they all require different forums in which to receive these messages. The Roman Emperors figured out thousands of years ago, as did the Egyptians and others before them, that gentiles (the nonbelievers) can best be served not by libraries and training manuals, but by circuses—events, entertainment, and diversions.

Give a stern lecture, and the echoes can be heard in the halls. Bored people learn nothing, and they cannot learn anything if they do not show up. Putting on a good show fills the house. A circus is a good way to motivate and influence a large number of people. No amount of memos or code in the employee manual can achieve the same effect.

The problem for a lot of companies is not only that they fail to take advantage of circuses for gentiles, but also they fail to recognize how circuses create a constituency called the believers. The believers are those who want to help advance the cause to which they have been called. Once a gentile becomes a believer, the circus is terrific for revitalizing and renewing interest, but a believer is someone who wants to help you, has bought into the act, and wants to advance the general cause.

Giving a believer circuses is like offering additional glasses of water to a goldfish. The best way to take advantage of those who wish to help is to give them support groups or councils, which ensure that the believers' energy gets channeled into action. A council of believers feeds on itself to stay motivated.

If the gentiles initially represent the largest, but least involved, constituency within the organization, the smallest group is likely to be the disciples. The disciples are those who buy so strongly into the vision that they cannot help but want to get others to share in this enlightenment.

The disciples do not simply want to help, they actually want to help rope others into the belief system. Generally speaking, disciples are far beyond the need for circuses and councils. They are part of the inner circle of those who wish to do your work with you. For them, the proper forum is the course curricula, training, and lessons. A formalized program provides them with the leadership tools needed to go out among the believers and the gentiles to turn the corporate vision into reality.

Rallying people this way has worked since the dawn of society and religion. As a *designer* with a mission, remember that what you say may often not be enough. How the message is delivered becomes as important as to whom it is said. Finally, there are the cynics. Cynics are those employees who remain unconvinced, no matter what. For them, the course of action lies in understanding the need to switch their mindset.

One of the most consuming wastes of corporate time is when two individuals are on opposite sides of an issue and fail to admit they are actually on two separate and conflicting sides in the first place. When a *designer* tries to move the organization forward, the team simply cannot afford the added weight of internal, nonproductive, or counterproductive baggage. That is what cynics represent. It is better to have 100 opponents than 10 on-board cynics.

4.6.2 From All Walks of Life *(who)*

Charles Schultz (1922–2000) created the comic strip Peanuts during the 1950s. Even though the comic is entirely in reruns, it still appears in over 2,600 newspapers in 75 countries around the world. As you might expect, when Charlie Brown and friends appear in Japanese newspapers, their words appear in Kanji. In Israel, the words are translated into Hebrew.

It is natural to expect translations of English writings into other languages and vice-versa. *Designers* do not always expect translations to go beyond mere translating into complete name changes. For example, in Mexico, the Peanuts comic strip is called The Radishes. In Denmark, Snoopy is called Nuser, meaning something cute, Charlie Brown is Soeren Brun, Lucy is Trine, and Linus is Thomas.

Culturally, some things or ideas work better in one country than in another, as is illustrated by the Peanuts comic strip and its characters. Creating a stereotype is not always fair, but like using the Myers-Briggs Type Indicator, a reliable image can be painted. So it is with how different cultures make decisions.

The United States has probably the most individualistic of all cultures. Employees are encouraged to emphasize individual initiative and achievement. However, every employee has become a replaceable cog in an organization's wheel. Typically, people from the U.S. do not have a difficult time saying *no*.

In the Central American country of Guatemala, employees take responsibility for their decisions, but make decisions in the context of team and enterprise needs. In Guatemala, development of strong friendships with coworkers is important. A person's ability to get along with colleagues is more important than the actual expertise a person possesses.

In Taiwan, Confucianism has a great influence on society. Confucianism generates a rigid ethical and moral system governing all relationships. Decisions are made by group consensus, which defers to those who have the most ethos, generally the oldest members of the team. Individuals must not bring shame to any team on which they participate as a member. Employees are careful not to cause someone to lose face. The Taiwanese often speak in vague politeness rather than saying *no*. The Taiwanese also have a strong authoritative structure that demands impartiality and obedience.

The English are another highly individualistic people who take responsibility for their decisions within the framework of the organization. Initiative and achievement are emphasized, resulting in strong individual leadership. The English do not find it difficult to say *no*. Friendships are few and meaningful.

In Brazil, nepotism is the influential family member's first obligation. The family is more important in Brazil than in any other Latin American country. Nepotism has been the single most important institution in the formation of Brazilian society.

Belarus, formerly part of the Soviet Union, continues to struggle between individual freedom and obligations to the collective unit. Traditionally, the extended family is the basic unit for decision-making. Although employees have a strong desire to contribute to the welfare of their teams, team leaders make the decisions.

In the Philippines, individuals act in the context of the team. Employees seek consensus of the group because individuals never feel they have the final say on anything. Filipinos like to get to know you and ask questions about your family and personal background. Rather than presenting their own ideas, they react more frequently to the input of others. It is difficult for a Filipino to be confrontational and give an outright *no*.

The *designer* of a global or international corporation must learn to communicate effectively in the accepted styles of the country and culture represented by individuals and teams.

4.6.3 Color *(what)*

Many enterprises have a global or international business presence and image. In Chapter 3, five of the six companies highlighted formally conduct business inside and outside the United States. Companies deciding to use the Internet as a marketing or sales vehicle can reach customers beyond their traditional borders—a positive opportunity for both the company and the customer.

Using the Internet, companies such as Equifax and Coca-Cola target customers formally by establishing specific Web sites in the various countries in which they conduct business. For example:

- Addresses ending in .com typically target American customers.
- Addresses ending in .it typically target Italian customers.
- Addresses ending in .com.br typically target Brazilian customers.
- Addresses ending in .co.nz typically target Kiwi (New Zealand) customers.

Creating a global image for any company is a complex undertaking. When a company sets up an office in a foreign land, the company must understand and abide by all the local laws and regulations. The company must understand the religious and cultural aspects of the country's citizens. Psychologically, the company must be able to adequately support its local employees and local customers, in accordance with what local society deems acceptable.

Trying to deal with a global psyche using a one-size-fits-all approach is likely to achieve less than optimal results. The way color is used in a worldwide context for example, is a profound issue. Color is often misunderstood or overlooked by *designers* of Internet applications. Although Equifax modifies Web page content on each country's Web site, it standardized its color scheme: black, red, and white. A question must be asked: "Are the colors black, red, and white homogenous, safe, and effective global business colors?"

Selecting a color scheme for a Web site is influenced by a customer's ability to see the color and the emotional and cultural inferences placed upon the color. Color can be used to entice, frighten, persuade, sell, and inspire. *Designers* use color to present art, information, products, services, and the corporate image. When *designers* attempt to convey a message to a global audience, the message must be made with awareness of the cultural significance of colors.

Jill Morton, an author, *designer*, and former faculty member of the University of Hawaii School of Architecture, is considered to be expert on color. Morton has conducted studies regarding the use of color on the Internet. Her studies indicate blue is the most globally acceptable color when designing for a worldwide audience. Blue has been determined to be an appropriate color for most types of Web sites, regardless of the target customer, goal, and location.

Men in some societies think pale pink is a feminine color and abandon Web sites automatically when pale pink is the predominant color. However, in Japan, pale pink and other pastel colors are acceptable to both genders. Purple can be polarizing in many cultures. Throughout European Catholic communities, purple is viewed as a symbol of death and crucifixion. In some Middle Eastern cultures, purple signifies prostitution, much as red connotes the same meaning in some Western cultures. Purple is also symbolic of mysticism and spiritual beliefs that go against Christian, Jewish, and Muslim paradigms: Wicca, New Age spirituality, and paganism.

When Disney launched its European theme park just outside of Paris, France in 1992, the initial sign designs used large amounts of purple. Overwhelmingly, visitors to Euro Disney found this morbid. The response was contradictory to the happy message Disney always tries to convey. Disney reworked its European advertising campaign, costing the company significant time and money.

Colors can appear to change depending upon how a *designer* applies them. Color is affected by texture, the actual amount of color used, and the juxtaposition with other colors. When adding texture, color can make smooth surfaces appear lighter and rough surfaces appear darker.

Different amounts of color can be used to create different effects. Using small amounts of purple in an international design might be fine, but lots of purple may cause problems. The balance of colors in the same design requires a fine eye to see which color dominates. The dominant color is the one the *designer* needs to think most about in terms of global cultures. See Figure 4-22.

COLOR AROUND THE WORLD

- In China, *red* is a symbol of celebration and good luck.
- *Purple* is a color rarely found in nature. In some cultures, the color is associated with mourning, new age, and alternative religions.
- *Blue* is the color of immortality in China. In Jewish culture, blue is the color of holiness. In Hinduism, blue is the color of Krishna.
- A calming and antidepressant hue is the color *green*. Green is associated with money in the U.S., but not in many other cultures.
- *Yellow* is a sacred and imperial color in Asian cultures. Yellow represents joy and happiness in several Western cultures. Women tend to respond positively to many values of yellow.
- In the United States, *orange* symbolizes an inexpensive product. For example, the infamous orange automobiles of the 1970s—the Ford Pinto and General Motors Gremlin. Orange should therefore be avoided when designing Web sites expressing sophistication, elegance, and luxury.
- Typically, *brown* is viewed as a neutral color and is associated with nature.
- In many cultures, *black* represents mourning. Black is also the color of dark and evil spirits. Paradoxically, black is also seen as a sophisticated and elegant color, especially in prosperous cosmopolitan areas.
- Salvation, holiness, and purity are often associated with the color *white*. However, white represents mourning in some Western and many Eastern cultures. White is a necessary color for contrast, so it is wise to mix white with colors having stronger, more obvious significance.

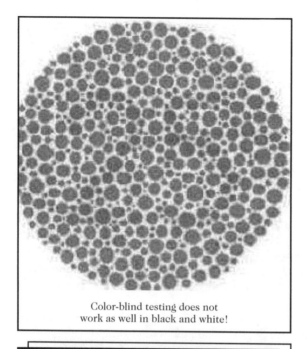

Color-blind testing does not
work as well in black and white!

Figure 4-22   Do you see the number 25?

In many Western and some Eastern cultures, white is considered a symbol of purity and cleanliness. In China and Japan, white is the color of mourning, and some consider the color bad luck. In India, if a bride were to wear all white, it would be believed to foreshadow unhappiness.

When negative colors are mixed with other colors, such as red, significance may change and negative connotations may be lessened or eliminated. In China, red is a symbol of good luck. Therefore, using red may attract lots of Chinese customers. Combined with white, red becomes even more powerful, and the negativity of white is neutralized.

Men and women react differently to color. When gender is combined with cultural issues, the design challenge becomes quite complex:

- Blue stands out for men much more than for women.[14]
- Men prefer blue to red, women red to blue.[15]
- Men prefer orange to yellow, women yellow to orange.[16]
- A woman's color taste is thought to be more diverse than a man's.[17]

To communicate effectively, *designers* must understand how gender plays a role in the perception of color. *Designers* must get to know the targeted audience as well as possible and spend time evaluating the approach to visual design. Currently, many *designers* do not think about color and culture.

To design a Web site for a global audience, the success of a product or service may depend on the color scheme used. Without careful consideration, color can weaken a corporate message, or worse, make it totally ineffective—shortening corporate longevity.

4.6.4 Processes *(how)*

Many businesses do not understand the reasons for their existence. During the 1990s, Royal Dutch Shell decided to study what makes it possible for some companies to stay around for a very long time. In this study, the youngest firms were 150 years old and the oldest was 750 years old. The study revealed four common longevity factors:

- A sense of cohesion
- Availability of cash
- Sensitivity to the environment
- Tolerance for the fringe

A sense of cohesion is derived from a clear leadership vision and the ability to communicate common understanding to all levels within the company.

The availability of cash is significantly different than today's focus on access to capital. Access to capital is an expensive, time and energy-consuming reach for required resources. The availability of cash requires leadership fortitude, in terms of denying bonuses and dividends in the name of long-term ability to move decidedly at key moments.

The sensitivity to the environment, in this case, refers not to the greens and the biological ecosystems, but rather to tuning the company to the world in which it does business. It seems logical to recognize that true survivors survive precisely because they develop an awareness of opportunities and threats and the dynamics that surround them. These longevity meisters all had a systematic tolerance for allowing some portion of the enterprise to focus on issues and opportunities other than the core competencies, which today get so much attention and focus.

Not surprisingly, none of the companies studied is still in the business in which it started. It is clear that these enterprises understood they were in the business of being in business, and whatever was required to stay in business, they would do. This is a far cry from today's highly focused companies that make the common mistake of forming entire enterprises around what they do, rather than who they are.

To be successful in a changing world requires not only adapting to change, but also actually evolving with change. Evolution is an externally driven activity. No animal gets up one morning with a burning desire for larger feet or more fur.

The CEO of Cascade Engineering does not simply remachine the Cascade Family to exist for the next 10, 20, or 100 years; Keller is continually leading the company's genetic transformations into a permanent change enterprise—an entity whose existence is change. It is the same issue that faces companies such as IBM and Intel.

The *designer* can create designs to do everything from stagnating change in the enterprise to helping change flourish.

4.6.5 Culture Shock *(where)*

People create their own culture. Norms and habits are established that become a way of life. Most companies require their workforces to be mobile and attend off-site meetings. Sometimes, when traveling to foreign lands,[18] a person's values conflict with other cultures. Experiencing difficulty when adjusting to a new culture is called **culture shock**.

Culture shock happens when your mind and body are disoriented and feel overwhelmed by unfamiliar surroundings. Culture shock causes psychological and physical discomfort. Within your own work culture, you know the language, traditions, non-verbal behaviors, values, and ways of reasoning. Many actions are done on autopilot. People tend to understand what is happening around them without thinking about a given situation.

For example, when meeting a work colleague, you probably do not have to think about the first words of greeting coming out of your mouth. When answering the telephone at work, you answer without wondering what to say, or if you will understand what the other person is saying. When invited to a meeting, you know when to arrive, what to bring with you, how to dress, and you probably understand what will happen during the course of the meeting. With a foreign culture, all these things are unfamiliar. This experience can become tiring and frustrating.

Culture shock causes some people to become inexplicably unhappy, and want to participate in work activities, or not want to speak the local language. People who do not understand culture shock have a difficult time trying to make themselves feel better. Preparing for culture shock and knowing how to overcome it can help reduce and minimize the shock's symptoms. See Figure 4-23.

Physical symptoms of culture shock include:

- Too much or too little sleep
- Eating too much or having no appetite at all
- Frequent minor illnesses
- Headaches

Psychological symptoms of culture shock include:

- Loneliness or boredom
- Homesickness; idealizing home
- Feeling helpless, overly dependent
- Irritability or even hostility
- Social withdrawal
- Unreasonable concern for health and security
- Rebellion against rules
- Crying
- Stereotyping host country's people

The number of symptoms experienced depends on the individual. Frequently, travelers experiencing culture shock develop negative attitudes toward the host culture and start noticing all the differences, rather than the similarities, between home and away.

Someone experiencing culture shock may share comments with co-travelers, such as: "It is awful the way they eat," or "Why do they care so much about being on time," or "Back home, things are much easier...," or "These stupid rules make no sense." People sometimes unconsciously encourage each other's unhappiness.

Learning how to deal with culture shock can be turned into a positive experience. Start by objectively analyzing differences found between your home and the host culture. Seek to understand why the host culture does things differently. Host customs are logical to the hosts, just as your home customs are logical to you.

Weaver ants are often eaten in Southeast Asia.

Figure 4-23   *Culture shock*

Sometimes pretending to be interested or happy can lead to the real thing. If you are in a meeting or attending a seminar that seems deadly boring, seek out one thing that is interesting to you and ask as many questions as possible. Create small, attainable tasks and goals. This is a good way to reclaim your sense of independence and self-assuredness in a foreign culture.

Humor tends to be one of the best remedies for almost any difficult situation. Developing an attitude that you can live with helps with the differences and confusions so that you can participate successfully and enjoy yourself.

4.6.6 Holidays *(when)*

Most origins of religion emphasize one of the following suggestions: human minds demand explanations, human hearts seek comfort, human society requires order, or human intellect is illusion prone. The following list illustrates these points:

Religion provides explanations:

- People created religion to explain puzzling natural phenomena.
- Religion explains puzzling experiences, including dreams and prescience.
- Religion explains the origin of things.
- Religion explains why there is evil and suffering.

Religion provides comfort:

- Religious explanations make mortality less unbearable.
- Religion allays anxiety and creates a more comfortable world.

Religion provides social order:

- Religion holds society together.
- Religion perpetuates a particular social order.
- Religion supports morality.

Religion is a cognitive illusion:

- People are superstitious; they believe anything.
- Religious concepts are irrefutable.
- Refutation is more difficult than belief.

The world has many religions. Judaism, Christianity, Islam, Baha'i, Sikhism, Hinduism, Taoism, Buddhism, Jainism, Society of Humankind, Zoroastrianism, Animism, Wicca, and Unitarian Universalism are but a few.

Depending on the religion, there is a belief in a single deity, dual deity, or no deity whatsoever. Many religions are inspired by sacred texts that inform believers how to conduct their daily lives and explain what morals and values are important.

Many of the religions use their own calendars, celebrating holidays, such as New Year's Day, on different days of the Gregorian calendar. Some calendars are lunar based, which cause holidays to be observed on different days each year when correlated to the Gregorian calendar. This is the case for the Islamic and Jewish calendars. The Islamic calendar is also 11 days shorter than the Gregorian calendar, which may sometimes allow Muslims to celebrate New Year's Day twice in the same Gregorian year.

In 2005, Jews celebrate the year 5765, Muslims the year 1425, and Buddhists the year 2546.

Religious holidays are very important in foreign countries. Knowing these religious observances honors and respects your friends and business associates worldwide. During the month of March, the following holidays are observed in various parts of the world. However, the actual Gregorian month the holiday is celebrated may vary based on the actual calendar used.

- Makha Puja—Buddhist observance
- Purim—Jewish observance
- Holi—Hindu observance
- Saint Joseph's Day—Catholic Christian observance
- Saka New Year—Hindu New Year
- Palm Sunday—Christian observance
- Id-al-Adha—Islamic observance

4.6.7 Faith (why)

Faith is the persuasion of the mind that a certain statement or situation is deemed to be true. The primary idea behind faith is trust. Faith is a strong, emotionally charged belief in certain ideas, even when the truth of that idea is not readily demonstrable in the ordinary world.

When information and events contradicting the faith are resisted actively in ways that seem irrational, or when information is taken as a threat rather than as an invitation to rational thought, we speak conventionally of blind faith.

Flexi-Van is a leasing company in the intermodal transportation industry, headquartered in New Jersey. Flexi-Van leases containers, chassis, trailers, and generator sets. Its story is not atypical. In 1982, Flexi-Van decided to rewrite most of its software applications and convert operations from a Honeywell computer to an IBM computer. To demonstrate how well things were going to executive management, the project managers hired many consultants to perform the programming.

The only problem was that nobody had gathered any requirements. Nobody knew what to program, and so no programming was done. The programmers sat for nearly a year doing very little. Because the executives were paying for programming staff, they believed programs were being generated.

Slowly, requirements were generated and turned into designs. The designs were handed over to the coders to program. Later in the year, a new manager of the IT department was brought in, and the deception was dropped to the lower-level managers. They started reporting falsely to the new manager how well things were progressing.

In April 1983, the new manager called a meeting. Everyone was brought into the conference room. On that day, the new system was supposed to go live. Unfortunately, no programs had been turned over for implementation, and the manager had become totally aware of this fact.

The manager relayed this story: "I was talking with so and so the other day, and he said I could get my new system if I could pull a rabbit out of a hat." The manager then bent down and reached under a table. He produced a black top hat and proceeded to pull out a live white rabbit by the ears. He then said in an earnest tone, "Here's the rabbit; I want my system."

For too long, the project was run on blind faith—every manager passing along a story of hope and goodness for which no metric could be measured or produced to back up the claims of progression. By the time the new manager realized what was happening, it was too late to complete a successful initiative.

4.6.8 Key Term

culture shock

4.6.9 Review Questions

1. Why is it important for *designers* of Internet applications to focus on color?

2. How is tuning the company to the world in which it does business similar to tuning an orchestra?

3. How does the CEO of Cascade Engineering enable change to flourish in his enterprise?

4. Why should the *designer* learn to communicate effectively in the accepted styles represented by individuals and teams?

5. Why should the designer be aware of both the religious and cultural aspects of an organization?

6. What happens when a project is run on blind faith?

SECTION 4.7 WHEN DEALING WITH BIRTH, DEATH, AND TAXES

QUESTIONS TO CONTEMPLATE

1. Why is it necessary for the *designer* to be a *corporate psychiatrist*?
2. How are the symptoms, illnesses, and life-altering experiences of a person similar to those of an enterprise?

4.7.1 Introduction

Corporations, just like human beings, suffer life-altering experiences. When a person suffers a life-altering experience, the advice generally given is, "Suck it up, get over it, and take a pill." In serious situations, the sufferer is offered sympathy. A corporation receives no such advice or solace. The following is a list of the stages of human life and the corporate counterparts:

Stages of human life	Corporate counterparts
Birth	Enterprise startup
Childhood	Early years
Puberty	Corporate awakening
Teen years	Corporate positioning and market share
Marriage	Acquisitions
Children	Spin-offs
Divorce	Partner dissolution
Loss of loved ones	Subsidiary sell off or shutdown; reorganization
Sickness	Business reversal
Catastrophic illness	Dramatic change in marketplace
Death	Close of the business

The corporation suffers and enjoys the same emotional shifts as people. The word trauma applies to both good and bad events. Psychiatrists claim that individuals are capable of withstanding only so many traumas a year. When that limit is exceeded, a person may no longer be able to cope, or may have a nervous breakdown. The same is true for the corporation. People going through bad times take those troubles to work. Likewise, corporations having difficult times force their employees to take those woes home. The corporation and the employee count on each other to provide a sense of emotional balance.

4.7.2 Life Stages *(when)*

In October 2000, Warren Selkow (b. 1942) awoke on a Wednesday night, shortly after falling asleep. He felt terrible. He was sweating and sick to his stomach. Selkow had a severe chest pain that he thought was indigestion. He was so concerned that he turned on his computer and searched Yahoo for heart attack symptoms. Selkow was suffering from all but one of the symptoms. By sheer luck, his younger son came home and asked him what was wrong. "I think I am having a heart attack," Selkow said to his son, who immediately took him to the local hospital emergency room. See Figure 4-24.

✔ Chest pain is unrelieved by rest and spreads or radiates through the upper body.
✔ Chest-area pressure or squeezing sensation.
✔ Shortness of breath or shallow breathing heart palpitations.
✔ Abnormally weak or fast pulse.
✔ Fainting or loss of consciousness.
✔ Feeling tired or fatigued.
✔ Sweating, often heavy, and often cold.
✔ Nausea or upset stomach.
✔ Gray facial color.

Figure 4-24 *Okay, let me see. Got it. Got it. Got it...Oh no.*

The emergency staff confirmed that he was having a heart attack and quickly administered drugs to stop the heart attack. Selkow's first thought was, *Phew...I am glad that is over; I can be back to work on Monday and no one will know.*

Early the following morning, he had an echocardiogram. "So what is it showing?" Selkow inquired of the technician. "I only do the tests; I do not know what they mean," she replied. Selkow had just heard one of the great medical lies. There is not a licensed, experienced medical technician in the United States who does not know what the tests indicate. They leave the bad news for the doctor to report.

BE PREPARED

In business, it is not uncommon to be summoned to the boss's office for an unscheduled meeting. However, an unscheduled meeting is rarely good news. Suppose an administrative assistant is asked, "What's going on?" If the news is bad, the assistant begins an immediate heart to heart discussion with the computer, or checks to see if there is lettuce on her shoe. Be prepared for the worst. Selkow needed to be but was not.

Within minutes of the test being completed, a nurse showed up and began puttering around the room, making small talk. Selkow's family, and indeed Selkow himself, did not think much about it. Thirty minutes after the test, the cardiologist came into the room, acknowledged Selkow's family, sat down, and without any prelude said, "You have a chronic, severe, and seriously leaking aortic valve, and if it is not repaired, you will be dead in six months."

Selkow's immediate unspoken thought was, *Say it ain't so, Joe.*[19] When he finally spoke up, he replied to the cardiologist, "This cannot be. I have a course to teach on Monday, and the following week, I must be in Atlanta to give a speech at the Business Rules Forum and attend a standards body meeting with the Business Rules Group." The cardiologist, without blinking an eye replied, "You may go to Atlanta, but you are not coming back." Selkow paused, and gave a brief response, "Oh."

Two weeks later, Selkow had open-heart surgery to replace his aortic valve with a mechanical valve, a four-way bypass, and a very large aneurysm above the aorta repaired. He is thankful to be alive. The important part of his story is not the surgery. The important part is the aftermath of the surgery and how it forced Selkow to change his lifestyle and alter his personal needs agenda.

Selkow changed his diet entirely, from a see-food diet (see food and eat it) to a seafood diet rich in high omega oils—no red meat, low sodium, low cholesterol, and no animal fats. He changed from a sports spectator to a daily walker and exerciser. He tried earnestly to put down his type A personality[20] as best he could and now tries to take things in stride. It was not easy for him. He has always been a friendly, outgoing person who greets you with a warm hug...but prior to the surgery, he could be quite arrogant and had an enormous ego.

FOCUS ON THE RECOVERY

Corporations live through the same type of crises. Organizational units initially feel the brunt of a problem. The proper reaction is to focus on the recovery, not the crisis. It is important to recognize that most business traumas are not terminal. The psychology must be placed on the healing, not on the blame. There is always blame enough to go around, and its entirely unproductive in both the short and long term. The advice is simple: get better, get over it.

Seventy percent of people who experience a heart attack only have one. The symptom Selkow did not experience when he had the heart attack was death. Many people do not believe smoking and obesity statistics apply to them. Selkow once waddled around 40 pounds overweight, eating fast-food, high-fat snacks and spending plenty of time as a couch potato. When catastrophe strikes, people do not believe it is happening to them so they do not seek aid. This denial may cause death.

Fifteen months later and during the writing of this chapter, Selkow once again found himself having open-heart surgery. The replacement aortic valve had sprung a leak. The authors wondered once again how the personal needs their friend and colleague would change when he returned to work.

Enterprises experience similar symptoms. The enterprise is not vigilant about all the things that threaten it. The *it can't happen here* attitude exists. A sudden convulsion due to either outside influences or external pressure may arise. The corporation waddles along as if nothing is wrong. When the realization finally strikes that something very serious is wrong, it may be too late.

Not all traumas are instantly terminal. Most are like cancer, gaining a small foothold. They are neither detected nor treated and eventually become terminal. Sometimes, like pancreatic cancer, the disease is recognized immediately as terminal. However, even when a person or an enterprise is found to be terminal, both people and organizations try their utmost to survive.

A mountain is the metaphor often used to depict a difficult situation. In the case of Selkow, life brought the mountain to him. On the other hand, some people go looking for the mountain. In both cases, the mettle of human endurance, self-motivation, and the sheer will to survive come to the forefront of their lives. And sometimes, these experiences actually happen on a mountain.

4.7.3 Persistence and Endurance *(how)*

Mountain climbers recognize that many of their activities are subject to regulation. Climbers work constructively with host governments to gain permission to climb. The climb team must adhere to the highest standards of efficiency, safety, and operational integrity and balance the interests of all involved.

The mountaineer who aspires to climb the world's highest mountain faces several other mountains before setting foot on Mount Everest. Getting permission to climb is one of them. Adventurers who organize their own expeditions need anywhere from three to seven years to arrange and prepare for the trip.

After reaching the Himalayan giant, mountaineers do not scramble up to the summit immediately. Like the paperwork and the permissions, climbing the mountain is an arduous task, often taking three to four months.

Mount Everest sits between Tibet and Nepal in the Great Himalayas. The Himalayan mountain range runs from the Indus River in Pakistan to the Brahmaputra River in southeast Tibet. It passes through India, Nepal, East India, and Bhutan. Mount Everest is named for Sir George Everest (1790–1866), who surveyed India for the British from 1806 to 1843. Before 1865, Mount Everest was known as Peak XV. The Nepalese word for Everest is Sagarmatha, meaning goddess of the sky. In Tibet, the mountain is called Qomolangma, meaning goddess-mother.

Peak XV in the Himalayas was determined to be the highest mountain in the world in 1852. The Great Trigonometrical Survey of India estimated the height at 29,002 feet. In 1955, the height of Mount Everest was adjusted from the original measurements. The mountain grew by 26 feet to 29,028 feet. Mount Everest grew another seven feet in 1999 after researchers analyzed data retrieved from the mountain in 1998. They discovered the mountain is actually 29,035 feet (8,850 meters) high.

The body of an Everest climber endures many physical changes. In a single day, a climber can lose seven liters of water just from breathing in the severe, cold weather and easily becomes dehydrated. In frigid temperatures, a climber's body weight drops three pounds every day. A climber's body no longer accepts food, and the mere thought of food becomes gross and horrifying. The climber can no longer sleep nor rest.

Dr. Beck Weathers (b. 1946) was part of an expedition team that climbed Mount Everest in 1996. He was an experienced climber. He was mentally fit, physically fit and emotionally fit. Prior to climbing Everest, Weathers had undergone radial keratotomy (RK) laser eye surgery to protect his eyes from the snow and ice. The surgery was performed to enable him to see more clearly in the strong winds of snow.

One group of people that leave nothing to chance are those that climb Mount Everest. They plan; they have an *owner* who has authority and responsibility to make decisions; they design the trip; they buy the right equipment carefully; and they practice. Everything is prepared at excruciating levels of detail, and all details are made explicit. Santa may check his list twice, but that is not sufficient for the Everest climber. Climbers do everything they can to mitigate risks. Weathers stated, "Climbing Everest is an option; getting back down is mandatory."

When Weathers designed his climb, he failed to resolve one particular *when* question. "When you are near 28,000 feet, what happens to an eyeball that has had RK procedures[21] performed on it?"

At midnight on May 10, Weathers and the other climbers set out from their high camp on the South Col. The South Col is a plateau, 26,000 feet up the side of the mountain. It is about 1,300 feet long by 500 feet across. To the south rises the rest of Lhotse mountain, to the north rises the rest of Everest, to the east, the Kangshung Face drops a sheer 7,000 feet straight down, and to the west, the Lhotse Face falls 4,000 feet.

On that day, Weathers became blinded by the consequences of his eye surgery after climbing for several hours. Low barometric pressure at high altitude caused his eyesight to fail. The RK surgery, reacting to the barometric pressure, fully dilated his pupils. The sunlight was blinding.

Weathers could not see. His guide told him to stop climbing and sit, not to move. The guide assured Weathers he would be back to collect him after he had been to the summit. So Weathers sat. He waited for over four hours for his guide in the snow, at 27,600 feet up the side of Mount Everest.

As he sat waiting, a violent storm came up, with blowing wind and snow. By 6:00 p.m., when he had been out in the cold for 18 hours, the blizzard really set in. Weathers gave up waiting and joined up with another group heading down.

By 6:45, Weathers was weak to the point that he could not walk on his own. By 7:00, winds were at 120 knots, and visibility was shrinking to only 3 feet. At 7:30, Weathers and his group reached the South Col, exhausted. They wandered over two hours, unable to find the tents, growing colder all the time. Ultimately, 11 climbers took shelter behind a boulder the size of a dishwasher. They were only 1,000 feet from their tents and safety.

At midnight, there was some letup in the storm, and the six who could still walk left Weathers and the others. They found the campsite and told those at the camp what had happened.

The next morning, a search team from the camp found Weathers' body. After they chipped away the 3 inches of ice covering his face, they found he was still alive. The would-be rescuers noticed that both of his right-hand gloves were missing. He was badly frostbitten, and he could not move. The searchers decided that even if he could be dragged back to camp, he would certainly die before he could be carried to base camp 9,000 feet below. They made the terrible decision to leave him.

His wife and family were notified of his death on the morning of May 11. At 4:35 p.m. the same day, Weathers stumbled into camp. He was horribly frostbitten; he had been comatose on the ice and in the storm for over 12 hours, but he finally forced himself up and set off, not knowing which way to go. Fortunately, he made the right choice of direction. The 7,000-foot drop of the Kangshung Face was only 30 feet away in the other direction. The climbers at the campsite bundled him into two sleeping bags and gave him hot water bottles. No one figured he would survive the night.

The storm returned with a vengeance. His tent collapsed. The wind was so fierce that it blew both sleeping bags off him. Somehow, he survived the night, and when the group started down the mountain that morning, they believed Weathers was near death and left him to die again.

At 10:30, he stood up. He got help getting into his climbing harness and joined the group going down. That night, Weathers walked into the lower Camp 2 on his own power. The next morning, the highest helicopter rescue in history took him to a hospital, where his right arm and both feet were amputated.

What do you think was the hardest thing for Weathers to do? Awaken from a night out in the storm at 26,000 feet? Endure a second night in a collapsed tent? Climb down from 26,000 feet? Or endure the psychological trauma of losing his limbs? It is a tremendous story of courage, persistence, and endurance, and of the majesty of battling your own personal psychology when you fail in design.

BASIC EQUIPMENT TO CARRY UP EVEREST

Thermal underwear, midwear, polar fleece jacket and pants, down suit or down jacket and pants, wind suit or jacket and pants, rain jacket, cotton long-sleeved shirt, balaclava, ski hat or padded hat, baseball hat, scarf, sox, finger gloves, ski gloves, high-altitude mitts and liners, snow gaiters, bivvi boots, trekking shoes, running shoes, climbing boots, neoprene over boots, base camp boots, headlamp, small flashlight, helmet, crampons, ice axe, ski poles, lip cream and sun cream, snow glasses, snow goggles, rucksack/backpack, day pack, large duffel bags, down sleeping bag, foam mattress, thermorest, water bottle, pee bottle, small plastic thermos bottle, climbing harness, locking carabineers, snap link carabineers, leashes for ascenders, ascenders, descenders, personal toiletries and medications, personal first aid kit, small kit bag, casual wear, pocket knife, walkman and spare batteries, music cassettes, books, camera equipment with film and batteries.

By the way, the batteries must be stored next to your skin; otherwise they freeze and will not work.

240

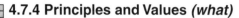

4.7.4 Principles and Values *(what)*

To help guide actions, decisions, and standards, many organizations or teams establish a set of guiding principles and values to operate in different business cultures and with different personalities. Corporate values shape the character of the organization and represent key beliefs that define corporate philosophy. Principles help govern day-to-day operations. They should not be negotiable. Principles should represent what an organization stands for, and what an organization will not stand for.

Principles and values demonstrate standards that govern the behavior of all employees to those inside and outside the enterprise. Enterprises are judged on their success in meeting these standards at all times and under all circumstances.

The following values are some beliefs that organizations use to condition employee behavior. They help explain why and how the principles are important and place the enterprise's values in a wider context.

- *Integrity*—A desire to achieve high ethical standards consistently in all business dealings.
- *Trust*—A belief that effective business relationships inside and outside the company are possible only with high levels of reliance on integrity and ability between parties.
- *Openness*—An aspiration to strive for honesty and straightforwardness, while recognizing that in complicated business arrangements, it is not always practical to be transparent on all matters.
- *Partnership*—A commitment to play a full role in stimulating the sharing of information, knowledge, experience, and skills both within the team and, where appropriate, externally.
- *Teamwork*—An aim to achieve value-enhancing collaboration between complementary businesses, and a common cause to pervade all activities.

The following principles are fundamental to conducting business and should not be compromised. All employees are responsible for observing these business principles, and managers are specifically required to promote these standards and ensure they are applied throughout an enterprise. All corporate decisions are made in line with the business principles.

- *Personal conduct*—An expectation of the highest levels of honesty, integrity, and fairness by all employees, regardless of position. Honesty, integrity, and fairness form the cornerstones of relationships inside and outside the company. Hospitality given and received as part of building normal business relationships is acceptable. However, employees are normally advised to avoid accepting gifts that appear to place them under an obligation. Typically, bribery of any form is unacceptable. A contact that leads to, suggests, or engages in personal activities that conflict with the organization is highly discouraged.
- *Work environment*—Organizations aim to provide all employees with safe conditions of work and competitive terms of employment. The welfare of staff is an essential principle. Organizations are usually committed to equal opportunities and the avoidance of discrimination. Sexual or racial harassment is not tolerated.

- *International operations*—In the countries where the enterprise does business, the enterprise seeks to play a responsible, constructive role, aligning its business objectives with the aspirations of the individual societies. The enterprise normally makes every attempt to comply with the applicable laws and regulatory requirements of the countries in which it is operating.
- *Health, safety, and the environment*—Organizations take their responsibility seriously to conduct operations with proper regard for the environment and the health and safety of those involved in its operations and the public at large.

- *Communication*—Organizations recognize the vital role that clear and effective communication plays in sustaining business relationships and safeguarding public confidence in its activities. Openness and transparency of operations, appropriate to the expectations of respective audiences, are key business goals subject to the demands of commercial confidentiality. Effective internal communication is of vital importance to the success of the organization and central to sustaining corporate values.
- *Third parties*—When operating in conjunction with third parties, or in joint venture arrangements, enterprises seek to promote the application of the enterprise's principles. Doing this effectively contributes to deciding whether to enter or remain in any third-party relationship. Business integrity is a key standard for the selection and retention of those who represent and work for an organization. Agents, representatives, consultants, and third-party contractors signify willingness to accept and comply with organizational policies and procedures and are retained only by abiding by them consistently.
- *Customers*—Customer satisfaction is the cornerstone of any business. An organization aims to develop and maintain profitable and lasting relationships with customers, offering safety, service, quality, and value supported by continuous innovation.
- *Community activities*—Many organizations seek to make a positive and meaningful contribution to community activities and to behave in a socially responsible manner. Organizations recognize that sustained commercial success is possible only in the presence of a healthy social environment.
- *Economic priorities*—Commercial organizations must provide an appropriate return for the shareholders to discharge its responsibilities and remain in business.

The enterprise recognizes many of its activities are subject to regulation. Enterprises and any subsidiaries work constructively with host governments and regulatory authorities to ensure such regulation is conducive to the highest standards of efficiency, safety and operational integrity, and balances the interests of investors and other stakeholders.

4.7.5 Going Door to Door *(where)*

For new designs to be accepted, they have to be sold. However, many people do not like to think of themselves as salespeople. Salesperson, in their eyes, is a belittling title; yet, selling is one of the *designer's* most important functions. New ideas are difficult to get accepted, and the more radical the idea, the more difficult the acceptance. New products or services are rarely accepted upon announcement. The *designer* is not only proposing something new, the *designer* is proposing change.

The more a *designer* knows and understands about the techniques of selling and the better those techniques are used, the more successful the *designer* is likely to be. Selling has four principal parts:

- Getting favorable attention
- Proving a need for the new product or service
- Obtaining necessary agreements and commitments for the product or service
- Closing the sale and beginning the work or installation

To sell a product, service, or idea, the *designer* must guide the participants through four mental processes:

- *Acknowledgement*—helps identify an area of concern. Acknowledgement is also very easy for people to do. The alternative to acknowledgement is admission. Few people admit to anything, but, generally, most people are comfortable acknowledging a problem area.
- *Agreement*—allows the participants to come to terms with the problem area and determine what is causing loss of time and money.
- *Commitment*—allows the participants to decide to do something about the problem area and give support to the effort.
- *Closing*—is the complete acceptance that there is a problem area, the problem is significant, the problem must be fixed, and the problem will be fixed.

The preceding four items must be reiterated on every issue. In this way, the *designer* fleshes out hidden agendas and resistance. The *designer* can keep score of the resolved issues and inform management of progress.

4.7.6 The Needy *(who)*

Abraham Maslow (1908–1970) was interested in studying how and why people reacted to events and aspects of everyday life. He came up with a concept of what he believed people needed to live and succeed in a normal and healthy lifestyle.

This concept is often organized in a table known as *Maslow's Hierarchy of Needs*. His table is based on five basic needs, which are included from lowest (most basic) to highest in the following list:

1. Physiological needs (food, water, warmth, air)
2. Safety needs (structure, protection, peace, comfort)
3. Love needs (love, friendship, acceptance, understanding)
4. Esteem needs (attention, self-respect, recognition)
5. Self-actualization needs (challenge, curiosity, growth)

As each lower level is met, the next higher level can be achieved. See Figure 4-25.

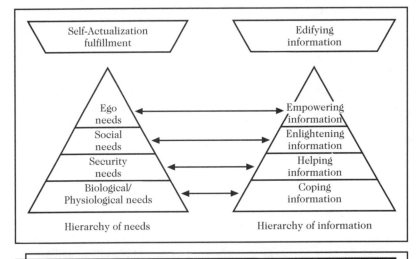

Figure 4-25   *Maslow's hierarchy of needs and information*

The Personal Needs Agenda

Every individual in the organization is part of a corporate culture, and every individual has a set of personal needs that are influenced by that culture. When these needs are not expressed and acknowledged, the individual is forced to operate with a hidden agenda. A hidden agenda is a desired result that is not shared with anyone. The personal agenda items can be expressed as follows:

- I am listened to and my opinion counts.
- My authority and responsibility (power) will not be either compromised or reduced.
- My position and image within the corporation will be enhanced.
- My additional work will be minimized.
- My accountability and risk are limited.
- I am getting my fair share of the budget pie.

In addition to each individual's personal needs, the individual has a set of business needs within the organization.

The Business Needs Agenda

If an enterprise is undertaking a new design effort, everyone needs to have a say. This need to have a say creates opposing and supporting requirements. The business needs for a new design include:

- Deliver the benefits as desired and promised.
- Work the way promised.
- Deliver the functionality required.
- Deliver the savings or payback, as promised.

- Be, at worst, benign in nature and cause no harm.
- Create a minimal amount of acceptable risk.

Recall that the *designer's* primary function is to design something new that satisfies the requirements of the management's mandate. The *designer* is most accountable to management, who will blame the *designer* for any failures. Conversely, the groups the *designer* must work with—the mid-level managers—are not accountable to the *designer*. The chain of command is blurred. The *designer* has responsibility, but no authority. This creates an untenable position.

Personal communication requirements necessitate that the *designer* becomes a sort of corporate psychiatrist. The *designer* must resolve all areas of contention and dissention that are caused by the personal and business needs of each participant. Over time, the needs of individuals may change as they grow older or gain more experience.

4.7.7 Survival *(why)*

Sigmund Freud (1856–1923) was born into a middle-class Jewish family in Freiburg, Moravia. Freud had a good education, winning a place at the gymnasium—a grammar school—at the early age of nine. In 1873, he enrolled himself as a medical student at the University of Vienna. His educational interests ranged from biology to physiology and anatomy.

Working under Ernst Brucke (1819–1892), he acquired a liking for physical science and established a neurobiological grounding. Faced with financial difficulties, Freud started working in the Vienna General Hospital in 1881. The following year, he became engaged, and during the four years he was engaged, Freud established a reputation for himself in neuroanatomy and neuropathology.

In 1885, Freud traveled to Paris and spent a few months under Dr. Jean-Martin Charcot (1825–1893) at the Sapêtrière, a hospital renowned for treating nervous diseases. This was a turning point in his life. Charcot's interests in hysteria and hypnotism fascinated Freud. He would take them eventually beyond tools of neuropathology, into tools of the investigation of the mind.

Freud returned to Vienna in 1886 and set up a private practice as a consultant in nervous diseases. It was during this time that he became increasingly absorbed by the treatment of neuroses. He learned about hypnosis from Dr. Ambroise-Auguste Liébeault (1823–1904) and Dr. Hippolyte Bernheim (1840–1919) and started using hypnosis instead of electro therapy. Freud was not happy with the results of hypnosis, and he persuaded Dr. Josef Breuer (1842–1925) to instruct him in a new procedure.

The procedure was based on the assumption that hysteria was the product of a psychical trauma that had been forgotten by the patient. The treatment consisted of inducing the patient into a hypnotic state to recall the forgotten trauma with the accompaniment of appropriate emotions. Gradually, Freud abandoned the use of suggestion in hypnosis, replacing it with *free association*, which he called psychoanalysis. In 1921, Freud began his work on personality in more earnest, producing *The Ego and the Id* in 1923.

The id is the unconscious part of the mind, which consists of natural instincts, urges, and drives that are repressed. It includes *internal events*, which stem from the influence of heredity. Although the id is the cause of all activity, the thoughts are often unconscious and repressed.

According to Freud, all instincts can be traced back to the existence of the Eros and the destructive instincts or death instinct. Within Eros is the contrast between the instincts of self-preservation and preservation of the species. Its goal is to bind the gap between *ego-love* and *object-love*. The second instinct, the destructive instinct, tries to destroy the connections made by Eros.

The ego is a defense mechanism that is partly conscious and contains the capacities to calculate, reason, and plan. As the id relates to internal events, the ego is occupied with the external world. Its task is to regulate and control instincts provided by the id. The prime function of the ego is determined by the individual's experiences.

The super-ego is the connection between the id and the ego. The super-ego is the mind's link to reality and society. It contains the influence of what is learned from other people. The super-ego, unlike the id, is not intuitive from birth, but acquired from childhood. Once established, one begins to feel guilt.

It is the ego that gives continuity and consistency to our behavior by providing a personal point of reference. The ego relates the events of the past that are retained in our memories with the actions of the present and future. This is represented by our imagination and our ability to anticipate. The ego, once developed, is capable of change throughout life, particularly under conditions of threat, illness, and changes in life circumstances.

Observations of the Eros between self-preservation and the preservation of the species become interesting for the *designer* when the species is viewed as the enterprise. The basic tradeoff is: "What can I do to get this piece of work off my desk so that I can move on to the next task" versus "What can I do that provides the best short- and long-term benefits to the corporation?"

This paradigm identifies many employees as intrinsically lazy. Laziness causes employees to produce deliverables in the quickest and easiest way possible, which often leads to all aspects of the design being primed with insufficient detail and many design decisions stemming from assumption.

The diligent *designer* places the highest priority on the preservation of the enterprise. This type of *designer* leads and commands those around her to define work at an excruciating level of detail and to drive out all areas of assumption. The resulting design provides a stronger basis for the enterprise to survive and adapt to change. The design becomes a complete record of the enterprise's anatomy.

4.7.8 Review Questions

1. Why do organizations establish a set of guiding principles?
2. Why is it necessary for the *designer* to be a good salesperson?
3. In what ways did Beck Weathers illustrate self-motivation? What lesson might the *designer* take away from the story?

4. What are the four mental processes the *designer* guides the participants through and why?
5. What items are included on a business needs agenda? A personal needs agenda?

4.8 SYNTHESIS AND CHAPTER SUMMARY

A major responsibility for the *designer* during the design process is to uncover and record the imposed business rules that are expressions of required constraints. The business rules are solicited from *owners*, stakeholders, and domain experts. They may also be found by reviewing existing documentation or by reverse-engineering computer programs.

Initially, the concepts of laws and rules were introduced in Chapter 2. Business rules are special types of rules and fall into one of two categories. The two categories:

- Implicit business rules
- Mandated business rules

Implicit business rules are culturally derived in the corporation. Implicit business rules are rules everyone in the company knows, but they are rarely written down. An example of a cultural business rule is: "Do not go over your manager's head." Like any explicit written rule, there is punishment for noncompliance, albeit applied subtly. The *designer* must understand the ripple effect of unwritten rules. The *designer* should make every attempt to make the business rules of behavior as explicit as possible.

Mandated business rules are imposed by outside market conditions, legislative requirements, and management directives. By definition, a violation of these rules results in some form of punishment. There are several forms of mandated business rules:

- *Absolute mandated business rules*—business rules from which there is no relief or exemption. These rules are always published in some form. Violation of these rules carries a harsh punishment. Punishments include: jail time, monetary fines, immediate termination for cause, and civil action or suit.

    Examples of these business rules include:
    - For all in-state retail sales, a sales tax must be collected and paid to the state.
    - Sexual harassment is not tolerated by any gender.
    - Insider trading of public stock is prohibited.
    - Only children aged 12 and under may participate in Little League Baseball.

- *Policy business rules*—business rules that provide guidance in following expectations.

    Examples of this type of business rule include:
    - Do not work overtime without getting approval from management.
    - All merchandise returns exceeding $100 require a manager's signature.
    - All products are shipped overnight via Federal Express, unless otherwise requested by the customer.

    In general, there are no exceptions to a business rule, only other business rules. For example, in the situation where the policy business rule is to fulfill orders in the sequence they are received, only if a customer has preferred status should that order be fulfilled immediately. An exception process may be required to handle a situation where insufficient inventory is on hand, or an item is backordered and the preferred customer's order cannot be filled immediately. In this case, one or more additional business rules are created for informing the customer that the order cannot be filled immediately, issuing purchase orders to bolster inventory, and reprioritizing fulfillment.

Individually or collectively, policy business rules state explicitly not only what may be done, but also how to get relief to violate the policy. Specification of relief is the principal distinction between policy business rules and absolute mandated business rules. With policy business rules, there is usually no sense of harsh discipline associated with its violation.

- *Guideline business rules*—unique forms of business rules. In some ways, guideline business rules are non-rule business rules. For example, some corporations set travel restrictions for their employees. A limitation may be placed on hotel expenses. The corporation may state that hotel room expenses may not exceed some set limit. This limit may be perfectly workable in most American cities. However, in larger cities, such as San Francisco, New York, London, and Paris, it may be impossible to find a hotel room for the corporate limit.

When staying in a larger city, the corporation may only require its employees to use their best judgment in spending corporate money. When the limit is exceeded, no managerial review is exercised and the expense report is approved. There are those who take advantage of the situation. Those who break the corporate trust may soon find themselves no longer members of the corporation.

Rules for stating a business rule include:
- Business rules should be explicit in nature so there is no equivocating or wiggle room. An example of this is in the game of Monopoly. GO STRAIGHT TO JAIL. DO NOT PASS GO. DO NOT COLLECT $200. In the business world, a very real business rule is: Do not steal. If you steal, you will be fired and you will be prosecuted.
- Business rules must have some form of enforcement and some sense of punishment for violation. The punishment may range from: *We would prefer you not do that again,* to *Do it and die.*[22] Some examples are: Expense reports must be accompanied with receipts or they will not be paid; Not paying union dues will cause expulsion from the union; and Falsifying expense reports will cause immediate termination.
- Requires a subject and a verb
- Requires an action
- Requires a time frame
- Requires an agent of action
- Must stand a test of reasonableness
- Must be performed somewhere
- Has a life span
- The more the rules stated above are included in the business rule, the more explicit the business rule becomes.
- There is no substitution for explicitness.

Like most aspects of actual design work, working through business rule discovery can be a tiring and complex activity. Most *designers* are completely unprepared to provide the necessary motivational and inspirational leadership. When the going gets tough, the great *designers* step in and provide the emotional backing to encourage continuation. This is part of the leadership requirement for the *designer*.

The *designer* recognizes all must win and feel good about what is being done. Compromise is part of the process of winning. Few like to compromise, so the *designer* must provide the emotional support for those asked to make big compromises. It is not enough for the *designer* to smooth ruffled feathers. The *designer* must make participants believe they played an active part in the design. The new design is basically the participant's idea, and the participant knows and believes this change is for the common good.

The *designer* must provide a winning attitude. If the example set is strong enough, the group adopts it. A good theme might be: If the Egyptians built the pyramids with no technology and only the will to do it, then we can do this.

4.8.1 Overcoming Corporate Fear, Dread, and Loathing

Life would be simpler for the *designer* if corporate staff said, "I don't wanna," when faced with new projects and making change. At least the *designer* would know immediately who would be impeding progress along the way. However, this is not what happens. The first thing the *designer* is faced with is passive aggressive resistance. The resistance is demonstrated in two other ways as well. The first type of resistance is *a condition* and the second type of resistance is *an objection*.

Conditions

Conditions are always caused by the failure to satisfy a business or personal need. A condition may be a showstopper. The conditions deal with understanding the project's value, provision of adequate funding, allocation of time, working relationships, and preparedness:

- Requirement fit is a condition caused when participants do not see or understand the need or value of the new project. Each participant must ask the following question, "Do I understand what needs to be done and does everyone share my understanding?" If the answer is no, progress is hampered severely. It is the *designer's* responsibility to help make sure everyone has a common understanding.

- There is just not enough money to pay for the new project. Often, new projects have major cost justifications. The corporation may not have the upfront capital required to fund the effort. If projects are placed on hold continually because of an inability to fund them, the corporation is potentially signaling a state of financial ill health. When financial health is a major concern, loss of support from customers, vendors, and financial investors is likely. For many corporations, failure to develop new projects leads to an inability to compete in the marketplace.

- How long does it take for a decision to be made, and how long does it take to complete the project? This condition expresses the impact of time on any undertaking. Projects having the best chance of adequate funding and support are projects demanded by senior executives.

- At some point in time, someone may not want to work with you, and you may reciprocate the feeling. Honesty is necessary to face up to relationship problems. Personal dislikes may be expressed as, "I cannot and will not do business with you." Relationship problems are hardly ever expressed, and yet can cause endless discussions and hinder the project. Recognize the condition, understand the condition, and tell management you are not capable of working with or for this individual. Management may not like the news, but it may understand.

- Preparedness is a condition to ensure progress. At the close of every meeting, the facilitator must make sure everyone knows what has to be done next, when the tasks must be done, and who is assigned to the tasks. Follow-up meetings should be scheduled, if appropriate. Failure to be prepared promotes a situation of stagnation and causes the project to grind slowly to a halt.

Most people invest emotional capital in a project, so the quicker these conditions can be identified, the easier it is to deal with the situation. Probably the best advice is: *Hey, it happens, get over it, take a pill, go cry, and move on*. The situation has nothing to do with you, and you should not take this personally—though it is recognized this is very difficult.

Objections

Contrary to popular belief, objections are good. The only time anyone has objections is when there is interest in the project. Objections are easy to overcome when you know how. For example, if the objection is that *it costs too much*, ask the individual, "It costs too much relative to what?" The answer to this question puts the objection in its proper context and will help further the discussion.

Additionally, understanding the individual's personality type can help you address the objection with appropriate language. Successfully overcoming objections ensures the success of the venture. The *designer* needs to make sure the appropriate domain experts or existing documentation is at hand to actively seek a solution to the objection. The reality is that the objection may yield to another compromise in the design.

4.8.2 The Proof Is in the Pudding

If you managed the resistance, worked through all the office politics, learned how to deal with the various personalities, dealt with all the issues of culture, accepted your mandate, handled the agreements and contention, and created a design, you have indeed survived.

Hopefully the final crafted design can be built. It probably took many hours to formulate and probably went through a multitude of iterations to accommodate continuous compromises to move the project forward.

Hopefully all the issues of assumption have been driven out and the design is detailed at an excruciating level. Documenting a design at an excruciating level of detail is not the same thing as analysis paralysis, where the *designer* does not know how to stop the design process. Documenting at an excruciating level of detail prevents reliance on *tribal knowledge*.

In the autobiographical fiction book *Roots*, Alex Haley (1921–1992) wrote, "The old griot had talked for nearly two hours up to then…'Kunta, went away from his village to chop wood and he was never seen again.' I sat as if I were carved of stone. My blood seemed to have congealed. This man whose lifetime had been in this back-country African village had no way in the world to know that he had just echoed what I had heard all through my boyhood years on my grandma's front porch…of an African who always had insisted that his name was 'Kin-tay'; who had called a guitar a 'ko'…"

With high employee turnover and people changing positions constantly within a company, the enterprise can no longer survive on griots (storytellers—the purveyors of tribal knowledge) and retained mental memories to keep the facts communicated and accessible. As Equifax Senior Vice President Mark Satterfield puts it, "We don't know what we don't know, and we surely don't know what we don't document."

During a lecture given at the University of Chicago by psychologist Mihaly Csikszentmihalyi, he commented, "Where do we have control over our lives? It's in the little things. Attending to details gives us immediate reward and increases our confidence to undertake bigger and bigger challenges. Details are the bridges that bring us closer to our best." Details lead to survival—especially excruciating levels of detail.

4.9 CHAPTER ACTIVITIES

4.9.1 Discussion Topics

1. What engineering principles constrain every design, and what can make the seemingly impossible become possible?

2. What were the two principal requirements for the design of the Oxcart project? In order for the *designers* to meet the two principal requirements of the project, only certain materials and fuel could be used. To accommodate the special materials, what engineering compromises had to be made?

3. Explain what is meant by the term industrial psychology.

4. Using the example of the Social Security Act of 1935, discuss the short- and long-term ramifications of design.

5. Why is it helpful for the *designer* to learn the culture of the organization?

6. Discuss why the Chapel of the Holy Cross in Sedona, Arizona is a monument to the compromise of design.

7. Choose three examples from the stages of human life, and compare and contrast them with their corporate counterparts.

8. Compare and contrast the status meeting and the brainstorming meeting, discuss the different preparation required for each.

9. Explain why the designer would not want people with either the eel or the backstabber personality characteristics on a project.

10. Explain the following management terms in the context of measurement: vision, mission, goals, objectives, strategies, and tactics.

11. Compare and contrast the differences between the internal and external influences of an enterprise.

12. Who benefits when the facilitator of a meeting states that there is no such thing as a stupid question?

13. Describe why design is a complicated and complex undertaking that demands attention to detail.

14. Using the analogy of the gentiles, believers, disciples, and cynics, discuss how the *designer's* challenge of rallying people can be aided by how the message is delivered.

15. In what way should the *designer* categorize a list to start a project? What purpose does this serve?

16. Explain why the *designer* needs to allocate resources.

17. Describe how metrics affect a project in relation to assets, process, location, people, events, and motivation.

18. Discuss the principal forces that constrain a design.

19. Using the example of Little League Baseball, explain the meaning of a mandate.

20. List six ways you would use to try to convince your manager that your fuel tank design is acceptable, even if it leaks.

21. Many people feel overwhelmed with responsibilities in enterprises today. Yet Covey's research indicates that less than 20 percent of human talent is being used. Discuss which organizational frame might alleviate these employees' feelings of frustration and why.

22. Explain how sharpening the saw and creating a synergistic organization has helped Fred Keller create a thriving, learning enterprise at Cascade Engineering.

23. Discuss why documentation is becoming critical to the enterprise today.

24. What is the designer's most important function?

25. Discuss why the designer should have a useful knowledge of individuals, teams, and the organization.

4.9.2 Critical Thinking

1. Write a one-page paper explaining the three different definitions of compromise. Provide additional examples of each type of compromise.
2. Write a brief paper to illustrate your interpretation of the phrase—The *designer* must understand the anatomy of the domain, or else become a mere decorator.
3. Using the Internet, find statistics regarding success rates of projects based on size, cost, team sizes, and deliverable functionality.
4. Make arrangements to visit a business in your community and observe the items listed in Section 4.5.2. Look around. Ask someone in the human resources department questions regarding the organization. Be prepared to share your description of this organization's culture with the class.
5. Using the Internet, look up GAAP and FASB to discover the standards set up for accurate reporting in an area of interest to you. In a one to two-page report, explain how these reporting requirements could place significant constraints on a project and the enterprise.
6. Write a short paper explaining how SWOT analysis may help the *designer* deal with politics.
7. Visit the Web site of a company of your choice, and using what you have learned about the use of color and cultures, analyze whether or not colors are being used to their fullest potential.
8. Thinking creatively, how would you redesign a common household appliance such as a DVD player? What features would you like to add and on what would you be willing to compromise?
9. If there are objections to spending time to drive out all areas of assumption and produce documents to excruciating levels of detail during the design process, *who* would be responsible for filling in the gaps and *when* would they fill the gaps? Write a short paper explaining your answer.

Endnotes

[1]Area 51 is a highly secure area for developing exotic aircraft and allegedly housing alien aircraft.

[2]The parts included the wiring, glazing, hydraulic fluids, seals, and the dome-shaped protective housing for radar antennas, called radomes.

[3]Roosevelt, President Franklin. Presidential statement signing the Social Security Act. Washington, D.C., August 14, 1935.

[4]Vilfredo Pareto (1848–1923)

[5]Bremner, Billy. Slogan taken from a popular soccer t-shirt.

[6]The original quote from Bolman and Deal has been adapted to use the word *designer* instead of *managerial*.

[7]Bolman, Lee and Deal, Terrence. *Reframing Organizations*. Jossey-Bass Incorporated. San Francisco, California, 1997.

[8]Ibid.

[9]Headcount refers to employees or temporary staff. Sometimes headcount can be specified as the number of FTEs—full-time employees.

[10]The Franklin Covey Company, headquartered in Salt Lake City, Utah.

[11]Covey, Stephen. *Change and Principle-Centered Leadership for the Twenty-first Century*. Adapted from presentation given at the sixth annual Worldwide Lessons in Leadership Conference. November, 2001.

[12]A journeyman player would be someone who is experienced and competent, but not as distinguished as the premier or impact player.

[13]Big brother is the watchful eye from George Orwell's book, *1984*.

[14]St. George, 1938.

[15]Jastrow, 1897.

[16]Birren, Faber. *Your color and yourself*. Prang Company Publishers, Sandusky, Ohio, 1952.

[17]Guilford, J. and P. Smith. "A system of color-preferences," *The American Journal of Psychology* 73 (4), (1959): 487–502.

[18]A foreign land could be across town, a different city, a different state or region, or a different country.

[19]On October 10, 1920, a case was filed in the Criminal Court of Cook County, Illinois alleging Shoeless Joe Jackson and seven other White Sox baseball players conspired to throw the 1919 World Series against the Cincinnati Reds for cash. Although the players were eventually found not guilty, they were indicted initially by a grand jury. When Jackson departed the grand jury room, a small boy clutched his sleeve and tagged along after him. "Say it ain't so, Joe," he pleaded. "Say it ain't so." "Yes kid, I'm afraid it is," Jackson replied. "Well, I never would've thought it," said the boy.

[20]Characteristics of a type A personality are:

- Always moving, walking, and eating rapidly
- Feeling impatient with the rate at which most events take place
- Striving to think or do two or more things at once
- Inability to cope with leisure time
- Obsession with numbers, measuring success in terms of how many or how much of everything they acquire

Characteristics of a type B personality are:

- Never suffering from a sense of time urgency with its accompanying impatience
- Feeling no need to display or discuss either achievements or accomplishments, unless such exposure is demanded by the situation
- Playing for fun and relaxation, rather than exhibiting superiority at any cost
- Ability to relax without guilt

[21]Radial keratotomy, a procedure involving a radial pattern of incisions used to correct eyesight.

[22]Figuratively speaking

254

TECHNOLOGY
IN COMMERCE

"The ultimate measure of a man is not where he stands in moments of comfort and convenience, but where he stands at times of challenge and controversy."
— *Rev. Dr. Martin Luther King, Jr. (1929–1968), Civil rights leader*

LEARNING OBJECTIVES

After completing Chapter 5, you will be able to:

1. Describe the *builder's* role.
2. Explain why topography is important to the *builder*.
3. List some of the opponents of an organization.
4. Contrast the pros and cons of standards.
5. Describe the supply chain for creating software.
6. Describe components that might be included in a major IT campaign.
7. Compare and contrast leading-edge, bleeding-edge, and trailing-edge technology.
8. Explain why trade-offs are necessary.
9. Understand the impact of legislation.
10. Understand the purpose of a knowledge management system.
11. Explain why time is important to the *builder*.
12. Describe why some corporations embrace technology and why others shy away from it.
13. Recognize the value of a schedule.
14. Identify and discuss the relationships between rules, standards, units of measure, metrics, and statistics.
15. Elucidate the significance of the open-source movement.
16. Understand the *builder's* motivation.
17. Explain why the *builder* is an agent of action.
18. Explain why designs from the *owner*, *designer*, and *builder* should be synchronized to the actual implementation.

5.1 INTRODUCTION

In June of 1812, the French Emperor, Napoleon Bonaparte (1769–1821), began a fatal campaign into Russia. As Bonaparte's troops returned home, they established a landmark in the destructive potential of warfare. Prior to entering Russia, Bonaparte controlled nearly all of continental Europe. He invaded Russia to prevent Russian trade with Great Britain and to force Tsar Alexander I (1777–1825) to submit to the terms of a treaty that Bonaparte had imposed upon the Tsar four years earlier.

Bonaparte amassed over 600,000 soldiers from the vassal states of Europe and France. The French Emperor entered Russia at the head of the largest army ever assembled. The Russians, under the military command of Marshal Mikhail Kutuzov (1745–1813), were not in a position to win through direct confrontation. Kutuzov began a defensive campaign of strategic retreat.

As Kutuzov's troops fell back, they devastated the land and harassed the flanks of the French. As summer wore on, Bonaparte's massive supply lines were stretched thin, and his force began to decline.

By September, without having engaged in a single battle, the French Army had been reduced to less than 200,000 troops. Over 400,000 soldiers were lost due to fatigue, hunger, desertion, and raids by Russian forces.

Despite the significant loss of French manpower, the Russians knew that without engaging in a major battle, Bonaparte would soon be in a position to seize Moscow. The Tsar insisted upon an engagement. On September 7, with the French Army 70 miles from Moscow, the two armies met at Borodino Field.

By nightfall, over 108,000 men had died. Neither side was in a position to declare victory. However, Kutuzov realized further defense of Moscow was useless and withdrew his forces. Kutuzov's action prompted the citizens of Moscow to begin a massive and panicked exodus. When Bonaparte's army arrived on September 14, the city was depopulated and bereft of supplies. That evening, the Russians set Moscow on fire, which meant the French soldiers would not have shelter to provide them with warmth.

Bonaparte waited in vain for Alexander to negotiate and eventually ordered his troops to begin marching home. Kutuzov's forces blocked the route south. The French troops were in no shape for battle and retreated along the devastated route of the invasion.

Having waited until mid-October to depart, the exhausted French army found itself mired in Russian winter. Temperatures dropped below freezing and Russian Cossacks took advantage by attacking stragglers and isolated units. For the French, food was scarce, and the march out of Russia was 500 miles.

In the end, only 10,000 men survived. Nearly 99 percent of the French soldiers did not return. The campaign ensured Bonaparte's downfall and Russia's status as a leading power in post-Napoleonic Europe.

Topography, the detailed and accurate description of a location, place, or region, is one of the major characteristics a *builder* must understand. A *builder* is the person or team that oversees the production of a product or service and ensures that it is built to the specification of the *designer*.

As a *builder*, Napoleon Bonaparte did not understand the topography of his Russian campaign. He could not manage his supply chain to bring the necessary food and other needed supplies for his troops. He was not able to manage the attacks to the flanks. He did not expect the Tsar to hold out on negotiations, nor did he anticipate the Russian winter.

Information technology faces a similar set of problems. The supply chain for creating software starts with obtaining and analyzing requirements. The results of the analysis can be used to create a design. In turn, the design can be passed along to a programmer to create code, which can then be tested, finally implemented, and used. Auxiliary supply chains for delivering pizza, coffee, software licenses, hardware, and networks supplement the primary software supply chain.

Whereas Bonaparte's campaign involved moving thousands of men across hundreds of miles, in IT, a major campaign can involve using limited resources to create hundreds of programs that perform transactions at a high throughput rate, which can recover from a disaster in minutes, rather than days or weeks. **Throughput** is the ability to quantify the movement of electrons from one location to another. Additionally, the IT campaign might need to process thousands of concurrent transactions.

Every war involves opponents. In business, opponents include the competition, government mandates, laws of nature, and technology. Unfortunately, opponents may also include a coworker who exhibits traits such as passive aggressive resistance, or any of the destructive traits discussed in Chapter 4.

Other obstacles to progress are part of the campaign itself. For example, IT campaigns are often slowed by rework in design or software, which is caused by failing to handle something appropriately. Rework can result from inadequate requirements, a poor design choice, incorrect coding, or undetected bugs. At moments of crisis, an IT campaign feels like a city set on fire, and the devastation can sometimes cause the project to be terminated—no food, no shelter, and maybe no job.

Just as Napoleon should have appreciated the topography of Russia more thoroughly, a *builder* in an IT project must thoroughly understand the topography of the project. The *builder's* responsibility is to plan appropriately for the implementation environment—the battlefield. The *builder* must assemble the right tools and people. The *builder* must work with the *designer*, when necessary, to adjust the design to accommodate the topography.

The *builder* must be familiar with all internal and external standards related to implementation. Standards are set to ensure compliance with certain required or necessary actions; without them, you risk project failure. When *builders* and their teams follow standards, their campaigns are usually successful. However, standards occasionally get in the way.

5.1.1 The Wheels of Progress

The Space Shuttle is one of the world's most advanced transportation systems. Many people can picture the shuttle sitting on the launchpad at Cape Canaveral, pointing straight up to the sky, strapped tightly to the twin solid rocket boosters and main fuel tank.

The solid rocket boosters are made by Thiokol in its Utah factory. The engineers at Thiokol comply with many standards when they build the rocket boosters. One consideration for *builders* is transporting the boosters to NASA's compound. The preferred method is by means of train, along a railroad line that runs from the factory through the Rockies. The boosters have to fit in the tunnels to be transported successfully.

A railroad gauge is the width between two rails. In the United States, the 1864 Union Pacific legislation enacted a standard railroad gauge of 4 feet 8½ inches. According to folklore, the British were responsible for this irregular standard. The U.S. railroad gauge is based on the width used in England, and many English expatriates built the U.S. railroads in the 1800s.

What prompted the English to use this particular gauge? The British industrialists who built the first railroad lines and the pre-railroad tramways used the same gauge. The tramways used the same jigs and tools used in building horse-drawn wagons. The wagons used the same gauge for wheel spacing.

Many old long-distance roads in England had wheel ruts, and wagon wheels were spaced to fit the ruts and therefore not break. Romans built these roads nearly 2,000 years ago for their legions. The Roman war chariots formed the ruts. The Roman chariot was just wide enough to accommodate two horses. See Figure 5-1.

| Figure 5-1 | *Some standards have lasting effects* |

In the United States, the standard railroad gauge is derived from the original specification for an Imperial Roman war chariot. The solid rocket boosters, a major design element for the Space Shuttle, were limited in width because of the rear girth of two Roman horses.

The gauge of U.S. railroads, despite being based on an obsolete technology, is a crucial detail in building the Space Shuttle and the International Space Station. Topography greatly affects the Space Shuttle project and requires *builders* to form and use many rules, standards, units of measure, metrics, and statistics for the 16-nation collaboration.

5.1.2 What Do You Mean, Did We Bring a Spare One?

In the early 1950s, German-born rocket pioneer Wernher von Braun (1912–1977) visualized building a 250-foot wide inflatable wheel reinforced with nylon to orbit over 1,000 miles above the Earth. He was convinced the wheel could provide a number of key uses, including navigational aid, meteorological station, military platform, and way station for space exploration.

In 1952, von Braun was technical director of the Army Ordnance Guided Missiles Development Group, and he later became NASA's director at the Marshall Space Flight Center. Von Braun's space station was designed to spin like a ferris wheel. The spin would create a centrifugal force and provide a false gravity on the space station. Inside the wheel, von Braun imagined three decks providing room for navigational equipment, communication equipment, an earth observatory, military command center, weather forecasting facilities, living quarters, and mercury-vapor generating turbines to power it all.

In the second century, Greek rhetorician Lucian (117–180) wrote fantasies about traveling into space in his account of a voyage to the moon. Fictional accounts of space stations appeared as early as 1869, when Edward Hale (1822–1909) published *The Brick Moon*. Hale described a manned satellite functioning as a navigational aide to ships at sea. During the Apollo era, Stanley Kubrick (1928–1999) popularized space stations in the movie *2001: A Space Odyssey*. The friendly HAL 9000[1] computer and his best friend Dave incited thoughts of a new society and the roles a sophisticated computer could play.

Had von Braun lived long enough, he would have been happy to see the International Space Station become a reality. The space station is not a weapon of war, as von Braun feared, but a cooperative effort of 16 nations, including the United States and Russia.

Here on Earth, dwellings provide shelter from the elements—wind, rain, heat, and cold. A home in Earth's orbit must shield occupants from solar winds and be capable of withstanding the steady rains of fast-moving, dust-sized meteoroids. A terrestrial house is normally insulated to keep the air inside cool or warm to suit its occupants. A major feature of a space home is keeping the air confined to the inside. A space home must be completely sealed.

At sea level, earthly structures support a constant gravitational pull of 1g.[2] In contrast, an orbiting structure must work in a 0g environment, and its components must withstand a 3g pull when launched out of Earth's atmosphere. A 3g pull means each component weighs three times its normal weight, placing a significant stress on each component. The environment and topography for building a structure for living in space pose a different set of challenges than building a home on Earth.

In Earth's orbit, a free-falling space home can take on a wider variety of shapes. Because of the free fall and absence of gravity, architecture and structures have no *this side up* to provide orientation. In the early part of the twenty-first century, the space station resembles an erector set more than von Braun's ferris wheel. Although von Braun's wheel concept was elegant, the design was constrained by the payload bays of current launch vehicles—NASA's space shuttles. Engineers had to contend with how to get the pieces on board the shuttle, and once in space, how to assemble the pieces into a unified body.

Modern terrestrial homes are typically built from plywood, strips of two-by-four pinewood (a standard set by the Levitts), dry wall, and a facade of brick, stone, stucco, or vinyl. Common materials in the space station are titanium, Kevlar, and high-grade steel. These materials make the structure lightweight, strong, and puncture resistant. Lightweight aluminum forms most of the outer shell.

The shell provides protection from high-speed impacts by tiny meteoroids and man-made debris. The space station travels through space at 27,000 kilometers per hour, and so even dust-sized grains present a considerable danger. Man-made debris, a drifting legacy of past space exploration, also poses a threat to the shell.

To ensure the crew's safety, the space station dons a bulletproof vest. Layers of Kevlar, ceramic fabrics, and other advanced materials form a blanket 10 centimeters thick around each component's aluminum shell. On Earth, police officers wear bulletproof vests made of Kevlar. The space station's protective shielding was tested by shooting high-velocity guns at it.

A typical window for a house on Earth has two panes of glass, each about $\frac{1}{16}$ inches thick. The space station windows use four panes of glass up to $1\frac{1}{4}$ inches thick. An exterior aluminum shutter provides extra protection when the windows are not in use. The glass is subject to strict quality control. Even minute flaws increase the chance of a fracture caused by a micrometeoroid.

The air pressure inside and outside of terrestrial homes is balanced. In the vacuum of space, no external forces press down on the building. However, the air inside the space station produces 15 pounds per square inch of pressure, with nothing on the exterior of the space station to balance the pressure. The structure of the components must handle both the 3g pull and the internal air pressure while in orbit.

A common berthing mechanism links the components. To ensure a good seal, the mechanism uses an automatic latch to pull together the components and tightens the latch with 16 connecting bolts with a force of 19,000 pounds each. The huge force ensures an airtight seal and keeps the internal air pressure from driving apart the components.

Without thermal controls, the temperature of an orbiting space station would soar to 250°F on the side facing the sun, while the other side would plunge to minus 250°F. The first design consideration for thermal control is insulation— keeping heat in for warmth and out for cooling.

On Earth, heat is transferred primarily by colliding air molecules and circular motions. These effects are known as conduction and convection, respectively. Space has no air for conduction or convection, but is dominated by radiation. Objects heat up by absorbing sunlight and cool off by emitting infrared energy, a form of radiation invisible to the human eye. As a result, insulation for the space station does not use the common fluffy mat of pink fibers. Instead, the station uses a highly reflective blanket made of aluminized Mylar, Dacron, and Kapton.

The insulation on the space station can prevent penetration of both solar radiation and bitter cold. The insulation works so well that it caused another problem for the engineers—controlling the internal temperature, which is always on the rise inside the insulated space station because of all the heat-producing instruments. So, in part, the very computers used to control the heat are also causing the heat.

On the space station, cold plates and heat exchangers are cooled by circulating water loops that remove excess heat. Air and water heat exchangers cool and dehumidify the internal atmosphere. Custom-built cold plates are attached to high-heat generating equipment.

Waste heat is exchanged via pipes containing ammonia. At standard atmospheric pressure, water freezes at 32°F. Ammonia freezes at minus 107°F. The heated ammonia circulates through huge radiators located on the exterior of the space station, releasing the heat as infrared radiation and cooling as it flows.

Environmental and life support systems control air quality and flow. In the 0g environment of outer space, hot air does not rise and cold air does not fall. Proper air circulation prevents cold spots that could produce condensation, electrical shocks, serious corrosion, and microbial growth. The Russian space station Mir had large corrosive fungi problems in the 1980s until its demise in 2001.

The space station has its own water treatment system, producing a higher level of cleanliness than our municipal systems on Earth. The space station recycles urine from the crew and laboratory animals and returns it to the drinking water supply, which is tested regularly.

The collective network of tubing and hardware for managing waste and supplying water and air is highly dependable, compact, lightweight, corrosion resistant, leak resistant, and microbe resistant. Titanium, stainless steel, and Teflon wrapped in metal mesh are materials used for the tubing. By comparison, household plumbing is typically made of inexpensive PVC[3] and copper.

On the space station, the toilets use sucking mechanisms to keep body waste away from the astronauts. On Earth, gravity or pressure from city water supplies creates flows in pipes. In outer space, liquids and gases stagnate on their own. The space station's plumbing system has dozens of pumps and fans to create pressure, coaxing liquids and gases into action.

Extreme conditions tend to be defined by environment and topography. Building and using a *house* in space require a different approach, a different set of tools, and different designs than building a house on Earth. When Bonaparte took on Russia, he was experienced in warfare, but did not adapt his experience to the new topography. He did not account for the environmental and topographical differences associated with Russia.

A small business like Movie Outpost may be able to use commercial software products, such as Intuit Quicken or Quick Books, to pay and keep track of bills. However, Cascade Engineering, Keane, Disney, Equifax, and Coca-Cola cannot use the same products. These companies still need to accomplish the same general processes that Intuit offers, but Intuit software cannot expand to provide the flexibility demanded by these larger companies. Even Intuit is too big to use Intuit software; instead it uses Oracle Financials.

Methods used to build simple software solutions are often different from those required to build complex software solutions. The complexity of a computer system is the result of its environment and topography, or **topology**.

Unlike *designers*, *builders* must anticipate and accommodate everything about the implementation environment and its topography. Recall from Chapter 2 that Cascade Engineering makes the dashmats for the Dodge Neon. Every Dodge Neon is built from the same design and uses the same dashmats. The *builder*, however, must account for the hundreds of environments in which a dashmat might be used.

For example, in cold-weather states, such as Minnesota, the grade of oil used in car engines is different from the grade used in Florida. California cars are equipped with different catalytic converters from the rest of the country. In Denver, the grade of octane in the fuel can be reduced because of the high altitude. Depending on how the car is driven, the driver may choose to use a different air pressure in the tires to achieve the *feel* the driver wants. The car must ride smoothly for the elderly grandmother from Texas, who never exceeds 40 mph, and the youth in Montana, who has a need to keep the needle on the RPM gauge pinned against the redline. In each environment, the car must perform.

The *builder* must make sure the product is usable under all expected conditions. On September 11, 2001, as news spread of the attacks on the World Trade Center and the Pentagon, millions of people turned to the Internet to find out the latest news. Using their browser of choice, people turned to Web sites such as CNN, MSNBC, BBC, and The New York Times. The systems choked on the public's demand for information. They could not respond. By mid-afternoon, each news site had reformatted its Web pages to exclude graphics in order to try to serve information to the stunned public.

One condition that *builders* of computer systems must consider is bandwidth, though bandwidth fluctuates from one network to another. The ability to **scale**, maximize throughput, process concurrent transactions, and recover from a failure are critical in complex computer solutions.

Equifax receives over 2.5 billion transactions a month, reflecting the spending and borrowing habits of the American population. Equifax has to process nearly 1,000 transactions per second for every second of the month.

Besides manipulating financial data and responding to commercial and consumer requests, Equifax spends time maintaining machines, applying fixes, backing up systems, and recovering from bad client data. If these auxiliary tasks take too much time, Equifax must process transactions faster than 1,000 transactions per second. In addition to handling this volume of data, Equifax must also accommodate all the processes that support a computer system.

Suppose each transaction coming into Equifax consumes 500 bytes of storage. Over the course of one month, the system requires 1,250,000,000,000 bytes (1.25 terabytes) of storage. Over the course of one year, that requirement amounts to 15,000,000,000,000 bytes (15 terabytes). If the system kept the information for seven years, that would equal 105,000,000,000,000 bytes (105 terabytes). One hundred and five terabytes is the equivalent of 5,250 20-gigabyte hard drives in a laptop computer. This amount of space does not include storage for indexes, unusable disk space, mirrored images, backup images, and archived images.

This is one system. Equifax has hundreds of systems. Managing this volume of information involves a unique set of issues, disciplines, and state-of-the-art storage techniques.

Prior to September 11, 2001, computer service companies would be asked if they had a disaster recovery plan. A simple answer of *yes* was usually satisfactory. Today, companies are asked "Can you fully recover from a disaster in 20 minutes, and can you prove it?"

Whether building the International Space Station, going off to war, or building a computer system, extreme operating conditions make the *builder's* decisions critical, including appropriate tool selection, design, building techniques, quality control, standards, metrics, measurements, and statistics.

Complex software solutions are becoming the norm for business and government computing. The environment, topography, and topology are domains of the modern *builder*. In other words, the *builder* must understand everything about where the product or service will be produced and used. The *builder* is an **agent of action** and plays a pivotal role between the *designer* and the *subcontractor*. An agent of action has three areas of authority and responsibility:

- Establishing an environment conducive to creating business transactions
- Giving permission to conduct business transactions
- Ensuring ongoing performance and viability of business transactions

SECTION 5.2 WHEN EVERYTHING LOOKS LIKE A NAIL

QUESTIONS TO CONTEMPLATE

1. What is meant by the concept of a hammer?
2. How do initial business events shape a solution?
3. Why should you design for the lowest common denominator?

5.2.1 Introduction

In 1961, President John Kennedy set a mandate and a goal for the American people. Kennedy's vision was to land a man on the moon before the end of the decade. On July 20, 1969, two men, Neil Armstrong and Buzz Aldrin, along with the efforts of thousands of people on Earth realized the assassinated President's vision.

Kennedy, a veteran naval officer from World War II, knew his vision was realistic even though nobody knew how it could be accomplished. By the time he became President, Kennedy was familiar with the intelligence, dedication, and work ethic of the American people and America's new economic growth. The Second World War stamped out the major forces of Nazism and fascism and catapulted the United States into a position of responsibility, transforming American life.

World War II's returning veterans survived the trauma of war and witnessed the death of friends and comrades in battle. Back in America, veterans wanted comfortable places to live and good jobs, which were both guaranteed by the GI Bill of Rights, one of the most important pieces of legislation passed in the United States.

William Levitt, with his father and brother, built Levittown and almost single-handedly passed the GI Bill through bribery, hectoring, and political force. The Levitts wanted to get rich by building and selling houses. William Levitt proposed that the GI Bill accommodate both housing and education. Legislators recognized the financial benefits the bill would offer to the Levitts, but they also wanted a bill that would provide education for veterans.

President Harry Truman is credited for the bill because it was passed during his term in office. Truman, a veteran of World War I, knew firsthand what it was like returning to America from a war. America went through boom times in the 1920s, only to have the economic bottom fall out by the end of the decade.

Truman believed that a weak educational infrastructure contributed to the stock market crash and the subsequent Great Depression. Adamant to prevent a reoccurrence of history, Truman believed that ignoring the lessons of history doomed the future to past mistakes. With help from Levitt, the President received support from Democrats and Republicans for the bill, and legislation passed quickly.

The GI Bill had far-reaching effects that no one envisioned, costing American taxpayers nearly $15 billion. It enabled millions of veterans to receive post secondary degrees and purchase their own homes. The American economy received the boost it needed within the first five years of the GI Bill becoming law.

Management expert Peter Drucker points to the implementation of the GI Bill as the start of the knowledge economy in America. Massachusetts Senator Edward Kennedy (b. 1932), in an address at Worcester State College on November 19, 1997, stated, "The economic payoff from the GI Bill has been remarkable. For every dollar invested, the nation received over twelve dollars in higher economic growth and greater revenues." Dr. Constantine Curris, president of the American Association of State Colleges and Universities, believed the amount the nation received might be higher.

The proverb, *If all you have is a hammer, everything looks like a nail*, is a statement of limitation. The veterans of World War II understood this limitation and helped reinvent the hammer—not an actual hammer, but the concept of a hammer stated in the proverb. A hammer is a very good tool for bashing a nail into something. However, if a hammer is the only tool in your toolbox, you have to treat everything like a nail because a hammer is generally limited to hitting something. The hammer in the proverb refers to having only one tool in your toolbox and using that one tool to address all your problems.

In the context of software, the hammer is sometimes called a golden hammer, which refers to a familiar technology or concept that is applied to many types of software problems. The solution to the problem involves expanding the knowledge of each *builder* through education, training, and study groups. Education exposes *builders* to alternative technologies and approaches and improves their overall knowledge. Examples of hammers include: fixed ways that individuals think about solving any type of problem, fixed procedures used to solve any type of problem, fixed techniques, or the use of a single programming language.

University of California, Berkeley Professor Thomas Kuhn (1922–1996) observed what was happening in America during the 1950s and published *The Structure of Scientific Revolution* in 1962. In his book, Kuhn defined the concept of a **paradigm shift**. Kuhn argued that scientific advancement is not evolutionary, but a "series of peaceful interludes punctuated by intellectually violent revolutions." In those revolutions, "one conceptual worldview is replaced by another."

A paradigm shift is a change from one way of thinking to another. It is a revolution, transformation, and metamorphosis. Agents of change drive paradigm shifts. The graduated veterans of World War II became the agents of change in the 1950s and 1960s. The *builder* is the **agent of change** in today's organizations.

5.2.2 Pulling the Trigger *(when)*

All business events have an initial starting action known as a **trigger**. The *builder's* trigger is a mandate received from the *designer* to begin a project. Generally, *builders* develop a preferred approach to a project. This preferred approach is likely to become the *builder's* hammer. The hammer may eventually limit the *builder's* ability to complete new projects successfully. For example, *builders* may start an IT project by constructing or configuring the following parts of a project:

- Application
- Business
- Database
- Hardware environment
- Telecommunications environment

To construct these parts, *builders* rely on their experience, general knowledge, business knowledge, IT knowledge, and organizational knowledge. This knowledge forms the *builder's* paradigm—the model he usually follows to create a solution. However, over relying on what he already knows can become a bias that constrains the *builder's* approach to a project—the hammer. The constraints become the *builder's* only tool—the hammer that makes everything look like a nail. In other words, the *builder's* bias may prevent him from using a new approach or technology.

The *builder* must construct the business events that start the processes of the enterprise. Each event usually starts another event in a measurable time frame and in an ordered sequence. Business events have triggers, sequences, and duration, and they establish the life cycle. The trigger, sequence, time frame, and duration contribute to creating business rules, defining units of measure, and establishing meaningful measurements and the context for statistics.

If the *builder's* hammer decrees that the first event or trigger of the business is to enter information into a system through a user interface, then all succeeding events are forced to comply. Once a *stake has been placed in the ground*, the *builder* has difficulty thinking of the problem in any other way. If any other event might be more important, or should occur before the data entry, the *builder* is unable to see this.

5.2.3 The Lowest Common Denominator *(who)*

A pioneer of pharmaceutical medicine, Dr. Wallace Abbott (1858–1921), began producing dosimetric granules in his North Side Chicago apartment in 1888. Based on the superior medical results achieved in his practice, he decided to take his business to his fellow physicians. He paid 25 cents to advertise in a publication called *Medical World*. The advertisement brought in $8 worth of business, and The Abbott Alkaloidal Company was born. In 1915, the company changed its name to Abbott Laboratories.

Since its origins, Abbott Laboratories has evolved into a diversified healthcare company that discovers, develops, manufactures, and markets leading-edge products and services. Abbott Laboratories now posts annual revenues exceeding $16 billion and has operations and offices throughout the world.

In the late 1980s, the Abbott's IT department received a $4 million budget and a mandate to redesign an order entry and inventory system within 18 months. Using the latest development technologies, including Texas Instruments' IEF case tool, the CIO was positive he could redesign the system on time.

All the software was written in 14 months and had a cost overrun of *only* $500,000. During beta testing, which allowed Abbott's IT department to pre-test the software with selected users, the users thought the system ran too slowly. IT responded by **denormalizing** the database design, which means that the same data may often appear more than once within the database. Users perceived that the new database design was faster, but not fast enough. Therefore, IT redesigned the process model to better match the new database design. The database denormalization initiative and code reconstruction added another $300,000 to the project, which was now in the twentieth month of development.

At this point, the users were happy with the system's performance, but complained the design was not task oriented—it did not reflect the tasks they typically performed. The IT department wanted to know why the users had not mentioned the problem before. "We tried to tell you twice before, but you would not listen," barked the users.

Despite being $800,000 over budget and two months late, Abbott's managers decided to continue, and the IT department went back to the drawing board. The user interface, reports, database, and application were redesigned and recoded. Almost one year and $1 million later, the system passed beta test and was ready to be implemented.

Abbott's Los Angeles office was selected as the first site for the new order entry and inventory system. Fulfilling a commitment to create entry-level jobs, Abbott Laboratories hired many order entry clerks who had less than a tenth grade education. The clerks could not use the user interface or pronounce the names of the products. They could not understand or read the commitment waivers, nor could they understand the concept of a controlled substance or a product shelf life.

In addition, the tasks the Los Angeles workers performed were different from the tasks performed by the test users. Tasks users performed in Los Angeles were different from those performed by the beta testers, and the level of expectation of performance was lower. The managers at the Los Angeles office asked the IT department to change the system to accommodate their needs.

After spending $6 million and three years working on a project, Abbott Laboratories still did not have a system. The system was reengineered and each work process was **normalized**, which means that the same work process was not duplicated elsewhere. The entire IT effort was restarted.

Failing to understand the topography of the corporation and to address the lowest common denominator (the weakest employee) sabotaged the system. Many systems have to be designed using the lowest common denominator principle. The system must first be built effectively for all users; after basic users' needs have been met, design features for advanced or power users can be addressed.

When a *builder* lacks knowledge and firsthand experience with a business problem, the hammer sees the nail (the problem to be addressed) as a past experience and treats the problem using previous ideas and techniques. Regardless of the information provided by the users for a system's requirements, an IT *builder* must spend at least several days in the field before designing a project.

5.2.4 Boy, You're Gonna Carry that Weight *(what)*

Every mistake built into the enterprise and IT systems adds costs to the operation of the business. The costs are weight.

The trigger for *A Christmas Carol*[4] is Jacob Marley's ghost warning his former partner, Scrooge, of his fate if he did not change. The novel begins, "Marley was dead: to begin with. There is no doubt whatever about that." Marley's apparition is bound with huge chains, of which Marley said, "I wear the chain I forged in life, I made it link by link, and yard by yard." Marley continues to say of Scrooge's chain, "or would you know, the weight and length of the strong coil you bear yourself? It was full as heavy and as long as this, seven Christmas Eves ago. You have labored on it, since. It is a ponderous chain!"

The *builder* forges heavy chains based on the errors and implicit assumptions built into the *builder's* mandate from the *designer*. In IT, the heavy chains are often exposed as legacy applications. Each error, no matter how small, becomes a link in the weight of the chain. Each error adds costs. Each cost increases the weight of the chain and thereby decreases the usability and flexibility of the legacy application.

The quality of stored data contributes to the problem of accuracy in the business. Data must be permanent, accurate, immutable, secure, and legible. IT systems rely on the computer network to ensure security. Accidental deletions, power surges, electrical storms, foreign objects on a disk, and internal or external sabotage may compromise electronic media. Backup and recovery systems are a major concern.

Companies such as Equifax observe that over 20 percent of working Americans change their addresses each year. Companies that keep names and addresses for marketing purposes witness rapid decay in the accuracy of data. Data decay also occurs because corporations change the meaning of historical data over time. Although data is permanent, its accuracy is not. The IT data hammer (data management) is weak and does not always do the job well. The IT data hammer adds great weight to the chain. The IT chain is a ponderous chain.

5.2.5 Build versus Buy *(how)*

Typically, corporations have policies for acquiring new applications. For example, a policy might be one of the following:

- Purchase commercial-off-the-shelf (COTS) software products that can be used as turnkey solutions
- Purchase COTS software products that can be customized
- Create custom software
- Use a combination of COTS and custom software, depending on the circumstance and cost

Decisions regarding software creation and selection require flexibility. Without flexibility, the policy becomes the paradigm and the paradigm becomes the hammer. The purpose of a policy is to provide a general statement of guidance. If the policy is used as a mandated rule and is never wavered, the policy acts as a force of limitation to the enterprise. When the *builder* is forced to comply with a policy, such as only purchasing turnkey COTS software, options for building may become limited. COTS software may restrict the flexibility of the business and prevent the *builder* from seeking creative solutions.

A REASON FOR COTS

Enterprises often use COTS software to adopt a business model that has been tried and tested—potentially minimizing risk and elevating quality. Gary Hamel, author of *Leading the Revolution*, states, "All too often a successful new business model becomes the business model for companies not creative enough to invent their own."

The fastest way to put together a jigsaw puzzle is to look at the picture on the box, find all the straight-edged pieces, and fit them together. The outer boundary of the puzzle then becomes clear. IT policies are like jigsaw puzzles. Organizations usually have some idea of the scope (the size of the jigsaw puzzle) and the boundaries (the outer limits of the jigsaw puzzle) of the project domain.

The difficult part of solving the puzzle comes next. Expert puzzle solvers assemble the pieces by color. The puzzle solvers then find pieces that connect to each other within the color and build small sections. Soon one small section fits to another and so on, until the total puzzle is completed. See Figure 5-2.

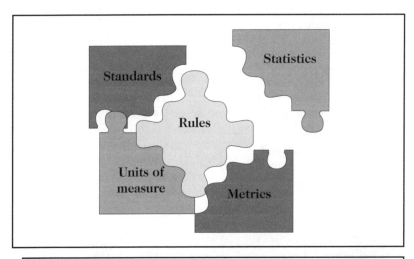

Figure 5-2   *Most enterprises are puzzles*

A policy that supports the goals and objectives of an organization provides guidance and a metaphorical picture of how to proceed. However, inflexible policies may or may not support the goals and objectives of an organization. An inflexible policy assumes the *builder* can figure out and assemble the puzzle with no picture on the box for guidance. The *designer* knows the colors for small-section construction and essentially provides the straight-edged pieces. Restrictive policies inhibit the *builder* from finding creative ways to solve the puzzle and can adversely affect construction.

5.2.6 Nothing but Net *(where)*

The nets (Internet, intranet, and extranet) are the new hammers of IT. Many recent IT policies require the use of net technologies for new or enhanced business applications. The policy has become: "If it is new, build it on the net." And, "If it needs to be fixed, fix it on the net."

However, this net-based policy can create problems for the enterprise. Because security can be a weak link on the computer network, nets increase the chance of liability to the corporation. Both eBay and Amazon.com have stated publicly in their SEC filings that their Internet systems are vulnerable to attacks by hackers. See Section 3.1.3. Both have reported hacker attacks and cannot guarantee the prevention of future attacks. SEC reports did nothing to reassure investors of these corporations' ability to survive in the future.

Amazon's and eBay's experiences underscore the importance of secure networks, which are part of an enterprise's topology. Topology can be characterized by a physical location, or a virtual location through the use of a computer network. The complexity or difficulty of the terrain increases the level of risk to a project. If not secured properly, net-enabled applications become like a bank with unlocked vault doors.

269

5.2.7 Hack *(why)*

An internal IBM paper[5] highlighted the impact of change on computer systems for Fortune 500 companies. Interviews with 108 chief executive, financial, and information officers revealed that more than 60 percent of their IT budgets were reserved for the maintenance of legacy systems. The paper also reported the following results:

- Sixty percent of the user interfaces did not match the work flow of the user, or were not task oriented, and required the user to do extra work to fulfill the requirements of the system.
- Eighty percent of the distributed reports were either not used, or not used for their intended purposes.
- Thirty percent of the reports were used to extract data for re-entry into systems not maintained by IT.
- The accounting department submitted the most requests for new reports and new systems.
- The sales department requested the least amount of reports and new systems.
- Users did not know how to uninstall a report once it was implemented.

The migration to the Internet is based on the idea of opening the enterprise to allow anyone anywhere to access information and conduct business. Current industry trends indicate that more companies are moving legacy systems to the Internet. New systems designed for the Internet have done little to relieve design problems experienced by systems of the early 1990s.

IT has brought the relief hammer to the Internet environment. Relief fixes simply try to satisfy user demand and provide only short-term solutions. The relief fix acts only to soothe an irritation; it does not cure the problem. The relief fix often makes the problem worse as time goes by.

Maintenance may become a nightmare after the relief fix has been applied. The relief fix is a cheap hammer that soon becomes more expensive to maintain. Adequate documentation is not usually part of the relief fix. The *builder* usually asks: *What did they do and why did they do this?* See Figure 5-3.

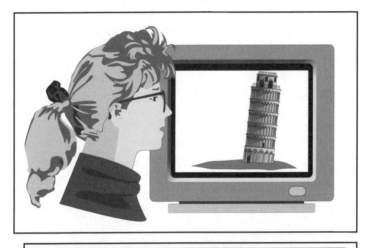

Figure 5-3   *What were those guys thinking about?*

IT often tries to build permanence into its systems. The concept of a permanent solution is as unacceptable as the idea of a relief fix to solve a problem. Time and experience have demonstrated both are unacceptable practices. Nothing is permanent.

Everything in nature erodes or dies over time. Every man-made creation either crumbles or becomes obsolete. The conceptual ideas of engineering and science will outlast anything made using those sciences. The laws of physics predict decay.

5.2.8 Key Terms

agent of action
agent of change
denormalizing
normalized
paradigm shift

throughput
topography
topology
trigger

5.2.9 Review Questions

1. Name three potential opponents of an organization.
2. What consequences can the *builder's* hammer have on the success of a new project?
3. Explain the meaning of a paradigm shift, according to Dr. Thomas Kuhn.
4. What is meant by the term knowledge economy?

5. Who is the agent of change in today's organizations?
6. What are some items that limit the *builder's* approach to a project?
7. Give an example of a business event, constructed by the *builder*, that starts the processes of the enterprise.
8. Explain what is meant by the lowest common denominator principle.
9. What are the *builder's* chains and how can they affect a project?
10. What problems are created for the *builder* when he is required to comply with a policy, such as being allowed to purchase only COTS software?
11. What extra precautions must be taken into consideration when working with Internet-enabled applications?
12. What makes relief fixes unacceptable?
13. Why is there no such thing as a permanent solution?

SECTION 5.3 WHAT ARE WE TO BUILD— RULES, STANDARDS, UNITS OF MEASURE, METRICS, AND STATISTICS

QUESTIONS TO CONTEMPLATE

1. What is the necessary interrogative for creating a measurement?
2. Are legislative mandates a burden or a help for managing an enterprise?
3. How are standards, units of measure, metrics, and statistics related?

5.3.1 Introduction

People measure everything, such as ambient temperature, the amount they drink, and the appeal of each person they saw today. Measurements are matters of survival, competition, and law. However, exercising the ability to measure is optional.

People interpret measurements based on experience, language, and culture. For example, an American identifies 24°F as cold because in his experience, an air temperature of 24°F has been cold. If he is not familiar with the Celsius temperature scale, he might also identify 24° Celsius as cold, though he has no experience with this particular scale. Measurements may be pushed through our emotional filters and influenced by our general attitudes.

Shared culture, language, and experience affect our understanding. More concrete objects are also subject to interpretation. Consider the following items:

- One bowl of rice
- An automobile
- A loaf of bread

What size is the bowl? What temperature is the rice? How many people is the rice expected to feed? What color is the rice? Chances are, as soon as you read *one bowl of rice*, you established a mental picture based on your personal experiences, culture, and emotional filters. A similar mental process would have occurred for the automobile and loaf of bread.

- One ounce of dried rice cooked and served with fresh tofu at the Lucky Dragon Chinese restaurant in downtown Schererville, Indiana
- A 1956 two-door Chevrolet Belair with a V8 engine and white-walled tires at an antique car show in Austin, Texas
- A large loaf of Jewish Rye bread without seeds, sliced and purchased at Adelman's Kosher Delicatessen and Restaurant in Brooklyn, New York

The additional details in these statements add to their emotional meaning. A person can now measure and compare the items. The following list identifies items that are routinely measured objectively. Portions of each statement are correlated to an interrogative. The more interrogatives that are correlated to the statement, the clearer the statement becomes:

- 90 minutes in a professional soccer game
  90 minutes (*when*—duration)
  Professional soccer game (*what*—type of sport)

- $2,000 subtracted from annual salary and invested in a 401(k) retirement account
  $2,000 and a 401(k) retirement account (*what*—monetary assets)
  Annual (*when*—duration)
  Invested (*why*—motivation)

- Two hours at 60 miles per hour to get to Hernando's Hideaway for Uncle Jake's birthday party
  Two hours (*when*—duration)
  60 miles per hour (*when*—speed)
  Hernando's Hideaway (*where*—location)
  Uncle Jake's birthday party (*what*—type of social gathering)

- Two men working four hours, using shovels, to dig a hole 3 feet wide by 6 feet deep by 6 feet long to be finished by 3 p.m. tomorrow for the interment of John Doe's remains in a casket at Camp Chase Confederate Cemetery in Columbus, Ohio, plot number 2255A, for $700
  Two men (*who*—manpower required)
  Four hours (*when*—duration)
  Dig a hole (*how*—process)
  3 p.m. tomorrow (*when*—schedule)
  Interment of the casket (*why*—motivation)
  Camp Chase Confederate Cemetery (*where*—location)
  Plot number 2255A (*where*—location)
  $700 (*what*—monetary fee)

These examples are objective and explicit. Each example includes *time* as part of the *measurement*, which is *essential to any objective measurement*. Each list combines two or more interrogatives. In the first example of a soccer game, two interrogatives were specified, so further meaning is left implicit. The last example of digging a cemetery plot addresses every interrogative (*what, how, where, who, when,* and *why*).

The examples in this chapter have left implicit the understanding of rules, standards, units of measure, metrics, and statistics. A shared understanding of these five things makes each example clear. For instance, we have a common understanding of a unit of time.

Time is measured in seconds. See Figure 5-4. Seconds combine or divide into minutes, hours, days, weeks, months, years, or fractional units such as microseconds and nanoseconds. The concept of an appointment or schedule is usually well understood. Without a shared standard and the rules that govern the standard, measurement would be impossible. Standards clarify how we think about comparisons, **rules of use**, and communication essentials.

The Ancient Egyptians created the 24-hour day. Each day consisted of 10 hours of daylight, 2 hours of twilight, and 12 hours of night. An early definition for one second was 1/86,400 of a 24-hour day.

In 1956, the Comité International des Poids et Mesures defined one second as 1/31556925.9747 of the tropical year for 1900 January 0 at 12h ephemeris time.

In 1967, the thirteenth Conférence Générale des Poid et Mesures defined one second as 9192631770 periods of the radiation corresponding to the transition between the two hyperfine levels of the ground state of the casium 133 atom.

 John Harrison's H4 chronometer weighs 1.45 kg and is 13 cm in diameter. Harrison's son William used the H4 to set sail for the West Indies on November 18, 1761. Arriving in Jamaica on January 19, 1762, the watch was found to be only 5.1 seconds slow. The H4's timekeeping was good enough to win the Board of Longitude's longitude prize.

Figure 5-4   *Rules of time*

ELEMENTS OF A RULE OF USE

- How the *element* will be used
- Where the *element* will be used
- Who the *element* will be used by
- When the *element* will be used
- Why the *element* was established

Examples of the *element* for a rule of use include standards, units of measure, metrics, and statistics, i.e., how the metric *element* will be used.

Once you measure, you need and want to remember. Recollection is achieved in a variety of manners.

IT'S FUNNY YOU SAY THAT; I'D FORGOTTEN ALL ABOUT IT

Tribal lore is a long-running historical narrative handed down from generation to generation. Without a written language and writing system, only verbal communication keeps history alive, including myths of creation, faith, and hope. Tribal lore is used to establish a sense of knowing and being. Tribal lore also gives perspective to current situations and troubles.

Ancient Egyptians invented a writing system using papyrus, brushes, and ink. The techniques of engraving on stone and clay gave way to writing on scrolls of paper. Scrolls gave way to books, journals, and electronic storage media.

Financial records are histories of how much money we made or lost, how much we spent, and how we measured everything. The earliest recorded law, *The Code of Hammurabi*, deals heavily with accounting. Without measurements and records, trade would be severely limited. Financial records allow us to measure our financial state over time and help us prepare for the future. Financial records also help us to prove our financial state for tax purposes.

Photographs, audio tapes, videotapes, and digital media provide a snapshot in time of our conditions and states of being. We create these records to help us remember *what* we were doing, *how* it was, *where* we were, *who* we were with, *when* we did something, and *why* we chose to do it. At a glance, we can measure and compare our past and our present.

To remember and measure, a level playing field needs to be created, which is associated with a game, and a game requires rules. Rules that need to be remembered and measured use standards, units of measure, metrics, and statistics. For example, a playing field might be a soccer field in sports, the trading floor of the stock market in business, or the communication protocol TCP/IP in information technology.

Rules governing standards, units of measure, metrics, and statistics help us interpret and understand outcomes. **Rules** also govern, constrain, or influence behavior. The context of a rule is essential for understanding the measurements.

Standards provide a uniform level of understanding, applicability, and use. **Units of measure** quantify a measurement, creating a common understanding. **Metrics** form a fact for observation. **Statistics** are used as a vehicle for comparison.

Rules

Rules govern, constrain, or influence behavior. To state a rule, consider the following guidelines for what a rule requires:

- Explicitness to prevent equivocating or wiggle room
- Method of enforcement and another method of punishment for violation
- Subject and a verb
- Action

- Time frame
- Agent of action
- Ability to stand a test of reasonableness
- Ability to be performed somewhere
- Life span

The more of these guidelines that are included in the rule, the more explicit the rule becomes. There is no substitution for explicitness.

Standards

Standards provide a uniform level of understanding. For example, you understand what one hour means because an hour is a defined standard. Standards may be grounded in science and physics and can be created to encourage reuse. Section 2.5 discusses how the Levitts established many of the general standards in construction.

Enterprises must have standards, which ensure compliance throughout the organization. An accepted standard should not be violated because standards are created from rules, and enforcement is a key characteristic of a rule. If a standard is violated, the end product may not work as expected and may be difficult or impossible to maintain. Standards create dimensions, application rules, and communication protocols. Section 1.2.1 illustrates how writing systems need many rules to create a language standard. The following are other examples of standards:

- 110 volt home electric lines
- Volume of one cup
- Length of a mile
- J2EE—Java 2 platform, Enterprise Edition

The standard for Java and J2EE was created by Sun Microsystems. The Java Virtual Machine makes applications written in the Java programming language 100 percent transportable between different hardware and operating system platforms. J2EE helps programmers and IT departments write Java programs once and then run the programs anywhere. With the exception of Microsoft, technicians did not try to alter or extend the standard. The standard was accepted, used, and opened up a new paradigm for information technology. (Microsoft is not a licensee of the J2EE standard.)

In the early 1980s, it was unclear which of three competing videotape standards—V2000, VHS, and Betamax—would dominate. In the end, the VHS system pioneered by the smallest firm, JVC, won out against the Philips V2000 and Sony Betamax. Although JVC was a smaller firm, the company was prepared to license its technology to competitors. Sony declined to let other manufacturers put their brands on its machines. In addition, JVC, in alliance with Thorn EMI and Telefunken, recognized earlier than Philips the importance of movie rentals.

A major corporation may impose standards on an entire industry. In the late 1960s, NCR, Sweda, Regitel, and GE-Honeywell battled to emerge as the vendor that set the standard for point-of-sale (POS) devices at checkout lines. IBM was also involved, but was considered insignificant by these corporations. The National Institute of Standards and Technology (NIST) acted as mediator to reach an industry-wide accord.

Unlike the other vendors, IBM recognized that POS was more than cash management and product ordering for retailers. Captured POS information ripples back through the entire supply chain. Tying the supply chain together was a breakthrough that changed the **value chain** of an enterprise. IBM realized it was in a unique position to supply organizations with both POS registers and **back office computers**—a fact not recognized by the other vendors.

In 1969, IBM representatives walked into the standards meeting at the NIST offices in Washington, D.C. and announced that the company had decided to use the Universal Product Code (UPC) bar code as the POS standard. IBM informed the group that they had signed contracts to manufacture the necessary hardware and had secured orders for over $300 million from several large retailers.

Prior to the meeting, IBM had worked through the issues of *what, how, where, who, when,* and *why,* and moved to develop the necessary hardware, software, telecommunication protocols, and business rules. When IBM presented the marketing case to managers representing companies all along the retail industry supply chain, IBM's discussion was to the point and on target, which helped IBM eventually secure agreement among the manufacturers, wholesale distributors, and retailers.

The breakthrough in technology and application for the UPC standard established the path for generations of point-of-transaction technologies, including the Automated Teller Machine (ATM).

Standards need:

- A name and a definition (*what*)
- A rule of use
  How the standard is used
  Where the standard is used
  Who the standard is used by
  When the standard is used
  Why the standard was established
- All the guidelines for stating a rule

In other words, standards need standards.

Unit of Measure

A unit of measure is based on a standard and quantifies a measurement, creating a common understanding. A unit of measure is the definition of something important to the business. That something is either perceived or tangible and is usually expressed as a number. For example, a consumer can choose from different brands, flavors, and packaging of soda in a grocery store. Grocery stores sell soda and need numerous units of measure including 8-ounce cans, 20-ounce bottles, 1-liter bottles, and cases. Retailers also purchase soda using a variety of different units, including a single can or bottle, a pallet, truck, or train car.

Each unit of measure requires a unique stock-keeping unit (SKU) or UPC. Each unit of measure has a different description, rule of use, and price. Each may require different store displays, handling, lead times for ordering, and storage space. Costs for facilities, infrastructure, labor, transportation, insurance, and utilities are distributed to each product unit. A different profit percentage may be associated with each UPC.

Each unit of measure requires a different set of business rules, which dictate how the appropriate information is reported, stored, calculated, analyzed, and used. Units of measure form the basis of metrics and statistics. Business rules dictate the process of store operations and information technology needed to support those operations. Units of measure require the following:

- A name and a definition (*what*)
- Determination of the number for the basic unit of measure (*what*)
- A rule of use
  How the unit of measure is used
  Where the unit of measure is used
  Who the unit of measure is used by
  When the unit of measure is used
  Why the unit of measure was established
- All the guidelines for stating a rule

Metrics

Metrics are a single piece of information requiring two or more units of measure from different interrogatives (*what, how, where, who, when,* and *why*). For example, one metric might measure the number of cans of soda sold in the last *n* minutes. This metric contains a unit of measure (*what*—quantity), the number sold (*how*— from a known selling process), and an historic time frame (*when*—*n* minutes, which is another unit of measure).

The metric may produce a measurement, such as 30 cans of soda sold in the last 30 minutes.

Metrics express the idea of measuring, recording, and reporting the facts of the business. Metrics is the term businesses and IT departments generally use to discuss the types of measurements required.

Metrics require the following:

- A name and a definition (*what*)
- A rule of use
  How the metric is used
  Where the metric is used
  Who the metric is used by
  When the metric is used
  Why the metric was established
- All the guidelines for stating a rule

Statistics

Statistics are a vehicle for comparison. While metrics produce measurements, they only provide a true sense of the financial state or progress of a corporation when the results of like metrics are compared. When like metrics are compared, the statistics derived from these metrics help management, legislative authorities, and the marketplace understand where the corporation is and how it is doing on its way to a future end-state.

Statistics are important in recording and reporting financial and asset risk management information, and in assuring regulatory compliance. Rule requirements apply to statistics, as well as standards, units of measure, and metrics:

- A name and a definition (*what*)
- Determination of the number for the basic standard (*what*)

- A rule of use

  How the standard is used

  Where the standard is used

  Who the standard is used by

  When the standard is used

  Why the standard was established
- All the guidelines for stating a rule

In October 2002, Delta Airlines announced that it was laying off 8,000 employees. Senior executives at Delta were forced into this tough decision because they understood the rules and standards they needed to follow. The airline's captured measurements and statistics showed they could not continue to operate with indifference. Rules, standards, units of measure, metrics, and statistics provide necessary meanings to frame how an organization must operate and how IT systems must be created.

5.3.2 Measure and Remember *(what)*

Healthcare is a heavily legislated industry, along with the airline, atomic energy, banking, and agricultural industries. Abuses of people and money in the healthcare industry were problematic prior to the Omnibus Budget Reconciliation Act (OBRA) of 1986 and the Americans with Disabilities Act (ADA) Regulation for Title III in 1994.[6] Healthcare suffers from a dearth of skilled and semi-skilled professionals and stringent financial constraints, including over 4,000 pages of financial mandates to follow.

Healthcare facilities must record measurements and statistics on the Internet for all to see and inspect. The record of healthcare administrators, including all kudos and complaints, becomes public knowledge. With the exception of athletes, actors, and politicians, few people have their performance records critiqued by so many.

The Lafayette-Redeemer Retirement Center in Philadelphia, Pennsylvania provides a good example of the constraints imposed on the *builder* by legislation. Before *builders* can start to construct anything, whether a physical site or information technology, they must thoroughly understand related legislation. After the *designer* has given the design and the mandate to construct to the *builder*, the *builder* is responsible for ensuring compliance with the design.

During construction, the *builder* must report on the processes used to ensure compliance and submit monthly reports to the organization. If federal funds are used in any phase of construction at Lafayette, the *builder* must provide well-documented construction records. In the healthcare industry, OBRA mandates the level of documentation required.

The *builder* must create the accounting standards and methods to report how money is spent. The *builder* must possess a good knowledge of generally accepted accounting principles and be comfortable with a general ledger and supporting journals.

The *builder* creates and applies rules, standards, units of measure, metrics, and statistics to ensure the business runs properly, information technology supports the business, and reporting requirements are satisfied. Satisfying reporting requirements dictates the rules for units of measure, metrics, and statistics.

Builders must also observe standard operating procedures, which specify an organization's preferred mode for accomplishing tasks in a given situation, such as the activities a person needs to perform to ensure data quality in a database. The level of enforcement at Lafayette for a standard operating procedure may vary based on the task, or the manager of those performing the task. For example, a standard operating procedure requiring employees to be at their desks, ready for work, by 8 a.m. may not be strictly enforced until a person abuses the rule. However, a standard operating procedure requiring that employees do not share computer passwords may be strictly enforced, and termination of employment may result following the first offense.

Standard operating procedures ensure the capture and storage of reporting information. Measurements for standard operating procedures tend to be Boolean—true or false. One rule at Lafayette stipulates that beds must be made by 10 a.m. Either the beds are made or they are not. In the business world of senior healthcare, that rule triggers many measurement reports that prove the beds were made, such as:

- Linen change and laundry charges
- Nursing aide schedules
- Employee payroll reports by skill level and hours spent by task
- Purchase of outside services for maintenance
- Housekeeping and maintenance for charge reports

All reports have measurement requirements that are associated with income or expense. If the reports are not accurate, do not comply with format standards, or are not submitted in the period required, the government is not obligated to reimburse the facility.

The first and most important unit of measure for most healthcare facilities, including Lafayette, is *the bed*. Every business has a first unit of measure and all the other metrics and rules of the business flow from that unit of measure. Other first units of measure include: *the account* in the banking industry, *the milk* in the dairy farming industry, and *the SKU* in the retail industry. Ultimately, the first unit of measure for an enterprise is arbitrary and is determined by management. What the *builder* at Lafayette must construct in business operations and IT systems to accommodate *the bed* includes:

- Location
- Person in the bed
- Care requirements
- Invoicing
- Scheduling
- Maintenance
- Security
- Food service
- Professional staffing certifications
- Employee background checks

All the *builder's* reports contain financial information. Controlling money and using it properly are the main motivations for OBRA. Mandated OBRA reports are used to create procedures to ensure correct reporting of finances. The *builder* must determine the most effective means of capturing financial information. The IT *builder* helps design the necessary facilities for automating the capture of financial information.

The *builder* has another level of reporting not mandated by the government. The *builder* must keep the *designer* informed of the progress and the need for any changes in the design. Just because it has been designed does not mean it can be built, as was the case with Babbage's analytical engine, mentioned in Section 4.1. The *builder* is the one who shoulders the burden of proof.

The *builder* must ensure that the design works, is practical and economical to operate, and delivers the benefits the *owner* seeks. The *builder* must ensure the design satisfies each mandate. If the design does not satisfy the *owner*'s requirements, the *builder* must demand a change in the design.

The *designer* may have to go back to the *owner* and explain why the *builder* has a problem with the design and discuss how revisions could affect the schedule and investments. Many times the *designer* places her career in jeopardy by delivering bad news.

The *builder* should understand the political implications of requiring a change and that he may be forced to proceed with the faulty design. The *builder* is usually told, especially in IT, "We'll deal with the problem later." If the *builder* proceeds with the faulty design, sooner or later, the system will fail. The failure usually occurs at the most inopportune time.

In 1994, the Holy Redeemer Health System bought a new retirement facility—Lafayette. The previous not-for-profit corporation owned the facility prior to 1994 and examined Title III of the ADA. The corporation concluded that it was not in a position to continue to make a profit, without retrofitting and renovating the facility. Corporate executives decided not to undertake the expense and sold the facility.

OBRA and ADA changed the face of healthcare and public accommodations. By early 1995, residents of Lafayette noticed many changes, including the increase of new occupants in wheelchairs and the daily noise made by construction. What the residents could not see was the upheaval caused by the legislation.

Holy Redeemer, a nonprofit organization, has 30 separate legal entities and business relationships with pharmacists, dentists, optometrists, opticians, audiologists, chiropractors, stress management experts, and gymnasiums for physical therapy. The *builder* must have a thorough understanding of the legal maze to establish uniformity of the rules, standards, units of measure, metrics, and statistics—all to satisfy management and mandated reporting.

The *builder* at Lafayette contends with a microcosm of the parent corporation. Each organization must count, account, store, save, compare, analyze, calculate, forecast, justify, document, and report. Each organization must be able to communicate and have: access to information, business procedures in place, needed facilities, adequate time, qualified people, and money to run the business.

5.3.3 Work, Live, and Play *(where)*

Location is one of the single most constraining factors facing the *builder* at Lafayette. The *builder* needs to know about all of the following:

- Location of the physical facility
- Size and layout of the site
- Water table of the site
- Natural resources on or near the site, like streams, parks, trees, and animals
- Ability of the location to support a structure
- Zoning laws
- Cultural offerings of the area

- Access to utilities, water, electricity, and natural gas
- Materials available for construction
- Access to site for construction equipment, construction workers, and telecommunication facilities

5.3.4 Have Patients, Dear *(who)*

Reams of legislation for OBRA and ADA at the federal, state, county, and city levels predicated organization at Lafayette. Lafayette is actually three separate legal entities. The entities are Residential Apartments, the Assisted Living Unit, and the Full-time Nursing Facility.

Residential Apartments are used by individuals who are independent and self sustaining. Cleaning services are provided once a week by Lafayette, and each year, the resident may schedule a spring house cleaning.

The Assisted Living Unit combines many of the features of the independent unit and adds a level of nursing care. Most residents in this unit require daily professional care and are mentally or physically handicapped in some manner.

The Full-time Nursing Facility is exactly what Americans view as *the home*. Residents in the Full-time Nursing Facility fall into one of four classifications, each requiring a different level of care:

- Mentally disabled and physically able (forever care)
- Physically disabled and mentally able (forever care)
- Physically and mentally disabled (forever care)
- Residents from either the independent or Assisted Living Unit who are suffering from an illness or accident and require more intensive nursing than is available in their everyday living facilities, but less than what is administered by a hospital (short-term care)

OBRA and ADA direct each state to set up offices of compliance and administration. The working mandate file in the administrator's office is over 4,000 pages long. Additionally, each state is given the authority to pass further legislation. States delegate responsibility for compliance and administration to counties, and the counties delegate to the cities.

The result is a large web of legislation, taxing authorities, registration fees, and licensing fees. A review of the legislation reveals it is almost impossible to be in full compliance. Outright contradiction exists in business rules from one governing body to another. The best that facilities like Lafayette can do is live up to the spirit of the law.

Lafayette invests more in training, facilities, and personnel than mandated minimums. Accountants for the Holy Redeemer state that legislative compliance and reporting consume 30 percent of the total resident charges, not including tax liability, permit, and licensing fees. In order to stay in business and make a profit, the healthcare industry's main concern is legal tax avoidance.

The three separate legal entities of Lafayette, the patients, patient care, and employee management are all governed, controlled, and reported by knowing precisely the necessary rules, standards, units of measure, metrics, and statistics. The *builder* must be familiar with all the organization's complexities to ensure that the *owner* achieves the necessary compliance to OBRA and ADA, and to create the necessary rules, standards, units of measure, metrics, and statistics. One paragraph from OBRA, defining compliance in IT terms, is:

> *In general, if a person desires to conduct any of the information transactions described in subsection (b) (1) with a health plan as a standard transaction, the health plan shall conduct such standard transaction in a timely manner and the information transmitted or received in connection with such transaction shall be in the form of standard data elements of medicare information.*

The language in the OBRA Act illustrates the complexities in understanding legalese, but it is necessary for the *builder* to understand.

5.3.5 I Told You So *(how)*

By the time the *builder* makes and applies the rules for the construction of the product or service, the following events have happened:

- The *planner* has tried to estimate project costs and may have listed concerns.
- The *owner* has reviewed the list of important considerations, including whether the project can be completed within a certain amount of time. The *owner* has also allocated the amount of money to invest in the project, determined whether the project is worth the time and expense, and set up many of the rules.
- The *designer* has made a design of the project, spread the budget (*what*) over the cost of process (*how*), location (*where*), people (*who*), and schedules (*when*). Most importantly, the *designer* has detailed the processes that can ensure the success of the project. The processes have determined the rules and forced assets, location, people, and time into agreement.

When the *builder's* activities start, the *builder* would like for the *planner*, *owner*, and *designer* to have eliminated every assumption and made everything explicit. However, this happens rarely. Assumptions are usually exposed during the actual construction. During construction, the assumptions can cause the process to disintegrate. Disintegration forces the *builder* to request a change from the *designer*.

Issues associated with location begin to validate the rules. The rules of every unit of measure, metric, statistic, asset allocation (*what*), process (*how*), technology (*where*), personnel requirement (*who*), plan and schedule (*when*), and reason (*why*) for the project are placed under great stress. Any assumption for a rule found to be incorrect may have a ripple effect on every other rule and cause the entire project to fail. When a rule breaks, the *builder* must reconstruct the rule. Retrofitting is expensive and can cause delays in the project.

When a rule is broken, the *builder* cannot assume the breakdown is caused by failure of the current process. The *builder* must assess whether the breakdown is caused by an incorrect measurement, or a misassumption about money requirements, location, people, or planning and scheduling. If the *designer* overlooked a detail, or reached an incorrect conclusion, a design assumption probably created a bad rule.

For example, in the lowest common denominator scenario in Section 5.2.3., Abbott Laboratories' situation was caused by the *owner's* lack of understanding of employee (*who*) issues. Abbott could not describe its organization to create a requirement for the new systems. When problems surfaced, the IT team looked at the databases (*what*) and processes (*how*) to fix the problems, but had not known to consider the *who* aspect. The lack of understanding of the organization among the *owner*, *designer*, and *builder* caused the rules to break.

In the construction of a product such as an airplane, production order changes are frequent. When the *builder* observes the need for a change, a change request is issued. The *designer* must review and approve this change request before any other step is taken. When the change has been granted, the *designer* must issue a change order. The change order is the authorization and mandate to make the change. Both the *builder* and *designer* notate the change on the documentation.

In the case of an airplane, Congress mandates rigorous controls for the manufacturing process. When a plane crashes for any reason, one of the first things the National Transportation Safety Administration does is review the building plans for the plane. If any aspect of the plane's design and construction has not been documented down to the last rivet, the consequences are significant, including fines and loss of license.

5.3.6 A Time to Plan *(when)*

After looking over the location and construction plans, the *builder* looks at the schedules. The schedules should include the Critical Path Method (CPM) prepared by the *owner* and the Gantt chart prepared by the *designer*. After reviewing the location, construction, and all the planning schedules, a *builder* typically says, "I sure wish those guys had talked to me before doing this."

Experienced *builders* can review plans and spot misassumptions immediately, or something worse. A common problem facing *builders* is design by hope, where *owners* and *designers* attempt to perform the design duties of the *builder*. Design by hope is a topic further covered in Section 5.4.7. When projects are designed by hope, the result is frequently less than desirable. Generally, *owners* and *designers* do not infringe upon the *builder's* job with malice, but *hope* to design the project themselves because of one or more of the following reasons:

- The investment required to complete the project has been underestimated.
- The processes or technology does not work as believed.
- The location is not appropriate for the designed structure.
- The business events have been poorly designed.
- The schedule cannot be met.
- Passive aggressive resistance is subverting the force of the *owner's* direction or mandate.

When everything that has been designed is explicit, based on explicit direction from the *owner*, the *builder* must create a group of additional plans:

- The rate the money is to be spent and payment schedules (*what*—assets)
- Detailed production or construction orders (*how*—process)
- A plan to create the construction infrastructure for the location (*where*—location)
- The design of the organizational units with mission statements (*who*—people)

- The detailed production schedule (*when*—time)
- The financial plan as to how costs can be controlled and profit can be made on the project (*why*—motivation)

ASSETS, PROCESSES, LOCATION, PEOPLE, TIME, AND MOTIVATION

- Assets (*what*)—the *builder's* asset management relates to accounting. Everything has a cost and is directly related to the rules, standards, units of measure, metrics, and statistics. Accounting is the purpose of measurement. The *builder's* authority and responsibility are to create the chart of accounts for the general ledger, design and implement the ledgers and journals, and establish the documentation for audit purposes.

  Builders establish the schedule for recording and reporting pertinent financial information. Laws mandate most organizational reporting.

- *Processes (how)*—builders must determine the exact order for both business and IT processes and the required time to conduct them. If the *builder* has underestimated how long any process or transaction takes, the result can be devastating to the project. Underestimation can cause long lines in service establishments, slow computer response, and collapse of the business system. Underestimation of time can cause cost overruns and set unrealistic expectation levels.

- *Location (where)*—builders must plan for the time and accessibility of the construction site. The plan takes into account the implementation for the necessary physical infrastructure required to support the construction, computer hardware, or network.

- *People (who)*—builders must plan how long each job function takes. The *builder* needs to create the organizational units to operate the business and construct the site. Each organizational unit needs a plan to hire people with the necessary skill sets, a compensation plan, and a mission statement.

- *Time (when)*—builders must create and implement a detailed production schedule to support the process schedule and the job function schedule.

- *Motivation (why)*—builders must create plans that demonstrate how costs are being controlled and how profit dollars are being generated.

5.3.7 Survival *(why)*

To create a measurement, someone must establish the rules, standards, units of measure, metrics, and statistics. Measurement provides a basis of comparison. Unfavorable comparisons cause changes in attitudes, beliefs, traditions, and ways of life. As we measure others, others are measuring us. Unfavorable comparison causes worry and discomfort. Worry causes us to think. Thinking causes us to seek information and develop knowledge. Knowledge gives us wisdom, which allows us to adapt and change for the better. Changing for the better gives us a competitive advantage, which gives us security and peace of mind. Security and peace of mind give us comfort.

People need to know how they are and where they are going. Memory and written records are vehicles used to accomplish the task of knowing how we got where we are; measurement and statistics help us understand where we are and how we are doing. An organization or enterprise also has the same needs to know how it is and where it is going—it's a matter of survival.

5.3.8 Key Terms

back office computers	standard
metrics	statistics
rule	unit of measure
rule of use	

5.3.9 Review Questions

1. Explain why *time* is such an important part of a measurement.
2. What do standards help clarify and create?
3. What term is used by business and IT to discuss what is measured and by how much?
4. What could happen if an organization does not compare *like* metrics?
5. Why is it important for the *builder* to report back to the *designer* regularly?
6. When are many assumptions usually exposed?
7. Why is documentation important during the production of any product?
8. What can happen if a *designer* underestimates how long any process or transaction takes?
9. What needs do people and enterprises have in common?
10. Name five guidelines for stating a rule.
11. What are two healthcare regulations with which the *builder* must comply?
12. What is the first unit of measure for the Lafayette-Redeemer healthcare facility?
13. What can cause a retrofit to be required?

SECTION 5.4 WHY DID THIS HAPPEN— TRADE-OFFS

QUESTIONS TO CONTEMPLATE

1. Why do trade-offs occur?
2. What are the various types of software licenses?
3. Why is it important to compare and contrast ideas, concepts, designs, and software?

5.4.1 Introduction

The Mata Atlantica rainforest is one of the most diverse and threatened eco-systems on Earth. This Brazilian rainforest has been decimated continuously since the Portuguese explorer Pedro Alvares Cabral (1467–1520) landed there on April 22, 1500. The rainforest has been logged for tropical hardwoods, mined for clay and sand, and cleared for cattle pasture and sugar cane fields. Previous *owners* permitted the stripping of vegetation and topsoil. The exposed sandy soils are vulnerable to erosion from wind and rain.

The Ford Motor Company chose to halt further environmental disturbance when it began building manufacturing facilities on 320 acres in Camaçari, Bahia, 40 km northwest of Salvador. Completed in 2000, Ford's facility cost over $1 billion to build. Ford wanted to find ways to make its facility an asset to both employees and the community.

A team of ecologists, environmental engineers, and landscape architects collaborated in building systems to help restore native habitats and regenerate the indigenous landscape. To accomplish the ecological aspects of the project, the team constructed wetlands with native plants to retain storm waters. The wetlands enhance on-site water quality and release water slowly into the surrounding ecosystem. The team used vegetated channels to slow the passage of storm water from the buildings while cleansing the water and creating native plant habitats. The water elements are also used to cool the buildings. On-site composting of organic materials from sanitary waste and food service waste builds soil and supports the regeneration of biomass.

The team chose local materials and construction methods for their adaptability to the regional climate. They oriented buildings to take advantage of prevailing winds and create shade from sunlight. They created a town center within the manufacturing complex. Non-manufacturing buildings are used for employee services and form a village at the core of the complex. The village includes medical facilities, training offices, administrative offices, a cafeteria, and a fitness center.

Trees and buildings are aligned to form shaded paths for pedestrians. Landscaped open spaces provide employees a place to enjoy workday breaks, while creating spaces suitable for recreational and community activities. Indigenous species of rainforest plants establish corridors that create habitats and connect the site to the surrounding environment. An adjoining site includes sports fields and employee gardens designed to encourage participation in the site regeneration.

Sometimes, corporations do not conduct business as usual. Ford Motor Company executives understood how building a manufacturing facility in the Amazon rainforest might be viewed by the public. Therefore, Ford traded investment dollars to be environmentally conscious in hopes of expanding its customer base.

5.4.2 Rationale *(why)*

Trade-offs in business and in the building of IT systems occur in several ways. Here are some examples:

- Seeking immediate gratification as opposed to doing what is best
- Choosing a short-term option over a long-term option
- Electing to implement a standalone product instead of seeking to implement an integrated product

- Producing a point-in-time-based solution instead of an infrastructure-based solution
- Taking an expense-based approach in lieu of an asset-based approach
- Optimizing the implementation at the expense of the enterprise versus optimizing the enterprise at the expense of the implementation
- Doing something quickly instead of doing it right

The reasons for choosing each trade-off are numerous and typically include: time, money, human resources, legislation, competition, and anticipated revenue. In 1998, the British Government passed the Data Protection Act, which specified new privacy laws for consumer data in the United Kingdom.

For many companies, the act provided a means and an excuse to retire old software systems that were built using short-term objectives and **point-in-time** solutions, which seek to solve an immediate need without consideration for future enhancement. The systems were generally disintegrated and cumbersome to maintain. Some companies, like Equifax and Experian, have taken the opportunity to reposition their software and data assets by redesigning and rewriting them.

Taking a quick-and-dirty approach or a short-term option is not always bad. Often this approach is a survival technique necessary for staying in business. However, when these approaches are sustained over many projects and over long periods, they tend to hurt the very enterprises they are attempting to enable.

Companies that view enterprise architecture as taking too long and costing too much often wish for the models of the enterprise. The models of the enterprise give the *owners*, *designers*, and *builders* an understanding of what they have. The models also provide clues into how modifications can be made to enable time-to-market at a reasonable cost. Some industries are fortunate to have an opportunity to stop using quick fixes and undo the errors of past ways. However, a company is bound to try the same trade-offs—*Hey, let's do it this way, it'll be cheap, and we can get it done by the end of the next quarter. This solution feels great*...See Figure 5-5.

Figure 5-5   *I'm bound to get a bonus for this*

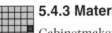
5.4.3 Materials *(how)*

Cabinetmakers make cabinets. Typically, they do not make their own tools: drill presses, chisels, hammers, screwdrivers, planes, bandsaws, and sandpaper. Some cabinetmakers elect not to make each piece of the final product, but to use pre-cut wood, manufactured moldings, mass-produced inlays, off-the-shelf knobs, screws, and hinges.

The *builder* of software applications does not typically design and construct all the components, programs, applications, and systems the enterprise uses. In the same way a cabinetmaker buys a drill press or a chisel, *builders* often choose to buy operating systems, programming language compilers, and text editors. In addition, *builders* may decide to buy some or all of the major components of the final application, including Web servers, application servers, database servers, utilities, payroll software, collections software, and enterprise resource planning software.

The *builder* must understand and know what types of software can be acquired and used. In addition, the *builder* must understand the various types of software licenses. If a *builder* chooses not to build 100 percent of the software needed, the *builder* must determine what software to buy, how to adopt or apply standards associated with the software, and how the software can be deployed.

Some software executables can be obtained free-of-charge, while others can be obtained with the **source code**. Some software is licensed by the site, based on the number of internal or external users. Some software is restricted for use or sale in certain countries. The *builder* must understand each type of software license. Organizations should examine license variations closely.

THE ORACLE TECHNOLOGY
NETWORK DEVELOPER LICENSE

One of the terms of agreement for downloading software in 2002 from Oracle's Web site is that you are "not listed on the United States Department of Treasury lists of Specially Designated Nationals, Specially Designated Terrorists, and Specially Designated Narcotic Traffickers."

Ironically, Oracle does not provide any mechanism to update your profile should you unfortunately be placed on one of these lists.

The open-source movement started in 1968 with ARPANET,[7] the predecessor to the Internet. ARPANET allowed researchers to share code and information. In 1969, Ken Thompson of Bell Laboratories developed the first version of the UNIX operating system. UNIX was distributed freely during the 1970s to universities and other research facilities.

In 1971, Richard Stallman joined an MIT[8] group devoted to free software. Stallman developed the first Emacs text editor and later founded the GNU[9] project, an organized effort that aimed to foster cooperative and open software development for the benefit of the computer industry. GNU remains active and is sponsored by the Free Software Foundation. Stallman found that many computer programmers agreed with GNU's open philosophy and wanted to help with the project.

At first, Stallman and his programmers decided to create an operating system similar to UNIX because the UNIX design was portable and widely accepted. Throughout the 1980s, developers collaborated on all major elements of the operating system—including software compilers, libraries for the C programming language, program debuggers, and text editors.

In 1994, Linus Torvalds, a programmer from the University of Helsinki in Finland, delivered the Linux kernel, the core component of the Linux operating system. The kernel was merged with existing GNU components, as well as other software created by contributors over the Internet. The goal to create a free UNIX-like operating system was conceived in 1984 and materialized 10 years later.

Through collaborative efforts, GNU contributors have produced many different software programs, including spreadsheets and word processing systems. An industry of GNU distributors emerged. These companies package, distribute, and sell software that is already freely available.

In 1997, community members for open-source software formed the Open-Source Initiative to define open-source software compliant licenses. The open-source definition provides a set of conformance guidelines for making free software available.

OPEN-SOURCE DEFINITION MANDATES

- *Free Redistribution*—The user must be free to sell or give away the software.
- *Source Code*—The program must include source code.
- *Derived Works*—The license must allow distribution of modifications and derived works.
- *Integrity of the Author's Source Code*—The license may restrict source distribution only if it allows patch files to modify the program at build time.
- *No Discrimination*—The license may not restrict use of the software based on any persons, groups, or fields of endeavor.
- *Distribution of License*—The license must be automatic.
- *License Must Not Be Specific to a Product*—The license must not restrict rights to a specific product.
- *License Must Not Contaminate Other Software*—The license must not place restrictions on other software distributed with the licensed software.

More than one dozen software licenses conform to the open-source definition. The term *open-source* is not a trademark, and vendors can include their own features and restrictions in their definitions of open-source. The most popular open-source license is the GNU General Public License. The license is designed primarily to protect the rights of software users to customize and distribute code freely, as they see fit.

Different types of software licenses, including open-source, commercial, and hybrids include:

- *General Public License (GPL)*—the license terms include the rights to use, change, and redistribute the code freely. GPL is also known as *copyleft* software. Copyleft is deliberately used as an antonym to *copyright*. GPL requires that the program be delivered with source code, and all derivative works also must be delivered with source code. Distribution terms do not allow distributors to impose restrictions when the software is modified and redistributed to others. Examples of the GNU copyleft license include the Linux kernel and GNU programming tools, such as a C compiler and Samba.
- *Berkeley Software Distribution (BSD) software license*—the license allows developers to change the programming code and sell it. Programmers are free to create their own proprietary versions. While many programmers return their work to the community, many open-source purists discourage spin-offs that result in proprietary software. Examples of products distributed under the BSD software license include BSD UNIX, Apache, BIND, and sendmail.
- *Commercial software license*—software that is typically proprietary and developed and sold for profit by a company. It is not typical for the source code to be included with the software executables.
- *Freeware software license*—software that is supplied with permission for users to copy, change, and distribute the program and its source code. The GNU project refers to free software as providing the freedom to do whatever one wishes to do with software. It does not mean a price of zero dollars. Freeware is a term that is generally discouraged from use and often refers to programs released only as executables. Freeware's definition has become ambiguous.
- *Mozilla public license*—the license was developed by Netscape Communications as part of its open-source release of Communicator 5. It is based on GPL, but allows private, derivative works. Mozilla source must be made freely available on the Internet. Additions to Mozilla may be licensed differently and do not need to be published.
- *Open-Source software license*—the license is defined by the open-source definition from the Open-Source Initiative. An open-source product must be free to redistribute; source code must be available; and modifications and derivative works must be allowed.
- *Proprietary software license*—the license permits software to be sold for a fee. Users are prohibited from modifying or redistributing the program.
- *Public Domain software license*—the license covers software that is not copyrighted.

- *Semi-Free software license*—the license is used for software not available free. The software is supplied with permission for users to copy, change, and distribute for nonprofit reasons.
- *Shareware software license*—the license allows software to be distributed openly, but requires a modest license fee from those who plan to keep and use the software. Shareware does not generally allow its source code to be modified.

Following are examples of some of the many open-source projects:

- *Operating systems*—Linux and BSD UNIX
- *Programming languages*—Perl, tcl, and Python
- *Web servers*—Apache, which provides a secure, efficient, and extensible server to provide HTTP services
- *Application servers*—JBoss, a J2EE-based application server
- *Database servers*—MySQL, a multiuser, multithreaded SQL database server
- *Utilities*—Samba, which allows UNIX to act as a file and print server on Microsoft NT and Windows networks
- *eMail*—Sendmail, which provides the Internet's e-mail infrastructure

Open-source software has found a niche as a low-risk way to extend or enhance an organization's current infrastructure software. Gaining entrance into business has not been easy for open-source software. Initially, Linux and other open-source software were rejected by corporate America.

Open-source software often solves the same business problems as commercial counterparts. Linux, for instance, has been shown to offer better services than some of its commercially available competitors. One of open-source's big benefits is that it a cost many organizations can justify.

cooperative development environment, open-source software can kly. Linux is the best example of a successful open-source project. the characteristics of a real UNIX operating system, like Sun user and multitasking features.

ies view Linux's lack of compatibility with Microsoft products and al user interfaces and documentation as deterrents. Linux is not Windows, and it requires end users to have different skills than Windows. See Figure 5-6. Vendor viability is a question for open-ecause a vendor does not usually develop it. Rather, groups of unrelated volunteers communicating over the Internet develop the software. In this case, the viability of the community is more of a question.

A *builder* must understand the trade-offs between open-source software and commercial software. If the *builder* plans to acquire a software product, the *builder* must understand the scope and semantics of the software license. Failure to understand the license might affect how the final software application can be used or sold.

	Linux	Windows XP
GUI	Varies based on the implementation: X.11, Free86, Gnome, KDE, or CDE.	Established Windows and Internet Explorer interface. The same interface can be used to navigate documents and files locally and on the Internet/intranet.
Price (US$)	The price ranges from zero dollars for an Internet download to $150 for a compact disc loaded with additional applications and utilities from Linux distributors. The license allows for unlimited seats.	$299 for a single license of Windows XP Professional.
Support	Distributors and support providers are available. Web-based help lines are generally very good.	There are many certified support centers and independent specialists.
Hardware Support	From Intel 386 to mainframe systems, including: Intel, Alpha, SPARC, and Motorola.	Intel Pentium processor or compatible.
Hardware Requirements	Very low requirements: 16MB RAM 20MB hard drive.	Minimum 300 mhz Intel Pentium processor or compatible. 128MB RAM. 1.5GB hard drive.

Figure 5-6   *Comparing Linux and Windows XP*

A *builder* should consider open-source software in the following circumstances:

- It provides functionality advantages.
- Product maturity, active development, and market presence is evident.
- Commercial or custom software costs are prohibitive.
- Source code needs to be modified or tuned.
- Internal resources have the skills to maintain and support the software.
- Licensing terms are appropriate.

A *builder* should consider a traditional approach to software purchasing in the following conditions:

- Strong and large selection of management tools is required.
- Strong vendor commitment of support and accountability is required.
- The corporation has a broad systems integration community.
- Environment needs high availability and scalability.
- Requirements exist for easy-to-use graphical interfaces.
- Need exists to protect intellectual property.
- Need exists to maintain a competitive advantage.

5.4.4 Web Services *(where)*

Since the mid-1990s, many Web sites have aimed to give visitors access to a myriad of information. In the beginning, content providers showed weather information, gave stock quotes, provided news, and offered mail services. Many companies then started purchasing the rights to use raw data and redistribute it in various viewable formats. After acquiring raw data, companies created expensive programs to convert provider-formatted data into a format that could be rendered to a browser in HTML. See Figure 5-7.

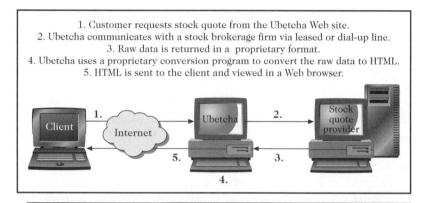

1. Customer requests stock quote from the Ubetcha Web site.
2. Ubetcha communicates with a stock brokerage firm via leased or dial-up line.
3. Raw data is returned in a proprietary format.
4. Ubetcha uses a proprietary conversion program to convert the raw data to HTML.
5. HTML is sent to the client and viewed in a Web browser.

Figure 5-7   *Steps for providing stock quotes on the Internet*

Smaller dotcoms found they needed to compete with dominant Internet portals such as AOL, MSN, and Yahoo. The model shown in Figure 5-7 proved tedious because disparate technologies used to source data from multiple vendors were often unmanageable from a logistics and cost perspective. Raw data transfer needed to become more cost effective. Easier ways to convert the data to a standard form were needed. See Figure 5-8.

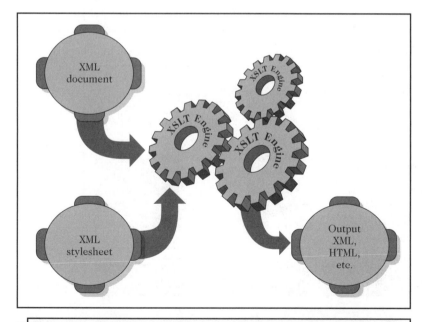

Figure 5-8   *Converting raw data to an Internet format*

The Web service emerged as the standard way to retrieve data without proprietary software and hardware. A Web service is a service provided via the Internet that can transfer data from the provider to the consumer, or requester, using the ubiquitous HTTP protocol in the data format known as XML. Extensible Stylesheet Language Transformations (XSLT) convert the data easily, without complex parsing programs.

More specifically, a Web service is invoked using HTTP and returns data to the consumer in XML. Sun Microsystems has defined a Web service as an "application that accepts requests from other systems across the Internet or an intranet, mediated by lightweight, vendor-neutral communication technologies." Microsoft has described it this way, "XML Web services let applications share data, and—more powerfully—invoke capabilities from other applications without regard to how those applications were built, what operating system or platform they run on, and what devices are used to access them."

Web services signify a shift in software development paradigms. Companies such as Concord EFS, located in Memphis, Tennessee, earn millions of dollars from credit card-processing Web services. Web services advocate segmenting large applications so that individual components can exist as Web services. Web services provide new avenues in distributed computing.

Web services and DLLs (subroutines of computer software) centralize application logic, such as business rules and database access. However, Web services can be accessed through the HTTP protocol, thus allowing any Web client to invoke a Web service. This is not the case with DLLs, which are typically invoked from clients within the same intranet. Additionally, Web services return data to a client in XML. DLLs typically return data through programming language-specific data types.

Web services benefit from the acceptance of HTTP as a protocol through which users access the Internet and XML as the de facto standard for data transfer.

Figure 5-9 illustrates the Web service. Notice the absence of leased lines and proprietary data formats.

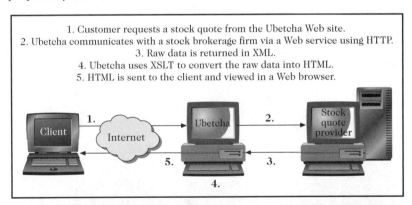

1. Customer requests a stock quote from the Ubetcha Web site.
2. Ubetcha communicates with a stock brokerage firm via a Web service using HTTP.
3. Raw data is returned in XML.
4. Ubetcha uses XSLT to convert the raw data into HTML.
5. HTML is sent to the client and viewed in a Web browser.

Figure 5-9 *Modified steps for providing stock quotes on the Internet*

The Java 2 Platform, Enterprise Edition (J2EE) is a set of specifications created by Sun Microsystems. Each specification dictates how various J2EE functions operate.

For example, the Java Transaction Service (JTS) specification identifies how to build a service that allows distributed transactions.

Companies such as IBM, Compaq, SAP, Oracle, Hitachi, NEC, and TogetherSoft have licensed J2EE. J2EE licensees can ship products that are J2EE compatible and bear the Java 2 Platform, Enterprise Edition brand, delivering on Java's *Write Once, Run Anywhere* capability. Microsoft is not a licensee, the consequence of a lawsuit resulting in a $20 million settlement. In 1997, Sun sued Microsoft for breaching its contractual obligation to deliver compatible products that implement Sun Java technology. In other words, Microsoft had not followed the Java standard.

J2EE's servlet technology allows Web service development. A servlet performs all processing, including calls to Enterprise JavaBeans that return data to the servlet. The servlets then formulate a response and package it in XML for return to the client.

Toward the end of 1995, Microsoft began to shift its attention to the Internet; the company arrived late to the market because of its focus on the Windows 95 operating system. At that time, Netscape was acquiring market share and Microsoft was struggling to launch its Internet browser.

Also at this same time, Microsoft scrambled to deliver technologies such as Active Server Pages (ASP). The company developed many technologies in **Internet time**—a rapid time-to-market, typically measured in hours or days instead of months or years. Some early technologies did not succeed. For example, Active Documents, an add-on to the Visual Basic programming language, enabled Visual Basic developers to create Web applications with no additional programming. Active Documents disappeared quietly and quickly because Microsoft realized the solution created a type of software hammer that would limit developers.

To capitalize on the Web service evolution, Microsoft launched the .NET initiative, which has a different architecture than its DNA (Distributed iNternet Applications architecture) origins. ASP.NET offers a full programming language environment, unlike its prior scripting-based environment. In .NET, Visual Basic became an object-oriented language. Other features not available in Sun J2EE include ASP.NET's capability to render pages in various HTML formats. Servlets can achieve the same task with manual coding.

For developers, both J2EE and .NET provide the tools to create Web services. While J2EE boasts multiplatform support, Microsoft has positioned its .NET offering to use a two-step compilation process, allowing Microsoft to provide runtime environments for different platforms.

In the .NET environment, developer-written code compiles into the Microsoft Intermediate Language. Then the Common Language Runtime (CLR) compiles the code into native code at execution. .NET includes C#, a programming language that is similar to Sun Java. Microsoft has also provided a facility to convert Java code to C#. CLRs are being targeted for Linux and BSD UNIX platforms. Currently, J2EE is the only development environment that offers platform independence.

In contrast to .NET, J2EE uses a single language—Java. .NET supports more than two dozen languages, including FORTRAN, COBOL, C++, and Visual Basic. Multilanguage support offers an advantage to organizations wishing to leverage developers' expertise. Microsoft's strategy is to relegate Java as just another programming language. Sun tries to position Java not just as a language, but as a platform.

In selecting a Web Services vendor, *builders* can use this rule of thumb: Use J2EE if there is not a commitment to a homogenous Microsoft platform. Ultimately, the *builder* needs to understand the Web services offered by both vendors and be able to weigh the perceived trade-offs in order to produce an Internet/intranet application design.

Part of the lawsuit between Sun and Microsoft involved changing a design, namely for Java. Microsoft had wanted to do it one way, but Sun would not allow it. Sun realizes that Microsoft has a strong foothold in the marketplace and that Sun may never attain a leading market share. However, Sun believes it can be a positive disruptive force in IT by bringing new *open* technologies to the forefront.

In general, enterprises need to change to be competitive. However, they also need to change to apply new technologies. The organization's enterprise architecture must be able to respond to new ideas, tools, and techniques as quickly as possible. The *builder* must always understand the tools at hand. The *builder* must also understand that inappropriate use of a facility, such as Web services, can lead to disaster. In the construction industry, Havens Steel is an example of a company that wanted to design and build things its way, which lead to a disaster.

5.4.5 Not Me *(who)*

In 1976, Crown Center Redevelopment Corporation began designing the Hyatt Regency Hotel in Kansas City, Missouri. The 750-room, 40-story tower hotel included a large conference center, which was to be connected to the hotel by three suspended walkways. The walkways would be enclosed in an atrium and would connect the second, third, and fourth floors of the hotel and conference center.

On April 4, 1978, Gillum-Colaco Enterprises agreed to provide the structural engineering services for the construction. In December, Havens Steel Company was chosen to provide steel for the hotel's atrium. The following February, Havens Steel changed the design of the connector of the second- and fourth-floor walkways from a single- to a double-rod design. See Figure 5-10.

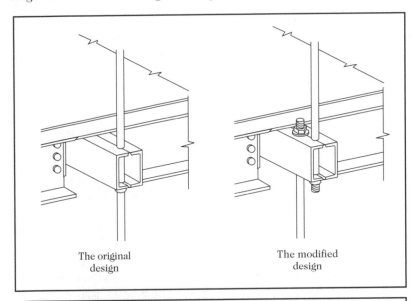

The original design

The modified design

Figure 5-10 *Comparing designs*

The atrium was splendid and large—17,000 square feet with a 50-foot high ceiling. The atrium's main feature was the three *floating* walkways. During construction, the atrium roof collapsed. The roof was reconstructed and inspected, and its safety was confirmed. In July 1980, the hotel opened for business. On July 17, one year later, the second- and fourth-floor walkways collapsed, killing 114 and injuring 200 others.

In the original design, single rods were intended to hold both the second- and fourth-floor walkways. When Havens Steel changed the design, rods connected to the fourth-floor walkway supported the second-floor walkway. The new design consisted of one hanger connection between the roof and the fourth floor and another between the second and fourth floors. The design change meant that a steel thread from the top to the bottom of the rod was no longer needed.

The design is analogous to two people holding onto a rope hanging from a tree. If each person can support his own body weight, and the tree and rope can hold both people, the structure is stable. However, if one person holds onto the rope, and the other person holds onto the other person's legs, the first person must support the combined body weight. The grip of the top person is more likely to fail. See Figure 5-11.

Figure 5-11. *Weight distribution*

The initial design was similar to two people hanging onto a rope, while the implemented design was similar to a second person hanging from the first person's legs. The first person's grip is comparable to the fourth-floor hanger rod connection. The failure of the grip caused the walkway collapse.

Around 7:05 p.m. on July 17, 1981, people in the Hyatt Regency Hotel in Kansas City, Missouri heard a loud crack. The second- and fourth-floor walkways collapsed while people danced on the walkways and atrium floor to the band playing *Satin Doll*.

Additional problems surfaced when investigators determined that both the first design and the applied design had not met Kansas City building code standards. The design had accounted for the support of only 60 percent of the minimum standard.

SIX REASONS FOR MOST STRUCTURAL FAILURES IN IT

- Lack of consideration for communication traffic acting on a particular connection
- Abrupt changes in the amount of transactions sharing CPU memory
- Failure to take security into account in the design
- Improper preparation of configuration variables
- Use of inflexible or unscalable software or programming techniques
- Failure to understand limits of hardware, networks, or COTS software

The U.S. Department of Commerce's Center for Building Technology worked to determine the exact cause of the accident and who was responsible for the fatal error—the *designer*, Gillum-Colaco, or the *builder*, Havens Steel. The Department of Commerce determined the flaw was contained in the design, and the construction techniques were not at fault. The construction was sound within the imperfect design. Therefore, Gillum-Colaco was determined to be completely at fault in causing the collapse of the walkways.

The Department of Commerce found the designs had been changed from a single-rod system to a double-rod system with Gillum-Colaco's approval, creating a weaker structure. It also cited that the design did not adhere to the Engineering Code of Ethics, which states that public safety is the most important part of a design.

As a result, the engineers employed by Gillum-Colaco, who affixed their seals to the drawings, lost their engineering licenses in Missouri and Texas. Gillum-Colaco also lost its certification to be an engineering firm.

As with any disaster, lessons learned from the walkway collapse can be applied to other situations. When walkways similar to the Hyatt Regency's design are undertaken in the future, the *builder* would know that the bridge should be suspended by one long bar rather than two. Engineers learned they had to overcompensate when bracing structures. The structure must withstand much more force than will realistically ever be needed. This engineering concept was known long before, but was reinforced by the Hyatt tragedy. The collapse of the walkway created a greater awareness of the need for preventive measures, such as stricter guidelines and better inspection procedures. One cannot cut corners when developing critical components.

5.4.6 Wait and See *(when)*

In the late 1980s, Sybase entered into a partnership with Microsoft to develop an OS/2 version, and subsequently a Windows NT version, of Sybase's successful UNIX database called SQL Server. After the partnership failed in 1994, both companies continued to use the SQL Server name to market database products. After several years, and starting with version 11.5, Sybase renamed its flagship database product

Adaptive Server Enterprise. The name change was created to prevent customer confusion and mask previous problems associated with earlier versions.

Sybase was founded in 1984, when the use of local area networks (LAN) enabled client/server computing. Seizing the opportunity, Sybase introduced its SQL Server relational database in 1987. With the commercial acceptance of LANs, Sybase executives accurately determined that many enterprises would take the opportunity to decentralize data manipulation and storage.

Since its inception, the Sybase SQL Server database engine has introduced unique features for database management with each major release. SQL Server was the first database to offer stored procedures. In the mid-1990s, Sybase introduced version 10 of the product,[10] which could allocate more memory to the data server without degrading its performance and allowed more than one database engine to take advantage of multiprocessor CPU machines.

Each SQL Server database engine ran as a UNIX process. When the database was deployed with more than one engine, one of the engines would be the master engine. The other engines were subordinate engines and were assigned tasks by the master.

Unfortunately, the version 10 multiengine architecture soon proved to be too limited. The database could not scale beyond four processors. In information technology, scale or **scalability** is the ability of a product to expand without the need for the base product to change. Some computers can scale or grow the number of processors on a single machine. Other forms of scalability include software that can utilize expanded hardware features. As in the Hyatt Regency catastrophe, the Sybase database engine could not support the weight of the enterprise. The database engine, the raw material for building data stores, was not designed to take the weight or throughput many corporations desired. In other words, Sybase's throughput rate was too slow for the needs of most organizations.

Sybase needed time to rework the database kernel in order to handle the scalability problem. In addition, Sybase was slow to get certification on Sun's new operating system, Solaris 2.4. The problem boosted the sales and reputation of Oracle, Sybase's major competitor.

Enterprises such as the Department of Justice in Bern, Switzerland abandoned Sybase. Wall Street all but abandoned Sybase too. The stock price plummeted from its high of $57 per share to less than $5 per share. The share price never recovered, and although many of the architectural problems were fixed in later releases, customers have stayed away.

A *builder* needs to understand the materials and structural thresholds, including databases, so he can create appropriate designs of the implementation. Sybase's defective materials (the database engine) cost the company its opportunity to be a dominant player in the database market. Corporations that used the materials (such as the database engine) were forced to spend hundreds of millions of dollars to redesign and redeploy using other vendors' databases.

Corporations cannot normally afford to wait while a vendor fixes a problem. Although many companies did wait to see whether Sybase could fix the problem, others migrated to other database servers when processing problems started piling up.

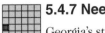

5.4.7 Need Proof *(what)*

Georgia's state legislators believed that 20 percent of Georgia's automobile drivers drove without the necessary automobile insurance and were, therefore, violating state law. Lawmakers agreed stricter enforcement was the key. However, police officers had no reasonable way to prove a vehicle had insurance coverage. Although insurance companies issued proof-of-insurance cards to policyholders, the cards were easy to counterfeit.

In April 2000, lawmakers signed into law Senate Bill 69, which mandated the setup of a database from which police officers could immediately verify a vehicle's insurance. Lawmakers gave the Department of Public Safety 16 months to get the database online.

From the beginning, the project had problems. At the root of the problem was Georgia's vehicle tag and title database. The database tracks automobile registrations for the state so counties know how much ad valorem tax to charge each year. The success of the bill relied on information stored in the state's tag and title database. In Georgia, cars are insured, not people.

The process required to accomplish the task was fairly *simple*. Figure 5-12 represents this process as a dataflow diagram. Each time an insurance company wrote a new automobile policy in Georgia, the name of the insurance carrier, the policy number, the policy expiration date, and the vehicle identification number were loaded onto a state-controlled computer. The information provided by the vehicle insurance company was cross-referenced with the tag and title database, which also tracked cars by vehicle identification number.

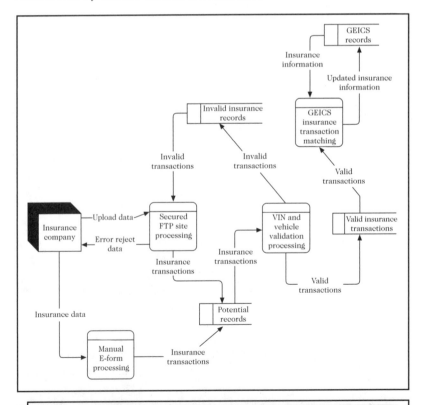

Figure 5-12   *GEICS dataflow diagram*

Police officers could already access mobile computers in their police cars to verify an automobile's registration; now they could access the insurance information too.

The bill made the Department of Public Safety responsible for putting together the insurance database. The agency already managed license suspensions for failure to have insurance, so to lawmakers, the agency seemed a natural fit. When the bill passed, the state's tag and title database resided within the Department of Revenue. Neither the tag and title database nor the Department of Revenue was mentioned in the bill. Bringing together the systems would take cooperation.

Unfortunately, the cooperation never came. The two agencies went back and forth over which should take control of the database, or whether an insurance field could just be added to the tag and title database. To compound the problem, the legislature had not provided funding for the project because it believed the existing state government budget could be used.

The agencies failed to contact the one agency that might have helped—the Georgia Technology Authority, which was created to bring agencies together to share data.

Within days of the original implementation date, Georgia's governor, Roy Barnes (b. 1948), signed another bill into law creating the Department of Motor Vehicle Safety. The new agency effectively brought the tag and title database and the responsibility for suspending driver's licenses under one roof. The yearlong tug-of-war over the insurance verification database was over.

Tom Burgess was appointed commissioner of the new agency, but decided he needed more information from the insurance companies, other than just the policy expiration date and vehicle identification number. Vehicle identification numbers are long and can be mistyped. Poor data quality would create unnecessary hassles for legally insured motorists. Burgess wanted other pieces of information to allow better cross-referencing to ensure accuracy.

The project has cost Georgia taxpayers hundreds of thousands of dollars. Lawmakers concluded this was a simple project and that they were equipped to make basic design decisions and forego understanding how all the information would flow. Believing they were equipped to make basic design decisions, these lawmakers provide an example of the *design by hope* term introduced in Section 5.3.6.

When people perceive something is easy, they are often inclined to seek additional shortcuts. The project lacked the appropriate planning, ownership, and funding.

5.4.8 Key Terms

Internet time	scalability
point-in-time	source code

5.4.9 Review Questions

1. Give three examples of trade-offs that might occur in business.

2. What are some of the reasons organizations choose to make a trade-off?

3. How is open-source code useful to organizations today? What is the most popular open-source software license called?
4. What are the open-source definition mandates?
5. Who develops open-source software and where does development occur?
6. What is a Web service and what is the primary language used to transport data?

7. How did *designing by hope* affect the Georgia automobile insurance project?
8. What caused the Sybase stock to plummet on Wall Street in the mid-1990s?
9. Why must the *builder* understand the materials, such as a database engine?
10. Why is overcompensation beneficial for constructing buildings or software?
11. How is the term scalability used in information technology?

SECTION 5.5 HOW TO SPEND MONEY

QUESTIONS TO CONTEMPLATE

1. After money has been budgeted, who is responsible for spending the money?
2. What is a bill of materials?
3. How many different ways can time be quantified?

5.5.1 Introduction

In the 1996 movie *Jerry Maguire*, Tom Cruise's (b. 1962) character tries to convince a client to continue using his services. The client, played by Cuba Gooding Jr. (b. 1968), is the demanding all-star athlete who instructs Cruise on what he must do to convince him to stay. "Show me the money," he tells Cruise. Soon, both characters are shouting the phrase over and over, louder and louder.

Throughout the enterprise, *planners* and *owners* try to justify spending money for building and maintaining software, or for any other project. In meetings to review project budgets, grumpy executives ask how much revenue the project will produce. In their exasperation, they scream, "Show me the money!"

In business, you have to spend money to *maybe* make money. After the budgets have been created and funded, the *builder* spends the money. The *builder* does not have to physically sign the checks or hand over the cash, but he is the one who says, "I'll have one of those and three of these."

Spending the money is part of the *builder's* responsibility, as is accounting for all expenditures. Planning, establishing priorities, finding the source of funding, and creating the design involve costs. However, until the design is created and approved, the enterprise has probably spent minimal dollars relative to the whole. When the *builder* is given the go ahead, he assumes the following elements are explicit:

- The amount of resources required for the project has been expressed, in terms of a currency, and committed for the project (*what*—assets)
- Processes are well understood (*how*—processes)

- All the sites to be used for communication and conducting business are known (*where*—location)
- The people interfaces have been discovered (*who*—people)
- The time frames and total time to completion are understood and acceptable (*when*—business event schedule)
- Someone had the authority, responsibility, and desire to proceed with the project (*why*—motivation)

By the time the *builder* has completed the design, the following project elements have been made explicit by the *planner*, *owner*, and *designer*:

- The resources have been detailed in a project budget (*what*—assets)
- Construction processes and toolsets are well understood (*how*—processes)
- All the issues of the construction site have been resolved, including communication networks and technology (*where*—location)
- The skill sets have been defined and are understood (*who*—people)
- Project milestones have been determined for each set of activities and tasks (*when*—project plan)
- The *builder* has been given the authority, responsibility, and management position to proceed with the project. The *builder* has become an agent of action (*why*—motivation)

Manufacturing is *big business* and manufacturing companies spend a lot of money to stay in business. Startup and ongoing costs can be huge. Manufacturing plants must be built, equipment must be built or purchased, administration buildings must be built or leased, personnel must be hired and trained, and raw materials must be acquired.

Small manufacturers run the risk of becoming so successful that they cannot obtain the capital required to expand and meet demand. Giant manufacturers, such as General Motors, Ford, Toyota, Deere, and Caterpillar, continue to fight a battle of reinvestment to adapt repeatedly to changing times.

Chrome Belt Manufacturing (CBM) provides an example of how the *builder* spends the money and demonstrates the complexities many large manufacturers face. The company is fictitious, but is based on automobile and electronics manufacturer General Motors and heavy equipment and engine manufacturer Caterpillar.

The following example applies equally to most types of businesses, including software developers such as Microsoft, computer manufacturers such as IBM, retailers such as Wal-Mart, and insurance companies such as State Farm.

5.5.2 Powerhouse to Powerless *(how)*

CBM is a huge enterprise with over 500,000 employees worldwide. In addition to its own 500,000 employees, CBM owns 125 other companies in the United States that are separate entities. These 125 other companies employ another 1 million people. The U.S. headquarters for major manufacturing operations is located in Muncie, Indiana, and the corporate financial headquarters is located in midtown Manhattan. CBM has many subsidiary companies, each with its own corporate identity. All the U.S. entities are incorporated in the State of Delaware.

CBM owns 85 corporations outside of the United States. These companies employ approximately 1 million people. With the exception of North Korea and Cuba, CBM conducts some form of business in many medium to large cities across the globe.

CBM is a heavy transportation equipment manufacturer and uses the corporate name Big Transportation Manufacturing (BTM). Other lines of business include plastics, electronics, agriculture, drugs, communications, and software development for commercial sale. The total sales for CBM's corporate empire are greater than the gross national product of most countries. CBM is an economic powerhouse, and its financial prowess provides political clout in all the world's capitals. CBM shares this economic power with about 100 other global corporations.

Edward Deming (1900–1993) said, "If you can't describe what you are doing as a process, you don't know what you're doing." In other words, *process, process, process; everything is process*. When Deming delivered his philosophy in the 1950s to the Big Four automakers (Ford Motor Company, Chrysler Corporation, American Motors Corporation, and General Motors Corporation), he was politely told: *Thank you, goodbye*. The Big Four believed they had a complete lock on the American automobile market.

Until the 1970s, the Big Four generally designed and built cars to become obsolete in seven years and to require repairs after about 12,000 miles. Frequent repairs ensured a good aftermarket for replacement parts.

The 1972 gasoline shortage in the U.S. had a sobering effect on the Big Four. The automobile market changed overnight. In 1972, the Japanese Honda Civic, a small car that got great gasoline mileage compared to Detroit's gas-guzzlers, was well built and reliable, and was designed not to become obsolete in seven years. The great Midwest manufacturing engine was turned into the *rust belt*. Economists argued busily among themselves about when the American economy would fail. As Mark Twain said upon reading of his death in May 1897, "The report of my death was exaggerated."

CBM took a big hit in those years. Because of its corporate name, BTM was accused of building inferior products, and critics pronounced the corporate name as *bottom*. Consumers quickly latched onto the slogan *rock bottom quality* to talk about any inferior product. CBM had to close plants, fire employees, construct new plants, and reconstruct existing plants using new machines, new tools, and new processes. Even CBM cried for Deming to come visit.

In the late 1950s and 1960s, many Japanese manufacturers recognized both quality and production problems. Japanese companies invited Deming to visit their facilities in Japan. The Japanese quickly believed in Deming's quality message and his *process, process, process* view. Deming's influence on Japan caused the world economic power balance to change.

Many Lakes Manufacturing (MLM), located in International Falls, Minnesota, is a subsidiary of CBM. By 1980, MLM started reconstructing and rebuilding itself to recover its lost market share. Prior to being overwhelmed by the acceptance of Japanese products in America, U.S.-based companies had been observing European products. American automobile manufacturers had already ceded the luxury top-end vehicles to Rolls Royce, Mercedes, Jaguar, and BMW. The American automobile industry was afraid of Volkswagen when Honda, Toyota, and Datsun (now called Nissan) caught the industry by surprise.

Kaizen, a term introduced into the Japanese vocabulary in 1985 by Masaaki Imai in the book, *Kaizen: The Key to Japan's Competitive Success*, combined Japan's quality innovations with product improvement. Kaizen means a gradual, unending improvement by doing little things better and by setting and achieving increasingly higher standards. Kaizen's principles enhanced Deming's original message. In the 1980s, Kaizen gave the Japanese another short-term competitive advantage.

Japan's homogenous society adapted easily to the quality messages of Deming and Imai, whereas the American heterogeneous society experienced more difficulty adapting to the quality messages.

MLM's *builders* were charged with constructing new processes and proving they worked. Depending on the *builder's* specific discipline, the processes included manufacturing, sales, marketing, accounting, human resources, logistics, quality assurance, and information technology. The *builder* also had to reconstruct the inventory control practices and prove they worked. All of this started with the *builder* identifying the first and most important unit of measure, the production order.

At MLM, when the production schedule manager receives a production order, the manufacturing process begins. The business rules the manager uses to start manufacturing depend on the point of entry and control for the production. In general, manufacturing is a complex undertaking; the point of entry and control is an arbitrary place the company chooses to start the entire manufacturing process. For example, when inventory is the point of entry and control, the rules for production may be different from the rules used when materials acquisition or product shipping are points of entry and control.

A unit of measure may be part of another unit of measure. Manufacturers of every product requiring more than one part for the total assembly have long used the concept of a **bill of materials**.

BILL OF MATERIALS CHARACTERISTICS

A bill of materials is a list of parts in a specific hierarchical sequence. The list contains the final product and every assembly and subassembly down to the smallest part used. Manufacturers use the term **product explosion** when determining all the parts required for any product. When a manufacturer wants to find all the products a particular part is used in, that is called a **product implosion**.

Product explosions help the manufacturer answer (*where*) questions like:

- What production facilities are needed?
- What raw materials are required?
- What are the number and order of manufacturing steps?
- What equipment is required?
- How many people are needed and with what skills?
- How much workspace is required?
- What monetary investments are required?

(continued)

Product implosions help the manufacturer answer (more *where*) questions like:

- Should we make or buy the part?
- What are the lead time requirements to ensure the part is available when the part is needed?
- Should the part be stored in inventory or should just-in-time concepts be employed?

The bill of materials helps create an expense breakdown detailing the step-by-step costs for the part (*what*). A bill of materials can be used to determine the exact application of the part (*how*). Bill of materials lists also help to identify the skills required for each functional step of the entire process, from order to delivery and maintenance (*who*). The list can also be used to determine the exact time line for each part (*when*), including:

- Workstation or location where the part is required
- Sequence of use for the part
- Time duration required to make, buy, move, store, and retrieve the part
- Iteration time frame for the continued reuse of the part

The list can be used to provide the rationale for the use of the part and justify other decisions regarding the part (*why*).

The *builder* must construct and account for all materials and processes for the project. Each piece of material and each process costs money—things the *builder* has chosen to spend money on.

5.5.3 Small Town U.S.A. *(where)*

Like dozens of small cities in the United States, International Falls, Minnesota owes its prosperity to a single manufacturer, MLM. Some of these other cities include Waterloo, Iowa; Decatur, Illinois; Ada, Michigan; and Wichita, Kansas.

MLM employs 4,000 people and drives the regional economy. In a remote location near the Canadian border, nearly 300 miles north of Minneapolis, International Falls is a cold place to live. The mean temperature in January is 1°F.[11] Summer temperatures average a mild 66°F. International Falls is also characterized by a dedicated, dependable, hard-working labor force and vast amounts of cheap power.

In any project, the *builder* has to consider power, which is an issue of infrastructure. Infrastructure is an issue of location. Infrastructure has costs and the *builder* must account for those costs. Here is a list of the other issues of infrastructure:

- Utilities
- Communication
- Zoning
- Local legislation
- Workforce availability

- Climate and weather
- Local culture
- Topography
- Geography
- Transportation accessibility
- Local education systems
- Local politics
- Security

Because these infrastructure issues are external to the corporation, they are considered to be **intrusions**. Most intrusions are ignored despite their potential disruptive tendencies. Intrusions can end or delay a project. The General Motors electric vehicle EV1 was subjected to legislative intrusions in 2002. The intrusions terminated the project. The EV1 is further discussed in Section 5.7.6.

The *builder* must understand the intrusions of climate and weather. Even in an IT data center, the *builder* must understand and control temperature and humidity levels. Local culture is often based on the weather. International Falls experiences 60 or 70 continuous days of subzero (Celsius) weather each year. The ground is so frozen, the dead cannot be buried until after the spring thaw, and then the permafrost must still be removed. Life here is only for the very hardy and adaptable.

Cold places place serious constraints on the *builder*. Equipment left outside in the winter becomes fragile. Iron and steel can crack in extreme cold. Bare hands must not be placed on exposed metal in the winter because skin instantly bonds to the metal and can cause severe medical problems. Physical and mental processes slow down when people are too hot or too cold.

The *builder* must know and understand all of these things, as he has at MLM. Because motorized vehicles must be kept running at all times, or be equipped with oil and engine block heaters when turned off, MLM's employee parking spaces have adapters to plug in automobile heaters. Battery jump-start services are always available. Employees working on loading docks are furnished with extra warm clothes. The loading docks are sealed off from the rest of the building to keep everyone else warm.

The *builder* must address many corporate infrastructure issues:

- Workspaces
- Utility provisions
- Telecommunications
- Corporate communication
- Special needs considerations
- Special workspaces
- Special technology requirements
- On-site security

These are internal intrusions to the organization, which can be as disruptive as external intrusions. Knowledge of an intrusion's disruptive nature helps the *designer* and *builder* focus their design energies.

The *builder* must construct the infrastructure to complete the site construction and run the business. The IT *builder* must construct the systems that support the construction and business operation.

5.5.4 They Work Hard for the Money *(who)*

The *designer* determines the business processes that are needed for the project, and the *builder* transforms the business processes into an organization chart. However, an organization chart rarely includes all the following facts for the organizational units:

- Charter (mission statement)
- Position descriptions
- Job descriptions
- Chain of command
- Staffing by position
- Staffing by job
- Skill requirements and definitions
- Annual budget
- Salary and benefits constraints

These are the same facts the Egyptians established 4,500 years ago. Organizational units have changed little in the intervening years.

The MLM *builder* has organized the 4,000 employees, as shown in Figure 5-13. On the surface, nothing is unique about MLM. The organization looks like many other manufacturing operations in America. MLM is a prototypical, well-run, and well-managed manufacturing organization.

The *builders* at MLM continually reconstruct the business operations and the information technology to provide optimum use of technology. MLM has the same number of employees today as the organization had in 1972, though its sales have quadrupled and profits quintupled. MLM has been able to pay a dividend every quarter since 1989.

5.5.5 On the Schedule and on Schedule *(when)*

At MLM, only scheduled tasks can occur, including when machines are turned on, when people are supposed to report to work, when materials and parts should be ordered, when bills are to be paid, when invoices are sent out, when IT systems are executed, and when employees are compensated. Everything at MLM must be scheduled, and the *builder* schedules everything.

When visitors tour the three-acre plant floor at MLM, they comment on the orderliness and neatness of the facility. There are no oil slicks on the floor, no litter, and no dust. The plant is well lit. The floors are sealed, and despite the noise of the machines, conversation in a normal tone is possible. All the workers seem to be satisfied and industrious. As the visitors pass each production line and work center, employees glance over and smile to acknowledge the guests.

No one is running around trying to find lost orders. Parts are not endlessly circling overhead looking for a home. Floor management is not immediately identifiable or noticeable. Inquisitive visitors often ask: "Where are the foremen and union representatives? Where is the contention that exists between labor and management?" MLM's CEO tells the visitors he does not know where those things are, but they are not at MLM. Figure 5-13 shows the MLM organization chart.

- CEO
  - Legal Department
    - Contracts Administration
    - Legal Affairs
    - Patent Application and Administration
    - Insurance Administration
  - CFO
    - Treasurer
      - Stock Issuance and Tracking
      - Dividend Payout and Tracking
    - Comptroller
      - Portfolio Management
        - Bond Manager
        - Stock Manager
        - Other Investments Manager
    - Pension Plan Administrator
    - Accounting
      - Bookkeeping
      - Accounts Receivable
      - Accounts Payable
  - CIO
    - Director of Operations
      - Computer Operators
      - Computer Technical Support
      - Computer Internals Experts
      - Network Administration
    - Director of Telecommunications
      - Telephone Support
      - Web Support
      - InterOffice Communication Support
  - Plant Manager
    - Production Scheduling
      - Shift Managers
      - Work Center Managers
        - Machine Operators
        - Service Operators
        - Expendable Supplies Management
      - Scrap and Rework
      - Die Making
      - Tool Setup
      - Numerical Control and Programming
      - Tool Safety
      - Employee Safety Compliance and Reporting
      - Time Keeper
    - Finished Goods Inventory
    - Raw Materials Inventory
    - Expediter
    - Shipping and Receiving
    - Quality Control and Assurance
    - Labor Coordination
    - Shop Maintenance
    - Equipment Maintenance
    - Purchasing Manager
      - Purchasing Agents
    - Materials Management Forecaster
  - Sales and Marketing
    - Marketing
      - Advertising
      - Public Relations
      - Telephone Marketing
    - Sales
      - Territory Managers
        - Salesmen
  - Human Resources
    - Recruiting
    - Benefit Administration
    - Salary Administration
  - Administrative Manager
    - Secretarial
    - Security
    - Office Supplies
    - Office Supplies and Miscellaneous Purchasing Agent
    - Facilities Management

Figure 5-13   *MLM organization chart*

At MLM, every worker believes the time allowed for each task is realistic, and the work can be done comfortably in the scheduled time frame. A reasonable time frame promotes the workers' satisfaction that their skills and efforts are valued and appreciated. The worker is given ample opportunity to learn and perfect new skills, and the learning is encouraged and paid for by MLM management. The *builder* was responsible for creating the environment where employees have a positive attitude and morale is high.

The *builder* constructs a detailed production schedule by using the *designer's* Gantt charts, which are based on the *owner's* Critical Path Method schedule. Coordinating these schedules creates organizational alignment.

The explicit production schedule details the sequence and time needed to accomplish each business event. Manufacturers have many ways to measure time:

- Order time
- Production time
- Work time
- Storage time
- Wait time
- Setup time
- Breakdown time
- Maintenance time
- Shipping time
- Elapsed time
- Idle time
- Lost time
- Testing time
- Break time

Anything that takes time must be scheduled. Everything takes time, and time always has associated costs. Associated costs aggregate into the total cost of the product or service being produced. Each time category may have associated equipment and personnel costs and storage space requirements. Equipment must be scheduled with the equipment operators. The facility must operate in accordance with Occupational Safety and Health Administration (OSHA) regulations.

The *builder* is responsible for setting the timing for each stop on the production line. The *builder* ensures the ergonomics, safety, reliability, dependability, practicality, and timing for the production line. The aspect of time (*when*) forces everything into alignment to make the operation run. Accurate schedules make sure there are no traffic jams or accidents. The *builder's* timings keep the operation operational.

The *builder* sets priorities for time and production orders using rules, standards, units of measure, metrics, and statistics. The *builder* determines the costs of time and sets how the costs are counted and accounted for. Accounting information is recorded, stored, analyzed, calculated, compared, and reported.

The MLM *builder* does exactly what Imhotep, Abbot Suger, General Leslie Groves, William Levitt, NASA, and Boeing did. The more the requirements change, the more important accounting and timing become. In some ways, nothing has changed in over 4,500 years.

5.5.6 Doling out the Cash *(what)*

To pay the bills, the *builder* must work with the purchasing and accounts payable departments because they help the *builder* keep the construction on schedule and report to the *designer* whether the money is being spent according to schedule. The *designer* reports to the *owner*, who schedules expenses for the next expense cycle.

Spending the money too soon may result in dishonored checks because the corporation may not have sufficient revenue. If an organization fails continually to honor its checks, vendors will demand that purchase orders are prepaid. Employees and temporary staffing agencies may demand establishment of an escrow account to ensure payment for services. Additionally, a corporation's credit rating might be downgraded by marketplace and regulatory authorities that watch a corporation's financial health. The *builder* must guard against even the rumor of financial trouble. Paying bills on time and having a positive cash flow maintain the corporation's financial health.

Timely payment offers additional benefits. Vendors may offer discounts for early payment of goods and services. The depth of discount is sometimes related to the cash flow of the vendor. Businesspeople recognize that cash in the bank today is worth more than the promise of cash in the future. In business, this is called days sales outstanding (DSO), which is a measurement that reflects the corporation's ability to collect monies owed. The *builder* must construct the appropriate accounting and review procedures to take advantage of the cash flow.

The *builder* first imposes the accounting and review procedures in the purchasing department, which arranges discounts, payment terms, and time for delivery. Vendors may offer discounts based on product volume and money spent. Purchasing procures goods and services at the best price and tries to stay within budget. Purchasing arranges payment schedules based on the budget and ensures the accounts payable department releases the funds when the obligations become due.

Purchasing and payables at MLM are major points of control. Purchasing is driven primarily by the production schedule, which demands compliance. If goods and services do not arrive at the appointed time, the production line stops and production is delayed. The result is many employees standing by the window drinking coffee and watching the outside thermometer. Lost time is an expense and an aggravation to management.

Some companies, such as Keane, account for lost time when the *builder's* project plans are produced. Although employees work a standard 8-hour day, Keane's experiences have shown employees are really only productive for 6.7 hours per day. Therefore, schedules are based on productivity of 6.7 hours in a single day for each employee. Lost time is not idle time because it is associated with people. Idle time occurs when the machine is not being used for any reason other than maintenance. If the machine is idle, the operator is usually assigned other work so no loss in personnel productivity occurs.

MLM's productivity rate is high, though the exact statistic is a closely held secret. MLM complies with ISO-9000 standards and received the Deming Prize and Baldridge Awards in successive years. MLM experiences less than four defects per million parts produced and consequently achieves Six Sigma, which is explained in Section 5.7.4.

311

The productivity rate provides a strong competitive advantage. MLM and its employees are proud to keep all information, buying practices, and operating procedures closely guarded. MLM is not worried about local competition. The *builder* constructed the accounting, purchasing, accounts payable, and operating procedures that also provide MLM with a competitive advantage.

5.5.7 We're in the Money *(why)*

The goal of commercial enterprises is to make money. The *builder* is responsible for spending the money and the *builder's* motivations are to define and construct the following:

- Metrics (*what*)
- Processes (*how*)
- Site (*where*)
- Organization (*who*)
- Schedules (*when*)
- Profit (*why*)

Because companies must make a profit year after year to remain in business, defining and constructing a profit is one of the most important aspects the *builder* needs to accomplish as an agent of action.

5.5.8 Key Terms

bill of materials	product explosion
intrusion	product implosion

5.5.9 Review Questions

1. What does the *designer* need to make explicit for the *builder*?
2. For what tasks is the *builder* responsible?
3. What was most important to Edward Deming?
4. What does Kaizen mean?
5. Who produces a detailed production schedule, a Gantt chart, and a CPM schedule?
6. What interrogative does the *builder* use to align the operations?
7. In an organization, the *builder* decides what to spend money on. What department negotiates the price, and what department releases the funds?
8. What is the difference between lost time and idle time?
9. What is the *builder's* motivation?
10. Name two types of external intrusions and two types of internal intrusions.

SECTION 5.6 WHO WILL WATER MY FLOWERS—TAKING CARE OF THE BUSINESS

QUESTIONS TO CONTEMPLATE

1. Why are methodologies significant?
2. What are the differences between data, information, knowledge, and wisdom?
3. When the *builder* is given an unrealistic budget and an unrealistic time frame for completion, what often happens?

5.6.1 Introduction

A business requires a way to measure its results and effectiveness. The enterprise needs structure, discipline, and organization to help manage the data and information it generates. Structure, discipline, and organization all require rules, standards, units of measure, metrics, and statistics. In addition, an enterprise must have a way of knowing what it knows and the knowing is called **knowledge management**.

Knowledge management, as an IT application, requires a methodology for facilitation. A knowledge management application uses technology to capture, catalog, retain, and retrieve data and information that may benefit decision-making. **Customer relationship management** (CRM) is an example of a type of decision-making knowledge management application.

In general, any type of methodology helps provide a structure. Structure helps provide discipline. Discipline helps provide rigor. Rigor helps provide standards. Standards help provide units of measure. Units of measure help provide metrics. Metrics help provide statistics. Statistics help demonstrate results. Results can be used to drive methods. This is a **causal loop** (see Section 5.6.6 and Figure 5-14).

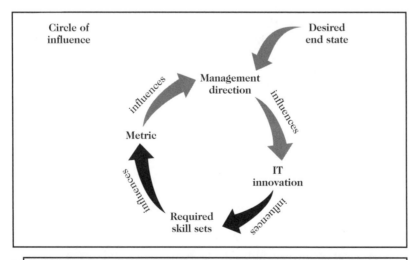

Figure 5-14   *Causal loop*

IT departments may decide to use a methodology developed in-house, one from an IT methodology book, or a commercial methodology. Each method recommends a set of deliverables and a suggested sequence to produce the deliverables. An understood and used method has typically been proven to be better than no method at all.

METHOD FUNDAMENTALS

The following elements are fundamental to all methodologies:

- *Background* sets up the situation for the project including: marketplace analysis, cash flow, legislative requirements, project necessity, and opportunity and risk.
- *Scope* defines all areas of reach and domain of the project. Scope may define explicitly what is considered to be outside the reach and domain of the project.
- *Goals* spell out the desired end state of the project.
- *Objectives* set out clearly what is required for success of the project. Objectives are used to establish metrics to measure success and progress.
- *Strategy* spells out the overall methods to accomplish the end-state.
- *Tactics* describe the specific way in which each task is to be approached and completed.
- *Implementation* sets the level of expectation and rules for the completion, installation, maintenance, and management of the business or system.

Most businesses and government agencies seek to find out more about what they know because knowledge provides effectiveness, competitiveness, and insight for dealing with customers or consumers. Businesses draw upon **data** and **information** to take the appropriate actions based on acquired **knowledge** and **wisdom**. Data is made up of raw facts. Information contains facts with context and perspective. Knowledge is information with guidance for action. Wisdom means understanding which knowledge to use for what purpose.

The following list demonstrates movement from data and information to knowledge and wisdom:

- I have a box that is about 3 feet wide, 3 feet deep, and 6 feet high.
- It is a very heavy box.
- The box has a door on it.
- There is a handle on the door.
- When you open the door, you find it is cold inside the box.
- People usually keep food in this box.
- There is a smaller compartment inside the box with ice and frozen food in it.

- When you open the door of the box, a light comes on.
- The box is usually found in the kitchen in a house.
- This box has a tendency to collect stuff on top of it.
- People do not often move this box, but when they do, there is usually lots of dust under it.

Somewhere along this list, you discovered that what was being described was a refrigerator. When you started reading, you did not know; you read on, and you still did not know. You read some more and still did not know, and then, you knew. Once you knew each statement described the refrigerator, each statement simply added to your level of certainty.

Different people might connect after a different number of statements. Statements could be provided in any order, yet at some point, the connection happens. The point is that what we know *we know* is due to patterns of association. The previous statements represent a **pattern**, and when the pattern connects, we know. Knowledge represents a pattern with which we connect.

There are patterns of association from data to information to knowledge to wisdom, as shown in Figure 5-15.

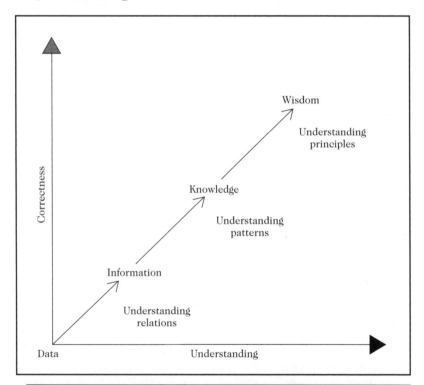

Figure 5-15   *Data to wisdom through correctness and understanding*

THE MARCH TO WISDOM

Data is the lowest level of abstraction. Data is stored entirely out of context and in and of itself is without meaning. Data requires a basic level of description and a rule of use so a person can understand it and a computer can store and use it.

Information recognizes and uses data by establishing relationships. Information is in context of something and is a subset of something larger. Somebody who works with information is known as a knowledge worker and can answer questions relative to a given situation.

Knowledge is the context for information and requires many relationships of information. Knowledge requires the storing of information and learning how best to interpret that information. Knowledge also infers that more solid conclusions can be reached because a wider view of an issue is being taken than on an information level.

Wisdom requires people to apply knowledge with an action to attain the best ends. Wisdom is a synthesis for the application of data, information, and knowledge. Wisdom is heightened when a systems thinking approach or holistic view is taken and actions are conducted with the understanding of their ramifications.

5.6.2 Human Memory *(who)*

Depending on someone else's information and knowledge is difficult. The most valuable asset of the corporation—knowledge—is locked away inside somebody's head. Some people in the organization are not capable of sharing knowledge. Psychologist Dr. Jonathan Lauter (b. 1956) states, "People have a hard time recollecting the past accurately. If predicting the future is hard, some people make predicting the past equally so." The following list provides possible reasons:

- People view knowledge as job security and to share would lessen employee value.
- People do not have very good memories and often forget things.
- People do not record or document to supplement their memories.
- People misplace things that were going to supplement their memories.
- People may lack the communication skills needed to transmit an idea.
- People often avoid recounting information if that information is associated with a traumatic situation or memory.
- People assume other people already have the information.

When people do not record and store what they know, knowledge becomes a matter of human memory. Some senior citizens say they know they are old when they have joined the CRAFT Club. CRAFT stands for *can't remember a frightful thing*. How and what we remember are based on interpretation and culture. Interpretation is based on emotional filters and experiences, and culture dictates what is important for us to remember.

Knowledge management applications are closed systems, which demand the persistence of data or a repeatable process. Airplane landing gears are an example of a repeatable process. Data stored on media, such as a computer's hard drive or a piece of paper, is persistent data.

In a closed system, changes that certain people considered and authorized previously are the only changes that the system allows. The domain of the closed system helps determine which *owners*, users, stakeholders, *planners*, and *designers* need to participate in the change process.

Manufacturing and production at Boeing Corporation use closed systems with well-defined change processes. The *builders* at Boeing must produce an airplane. This mandate is constrained by the *planner*, *owner*, *designer*, physics, and the Federal Aviation Authority. Airplane producers must account for the use of everything in an airplane down to the last rivet.

The *designer* might specify a ³⁄₁₆-inch coated steel and aluminum stem rivet. However, the *builder* might discover that a ⁵⁄₃₂-inch rivet works just as well, or so the *builder* believes. However, the *builder* cannot arbitrarily replace an item in the design specifications. Instead, he must request a change. The *designer* must review the request for change, consult others in the domain, and if warranted, issue a change order. Each piece of documentation is cataloged and recorded.

Information technology should be a closed system with a defined change management process. Managing change in IT is no different from managing change in building an airplane.

The *builder* must make sure all employees understand that they are working in a closed system. The *builder* uses rules, standards, units of measure, metrics, and statistics to ensure the safety and integrity of the closed system. A knowledge management application succeeds when the resulting measurements persist (are kept for later reference). If a knowledge management application fails, one of the corporation's most valuable assets is lost.

5.6.3 Managing the Body of Knowledge *(what)*

An entry (*what*) in the general ledger records costs associated with processes (*how*), location (*where*), and people (*who*). To associate costs with processes, location, and people, you must have a schedule (*when*). To have a schedule, you need motivation (*why*). Take away any interrogative and the entry will not appear in the general ledger. The phrase, *If it is not in the general ledger, it does not exist* is a truism for business and government.

Accounting is the accumulation and result of the interrogatives *how* (process), *where* (location), *who* (people), and *when* (schedule). Costs are associated with each interrogative. The *builder* must record, track, and store the costs, using the domains of each interrogative. The accountant is responsible for maintaining accurate information and numbers, and must prepare and submit all financial reports stipulated by the *designer's* mandate.

The *builder* requires a **repository** that combines the features of a dictionary, the-saurus, and encyclopedia. The repository must store and allow instant access to pictures, models, plans, schedules, drawings, numbers, historical information, documents, documentation, video, and audio. The repository must maintain relationships from one piece of data or information to another piece of data or information. The relationships are established by the interrogatives (*what, how, where, who, when,* and *why*) and perspectives (*planner, owner, designer, builder, subcontractor,* and *functioning enterprise*) of a project. The repository needs rules, including the following:

- Information must be accessible to all personnel and controlled by levels of security.
- Relationships for data and information must be kept intact.
- Relationships for data and information must be governed by rules.
- Both real data and metadata must be stored. Real data includes financial statements and documents. Metadata includes rules about standards, units of measure, and metrics.
- All users must have a consistent view of the same data.

The knowledge management manager has overall authority for the repository. However, the accountant must conduct audits to ensure the repository's integrity.

5.6.4 Drowning in Information *(how)*

I can't keep up. I just cannot keep up! Many people have this feeling on a regular basis. Information overload contributes to the *cannot keep up* distraction and is only going to get worse. Not only does a body of knowledge about any subject continue to grow, the number of subjects to know about also increases. According to innovator Stewart Brand (b. 1938), "Many people may discover that about 20 percent of the new things they learn will cause about 80 percent of the things they thought they already knew to be invalidated." New discoveries have ripple effects far beyond what is originally anticipated. A new theory or practice in any one area can apply suddenly to other fields.

For years, physicians believed stomach ulcers were caused by diet and stress. The practice of gastric treatment was based on this belief. A regular remedy was to have the ulcer surgically cut out from the stomach. However, the Centers for Disease Control (CDC) in Atlanta, Georgia reports nine out of ten ulcers are caused by a bacterial infection called Helicobacter pylori (*H. pylori*). *H. pylori* are a spiral-shaped bacterium attached to or just above the gastric mucosa. The organism can live in the stomach indefinitely, but may not cause clinical illness for many years. The bacteria can now be controlled with antibiotics.

Australian doctors Barry Marshall and Robin Warren discovered the ulcer-causing bacteria in 1983. Once the antibiotic was developed and approved, surgery became unnecessary. Therapy for *H. pylori* consists of one to two weeks of antibiotics, such as amoxicillin, tetracycline, and metronidazole. The ripple effect of ulcer antibiotics has been dramatic because it changed the economics of the healthcare system. The burden on hospital facilities has been eased. Patients are diagnosed sooner and cured faster, and physicians have time to treat other serious diseases. The relative value of something is determined by point of view.

In-depth information means the difference between success and failure in the marketplace. An organization needs to know the answers to the following questions:

- Who is the customer?
- What is needed to ensure customer loyalty?
- How effective and efficient is the supply chain?
- What is the immediate value of money in any given country at any given time?
- What is the political climate of a city, state, region, or country?
- What regulations, level of compliance, and enforcement are required?

Futurists like Mitchell Kapor (b. 1950), Brian Eno (b. 1948), Esther Dyson (b. 1951), and George Gilder (b. 1939) maintain that world governments are not prepared for explosive rates of information expansion. National and international laws are challenged at every level. Third world nations and economically and educationally depressed areas either will be consumed by the rich and smart, or will rise up in rebellion. Futurists conclude there will be no middle ground.

Interrogatives provide a template to help understand the impact of new technology and information on enterprise architecture and the organization's business operations. The template helps measure the ripple effects throughout an organization. Corporations that are the fastest to understand the impact of new technology and information and translate the technology and information to new products and services are likely to become future economic giants, or at least survive.

5.6.5 Shake, Rattle, and Rebuild *(where)*

Since 1989, California has spent billions of dollars on public works, such as highways and government buildings, and started rebuilding every public structure and accommodation to withstand an 8.0 earthquake.[12] *Pardon our dust and sorry for the inconvenience, retrofitting underway for your protection and safety* signs remind the public why they are being inconvenienced. Retrofitting teaches Californians the value of good plans and the uselessness of bad plans. Californians are also being educated in the value of long-term recovery instead of short-term relief.

The Webster Street Tube connects Oakland to Alameda in the San Francisco Bay area. Alameda is an island that is 4 miles long and 2 miles wide, with a wide beach running almost the length of the island. At the turn of the twentieth century, Alameda was a vacation area for the affluent because summer temperatures rarely exceeded 80°F.

The Webster Street Tube, a tunnel under the estuary to the mainland, was constructed in 1927, a time of economic prosperity in America. The subterranean section of the tube is 4,700 feet from portal to portal. In 1947, a second tube was built. Today, this twin tube is called the Posey Tube. The tubes are unique in that they are under nearly 50 feet of water in an earthquake zone.

In 2001, Alameda residents learned they would enjoy a retrofitted Webster Street Tube. The tube was closed to all traffic from 9 p.m. to 5 a.m. five nights a week. The cost for the retrofit was budgeted at $4 million. The work begun and was scheduled to take two years. The work stopped in February 2002. The *builders* and *subcontractors* discovered many things were not where they were supposed to be.

Both tubes have seven connection points and a bend in the Webster Street tunnel is 3 percent greater than the design specifications indicated. Workers broke into the walls where construction plans indicated the location of the seams. To everyone's surprise and no one's delight, the joints were not there. Literally, by trial and error, each joint was found several feet away from its specification.

The detailed drawings showed explicitly how the joints were constructed. However, no joint met the specification. Each joint was different from every other joint, indicating a trial-and-error process was used in the joint construction. Plans were not changed to reflect the final construction techniques.

Information technology practitioners also allow their designs to become out of synchronization with production software. To ensure everything stays synchronized, the IT *builder* must try to attempt to eliminate the following types of problems:

- Not performing the testing required to prove an application works the way it was designed.
- Changing the design specifications to conform to the requirements imposed by technology and not informing the *designer* the change was made.
- Reconstructing the database to achieve better throughput and transaction processing without fully understanding how that change may affect other systems.
- Changing the design of the user interface based on *builder* preferences.
- Not explaining change or listening to feedback from stakeholders and user communities.
- Not adhering to coding standards.
- Not recording information as a means of job security.
- Not documenting the application.

In the Webster Street Tube project, the information, as originally conceived, was stored and accessible for use. The construction changed the plans and the changes were not recorded, making the designs incorrect. Incorrect information may be worse than no information at all.

5.6.6 Give Me a Break *(when)*

Schedules establish dates for producing deliverables. Schedules create deadlines. Deadlines create tension. Tension creates a sense of urgency. Urgency stimulates creativity. Creativity creates a need to know. A need to know seeks opportunities. Opportunities find new ventures and projects. New ventures and projects need schedules. Although no schedule is foolproof, the cycle and logic illustrated are a causal loop that has become a **closed loop** because of its cause and effect linkage.

Builders receive deliverable schedules from *designers* that may be unachievable. The *designer* may establish unrealistic schedules to satisfy the *owner*. The *owner* may have unrealistic expectations about when the company can accomplish a project. Delivery dates calculated without consulting the *builder* can have disastrous results. If there is a mandated completion date, or a limited window of opportunity to get a new product or service to market, the *builder* must be consulted as soon as possible.

Unrealistic delivery dates encourage the *builder* to take shortcuts. Shortcuts taken in the name of expediency inevitably cause hardship in the future. The Webster Street Tube is an example of *tomorrow's* maintenance nightmare.

IT projects rarely have realistic delivery dates. Executives think IT projects take too long and cost too much. The IT *builder* must work within the limits of the imposed schedule, forced by unrealistic levels of expectation. If the schedule (*when*) is too short, other aspects (*what, how, where, who,* and *why*) of the project must be increased:

- More money (*what*)
- Altered processes (*how*)
- Amendments to location (*where*)
- Reassigned tasks (*who*)
- Redefined goals and objectives (*why*)

When the IT *builder* has an unrealistic budget (too little money) and an unrealistic schedule for delivery (too little time), the project often produces less than desirable results.

The building of the Great Pyramid was an example of a project with a finite completion date, a date that forced every other aspect (*what, how, where, who,* and *why*) of the project into alignment to make the delivery date (*when*). The Pharaoh furnished enough money (*what*), the processes (*how*) were standardized, the location (*where*) was well prepared, adequate people (*who*) were recruited with the right skills, and the motivation (*why*) was achieved.

The building of the Cathedral of Chartres illustrates how a well-conceived plan and schedule were sabotaged by unrealistic levels of expectation regarding:

- Amount of money (*what*) required
- Processes (*how*) required
- Location (*where*) to support the structure
- People (*who*) with the right skills
- Schedule (*when*) was appropriate
- Abbott Suger's original goals (*why*) assumed the *what, how, where, who,* and *when* were understood

5.6.7 Change *(why)*

Profit is a strong motivation for the *builder*. Every perspective has a motivation, though each is different:

- The *planner's* motivation is the requirement to ensure nothing is over-looked. All possible scenarios should be scoped, itemized, and prioritized.
- The *owner's* motivation is to be successful in business and make money.
- The *designer's* motivation is to satisfy the mandate of the *owner*.
- The *builder's* motivation is to make a profit.
- The *subcontractor's* motivation is to make a living.
- The corporate motivation for the *functioning enterprise* is to achieve the desired end and ensure people keep their jobs.

All the motives are an issue of survival.

A *builder* survives if he can deliver the goods to make a profit. A *builder* that does not make a profit will not stay employed. The *builder* cannot directly make sales nor make customers buy. The *builder* can control costs on the supply side of the supply and demand equation. In this way, the *builder* has the authority and responsibility to ensure the effectiveness of the organization's supply chain.

Accommodating change is one of the biggest challenges facing the *builder*. The subtleties and complexities of change exacerbate the challenges. Though inevitable, change poses a threat to the continued ability to make a profit. In the play, *Fiddler on the Roof,* the song *Sunrise, Sunset* illustrates how change creeps up. "Is this the little girl I carried? Is this the little boy at play? I don't remember getting older, when did they?" In IT, this effect is known as scope creep.

Change occurs as either evolution or revolution. Evolutionary change is slow, occurring over a relatively long period of time. Revolutionary change is dramatic, almost instantaneous, and causes a paradigm shift, which changes all the rules of accepted behavior, accepted practices, and accepted ideas. A paradigm shift can change the culture.

Change is the biggest threat to continued profits. Because profits ensure surviv-ability, the *builder's* task is to ensure the survivability of the enterprise.

5.6.8 Key Terms

causal loop	knowledge
closed loop	knowledge management
customer relationship management (CRM)	pattern
data	repository
information	wisdom

5.6.9 Review Questions

1. Why are structure, discipline, and organization important?
2. What do games, languages, project development, and marketplace evaluation have in common?
3. List six items all methodologies have in common.
4. Give an example of a knowledge management application.
5. How does a knowledge management application benefit the enterprise?
6. What are two characteristics demanded by a closed system?
7. Accounting is the accumulation of which interrogatives?
8. List five rules needed by a repository.
9. Why is it important to reflect changes in a design that occur during construction?
10. How do unrealistic budgets and time frames affect the *builder*?
11. Which two types of changes do enterprises experience?

SECTION 5.7 WHERE THE EDGE IS BLEEDING— ADOPTING RADICALLY NEW TECHNOLOGY

QUESTIONS TO CONTEMPLATE

1. How do organizations try to take advantage of using new things?
2. When is technology a risky undertaking?
3. Why is knowledge a critical factor when applying technology?

5.7.1 Introduction

Technology continually changes the way we live and work. Organizations hope investments in technology turn out to be valuable, relevant, and effective. Technology tools must be shaped to meet common goals and requirements of the organization. The investment in technology should provide tangible benefits to productivity or cost savings. Prior to making a decision to invest in a new technology, organizations must develop a process to identify and weigh what value is added by making the investment decision. According to Equifax's CEO and chairman Tom Chapman (b. 1943), "Technology is a weapon, it is not a crutch."

Some organizations put the entire corporation at risk so they can be at the forefront with new technology. Other organizations prefer to be more conservative and justify the expenditure on technology through observing what others are doing in the industry. Still other organizations prefer to avoid making any investment in new technology. Sometimes an organization's inaction can also place the entire corporation at risk.

Bleeding-edge organizations tend to be technology centered and big risk takers. The approach to technology is to multitask and have different people and teams working on different projects and business change at the same time. The bleeding-edge approach means organizations must receive immediate feedback to changes. People in these organizations are empowered to make decisions and take the lead. Bleeding-edge organizations are usually faster, smaller, and more tolerant of risk. Because of these characteristics, these organizations are better able to react to or achieve rapid change.

Hauppauge School District in Hauppauge, New York, is an organization at the bleeding-edge of school security technology. The district uses handheld computers and data retrieval software to track class attendance. Security personnel and school administrators use these devices to access student schedules if a student is walking through the building without a pass. Student information is downloaded instantly from an administrative directory to a Microsoft Access database and transferred to a Palm Pilot for review and possible action against the student. Class schedules, parking permits, names of emergency contacts, and medical information can also be retrieved by scanning the bar code on the back of the student's identification card.

Because safety is a priority in this Long Island district, security measures have been upgraded and installed following a comprehensive technology bond issue passed by residents of Hauppauge. The district uses Palm Pilots, more than 75 interior cameras in the 1,200-student high school, six exterior cameras, 32 interior cameras in the middle school, and 16 cameras in three different elementary schools.

Cameras are linked through fiber optics to the middle school, where security personnel track surveillance 24 hours a day, seven days a week. During the school day, security officers staff a video room and dispatch information to administrators throughout the school property. Small monitors are located on the desks of principals and assistant principals who believe that lack of size is no excuse to install only minimum security measures in the 3,500-student school system.

A **global positioning system (GPS)** receiver tracks the whereabouts of administrative and security staff, including their vehicles. Administrators can access GPS updates using the Internet or a pager. The district also uses access control and security radios that track and log radio activity. Computer labs are secured with custom cables, locks, and cable traps to prevent theft. The president of the Suffolk School Security Alliance says that he expects many more changes in school security technology because the district wants to stay ahead of the curve.[13]

Other organizations do not want to be too far behind or too far ahead of competitors. **Leading-edge** organizations like to stay current with technology. These organizations are usually focused on full service and overall value, rather than competing on price or innovation. Leading-edge organizations use technology to improve customer service, quality, and productivity. Before investing in technology, these organizations prefer to look at previous models of usage. When they do invest in technology, they prefer to justify the investment by showing how the technology adds value to the business.

One of the first companies that demonstrated using technology as a tool to disseminate information to management was Frito-Lay, a company based in Texas and currently operated by PepsiCo. To disseminate information, Frito-Lay provided its 11,000-route sales force with tools that allow them to see how decisions about in-store displays, product mix, and promotional spending affect company profit. This was leading-edge technology in the 1980s. Today, this process has now moved to the Internet, where information flows between companies for complex supply chains.

Trailing-edge organizations do not view IT as a strategic necessity. They tend to view IT as an expense and have historically competed in business areas with non-strategic IT requirements. They tend to operate through centralized decision-making and are low risk takers. Trailing-edge organizations run the risk of putting themselves out of business by using technologies that are either difficult or impossible to maintain and support.

Some school districts are good examples of trailing-edge organizations, especially those that view technology as an expense. In the early 1980s, Apple Computer positioned itself as a leader in educational technology. Thousands of Apple computers were placed in public schools across the country at a low cost to the districts. Those computers remained in classrooms for many years after software and compatible equipment was no longer being developed for those machines.

Often students and parents expressed frustration that families had better technology available at home than the students were able to access at school. Most of these school computers were scrapped eventually. Some organizations can transform by phasing out trailing-edge technology.

Founded in 1792, State Street Bank and Trust, headquartered in Boston, Massachusetts, has evolved from a local merchant bank with trailing-edge technology into a global financial services company delivering technology and information solutions for investors around the world. When Marshall Carter (b. 1940) became CEO in 1992, he described the bank's technology as, "basically a humongous bookkeeping machine."

With a new focus on asset management, State Street has positioned itself to gather and analyze enormous amounts of data from around the globe. Carter decentralized decision-making and made each department responsible for its technology. The company also provided user-friendly, PC-based, Internet-enabled tools to let the bank's customers access and manipulate data for themselves. Carter's direction and leadership created an organization whose assets under management grew from $100 billion to $600 billion during his tenure.

The company views technology as its core business. Technical experts and business experts work hand in hand. The IT community is structured in a way that fosters and depends on this teamwork. New leading-edge technology connects State Street's clients to the marketplace in unique ways and provides valuable investment information.[14]

Net Asset Value (NAV) Alert is one example of the leading-edge technologies implemented by State Street to create solutions to its business challenges. NAV Alert is a work system used to enhance the collaborative use of a mainframe accounting system. The system automates the validation and reconciliation process of computing a mutual fund's net asset value. The system provides instantaneous access to fund data and generates exception conditions. NAV Alert uses **real-time**, **event-driven** notification alerts and enables accountants across the world with a spreadsheet to see the same view of the same interactions at the same time.

When David Spina (b. 1943) took over as State Street's chairperson and CEO in 2001, the company had over 19,000 employees in 23 countries and clients in 75 countries. Leading-edge technology has enabled this organization to prosper. Innovative use of technology does not guarantee a profitable return for all companies.

The IT *builder* is often charged with advancing an organization's ability to absorb information technology. Regardless of a corporation's attitude toward technology, from trailing-edge to bleeding-edge, the *builder* plays an integral role. The *builder* needs to make sure the organization can maximize its use of technology, help the organization and information technology department minimize risk, define standards, units of measure, and metrics to assist in defining the quality of the technologies used, and make sure the organization is aware of the appropriate level of training required.

The *builder* helps determine how the organization responds to regulations and threats from competitors. The *builder* needs to understand the organization's goals and objectives and make sure the use of technology is aligned appropriately. The *builder* needs to understand how technology can be used as a strategic advantage. The *builder* must also understand the corporate topography and environment to ensure technical success.

5.7.2 Creating an Advantage *(where)*

Webvan, a dream announced by Louis Borders in April 1999, was to be the biggest and boldest of Internet retail establishments. Borders, who also started the Borders book chain, believed that once customers opened their doors for grocery delivery, with the help of technology, the company could overturn the retail establishment and sell anything and everything. The idea was to beat the competitors with efficiency of delivery through its automated high-tech warehouses. Each warehouse was worth about $30 million. After its San Francisco area service opened, the company, signed a $1 billion contract with Bechtel to build another 25 warehouses.

The company gathered more funding than any other Internet retail company, with the exception of Amazon.com. In its **initial public offering**, in November of 1999, Webvan raised $375 million. Webvan expanded to Atlanta, Georgia, where orders continued to pile in and expansion plans moved ahead. Then in late 2000, the American economy took a turn and money began decreasing. Webvan had already signed site leases worth millions of dollars throughout the country.

The entire idea had been created in a vacuum, and delivery on this scale had never been accomplished before. The company wanted to be on the forefront. In September 2000, the merger with HomeGrocer, a company facing diminishing cash reserves itself, was intended to eliminate a rival and enable Webvan to reach its long-term goal more quickly. The merger of HomeGrocer allowed Webvan to acquire an additional $150 million and to gain an established market in six more cities. Together the two companies raised $1.4 billion in venture capital and public stock.

However, the merger was followed by a number of poor management decisions. The company was so focused on meeting its long-term goal of delivering anything and everything to anyone, anytime or anywhere, that the day-to-day goal of pleasing grocery customers was ignored. Even though the company was running out of money, management embarked upon an aggressive rebranding campaign to make sure the company was not thought of only as a grocer. It also created and marketed a new logo, which showed a bag of groceries behind the words "webvan.com."

After the HomeGrocer merger, Webvan bagged its logo. With its new nondescript logo, Webvan soon disappeared.

Webvan felt obligated to shareholders to roll out to 26 cities, so management continued to follow the aggressive expansion plan, even before proving the business model. However, the company failed to understand its market, particularly how wired the service area was. It failed to understand the density of its customer base. It failed to understand how many deliveries it would be expected to make in a day. It simply did not polish or understand operations.

Webvan did not understand how to achieve its vision. Operations and technologies were not connected to the people doing the rollouts. The company never took the opportunity to develop an efficient complex supply chain while serving 10 U.S. markets—Atlanta, Georgia; Dallas, Texas; Chicago, Illinois; Seattle, Washington; Portland, Oregon; and the following areas in California—Sacramento, Los Angeles, San Francisco, Orange County, and San Diego—prior to its closing, in 2001.

Webvan went from a company worth $1.4 billion to a company $25 million in the red in less than 30 months. When investors asked Borders about whether Webvan would be a billion-dollar business, he commented, "Naw, it's going to be a $10 billion dollar business. Or zero." His prediction was right.[15]

5.7.3 Betting the Farm *(how)*

FoxMeyer Drugs was the nation's fourth largest producer of pharmaceuticals and a $5 billion company until the organization attempted to install the SAP R/3 enterprise resource planning (ERP) software. With the goal of increasing technology efficiency, FoxMeyer conducted market research and product evaluation and then purchased SAP R/3 in December 1993.

Andersen Consulting, now known as Accenture, was retained by FoxMeyer to perform the SAP installation. SAP sales representatives had assured FoxMeyer its software was well matched to the needs of a high-volume distribution company. In the end, FoxMeyer was unable to process most of its customer orders with the R/3 software. The company went into bankruptcy in 1996 and sued both SAP and Andersen for $1 billion.

In the lawsuit, FoxMeyer claimed SAP lied repeatedly about the capabilities of the R/3 software. FoxMeyer also claimed Andersen used FoxMeyer as a training camp for its inexperienced staff. FoxMeyer was one of the first big users to take a chance on SAP R/3 software. Legal documents indicate FoxMeyer knew the R/3 software had not been used previously with distribution companies. Perhaps FoxMeyer should have been more guarded. Negligence and neglect can be prevalent in IT projects, and FoxMeyer demonstrated the risk of moving forward with speculation.

Ironically, an article in *Computerworld*, September 5, 1994, quotes FoxMeyer's chief information officer, Robert Brown, as saying, "We are betting our company on this." FoxMeyer placed the bet and lost the business.

5.7.4 Defining Quality *(what)*

Most organizations are concerned about quality. Competition has never been tougher, and quality makes a difference in success and failure. In the 1980s, Deming and Dr. Joseph Juran (b. 1904), along with Philip Crosby (1926–2001), revisited the discussion of quality in the United States and this time, their message was heard. Each had his personal approach to the topic, but the messages were similar. The product or service being offered should meet the needs and wants of the user. These quality movement leaders believed that if organizations worked toward meeting this objective, the results would be returning customers, satisfied employees, and increased market share.

Deming's quality management style complements the systems thinking approach discussed in Section 3.1.5. For example, suppose an organization discovers that a defective product is being produced and the error of an inexperienced employee caused the defect. The first question to ask is, "Why was the error made?" Perhaps the organization discovers a lack of training caused the error? The next question to ask could be, "Why did the employee not receive enough training?" The answer might be that not enough money was budgeted for training. The next question could be, "Why wasn't an adequate amount of money specified for training?" The answer might be that training was not a top priority. The resulting lack of training should indicate to management that priorities need to be changed to improve product quality. This scenario is an example of a causal loop, resulting in a product of poor quality.

Juran is probably best known as the person who added the human dimension to quality, moving the term from its statistical origins to what is now called **Total Quality Management (TQM)**. After continuously trying to improve product and process quality, Motorola coined the phrase Six Sigma Breakthrough to help the company target and achieve breakthrough results. The tools and techniques used by Motorola in the 1980s are the fundamentals of the quality management documented by Juran. These fundamentals were used to launch the Japanese Quality Revolution in the 1970s and the American Quality Revolution in the 1980s. Today, the term **Six Sigma** commonly refers to a goal or philosophy of eliminating waste and improving quality, cost, and time performance in any organization.

Crosby believed a high-quality product to be one that conforms to design specifications. Crosby created the concept of **Zero Defects**. He believed an organization should instill a commitment to quality from upper management throughout the entire organization. The two messages he delivered are, "The system for causing quality is prevention, not appraisal," and "Do it right the first time." Crosby believed quality is free and cost is associated with defects.

A fundamental problem in software development is that programmers make mistakes. In *Computerworld*, January 2002, Mary Ann Davidson, chief security officer at Oracle Corporation, sends Crosby's message, "Do it right the first time," to her staff of developers. Beyond that, she believes, 90 percent of what is required is *sheer corporate will*.

Chairman and chief software architect Bill Gates (b. 1955) announced in a 2002 memo to the entire Microsoft workforce that the company's emphasis was on developing high-quality code that is available, reliable, and secure—even if it comes at the expense of adding new features. In the memo, Gates coined the term Trustworthy Computing. Gates now says that when facing a choice between adding features and resolving security issues, Microsoft needs to choose security.[16]

WE CAN AND MUST DO BETTER

From: Bill Gates
Date: Tuesday, January 15, 2002
To: Microsoft and Subsidiaries: All FTE (*full-time employees*)
Subject: Trustworthy Computing

Every few years I have sent out a memo talking about the highest priority for Microsoft...Over the last year, it has become clear that ensuring .NET is a platform for Trustworthy Computing is more important than any other part of our work. If we do not do this, people simply will not be willing—or able—to take advantage of all the other great work we do. Trustworthy Computing is the highest priority for all the work we are doing. We must lead the industry to a whole new level of Trustworthiness in computing...

No Trustworthy Computing platform exists today. It is only in the context of the basic redesign we have done around .NET that we can achieve this...Key aspects include:

- Availability—our products should always be available when our customers need them...
- Security—the data our software and services store on behalf of our customers should be protected from harm and used or modified only in appropriate ways...
- Privacy—users should be in control of how their data is used...

In the past, we have made our software and services more compelling for users by adding new features and functionality, and by making our platform richly extensible. We have done a terrific job at that, but not all those great features will matter unless customers trust our software...If we discover a risk that a feature could compromise someone's privacy, that problem gets solved first. If there is any way we can better protect important data and minimize downtime, we should focus on this. These principles should apply at every stage of the development cycle of every kind of software we create, from operating systems and desktop applications to global Web services...

According to Watts Humphrey, Software Engineering Institute[17] fellow and a former director of programming quality at IBM, if flaws in coding are not repaired, they provide hackers an entry into systems. Humphrey believes Microsoft needs an engineering cultural change. He believes engineers rely too heavily on finding problems during the testing phase, rather than preventing them in development. Crosby sent the same prevention message in the 1980s.

Another Microsoft employee, Pierre DeVries, says that Microsoft requires a new mindset, in addition to improving the software development processes and the quality of the product. Microsoft is committed to training all developers working on the.NET initiatives to write secure software.

A software engineer from Intrasphere Technologies in New York says that IT managers have been choosing between secure and reliable software and cheap and easy software—a choice that has required companies to make an uncomfortable trade-off.[18] Gates challenged his company to change that idea. An organization that competes to keep and win business today needs to have quality products and services.

5.7.5 Training *(who)*

Companies across the world have experienced projects that fell out of alignment with business goals, or that were conceived or executed poorly. At the *heart* of good decisions lies the role of individual communication.

A $100,000 database server sits in a storage room at Concord Hospital in central New Hampshire—it has never been used. The Tracemaster Electrocardiogram (ECG) Management System was supposed to allow nurses and physicians to access information from patients' ECGs from workstations throughout the hospital.

The 295-bed hospital serves 117,000 people in New Hampshire's capital city and approximately 20 surrounding communities. Historically, individual clinical departments acquired medical equipment for their units. *Builders* from the cardiac unit recommended that it purchase the database server. In the past, each clinical unit would plan responsibly and train the people who needed to access any specialized equipment.

Today, however, customer needs include shared information. Therefore, the hospital's approach to training has become blurred. The Tracemaster data would be useful to healthcare professionals in other areas of the hospital too. Now, not only the people in the cardiac unit need to be trained to use the equipment, but many other nurses and physicians as well.

Today, the information in the cardiac unit is transcending clinical systems. Information is no longer purely clinical. Information systems and clinical systems must be integrated because information needs to be accessed through multiple locations in the hospital for multiple purposes.

Due to the Health Insurance Portability and Accountability Act (HIPAA) of 1996, Concord Hospital must meet the first compliance date of 2003 for its systems. These medical regulations are designed to make healthcare more efficient and create standards for electronic data exchange specifications among the many types of organizations that handle patient information. Regulations aim to ensure the privacy and security of data through technology standards.

Gary Light, chief technology officer at the hospital, says that the state-of-the-art server sits in the storage room because "We needed to pull back and think a lot of things through. We did not want to just drop this on people's desks."[19]

More questions had to be answered: *What* do we want to do with this information? *How* will nurses and physicians access the information? *Where* will the software be installed? *Who* will manage security? *When* will the users be trained and by whom? *Why* make this investment? The Tracemaster is needed to solve a specific problem, yet holistically, the Tracemaster needs efforts and answers from the entire enterprise to make its use a reality. The staff at Concord Hospital needs to apply the thought processes associated with enterprise architecture to gain long-term benefits from the $100,000 database server.

The complexity and total cost of integrating the system into the network, installing the software on workstations, and training users were underestimated.[20] New technology is useless if employees do not know how to use it.

5.7.6 External Influences *(when)*

General Motors Corporation (GM) took the world into the next generation of advanced technology vehicles with the EV1. GM's EV1, a car of the future, was environmentally friendly, and in the late 1990s, was one of the most efficient production vehicles in the world. The EV1 looked like a sporty sedan with a long heavy-duty electrical cord extending from the front center of its hood.

The second-generation EV1 runs on high-capacity batteries and, depending on the topography and environment, has a driving range of 55 to 95 miles. A more advanced technology nearly doubles the range of the first-generation battery pack. This nickel-metal hydride (NiMH) battery pack also offers a longer battery life. Batteries can be safely charged inductively in all types of weather. The NiMH pack stores more energy and takes approximately six to eight hours to charge. The battery pack is 98 percent recyclable, and the vehicle's aluminum structure is completely recyclable.

GM's electric vehicle three-phase alternating current (AC) induction motor delivers 137 horsepower. No emission testing is needed because the motor is a zero emission vehicle. The car does not have an engine because it does not need one. Because the car has no exhaust, no tailpipe is required. The car does not have valves, pistons, timing belts, or crankshafts. EV1 requires no tune-ups, gasoline, or oil changes. That means cleaner air and less dependency on foreign oil. Running at an electronically controlled top speed of 80 miles per hour, the EV1 was the most aerodynamic production vehicle in its day. The back wheels are 9 inches closer together than the front wheels, giving the car the shape of a teardrop from above.

The EV1 has low-rolling resistance Michelin tires, weighing only 8.5 pounds. The electric car has a braking system that regenerates energy and sends the power back to the batteries. The EV1 also has seven on-board computers that control everything from the interior temperature of the car to the battery pack.

Instead of gasoline, you need to have a 220-volt MagneCharge inductive charging system installed in your garage. By inserting the charge paddle in the front of the car, the master computer in the car informs the charger how much energy is needed. All this can be done while you are sleeping. GM formed partnerships with many different companies in California and Arizona to build an electric car-charging infrastructure and had installed more than 1,100 chargers in retail centers, restaurants, beaches, airports, key workplaces, and Saturn retail facilities.

GM offered the vehicle only through a leasing agreement because electric vehicle technology was so new. Saturn covered all routine maintenance, including batteries and tires, under its three-year, 36,000-mile warranty.

In June 2001 the California Air Resources Board (CARB) decided to support a single *conductive* standard for EV chargers in the state of California. As a result of the *external legislative intrusion*, GM decided to no longer invest in the *inductive* charger infrastructure and terminated production of the Gen2+ model chargers and further investment in public infrastructure activity. There is no longer a supplier for the unique Gen2+ components, nor a way to retrofit existing inductive chargers to the mandated conductive chargers.

331

GM decided eventually not to issue or reissue leases for the EV1. In February 2002, GM notified CARB that it was no longer considering offering a future fleet of EV1s because the cost to maintain the fleet far outweighed any future benefit. Because of the technology involved in this project and the vehicle's need for continuous warm sunshine, GM could not reasonably lease its product in any state other than Arizona or California.

When California state legislators decided to adopt conductive charging as one of the prerequisites of qualifying future zero emission vehicles, GM's investment in an inductive charging infrastructure was diminished significantly. Therefore, GM decided to not only *pull the plug on inductive charging, but also on the EV1*. The external influence of government regulation plays a significant role in a product's viability.

5.7.7 Friend or Foe *(why)*

Technology can sometimes be regarded as a friend and other times a foe. Some companies prefer to remain conservative and purposefully stay away from new technology. Although Hobby Lobby, an arts and crafts store established in 1972, maintained a simple Web site connecting it to customers, the risk of investing in automated systems did not promise a more profitable operation, so the company remained comfortable minimizing the use of technology.

In 1997, Ken Haywood, vice president of Hobby Lobby operations, said the company considered "its people a positive and its systems a negative."[21] The company had always been conservative when making decisions about information technology. The senior management team expected employees to use their brains; store managers knew within a few hours what product had come in and what was on the shelves of their stores.

The company grew from a 300-square foot store in Oklahoma City, Oklahoma, to 126 stores within an 800-mile radius of the same city by 1997. The first store manufactured miniature picture frames. All stores were served by a 1 million-square foot distribution center that carried 37,000 unique items or stock-keeping units (SKUs). Buying decisions were made at this distribution center.

Individual stores transmitted orders electronically every week and usually received merchandise within 24 hours. The company supplied all stores without a warehouse management system or bar coding—a surprising fact considering Hobby Lobby had $450 million in sales in 1997.

The company did not see any value in adopting point-of-sale (POS) systems. All orders were filled using picking lists that were generated by the electronic orders. Orders for 25 of the stores were filled daily, relying on 150 people over two shifts to fill carts. The company realized its industry was significantly behind in technology compared to other industries. Hobby Lobby also knew most of its vendors did not transmit data electronically, or use bar coding.

Senior vice president Steven Green said that the company operated on a keep-it-simple philosophy. The company preferred to stay a step behind other organizations in the industry and let them work out any technology bugs. This conservative philosophy toward technology was profitable for Hobby Lobby in 1997.[22]

For companies to remain competitive in today's changing economy, remaining a foe of technology is not usually a profitable choice. Hobby Lobby maintains its trailing-edge philosophy only in non-strategic areas of the company. Since 1997, Hobby Lobby has used and upgraded frequently to newer technologies for its warehouse management systems to serve customers more efficiently. Laser-driven conveyor systems cross-dock products directly into the trailers backed against the loading docks of the warehouse. Hobby Lobby knows that it is in a consumer-based business. It also knows that new technology, unless it translates into customer satisfaction and approval, will not improve the business acumen.

Being more aggressive with the strategic use of technology, the company has experienced phenomenal growth. Hobby Lobby operates over 280 stores in 24 states and now tracks over 60,000 SKUs, with sales in excess of $1 billion. Hobby Lobby headquarters are located in a 1.7 million-square foot manufacturing, distribution, and office complex. The IT *builders* at Hobby Lobby have worked hard to minimize risk and still advance the company in adopting and accepting new technologies as friends instead of foes.

For organizations that are leading in a marketplace or industry, technology might be regarded as a foe. Organizations not in first place often view technology as a friend. The reason for the opposing viewpoints is that while new technology always poses some level of risk, a leading organization has much to lose if the new technology fails. For enterprises trying to get into first place in an industry, the rewards of jumping into first place often outweigh the risks of staying in second or third position.

333

5.7.8 Key Terms

bleeding edge	real time
event driven	Six Sigma
global positioning system (GPS)	Total Quality Management (TQM)
initial public offering	trailing edge
leading edge	Zero Defects

5.7.9 Review Questions

1. What guidelines should the *builder* use when considering technology tools?
2. Describe your understanding of the term *bleeding-edge* technology.
3. Even though State Street Bank is in the banking industry, what does it consider its core business to be?
4. How could a GPS system benefit an enterprise?
5. List four things that caused Webvan to fail in its endeavor.
6. What risk did FoxMeyer Drugs take willingly when it embarked on an SAP implementation?
7. Who are three individuals who led the quality movement in the United States during the 1980s?
8. Who coined the phrase Trustworthy Computing and what does it mean?
9. Why did Concord Hospital decide not to use its new database server and keep it stored in a closet?
10. What external influence caused General Motors to pull the plug on the EV1?
11. What has been Hobby Lobby's approach to technology?
12. What types of organizations might consider technology a friend?
13. How do organizations try to take advantage of using new things?

5.8 SYNTHESIS AND CHAPTER SUMMARY

The *builder* creates designs for the implementation site that transform the *owner's* design and the *designer's* design. Understanding the topography and topology of a project is important for the *builder*...even for an iceberg cowboy.

On April 15, 1912, an iceberg 400 miles south of Newfoundland, Canada caused the Titanic to sink on its maiden voyage across the North Atlantic Ocean. Today, icebergs threaten multibillion-dollar offshore oil rigs in the same treacherous waters.

The ocean waters off Newfoundland are known as iceberg alley. Each spring, 400 to 900 icebergs of varying shapes and sizes drift by and glide into the surrounding waters of the Grand Banks. Once south of the banks, the icebergs melt in the warm Gulf Stream.

In 1993, during a heavy iceberg season, four European shipping vessels ended up in dry dock with gaping holes after encounters with icebergs. In 2001, a shrimp trawler crashed into jagged ice and sank within five minutes. Ships crossing the Atlantic usually know the location of ice and avoid it. However, icebergs can move in erratic paths and stormy weather can complicate matters. Hundred-foot waves have been known to pick up icebergs and bring them crashing down onto boats.

Techniques people have tried for removing icebergs include: whacking them with sledgehammers, shooting them with shotguns and rifles, and dynamiting them. Dynamite does not vaporize the iceberg; instead, hundreds of smaller icebergs are created after the boom. On one occasion, the Canadian Coast Guard dumped black ash on top of several icebergs, hoping the dark covering would absorb more sunlight and accelerate the melting process. The icebergs melted so quickly, they became unstable and rolled over. The black ash ended up on the bottom and washed away.

Concern about icebergs intensified as Newfoundland's oil industry grew. In 1997, the $5 billion Hibernia fixed oil rig project began operations on the Grand Banks, and in January 2002, the adjacent $1.8 billion Terra Nova floating oil rig project started. The oil industry concluded that the only reasonable way to prevent collisions with oil rigs was to intercept and redirect the ice.

Jerome Baker is an iceberg cowboy, complete with lasso. Baker arms himself with a 270-foot, 9,600-horsepower boat, and an 8-inch thick, 4,000-foot floating polypropylene lasso. He ropes, wrangles, and tows million-ton icebergs out of the paths of oil rigs, saving them from close encounters of the crushing kind.

Looking for ice, Baker's 10-man crew patrols the Grand Banks within a 60-mile radius of Hibernia and Terra Nova. Baker uses high-powered water cannons to blast smaller ice chunks, known as bergy bits, away from the oil rigs. Larger icebergs are wrangled with the lasso and towed until they drift safely away from the production sites.

According to the U.S. Coast Guard, bergy bits can be 13 feet high, 46 feet long, and weigh 100 tons. Medium-sized icebergs, the most common on the Grand Banks, are usually 150 feet high, 400 feet long, and weigh 2 million tons. Large icebergs can weigh up to 4 million tons and require three boats to tow them. Ninety percent of an iceberg's mass is hidden underwater.

Roping an iceberg is hard to do. Melting icebergs can break apart and roll over, causing huge waves that can swamp a boat. Often the lasso slips off. Fog, 50-foot waves, and freezing water further complicate the job of an iceberg cowboy. Towing an iceberg 20 nautical miles can take Baker 30 hours. See Figure 5-16.

Figure 5-16 *It is a ponderous chain*

In the event of an exceptionally large iceberg, work on the Terra Nova is halted and the rig is moved out of harm's way. Hibernia, which is permanently fixed to the ocean floor, was built to withstand a 6-million-ton iceberg collision with repairable damage.

Because of the topography, weather conditions, and the shape and weight of the iceberg, the *builder* has many designs for dealing successfully with the iceberg. Baker cannot treat every iceberg with the same method each time. He must not view his lasso as a generic hammer. Baker has made being an iceberg cowboy a science and has created a series of rules, standards, units of measure, metrics, and statistics to make sure he is successful.

Baker has also had to understand trade-offs in terms of crew safety, oil rig safety, and getting the job done. Baker is continually looking for new ways to be successful and accomplish the task at a reasonable cost. Baker has to work with meteorologists, ice management planners, the Canadian Coast Guard, and the International Ice Patrol to make sure he is taking care of business.

Early Mariners

At sea, with no land in sight and only stars for guidance, the success of early sea voyages depended on the data, information, knowledge, and wisdom of the captain and his navigator. Essentially, all long-distance sea voyages were dangerous, but became easier as new technologies, standards, and metrics found their way on board the wooden vessels.

Today, satellite technology allows global positioning systems (GPS), like the one used by Hauppauge School District, to guide and track people or vehicles over both short and long distances. Some vehicles, like airplanes, are equipped to navigate between two points on automatic pilot, thanks to GPS.

The first technology to reasonably enable circumnavigation was the chronometer. The chronometer was invented by John Harrison (1693–1776) in the mid-1700s. Harrison's bleeding-edge technology allowed him to determine longitude (imaginary east-west lines circling the globe). Longitude was so important to the British

Government that it offered £20,000 in 1714 for a solution capable of calculating longitude to within half a degree (2 minutes of time).

Harrison's accurate chronometer could cope with the rocking motion of a boat and resist the variations in temperature and humidity (environment) experienced on long voyages. If a ship's chronometer lost more than a few seconds a day, the vessel could sail many kilometers off course.

Harrison's mainspring was the prevailing paradigm until Juergen Staudte (1937–1999) invented a method for mass producing quartz crystals[23] for watches in the early 1970s. Swiss watchmakers, when presented with the technology, rejected the idea, like the Big Four rejected Deming in the 1950s. Quartz crystals broke the Swiss paradigm. The Swiss were confident they could make the next breakthrough in timekeeping technology. In less than two years, Japanese watchmakers stole the marketplace. The Swiss, just like the American automobile manufacturers, focused on European competition, instead of competition from everywhere.

Topography and topology are significant for the *builder* to understand. The *builder* is responsible for designing the physical location and has the authority, responsibility, and management privileges over the *subcontractors* who perform the actual construction tasks. The *builder* proves the assumptions of the *designer*, and if the *designer* has made any misassumption, the *builder* and *subcontractor* usually discover the error during construction. Misassumption may cause anything from mild irritation to catastrophic consequence. Many IT departments are resigned to this paradigm, which is why they typically test only software and not the designs.

The laws of applied physics may have differing consequences depending on the topography. A stone dropped on Earth falls to the ground. A stone dropped from inside a spacecraft may travel in any direction. The *builders* of the International Space Station are not constrained by earthbound rules of physics. Equipment can be placed anywhere to maximize available space efficiently.

Considerations for ships rocking in the water and varying ambient temperatures are properties of location (*where*). Time (*when*) is a property of distance (*where*) and speed (*how*) and can be calculated once a uniform set of rules, standards, units of measure, and metrics are adopted. The importance of distance (e.g., yard, meter, mile, and light year) and time (e.g., second, minute, hour, and millennium) is predicated on the rules of physics. The formulas for the calculation of time, distance, and speed are interchangeable and form the basic set of metrics to determine where you are.

Knowing Time and Place

An enterprise's position on the map or in the marketplace is only as accurate as the last map reading. Technically, you can only know where you are in the past and never know where you are in the present. For example, the GPS on a Boeing 777 reads the plane's position several times a minute. The data is fed into the aircraft's automatic pilot, which tracks and calculates the airplane's course. In addition, the automatic pilot takes into account other factors like wind speed, ground speed, weather conditions, engine performance, and fuel burn rate.

Based on these real-time readings, the aircraft automatically makes the necessary *tactical* changes required to stay on course. In general, the plane is never on course and continually makes tactical changes to get to the destination. Continual tactical changes are a fundamental concept in business. Business goals and objectives are hard to reach in a straight line. Continual tactical changes by the business are necessary for taking into account current factors like wind speed, ground speed, weather conditions, engine performance, and fuel burn rate. For an IT project, remaining money in the budget, remaining time in the budget, current project phase, current conditions in the marketplace, proposed legislation, and activities within other departments of the enterprise are all factors to be considered prior to making tactical changes.

Taking frequent readings of one's position helps the *builder* manage the construction process and allows the *builder* to alert the *designer* should the project appear to be going off course. The *owner* and *designer* are then able to help the *builder* make the necessary tactical decisions to put the project back on track.

Taking a positional reading every four hours will not be detrimental to a sailing ship, even when traveling at full speed. However, an aircraft traveling at 600 miles per hour would be in serious trouble. Each enterprise and each project needs to determine the appropriate latency between readings. For many IT projects, the latency is once a week. For IT projects that follow a methodology called Scrum, the latency is once a day. For Wall Street analysts reporting on an organization, the latency is often once a quarter.

Where Are We Going

Time can be considered the most important component of a metric because time is essential to establishing an objective measurement. Corporate reporting is relative to time and is based on two financial documents—the income statement and the balance sheet.

CORPORATE REPORTING

The income statement can be produced according to any arbitrarily established reporting period. Automobile dealerships produce a daily operating control (DOC) statement that is a day-by-day report of the financial condition of the business. Most companies produce monthly, quarterly, and yearly statements. The income statement reports total sales, cost of goods sold, gross profit (before taxes), and net profits (after taxes). The income statement covers a period of time, like a month, a quarter, or a year and shows sales, expenses, and profits. An income statement may also show the distribution of profits to stockholders, but this distribution report is not a requirement of the income statement.

The balance sheet balances the financial accounts of the corporation for a particular point in time. The balance sheet shows assets, liabilities, and owner's equity on a given day.

IT departments are also dependent on two reports, the project plan and the deliverable acceptance report.

- The project plan stipulates the project, the activities, tasks, milestones, and associated deliverables. The project plan's schedule helps establish the budget for a project and, when updated, helps the *builder* keep track of dollars and time spent.

- The deliverable acceptance report tracks each accepted deliverable and which stakeholder accepted the deliverable as sufficiently meeting expectations. Tracking deliverables during the project helps apply value to the work already completed, serves to minimize scope creep, and aids change control.

Once constraints are placed on the project, the *builder* begins to make trade-offs. Too little money and too little time force the IT *builder* to apply trade-offs on all the wrong things for all the right reasons. Documentation and extensive testing are the first of many things scrapped to save time.

A key to enterprise survival is adaptability. Measuring the right things the right way starts with understanding and establishing the right rules, standards, units of measure, metrics, and statistics. Reporting statistics helps the enterprise define what must be adapted in the value chain, supply chain, marketplace, and mandatory compliance to stay on course.

Managing risk can be mitigated by not treating every problem, issue, opportunity, and project with the same old tools, techniques, and methods—the hammer. The *builder* must establish the discipline of systems thinking and focus holistically to tackle each situation appropriately.

Microsoft formerly advertised itself with a question, "Where do you want to go today?" The slogan suggested that Microsoft has the answers. Further, Microsoft's advertisements usually pictured people sitting eagerly at a computer, suggesting that whatever the question, the answer lies in digital, computer-ready information (probably with a preference that the information is served up using .NET Web services).

Even though Microsoft's advertisement asked where you want to go, Microsoft was not offering to take you anywhere. The question would be different coming from Microsoft's Seattle neighbor, Boeing. No doubt, Boeing and the airline carriers regret Microsoft's redefinition of the word *go* as *stay*. Stay where you are, the advertisement suggested, and technology will bring virtually anything you want directly to your home or office.

The *builder* is tasked with making reality the basic message every enterprise needs to ask every day—"Where can we go today?" The *builder* must develop an understanding of the appropriate use of tools and must keep an eye on future tools, techniques, and methods. The *builder* must create the rules, standards, units of measure, metrics, and statistics to act as an enabler to the enterprise. The *builder's* appropriate use of data, information, knowledge, and wisdom determines the necessary actions to take when choices force a trade-off.

The *builder* must develop the skills to know what to buy and how to appropriately spend the enterprise's fiscal resources. The *builder* must make sure the corporate memory is retained in a repository and a knowledge management application. Finally, the *builder* must make sure that what is constructed can be used and that people will be trained how to use the product. Then the *builder* can say, "We're here; where to next?"

The *builder* is an agent of action and is responsible for making sure the project can be accomplished. However, the *subcontractor* performs the actual work of construction. The *subcontractor* is discussed in detail in Chapter 6.

5.9 CHAPTER ACTIVITIES

5.9.1 Discussion Topics

1. Describe the role of the *builder*.
2. Why are the transportation capabilities of the Space Shuttle so important to the building of the International Space Station?
3. Describe the supply chain for creating software.
4. Why are the environment, topography, and topology all important for the *builder*?
5. Describe why some corporations embrace technology and why some shy away.
6. Why is it important for the *builder* to work with the *designer*?
7. How can a *builder's* lack of knowledge about standards affect an implementation?
8. Compare and contrast building a dwelling on Earth and building a dwelling in space.
9. In addition to handling the volume of data, discuss what other processes and considerations the *builder* must take into account at companies like Equifax.
10. Explain why a company like Ford decides not to conduct business as usual in the Amazon rainforest.
11. Discuss the pros and cons of a quick-and-dirty approach or a short-term option.
12. Explain why a *builder* must know what software can be purchased and understand how the software could be used.
13. Explain why the *builder* would benefit from knowing about open-source definitions and projects.
14. Discuss reasons why the *builder* should consider using a traditional approach to software purchasing versus an open-source software solution.
15. What kinds of problems did the Sybase SQL Server database engine cause for many corporations?
16. What factors establish the *builder's* paradigm? How can projects be affected by that paradigm?
17. Discuss the topography of Abbott Laboratories, and explain how characteristics of that topography affected the IT project described in Section 5.2.3.
18. Why are standards essential to measurement?
19. What challenges do the levels of complexity at Lafayette present to the *builder*?
20. Prior to the time when the *builder* starts his design, what is the role of the *planner*? The *owner*?
21. Explain why the first unit of measure is important to the *builder* and give some examples.
22. What is meant by a ripple effect and how does it affect an enterprise or a supply chain?
23. Identify and discuss the relationships between rules, standards, units of measure, metrics, and statistics.
24. What is the *builder's* motivation?
25. Explain why the *builder* is an agent of action.
26. Discuss why designs from the *owner*, *designer*, and *builder* should be synchronized to the actual implementation.
27. Explain the statement: *Time* as part of the *measurement* is *essential to any objective measurement*.
28. What are critical components of a knowledge management system? Explain why a knowledge management system is considered a key corporate asset.
29. Explain the following terms: schedule, event, trigger, and time.
30. Corporations that upgrade continuously or change technologies face a huge training issue for employees. Why should training be taken into account before upgrading or changing to a new technology?

5.9.2 Critical Thinking

1. Describe how the lessons learned through the Hyatt tragedy could be applied to an IT project.
2. Using the *Wall Street Journal* or the Internet, find an example of an organization that has experienced a paradigm shift. Be able to present and justify your example to the class.
3. Visit an organization in your community and find out what types of policies are in place regarding the acquisition of new applications. Be prepared to share your findings with the class.
4. Using two or more interrogatives, create five examples of objective routine measurement that eliminate implicitness and focus on explicitness.
5. Visit a local healthcare facility and interview a healthcare administrator. Determine the impact of OBRA and ADA on the facility and learn about the first unit of measure. Find out what other standards are followed and what measurements are captured on a daily basis. Produce a report about the key rules, standards, units of measure, metrics, and statistics the facility uses.
6. Using the Internet, answer the following questions about the Free Software Foundation and the GNU project:
   - *What* do they provide?
   - *How* can developers help the organization?
   - *Where* are they going?
   - *Who* are they?

- *When* were they formed?
- *Why* do they continue to exist?

7. Document the benefits of using commercial-off-the-shelf software (COTS) for enterprise resource planning (ERP), customer relationship management (CRM), or supply chain management (SCM) from such vendors as SAP, PeopleSoft, Baan, and J.D. Edwards. Explain why companies would choose to develop their own ERP, CRM, or SCM systems.
8. Find out what legislation prevents American companies from exporting or licensing products into certain countries. Identify which countries have embargos and how this might affect a company like CBM. Additionally, determine which countries have legislation prohibiting import of software supporting only the English language.
9. Discuss the infrastructure issues with which the *builder* at MLM had to deal. Distinguish between internal and external intrusions.
10. In Section 5.6.1, a list of statements describe a refrigerator. With a partner, create two lists—one describing a window and one describing a door. What are the differences between the two lists, if any?
11. Prepare a one-page paper comparing and contrasting organizations that might be labeled bleeding-edge, leading-edge, and trailing-edge technology organizations.

Endnotes

[1] The name HAL was derived from the International Business Machines (IBM) acronym. The letters in HAL represent those that precede I, B, and M. In the 1980s, IBM actually released an enterprise server mainframe computer called the 9000.

[2] g stands for gravitational force.

[3] PVC—polyvinyl chloride, a common thermoplastic resin used in a wide variety of manufactured products, including rainwear, garden hoses, piping, phonograph records, and floor tiles.

[4] Dickens, Charles. *A Christmas Carol*. New York, NY: Bantam Classics, 1999.

[5] Selkow, Warren, Raymond Payn, Michael Heiburg. *One Hundred and Eight Surprises*. 1993.

[6] The Americans with Disabilities Act was first passed in 1990. Title III amended the act to include nondiscrimination on the basis of disability by public accommodations and in commercial facilities.

[7] ARPANET—Advanced Research Projects Agency Network.

[8] Massachusetts Institute of Technology, a university located in Cambridge, Massachusetts.

[9] GNU stood for Good News it's not UNIX.

[10] The previous version was called SQL Server 4.9. The number assigned to a version is often viewed as a marketing ploy. Version 10 sounds twice as good as Version 5. At the time, Oracle was marketing their database as Version 7, and Microsoft was marketing SQL Server Version 6.5. Version 10, positioned Sybase's numbering scheme ahead of Oracle, IBM, Informix, and Microsoft. Psychologically, the higher the number, the more mature and refined the product.

[11] The mean temperature of Anchorage, Alaska in January is 15°F.

[12] Seismologists use a magnitude scale to express the seismic energy released by an earthquake. The most common magnitude scale is the Richter scale.

[13] Adams, Carey. Ahead of the Curve. *Access Control & Security Systems Integration* v.43 no.5, April 2000.

[14] Melymuka, Kathleen. Old Bank, New Ideas. *Computerworld*, February 15, 1999.

[15] Stross, Randall *Eboys: The First Inside Account of Venture Capitalists at Work*. New York, NY: Crown Business, 2000.

[16] Gates, Bill. Memo from Bill Gates. January 2002.

[17] A research and development center operated by Carnegie Mellon University.

[18] Hulme, George V. Software's Challenge. *Computerworld*, January 21, 2002.

[19] Personal interview with Gary Light, Chief Technology Officer, Concord Hospital. May 2002.

[20] Hayes, Mary. A Delicate Balance. *Informationweek*, April 2002.

[21] Andel, Tom. Fear of a Hatchet May Inspire a Scalpel. *Transportation and Distribution*, v.38, February 1997.

[22] Personal interview with Steven Green, Senior Vice President, Hobby Lobby. May 2002.

[23] Quartz crystals were first used as a time standard by Warren Marrison (1896–1980), who invented the first quartz clock in 1927.

341

WHERE
WHO
What
WHEN
HOW
Why

CHAPTER 6
SYSTEMS DEVELOPMENT

"There will be no foolish wand waving or silly incantations in this class. As such, I don't expect many of you to appreciate the subtle science and exact art that is potion-making [enterprise architecture]. However, for those select few who possess the predisposition, I can teach you how to bewitch the mind and ensnare the senses. I can tell you how to bottle fame, brew glory, and even put a stopper in death. Then again, maybe some of you have come to Hogwarts in possession of abilities so formidable that you feel confident enough not to pay attention."

— Professor Severus Snape, Potions Master,
Hogwarts School of Witchcraft and Wizardry
From the movie Harry Potter and the Sorcerer's Stone
Based on the novel of the same name by Joanne Rowling (b. 1965)

LEARNING OBJECTIVES

After completing Chapter 6, you will be able to:

1. Explain what impact a mentally and physically unfit *subcontractor* may have on information technology applications.
2. Discuss why the *subcontractor* must have endurance.
3. Explain why the enterprise data center should be organic.
4. List four basic challenges *subcontractors* face in software development.
5. Discuss information technology career opportunities, requirements, and predictions.
6. Compare and contrast security options used by the *subcontractor*.
7. Explain how the enterprise benefits from the programmer knowing and using efficient and creative techniques.
8. Discuss how databases are an asset to the enterprise.
9. Explain the purpose of a service level agreement.
10. Discuss how knowledge of patterns and antipatterns helps improve software structure.

(continued)

11. Explain how the development techniques of the *subcontractor* relate to data integrity, data quality, and data identification.
12. Explain how faster computer chips and slower software affect the enterprise.
13. Discuss the importance of long-term thinking for applications and the enterprise.
14. Explain what happens when the *owner* does not make business rules explicit.
15. Explain why any change to a project should be estimated in terms of time, cost, and effort.
16. Compare and contrast three ways business changes are implemented in an IT project.
17. Discuss safety factors in IT, which can make change easier.
18. Explain the benefit of defensive development to the *subcontractor* and the enterprise.

6.1 INTRODUCTION

Michelangelo di Lodovico Buonarroti Simoni (1475–1564) towered above his contemporary athletes of the imagination. Michelangelo was an artisan...a *subcontractor*. A *subcontractor* is responsible for creating, building, or assembling parts for an end product or service.

Michelangelo's product was art, and as a craftsman, his skill was supreme. He brought passion to the sculptures, paintings, and drawings he produced. Michelangelo defined art as that which has tumescent substance—*The closer you see painting approach good sculpture, the better it will be.*

COMPUTER...SCIENCE OR ART?

When artists such as Michelangelo create a sculpture, the art (or physical appearance) is the result of applying science. Michelangelo's art is the result of understanding and applying science, especially physics, in order to achieve an aesthetically pleasing result.

To create an object d'art, Michelangelo understood:

- The hardness of the marble
- The weak spots created by the marble's grain
- How and why to vary the force the hammer strikes the chisel
- How and why to vary the angle the hammer strikes the chisel
- The angle to place the chisel on the marble

The computer programmer creates a work of art (the physical appearance of the program). The program is the result of applying science. Computer science is subject to physics and mathematics, such as the speed of electrons moving along

(continued)

344

a piece of fiber optics, or through a silicon chip, and various branches of logic, including fuzzy, predicate, Boolean, and first order.

The Zachman Framework promotes communication and understanding. Something that is pleasing to the eye is easier to grasp, whether it is a painting, ammatically correct sentence, or a computer program. As long as you understand the language of the writing system, artistic qualities facilitate understanding.

Computer hardware and software are rooted in science. The application of the sciences should, in many cases, have an artistic value. The artistic value desired is that the product or service *speaks to me*. I can understand what I see.

To create an object d'art, the programmer understands:

- The language's syntax
- The language's weak spots
- How to use memory allocations effectively
- How to persist data to a database effectively
- What type of logic structure to use
- Why structure is important in a program
- Why documentation in a program is important

An artist can produce work for his or her own gratification or for a larger audience. When Michelangelo produced the David, the statue had to be right the first time. Some products or services have to be right the first time; others can evolve. Regardless, the work will be abandoned if it does not communicate.

The purpose of the *subcontractor* being analogous to the artist is that the final product should have an aesthetic quality.

Michelangelo was the greatest sculptor of the sixteenth century, as Donatello (1386–1466) was in the century before him, and Bernini (1598–1680) was in the century after him. Many people admire the products of his genius, but few consider the magnitude of his undertakings, the problems he encountered, and the setbacks, or even failures, he may have experienced.

Two of Michelangelo's most famous sculptures, the Pietà in Rome shown in Figure 6-1, and the David in Florence, are spectacular accomplishments that obscure the mundane facts of their creation. Before these sculptures became admired, sublime marvels, they were inert and spiritless stones. Strong and dexterous hands fashioned the raw and resistant marble. Those same hands were often tired and bruised. To complete his sculptures, Michelangelo exhibited the capacity for great mental and physical endurance.

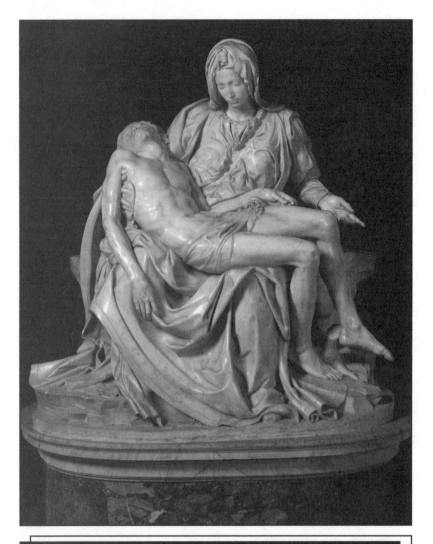

Figure 6-1   *Michelangelo's sculpture: The Pietà in Rome*

Carving marble is difficult. The work is loud, dirty, and unforgiving. Michelangelo's rival, Leonardo da Vinci, considered painting a more noble enterprise and described the actual process of sculpture as a "most mechanical exercise." In his notebooks, da Vinci wrote:

> *The sculptor in creating his work does so by the strength of his arm by which he consumes the marble, or other obdurate material in which his subject is enclosed: and this is done by most mechanical exercise, often accompanied by great sweat which mixes with the marble dust and forms a kind of mud daubed all over his face. The marble dust flours him all over so that he looks like a baker; his back is covered with a snowstorm of chips, and his house is made filthy by the flakes and dust of stone.*

Each time the sculptor's lump hammer collides with the end of the chisel, metal is striking metal, which, in turn, strikes the marble. Chips fly in all directions and soon the dust lies thick. Modern stone workers wear goggles, but Michelangelo did not. He wanted to see the stone, to see each mark, to make tiny adjustments to the angle of his chisel, and to the force of his blow. One wrong stroke could cause an *uh-oh*. Only after tens of thousands of perfectly directed hard and soft blows does an inert marble figure come to life.

Michelangelo became one of the greatest marble sculptors of all time. Michelangelo also became a great painter, architect, and poet. Few artists and craftsman have been as prolific as Michelangelo. Fewer still have succeeded in creating enduring masterpieces in so many different media.

If during his lifetime, Michelangelo had only carved David, or painted the ceiling of the Sistine Chapel, or erected Saint Peter's, he would have been guaranteed a place in history. Rather, Michelangelo made all three works, and each is an achievement in human endeavor.

In his sixties, Michelangelo was able to chisel off more chips of hard marble in 15 minutes than the number of chips three young stone carvers could chisel in three or four hours. Moving with fury and precision, Michelangelo's honed skill allowed him to knock off large chunks of marble, three to four fingers thick, with a single blow of his hammer and chisel. Michelangelo not only mastered his craft, but also mastered his body. He maintained his health, his strength, and his power—he had endurance.

OH GREAT ONE

A database administrator (DBA) working at Bethlehem Steel in Bethlehem, Pennsylvania started a typical day by reviewing new database queries created by the developers in the DB2 (Database2) database catalog. The DBA noticed some queries he could improve. He spoke with the developer, who had been working on the program for three weeks and was struggling to finish the program.

The DBA knew the program would have to be restructured to perform well in production. In 1 hour and 10 minutes, the DBA wrote a program from scratch that worked. The program would outperform the developer's program—even though the developer had not yet completed her version of the program.

In most disciplines, a skilled craftsperson can produce better quality work in less time than one with fewer skills.

Endurance

Endurance is often associated with athletes. Endurance athletes who compete in long-distance events, such as the Ironman[1] and ultra-marathons,[2] require a great deal of stamina and strength to perform well. Strength training helps build physical strength, which, in turn, minimizes the risk of injury, helps improve resistance to fatigue, and helps improve endurance.

The ability to resist fatigue allows an athlete to hold a set pace for longer periods, or to increase speed over a given distance. Strength and power training is beneficial for all athletes. Benefits from consistent strength training are not immediate and may take up to two months to appear. See Figure 6-2.

Training for a 100-mile race can take 10 months. Keep in mind that each person is an *experiment of one*—no single training schedule is a panacea for every athlete.

During the first six months, build base mileage:
- Run 100 miles per week
- Run 25 of those miles at a 10K pace
- Weight train

Reserve the next month for transitioning to very long training runs:
- Run 120 miles per week
- Run 40 of those miles at a 10K pace
- Weight train

The next two months are used for intense training:
- Run 170 miles per week
- Run 80 of those miles at a 10K pace
- Weight train

The final month and race day:
- Run 70 miles the first week
- Run 50 miles the second week
- Jog lightly the third week
- Rest for two days
- After the race, soak your feet in Epsom salts—you deserve it!

Figure 6-2 *Intensive*

Yawn...Oops

In general, organizations are partial to installing new information technology applications over a holiday weekend. In the United States, Memorial Day and Labor Day weekends are good three-day candidates. Thanksgiving is *wonderful*...it provides four days. Typically, the extended weekend periods mean the office is empty of administrative and operational staff. An empty office means less people are affected if an installation runs into a problem. Developers (*subcontractors*) are often expected to come into work and not sleep or leave until the new application is *alive and kicking*.

When a production system fails and *goes down* in the middle of the night, mobile phones and pagers sound the alarm, and on-call developers must return to work immediately. Forced back to the office, developers must fix any hardware or software problems, despite the consequences of family demands and sleep deprivation. The problem must be fixed, regardless of how long the process takes.

IT projects are known for having unrealistic schedules. Many projects start by requiring overtime from developers. Within a few weeks, working on the weekend becomes mandatory. *Subcontractors* have been known to miss the experiences of seeing their children grow up, while being summoned to pound the keyboard and watch the desktop monitor...night and day, week after week, month after month.

The *subcontractor* is forced to be an endurance athlete, but without the necessary training. *Subcontractors* are taught the art, craft, and science of their work, but are not necessarily taught how to develop endurance. An IT *subcontractor* required to work late into the evening is not likely to experience a balanced and nutritious diet. Many corporations believe that feeding *subcontractors* a diet of pepperoni pizza, soda, popcorn, and candy bars is essential to provide *food for thought*. See Figure 6-3.

Figure 6-3	*It's the usual, ma'am*

Like athletes, developers suffer from mental and physical fatigue when working long hours or participating on stressful projects. Very little is done to help train *subcontractors* to manage the endurance aspect of their careers. Like Michelangelo, carving beauty into stone where one strike can ruin everything, developers craft systems that become the business itself. When a system fails, the business can stall and even completely fail.

IT *subcontractors* are apt to think about their work at home. Many developers experience an *ah-hah* moment while taking a morning shower, or find themselves waking at 3:08 a.m. with a potential solution in their mind. The *ah-hah* moment is a realization of how to solve a nagging technical problem.

Luge athletes picture a course in their minds as part of practice; similarly, the IT *subcontractor* creates a mental model of the task at hand. However, the IT *subcontractor* performs the work without appropriate endurance training. Mentally and physically unfit *subcontractors* may be the primary reason why information technology applications contain so many bugs.

Microsoft Office 2000 consisted of 30 million lines of code and went into production with over 200,000 known bugs.[3] The ratio of bugs to lines of code produced by Microsoft's *subcontractors* is probably quite good by industry standards. However, many problems may have been introduced because the *subcontractor* was not an endurance athlete, even though the individual was considered the Michelangelo of the domain.

A person assigned to an IT project resembles an athlete registered for a 100-mile race who is not given any training guidelines for the event. In the end, *subcontractors* are defined by the artistry of their work and their tolerance for endurance. The *subcontractor* is taught the art and science of information technology, but not how to maintain a physically and mentally fit mind and body for applying the art—that too is *food for thought*.

SECTION 6.2 HOW TO SPACKLE—THE ART OF PROGRAMMING

QUESTIONS TO CONTEMPLATE

1. How does the *subcontractor's* job resemble a work of art?
2. How are patterns used in software?
3. What can help bridge the gap between *planners*, *owners*, *designers*, *builders*, and *subcontractors*?

6.2.1 Introduction

Computer programming is a genuine creative art. A computer program instructs a computer to do something specific for a special purpose. A program is created in an artificial language—a language designed and written by people, but translated into instructions on which a computer can act.

Like all human languages and writing systems, every computer programming language has its own conceptual biases, limitations, and unique possibilities. A developer's choice of programming language, use of that language, and specific program content are used to create, define, and delimit a unique window of the computer's broader capability. The unique window becomes the **application program**, which allows end users to actively or passively interact with the computer.

Once written, a computer program presents its user with an unchanging series of special-purpose features. The features have been crafted either by a developer's personal discretion, or by mandates from business personnel. The program is a fixed subjective creation drawn from infinite possibilities. The program is a specific image painted between the viewer and an underlying blank canvas. The program is an *object d'art*. Ultimately, the program should help move the enterprise toward a larger market, rather than achieve a particular aesthetic result or creative solution.

Learning a programming language's syntax is generally easy for software developers. Hence, the actual creation of a program is thought to be relatively easy. After all, most people can understand the following concepts, which underlie the logic of all programming languages:

- If this is true, then do that.
- While this is true, then continue doing that.
- Read this, write that.

Programming a computer can seem rather trivial. After all, the computer's alphabet has only two characters: zero and one. How difficult can programming a computer be?

Have you ever tried spackling a wall? It is a cinch. Place a dollop of spackle on a spackling knife. Then spread the spackle on the wall. One minor problem is the spackle never seems to come out flat and smooth against the surface of the wall. How can this be? Television personalities on home improvement shows make spackling seem so easy. With a motivating smile and gleaming white teeth, they tell us the process is a simple one. However, spackling takes practice; it is a true art form. Programming takes practice too, and is a true art form. However, you cannot create art without an understanding of the underlying sciences supporting the art form.

Subcontractors find the *megahurts* in that computers always seem to do what they are told and seldom do what was intended. Four basic challenges face the *subcontractor* in software development. Each of the following challenges requires knowledge of an appropriate technique, science, and discipline:

- Make the software run.
- Make the software right.
- Make the software fast.
- Make the software small.

Subcontractors also need to think in the large, or see the big picture, which means to consider the ramifications of their work. For example, developers had to rewrite many systems during the middle and late 1990s to solve the Y2K problem, which happened because programmers stored two-digit years instead of four-digit years. The reason most cited for this blunder was that a two-digit year stored in 2 bytes takes up less hard drive space than a four-digit year stored in 4 bytes. Whereas this is a true statement, storing a two-digit year in character form consumes more hard disk space than a four-digit year stored using binary notation.

For example, the date May 3, 1953 would have been stored in 6 bytes as 050353 (two-digit month, two-digit day, and a two-digit year), or with the following binary equivalent in ASCII:[4] 00110000 00110101 00110000 00110011 00110101 00110011. Each zero or one represents a **bit** and 8 bits represent a **byte**. One byte represents one character.[5]

Alternatively, the date could have been stored with a four-digit year, 19530503 (year, month, and day), as the following string of binary numbers and only consume 4 bytes on a hard drive: 00000001 00000101 00000011 00000111. The 4 bytes are sufficient to hold a six-digit year.

Storing a date in year, month, and day sequence instead of month, day, and year sequence is part of the attention to detail that the *subcontractor* must learn as an artist. One of the major problems caused by *subcontractors* is their preference to store data in the format it will be presented to the knowledge worker. Data presented for viewing does not have to be stored on a hard drive in the same format or sequence. This, too, is part of the artistic know-how of the *subcontractor*.

Three primary reasons why programmers stored dates with two-digit years in 6 bytes are:

- Dates stored in character format are easier to read in core dumps should the program fail to execute properly
- Dates stored in character format are easier to read in a sequential file
- Ignorance of other techniques

Subcontractors in IT often make decisions based on what is convenient for them in lieu of what is best for the organization. The Y2K debacle was a common industry example. On the other hand, an example of an efficient programming technique is Gray code. Most people who are taught to count in binary use the technique in Table 6-1.

Decimal	Hexadecimal	Binary
0	0	0000
1	1	0001
2	2	0010
3	3	0011
4	4	0100
5	5	0101
6	6	0110
7	7	0111
8	8	1000
9	9	1001
10	A	1010
11	B	1011
12	C	1100
13	D	1101
14	E	1110
15	F	1111

Table 6-1   *Decimal, hexadecimal, and binary equivalents*

Between the numbers 7 and 8, all four bits are forced to change. Each time a bit is changed, the computer uses more time. Minimizing the number of bits a computer has to change results in a faster computer. Gray code uses a sequence that requires a computer to change only one bit as numbers increase sequentially. Gray code is one way to increase the speed of a computer. See Table 6-2.

Decimal	Hexadecimal	Binary	Gray code
0	0	0000	0000
1	1	0001	0001
2	2	0010	0011
3	3	0011	0010
4	4	0100	0110
5	5	0101	0111
6	6	0110	0101
7	7	0111	0100
8	8	1000	1100
9	9	1001	1101
10	A	1010	1111
11	B	1011	1110
12	C	1100	1010
13	D	1101	1011
14	E	1110	1001
15	F	1111	1000

Table 6-2   *Decimal, hexadecimal, binary, and Gray code equivalents*

Computer programming is an art and the *subcontractor* is the artist. The broader the *subcontractor's* knowledge, the larger and more versatile the artist's palette becomes. However, as with most art forms, there are great artists, good artists, and those that should find something else to do. The enterprise is dependent on the quality of the programmer's technological and artistic skills.

6.2.2 Programming Languages *(how)*

A significant design detail in the art of computer programming is the style and vocabulary used in a program's construction. A *subcontractor* should strive to make the finished program an artifact that can be understood readily by both seasoned and novice *subcontractors*.

If one of the four challenges to software programming is making the software right, then *right* should be thought of as having two key goals. The first goal is to produce a program that runs error free under all conditions. The other key goal is to construct software so that another *subcontractor* with an undetermined level of skill can continually modify the program.

Constructing a program that is understandable and maintainable requires discipline and promotes the *subcontractor* far beyond what the *labels* developer and programmer convey. A talented programmer is an artist. An IT artist creates software with a recognizable style and signature. In the same way that one can look at a building and know that Frank Lloyd Wright (1867–1959) was the architect, look at a painting and know that Edvard Munch (1863–1944) was the painter, or look at the Norwegian Fjords and know that Slartibartfast[6] was the designer, one can also look at a computer program and identify the programmer.

Subcontractors who maintain software have limited time to study the program. Recognizable signatures, styles, patterns, and vocabularies contribute to help those who maintain software. The following is a selection of helpful artistic design principles for writing software:

- Appropriately name all variables—avoid single-letter variable names and creative spelling.
- Appropriately name all methods—avoid ambiguous and abstract words like *it*, *everything*, *data*, *handle*, *stuff*, *do*, *routine*, and *perform*. For example, methods named *PerformDataFunction* and *DoIt* do not promote understanding.
- Document acronyms close to where they are used.
- Use a formal notation for when to capitalize letters.
- Avoid using names that are later used in a different context.
- Avoid using accented letters.
- Use a single language to name variables and methods. For example, if you use Spanish names, do not intermix Portuguese names. Or if you are using American English, do not intersperse British English.
- Do not use extended ASCII characters such as ß, ∂, and Ω.
- Avoid irrelevant names or names that connote emotional meaning.
- Follow published and accepted standards.

- Use fonts that help distinguish 1 (one) and l (lowercase ell), 2 (two) and Z (zee or zed), 5 (five) and S (ess), 0 (zero) and O (oh), and m (em) and rn (ar and en).
- Do not reuse global names as private names.
- When using Hungarian notation, do not change the variable type.
- Provide ample comments and documentation.
- Use documentation to describe *why* something is being done instead of just *what* is being done.
- Keep comments and code synchronized.
- Document the units of measure a variable's value uses.
- Create reusable modules rather than cut and paste lines of code from existing software.
- Avoid overly nested logic.
- Provide for exception (error) processing.
- Create test cases.
- Test all logic.
- Evaluate the performance of all logic.
- Follow **best practices** for the specific programming language being used.
- Limit the number of programming languages used in an application.
- Do not mix techniques. For example, an SQL (structured query language) outer join can be accomplished several ways. For consistency, use only one method.

Ultimately, the *subcontractor* has many ways to express creativity. Even if a program is difficult to write, the program should not be difficult to read.

6.2.3 Creativity *(what)*

As artists, developers should be given a mandate to go as far as their imaginations take them. Should not developers who create works of design have the same freedom of thought and expression that societies tolerate for painters, dancers, authors, and thespians? Many businesses and government agencies require a specific dress code for developers. Developers are also required to abide by mandatory work hours, regardless of the actual number of hours worked.

Authors talk of having writer's block, painters talk of being uninspired, and dancers talk about a movement not *speaking* to them. The sympathy and understanding awarded these artists are not extended to the developer. Developers do not have the luxury of sitting around, trying to stimulate the creative process.

Creativity cannot always be summoned or demanded. Creativity may make an entrance at odd hours, or out of context to the developer's surroundings. The hours of creative thought are typically never recorded or captured on a project plan. Off-hours creativity is never measured, though it is a common artistic trait. The actual amount of time required to create a program, or even a network, will never be known.

The network developer can be viewed as the composer of a symphony. The network developer coordinates various instruments of the network. Each instrument must work in harmony to produce a technological symphony. The art of maximizing bandwidth and other network resources, coupled with the skill of coordinating disparate network entities, helps illustrate the artistic effort required to get a series of *bits* to dance in sequence from node to node.

Stifling the creative energies of developers helps ensure *subcontractors* remain stuck in the backwaters of the industry. In the Renaissance period, nonconformists like Michelangelo extended the envelope of knowledge and beauty. In the early 1990s, renaissance methodologist Kent Beck (b. 1961) wanted to create a reliable way to develop software. Beck contemplated what made software both simple and difficult to create. In March of 1996, Beck began a project at DaimlerChrysler, using some different concepts of software development. The result was the Extreme Programming (XP) methodology.

 ## 6.2.4 Extreme Programming *(why)*

In XP, Beck focused on four dimensions for improving software construction:

- Improving communication
- Seeking simplicity
- Receiving constant feedback
- Proceeding with courage

Communication, simplicity, feedback, and courage are four values sought by XP *subcontractors*.

XP has been proven successful at companies like Bayerische Landesbank, Credit Swiss Life, DaimlerChrysler, First Union National Bank, Ford Motor Company, and the financial organization, UBS. XP's success can, in some ways, be attributed to its emphasis on customer satisfaction. The methodology is designed to deliver software when needed.

XP empowers developers to respond confidently to changing customer requirements, even when the changes are occurring late in the project's life cycle. XP emphasizes teamwork. Managers, end users, and *subcontractors* are all part of the team dedicated to delivering quality software. XP *subcontractors* seek ways to keep their designs simple and clean. *Subcontractors* receive feedback by testing software, starting on day one. *Subcontractors* deliver software to end users as soon as possible and implement changes as suggested.

XP is based on the idea that software engineered to be simple and elegant is more valuable than software that is complex and hard to maintain. XP emphasizes testing to provide safety nets for *subcontractors* and end users. Tests are created initially, before a single line of code has been constructed. If bugs are found in the program code, new tests are added. All testing is automated to facilitate retesting.

XP embraces change, allowing the end user to modify requirements during construction. Continuous feedback is provided by the end user, allowing for functionality to be changed and satisfaction improved. Source code quality is very important. Just because end users are not typically shown the source code, *subcontractors* should still put effort into creating a work of art.

Figure 6-4 illustrates the XP methodology.

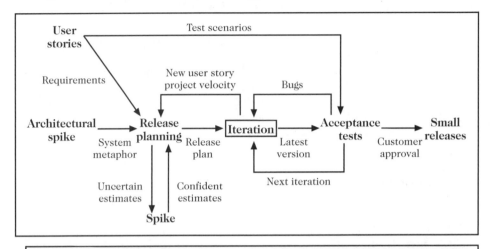

Figure 6-4 *Extreme Programming (XP) workflow*

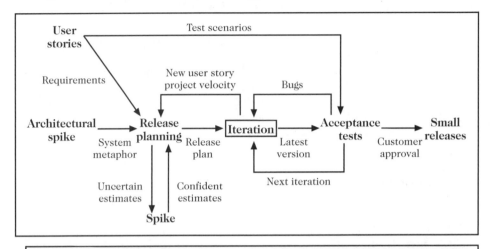

Rules and practices of XP include:

Plan
- Write user stories.
- Create the release-planning schedule.
- Determine and discover how to create frequent small releases.
- Create rules, standards, units of measure, metrics, standards, and statistics for the project.
- Divide the project into iterations.
- Start each iteration with planning.
- Move people around to broaden the knowledge base.
- Start each day with a stand-up meeting.
- Fix the XP process when it breaks.

Design
- Keep it simple (KISS principle).
- Choose a system metaphor—a pattern that can be used to understand the project.
- Use CRC[7] cards for design sessions.
- Create spike solutions to reduce risk. Spike solutions focus on problem areas, ignoring other concerns.
- Avoid adding additional functionality early—stick with Refactor whenever and wherever possible.

Code
- The end user is always available.
- Code must be written to agreed upon standards.
- Code the unit test first.
- All production code is pair programmed.
- Only one pair integrates code into the application at one time.
- Integrate new code into the application often.

- Use collective code ownership. See Figure 6-5.
- Leave program optimization until the end of the process. Focus on functionality.
- Do not work overtime—recognize people do not have the mental and physical endurance to produce quality work after a given number of hours.

Test
- All code must have unit tests.
- All code must pass all unit tests before formal release.
- When a bug is found, tests are created to catch the bug.
- Acceptance tests are run often and progress metrics are published.

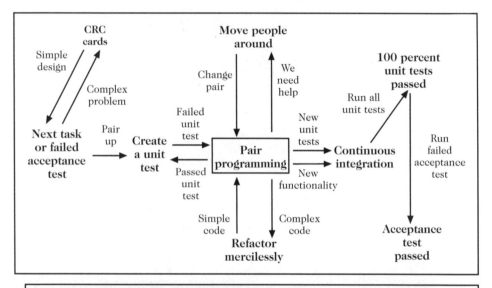

Figure 6-5 *Collective code ownership in XP*

In XP, Beck set out to change the patterns for developing computer software. XP's success in smaller projects is fostering its use in larger software projects.

6.2.5 Software Patterns *(where)*

During youth and through education, you became a pattern expert. You can spot a *family* when you see one, or design a family to fit a story. In some cultures, a family may have two parents and one or more children. In this scenario, each child has a set of parents. The pattern can be given a name: family. The pattern has participants who play one of two **roles**: parent or child. The pattern has multiple bidirectional **relationships**. See Figure 6-6.

Patterns are defined by their standard roles and relationships. Patterns are reused by applying them to specific situations, filling those roles, and establishing the relationships. A definition for a pattern in software is a set of standard roles, and relationships that are designed to become a reusable solution for a recurring design problem.

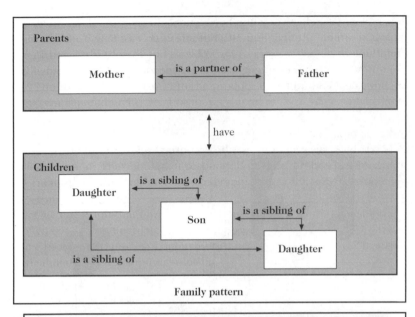

Figure 6-6 *The roles and relationships of patterns are easily portrayed in a diagram*

A role denotes standard behavior that something should perform. A relationship connects two role players and allows them to collaborate. Relationships can be unidirectional (one way) or bidirectional (two way). See Figure 6-7.

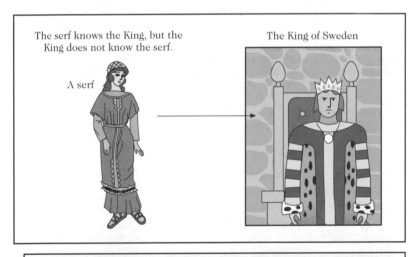

Figure 6-7 *The King of Sweden is an example of a unidirectional relationship*

An application is a collection of interacting elements. A software pattern is how some of those elements are organized in a standard manner, according to the roles and relationships of the pattern. In this context, pattern does not mean the presence of recognizable, ordered, or repeating elements, such as a snowflake, Morse code, or a stock market graph.

Software patterns are similar to everyday patterns we see in life, but have more structure. For example, software patterns should be given one:

- Easily understood name
- Description of the problem the software pattern solves
- Description of how the software pattern provides a solution
- Description of pros and cons for using the software pattern

Software patterns are information rich. Additionally, describing the pattern visually with a model is also helpful, as shown in Figures 6-8 and 6-9. Figure 6-8 illustrates a pattern called the Singleton pattern.[8] Figure 6-9 shows a portion of the programming code that supports the pattern. In the Singleton pattern, the roles are *single instance* and *client*. The relationship is the client *has a* single instance.

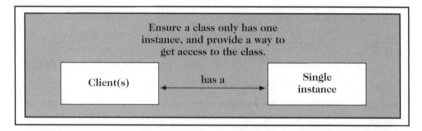

Figure 6-8   *A model showing the Singleton pattern*

```
Public class ConnectionPool {
    protected static ConnectionPool singleton = new ConnectionPool();
    protected ArrayList pool = new ArrayList();
    public static ConnectionPool getInstance() {
        return singleton;
    }
    public Connection acquireConnection() {
        if (pool.isEmpty()) {
            return createConnection();
        } else {
            return (Connection)pool.remove(pool.size() - 1);
        }
    }
    public void releaseConnection(Connection conn) {
        pool.add(conn);
    }
    protected Connection createConnection() {
        // Do some work here....
    }
    protected ConnectionPool() { }
}
```

Figure 6-9   *Java programming code based on the Singleton pattern*

An IT *subcontractor*, who bases a program on a proven software pattern, should not feel the pattern limits his freedom as an IT artist. If a *subcontractor* alters program code to make it simpler without altering the program's functionality, the *subcontractor* is refactoring.

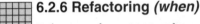

6.2.6 Refactoring *(when)*

Software **refactoring** is a form of code modification. Refactoring improves a program's structure to support subsequent extensions. The goal of refactoring is to simplify maintenance of the program over the long term. Refactoring a program does not involve adding new functionality or altering the program's capabilities. Refactoring simply recognizes the program was not created by an artisan, or that improved techniques have been discovered since the program's creation. Refactoring is a transformation from the complex and ugly to the simple and refined.

Good software structure is essential for application extension and maintenance. Software development can be a chaotic activity. Often the program's structure strays from the *builder's* planned design. When refactoring a program, any structural changes are best applied before considering performance optimization.

Optimization sometimes involves compromises to a program structure. Changes that a *subcontractor* makes to a program structure to optimize performance de-optimize the *designer's* or *builder's* program design. The concepts of optimization and de-optimization are discussed in Chapter 7. Ideally, only small areas of a program need to be optimized. Refactoring prior to optimization helps partition optimized code away from the majority of the software.

Examples of refactoring transformations include:

- Superclass abstraction
- Conditional elimination
- Aggregate abstraction

These changes are called refactoring because they have no effect on program correctness. When used properly, refactoring is a normal activity in the programming process. Refactoring recognizes that people with different levels of skill participated in creating an application.

Refactoring raises the quality of work over time. Refactoring recognizes that programming is an art form and that a good program has aesthetic qualities. Refactoring is a solution for coping with an antipattern.

6.2.7 Antipatterns *(who)*

Antipatterns represent a concept in a series of revolutionary changes in computer science and software engineering. As the Standish Group statistic used in Chapter 1 illustrates, many software projects fail. Often, failure to produce quality software can be attributed to a recurring reason. Using a technique that consistently produces less than satisfactory results is *stupid* and may be formalized as a negative solution.

Antipatterns are documented ways to learn from previous mistakes of others. By focusing on repeated software failures, antipatterns attempt to understand, prevent, and recover from those mistakes. Antipatterns are tools to bridge gaps between *planners, owners, designers, builders,* and *subcontractors.* Antipatterns are natural extensions of design patterns.[9]

Antipatterns provide an industry vocabulary for common defective processes, techniques, and implementations. Documented antipatterns strive to bring together the forces causing the negative solution, describe the unsuccessful process, and address the problem's core issues. Examples of antipatterns are: Golden Hammer, Spaghetti Code, and Cut and Paste Programming.

In software development, antipatterns are pervasive. To solve a problem, two of the options a *subcontractor* can use are to make something up or use a pattern that worked previously. A pattern can become an antipattern when the pattern starts producing more problems than the pattern actually solves.

Antipatterns are based on a rhetorical structure that differs from simple patterns. Antipatterns begin with a compelling, problematic solution. From the problematic solution, someone determines and records the problem's root causes. The antipattern is the result of incorrectly trying to resolve a specific problem in a specific context.

Once an antipattern has been identified correctly, the code can be refactored to remove the problem. Examples of antipatterns include:

- *Golden Hammer*—When a familiar technology or concept is applied obsessively to many different types of software problems, the solution becomes a hammer because everything is viewed as a nail. The problem's solution involves expanding the knowledge of each *subcontractor* through education, training, and study groups. Education exposes *subcontractors* to alternative technologies and approaches and improves their artistic range.
- *Spaghetti Code*—Ad-hoc software structures make program code difficult to extend and optimize. Frequent code refactoring can improve software structure, support software maintenance, and enable iterative development.
- *Cut and Paste Programming*—Program code that is reused by copying source statements and can lead to significant maintenance problems. Alternative forms of reuse, including black-box reuse,[10] help reduce maintenance issues by having common source code, testing, and documentation.

Form may follow function, but in a fast-paced business environment, transforming computer code into an artistic form is a way to implement new software expediently. Proficiency allows the business to introduce new products to the marketplace even faster. *Subcontractors* need to follow rules of science in creating a program, but future productivity may be based on art rather than science, engineering, or technology.

6.2.8 Key Terms

application program	refactoring
best practice	relationship
bit	role
byte	

6.2.9 Review Questions

1. On what two goals should the *subcontractor* focus when striving to make software *right* during software development?
2. How is the Golden Hammer an antipattern, and what are the possible solutions?
3. Why is refactoring important for the enterprise?

4. Explain how antipatterns can bridge the gap between the *planner, owner, designer, builder,* and *subcontractor*?

5. Kent Beck focused on what four dimensions of improvement for software construction?
6. Why must the *subcontractor* strive to make the finished program an artifact that can be understood readily by seasoned and novice *subcontractors*?

SECTION 6.3 WHY THIN IS IN

> **QUESTIONS TO CONTEMPLATE**
>
> 1. Why should business rules be separated from the process?
> 2. How does form affect a program?
> 3. What is the benefit of a rule book?

6.3.1 Introduction

Do ends justify the means or do means justify the ends? Which is more important, the outcome (end) or the process (means) by which the outcome was accomplished? In today's highly competitive marketplace, most managers might argue only the end result counts.

The *subcontractor* produces the applications for obtaining the organization's operational results, which creates a compensation paradox. Should the *subcontractor* be compensated for turning out a system as fast as possible or for excellence of practice?

Obviously both are important, but organizations probably let one outweigh the other. In many cultures, the emphasis is on form and not solely on results. For example, Japanese Samurai archers practiced form using a highly meditative martial art called Kyudo. The goals of Kyudo are truth, goodness, and beauty.

A master archer, if asked the question, "What is truth," would, without saying a word, pick up a bow and arrow and shoot. The level of the archer's mastery would be allowed to serve as the gauge of the archer's progress. Progress translates into the archer's knowledge of reality—or truth.

In Kyudo, the archer does not try to hit the target by staring at it. Kyudo teachings deal with precision, discipline, and the archer's relationship with the mind, body, and weapon. When an archer shoots at a target, the archer tries to visualize the target as a reflection or mirror of the mind. When the archer releases the arrow, it cuts the archer's ego so that the archer can see his own mind.

Secondary traits of the successful Samurai archer include sincerity, courage, patience, alertness, and commitment. Centuries ago, the intense training each archer received and the proficiency of form proved devastating to the Samurai's enemies. The importance of form is still prevalent in Japanese culture.

The Olympic Games illustrate examples of both form and result. All athletes competing in the games are physically conditioned. Conditioning is a precursor to form. Regardless of form, a runner is judged on an objective basis and awarded medals solely for speed. On the other hand, gymnasts are judged subjectively, and points are deducted based on form.

In business, form requires rules of practice. The *subcontractor's* rules of practice cultivate the *subcontractor's* artistry and help create the programs that support the rules of business. The rules of practice help to translate the rules of business into a successful service or computing product.

Most aspects of business software are based on rules. When creating business software, speed is the goal in virtually every organization that produces software. If an application can be delivered in one day and work as required, little if any consideration is given to the application's form. However, because most applications are modified eventually, some degree of form pays off. One area of focus for form is how the *subcontractor* decides to handle business rules.

363

6.3.2 Rule Books *(why)*

In professional sports, the game of soccer has relatively few rules. There are 17 categories of rules or *laws*, as the Federation Internationale de Football Association, the worldwide governing body of the sport, prefers to call them. The specifics for each rule are detailed in a rule book.

The team's owners, coaches, players, and referees all abide by the rules. If they fail to abide by the rules, there are rules to handle that too. When dealing with business rules, there are no exceptions to the *rule*; exceptions are just other rules. A rule is a rule is a rule.

An organization has several rule books. The human resource department has a rule book that governs employees' behavior and lets employees understand what they can expect from their employer. Public corporations have rule books provided by the SEC, governing financial reporting and insider trading restrictions.

Sporting authorities have good rule books. Industries that are regulated heavily, like banking and insurance, usually have good rule books for most of their business applications. All organizations have rule books, though they probably cannot produce one upon request. For most organizations, the rule book is hidden and strewn about inside hundreds of application programs and configuration files. When rules are hidden, they become forgotten or misunderstood.

One way to determine form in a computer application is to determine how business rules are handled. Can the business rules be fully accounted for? Can the business rules be modified easily? Is each action that is associated with a business rule known and understood? Which business rules are codified in an application? Which business rules are empowered to a user? A formal rule book can help answer all these questions.

A typical program moves data from one location to another and performs a series of business rules upon the data. Movement of data should be separated from rules. Separating rules from an actual process has many benefits. For example, Figure 6-10 contains two soccer scenarios.

Figure 6-10   *Finding the process that works*

In the scenarios presented, the referee has awarded the team in white a direct free kick just outside the penalty area. In scenario one, the kicker shoots the ball directly into the goal and scores. In the second scenario, the kicker passes the ball to a team player, who shoots and also scores.

In both cases, the rules of the game remain intact and unchanged. However, the two scenarios represent two different processes. In the game of soccer, the rules are separated from the actual play, so a team can easily change and adapt the type of processes they need for a given situation. If one process never seems to work well, the process can be discarded with no impact.

In many software programs, the rules are embedded directly into the process. When an enterprise needs to change a business process, the rules have to be handled too because the rules are intertwined directly with the process. In many instances, enterprises need to revise processes, not rules. If the rules are separated from the process, the enterprise may be able to change its processes constantly with minimal cost.

For example, many online shopping portals frequently revise the look and feel of their Web sites. However, the rules for adding or removing items to and from the shopping cart, calculating tax, and applying shipping and handling charges remain the same. The navigation processes change; the rules do not. Separating the rules from the process may yield the ability to react and change with speed and agility.

6.3.3 Getting Thin *(how)*

One of the first computers was the Electronic Numerical Integrator and Computer (ENIAC). ENIAC had no monitor and could only remember 20 numbers at a time. In the 1940s, the University of Pennsylvania demonstrated ENIAC's capability to count from 1 to 5,000 in just ⅕ of a second. The feat shocked the world out of the mechanical age and into the world of digital processing.

Assembling the original set of wires, vacuum tubes, resistors, and switches took about 18 months. Fully operational, the computer used about 174 kilowatts of electricity every second—enough to power a typical home for about 10 days. Costing nearly $500,000, the motivation for building ENIAC was World War II.

The liaison between the U.S. Army and the ENIAC team, Herman Goldstine, said, "The electronics people said there were too many vacuum tubes and it would never run. The mathematics people said there were no problems complex enough that computers were needed." In the end, the U.S. Army provided both the complex problems and the money.

John Mauchly (1907–1980), one of two masterminds behind ENIAC, knew the army was having difficulty working out the complicated firing tables needed to help gun crews aim the new artillery being used against German forces. The 32-year-old Mauchly told army officials that in a matter of minutes, his proposed machine could complete a job that took someone using a mechanical desktop calculator 40 hours.

ENIAC was completed just as the war was ending, too late for those artillery tables. However, ENIAC fulfilled another military purpose—doing millions of calculations on thermonuclear chain reactions, predicting the destruction that could be caused by the hydrogen bomb.

Two critical concepts for future computing evolved out of ENIAC. One was the idea of a *stored program* and the other a programming tool known as the *if statement*. Today's computers can store numerous programs, but for ENIAC, engineers had to drag around 18-kilogram trays of wires and vacuum tubes to change settings and perform simple tasks. They realized quickly that stored programs need more memory. The *if statement* was just as important because it permitted the computer to choose between different outcomes based on different inputs.

With these concepts firmly in place, the *stored program* and the *if statement* yielded the birth of the *fat process*. Ever since that time, programmers have relished the idea of trying to put as much logic into a process as time and design allow. Even today, some programmers create huge Java and Visual Basic programs that perform multiple, sometimes hundreds of, different and occasionally unrelated functions in a single program or class. Not all programmers produce inflexible fat programs, but not all programmers are proficient *engineers* or *artists* either.

Since ENIAC, many *designers*, *builders*, and *subcontractors* have learned to remove more elements from the stored program. Removing elements to create components reflects the engineering traits of programming. Operating systems are separate from application programs. Application programs are independent of storage devices and no longer need to keep track of the number of revolutions a disk spins and the speed at which a read/write head moves.

Peripherals and drivers have been separated from the application. Structured techniques, modularized techniques, and application program interface techniques have helped minimize the amount of code in one place. The thinner application programs can become, the more agile the enterprise can become. By learning to separate business rules from the process, the *subcontractor* can continue to help forward the **thinning process**.

6.3.4 Rules Rule *(what)*

As the dependence on technology continues to increase, what enterprises choose to automate becomes a major factor in how quickly they can react to changes in the environment.

Historically, applications have been designed in terms of database structure and organization of process. Little attention was paid directly to designing business rules and policies. Even today, many enterprises struggle to define all the business rules during analysis. In many cases, rules are discovered and created by the *subcontractor* as the program is developed.

In many application programs, business rules are hard to locate and adjust in order to meet ongoing changes to business requirements. Software applications frequently become an impediment to the changing business. Development approaches have to start focusing on flexibility and become more component based.

From the *owner's* point of view, a business rule is defined as "A statement that defines or constrains some aspect of the business. It is intended to assert business structure, or to control or influence the behavior of the business."[11] Examples of business rules include:

- A customer cannot order goods on credit unless they have an approved credit account.
- Goods cannot be sold to a customer on credit beyond their credit limit.

From a *subcontractor's* perspective, all business behavior can be described as constraints on creating, updating, and deleting data. The previous business rule examples can be stated from a constraint on data as follows:

- A credit order cannot be stored unless the approved credit flag is true.
- If the sum of the outstanding amount and current order amount exceeds the credit limit, the order cannot be stored.

Following are some of the benefits that a business rules approach to software development can bring:

- Applications can be customized precisely to fit business needs, at an affordable cost. Transparency of the business rules gives business users better visibility and control over the business policies enforced by the application.
- The ease of altering business rules can reduce the long-term cost of ownership.
- Business rules can provide a more complete and accurate analysis of business requirements, resulting in better communication between business users and IT workers.
- Architectures developed around the business rules paradigm tend to be more flexible and are designed for change.

In 1997, the Business Rules Group, an independent IT standards body, published a framework for classifying business rules. The taxonomy included:

- Structural constraints
- Derivation rules
- Action assertions

Taxonomies for business rules can help *subcontractors* better understand the business aspects of an application. The Business Rules Group taxonomy helps business users better organize their thoughts for an application too.

6.3.5 Conflicting Rules *(when)*

What is the color red? Depending on the domain and the context, one person might see red as the attribute of a specific object. For example, that Ferrari over there is red. Another person might see red as a thing that itself has properties. For example, this red has a hue (the color itself), a saturation level (the color's intensity), and luminance (the color's brightness). Another person may see red as a general object with properties and behaviors. For example, the red object gets soft when heated and hard when cold.

How a *subcontractor* determines to interpret *red* can have distinct effects on the application. An organization places rules on red and the *subcontractor* is the final arbiter and practitioner of the business rules in a software application.

The *subcontractor* requires explicit definitions for each business rule. When ambiguity of a business rule is permitted, the *subcontractor* has no other choice but to fill in the gaps. In practice, *subcontractors* often decide how an enterprise operates.

Two questions must be asked:

- Why are the rules well understood and practiced in the manufacturing industry?
- Why are the rules neither well understood nor well practiced in information technology?

The *subcontractor* in information technology is usually left to guess how to interpret things like the color *red*. *Subcontractors* often lack the skills to know how to ask either the *designer* or *builder* for the true meaning of *red* and, therefore, assume all the rules of use and application.

In IT, the *subcontractor* ends up with all the knowledge of how things work. Management willingly abrogates all responsibility to the *subcontractor*. *The tail now wags the dog.* A large portion of the enterprise's knowledge is isolated in individual *subcontractors*. The system is the enterprise.

Unless the *subcontractor* guesses right, the system will not deliver what the enterprise requires. Conflicts of business rules are a common problem in large enterprises. Conflicts of rules increase when organizational units within an enterprise are viewed as independent operations, not accountable to the whole.

Sometimes newly installed applications cause other applications to break. The result of an action associated with a rule in one application causes a condition to be violated in another application. The puzzling part is when an application has been operating for a period of time with no mishap, and suddenly the sky seems to fall (just like on Chicken Little and Turkey Lurkey). The problem is symptomatic of enterprise-wide integration tests not being performed adequately.

When the conflicts of rules have been eliminated, the rules become consistent across the enterprise. The enterprise achieves a level of stability and all organizational units work well together.

6.3.6 Consistent Rules across the Enterprise *(where)*

In an enterprise that spans many geographic areas, common rules may be fired from any number of events from multiple places. Firing a rule implies that a situation occurs meeting a specific condition the rule is checking for and that an appropriate type of action can then be enacted. If the processes of the geographic areas are integrated for a common supply chain, the rules need to work in concert.

Additionally, many software applications are **architected** to have components run on different computers in a single location. These architectures also form a supply chain, where the rules need to work in concert. No matter how physically far apart the rules are when fired, the rules need to be consistent and integrated.

For example, suppose you are writing an application for property insurance. The company has a number of insured clients who already purchased policies protecting buildings against some form of loss. Coverage is specialized into four types:

- Building coverage
- Personal property coverage
- Debris removal
- Special provision

At the heart of these specialized coverages are the business rules. *Subcontractors* typically find countless rules governing a business application. The rules are often scattered across tiers: presentation tiers, logic tiers, and database tiers. Each tier may have its own set of rules. Examples of business rules for the logic tier include:

- Policies cannot have duplicate coverage.
- In order to add personal property coverage to a policy, the policy must already have building coverage.
- InflationGuard is additional coverage that can be used if building coverage is part of the policy and the policy does not already contain debris removal coverage.
- Policies should not have coverage with overlapping dates.

Policies, coverage, and rules associated with individual coverage are often changing because of external influences such as competition and legislation. The business needs to change rules to ensure market share and profit, and thereby survive. The business can achieve these objectives by changing business processes prudently to accommodate rapidly changing needs and help stave off the competition.

To rapidly change the design of business requirements, *subcontractors* need to locate and modify rules without incurring side effects. Sometimes an organization may need to restore a previous condition of the rule at a later time, i.e., when a promotional offer expires.

The requirement for variation and change involves the requirement for **plugability** and adaptability. But first, the rules must be well organized. If rules are scattered throughout the application, changing them without side effects can be a cumbersome manual endeavor, increasing project time and cost. In some cases, this manual process is actually infeasible and business process adaptability is compromised.

Instead of enforcing the rules by using a set of hard-coded *if statements* that are difficult to identify, change, and deploy, *subcontractors* may begin by locating rules in a rule method. Each method handles one rule. As organizations continue to make changes, the rule method is refactored into a rule object with methods for conditions and actions.

As these conditions and actions increase in number, new conditions have to be added, updated, and deleted. Each condition is separated into its own class that belongs to the rule object. All IT projects have business rules. If the *subcontractor* wants to avoid doing the same thing repeatedly on multiple projects, the *subcontractor* can set up components, which allow rules to be shared throughout the enterprise.

Business rules seldom change completely. Usually new conditions are added to old conditions. New or modified actions need to be replaced or combined in new ways. Therefore, the technique to **componentize** rules for plugability emerges, leading to an enterprise having adaptable components.

Components provide the ability to rapidly change, extend, recombine, reuse rules, reuse rule constituents, and reuse components. For example, being able to plug in some conditions to check for a new type of property insurance would be convenient (i.e., personal property). If the new conditions apply, the application would perform some action. The action can be as simple as displaying a warning message to a user. The message might inform the user that overlapping coverage has been entered and cannot be inserted into the same policy.

Reusable rules in components help create consistency across any enterprise, including the insurance industry. In many instances, the enterprise is obligated to perform at a certain level. Predictability in the business rules helps the enterprise establish confidence that it can afford to be measured and held accountable.

6.3.7 Service Level Agreements *(who)*

Many organizations use internal and external **service level agreements** for operational computer applications. A service level agreement typically exists between two parties—a provider and a subscriber. Depending on the nature of the agreement, each party may play both provider and subscriber roles. Agreements specify that hardware, software, and personnel are available during specified periods, or perform at a certain level.

Availability measures how much an application can be used for its intended purposes during specified times required by the business. Performance measures **latency** for an application or person to start and finish a task. The service level agreement specifies penalties awarded to the subscriber when the provider fails to meet promised availability and performance levels.

Subcontractors fabricate and assemble the applications for the enterprise. The availability and performance of the application are directly attributable to the level of quality provided by the *subcontractor*. For example, if the application goes down, the problem was caused by the *subcontractors* who created the application. The type of *subcontractors* who create the application include:

- Programmers
- Testers
- Configuration specialists
- Implementers
- System administrators
- Database administrators
- Network administrators

A *subcontractor* is needed to fix any problem associated with the application in a timely fashion. Essentially, the service level agreement becomes the business rules that are applied directly to the *subcontractor*.

6.3.8 Key Terms

architected

componentize

latency

plugability

service level agreement

thinning process

6.3.9 Review Questions

1. Who is indirectly responsible for the availability of the service level agreement and what it specifies and why?
2. How does minimizing the size of a component assist in increasing agility for the enterprise?
3. Explain the difference between form and results.

4. What is a rule book?
5. What is the benefit of stating business rules explicitly before the *subcontractor* needs to write a program?
6. What do reusable business rules provide?

SECTION 6.4 WHAT ASSET—DATABASES IN BUSINESS

QUESTIONS TO CONTEMPLATE

1. How are databases an asset to the enterprise?
2. How are data integrity, data quality, and data identification associated with the *subcontractor's* development techniques?
3. How is the amount of online data related to corporate memory?

6.4.1 Introduction

Persistent data is a major asset of any enterprise. Whether recorded on paper or encoded on magnetic platters, enterprises cannot survive without data. For many businesses, stored data defines the organization. The knowledge base for many businesses is limited to the stored electronic data that is immediately accessible. However, some organizations are oblivious to the fact that corporate knowledge is limited to the amount of data kept online (immediately accessible).

The process of archiving data involves moving data physically from one location to another. Typically, archiving moves data from a hard drive to a cartridge tape. Archiving data from immediate accessibility is a common activity in most organizations. Depending on the organization and regulatory restrictions, data is usually kept online from six months to seven years. Mortgage and life insurance applications obviously need to keep data online for longer periods.

Reasons for archiving include reduction of required hard drive space and improvement of database performance. If an enterprise elects to keep only two years worth of data online, the enterprise's view of the world is limited directly to the information and knowledge it can derive from those two years. Archiving immediately nullifies the value of the data asset that was archived. Data is valuable only when accessible.

As an **organic entity**, the enterprise changes constantly. Executives, managers, and employees come and go, and so do customers. Enterprises must be redefined constantly and articulate how to change shape and form in an evolving economy. An enterprise can do nothing without data. Employees cannot be paid, products cannot be built, and decisions cannot be made. Data is elementary to everything, and yet its asset value is often ignored.

Corporate memory is only as good as its access to data. Before data can be accessed, the data must be stored. *Subcontractors* are often members of teams that focus on either getting data in or getting data out. Understanding the polarizing tendency between getting data in and getting data out can help the *subcontractor* understand the subtleties of handling the corporate memory. The easiest techniques and structures for storing data may not have easy techniques for reading or updating the data and vice versa.

Data is one of the enterprise's raw materials. Whether data is structured or unstructured, the data has value. However, the true value of data is enhanced when data can be manipulated. Successful manipulation requires a degree of quality.

A lack of data quality costs the enterprise money. Inventory outages occur, misdirected mail is returned, effort is wasted, rework is incurred, and sales are lost. These are all examples of what can happen when data quality is weak. Quality implies differences, differences imply distinctions of value, and distinctions of value imply market value. Market value has a monetary value to the enterprise.

Data quality requires a process of learning from mistakes and committing to business results. The quality of data is often related to the *subcontractor*. Through the structure of the database design and the programs that populate and read the database, the *subcontractor's* work directly heightens or weakens data quality. The *subcontractor's* main tool for managing the data asset is the database.

6.4.2 There's Gold in Them There Hills *(what)*

Data stored for access by computers is often stored in a filing system known as a **database**. Databases are founded on many different models and offer a set of specific features, each of which is designed for a specific problem, need, or industry. Common types of databases include:

- *Relational*—the most widespread database model. Relational databases are founded on set theory and predicate logic.
- *Object-oriented*—based on the object-oriented philosophy. Object-oriented databases allow users to create objects and specify how objects are related.
- *Object relational*—a relational database infused with object-oriented features. An object relational database allows data to be manipulated in the form of objects, as well as provisioning a traditional relational interface.
- *Distributed*—a model for databases that are spread across several systems. The topology of the systems may be networked across cities, states, countries, and continents, under the oceans, on the oceans, in the air, and in outer space.

- *Multimedia*—a model for storing different types of files including, text, audio, video, and images in a single database. Multimedia data such as word processing documents, video, and audio are regarded as unstructured data.
- *Network*—a rarely used type of database that uses linked records to organize data.
- *Hierarchical*—used mostly on IBM mainframes and predates most database models. Though still in use, many businesses are phasing them out.

Database manufacturers attempt to produce databases that adhere to formal ANSI and ISO standards in addition to their own proprietary standards. Overall, standards simplify the *subcontractor's* process of exchanging data between databases and applications, and between different manufacturers' databases.

MANUFACTURER INDEPENDENCE

Portions of some ANSI and ISO standards create disparity among database products. For example, all commercial databases supporting SQL comply with ANSI and ISO standards to varying degrees. The ANSI and ISO standards allow manufacturers to comply at different levels.

In addition, a number of items in these standards allow manufacturers to make individual decisions and still comply with the standards. Defining fields with a TIMESTAMP data type is an example of both compliance and disparity. TIMESTAMPs are designed to store dates and times.

The ANSI and ISO standards allow database manufacturers to pick the precision of subseconds stored. Consequently, IBM's DB2 stores subseconds to a precision of six decimal places, Microsoft's SQL Server stores subseconds to a precision of three decimal places, IBM's Informix stores subseconds to a precision of eight decimal places, and Oracle does not store subseconds.

In addition, Oracle can support B.C.E. years, whereas other manufacturers cannot. Each manufacturer complies with the ANSI and ISO standards, yet the TIMESTAMP feature is not readily interchangeable. A *subcontractor* must understand these subtle differences fully because migrating from one database manufacturer to another significantly affects business operations, often requiring considerable amounts of rework.

Standards help reduce development costs for the database manufacturers and training costs for organizations using the databases. Transferable *subcontractor* skills benefit all enterprises. Three key standards for accessing databases include SQL, ODBC, and JDBC.

STRUCTURED QUERY LANGUAGE (SQL)

SQL was invented by IBM's Donald Chamberlain and Raymond Boyce in the early 1970s. SQL is a language designed to read and write data based on the constraints of the relational model. The language has formally been expanded to support object relational databases also.

OPEN DATABASE CONNECTIVITY (ODBC)

ODBC is an application programming interface used to connect application programs and databases. Designed by Microsoft, ODBC is a way for programs to connect to a database without having to use database specific commands and features.

ODBC commands are used in computer programs, which are then translated into appropriate commands necessary for a specific database system, typically SQL. ODBC allows programs to be ported between manufacturers' databases with minimal code changes.

JAVA DATABASE CONNECTIVITY (JDBC)

JDBC is an application programming interface from Sun Microsystems. JDBC is used to connect a Java program to a database, either directly or by connecting through ODBC. The connection technique depends on whether the database manufacturer has created the necessary **drivers** for Java.

In most cases, enterprises have only one chance to get a database structure right. After applications are built and implemented, augmenting the database structure often becomes the greatest impediment to change because of its cascading effects.

For example, when an application program requires a change, only that one program is changed. When the database structure is changed, every program referencing the database structure may require a change. The number of application programs requiring modification can range from one to hundreds.

6.4.3 Take the Fifth *(how)*

When a production database requires a change, developers usually choose a solution that has the least effect on existing programs, as well as the *subcontractor's* time and effort. Over time, adaptations are built on adaptations. Soon the database structure and supporting application programs become a maintenance nightmare. Often the result reduces data quality, decreases flexibility, and diminishes the overall value of the data asset. Figure 6-11 shows the potential ripple effect of change. Changes occurring in or near the bullseye can be the most costly and have the greatest effect throughout the application.

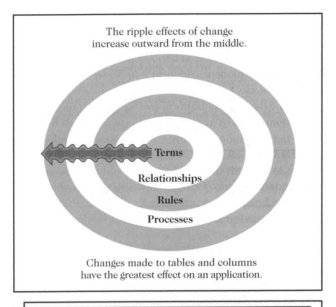

The ripple effects of change increase outward from the middle.

Terms

Relationships

Rules

Processes

Changes made to tables and columns have the greatest effect on an application.

Figure 6-11   *Ripple effects*

Creating a **normalized** relational database structure is the first step in building a long-term database. Normalization is a common-sense process that can lead to flexible and efficient database structures that are easy to maintain. However, achieving an acceptable level of database performance often requires using optimization techniques that warrant breaking the rules of normalization.

Relational theory and normalization techniques began in the early 1970s, when Dr. Edgar Codd's (b. 1923) papers, *A Relational Model for Large Shared Databanks* and *Further Normalization of the Data Base Relational Model*, were published. The papers introduced the relational model and the topic of data normalization, so-named because, at the time, President Richard Nixon (1913–1994) was *normalizing relations* with China.

A Microsoft Excel workbook is made up of one or more worksheets. Each worksheet has a series of column headings. In a relational database, a table is similar to a worksheet, and a column is similar to a column heading. In relational theory, a table is known as a relation and a column is known as an attribute. The formal process of normalizing determines which columns belong in which tables in a relational structure. The purpose of normalization ensures that common sense and intuition are applied consistently to the entire database design. A normalized relational database provides several benefits:

- Eliminates redundant data
- Structures data so the database is easier to extend
- Provides data integrity

Normalization helps realize benefits from a relational database. The language of normalization can be intimidating. In *An Introduction to Database Systems*, Christopher Date writes, "a relation is in third normal form (3NF) if and only if it is in 2NF and every nonkey attribute is nontransitively dependent on the primary key." The language leaves many people confused and scratching their heads.

Initially, papers written on relational database theory and principles of normalization were articulated by people familiar with set theory and predicate logic and written for other experts. The result is that many *subcontractors* think normalization is difficult to learn.

However, the principles of normalization are generally simple. Michael Hernandez, in *Database Design for Mere Mortals*, describes the same aspect of normalization that Date described—"A table should have a field that uniquely identifies each of its records, and each field in the table should describe the subject that the table represents."

Hernandez simplified the definition by removing many intimidating words. During your childhood, you probably heard your mother say, "a place for everything, and everything in its place," which summarizes the intent of normalization succinctly.

Designing a database structure and implementing a database structure are different tasks. When a designer forms a structure for data, the design should be described without reference to the specific database planned for the implementation, such as DB2, SQL Server, or Oracle. In addition, the designer should not need to make concessions to the design based on performance needs. However, the *builder* and the *subcontractor* are responsible for creating designs for a specific database such as DB2, SQL Server, or Oracle, and doing all they can to optimize performance.

Implementing a database not initially designed by a *designer* can lead easily and quickly to flawed structures that are difficult and costly to modify.

Data normalization is a technique used during **data modeling** to ensure there is only one way to know a fact or piece of information. The goal of normalization is to control and eliminate redundancy and mitigate the effects of modification anomalies associated with inserts, updates, and deletes.

NORMAL FORMS

There are six generally recognized normal forms of a relation:

- First normal form (1NF)
- Second normal form (2NF)
- Third normal form (3NF)
- Boyce/Codd normal form (BCNF)
- Fourth normal form (4NF)
- Fifth normal form or project join normal form (5NF or PJNF)

The normal forms are hierarchical and loss-less because each normal form builds upon its predecessor and is reversible. 5NF is often regarded as the purest normal form. See Figure 6-12.

(continued)

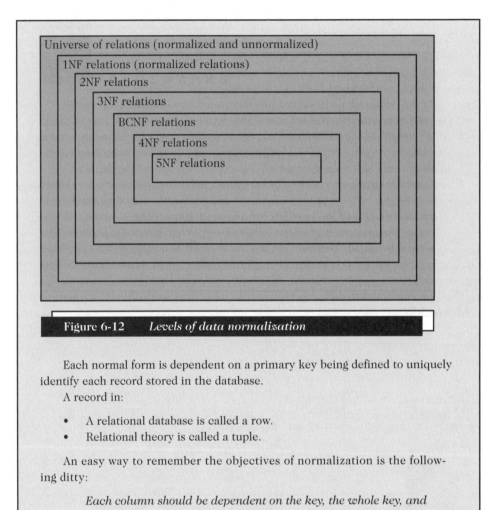

Figure 6-12   *Levels of data normalization*

Each normal form is dependent on a primary key being defined to uniquely identify each record stored in the database.

A record in:

- A relational database is called a row.
- Relational theory is called a tuple.

An easy way to remember the objectives of normalization is the following ditty:

Each column should be dependent on the key, the whole key, and nothing but the key...so help me Codd.

Using statistics from the United States 1990 census, you can extrapolate that over 50,000 people are named John Smith. The federal government needs to keep track of each distinct person named John Smith for reasons of collecting taxes and paying benefits, but mostly collecting taxes. How does the federal government keep track of each John Smith?

In the U.S., individuals are given a social security number to provide unique identification by the government. All 50,000+ John Smiths have unique social security numbers. In a database table that contains U.S. taxpayers, the social security number can be the primary key—a value that uniquely identifies a row in a table.

If the social security number becomes the primary key in a database, all activity against the database can locate the correct John Smith, assuming the appropriate social security number was provided.

In some cases, an artificial or surrogate key must be created for the database design to uniquely identify something that does not have a unique identifier. For example, a Snickers bar has a universal product code (UPC). However, the UPC identifies a kind of chocolate bar; the UPC does not identify each individual bar of Snickers chocolate. See Figure 6-13.

Figure 6-13   *Three bars of candy*

A register receipt for three Snickers bars does not identify which specific bar of chocolate belongs to which line item. See Figure 6-14. Each bar would have the same written description (SNICKERS), the same identifier (401020), the same price (49 cents), and the same tax/non-tax indicator (F).

Each organization determines whether it must uniquely identify a product, service, or thing. Some organizations do not need to identify specific individual items. In the Meijer receipt, Meijer does not need to uniquely identify products sold. Some organizations do need to identify specific individual items, but may not always be able to do so. Then an organization invents a surrogate identifier, such as a social security number or a line item number on a receipt, to keep track of things.

If one of the Snickers bars was later returned for a cash refund, knowing which physical bar was represented by which line item would never be known. For the purpose of this business transaction, knowing the specific line item is unimportant. For other types of business transactions, such as returning computer software, knowing the line item on a receipt is important.

Every copy of Microsoft Windows has a unique serial number. Therefore, each CD containing the software can be identified as to where and when it was manufactured. Potentially, the serial number can also identify who created the CD.

5531 28TH ST. S.E.
GRAND RAPIDS, MI.
Web: http://www.meijer.com
(616) 949-7200
Store# 50

Cashier: BARB R.

02/11/03		10:00:38	
GROCERY			
SNICKERS	401020	.49 F	
SNICKERS	401020	.49 F	
SNICKERS	401020	.49 F	
Grocery Sub (before tax)		1.47	
Order Sub-Total (before tax)		1.47	
TOTAL TAX		.00	
TOTAL		1.47	
CASH	TENDER	20.00	
Payment Total		20.00	
CASH	CHANGE	18.53	

Figure 6-14   *A receipt for the candy*

Database normalization is a good design practice. Data integrity, data quality, and data identification are directly related to good development techniques used by the *subcontractor*. However, business data and the design practice do not always fit together naturally. In some cases, the relational ditty should be: It would have been nice if the business data had a key, a whole key, or even a little key...forgive me Codd.

6.4.4 Distributed Data *(where)*

All technology has limits and computer systems are no exception. Limitations in computers can be caused by the amount of memory the system can address, the number of hard drives that can be connected, and the number of processors that can be used in parallel. As an enterprise stores more data, the likelihood increases that a single system will no longer be able to adequately cope with getting data in and out.

The *subcontractor* must develop the rules, standards, units of measure, metrics, and statistics for monitoring the system to prevent it from failing. The *subcontractor* plays an integral role in keeping the enterprise's systems healthy.

Bigger, better, and faster computer systems can be built as technology improves. However, upgrading systems every few months is generally not cost efficient or cost effective. Deploying several **database servers** to appear to the user community as a single database server is often more pragmatic and affordable.

Using multiple smaller database servers can allow commodity computers to be purchased and used instead of more expensive specialized computers. Commodity hardware is generally cheaper to buy. Using more than one database server has the advantage that newer machines can be added without needing to immediately discard older machines.

Databases that work across multiple database servers are called distributed databases. Software allows multiple database servers to split up database requests and tasks. Distributed databases are stored on two or more computers, called nodes. These nodes are connected using a network. There are two classifications for distributed databases, homogeneous and heterogeneous.

Homogeneous databases all use the same database software and have the same applications on each node. They have a common schema or file structure and can have varying degrees of local autonomy.

Local autonomy specifies how the system appears to work from a user and *subcontractor* perspective. For example, a system with little or no local autonomy has all requests sent to a central node. From the central node, requests are assigned to a node that holds the data or application required. This is the typical model seen on the Internet. Popular sites are mirrored so that several nodes can hold exactly the same data and applications in order to accelerate throughput and access times.

The disadvantage of this model is that the central node has to support high volumes of network traffic. Additionally, computers require lots of processing power to keep up with requests for routing data back from nodes to users.

Heterogeneous databases, in contrast, have a high degree of local autonomy. Each node in the system has its own local users, applications, and data. The heterogeneous database handles all the processing itself and connects to other nodes only for data it does not have.

Heterogeneous types of distributed databases are often called **federated systems**. Federated systems are becoming more popular because of their scalability, reduced cost when adding extra nodes, and ability to mix software packages. Unlike the homogenous systems, heterogeneous systems can include different database software. Heterogeneous systems are appealing to organizations because they can incorporate legacy systems and legacy data into new systems.[12]

Using many distributed databases can help keep the organization operational in the event of a failure, since they can be designed with no single point of failure. As organizations grow, so does the requirement to house more data, and the job of the *subcontractor* becomes increasingly difficult. Sometimes *subcontractors* need to learn and adopt new approaches to handle the complexity.

6.4.5 Data Greenhouses *(who)*

In 1609, Galileo produced a telescope capable of magnifying objects 20 times. Galileo's many other innovative devices, including the hydrostatic balance and pendulum clock, did not have the same negative personal and professional effects caused by his telescope.

Unfortunately for Galileo's career, his book, *Dialogue Concerning the Two Chief World Systems*, documented the fact that the earth was not at the center of the universe. Galileo's point of view was not well received by the establishment. Galileo was ultimately forced to spend his remaining days under house arrest. In time, Galileo's proof became accepted by society.

Unlike Galileo, today's futurists often see their predictions realized in our culture's rapidly moving business and technology environments. Information technologists often deploy one database for each transaction processing application in the enterprise. The technologists then deploy many different databases for *decisioning* applications, such as data warehouses, operational data stores, business intelligence, and customer relationship management.

For example, Carnival Cruise Lines provides vacations on ships. In 2002, the following scenario was possible. Damon, a potential customer going to Carnival's Web site found a vacation deal for $1,000. Damon decided to compare prices by calling a travel agency. The travel agency offered Damon the same trip for $900. Damon believed this was a great deal and booked the vacation.

When Damon navigated the Web site, he entered his name, address, and telephone number. Because Damon did not purchase a vacation online, Damon's information was later routed to a call center operator, who called Damon and offered him the same vacation for $750.

The call center had no idea Damon had already booked the vacation through a travel agency. Carnival's enterprise was distributed and unconnected. Damon was left confused and annoyed. In the future, Damon would have no idea how to get the appropriate price for his vacation and, in all likelihood, would probably stay away from Carnival Cruise Lines. Carnival recognizes this is a business problem and is reorganizing its database to be more integrated...*just in case Damon calls again*!

Data greenhouses blend everything an enterprise needs to operate and analyze its business into a single distributed database. Through appropriate design and use of technology, organizations can achieve a single view of the enterprise.

A data greenhouse approach is viewed as heresy to the establishment and runs contrary to prevailing opinions. Fortunately, today's inquisitions do not result in house arrest. Creating a single database allows a business to eliminate many data processes, including extracts, transforms, and loads. In addition, data greenhouses may help reduce the number of required database licenses and support personnel. See Figure 6-15.

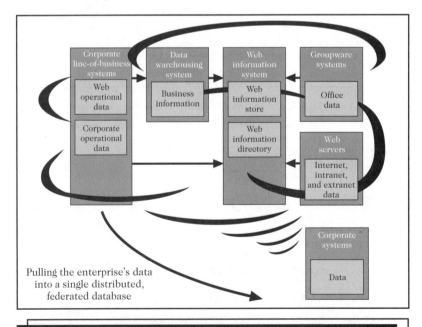

Figure 6-15   *The data greenhouse*

Distributed technology provides ways to integrate disparate data sources and applications. Federated system enablers create and sustain flows of data between the many heterogeneous applications found in business organizations.

The near real-time data demands of enterprises cause *subcontractors* to rethink old solutions and provide new options. Often new options are complex and require the artistry of a skilled developer to make them practical, so they can become a reality.

6.4.6 Data Centric *(when)*

The database structure should be designed independent of applications the database ultimately supports. However, the subcontractor must determine which processes to use to get data in and out of the database. Placing the focus on processes in a data centric environment helps keep the value in the data asset.

Subcontractors should focus on process first and data second. If the data is determined to be bad, then no matter how good a database design is, the value of the data diminishes and ultimately becomes useless. Data loses value because the results obtained from bad data become meaningless.

A data centric approach implies the database structure is highly independent of past, current, and future processes. However, data centricity cannot take into account the changing nature of data and database structures over time, or the impact that data has on the supporting business applications and users.

The types, quantity, and sources of data can all change over time. Enterprises that do not focus on defining processes that allow for the addition of new data sources and the removal of old data sources, or account for the changing meaning of data, witness a decay of the quality and value of the database. Degradation occurs because users cannot access the right type of data.

Subcontractors should focus first on designing processes to allow different data sources to be added and removed, and only then focus on ensuring the data quality. Dealing with growing volumes of data is one of the biggest problems facing the *subcontractor*. Seeking products that use algorithms to highly compress stored data is one method, but maintaining database integrity, quality, backup speeds, recovery speeds, security, flexibility, and throughput remain critical issues with which the *subcontractor* must deal.

The *subcontractor* is required to maintain as much data online as possible, without affecting any operational aspect of the enterprise. When the techniques applied by a *subcontractor* maximize the amount of data stored online, the knowledge base of the enterprise expands.

6.4.7 Feed Me, Feed Me *(why)*

Retaining data is both valuable and risky. Enterprises consider legal, industry, and internal factors when establishing data retention policies and practices. Policies for data retention are usually motivated by the following factors:

- Data management that supports the business
- Business continuity
- Concerns about judicial discovery and legal liability

Data availability and retention have taken on greater significance in the wake of the Microsoft antitrust case, the Enron debacle, and the September 11, 2001 attacks on the World Trade Center and Pentagon. Enterprises need to find the right balance to retain data for later use. Stored data represents the history and knowledge of the enterprise. An enterprise can only recall the past if it actually has the data.

To find the right balance, enterprises must start by understanding what data they have. Lea Anne Armstrong, director of distributed servers at Boeing, commented in *Computerworld* that Boeing is only able to estimate its amount of data. Armstrong believes Boeing has somewhere between 50 and 150 terabytes of data.

The difference between 50 and 150 terabytes is significant enough to warrant different strategies and tactics for managing data. When an enterprise cannot quantify or identify data it owns, the enterprise is, in reality, suffering from amnesia. The data exists physically in the corporate memory. However, the enterprise has forgotten what the data is and where it is stored. Placing a value on forgotten or unknown data assets becomes, for all practical purposes, an impossible endeavor.

In 27 states and several countries, Boeing has many mainframes running MVS and thousands of application and database servers running Unix and Windows. Much of its business data resides on relational database technology from IBM, Oracle, and Microsoft. Boeing's diverse terabytes of data place concerns on data integrity, backup, security, and availability.

The *subcontractor* is responsible for designing the final database structures and programs. The *subcontractor's* work must include assurances for data integrity, writing backup procedures and scripts, configuring and creating security mechanisms, and making sure everything integrates appropriately to support high availability. Many companies would like to achieve uninterrupted uptime 24 hours a day, 7 days per week, 365 days per year.

In reality, most companies cannot afford the infrastructure to be operational $24 \times 7 \times 365$. Although technology plays a large part in uptime, much of the availability relies on the knowledge, artistry, endurance, and skill of the *subcontractor*.

Data Management

Data retention should include all media types: database, paper, fax, e-mail, instant messages, and other media types not yet born. Enterprises seek to retain data for several reasons:

- Current and past projects need to be documented as part of the business record.
- Data represents a significant business investment and when properly stored and leveraged, it can enhance the business.
- The enterprise is compelled by law or statute to keep certain records for a certain period of time.

Decisions about what data should be kept and for how long should be consistent with corporate culture and regulations. Considerations include:

- Keeping data for the required number of years in case a regulatory body asks to see the data
- Keeping data relevant to interactions with a given customer to create a richer relationship with that customer
- Creating an enterprise knowledge base that can be **mined** and leveraged in the future

Long-term storage has many implications, including the ability to reread archived storage media. In the past, some people backed up key files on their personal computers with 5¼ inch floppy disks only to find that their next computer did not have a 5¼ inch drive. Some people have backed up data to tape or compact disc and find the media cannot be read at a later time. These same problems occur on mainframes and midrange computers.

Other problems enterprises encounter include updating a backup with changes made to the online database structure. Because the backed up structure no longer matches the online structure, the archived data may not be restorable. Another scenario involves an enterprise deciding to upgrade its database software. Previous database backups and archives taken on the older version may not be supported on the newer version.

Media failure, changes to database structures, and changes to database versions are reasons why archiving is a dangerous undertaking. The more data an enterprise can keep online, the better the *subcontractor* can handle a database recovery. The *subcontractor* is responsible for articulating data vulnerabilities to the *planners*, *owners*, *designers*, and *builders*.

Business Continuity

In the case of a hard drive failure, a fire, or other disaster, the question of business continuity must be addressed. The enterprise must consider what data is needed and where the data should be positioned so business can resume quickly. Vital data includes:

- Data necessary to resume operations in the event of a business interruption
- Data required to reinstate the legal or financial status of the enterprise
- Data that preserves the rights of the enterprise, its employees, stockholders, and customers

Preservation of vital or reusable data can represent a daunting task. Additional business sites may be required, hard drives may need to be mirrored or shadowed, or data may need to be archived to an off-site facility.

In the United States, the insurance industry is moving away from paper-based documentation and physical storage in filing cabinets toward a paperless workplace. The paperless workplace uses images and document technologies for housing data.

Renee Zaugg, an operations manager for Aetna Incorporated, an insurance company headquartered in Hartford, Connecticut, reported in *Computerworld* that the company stores over 175 terabytes of data on 14 mainframes and over 1,000 Unix servers. Aetna uses database technology from IBM, Oracle, and Sybase. Over 10 percent of Aetna's data is available to customers across the Internet.

Judicial Discovery and Legal Liability

After the controversial Iran-Contra hearings in 1987, involving Oliver North (b. 1943) and other members of President Ronald Reagan's (b. 1911) staff,[13] many corporate executives were asked not to take notes during meetings. Instead, executives were asked to manage by mentally retaining information. The directives were an assurance against having documents subpoenaed.

As the Internet arrived in corporate America during the 1990s and global e-mail became popular, the directives fell by the wayside. Incidents in 2001 involving

Enron and Microsoft have caused some legal departments to urge businesses to delete all e-mail messages within weeks of being created and read. In cases where documents have been shredded to cover up wrongdoing, some enterprises and local governments have decreed nothing may ever be deleted.

Many corporations believe keeping everything allows the opportunity to re-create the original context of the transaction or electronic conversation. A single message can easily be taken out of context and misunderstood.

At What Cost

Often IT managers fail to communicate ways to account for the on-hand data asset. In 2002, Meta Group Incorporated created some generalized statistics on how much it costs companies in specific industry sectors, which were unable to access data assets. Essentially, the data asset has two sides. One side is what the data is worth in an operational mode. The other side is what the data is worth when the enterprise cannot operate. See Table 6-3.

Industry sector	Loss of revenue per hour	Revenue employee per hour
Energy	$2,817,846	$ 569
Telecommunications	$2,066,245	$ 187
Manufacturing	$1,610,654	$ 134
Financial institutions	$1,495,134	$1,080
Information technology	$1,344,461	$ 184
Insurance	$1,202,444	$ 371
Retail	$1,107,274	$ 244
Pharmaceuticals	$1,082,252	$ 168
Banking	$ 996,802	$ 131
Food and beverage processing	$ 804,192	$ 153

Table 6-3   *Revenue loss*

6.4.8 Key Terms

data modeling

database

database server

driver

federated system

heterogeneous database

homogeneous database

mined

normalized

organic entity

persistent data

6.4.9 Review Questions

1. What possible advantage would a company that stores 10 years of data have over a company that stores only two years of data?

2. Explain why data quality can often be tied back to the *subcontractor*.

3. How can standards help *subcontractors* exchange data?

4. What is the purpose of normalization?

5. What is considered to be vital data?

6. What is the cost justification for a federated system?

SECTION 6.5 WHERE IS THE COMPUTER?

QUESTIONS TO CONTEMPLATE

1. Why must the *subcontractor* be a good communicator?
2. Why are change and technology inextricably tied together?

6.5.1 Introduction

Information travels faster and faster today, unifying the world and creating new and improved ways of conducting commerce. In today's global marketplace, organizations must maximize productivity by relying on efficient flows of data to remain competitive. The enterprise's computer network must facilitate the increasing productivity of its people. The *subcontractor* is responsible for putting together and keeping operational the data center, hardware, hubs, routers, switches, and network.

The *owners*, *designers*, and *builders* need to make the following decisions about the data center: amount of floor space needed, location, and type of servers to be used. *Subcontractors* are often responsible for designing how the equipment is going to be laid out in the data center.

The *subcontractor* probably starts by painting a mental picture of where equipment should go, and then sketches a rough plan on paper or a whiteboard, similar to how an artist creates a painting. The *subcontractor's* decisions must allow systems to stay up and running under most circumstances, including build outs of delicate fiber runs and multiple redundant power gridlines.

Subcontractors are responsible for putting together fire suppression equipment, cooling systems, storage units, and command centers resembling the Millennium Falcon in the *Star Wars* movie. Another detail with which the *subcontractor* contends is rack placement for housing all types and sizes of servers and routers.

As an artist, the *subcontractor* plays with colors. See Figure 6-16. First, the cabling—color-coding schemes help identify cables and organize the routing process. Because computer resource needs grow, the artist sees the importance of neatness and color. Neatness assists in troubleshooting when problems arise. Being able to quickly determine where a color-coded cable is supposed to terminate and seeing where the cable actually terminates can save valuable time.

Visually tracing a cable from one end to the other may assure the *subcontractor* that data and power cables are running perpendicular to each other, preventing electromagnetic fields from affecting the data cables. Color also reduces installation errors and simplifies inventory management as well as job site inspection. The orderliness of the artist's canvas helps prevent problems later.

The *subcontractor* uses knowledge of the art and science of information technology to build a network capable of meeting an enterprise's dynamic needs. When assembling a data center, the *subcontractor* considers many issues. An artist (*subcontractor*) with an empty palette and blank canvas is limited by information, knowledge, wisdom, and creativity.

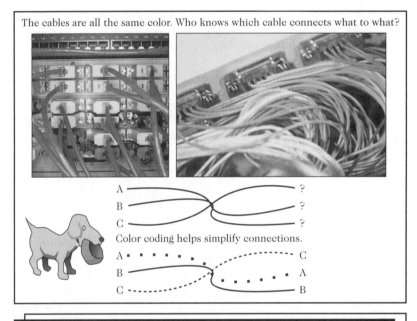

Figure 6-16   *Color cabling—not much help to a dog*

6.5.2 Lights Out *(where)*

Organizations use data centers or specially configured computer rooms to handle **mission-critical** operations. A **data center** generally refers to a location where application and data servers are housed. A data center consists of the facilities and premises that are required to operate an organization's computer systems. Some data centers are more elaborate than others.

Data centers may be staffed continuously with employees working in shifts, while others are not staffed—a situation known as *lights out*. A **lights out** operation in a data center environment refers to automating manual activities. Automation limits the need for human intervention and helps deliver consistent results. In an unstaffed data center, the lights are out because no lights are needed—computers do not need to see. Many lights out data centers can be maintained remotely, enabling data centers to be located in remote areas away from potential threats to business operations.

POWER STRUGGLE

At Meijer Corporation in Walker, Michigan, the data center is always staffed. There has been only one period of time in its history that there was not at least one person in the data center and that was for only 1 hour and 20 minutes during a gas leak on the premises.

Upon entering Meijer's data center, visitors see the command center. The limited-access room has automated systems to monitor server activity, Web traffic, human traffic, and network performance. Monitoring utilities alert engineers to small variations in performance long before a system failure might occur. The company is able to repair, back up systems, or reboot without affecting production.

Internet routers handle traffic from multiple T1 and T3 lines. The routers are equipped with redundant supervisor modes and power supplies that intervene if the network fails. Traffic can be moved to another router so network performance is not affected.

Air conditioning units are integrated into Meijer's data center. With such a high density of electronic equipment, air is circulated and filtered by forcing the air beneath the tiles in the floors and through vents located near each server bank. The air conditioning units maintain a comfortable temperature for servers even though the air may feel a bit cool for people.

Meijer has two external power sources. The external power feeds to the data center are regulated and monitored by an uninterruptible power supply (UPS). The UPS unit protects servers from power surges and dips. When necessary, power is drawn from batteries if a power interruption occurs. If a UPS system detects a power loss, diesel generators begin feeding power within seconds. Meijer tests its generators once a month. The generators produce enough electricity to maintain the climate control systems and keep the computer systems operational for 24 hours.

The data center often includes a server room, archives, storage facilities, print facilities, computers, power supplies, cooling mechanisms, and robot systems storing and retrieving tapes and cartridges. Centralizing mission-critical hardware can save manpower by enhancing availability and standardizing administration. The obvious drawback is that a catastrophe to a data center can have devastating effects on an entire enterprise.

Data centers frequently span two areas—the main computer room and a remote facility that is connected via a wide area network (WAN) to the components in the computer room. The main computer room usually contains database, application, and file servers; communication equipment; and all supporting hardware. Distributed servers, however, can be located almost anywhere in or outside of the main computer room. Regardless of where a computer is located, organizations must be able to recover from major threats including:

- Environmental disasters
- Organizational shortcomings
- Deliberate attacks
- Technical failures

Enterprises must be sure the computers and networks can adequately handle the company's data processing. Headquartered in New York City, TIAA-CREF is a leading financial services organization, a major institutional investor, and the world's largest retirement system, with more than $290 billion in assets under management.

TIAA is the Teachers Insurance and Annuity Association, one of only three U.S. firms to hold triple-A ratings from all four major independent analysts of the insurance industry. CREF is the College Retirement Equities Fund, an open-end, diversified management company. By the end of 2003, TIAA-CREF will spend over $17 million on a new data center in Charlotte, North Carolina. This enterprise is focused on the technology that keeps the data moving through system upgrades, storms, routine maintenance, and accidental shutdowns.

TIAA-CREF's UPS was built into the data center's design because the data center runs mission-critical operations. Many organizations are concerned about the quality of power supplies. According to Sara Bradford, an industry analyst with Frost and Sullivan, the power from utility power grids is "only 99.9 percent reliable." This equates to nearly nine hours of downtime a year. Therefore, organizations like TIAA-CREF are choosing UPS and other power equipment for better reliability. Bradford says, "Alternative power sources can give organizations 99.99999 percent reliability,"[14] equivalent to just over three seconds of downtime a year. TIAA-CREF cannot tolerate power outages because millions of dollars could be lost every hour.

When building a data center's power supply, the *subcontractor* must consider many details. Because power equipment is very large and heavy, the *subcontractor* must consider the load on the flooring. The power unit also has to meet strict electrical and environmental codes. With the density of this electronic equipment and faster processors, effective cooling systems are critical. Installing these power systems sometimes requires heavy-duty cranes and on-site assembly, with the building being constructed around them.

Many computing systems in today's organizations operate around the clock $(24 \times 7 \times 365)$, with little time for maintenance and upgrades. The organization's data center, in reality, encompasses much more than a room full of hardware and software; it must keep the company running. The data center's UPS system must be able to handle higher voltages and more kilowatts as enterprise demands increase. The data center extends to the organization's entire network, including workstations, desktops, and the computer room. The *subcontractor* must build a data center for today and tomorrow that is focused on connectivity to the outside world.

6.5.3 Organic *(why)*

Change and technology are inextricably tied together. As an organization's needs increase or change organically (naturally), the technologies and techniques that service those needs must also be able to grow organically and adapt to these new needs.

Ideas for organic computing are borrowed from biology. Among the key ideas for organic computing are flexibility, robustness, growth, development, self-organization, reproduction, evolution, autonomy, embodiment, and distributed and collective behavior. The *subcontractor* must help set the philosophy, goals, and objectives to allow the data center to evolve naturally over time.

If the data center was being built to accommodate the needs of the organization for only one moment in time, then limiting the focus to initial requirements would be acceptable. However, accommodating one moment in time is not worth the sizable investment required to build a data center. For the facility to be useful over time, the data center should be viewed as a living, breathing, and constantly evolving creation—an organic entity, not a static entity.

The *subcontractor* must communicate the need to expand to accommodate for future growth of the dynamic organization. Organizations are becoming more demanding, competition is fierce, and markets are changing rapidly. New solutions are needed to handle the rapid increases in the amount of data that enterprises need to collect and analyze. The solution must also handle growth in the number of users, both internal and external to an organization, who need access to this information. These new solutions must make transformation easy for IT professionals to provide new functionality as quickly as needs change.

In other words, the data center must be **scalable**. The facility should be able to scale (grow) quickly and adapt to provide additional functionality, enabling high performance and added value to the organization. The *subcontractor* must help set the philosophy to embrace and manage that change, rather than suppress it.

Like anything else that is organic, the organic data center is never *done*—instead the facility is dynamic. The *subcontractor* must think incrementally to build a data center that can adapt easily to changing requirements. By identifying current needs of the organization and considering where the organization is headed, the *subcontractor* is better prepared to build a data center that changes naturally and grows incrementally over time, without applying radical or potentially disruptive changes.

Corporations are taking advantage of better networking equipment and lower costs for high-end components, such as switches and administrative tools that manage a smaller number of servers in central locations like data centers. Server consolidation may indicate a transition from *more is better* to *rightsizing*. Rightsizing is a term Goldilocks may have used—not too big (hot or hard), not too small (cold or soft), just right.

Wyndham International Incorporated, a global hotel chain with headquarters in Dallas, Texas, decided to think small and *rightsize* its data center servers. The company trimmed the number of its client/server networks by putting the guest management application on two powerful Unix servers. The application controlling guest billing, arrival, and departure formerly required 165 servers placed in 100 locations.

Several years ago, IT departments thought the best way to reach high performance and availability was to position single-purpose servers in many different locations. Today, other approaches must be considered. Finding a balance between a widely distributed and a consolidated approach is usually best. The real answer is to be as centralized as the situation allows. Companies usually consider server consolidation as a cost-saving measure. Wyndham expects its hardware bills to be nearly

40 percent lower after the server consolidation. The hotel chain also expects to decrease travel and training costs significantly.

According to a Framingham, Massachusetts market research firm, IDC, the worldwide server market continues to grow, with the highest sales growth in consolidating friendly, rack-mounted servers. By placing fewer servers in a central location, networks become more manageable. Instead of needing several network managers, organizations can operate with fewer administrators at a data center. However, if a centralized server goes down, many people suffer. To avoid interrupting business operations, you must ensure your data center is reliable and available, in addition to scalable.

Reliability refers to the extent a system or component can operate as specified. Redundancy is the most important way to gain reliability in a data center. Redundancy is the practice of providing equipment not necessary under normal operating conditions, but that can be substituted for failed equipment as needed.

Another important factor directly related to reliability is availability in a data center. Availability refers not only to loss of service, but also to the repair time needed to restore service. Because power is the lifeline of a data center, availability refers to the time period in which a power supply can meet equipment needs for the organization. For example, if a power cord is damaged that supplies current to a server rack, the system loses service or availability.

Availability is sometimes expressed as a decimal. Because high-reliability companies like TIAA-CREF handle business transactions and could lose millions of dollars if service was interrupted, these sites need 99.99999 percent, or seven nines (.9999999) availability. This decimal translates into a given number of seconds of service being unavailable during the year.

To provide high availability, the *subcontractor* must understand the effect each piece of equipment has on overall availability and specify components that reduce the possibility of failures as the data center grows organically. In a 24×7 business environment, reliability is essential. Planning for adaptability and scalability allows an organization to carry on business as usual during periods of change and growth. Planning, acting intuitively, and observing historical data can help improve the *subcontractor's* ability to react when unpredictable and predictable Web site demand occurs.

6.5.4 Capacity Planning *(when)*

The Internet has caused a considerable amount of change and growth affecting all businesses and commerce paradigms. Most successful e-business sites are potential candidates for being overwhelmed by large numbers of customers bringing the site operations to a halt.

Whether Internet spikes are caused by breaking news about a terrorist attack, free shipping during a holiday season, or a stock market plunge, organizations are struggling with decisions about how to handle spikes in Internet traffic. Despite planning and testing prior to major online events, some Web sites experience traffic beyond the wildest expectations. Availability, reliability, and security create significant challenges in the e-business world for the *subcontractor*.

In-house enterprise and e-commerce applications also experience spikes. What does the *subcontractor* do when customers visit an organization's Web site 100 million times during the first month, particularly when only 25 million hits were expected? Triggers like a **bursty**[15] Web site can cause the *subcontractor* to go back and do things differently.

The *subcontractor* must match application capacity to user load. The challenge of estimating growth for an application used exclusively in-house and an Internet e-commerce application is how closely the *estimated* number of users matches the *actual* number of users.

Applications that are only used by in-house staff are tracked more easily for growth usage. For example, if a company currently employs 10 people, and a new person is hired, the IT department can anticipate an approximate 10 percent increase in network usage for the applications the new person is likely to use. On the other hand, it is difficult to anticipate the number of new Internet users that will use your company's Web site even if you know how many people recently became Internet active.

Because the number of employees in a company is generally known, the *subcontractor* can estimate what percentage of employees needs to access each application at one time. An e-commerce application is different. Demand depends on the number of customers who want to access the Web site concurrently. Predicting how many people will use the site at the same time is difficult because *only* the number of Internet users in the world limits demand.

In addition to predicting the number of users, the *subcontractor* also needs to consider other triggers that might affect Internet traffic. For example, companies that are running television advertisements during the live broadcast of the National Football League's Super Bowl need to invest in improvements to their networks, hardware, and databases to ensure that their Web sites are not overrun by the expected surge in traffic.

The success of an organization's e-business depends on an environment that supports business objectives. The *subcontractor* must build systems that can grow quickly enough to handle spikes in demand, while offering stability. **Capacity planning** assists the *subcontractor* in meeting business objectives and involves planning which software and hardware the application uses so that the Web site has sufficient capacity to meet anticipated and unanticipated demand.

The *subcontractor* must determine load levels by considering new applications and services, changes in the e-customers' behaviors, and the current workload. Planning for e-commerce applications depends on the type of site being used. Five general categories of Web sites include:

- Online shopping
- Customer self-service
- Publish and subscribe
- Business-to-business
- Trading

WEB SITE CATEGORIES

Online shopping sites are retail sites where the consumer can purchase products. The site may include a catalog that changes frequently or infrequently. If catalog information is static, page layouts need not change. However, if catalog content is dynamic, with cyclical changes, pages need to be updated frequently. Search traffic on online shopping sites is usually high, and when users decide to make a purchase, many additional security issues are raised such as privacy, authentication, and integrity. These transactions also depend on other systems.

Customer self-service sites allow individuals to perform services themselves, such as making travel arrangements, checking bank balances, tracking packages, and accessing telephone bills. Transaction traffic for self-service sites continues to grow. These Web sites usually pull information from a variety of sources, making consistency of data critical. If customers are banking online from home, security is a high concern for the *subcontractor*. However, search traffic for the self-service Web site is lower than a publish and subscribe site.

Publish and subscribe sites contain information that changes frequently. Event sites, search engines, newspapers, and media sites are examples of sites requiring frequent page layout changes. Traffic volumes are especially difficult to plan. Unlike self-service and shopping sites, page content is usually current and not linked to other systems. Because transactions are few, security is not of great concern to the *subcontractor*.

Business-to-business sites are established to conduct commerce in a real-time mode using highly secure connections. Critical data consistency is necessary due to the complexity of transactions linking multiple systems. Business-to-business sites frequently allow collaborative use of information connecting multiple data sources.

Trading sites have time-sensitive, complex transactions. These sites allow users to buy and sell products and services. Content is usually very dynamic, particularly on auction sites. Transactions taking place between users generally interact with a back-end server and are linked closely with other systems. Security is another area of high consideration for the *subcontractor*.

By monitoring activities such as products or services delivered, number of customers, number of transactions per period, navigational activities, third-party services, workload parameters, and performance indicators, the *subcontractor* can more accurately predict Web site usage, and therefore adapt its capacity. The *subcontractor* must stay current and stay ahead of technology choices and changes to establish an infrastructure that allows the organization to stay competitive.

Capacity planning, whether proactive or reactive, helps the *subcontractor* develop a greater aptitude for change when unpredictable growth and unknown problems occur. The subcontractor should understand the Web application environment, including the number of page requests and concurrent connections the application can handle. Any assumptions made by the *subcontractor* (or even the *designer* or *builder*) should be updated after the Web site usage measurements have been captured and reviewed.

Response time is also a very important requirement for Web sites. If users perceive that a site does not respond to their requests quickly, they will shop elsewhere. System stress, which is sometimes caused by a bursty Web site, is difficult to predict as processes compete for the same resources and load increases. The *subcontractor* must take care that increased load does not cause an application to become unstable.

Networks must operate significantly below their rated capacity so throughput is not reduced due to frequency of data transmission collisions. A data collision is the simultaneous presence of signals from two nodes on the network. A collision can occur when several nodes on a computer network think the network is idle and both start transmitting at the same time. The collision creates a need for the data to be retransmitted.

The *subcontractor* should test performance and scalability after installing and configuring the hardware and software for an application. Some resources tracked during performance testing include network, CPU, memory, threads, database connections, and hard drive input and output.

After completing these tests, the subcontractor should analyze the results to make meaningful comparisons between prospective configurations. The *subcontractor* must take responsibility to help the organization meet its objectives. If requirements are not being met, identify bottlenecks, eliminate application defects, reconfigure parameters or options, and repeat the process.

The quality of service an e-business site provides to customers depends on several interrelated factors discussed previously, including the architecture of the site and network capacity. In addition to these factors, system software structure also affects site operations.

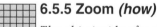 6.5.5 Zoom *(how)*

The chip inside of a computer determines the computer's speed, which is the rate that the chip can process instructions the computer receives. Computers bought today are much faster than computers purchased two years ago. Five years from now, computers will be faster than they are today. Chips are powerful devices that can make the computer do amazing things.

The increasingly complex uses of the computer depend on a fast chip. Gordon Moore (b. 1929), a founder of Intel Corporation, helped pioneer the field of computer chips. In 1965, Moore predicted the number of transistors on a chip would double every 18 months and that the chip would become not only more powerful, but also cheaper. His prediction was the origin of Moore's Law, which has now been extended and applies to anything that grows geometrically in the industry.

Tiny on-off switches called transistors are components used to help increase a chip's speed. In 1977, PC chips had 2,300 transistors. In 2002, PC chips had about 7 million transistors. By 2012, *PC Magazine* estimates a chip on your home PC will have 100 million transistors.

Due to the expanded power of the chip, the computer industry has grown rapidly and created a cycle—a causal loop. Newer, faster chips encourage manufacturers to

393

design and build new computers. New computers encourage developers to create new software that drives the economy. To meet the demand for new software, the *subcontractor* often hurriedly creates a product that comes to market with many flaws.

Organizations tend to replace hardware every few years, even though the hardware still operates according to its original specification. New machines are needed to run new software. New versions of software tend to be bigger and slower. Software developers seem to feel no obligation to write efficient code because processors continue to get faster, disk capacity gets higher, and memory is inexpensive. This is not a good trait for a developer.

GATES' LAW

"The speed of software halves every 18 months." This often-cited law is an ironic comment on the tendency of software bloat to outpace the every-18-month doubling in hardware capacity per dollar predicted by Moore's Law.

Oracle's database for the Windows platform provides an example of software bloat:

- 1986—Oracle version 5 for MS-DOS was distributed on several 5¼-inch floppy disks.
- 1992—Oracle version 7 for Windows was distributed on 15 3½-inch diskettes.
- 1999—Oracle8i for Windows was distributed on a CD.
- 2001—Oracle9i for Windows was distributed on three CDs for the base product alone.

Coupled with a corollary of Parkinson's Law, "Data expands to fill the space available for storage," Moore's Law and Gates' Law provide a stochastic steady state—another causal loop.

Although the number of instructions per second that today's machines can perform is thousands of times faster than the computers of just several years ago, these machines are really no faster in terms of performing work. Due to sluggish software, the enterprise does not benefit from faster chips. Machines take longer to boot up and applications take longer to start. The result is that completing a task takes just as long or longer now than the task took to accomplish on the older machine.

Each new version of Microsoft Word requires extra speed and extra processing power. As a *subcontractor*, you need to avoid developing slower, flawed software. Rather than writing slower and fatter code, you should attempt to make the code lean to take advantage of the faster and more powerful hardware.

You can also take advantage of faster computer chips by understanding the dynamics of a particular chip. Learning the many efficient techniques for moving data through a computer's memory should be essential to the performance-oriented *subcontractor*.

An elementary example of memory management involves moving data by reference instead of by value. Suppose the following string is stored in the computer's memory:

Dr. Richard Feynman was born in Brooklyn, New York in 1918 and died in Palo Alto, California in 1988. During his lifetime, Feynman worked on the atomic bomb; he learned to play the bongo drums; he cracked safes; he deciphered Mayan hieroglyphics; he proved that frozen O-rings caused the Challenger space shuttle to explode; he discovered something called quantum electrodynamics, for which he received the Nobel Prize in 1965; and most importantly, he figured out why ants walk in single-file lines.

If this fact is stored at memory address x'0453D1CD', then a computer program can send the memory address, rather than the entire copy of the fact to either another computer program or a different area of an existing program. See Figure 6-17.

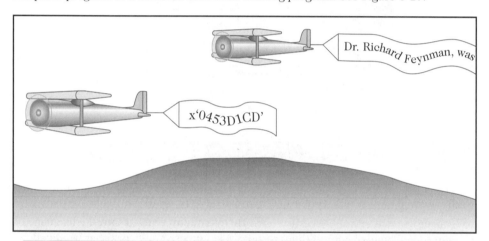

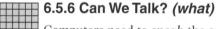

Figure 6-17   *Smaller messages get to their destination quicker*

Moving data efficiently in memory, to and from storage, and across the network are critical performance elements. The network programmer is responsible for understanding the appropriate protocols and techniques for moving large volumes of data from node to node.

6.5.6 Can We Talk? *(what)*

Computers need to *speak* the same language before they can communicate over a network. What allows them to communicate? Data has no meaning until it has been used in a known context. In Chapter 1, you learned the importance of writing systems, which create a common alphabet. With a common alphabet, you can develop words and then sentences that can promote understanding. The *subcontractor* develops the writing system for machines so that computers can *speak* the same language and communicate.

The common alphabet for computers is made up of zeros and ones. These characters become a bit stream—the sentence. The sentence is known as a protocol. Protocols become the method for carrying the alphabet and interpreting the data when it gets to its destination. If one system uses a protocol that is different from that of another system, the two systems cannot communicate, even though they may be physically located on the same network. See Figure 6-18.

Figure 6-18   *Before they talk, they first shake hands*

The most widely used protocol today is Transmission Control Protocol/Internet Protocol (TCP/IP). Originally designed as a protocol to allow U.S. military networks to recover from catastrophic failures, TCP/IP eventually evolved into the language of the Internet. The idea behind the Internet was to create a network that would allow military installations to communicate even if one or more of these sites was destroyed in a war.

Flexible addressing schemes and error correction capabilities ensured that routers could decide on the best path to send the data so that the information was received. Although TCP/IP is the most widely used protocol today, it is also the slowest. Additionally, many protocols used by the Internet were never designed for security.

The responsibility for security now rests with the software developer. The demand for security has changed the development, testing, and marketing of software. The Internet infrastructure facilitates new industries and consolidates national and international businesses with the use of **digital certificates**. Digital certificates and digital signatures are used frequently for authentication. See Figures 6-19, 6-20, and 6-21, which illustrate examples of digital certificates.

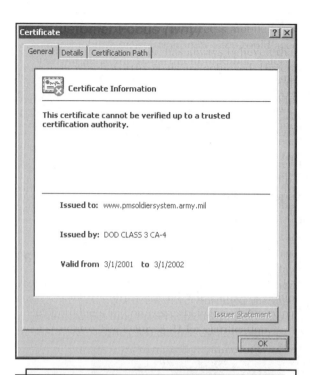

Figure 6-19 *An expired digital certificate*

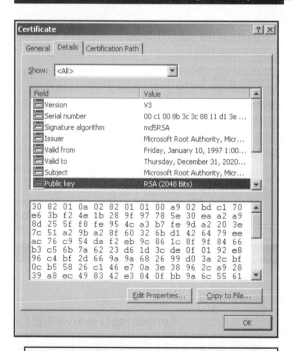

Figure 6-20 *Digital certificate and its public key*

Systems Development

03004902	A7DD7A04	12G01621	G002C5BD	83EFA503	G0030200
01008800	80536C00	036825G0	024FG002	9ED34C00	446A2500
A0D14C00	1F6D2585	01807C00	80536C00	036825G0	024FG002
9ED34C00	446A2500	A0D14C00	1F6D2585	4F553D53	616C6573
2F4F3D45	71756966	6178434E	3D53616D	20466572	6C697369
2F4F553D	53616C65	732F4F3D	45717569	66617842	56040031
2E300042	43010003	42410100	30424C02	0076024E	4E5000F3
EF2993DD	8B957AED	B33ABA7E	D2AB3819	012F0482	581C7F85
7AE69F7F	568F8FB7	883ADBA9	EB09AEDE	04806CAC	A68159CD
BEB25F1A	70805DAA	80942A3F	0A4DA951	8E5CD5F7	CE80B418
14F010D0	E7210045	4E04005D	4CG0014D	40180087	6F196EF3
BC017680	00505552	53414623	1696855D	DF52A4C6	0C76E2C9
1BD84662	157500F7	92F752DE	2CCD8235	217D41C9	FFB30185
D3892560	91B3C568	1F6C27C1	3E4D2283	0527D4E9	2A749EE4
552664D2	F6AD5E4B	BBC17A4F	AEA0F5A6	2E0B4256	0400312E
30004243	01000342	41010030	424C02G0	01024E4E	440011B2
EE43CE36	A88437A0	38945443	3A1DD146	D707A21E	3A966641
13818A51	814F331A	A8DE63D3	3A67474C	4C0D9F84	D68DEA4A
0E201BE6	5A1E09B9	168A6849	2BA1G003	454E0400	F37EG001
4D410800	A7591E19	0A90E3DE	74005055	52534146	117DAE36
E6A17C1A	06EF4CB2	7296516F	F2A04F3A	4B7EFB3	D63D8BBD
65C69EBE	D998F323	D4962DF0	5616F31F	1D0E8C66	1C1421D1
76DC715B	B2FB04EA	7809E53B	7883D557	E90C1738	9D415FE5
634317					

Figure 6-21 *A digital signature represented as a string of hexadecimal characters*

Authentication is the process of identification, usually giving a guarantee that the two parties involved are interacting with whom they think they are interacting. In Section 3.7, you learned how Equifax created a patented software process to determine the identity of a particular consumer.

A digital certificate is an electronic message attachment used to verify the sender of the message. Digital certificates can be used to legally bind someone in an agreement. To apply for a digital certificate, you must submit personal information to a trusted third-party organization, called a **certificate authority**, that guarantees the identity of the sender. After information is verified, the organization's server issues certificates for users and services. The digital certificate can act as your signature for legal documents.

Public key infrastructure (**PKI**) is a system where a person's online identity is validated by a digital certificate. For example, in the healthcare industry, certificates are issued to healthcare professionals and plan members through the organization's certificate authority. The organization determines what access privileges the holder is allowed to have and the length of time the certificate is valid.

The holder presents this proof of identity to reliant applications so private information can be accessed. Digital certificates can also generate **digital signatures**, which are unique codes attached to an electronically submitted message. Digital signatures can be used to verify the authenticity of the sender of the message and to verify data integrity.

A problem with digital certificates is that they only identify a machine, not a person. Because the owner's certificate is stored on a computer, the owner must protect that certificate. When the certificate owner sends an encrypted e-mail message, the person receiving the owner's public key can decrypt and read the message. If another individual sits down at the machine, that person could potentially gain access and conduct unauthorized business.

One way of addressing the weakness of digital certificates is by combining them with biometric technology. The incorporation of a bioprint (e.g., unique photo, voice, or fingerprint) with the digital certificate could confirm the identity of the sender, not just the machine. Biometric data could secure the digital certificate, no matter where it is stored. A combination of the digital certificate and biometric identification could be advantageous to the healthcare industry as organizations move toward greater compliance with HIPAA mandates, discussed in Section 5.7, which require auditing the trail of patient information transmitted electronically.

Additional protocols the *subcontractor* must be familiar with to communicate across the World Wide Web and secure a Web site include:

- Secure Sockets Layer (SSL)
- Transport Layer Security (TLS)
- TLS Record Protocol
- TLS Handshake Protocol
- Secure Electronic Transactions (SET)

These protocols handle encryption, compression, privacy, payment information, and non-repudiation. Non-repudiation is an attribute of a secure system that prevents the sender of a message from claiming a message was not sent.

The *subcontractor* must know about available options for providing security for the organization. Authentication, privacy, availability, and data integrity are all critical components of a successful business. The *subcontractor* must be aware of trade-offs between performance and security to balance business needs.

6.5.7 Networks *(who)*

The *subcontractor* transforms the ideas and designs specified by the builder to construct the network, enabling knowledge workers to do their jobs and customers to transact with the enterprise. The *subcontractor* is responsible for assembling the network and providing a critical product and service for the enterprise.

A network is actually a collection of computers that use a common language to communicate. These works of *art* allow users to communicate and share data, printers, and applications. An understanding of networks is incomplete without understanding the Open Systems Interconnection (OSI) reference model. See Figure 6-22.

The seven-layer OSI model is a set of guidelines for companies to use when developing network products. Without this standard, the entire networking suite would have to be replaced for any new application, protocol, or network card that was introduced. Software manufacturers can develop products that communicate and work at one or more layers of the model and be assured those products will function with products developed by other vendors conforming to the model.

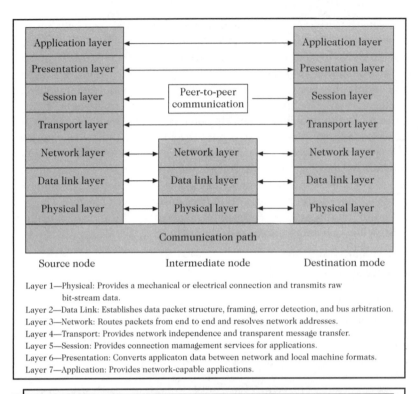

Application layer		Application layer
Presentation layer		Presentation layer
Session layer	Peer-to-peer communication	Session layer
Transport layer		Transport layer
Network layer	Network layer	Network layer
Data link layer	Data link layer	Data link layer
Physical layer	Physical layer	Physical layer

Communication path

Source node   Intermediate node   Destination mode

Layer 1—Physical: Provides a mechanical or electrical connection and transmits raw bit-stream data.
Layer 2—Data Link: Establishes data packet structure, framing, error detection, and bus arbitration.
Layer 3—Network: Routes packets from end to end and resolves network addresses.
Layer 4—Transport: Provides network independence and transparent message transfer.
Layer 5—Session: Provides connection mamagement services for applications.
Layer 6—Presentation: Converts applicaton data between network and local machine formats.
Layer 7—Application: Provides network-capable applications.

Figure 6-22   *Seven-layer OSI model*

The OSI model helps remove some of the complexity for building a network, but as with Michelangelo's work, few people take time to consider the magnitude of the tasks involved in sculpting a network. Thinking holistically, the *subcontractor* considers everything from individual user needs to mission-critical applications. The *subcontractor* must understand the complex interconnectivities and the fragile balance the network creates among users and across systems.

As previously stated, the *subcontractor* has to stay current and be constantly aware of available technology to ensure the organization's competitiveness, while focusing on the organization's willingness to accept technical risk. People generally go about their daily tasks, unaware of the intricacies of the functioning network, until something goes wrong.

Recall that the *subcontractor* is responsible for implementing solutions that align the security needs of the business with the technical capabilities of the organization. The goal is to establish secure connections to any user, anywhere, at any time. One tool used to protect the network from outside attacks is a firewall.

A **firewall** can be hardware, software, or both, and it controls the type of information allowed to pass from a public network to the private network. A firewall can provide a managed entry point to many systems behind it. There are six types of firewalls:

- Embedded
- Enterprise software-based

- Enterprise hardware-based
- Small office/home office (SOHO) software
- SOHO hardware
- Specialty firewalls

The designer and builder must decide which type of firewall suits the needs of the business. The *subcontractor* implements and configures the firewall.

Embedded firewalls are embedded into either a router or a switch and are sometimes referred to as choke-point firewalls. These routers can be configured to block the flow of packets from one network to another. Because embedded firewalls work at the IP level, they cannot protect the network from application level attacks, such as viruses, worms, or Trojan horse programs.

Software-based firewalls are installed on top of an existing operating system and hardware platform, available in both enterprise and SOHO models. Hardware-based firewalls include a hardware device with software already installed inside. Sometimes known as appliance firewalls, these firewalls also come in both enterprise and SOHO models. Specialty firewalls have a particular application focus, such as servers that filter content.

Very large organizations sometimes create a security perimeter network called a **demilitarized zone (DMZ)**. See Figure 6-23. Generally, these organizations probably want to separate their firewalls from all other applications.

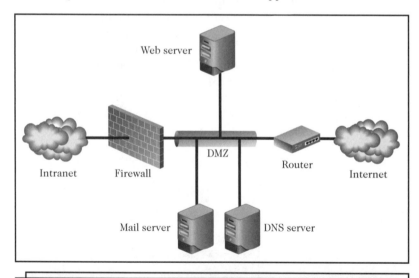

| Figure 6-23 | *A security perimeter network — DMZ* |

The *subcontractor* must consider how many users need to be protected and how many firewalls the network needs. More supported users usually require more processing power and memory in the firewall. Logging capabilities are also very important to the *subcontractor* in order to trace intrusions, should they occur. Firewalls should allow filtering minimally by: IP address, connection types, domain names, network numbers, and date and time. Software firewalls allow more flexibility than hardware firewalls because the choice of operating system you want to run the firewall on is yours.

On the other hand, hardware firewalls can be deployed rapidly because everything comes prepackaged. Most firewalls come with **network address translation (NAT)** capabilities, which means private IP addresses can be translated into legal public addresses (addresses are strings of numbers such as 156.12.324.12. A legal public address is one assigned by an accredited registrar or the Internet Network Information Center). NAT helps hide the internal topology of a network by mapping an internal IP address to a different external public IP address, thus keeping the network more secure.

Firewalls can also be used as **virtual private network (VPN)** endpoints. VPNs send data through an encrypted tunnel and keep the information private and away from the rest of the world. Using a VPN is the best way to ensure data integrity and privacy, since firewalls act only as a blocker, letting certain traffic in and out.

Once textual traffic is on the Internet, anyone can view the information in clear text. Passwords, as simple as they seem, can help secure the network if they are used properly. Real-time data can be analyzed using **intrusion detection systems**. These systems monitor the network and can detect, log, and even stop unauthorized access when the breach occurs. The *subcontractor* must assist in establishing the philosophy that recognizes that security measures set today for the network will probably need to change in the near future.

Organizations understand the urgent need to assess and upgrade security to protect the enterprise's data. Data, like a data center, is organic. Depending on who is using the data, its form and location change from one moment to the next. One second it is here, and the next second it is there. The *subcontractor* must communicate with others to understand *who* needs what data, *how* the data is used, *where* the data exists, *when* the data is needed, *why* the data is needed, and *what* it may become in order to keep networks carrying the data secure and efficient.

Using knowledge based on experiences, communication, patterns, and trends, the *subcontractor* learns to predict, adapt, and make intuitive security decisions to sculpt networks so that people can perform their work and help organizations strive to gain a competitive advantage.

6.5.8 Key Terms

authentication	firewall
bursty	intrusion detection system
capacity planning	lights out
certificate authority	mission-critical
data center	network address translation (NAT)
demilitarized zone (DMZ)	public key infrastructure (PKI)
digital certificate	scalable
digital signature	virtual private network (VPN)

6.5.9 Review Questions

1. How do network reliability, availability, and scalability affect the enterprise's health?
2. What effect can a bursty Web site have on the enterprise?
3. Why is capacity planning beneficial to the *subcontractor*?
4. How can the *subcontractor* benefit by learning efficient techniques for moving data through the computer's memory? How does the enterprise benefit?
5. What options are available to the *subcontractor* for providing security to the enterprise?
6. How does the OSI model assist the *subcontractor* in enabling the enterprise to communicate worldwide?

SECTION 6.6 WHEN A CHANGE IS NEEDED

QUESTIONS TO CONTEMPLATE

1. What challenges does obsolescence in hardware and software create for the *subcontractor*?
2. Why is change management important to the enterprise?

6.6.1 Introduction

The project's deadline looms ever closer. Once more, Chelsea, a seasoned developer, notices her coffee cup is empty, but this time she is not sure when she took that last sip. The soda machine next to the photocopier has been empty for the past three hours, and Chelsea has not seen daylight in weeks. The application is starting to stabilize and come together, but completing the application is getting down to the wire.

The telephone next to her monitor rings. The telephone's single ring indicates an inside call. Thoughts of not answering cross Chelsea's mind, but she picks up the telephone anyway. "I've been thinking..." the voice on the other end starts—three innocent words that make Chelsea open her mouth and mimic a loud prolonged scream. She realizes she is not going to like what comes next.

They want changes. They want lots and lots of changes. And they want them now. The changes are really important and they are so sorry they did not request them until now.

She wonders, should I agree? Should I find someone else to handle this? Should I tell them to go jump off a cliff? Should I just be polite, promise to think about it, and hope they forget? But she knows, *they* never forget!

Change is inevitable. Some organizations handle change better than others, but the need to change happens. Organizations hope new or modified features can be incorporated readily into existing systems. Sometimes the magnitude of a change means existing work has to be scrapped and started over. Occasionally, organizations

cannot figure out how to incorporate a change because no one on the IT staff is familiar with the system, and the system has no documentation.

Long-term thinking for the survival of an application is often secondary to
quickly releasing the software. Frequently, members of the project team do not take
time to compensate for the rushed approach. The Long Now Foundation is helping
to redefine how people and organizations need to think for the long term. The foundation is building a clock to last for 10,000 years—a daunting objective when you
consider civilized man has only been around for 7,000 years.

In 1993, Daniel Hillis (b. 1956) conceived the idea of a three-story clock that
would run for 10,000 years in a remote desert location. Hillis devised the project as a
way to get people thinking past the mental barrier of the year 2000 millennium.

As an inventor, scientist, and computer designer, Hillis looks beyond the normal
five to thirty-year technological cycle. Designers and builders have not always been
shortsighted. When oak beams in the hall at New College, Oxford, England had to be
replaced in the nineteenth century, wood was used from oak trees planted in 1386—
the same year the hall was built. The fourteenth century builders had planted the
trees in anticipation of the time, hundreds of years in the future, when beams would
need to be replaced.

The remote location selected for the Long Now Clock site is near Ely, in the
Nevada desert, on 80 acres dotted with ancient bristlecone pine trees and sheer
limestone cliffs. The foundation chose the dry climate and geological stability of the
high desert of the southwestern U.S. to help ensure the clock's materials would last
thousands of years.

Survivability of materials is not the only engineering challenge in building a
machine to last 10,000 years. Its meaning, function, and maintenance features must
also be clear to anyone who encounters the clock in the year 12,000. The meaning
and function of Stonehenge, built by Druids on Salisbury Plain in England, have
been lost in less time. The Long Now Foundation's objective was to create something
that could be understood transparently by future generations—unlike Stonehenge.

The Foundation included the following general design principles for the clock:

- *Longevity*—With occasional maintenance, the clock should reasonably
  be expected to display the correct time for the next 10,000 years.
- *Maintainability*—The clock should be maintainable with bronze-age
  technology.
- *Transparency*—Close inspection should reveal operational principles of
  the clock.
- *Evolvability*—When necessary, the clock should be improved upon
  with time.
- *Scalability*—Using the same design, working models of the clock from
  tabletop to monumental size could be built.

More specific rules followed from the general design principles. To promote
longevity, designers shied away from sliding friction (gears). To encourage maintainability and transparency, they decided to use familiar materials to make it easy to
build spare parts. Most importantly, they decided to include a manual of instructions. For scalability and evolvability, they proposed to use parts of a similar size,
separate processes, and make interfaces as simple as possible.

The design accommodates future maintenance providers by giving them easy access to all key parts. It is a skeleton clock—no case, no louvers, and no covers.

The clock's face displays a Gregorian calendar, the sun's position, moon phase (with the current star field in the middle), and the precession of the equinox (the axial wobble of the earth that occurs every 25,792 years). See Figure 6-24. Hillis' original designs called for the clock to tick once a year, bong once a century, and cuckoo once a millennium. Originally, the clock was going to be powered by seasonal temperature changes, but the designers opted for human winding because that would foster responsibility and invite involvement.

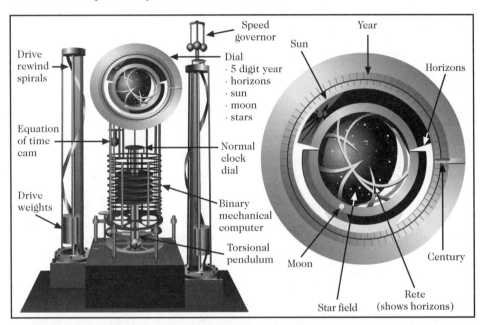

Figure 6-24   *The Clock of the Long Now*

Any computer user who has tried to find software to translate Novell WordPerfect 4.0 or Microsoft Word 2.0 files is probably already familiar with problems caused by increased obsolescence in hardware and software. Difficulties in dealing with incompatible file formats, caused by data stored across various platforms, are just the tip of the iceberg for both government and commerce in dealing with data longevity. DECtape and UNIVAC drives, which for years recorded huge amounts of government data, have vanished, as have software programs such as FORTRAN II.

Remote sensing data from NASA captured during the 1950s and 1960s has been lost to technological advancements. The data was recorded on giant magnetic tapes and used tape readers, which were eventually phased out of usage. When **data archaeologists** wanted to see the data, NASA reconstructed a reader. Unfortunately, nobody preserved the data's organizational structure. NASA was unable to make heads or tails of the recorded bits.

The overall goal of the Long Now Foundation is to transform our idea of time—to shift our view from next week or next year and immediate profit or short-term goals toward the perspective of tens of thousands of years.

In some of his original design work, Hillis used a Microsoft Excel spreadsheet to predict which clock dials would be indexed at what times. He soon found that Excel was not Y10K compliant. Hillis could not format the date function past the year 9999. Sooner or later, someone is going to submit another change request. Are you going to answer the telephone? *It's ringing.*

6.6.2 Could You Just Add this One Last Thing? *(when)*

When a project receives a series of change requests perceived to be so small and inconsequential that nobody readdresses the project plan or re-estimates the development effort, the project has entered into the realm of **scope creep**.[16]

Scope creep can be hard to manage. Most projects are affected by this symptom. Since the beginning of time, every project has probably been faced with an innocent request to make a few minor alterations. At some point in the project's life cycle, someone realizes, *this is not what we set out to build.*

Scope creep is a natural phenomenon. As a product takes shape, the vistas of possibility grow wider for the product's *owners* or users. A user often perceives that adding one more small feature should not take too long or affect the schedule.

There is nothing wrong with wanting to change something. However, change of any form should be managed and planned appropriately. Any impact the change has on a project should be estimated in terms of time, cost, and effort.

Time can have a positive or negative effect on the project's schedule. Cost can have a positive or negative effect on the project's budget, estimated operational costs, and estimated revenue. Effort can have a positive or negative impact to the number of people required to complete the change. Time, cost, and effort are interdependent. However, changing one affects the other two.

Before a project starts, everyone involved should understand how the project's managers will handle change. Controlling change so that the *owners* do not become dissatisfied is part of creating a successful product. IT departments should not try to address more work than is actually possible. Additionally, the organization should not put itself in a position where failure might result in losing money or personnel. To help control change successfully, answer the following questions:

- Is the change request really a change?
- What exactly does the change request involve?
- What impact does the change have on the project in terms of time, cost, and effort?
- What are the available options? What are the available solutions?
- How will you show the *owner* what will change and be affected?

People in service businesses have generally perfected techniques for identifying and managing scope creep. Painters, carpenters, builders, car mechanics, and landscapers know where the boundaries of their services lie. In general, IT professionals find boundaries difficult to manage.

Michael and Brian are brothers and professional house painters. They were on their way to arrive promptly at their next job. Several weeks earlier, they had given the homeowner a detailed estimate and everyone had agreed on this start date. The brothers showed up on time, had their tools ready, and quickly worked up a plan. The brothers began applying the first coat of paint within 15 minutes of arrival.

Erin, the homeowner and an IT professional by trade, was impressed at how flawlessly the brothers seemed to execute their plan and wished silently that her projects at work would go this smoothly. Erin could tell Michael and Brian were professionals and was confident the house would look great when they were done.

During the next few days, the brothers continued to impress the homeowner. Every day, Erin walked around the house and inspected their work. At times, Erin discovered minor repairs that needed to be made unrelated to the painting. Even though the repairs were minor, Erin believed she did not have the necessary expertise and that the repairs would take her too long to complete. Besides, the brothers already had the necessary tools and a 30-foot extension ladder; Erin was not crazy about heights. When Erin decided to ask the brothers about the repairs, they replied, "No problem." A little while later, Erin saw them working on the minor repairs she had pointed out.

"Too bad," Erin thought to herself, "They are good painters, but they do not know how to manage scope at all. They could lose money this way. Maybe I will talk to them about scope management at the end of the job."

Erin asked Michael and Brian about a small but persistent roof leak. The brothers responded that they were not roofers, but were happy to offer suggestions regarding the possible problem. Although the brothers gave advice, they would not volunteer to do the work. Finally, Erin asked flat out, "Will you fix the leaky roof?"

That was when Erin discovered the brothers' scope management skills. Michael went up into the attic and examined the whole roof. He told Erin that he found several leaks and reminded her that the roof was not part of the original estimate. "We can fix the roof for $431," Michael said. Erin accepted the offer. The brothers bought the necessary materials and fixed the leaks.

Michael and Brian knew what they had to manage. They knew how to recognize change, how to react to change, and how to recognize new opportunities.

6.6.3 Agile—Being Able to Change Quickly (why)

Simulating a combat mission, 40 Army Rangers parachute into the forests at Fort Polk, Louisiana. Each ranger is outfitted with the *Land Warrior*, a computer system full of high-tech firearms and communication gear. Once on the ground, the troops used Land Warrior's satellite-mapping device and found each other in 30 minutes. Using traditional flashlights and paper maps, the process would have taken two or three hours.

One of the Rangers peered through a heat-sensing thermal sight on his M-4 rifle and spotted pretend enemy snipers in the dark 300 meters away. The Ranger opened fire and killed them. The Rangers finished their mission twice as fast as a typical platoon.

In 1996, soldiers who used an earlier version of the Land Warrior system disliked the equipment so much they ripped it off their backs. The Land Warrior system developed by Raytheon cost $2 billion and was in the process of being shelved. Then in 2001, a team of Silicon Valley engineers from Pacific Consultants, Exponent, Pemstar, and Computer Sciences resurrected the project and completely overhauled the Land Warrior in six months.

Choosing to ignore rigid Army specifications, the companies brainstormed ideas. They lightened the Land Warrior computer harness, wrote new software, and worked closely with soldiers. By 2004, the reworked Land Warrior will be available for actual combat missions. See Figure 6-25.

Figure 6-25   Land Warrior

The engineers used many commercial products to change the Land Warrior, including Microsoft software and Intel computer chips. Commercial products allowed the development to go quicker and cost less.

When the Army put the development of the Land Warrior out to bid, it hoped the Land Warrior would revolutionize combat by creating a digital soldier. Infantrymen would use a computer and radio harness, voice communication and wireless e-mail, a satellite-mapping system, and other sophisticated electronics.

According to the General Accounting Office, the first prototype produced by Raytheon weighed 40 pounds. During testing, soldiers who rolled on the ground got stuck on their backs like tortoises. The helmet was so heavy, troops who were crawling could not lift their heads to fire rifles. The thick helmet cable would snag in bushes and fall off.

Early versions of the Land Warrior's software rarely worked, and batteries for computers and radios lasted far less than the desired 12 hours. The system failed water tests and leaked badly. During jump exercises, the bulky computer packs would not fit under a soldier's parachute.

In 1999, the Army brought in consultants from Exponent. Exponent felt Raytheon had followed Army specifications for the project too closely. In three months, Exponent created a new prototype. Off-the-shelf electronics purchased from retailers such as Best Buy and Fry's Electronics were used. Microsoft Windows CE operating system and generic wireless cards allowed the new Land Warrior's computer to send data.

Developers wrote new software using common languages, such as C++ and Java, instead of less common languages, such as ADA, used by the government and its normal contractors. By 2002, the Land Warrior weighed only 12 pounds and the vest and body armor fit snugly around a soldier's torso. The operating system had been upgraded to Microsoft Windows 2000, and the applications were nearing the project's goal of 10 days of usage without a breakdown.

Engineers from the Silicon Valley companies used agile techniques to get the job done. The companies purchased off-the-shelf components and used existing technologies. Engineers spoke with the system's users (soldiers) to learn how it would be used. Choosing to follow a path that allowed rapid and relatively inexpensive ways to change the Land Warrior, the engineers' agile approach succeeded where Raytheon's approach failed.

6.6.4 Components *(how)*

Implementing business changes into an IT project generally happens in one of three ways. Changes to hardware or software can be:

- Made to order
- Provided from stock
- Assembled to order

Made-to-Order Projects

Most product-oriented industries, including most IT departments, conduct business in a made-to-order environment. IT managers, analysts, and developers wait for someone to say the magic words, "I've been thinking..." These words indicate the wheels of change are in motion and IT departments know they can now get to work. Fortunately, most IT departments have a backlog of work, so waiting around is not typically a problem.

Organizations that manufacture a product made to order are often referred to as job shops and are known for producing custom work. In a job shop, a customer might contact the sales department and request that it build something such as a digital-kumquat. The salesperson politely asks the customer, "What exactly is a digital-kumquat and what does it do? If we are going to manufacture this custom-built digital-kumquat, you will have to give us the **functional specifications**."

When the customer then defines the digital-kumquat's functional specifications, one of the manufacturer's engineers designs the digital-kumquat to meet these specifications. Next, a manufacturing engineer figures out how to build the digital-kumquat designed by the engineer. If the manufacturer has a plant, raw materials, machine tools, and employees, the digital-kumquat can be fabricated and assembled.

IT departments work in the same way. When the customer (*owner*) calls and says, "I've been thinking...can you build me an Internet-enabled-kumquat (an application or feature of an application) for me," IT asks, "What exactly does an Internet-enabled-kumquat do? If we are going to develop this custom-built Internet-enabled-kumquat, you will have to give us the functional specifications."

The *owner* defines the functional specifications. An analyst (*designer*) in IT designs the Internet-enabled-kumquat to meet the functional specifications. Then a manufacturing engineer (*builder*) has to figure out how to build the Internet-enabled-kumquat designed by the analyst. If the IT department has a plant (a building to house desktop computers and a computer room with networked servers), machine tools (operating systems, utilities, compilers, and databases), raw material (data), and employees (system administrators and operators), the machinists (*subcontractors*) can fabricate and assemble the Internet-enabled-kumquat (application). Typical IT departments follow the job shop model.

Provided-from-Stock Projects

A provided-from-stock strategy may solve some of the problems associated with made-to-order products, such as long lead times. In a standard production environment, a provided-from-stock strategy uses pre-manufactured, standard products. These products may be produced in-house and stored in inventory or acquired through a vendor. In either case, the products have been built prior to an order. In IT, provided-from-stock projects usually involve COTS packages, such as operating systems, office productivity tools, enterprise resource planning software, or accounting applications.

If you have finished goods or applications on the shelf when an *owner* calls and says, "I've been thinking...I need an Internet-enabled-kumquat," the organization might be able to deliver the application off the shelf. Minus the implementation time and any parameter configuration settings, the lead time goes to zero.

Per unit implementation cost can be low because the engineering, manufacturing, tooling, and testing can be spread across a series of implementations. Reliability and availability can increase because the same code is reused.

The major drawback to the provided-from-stock model is flexibility. As the automobile manufacturer Henry Ford once said, "A customer can have any color they want as long as it's black." Flexibility is the price an owner pays for immediate delivery, low per unit implementation cost, high reliability, and high availability. Often, in information technology, the customer is forced to change operations to fit the application.

Most organizations would prefer to have the flexibility of custom applications, but with the same characteristics as provided-from-stock packages, including immediate delivery and low per unit product cost.

Assembled-to-Order Projects

All too often, IT departments have to deal with *owners* who are unable or unwilling to define the characteristics of an application they want until they are ready to take delivery. An *owner's* preference is to have a custom-built application mass produced in a quantity of one for immediate delivery.

If organizations do not like waiting for made-to-order applications and provided-from-stock applications are too limiting, the development concept has to change to use an assembled-to-order paradigm. An assembled-to-order strategy involves mass customization of one. Assembled-to-order strategies are based on using components (parts). Components are developed and placed in inventory. Each component is not a finished product or application—it is just a component (a piece that becomes part of the finished product).

When an *owner* places an order for an application, delivery time includes only time to identify the components and assemble them into the finished product. Assembled-to-order concepts fit well with object-oriented programs. Components such as reading the customer database or writing to the customer database are prefabricated, reusable programs that simply require assembly into a final application.

The assembled-to-order concept presumes that the *designers*, *builders*, and *subcontractors* are designing and building the components so they can be assembled into more than one finished application. That is, the components are being engineered so that many completed applications can use them.

Table 6-4 shows correlations between made-to-order and assembled-to-order products.

Made-to-Order	Assembled-to-Order
One of a kind	Mass customization
Custom products	Standard/custom products
Short-term	Long-term
Project-oriented	Process-oriented
Implementation dominant	Integration dominant
Single purpose engineering	Reusability
Expense-based	Asset-based
Order controlled (cost/order)	Part controlled (cost/part)

Table 6-4   *Correlations between made-to-order and assembled-to-order*

If an organization uses a made-to-order model, the only way to handle change and reduce the time to market is to reduce the complexity of the product. At some point, simplification may result in a trivial product, severely limiting advantages the organization might yield through software.

If an organization uses a provided-from-stock model, the organization can drastically reduce its time to market, but the organization may have to change to fit the package. Trying to customize a package to fit the organization can take longer and cost more than using a made-to-order approach.

The most desirable results are achieved through component-based development with the intention that the components are designed and built for reuse. Component-based development requires both an engineering and artistic flare.

6.6.5 Side Effects *(where)*

Automating processes through software is a major investment of time, cost, and effort. Enterprises make this investment to stay alive. Such investments often reflect the long-term strategy of an organization, not just the development of the initial software. Many initial decisions have pervasive consequences for decades to come.

The use of a two-digit year field is such a decision that had far-reaching negative consequences. The hardware, operating system, language, approach, skill level, and foresight that an application uses reflect decisions that can ultimately affect the changeability of the application.

People are natural learners, so the competence of an application's maintenance team tends to grow over time. However, the increase in learning masks the deterioration of the program code itself, creating side effects. When design integrity breaks down, documentation is not kept up to date or up to standard, and the coding style becomes unfathomable. This compromises the quality of the software and potentially the application itself. The changeability of an application deteriorates due to the addition of faults and performance inefficiencies.

One measure of changeability is the ripple effect. One way to measure the ripple effect is by monitoring the number of separate areas that have to be altered to accommodate a single change to the application. Gerald Weinberg, author of *Quality Software Management: Volume 1 Systems Thinking*, describes a hardware manufacturer that found each change led to about 300 other changes in the operating system—"equivalent to a nuclear reactor, one that was on the verge of turning into a nuclear bomb."

Ivar Jacobson, Magnus Christerson, Patrik Jonsson, and Gunnar Overgaard, in their book *Object-Oriented Software Engineering: A Use Case Driven Approach*, comment that after the first release of an application, the real development starts. An application normally develops through changes incorporated in newer versions. Most software never remains at version 1.0. Most software gets replaced eventually. Developing applications to be maintained successfully is a cost-effective option for any enterprise.

6.6.6 Top Down *(who)*

Managers and *subcontractors* working on a software project can act as if they are rehearsing a fiasco scene in the engine room of the Star Trek Enterprise:

> *"You'd better hurry," Spock (the manager) says helpfully with one eyebrow raised, "By my calculations, we have 8 minutes until impact."*
>
> *"Sorry," Scotty (the subcontractor) says in his Scottish brogue, "we can't fix it in under 14 minutes. Not and maintain a safety factor."*
>
> *"You don't have time for a safety factor," says Spock, who turns on his heel and walks away.*

The safety factor in IT includes artifacts such as models, documents, and documentation from the *planner*, *owner*, *designer*, *builder*, and *subcontractor*. Without the artifacts, making any change becomes more difficult. Sometimes any type of change can become impossible.

Organizations need to develop a culture that embraces working at a speed to produce a maintainable product. The list of trade-offs in Section 5.4.2 also applies to the change paradigm for software:

- Seeking immediate gratification as opposed to doing what is good for you
- Choosing a short-term option over a long-term option
- Electing to implement a standalone product instead of seeking to implement an integrated product
- Producing a point-in-time based solution instead of an infrastructure-based solution
- Taking an expense-based approach in lieu of an asset-based approach
- Optimizing the implementation at the expense of the enterprise versus optimizing the enterprise at the expense of the implementation
- Doing something in a quick-and-dirty manner instead of doing it right

In the Star Trek episode *The Naked Time*, Scotty says, "I can't change the laws of physics; I've got to have 30 minutes." Without adequate artifacts, a *subcontractor* might not be able to find the appropriate program to change, follow the logic of the program needing to be changed, or identify the potential ripple effects of any changes to a program. The artifacts are the laws of physics for the *subcontractor*.

Not all applications in an organization are changing constantly. Not all applications require a permanent full-time staff to maintain them. However, stable applications soon become nightmares to maintain when they do not include appropriate models, documents, and documentation.

Subcontractors may leave the organization, get promoted to management, or forget their work over time. Often, fresh sets of eyes are trying to do the equivalent of decoding hieroglyphics. The work can become difficult very quickly and can lead easily to unmotivated employees whose work is a **kludge** (pronounced klooj). A kludge is a clumsy, inefficient, inelegant, or unfathomable solution for the problem—not artistic in nature and not an elegant solution. Elegant solutions come about by training, experience, and following best practices. Best practices come about by establishing rules, standards, units of measure, metrics, and statistics.

Letting knowledge persist in a model, document, or documentation makes the *subcontractor* effective. Can you imagine the captain of the *Titanic* calling for the blueprints after the ship hit its fatal iceberg and being told, "We didn't have the time to produce them." The blueprints allowed the captain to understand how the ship would continue to take on water, which would eventually cause her to sink. Seven hundred and thirteen people survived because the captain was able to order the evacuation of the *unsinkable* ship.

6.6.7 Being Defensive *(what)*

Using a forward-thinking mindset to anticipate problems is one way a *subcontractor* works to produce an application. Defensive development can reduce the amount of work a future unknown change might require. The *subcontractor* can use various artistic techniques to achieve a defensive approach. The following are some suggestions from the software architecture and programming fields that can help the *subcontractor* work defensively:

- Use abstract interfaces to components instead of interfaces that expose the components' implementation details. The book *Design Patterns*, by Erich Gamma, Richard Helm, Ralph Johnson, and John Vlissides, presents several patterns of abstract interfaces including AbstractFactory, Adapter, and Bridge.
- Instead of hard-coded literals, use a named constant to declare an attribute's size.
- Use late binding strategies for data structures and for executing programs. Early binding happens at compile time and late binding happens at execution time. Delayed binding can help a program be version independent.
- Use relational database tables to base a program's logic on values stored in the table. An extension of this approach uses metadata, which describes what a value means, or what is available.

413

- Create reusable components rather than duplicating code, even if the component has only one or two lines of code.
- Keep components small and as simple as possible. Keeping components simple can result in ways to use a component in the unforeseeable future.
- Separate unrelated pieces of logic into separate components, even if the logic is relatively simple to follow and understand.
- Separate logic for general processing from logic for specialized processing. Distinguish between components or logic for use throughout the enterprise, in a specific application, or in a specific version of an application.
- Create documentation for everything.

Defensive development does not refer to any specific methodology. See Figure 6-26. Defensive development is a general practice used to develop software that acknowledges that an unknown change to the application will be required in the future. A defensive style of coding creates a program structure that readily accommodates change.

Figure 6-26   Sports

For example, if a computer application handles the sports basketball, soccer, and baseball with a specialized program or data structure, then when the time comes to add hockey, a new program or data structure will need to be written and added. A defensive approach would abstract each explicit sport as a common activity called sport. If sport is made generic, it may be possible to add hockey without adding any new programs, logic, or data structures.

6.6.8 Key Terms

data archaeologist

functional specification

kludge

scope creep

6.6.9 Review Questions

1. What challenges does obsolescence in hardware and software present for the *subcontractor*?
2. Why must the impact of any change on a project be estimated in terms of time, cost, and effort?
3. Why are agile techniques important to the *subcontractor* and beneficial to the enterprise?

4. When automating a process through software, list some choices the *subcontractor* makes that can affect the changeability of the application.
5. Why must the enterprise develop a culture that embraces speed, but also maintains product quality and maintainability?
6. What is meant by defensive development?

SECTION 6.7 WHO WANTS THIS JOB—A LOOK AT CAREERS IN IT

QUESTIONS TO CONTEMPLATE

1. What kind of skills are needed to work in the IT industry?
2. What challenges and opportunities are available in IT?

6.7.1 Introduction

Careers in information technology cover a wide spectrum including management, architecture, data, software, hardware, and support services. According to the U.S. Department of Commerce's *Digital Economy 2000*, the financial services industry is the biggest consumer of IT products and services in terms of expenditure, followed by communication, manufacturing, wholesale, business, retail, real estate, and transportation services.

The U.S. Department of Labor predicts the fastest-growing occupations through 2010 will be computer systems analysts, engineers, and scientists. The U.S. Bureau of Labor Statistics forecasts that by 2008, an additional 2 million workers will be needed to fill information technology positions across all industry sectors.

Backgrounds of IT professionals vary greatly by education level and primary career choices. Many professionals migrate to IT because of the field's diversity and challenge. For example, at Spectrum Health in Grand Rapids, Michigan, nurse clinicians and therapists have joined Spectrum's IT department to help provide their industry expertise in delivering technology solutions to customers.

Most organizations rely on computers to survive and remain competitive. Organizations need employees who have higher-level skills and the knowledge required to keep up with changing technology and changing business needs.

IT hiring in defense, pharmaceuticals, and healthcare has been expanding since the turn of the century. The healthcare industry spends billions of dollars per year to comply with government regulations for protecting the security and confidentiality of medical records (i.e., HIPAA, which is discussed in Section 5.7.5).

Terrorist events have stimulated development of more sophisticated weapons and security systems by the U.S. government. The twenty-first century has ushered in a new era of security awareness, promoting the passing of the USA PATRIOT Act.[17] Strict security and privacy regulations in finance, development of stronger user awareness policies, challenges of wireless access, expansion of business-to-business exchanges, and the increased role of application service providers mean even more job opportunities in information technology. IT workers who understand their company's entire enterprise should be equipped to point out the security breaches that could threaten any part of the financial bottom line.

Information technology employment opportunities continue to grow because this field changes rapidly. Organizations need new applications that enable employees to perform their jobs better. New applications are also needed that allow **internal** or **external customers** to better interact with the enterprise in a real-time environment. A real-time environment implies that an application's transaction can be completed with a minimal time lag between the request and the response. In business, the time lag or latency associated with a real-time environment is usually between 1 and 10 seconds. Rewarding career opportunities await those who have the right knowledge and skills as society becomes wireless and the Internet, e-commerce, and e-government presence expands.

6.7.2 Never Mind the Title, Let's Get on with the Work *(who)*

In 2002, Thomas Siebel, CEO of Siebel Systems Incorporated, a customer relationship management software vendor, testified before the U.S. House of Representatives that unintegrated databases and an unsophisticated culture contributed to the U.S. government's inability to avoid the terrorist attacks of September 2001.

Siebel and several other IT vendor executives argued for a person to be responsible for promoting greater interagency cooperation within the government to provide useful citizen services more quickly. Siebel argued that the responsibility should be given to a federal chief information officer (CIO) and that the government should create such as position.

The executives further argued that the CIO's focus would be to promote greater collaboration by forming procedures to evaluate technologies and applications that could be deployed throughout the government.

Political discussions about the appointment of a federal CIO ensued, but focused more on the job title than on the job's responsibilities. An equal number of government representatives were for and against the proposition. Even Mark Forman, the person who would eventually assume the position, was opposed to creating the new position and title.

Forman believed the Office of Management and Budget (OMB) was already "doing the job." He favored OMB's deputy director for management taking on additional responsibility associated with the federal CIO role. Opposing politicians argued that the two positions needed different skills. These opponents believed the federal CIO would concentrate on technology, while the deputy director would concentrate on finance—different titles, different skills, and different job descriptions.

Although many of the government's discussions revolved around the type and title of the position that should be created, and to whom the person should report, the real focus should have been on the job description and responsibilities.

For many organizations, whether they are government, for profit, or nonprofit, the phrase *Never mind the title, let's get on with the work* applies. Forman was eventually given the role of federal CIO, but it was called associate director for information technology and e-government.

In his position for the OMB, Forman heads up the effort to make government more responsive to citizens. Forman strongly believes, "Our focus isn't on titles, but on how to get the work done."[18]

When looking for employment opportunities in newspapers, trade journals, and on the Internet, organizations use different job titles to describe various combinations of technical, non-technical, and soft skills for the multitude of IT job positions. Differing job titles may include the same, similar, or different skill combinations, which may confuse job candidates.

Most organizations post a job when a specific position needs to be filled. Therefore, the postings usually list specific skills needed for one particular project. Some organizations list desired skills for future projects. Skill sets and descriptions can differ for the same job title due to the work that needs to be accomplished and the organization's biases and culture. Table 6-5 illustrates examples of job titles and descriptions for senior management in information technology.

The size of an IT organization helps determine each person's job function and description. In a small organization, a CIO may be involved exclusively in strategic planning and managing day-to-day operations, and even be expected to help with development. In a mid-sized organization, a CIO may be focused on managing day-to-day operations, but also do some strategic planning. In a large organization, the CIO may be involved exclusively in strategic planning. Ultimately, the job description helps determine the nature of the job, not the job title.

Job title	Description
Chief information officer, chief technology officer, or vice president of information technology	Information technology executive responsible for technology direction and technology budget in the enterprise
Director of information technology	Information technology executive responsible for technology direction and technology budget in a business unit or division
Director of systems development	Systems development executive responsible for directing systems management and applications programming, from handheld devices and desktop machines to large-scale mainframes
Director of networks	Networking executive responsible for managing voice and data communications for the enterprise
Director of information technology operations	Operations executive responsible for directing the data center and systems operation groups
Internet technology strategist	Oversees integration of Web reporting, workflow, e-mail, streaming media content, and Internet security processes
Web architect	Responsible for the development of Web-enabled customer applications, maintains Web servers and back-office infrastructure linkage
Enterprise architect	A senior designer whose skills blend all forms of information technology architecture and disciplines; responsible for modeling, model integration, and making sure the information technology department produces applications aligned to the business. Focuses on ways to create flexible and reusable resources for the enterprise. Helps the enterprise incorporate change and work toward responsive solutions.
Business analyst	Supports internal business processes to improve efficiency and decision-making, reduce redundancy, and ultimately enhance business results

Table 6-5 *Sample senior management positions*

6.7.3 Technical Skill Sets *(what)*

Due to the changing nature of information technology, employers in all areas demand higher levels of skill and expertise. The types of technical skills needed vary depending on the job description, and more importantly, on the project at hand. The increase in time, cost, and effort to design, develop, and implement e-commerce infrastructures means businesses and governments are demanding knowledge skills in database, Internet-enabled applications, and application integration areas.

Hardware and software technical skills in areas such as computer forensics, intrusion detection, firewalls, authentication, authorization, and security auditing are advantageous. Security professionals now need network engineering and operations skills, regardless of their specialties. Other worthwhile technical skills are listed in Table 6-6.

Client/Server

Technology	Examples
OLTP servers	Oracle, Sybase, SQL Server, Informix, DB2
Front-end	Visual Basic, Visual C/C++, X/Motif, Developer 2000, Delphi, PowerBuilder
ER analysis and modeling	ERWin, Designer 2000, S-Designer
Data warehousing	COGNOS, Sagent, Informatica, Business Object, ETL
Middleware	Visibroker, Java Message Queue, Tuxedo, Forte
Languages	C/C++, Pro*C, PL/SQL, CICS/COBOL, Crystal Reports
Configuration management	PVCS, CCC/Harvest, ClearCase, Purify

Internet Technology

Technology	Examples
Internet/WWW planning	Netscape Server, Oracle Web Server, Microsoft IIS, Java Web Server, MTS, JRUN
Web development languages	C#, Java, Visual J++, JavaScript, VBScript, Perl, ColdFusion, CGI, ASP, Dreamweaver, JSP, Servlets, Corba, RMI, SOAP, SSL, DHTML
Web development tools	EJB, XML, XSL, SWING, JSP, Java Beans, JDBC, JMS, ActiveX, BroadVision, Lotus Notes-Domino
Web IDE	Visual Age, JBuilder, JADE, JDeveloper, Visual Café, PowerJ, MS Front Page
Application server	WebSphere, WebLogic, Oracle Application Server, WebObjects, Together/J, Versata, iPlanet, Apache Web Server
Network management	IBM SystemView, HP OpenView, Microsoft SMS, Zen Works, Cisco Works, 3Com Transient, Nortel Optivity, TCP/IP, DECnet, UUCP, Citrix

Object Technology

Technology	Examples
OO design and modeling	Rational Unified Process, Rational ROSE, UML, Power Designer
OODBMS	Object Store, Versant
Object broker/implementation	Visibroker, EJB, CORBA, COM/DCOM, ORBIX

Systems

Technology	Examples
RTOS	VX Works, ThreadX, RT Linux
Unix	Solaris, HP-UX, AIX, Linux, DGUX, IRIX, SCO
Windows	Windows 9x, Windows NT, Windows 2000, Windows XP
Novell	Novell Netware

ERP/CRM

Technology	Examples
ERP	SAP and ABAP/4, PeopleSoft, BaaN, Oracle Applications, J.D. Edwards
CRM	Siebel, Vantive, Clarify, E.piphany

| Table 6-6 | *Sample technical skills* |

When you look at an employment advertisement on the Internet or in the newspaper, you may see specific technical requirements posted for the job listing. Often these postings seem like they require a *jack-of-all-trades*. The employer may be including an optimal skill set as well as the minimal skill set required. Because needed skills vary from project to project, employers find it difficult to limit the skill sets listed in a job posting.

6.7.4 Release 2.0 *(when)*

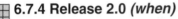

As technology evolves, IT workers must constantly strive to stay up to date and acquire new skills to remain competitive in their field. Vendors like to release new versions of hardware or software every 12 to 18 months. Some IT organizations like to be on the bleeding edge of technology and use new products while they are still being beta tested.

However, most organizations watch for a product to reach general availability (GA) status and then wait a few months before adopting the product. Trailing-edge organizations are very slow in moving to new technologies and only upgrade when they can no longer obtain vendor support on a given hardware or software product.

Hardware and software vendors frequently offer training workshops to promote new products. Employers, colleges and universities, private training institutions, and professional computing societies also offer continuing education and professional development seminars. Some companies provide informal on-the-job training, while other companies pay for higher education and formal off-site training for employees.

By increasing the education and training of technology workers, organizations may be able to offer improved services to customers. The employee may also benefit from new opportunities and career advancement.

Technical or professional certification can be one way of ensuring the quality or competency of IT professionals. However, certification alone does not necessarily mean an individual is capable or has better qualifications for the job. The Institute of Certification and Computing Professionals (ICCP) and the Institute of Electrical and Electronics Engineers (IEEE) Computer Society both offer voluntary certification.

ICCP requires individuals to pass a core examination for general knowledge, plus exams in two specialty areas, or in one specialty area and two computer programming languages. The Certified Computing Professional designation is only available to those who have at least two years of experience and a college degree.

The IEEE also offers software engineer certification to those who successfully pass an examination. This professional certification is not always mandatory, but may be advantageous for someone looking for a job. Technological advances come so rapidly in the computer field that continuous study is necessary to keep skills and certifications up to date. By the time you master version 1.0, version 2.0 will become available. The desire for learning is critical to enjoying an IT career.

6.7.5 Have Laptop, Will Travel *(where)*

IT workers can work anywhere, but that is not always the best choice. Giving people more mobility and access to more information can lead to greater productivity, but can also lead to more pressure and longer hours. The challenge for IT managers is to quickly capitalize on the opportunities in a world of *doing more with less*, without burning out the workforce that remains. According to preliminary findings from the *Information*

Week 2002 annual salary survey, more than half of all IT workers and more than 60 percent of IT managers say their jobs are more stressful than the previous year.

Businesses give their employees a variety of tools designed to make workers more productive. For example, Eli Lilly and Company, a pharmaceutical organization headquartered in Indianapolis, Indiana, begins with a basic management philosophy that its workers are hard working and dedicated. Although telecommuting can complicate the issue of balancing productivity and lifestyles, Lilly takes advantage of a fully networked economy by allowing all of its knowledge workers to occasionally work from home.

GMAC Commercial Mortgage has set up technologies that it hopes will make all employees more productive. One technology is the use of software that allows employees to check their e-mail, work schedule, and meeting schedule by telephone. They can then log on to a virtual private network to respond to messages.

One employee says this technology saves him 30 minutes per day. He makes the call on the drive in. According to audit logs, employee use of the system spikes during drive time and at lunchtime—the employer is benefiting from the employees working more hours. Employees do not seem to mind the fact that they work longer hours because the increased flexibility of schedule allows them to reach their goals when they choose.[19]

Laptops allow IT workers to travel all over the world and remain connected to their offices and work environments. However, telecommuting also causes isolation from people and colleagues. Personal contact enables people to make connections with each other that are different from an e-mail message or a telephone call.

Face-to-face meetings and work environments are generally considered more effective and rewarding both professionally and psychologically. In addition, agile development techniques like XP and Scrum work better when people can physically collaborate together—regardless of where they choose to actually collaborate.

6.7.6 Rich Reward *(why)*

Anna Kilinski, a college graduate, had a clear vision of how she wanted to leave her career mark. Entering the University of Alabama as a healthcare management major, she soon discovered that a minor in computer science could give her a competitive edge. While taking computer science classes, she realized she wanted to pursue the business applications of technology and changed her major to management information science during the following year.

Kilinski likes to be challenged continuously and is excited about the opportunity for career-long learning. She finds information technology to be interesting because the area is changing constantly. She likes having the opportunity to work on smaller projects alone and collaborate on larger, team-oriented projects, where her decisions rely on other people's input. As an IT professional, she enjoys working with people who have different backgrounds and career goals.[20]

Because the information technology industry allows people to focus on relationships among technology, information, people, the organization, and society, it attracts people with all levels of education and experience, and from all walks of life. IT workers use both logic and creativity to solve business and technical problems and to use computers and related technology to achieve and sustain success for organizations, society, and the individual.

According to a study conducted by David Foote, president and chief research officer of Foote Partners, LLC, a management consultancy and IT workforce research firm in New Canaan, Connecticut, people who apply for IT jobs like solving problems. They are motivated to become better IT professionals, and therefore tend to be interested in professional development. They want continued training that prepares them to work on projects with emerging technologies. Those who seek careers in IT work hard and expect to be recognized for delivering products or services using their business knowledge and technical skills.[21] IT professionals benefit from being self-motivated, artistic, creative, communicative, abstract thinkers, and system thinkers, with plenty of patience and endurance.

6.7.7 Soft Skill Sets *(how)*

As work environments evolve, organizations are recognizing the importance of soft skills. Being a *computer geek* or *propeller head* is no longer sufficient to survive in a corporate IT environment. Restructuring of corporate cultures from vertical to horizontal alignments requires people to work together more closely.

Organizations are becoming flatter in nature; layers of management are disappearing, and people are required to work smarter, faster, and cheaper. People interact closely with one another. Tasks and activities are usually team driven, where differences in personalities become more obvious. IT workers therefore need to learn how to interact productively with others. By recognizing the 16 personality types associated with Myers-Briggs, discussed in Section 4.3, IT workers may be better equipped to understand and communicate effectively with coworkers.

Spectrum Health is the largest healthcare system in southwest Michigan. Jane Gietzen, information management resources manager, realizes the importance of getting the right people for the job in order to properly meet the needs of the organization's internal and external customers.

Patients and families are cared for at one of Spectrum's hospitals, nursing homes, primary care practices, outpatient surgery centers, urgent care centers, and through partnerships with organizations like Priority Health that provide outreach services. With a staff of more than 10,000, Spectrum Health earned *U.S. News and World Report's* Best Hospitals specialty honors in 1999, 2000, 2001, and 2002.

Gietzen makes sure employees have the proper tools and strategies to complete IT projects on time. She tries to streamline workflow by matching the right talent to the right task and to bridge the communication gaps that cause projects to fail and profits to fall.

To make projects succeed, Spectrum's IT job requirements include effective written and verbal communication skills. Employees are expected to make quality, independent decisions and work toward collaboration.

Most contemporary organizations value the ability to work effectively and efficiently with others under tight deadlines, high volumes, and multiple interruptions. Doing so means that organizations also value trust, confidence, empathy, adaptability, and self-control among employees. A team-driven workplace requires a positive relationship among coworkers to meet the group's objectives.

According to Hendrie Weisenger, Ph.D, "There is now hard data that shows such skills as listening and building consensus actually do affect the bottom line. The soft skills have become the hard skills."[22] If project teams are to function efficiently, individuals must help each other move from conflict to collaboration, improve listening and communication skills, and focus on organizational goals—not individual differences. Without effective communication, projects are delayed, cooperation decreases, and results falter.

6.7.8 Key Terms

external customer

internal customer

6.7.9 Review Questions

1. What industries are the biggest consumers of IT products and services?
2. Why would the size of an IT organization be an important issue when considering employment?
3. Why do employment advertisements for the same job title sometimes have different requirements?
4. Why do many job postings seem to be asking for an IT Superwoman or IT Superman?
5. Why should a *subcontractor* be a creative problem solver?
6. How do soft skills affect an IT employee's effectiveness in the workplace?

6.8 SYNTHESIS AND CHAPTER SUMMARY

Once someone proposes an idea or need for a software application in an organization, nearly all organizational activity supports the *subcontractor*. The *planners*, *owners*, *designers*, and *builders* produce artifacts (e.g., models, documents, and documentation) so the *subcontractor* can create *works of art* and modify those works later.

The *subcontractor's* responsibility is to fabricate and assemble the final product or service and then produce the necessary product documentation. The *subcontractor's* unrelenting taskmaster is reality. No amount of arguing about the elegance or aesthetics of a piece of work and no amount of pleading that the product *should* work will result in a finished product. Reality turns a deaf ear to the *subcontractor*. The final product either works reality's way, or the product does not work at all.

If the *subcontractor* is producing a software program, that program becomes the ultimate design document for the program. However, the program is out of context with the whole application. The program has a function to perform; the program is not the application. The program becomes just one of the application's parts. An application has many parts: multiple programs, utilities, databases, and configuration files. Although the program documents the program, the program does not document the application, nor does the program necessarily document how the program fits into the contextual whole of the application.

All models, documents, CPM charts, Gantt Charts, organization charts, network diagrams, and lists support the *subcontractor*. If the *subcontractor* is producing code, then the code is the ultimate description of what the program really does. The program is a design document; however, the program should be augmented with structure and additional documentation to provide for easy reading. Often, following the logic in a program can make it easy for another *subcontractor* to rationalize what is going on, but the structure does not reflect *why* the what is going on.

Although the *subcontractor* produces a work of art, appropriate standards and best practices must be followed. Not all works of art have enduring qualities, and some works are best left hidden in a drawer. Some types of creativity are best left for thespians, authors, sculptures, and poets. The art in writing a program is to make the code appear normal—standards and best practices help define *normal*. For example, the following pseudocode written in C, shown in Figure 6-27, is easier to follow than the same pseudocode shown in Figure 6-28. The only difference between the two is the style of indentation.

```
function()
{
        statement;
        statement;
        if (expression) {
                statement;
        function();
        }
        function();
}
```

Figure 6-27   Normal indentation

```
                        function()
                                {
        statement;
        statement;
        if (expression) {
statement;
function();
}
                function();
                                }
```

Figure 6-28   Abnormal indentation

Safety Factor

In recent times, many major corporations have been shaken up for one reason or another. During the accounting scandals of 2001 and 2002, organizations such as Enron Corporation, WorldCom Incorporated, Merrill Lynch & Company, Arthur Andersen, and Computer Associates International Incorporated had to change.[23] Apart from correcting accounting procedures, these companies laid off tens of thousands of employees from all sectors of the businesses. In addition, some of the employees who were lucky enough to keep their jobs left as soon as they found new opportunities.

Unless an organization is closing down a business unit, organizational downsizing involves only the removal of personnel from the payroll. Most, if not all, of the job functions and job responsibilities remain. The remaining staff has to pitch in and fill the void by taking on additional work and responsibilities. This is the nature of corporate downsizing and rightsizing.

If you were a *subcontractor*, how would you pick up the pieces for an application where all key personnel, *owners*, *designers*, *builders*, and *subcontractors* have left? Agile processes rely on people to provide the short-term and long-term intellectual capital to explain an application from design to implementation and maintenance. When a production bug appears, you cannot say to management, "Tsk, tsk, that'll teach you for letting Kimberly, James, and Donna go." Production problems have to be fixed and they have to be fixed now. To protect itself from this type of problem, an organization needs to invest in an insurance policy.

INSURANCE

Modern societies are accustomed to purchasing insurance policies to hedge against uncontrollable or unforeseen future events. Many people and organizations are eager to protect their financial interests in vehicles, airplanes, ships, trains, goods-in-transit, buildings, health, and life. The possibilities of sudden unexpected indebtedness are endless. Purchasing an insurance policy helps minimize worry.

In most cases, insurance is a binding agreement between the insurer and the insured. In the event of a covered circumstance where the insured is financially affected, the insurer agrees to pay a predetermined sum of money to the insurance policy's beneficiary. For accepting the burden of payment, the insurer collects a fee known as an insurance premium. Insurance is one way of controlling the financial aspects of an unknown future.

Companies that experience difficulties often cannot perform at previous levels of achievement. Companies may continue to operate in a weakened state, file for bankruptcy protection and continue to operate in a weakened state, or find another corporation to acquire the remaining debt, assets, customers, and employees. Under any of these conditions, many software applications are shelved, not because they are worthless, but simply because no one has the time or money to understand how they work.

A *subcontractor* who takes the time to provide the appropriate amount of excruciating detail for his work products provides an organization with an insurance policy. Producing documentation may seem boring at times and not worth the effort, but, ultimately, the *subcontractor* is being paid to produce a product that meets *all* the organization's requirements.

The *subcontractor* is vital to the survival of the enterprise. Even when the *subcontractor* finds tasks such as documentation less appealing than other tasks, forcing the *subcontractor* to produce specific levels of quality in all aspects of his job *is the enterprise's insurance premium.*

The price of the insurance premium is worth every penny. An organization may never need the models, documents, and documentation at excruciating levels of detail, but that is the very nature of insurance. One hopes never to need the insurance, but it is nice to have when needed.

From the *subcontractor's* point of view, performing extra tasks of documentation may seem draining and tiring. The *subcontractor* needs *endurance* to overcome these mental roadblocks. The *subcontractor* needs to demonstrate *artistry* to produce something worth looking at and reading. Neither endurance nor artistry happens by accident. The *subcontractor* needs to train for both.

ENDURANCE THROUGH ERGONOMICS

To develop endurance, an IT professional needs to do more than calisthenics and eat a balanced diet. An ergonomic workplace is equally as important to the health and well-being of the *subcontractor*.

In an ergonomic work environment, each *subcontractor's* monitor should be positioned centrally to the body at a viewing distance of at least 50 cm, depending on the size of the screen. The top of the screen should be at or slightly below eye level to avoid neck and back strain. Steps should be taken to avoid glare on the screen. See Figure 6-29.

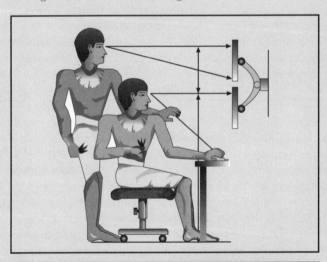

Figure 6-29   *Ergonomics*

(continued)

When using the keyboard, the wrist is often in an unnatural position, namely at an angle with the lower arm. This unfavorable position is often mentioned as a cause of carpal tunnel syndrome. When using keyboards, elbows should be positioned comfortably at a 90-degree angle, with wrists remaining straight.

If an enterprise wants a future, the enterprise must plan for the future in the present. Because an enterprise cannot predict the future, insurance is helpful. However, unlike a traditional insurance policy that has a monetary insurance premium, the enterprise's insurance premium involves time, cost, and effort.

Make a Comment, Make a Point

Good comments strive to tell the reader (a *subcontractor*) *why* the code was written, as opposed to *what* the code is doing. Figure 6-30 illustrates a *what* comment.

```
//Assign the value of 4 to x.
//
x = 4;
```

Figure 6-30   *Comments: Style 1*

Figure 6-31 illustrates the type of mistake a *subcontractor* makes when he is still trying to learn the language's syntax (or writing system).

```
/**
 * Calculates tax.
 * @param amount - a float
 * @param rate - a float
 * @return a float
 */
public float calculateTax( float amount, float rate );
```

Figure 6-31   *Comments: Style 2*

Figure 6-31 added no meaning to the method's usage. What are the expected input values? What are the expected outputs? Examples of usage should be provided too. See Figure 6-32.

```
/*
 * Given an amount of money (significant to two decimal places),
 * and the percentage of tax to apply (known as the rate),
 * the method returns the amount of money that when added to the
 * given amount, yields the original total with taxes included.
 *
 * The amount and rate supplied must be greater than zero. The rate
 * must not exceed one. The method returns a –1 if either amount or
 * rate are invalid.
 *
 * For example:
 * <CODE>
 * float tax = calculateTax( 123.45, 0.07 );
 * </CODE>
 *
 * The value of 'tax' will be 8.64 (7 percent of 123.45)
 *
 * @param amount - the amount of money to calculate taxes
 * @param rate - the percentage of tax to calculate on the given amount
 * @return the cost for tax on the given amount, significant to two decimals
 */

public float calculateTax( float amount, float rate );
```

Figure 6-32   *Comments: Style 3*

Sometimes, poor comments lead to poor applications.

You Have Got to Be Kidding

CompuServe, the Internet Service Provider, has been in business since 1969. In 1998, AOL acquired CompuServe. In 2001, AOL then acquired Time Warner and became the world's largest multimedia company with annual sales exceeding $38 billion.

On July 11, 2002, an e-mail was sent to CompuServe requesting the telephone access numbers for its service in the United Kingdom. See Figure 6-33.

```
----------original message----------
From:  HappyCamper1125@cs.com
To:  ukcssvc@cs.com
Subject: UK access numbers

What are the United Kingdom access numbers for Compuserve? Is  there just
the one: 0845 303028?

Thanks
```

Figure 6-33   *E-mail inquiry*

The reply, shown in Figure 6-34, contains the following statement, "Please note that we do not have access to previous correspondence. Therefore, if replying please help us to help you by including any information relevant to your question."

```
Return-Path: <ukcssvc@cs.com>
Message-ID: 5048333.1026732086600.JavaMail.smapil@smapi1op.office.aol.com>
From: ukcssvc
To: HappyCamper1125
Subject: Re: Uk access numbers
Mime-Version: 1.0
Content-Type: text/plain; charset=utf-8
Content-Transfer-Encoding: 7bit
Date: Mon, 15 Jul 2002 7:21:27 AM Eastern Daylight Time

Thank you for your enquiry.

* Please note that we do not have access to previous correspondence.
Therefore, if replying please help us to help you by including any information
relevant to your question. *

Yes, the CSGlobalnet number 0845 3030208 is the sole access point in the
UK. It is charged at the "local rate" from anywhere in the UK.

If you need any additional help or information, please don't hesitate to
get back to us using the contact details below.

Warm regards,

Roger Chamberlain
CompuServe Technical Support

For CompuServe Support: GO MEMBER or call 0870 6000800
For AOL Tech Support: Keyword: TECHCHAT or call 0800 376 5432
```

Figure 6-34   E-mail response

Do you think the business *owners* and users established the following software requirement for their support center?

To our beloved IT department...We are in need of some software to help support our customers in need. For us to truly help them, our customers, please make sure we cannot track their correspondence. We know the correspondence will contain an e-mail address, and we could possibly use the address as a primary key for the database. You see, each e-mail address uniquely identifies a customer. Oops, sorry, we shouldn't be telling you how to do your job. By the way, if you immediately archive the e-mail after we've read it, we'll forget we ever saw it and we'll never know our customer had a question. Therefore, we can pretend like nothing ever goes wrong. Thanks, we know you won't let us down.

Although the requirements are stated tongue-in-check, why would a premier Internet Service Provider use an application that obviously lacks basic functionality? In all likelihood, the *owners* clearly stated the business requirements. As stated in Section 6.4.3, implementing a database not initially designed by a designer can lead easily and quickly to flawed structures that are difficult and costly to modify—probably the root cause of the problem.

According to Katie Watts, a CompuServe customer service representative, "The database we use isn't able to search through messages that have been sent from everybody, only our own replies."

Do the traits of CompuServe's *subcontractors* include sincerity, courage, patience, alertness, and commitment like the Samurai archer? Did they understand the underlying sciences of software? Were they proficient craftsmen and skilled in their art? Did the *subcontractors* understand the engineering principles of databases, programs, and networks? Alternatively, were they just tired?

The resulting application is limited for a reason. The *owners'* desire for a cumbersome and ineffectual application is probably not one of the reasons.

Learn and Apply

Ronald Davis (b. 1961) is a data strategist for Equifax. Davis believes form is essential in his work. His experiences have shown that simplicity and extensibility are key to achieving desirable long-term results. Davis, an avid amateur golfer, has applied what he once learned in a golfing clinic to his work.

Davis states, "Most golfers are taught to look at the golf ball during a swing. Most everybody has heard the phrase, 'Keep your eye on the ball.'" He remarks that the advice is poor and all golfers should ignore it. "In all the years that I've been golfing, I have yet to see the ball move until I strike it. By relying on the ball to keep its position, I can shift all my attention to my grip, ball position, alignment, and posture."

At work, Davis seeks to gain a comprehensive understanding of the business requirements. After years of practice in how to ask the right questions (*what*, *how*, *where*, *who*, *when*, and *why*), Davis has learned to view requirements as a golf ball, and now views the requirements as having stability. Having stabilized the requirements, Davis can shift all his attention to people, innovation, growth, and technology.

Davis further discussed the golf clinic he attended. He had to learn to swing the club very slowly. In fact, he now takes as long as 23 minutes to complete a swing. The slow swing allows him to feel his muscles in every position of the swing. His nervous system memorizes the feel, and he is now able to consistently hit the ball over 250 yards in a straight line blindfolded. Davis applies this lesson to business data, which he views as the backbone or skeleton of Equifax's operation. According to Davis, "In the same way the human skeleton supports the weight and all movements of the body, Equifax's data has to support all processes, rules, and products of the enterprise."

He further explains, "Ronald Ross developed a human body analogy to data, process, and rules in his book, *Business Rules Concepts*. The muscles perform the processes, but require the nervous system to send the appropriate messages by reacting to rules at the right time, and to the right muscle to achieve the right process."

In his job as a data strategist, Davis is concerned about more than just data:

> *I have to make sure the developers can get data in and out of the database. I have to work with the hardware and network people to make sure we can appropriately distribute our data and have the appropriate bandwidth to support our product line. I need to work with our programming staff to make sure they develop the appropriate security needs. I also need to make sure the programming staff creates the appropriate user interfaces and*

make sure the data is going to be interpreted by our customers appropriately. I also need to understand the timing of everything that happens in the application and what causes each event to transpire. Finally, I need to make sure the business strategies and tactics are supported by the business rules and that we are achieving the results our CEO needs.

DATA STRATEGIST TURNED SYSTEMS THINKER

Ronald Davis' job title is data strategist. However, his job responsibilities cause him to work across all the disciplines in the enterprise.

What—data and database
How—getting data in and getting data out
Where—hardware, network, bandwidth, and distribution (topology)
Who—security and user interfaces
When—timing and event
Why—strategies, tactics, and business rules

In his golf game, Davis learned to accept his limits and set aside his ego. He knows he can hit the ball 250 yards. However, if a pond lies 250 yards in front of him, he now elects to hit the ball short instead of trying to hit the ball 280 yards and over the pond. In IT, Davis has learned that taking controlled incremental steps is best, instead of allowing his ego to strive for more than is possible. "In golf, I'm finishing most holes at par. At work, my applications are coming in at par too."

Trying to always hit the ball as far as you can is how Davis sees many IT professionals. "Golf and information technology are mental games—not physical. I have a certain amount of time, money, and resources to complete a project. I view coming in on time, on budget, and meeting the expectations of my users as hitting par. I have spent countless hours learning how to hit the ball on the sweet spot [of the golf club's head]. I have worked hard to find the sweet spot in delivering IT systems. I have developed my form by asking good questions, learning the business rules, keeping things simple, accepting change as a normal part of business, thinking holistically, learning new algorithms, keeping one eye on the future, and listening to others."

Davis is more excited than ever about his IT career. With regard to the challenges and changes that will occur in business and IT over the coming years, Davis just says, "Bring it on."

To meet these future challenges and changes in business and IT, the *subcontractor* must have a roadmap, even though there may not be any roads. Change is inevitable, but also unpredictable.

Dog-Day Afternoon

In 1971, Mr. Haim Beckman was the headmaster of Rosh Pinah Primary School in Edgware, England. One morning, Beckman informed an assembly of impressionable students between the ages of seven and eleven that by the time they graduated from college, there would probably be just two jobs left in the world. One of the two positions would be filled by a man. The other position would be filled by a dog. The man would be employed to feed the dog, and the dog would be employed to stop the man from touching any of the computers. See Figure 6-35.

Figure 6-35 *Back away slowly and refill my bowl, please*

One day, computers might be able to program other computers for all the needs of an enterprise. Until such a time, the *subcontractor* is going to be an integral part of every enterprise—fabricating and assembling the final products or services.

For the enterprise to get the most value from IT systems in the future, integration, flexibility, adaptability, and creativity are required. In a customer-centered world, the *subcontractor* must enable the enterprise to move and use data from any point in the value chain at any time.

The *subcontractor* must craft the infrastructure to access disparate data sources and then create the structure to distribute meaningful information. All applications must work together and share information easily and efficiently. This integration requires technological innovation derived from the *subcontractor's* expertise in the art, craft, science, and engineering of computer systems.

Norman Augustine, former chairman and CEO of Lockheed Martin, once stated, "In truth, we are on a journey with no final destination and no resting points."

6.9 CHAPTER ACTIVITIES

6.9.1 Discussion Topics

1. How can moving from one career path to the IT team of an organization be advantageous to an individual and the organization?
2. How can studying employment advertisements in trade journals, newspapers, or on the Internet be advantageous to you?
3. Brainstorm together and list the reasons an employer might provide or pay for training and education for IT employees.
4. Explain why an IT worker needs to be a career-long learner.
5. How does the *subcontractor* benefit from the OSI model?
6. Discuss why the *subcontractor* would choose one type of firewall over another. List some items the *subcontractor* should consider before choosing a firewall.
7. What are examples of questions the *subcontractor* needs to ask to construct an efficient and secure network for the people who use it?
8. Explain why writing systems are important to the *subcontractor*.
9. How does the fact that change and technology are inextricably tied affect the role of the *subcontractor*?
10. Discuss why a data center or an organization should be thought of as a living, breathing, changing creation.
11. Discuss different triggers that might affect a *subcontractor's* decisions.
12. Explain the implications of the phrase, "Faster and faster chips, slower and slower software."
13. Give examples and explain the importance of following artistic design principles when writing software.
14. Explain the philosophy of software development when using Extreme Programming (XP).
15. How are patterns used in software?
16. Explain the meaning of the statement, "The broader the *subcontractor's* knowledge, the larger and more versatile the artist's palette becomes."
17. What is the effect on the *subcontractor* when the database structure needs to be changed?
18. Explain how the Long Now Foundation is helping organizations redefine thinking processes through the clock project.
19. Discuss how and why refactoring can raise the quality of work in the enterprise over time.
20. When long-term thinking is secondary to a speedy implementation of a release, how is the *subcontractor* affected? How is the enterprise affected?
21. Compare the three ways that business changes are implemented in an IT project.
22. Discuss what impact defensive development can have on the *subcontractor* and, ultimately, on the enterprise.
23. Why should business rules be separated from business processes?
24. How does form affect a program?
25. How does a rule book benefit the enterprise?
26. When the *owner* does not make business rules explicit, what happens?
27. What is the purpose of a service level agreement?
28. How are databases an asset to the enterprise?
29. Discuss why Ronald Davis, the data strategist, finds stabilizing business requirements helpful in his work.

6.9.2 Critical Thinking

1. Government mandates can greatly affect industries and employment opportunities. Choose one of the mandates previously mentioned in the text, or another of your choice. What effect did the mandate have on a particular industry? Was the effect positive or negative for IT positions? Why? What effect did the mandate have on a specific organization? Why? Share your findings in an electronic presentation with the class.

2. Choose any job title that interests you in the IT industry. Using a newspaper, a trade journal, or the Internet, research the education requirements, experience requirements, personal characteristics, and job responsibilities for that particular job title. In a table, document the information you gathered from three different sources. Provide handouts for the class and give a verbal presentation of what you learned. Identify any descriptions that require an IT Superwoman or an IT Superman.

3. Organizations need to respond quickly to major threats, such as environmental disasters, organizational shortcomings, deliberate attacks, and technical failures. Using trade journals or the Internet, research how a major organization responded to a major threat. In a two to three-page paper, summarize the incident and describe why you believe the organization acted appropriately, indicating if there are other steps you believe might have been appropriate.

4. Using the Internet, research two types of Web sites discussed in this chapter. Compare and contrast security challenges the *subcontractor* would have with these two Web sites. Be prepared to share your information with the class.

5. Using available resources, illustrate how design principles applied to the Clock of the Long Now relate to enterprise products or services. Write a one to two-page paper to share your thoughts.

6. Research and document two antipatterns not listed in this book. Write why each antipattern is considered an antipattern, and discuss why *subcontractors* would benefit from learning to recognize and cope with each of these antipatterns.

7. Visit the human resources department of a local business and using the six interrogatives, discover what the organization's philosophy is regarding employees working anywhere. How does the organization's philosophy affect the *subcontractor*? Determine what impact the philosophy has on teams that depend on highly collaborative work. Present your findings in an electronic presentation, a two to three-page paper, or in a class discussion.

8. A software program is refactored to enhance its readability and structure. Why do some programmers write sloppy code? Should programmers be artists, craftsmen, or engineers? Should there be a minimum qualification level for programming? Who in an enterprise should be responsible to measure the artistic aesthetics of a program? Answer these questions in discussion groups.

Endnotes

[1]The Ironman competition is a triathlon event consisting of a 5-mile swim, a 100-mile bicycle race, and a 26.2-mile footrace. Many athletes who pass the finishing line do so in less than 9 hours.

[2]Ultra-marathons are footraces, typically ranging from 100 to 200 miles in distance. A 200-mile race can take athletes 18 hours to complete. That averages to 5 minutes and 30 seconds per mile. The world's longest certified footrace is the Sri Chinmoy 3,100-mile race. The race has a 51-day cutoff and the winner usually finishes in under 49 days.

[3] Gilder, George. *Telecosm: The World After Bandwidth Abundance*. New York, NY: Touchstone Books, 2002.

[4] ASCII is an acronym for American Standard Code for Information Interchange. ASCII was developed by the American National Standards Institute between 1963 and 1968. ASCII was established to achieve compatibility between various types of data processing equipment.

[5] Some character sets like Japanese Kanji require 16 bits and two bytes to represent one character.

[6] In the book *The Hitch Hikers Guide to the Galaxy* by Douglas Adams, Slartibartfast is introduced as the designer and creator of the Norwegian Fjords. Slartibartfast helps the main character, Arthur, stumble across the true meaning of Life, the Universe, and Everything, including the importance of mice and the origins of Earth and its successor.

[7] Class, Responsibilities, and Collaboration cards help identify objects in a system.

[8] Gamma, Erich, and Richard Helm, Ralph Johnson, and John Vlissides. *Design Patterns*. Reading, MA: Addison-Wesley, 1995.

[9] Design patterns for software provide an effective form for software creation. Proponents of software patterns have helped codify a concise terminology for conveying sophisticated computer science thinking.

[10] Black box denotes that the actual method of processing is unknown. White box is the opposite and denotes a method of processing that is known.

[11] Business Rules Group. *Defining Business Rules—What Are They Really?* July, 2000.

[12] Legacy systems and legacy data can refer to applications and data existing on a given platform like a mainframe; age of the application, such as two years old; or the programming language or database system used—for example, a system written in COBOL, or using Microsoft Access version 1.0.

[13] Oliver North used an IBM e-mail program called PROFS. Even though North deleted the electronically stored messages and shredded the printed copies of his incriminating messages, he had not realized they were stored on a backup copy. The backup copies were restored and made available to the courts.

[14] *Failure Isn't an Option for Power Supplies*. Information Week. May 27, 2002.

[15] When a Web site experiences a surge of data transmission packets across the network, the Web site is said to be *bursty*. For example, when a transmission protocol such as TCP attempts to address the sudden demand of a bursting connection, congestion and retransmission may occur. Large multimedia files are considered bursty since they often move large amounts of data across the network to satisfy a download request.

[16] The last part of the sentence should be read trying to imitate Rod Serling (1924–1975).

[17] Uniting and Strengthening America by Providing Appropriate Tools Required to Intercept and Obstruct Terrorism (USA PATRIOT) Act of 2001.

[18] Chabrow, Eric. *Never Mind the Title—Get On With the Work*. Information Week. April 15, 2002.

[19] Khirallah, Diane. *The Tug of More*. InformationWeek. April 8, 2002.

[20] Goffe, Leslie. *IT's Future Is In Good Hands*. Computerworld. May 21, 2001.

[21] Foote, David. *As 2002 Dawns, Job Market Has Some Bright Signs*. Computerworld. January 7, 2002.

[22] Weisenger, Hendrie. *The Power of Positive Criticism*. New York, NY: Amacom, 1999.

[23] Enron collapsed into bankruptcy amid an investigation surrounding off-the-book partnerships used to hide debt and inflate profits. WorldCom hid $3.85 billion in expenses, allowing WorldCom to post net income of $1.38 billion in 2001, instead of a loss. Merrill Lynch paid $100 million to settle a probe by the attorney general of New York State because it tailored stock research to win investment banking business. Andersen was found guilty in federal court for obstructing justice in the government's investigation of Enron. Computer Associates paid $638,000 in penalty charges to settle charges with the U.S. Justice Department that it violated pre-merger rules after announcing it would acquire Platinum Technology Incorporated.

435

What WHERE WHO HOW WHEN Why

THE ZACHMAN FRAMEWORK FOR ENTERPRISE ARCHITECTURE

"Put it before them briefly so they will read it, clearly so they will appreciate it...and, above all, accurately so they will be guided by its light."

— *Joseph Pulitzer (1847–1911), Journalist and newspaper publisher*

LEARNING OBJECTIVES

After completing Chapter 7, you will be able to:

1. Explain the difference between a conceptual view and a contextual view of the enterprise.
2. Describe the viewpoints of the *planner*, the *owner*, the *designer*, the *builder*, the *subcontractor*, and the *functioning enterprise*.
3. Categorize the perspectives and explain the significance of each category.
4. Compare a primitive model to a composite model.
5. Explain how the Framework helps simplify the complexity in an enterprise.
6. Discuss why reuse is important to the enterprise and how the Framework can facilitate reuse.
7. Explain the importance of understanding the difference between architecting the enterprise and designing an implementation.
8. Discuss how the characteristics of the Framework make this tool useful to the enterprise.
9. Explain why the values, principles, and practices of the Framework expedite reduced time to market for new products or services.
10. Discuss how enterprise boundaries affect integration, interoperability, and reusability.
11. Describe why placement on the Framework for an activity you may perform does not depend on your job title.
12. Describe the importance of senior management being knowledgeable about some technologies.
13. Explain how vertical and horizontal integration sometimes add constraints and force de-optimization of an original design.
14. Explain the concept of a sliver in the Framework.
15. Use the terminology of the Framework to describe the Framework's major concepts.

(continued)

16. Discuss how the laws and rules of the Framework can assist practitioners in applying the Framework to an enterprise.

17. Explain how transformation in the Framework can help you develop a comprehensive understanding of a subject.

18. Explain how flexibility of the Framework allows the enterprise to benefit from the classification schema, no matter which method of practice the organization follows.

19. Understand that the primitive model or artifact produced is a result of the information at hand and personal biases.

20. Understand that enterprise architecture is a business issue, not a technical issue.

21. Explain why establishing a level of importance of the perspectives is important to the practitioner of the Framework.

22. Discuss how the Framework is conducive to thinking, reasoning, and communicating about the complex issues of the enterprise.

23. Explain how the Framework can help design a *functioning enterprise* if the Framework does not mandate producing design artifacts.

24. Understand how information persistence assists project teams in collaboration.

25. Understand why the Framework is neutral to methodology and technology.

26. Discuss why the Framework does not have a fixed starting point for any enterprise architecture activity.

7.1 INTRODUCTION

The *planner, owner, designer, builder,* and *subcontractor*—these five perspectives can be used to create and modify anything. Whether you choose to offer a service, build and sell a product, receive an education, or readjust the purpose of your life, these five perspectives are holistic and ubiquitous. So far, each chapter in Part II has addressed one of these perspectives. Chapter 7 covers the final perspective: the *functioning enterprise.*

Once something is created, it becomes ready for use. The physical creation is the final product—the materialization or realization of what you want. The perspective of this final product is called the *functioning enterprise.* To describe the *functioning enterprise,* this chapter explains the Zachman Framework for Enterprise Architecture, which is the materialization and realization (the actual product) of this textbook.

In the first five chapters of Part II, the first five perspectives of the Framework were explained without explicit reference to the Framework. Each chapter discussed major purposes and issues related to one of the perspectives. Each perspective was examined with specific aspects: the *what, how, where, who, when,* and *why* divisions of each section. By reading the first five chapters of Part II, you have already explored the major components of the Framework.

One advantage of demonstrating the Framework without discussing it directly is that you can see how work can proceed in an enterprise without everyone understanding how all the pieces fit together. Another advantage of using this method is that you can see how *natural* the Framework is. You have always used the Framework or parts of it, though you probably did not call it the Zachman Framework.

There are advantages to some people knowing how everything relates and fits together, including every intricacy of the enterprise. Realistically, not everybody needs to have a holistic view of the enterprise, especially in large organizations. Many people specialize in their careers. Because specialists often focus within an area of interest, their participation in an enterprise is confined to that area. Whether a person's participation in the enterprise is broad or narrow, the Framework can help everyone think, reason, and communicate about an issue. The Framework is heuristic.

This chapter is about the Framework, a *functioning enterprise*. A *functioning enterprise* could also be a computer application, delivering mail, attending a class, participating in a marriage ceremony, or undergoing heart surgery. In general, the *functioning enterprise* is anything that first requires answers to these questions:

- *What* do I need?
- *How* am I going to do this?
- *Where* will I do this?
- *Who* will help me do this?
- *When* should I do this?
- *Why* do I want to do this and how will I know when I have succeeded?

7.1.1 A Classification Schema

Figure 7-1 shows the Zachman Framework for Enterprise Architecture. The Framework is a two-dimensional classification schema that describes an enterprise. The Framework contains six rows and six columns. At the intersection of each row and column is a cell. Each cell represents a fundamental piece of knowledge relative to the row and column and is known as a primitive.

Having complete knowledge of each primitive is relative to understanding the *functioning enterprise*. What you can create, you can understand. A comprehensive knowledge base (knowledge of all the primitives) helps you determine whether the *functioning enterprise* is working appropriately. An appropriately *functioning enterprise* is one that is aligned, flexible, integrated, and responsive. These concepts are explained in this chapter.

	Data *What*	Process *How*	Network *Where*
Scope (contextual) *Planner*	List of things important to the business Entity = class of business thing	List of processes the business performs Process = class of business processes	List of locations in which the business operates Node = major business locations
Business model (conceptual) *Owner*	e.g., Semantic model Entity = business entity Relationship = business relationship	e.g., Business process model Process = business process I/O = business product/service	e.g., Logistics network Node = business unit group Link = business connection
System model (logical) *Designer*	e.g., Logical data model Entity = data entity/object Relationship = data relationship	e.g., Application architecture Process = application system I/O = user views	e.g., Distributed system architecture Node = IT function (process, storage, etc.) Link = Line characteristics
Technology model (physical) *Builder*	e.g., Physical data model Entity = segment, row, record Relationship = pointer/ key/etc.	e.g., System design Process = computer process I/O = screen/device formats	e.g., Configuration design Node = hardware/system software Link = line specifications
Detailed representations (out-of-context) *Subcontractor*	e.g., Data definition Entity = field, data types Relationship = address, access methods	e.g., Program Process = language statements I/O = control block	e.g., Network architecture Node = address Link = protocols
Functioning enterprise	e.g., Data	e.g., Process	e.g., Network

Figure 7-1 *The Zachman Framework for Enterprise Architecture*

7.1.2 Black Holes

A black hole is a region of spacetime where the pull of gravity is so strong, nothing can escape, not even light. In 1783, Cambridge University don Reverend John Mitchell (1724–1793) presented the first discussion on black holes. Mitchell's work was based on Newtonian physics, which stated time was absolute and continues no matter what.

Role *Who*	Timing *When*	Motivation *Why*	
List of business responsibilities	List of events significant to the business	List of business goals/strategy	Scope (contextual)
Responsibility = major organizations	Time = major business event	Ends = mission/goals	*Planner*
e.g., Work flow model	e.g., Master schedule	e.g., Business plan	Business model (conceptual)
Responsibility = work unit /structure Work = business resources	Time = business event Cycle = business cycle	Ends = goals Means = tactics/plans	*Owner*
e.g, Human interface architecture	e.g., Processing structure	e.g., Business rule model	System model (logical)
Responsibility = system privilege Work = access requirements	Time = system event Cycle = precedence/timing	End = structural assertion Means = action assertion	*Designer*
e.g., Presentation architecture	e.g., Control structure	e.g., Rule design	Technology model (physical)
Responsibility = access authorizations Work = access group	Time = execute Cycle = processing calendar	End = condition Means = action	*Builder*
Security architecture	e.g., Timing definition	e.g., Rule specification	Detailed representations (out-of-context)
Responsibility = access object Work = access profiles	Time = interrupt Cycle = job schedules	End = subcondition Means = step	*Subcontractor*
e.g., Organization	e.g., Schedule	e.g., Strategy	Functioning enterprise

Scientists started to grapple and speculate about black holes. In 1916, German astronomer Karl Schwarzchild (1873–1916) found a solution to Einstein's theory of relativity that represented a spherical black hole. Surprisingly, Einstein never believed in black holes.

Even today, everything that happens inside or on the other side of a black hole is based on theory, speculation, and imagination. Because light cannot escape, astronomers have a difficult time seeing what is going on inside the blackness. Regardless of what is inside the black hole, astronomers can observe the black hole's presence. Black holes exist, but beyond that, nothing is known for sure.

When you see the Framework's 36 cells, you might wonder what happens inside each cell. At first glance, some cells may seem unnecessary, or not as important as other cells. However, in the same way science can predict the presence of something like a black hole, the science of the Framework dictates the presence of each cell. Each cell exists even if you do not know what is inside the cell.

The more you work with the Framework, the more impressive its logic becomes in helping you understand areas that are not known or well understood. In business, not knowing something can introduce risk. Realizing that you do not know something can help you mitigate risk. To mitigate risk, you can try to discover what you do not know currently. You can then record what you know now—for all to share.

Peter Senge, author of the *Fifth Discipline*, often refers to mental models, which are images, assumptions, generalizations, and stories that people have in their minds. If two people have different mental models, they can observe the same situation and then describe it differently. The discipline of mental models brings these mental models to the surface so that people can talk openly about their viewpoints.

To share a mental model adequately, the model should be made explicit. The Framework provides a classification schema to organize what needs to be communicated. Anything made explicit becomes an asset to the enterprise and part of its knowledge base. You can share and reuse explicit knowledge. The knowledge an enterprise needs to share can range from the simple and mundane to the highly complex and sophisticated.

7.1.3 The Argument for Enterprise Architecture

You can use the Framework to organize simple pieces of information. However, because most issues and actions in an organization today are highly complex, the benefits of using the Framework might best be realized when tackling a complex issue. Complex issues require architecture. Each of the following arguments discusses the need for enterprise architecture.

Argument One

Since the dawn of civilization, human history has established that the key to managing complexity and change is architecture. If what you want to build becomes so complex that you cannot remember everything at the same time, you have to write it down. Recording information is the basis of performing architecture.

When you want to change what you have built, you start by reviewing what you wrote down. Documentation is the baseline for managing change. In the information age, you create an enterprise architecture because organizations are becoming increasingly complex and demand change constantly.

Argument Two

The Framework is a normalized classification schema. This means one fact or concept appears in one place. Having one fact in one place makes the Framework a good analytical tool. If rows or columns were added or changed, the Framework would become denormalized and cease to be a good analytical tool. The Framework provides a semantic structure that does not imply anything about the methodologies, techniques, or tools used to record the architecture.

Approaches to recording the architecture can start at the *planner* row and work downward through the Framework's perspectives. This type of technique is known as **forward engineering**. Another approach is to start with the *functioning enterprise* row and work upward through the Framework's perspectives. This type of technique is known as **reverse engineering**.

Alternatively, you could start at the *designer* row and work in both directions at the same time. The method of practice relative to the domain of the *functioning enterprise* can be used to establish the rules of use—which perspectives to use, which aspects to use, and in which directions to work.

Argument Three

You can use the Framework to help you think, reason, and communicate about anything—an entire enterprise, or just a portion of the enterprise. An enterprise is a domain. The enterprise domain includes every area of interest to the enterprise and can be partitioned into smaller specific areas of interest.

The broader the enterprise domain is defined, the greater the benefits the organization can expect to receive relative to integration, reusability, and interoperability of the *functioning enterprise*. However, the broader the enterprise domain, the more complex the analysis is likely to become.

Conversely, the narrower the boundary around the enterprise domain, the simpler the analysis becomes. However, the organization's advantage relative to integration, reusability, and interoperability can be diminished.

If the enterprise domain boundary is drawn beyond the control of the organization, not everything that you think, reason, or communicate about can be changed. For example, you cannot change federal law. Even if you cannot control everything directly, you can seek to understand everything.

If the boundary for the enterprise domain is drawn more narrowly than the organization's control, the organization may disintegrate the enterprise. A disintegrated enterprise can only build legacy products and services, which are those that cannot be readily integrated or reused with the enterprise as a whole—even when the product is new.

Argument Four

Definitions are important to architecture. If the *functioning enterprise* needs to save data or information, the enterprise must be aware of the contextual meaning of this data or information. Saving something means that it persists. Data for a computer application often persists in a database. Stories often persist in books or electronic media.

For example, if a computer manufacturer uses a database to store information about its products, the amount of memory in a particular product might be stored in a database field called *MEMORY_SIZE*. Additionally, the manufacturer might store the computer chip's speed in a database field called *CHIP_SPEED*.

In 1985, the manufacturer may have stored the memory size in kilobytes, such as 640. The knowledge that the unit of measure was in kilobytes was external to the number stored. The knowledge worker was left to infer that 640 meant 640 kilobytes. In 2003, the same manufacturer using the same database field might store 384. Again, the manufacturer now depends on each knowledge worker to interpret the unit of measure as a megabyte.

If you were asked to analyze the type of products built by the manufacturer, you might decide to use the company's database. In reviewing the memory sizes of the various products stored in the database, you would have no way of knowing when the meaning of the database field changed. In this example, the implied definition changed from kilobytes to megabytes. Tomorrow, the manufacturer may change the definition again to gigabytes.

A more drastic type of meaning change may have occurred with the chip speed field. In 1985, the manufacturer may have stored the speed in terms of MIPS (millions of instructions per second). Today, the manufacturer may store the chip's speed based on the megahertz unit of measure.

Analyzing things that seem to have clear and consistent meanings can produce anomalies and errors. Architecture can help avoid scrapping what you have and starting again. When modifying a building, you must be careful not to disturb a load-bearing wall. Incorrectly affecting a load-bearing wall can cause an entire structure to crumble and fall. Databases have elements that are load bearing too. Altering the meaning of these elements can cause an entire application to crumble and fail.

Argument Five

The Framework does not mandate that each artifact must be produced at a sufficient level of detail before the *functioning enterprise* starts to operate. However, remember that anything not made explicit is implicit. Everything that is implicit is an assumption. Assumptions imply that you are willing to accept the risk that all or part of the work must be scrapped and restarted.

Argument Six

When artifacts are not produced from an enterprise perspective, the organization is inhibited in its ability to share and be consistent with information, processes, networks, workflows, schedules, and rules. Disintegration is one cause of management frustration.

Argument Seven

If you do not observe the engineering design principles related to the cell's artifacts, you will not realize the engineering design objectives of alignment, integration, flexibility, interoperability, reduced time to market, quality, seamlessness, adaptability, user-friendliness, usability, and reusability.

Argument Eight

If the enterprise cannot find, share, and reuse a cell's artifacts, it can only operate in a made-to-order mode. An organization cannot appreciably reduce its product or service time-to-market until it can reuse things out of its inventory. The goal is for each organization to create products and services based on *mass customization* of one. In other words, the organization operates using an assembled-to-order paradigm.

Argument Nine

If you are not building, storing, managing, and changing primitive models, you are not creating architecture. You are creating implementations. The idea is to create an implementation based entirely on primitive models so that each implementation can be built readily and changed later. Then every implementation can continue to support each of the engineering design objectives mentioned in Argument Seven.

Argument Ten

Statistics gathered by the Zachman Institute for Framework Advancement indicate that developing software by taking an approach based on enterprise architecture instead of a traditional approach toward computer software produces *functioning enterprises* ten times cheaper and six times faster. Enterprise architecture is based on the idea that something should be engineered before it is manufactured and implemented.

Argument Eleven

Enterprise architecture enables senior business managers to use business controls for corporate governance and accountability throughout every facet of the enterprise. Business controls are not just needed for the operations of the enterprise, but also for the plan, design, and construction of the enterprise.

7.1.4 The Game

If you are conferring with someone about the Zachman Framework and something is said that is inconsistent with any of the 11 arguments, then one of you does not understand either the logic of the Framework or the implications of that logic.

Like backgammon and Chinese Go, you can start using the Framework in a short period of time, but the strategies can take a long time to develop. The Framework provides a holistic view of any situation and can help simplify complexity in order to achieve success. However, each complex situation may require its own set of strategies. Like most things in life, as your experience grows, so does your level of understanding. The Framework is no exception.

SECTION 7.2 WHEN YOU WANT CLARITY

> **QUESTIONS TO CONTEMPLATE**
>
> 1. What is the significance of the rows and columns of the Framework?
> 2. What are the values, principles, and practices associated with the Framework?
> 3. How can an infinite amount of composite artifacts be produced from a fixed set of primitive artifacts?

7.2.1 Introduction

The Zachman Framework for Enterprise Architecture is a classification schema for organizing descriptive representations (artifacts) of an enterprise. Recall that artifacts may include models, pictures, diagrams, or textual documents. Although every artifact an enterprise produces can be organized into the Framework's classification schema, every artifact is not significant or valuable to an enterprise. Using the Framework involves distinguishing artifacts of value from artifacts of noise.

An artifact of noise yields little or no value and may often distract attention from the enterprise's core issues and problems. For example, if your core business is producing aircraft and you need to model the scheduling of parts for delivery, modeling the schedule for when the vending machine should be refilled is probably an artifact of noise to the central purpose of the business. Artifacts of value help to manage the enterprise and make it real and operable. For example, a model of when parts need to be delivered for producing an aircraft is an artifact of value.

The holistic view of the Framework can help you determine the worth of an artifact. An artifact of value should help promote thinking, reasoning, and communicating about the topics of interest within the enterprise. If the artifact is not contributing to this cause, it is probably not significant to the enterprise.

The primary structure of the Framework is a matrix with rows and columns, but the organization of the Framework itself is a logical structure, formed from the six interrogatives of the English language and six primary perspectives identified in disciplines requiring thought and action.

Chapter 6 discussed the concepts of normalizing data, which removes redundancy in a design by making sure each data element is described and used in only one place. Normalization is not exclusive to data. In the object-oriented paradigm, objects can be normalized too.

In object orientation, behavior can be described and used in only one place. The Framework's logical structure is also a normalized structure. The six perspectives and the six aspects provide a classification schema to ensure each fact about an enterprise is described and used in only one place.

Abiding by the Framework's normalization, you can focus on discrete elements of a problem without losing context. The Framework's classification schema helps divide the enormous amount of knowledge in an enterprise into manageable and logical chunks.

A HERCULEAN EFFORT

In Greek mythology, the hero Hercules was a son of Zeus. Unfortunately, Hera, his stepmother, was less than thrilled when she found out he was Zeus' son. Hera put a curse on Hercules, which caused him to kill his wife and children. For this crime, Hercules was required to serve his cousin, Eurystheus, in ten labors.

For the second labor, Hercules was demanded to kill the Lernean Hydra. The hydra was a monstrous serpent with nine heads and lived in the murky waters and swamps near a place called Lerna. Over the years, the hydra had established a nasty habit of terrorizing the countryside by attacking people with poisonous venom.

(continued)

The monster was not easy prey. One of his nine heads was immortal and therefore the monster was technically indestructible. However, as with most endeavors, things thought to be indestructible are proven otherwise by some other unforeseen technicality. With his trusty nephew, Iolaus, Hercules set off to hunt and destroy the nine-headed menace. By the springs of Amymone, they discovered the lair of the loathsome hydra.

By shooting flaming arrows, Hercules was able to lure the monster from the safety of its den and seize it. However, the monster was not so easily overcome. The hydra wound one of its coils around Hercules' foot and made escape impossible for the hero. Hercules attacked the many heads of the hydra with his club, but as soon as he smashed one head, two more would burst forth in its place.

Fortunately, for Hercules, his nephew quickly surmised that holding a lit torch to the tendons of a headless neck prevented the hydra's growth of replacement heads. Soon the pair gained the upper hand on the beast and destroyed all the mortal heads. The immortal head was then chopped off (the technicality) and buried at the side of the road leading from Lerna to Elaeus.

Just in case of any *uh-ohs*, Hercules covered the buried head with a heavy rock. As for the rest of the decapitated hydra, Hercules slit open the corpse and dipped his arrows in the venomous blood. Hercules declared victory and moved on to the next *project*, the Hind of Ceryneia.

447

Most people are not trained to resolve problems or think about issues in a normalized manner. As a result, solving one problem often leads to another problem. In a similar vein to the myth of Hercules and the Lernean Hydra, when Hercules solved one problem, two more cropped up. Mapping out the enterprise in a normalized manner and in accordance with the Framework's logic helps to control nasty ripple effects.

In the mid-1980s, AT&T Consumer Products, a former division of AT&T, developed a series of new applications. AT&T Consumer Products managed and distributed leased telephones and needed the applications because of the divestiture of the national telephone company in 1983. The programs and database they developed were designed for one purpose—to provide a monthly bill for customers.

Solving the problem of monthly bills, however, created a more serious problem for others in the enterprise. Because the AT&T application was designed only to produce bills, it deleted customer records when that customer stopped leasing a telephone. The deletions helped keep the database a manageable size, but the marketing and sales group had no way to try to win back the lost customers—the data was gone. The *designers* did not understand that a solution in one area could cause a problem in another area.

7.2.2 Presentation *(when)*

The Framework is a hieroglyphic, which is a picture or symbol that represents words and ideas. Similar to the hieroglyphics used by the Ancient Egyptians and Mayans of Central America, you can decipher the Framework's hieroglyphics to tell a story. The story is one of ubiquity and completeness.

Unlike other architectural frameworks, such as the U.S. Department of Defense's C4ISR, the International Standards Organization's RM-ODP, and the IEEE's P1471, which are aimed at computer-based and information technology systems, the Zachman Framework is intended to be generic based on its structural logic.

The Framework tells a story of completeness because its six perspectives and six aspects form a holistic representation of the enterprise. See Figure 7-2.

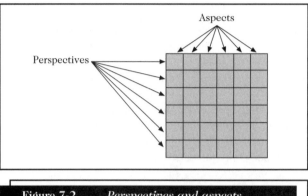

Figure 7-2   *Perspectives and aspects*

Like a good software pattern, each cell has a descriptive template. Each cell in the Framework is illustrated with a sample icon, an appropriate primitive model description, and a primitive component. Figure 7-3 shows a sample icon.

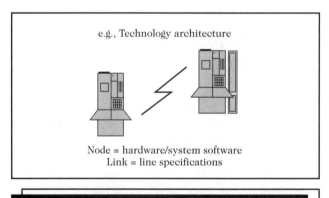

e.g., Technology architecture

Node = hardware/system software
Link = line specifications

Figure 7-3   *A single Framework cell*

Each cell is the intersection of a perspective and an aspect—the rows and columns of the Framework. The Framework hieroglyphic implies that if knowledge from each cell is made explicit, the *functioning enterprise* will be:

- Operational
- Aligned to each part of the enterprise
- Flexible
- Adaptable
- Able to embrace change

7.2.3 Perspectives *(who)*

Recall that the two-dimensional classification schema's axes are known as perspectives and aspects. Whereas the perspectives represent viewpoints into the classification schema, the aspects represent subject areas.

The Framework's perspectives are the *planner, owner, designer, builder, subcontractor,* and *functioning enterprise.* The process of recording architecture began over 4,500 years ago with the Ancient Egyptians. Since that time, the six perspectives represented in the Framework have provided a comprehensive set of viewpoints for an enterprise.

The perspectives are independent of geography, culture, language, politics, and technology. From the time of the pyramid builders in Egypt to the house builders of Levittown; from the exit of the Dark Ages in Europe to Boeing's digitally designed 777 aircraft; from the Italian Renaissance to the landing on the moon; and from the Manhattan Project that brought closure to World War II to the omnibus-like travel into outer space and the international space station, each of the six perspectives are common—identifiable, verifiable, and ratifiable.

Each of the six perspectives can be categorized as:

- Principal
- Empirical
- Certifiable

Enterprise architecture is about applying a discipline of design prior to constructing something. Rows 2, 3, and 4 represent the major design perspectives of the Framework. That is why they are categorized as principal. Row 5 is empirical because we know we want to build what we design. Row 1 is also empirical because we know we should plan and establish scope prior to undertaking a design. Row 6 is certifiable because this is the actual enterprise in action and should be guaranteed to work in the way that the *planner, owner, designer, builder,* and *subcontractor* envisioned.

The principal perspectives of the Framework are the *owner, designer,* and *builder* because these are primary perspectives of architectural design. Each perspective is contextual in that the problem area is viewed as a whole. For example, if you want to want to run a restaurant, then your problem area may consist of the type of restaurant, the menu, the acquisition and preparation of food, handling receipts, payroll, and so on. Needing to view the entire problem area holistically is a trait of the principal perspectives.

- The *owner's* perspective is identified as Row 2 of the Framework. See Figure 7-4. The *owner* is often the intended recipient of the final product or service. The artifacts produced for (or by) the *owner* represent the desirable characteristics of the product or service. The artifacts show what the *owner* is going to do with the product or service once it's in possession. The *owner's* perspective is a conceptual view of the final product or service.

449

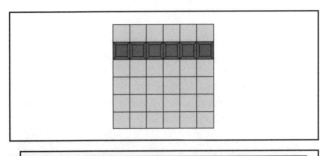

Figure 7-4   *Row 2 — The Owner*

- The *designer's* perspective is identified by Row 3 of the Framework. See Figure 7-5. The *designer* is the engineer or architect of the final product or service. The *designer* is the intermediary between what the *owner* wants and what is physically and technically possible for the *builder*. The artifacts produced by the *designer* represent the laws of nature, the system, or the logical constraints of the product's or service's design. The *designer's* perspective is a logical view of the final product or service.

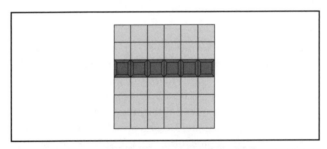

Figure 7-5   *Row 3 — The Designer*

- The *builder's* perspective is identified by Row 4 of the Framework. See Figure 7-6. The *builder* is the manufacturing engineer or general contractor of the final product or service. The *builder* applies the physical constraints of what is possible to the *designer's* artifacts and understands the implementation environment, including how the product can be built and used. The *builder's* perspective is a physical view of the final product or service.

The empirical perspectives are the *planner* and the *subcontractor*. The *planner's* perspective, like the *owner*, *designer*, and *builder*, is contextual regarding the problem area. The *subcontractor's* view, however, is regarded as out of context. The out-of-context artifacts depict the product disassembled into parts, so that the product or service can be manufactured piece by piece and then assembled into the final product.

- The *planner's* perspective is identified by Row 1 of the Framework. See Figure 7-7. The *planner* establishes the context for the enterprise's universe of discourse, the inner and outer limits of the enterprise, and the list of relevant constituents. These constituents must be accounted for in the artifacts for the other perspectives. The *planner* provides the scope for all products and services.

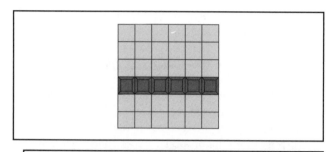

Figure 7-6   Row 4 — The Builder

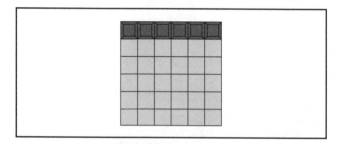

Figure 7-7   Row 1 — The Planner

• The *subcontractor's* perspective is identified by Row 5 of the Framework. See Figure 7-8. The *subcontractor* creates the detailed descriptions that disassociate the parts or pieces of the complex object for purposes of manufacturing. The *subcontractor* is out of context and seeks to fabricate and assemble all the necessary components. If the *subcontractor* is a carpenter, this might involve building the deck on a house. If the *subcontractor* is a programmer, this might involve coding a component to access a customer's name and address from a database.

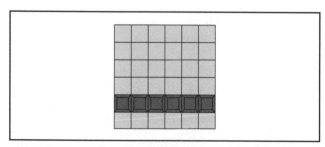

Figure 7-8   Row 5 — The Subcontractor

The certification perspective is the *functioning enterprise*. This perspective is not an artifact of the real thing because the *functioning enterprise* is the real thing.

- The *functioning enterprise's* perspective is identified by Row 6 of the Framework. See Figure 7-9. The *functioning enterprise* is the physical materialization of the product or service and is the result of what was articulated through artifacts (descriptive representations and models). Certification is a formal declaration from the *designer*, *builder*, and *subcontractor* to the *owner* that the *functioning enterprise* is as the *owner* described. Therefore, the *functioning enterprise* should resemble the *owner's* perspective, with the other perspectives attempting to make what the *owner* desired a reality. Row 6 is therefore the reality and is what the users of the enterprise's product or service experience physically.

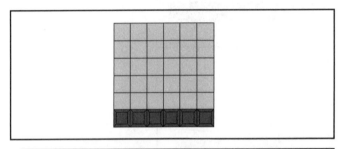

Figure 7-9   Row 6 — The Functioning Enterprise

The Framework's viewpoints or perspectives are represented horizontally as rows. The Framework's subject areas or aspects are represented vertically as columns.

 ## 7.2.4 Aspects *(what)*

The Framework's aspects or columns are based solely on the six primary interrogatives of the English language: *what*, *how*, *where*, *who*, *when*, and *why*. Interrogative variations such as *whom*, *whomever*, *whose*, and *whatever* are not considered distinct aspects of the Framework. Interrogatives such as *which* and subclasses such as *whether*, *if*, and *did* are also not distinct aspects of the Framework.

The Framework is limited to the six primary interrogatives because they can address every type of question. As such, the six primary interrogatives are normalized. If additional interrogatives are added to the Framework, a fact could show up in more than one place. If the Framework were denormalized, it would not be as adequate a communication vehicle.

The entire classification schema is normalized. Every fact about an enterprise can be mapped to only one place in the Framework. Because the normalized structure of the Framework is based on logic, the Framework creates a science (a methodological activity and discipline) and its structure is engineered. A series of laws and rules are described in Section 7.3.

The six aspects of the Framework—*what*, *how*, *where*, *who*, *when*, and *why*—represent the independent variables in a complete, normalized domain:

- *What*—is it made of?
- *How*—does it work?

- *Where*—are the components located?
- *Who*—performs what function?
- *When*—does something happen?
- *Why*—do things happen?

The Framework's aspects indicate the primitive units of measure for evaluating an enterprise in action. The six units of measure are inventory, yield, capacity, performance, duration, and state:

- *What*—inventory—for the things of interest
- *How*—yield—for each process
- *Where*—capacity—for each node
- *Who*—performance—for each work function
- *When*—duration—for the response time and cycles
- *Why*—state—for desire and is associated with quality

An enterprise's reporting requirements help establish the exact units of measure and metrics required. Management science defines how the metrics will be captured and reported. One of the purposes of a management science is to provide the laws of control. These laws establish the domain and the context of an activity performed in the enterprise. Because the Framework is normalized, it can help determine the appropriate methods for reporting each metric an enterprise needs. The reporting of metrics is a prerequisite to a successful enterprise.

The six aspects offer a practical way to simplify the subjects in an enterprise. Simplifying helps you manage complex problems. However, after you separate complex problems into simplistic or manageable chunks, assembling them back to the whole can create so many interrelationships that the problem can seem even more complex.

The Framework suggests that the enterprise can be managed with as little as 15 interrelationships (composites):

1. *What* and *how*
2. *What* and *where*
3. *What* and *who*
4. *What* and *when*
5. *What* and *why*
6. *How* and *where*
7. *How* and *who*
8. *How* and *when*
9. *How* and *why*
10. *Where* and *who*
11. *Where* and *when*
12. *Where* and *why*
13. *Who* and *when*
14. *Who* and *why*
15. *When* and *why*

The total number of possible composite artifacts for a single row is 63. The formula is $2^c - 1$, where C represents the number of columns—in this case, six. Figure 7-10 represents the cells in a helix, which shows how all the cells can interrelate.

Interrelationships are called composites. Viewing the intersection of a single perspective and a single aspect is known as a primitive. Primitives and composites are further discussed in Section 7.2.4.

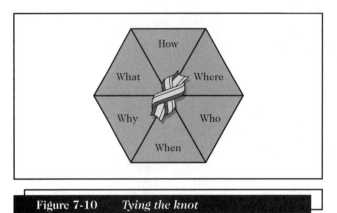

Figure 7-10   *Tying the knot*

What is the first column of the Framework and denotes the material composition of the enterprise. See Figure 7-11. Every term and the relationships between every term (a fact) that an enterprise uses should be defined in artifacts associated with Column 1. For example, *employee* and *information technology* might be terms of the enterprise. An *employee works in information technology* might be a fact of the enterprise.

Figure 7-11   *What — Identifying things that matter*

When a *functioning enterprise* is a computer system, the terms and facts are often represented by a database management system, such as Oracle and Microsoft SQL Server.

How is the second column of the Framework and denotes the transformations caused by the processes of the enterprise. See Figure 7-12. A transformation is an input to a process that is altered in some way to form an output. In a computer system, Column 2 is often an application program.

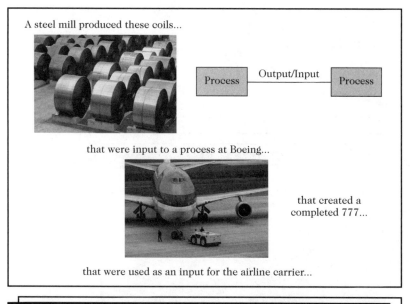

A steel mill produced these coils...

Process — Output/Input — Process

that were input to a process at Boeing...

that created a completed 777...

that were used as an input for the airline carrier...

Figure 7-12   *How — Process begets process*

455

Where is the third column of the Framework and denotes the connectivity between the enterprise's node points. See Figure 7-13. From the viewpoint of the *planner* and *owner*, the *where* column is often based on relative positions of each node and forms the enterprise's geometry. The *planner* and *owner* are interested in the logistics for creating and distributing the enterprise's products or services. In a *functioning enterprise*, the connectivity might be a computer network.

Who is the fourth column of the Framework and denotes the collaboration, responsibility, or workflow of the organization and its people. See Figure 7-14. The focuses of this aspect are performance, worker interactions, and security.

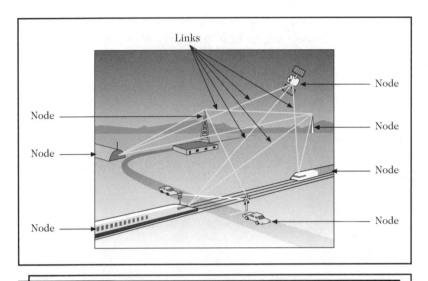

Figure 7-13   Where — Being connected

Figure 7-14   Who — Organization begins with leadership

When is the fifth column of the Framework and denotes the dynamics and timing of the enterprise. See Figure 7-15. This aspect focuses on the triggers that cause events in the enterprise and the schedule that handles each type of event.

Why is the sixth column of the Framework and denotes the strategy, plans, direction, values, and guidance. See Figure 7-16. The focus of this aspect is the motivation for the purpose and survival of the enterprise. In the *functioning enterprise*, the motivation is seen by the cause and effect of every strategy, tactic, policy, and rule.

7.2.5 Cell Basics *(where)*

Each of the six perspectives of the Framework is primitive and collectively they are comprehensive. The six aspects are also individually primitive and collectively comprehensive. Therefore, each cell in the Framework is primitive and the total set of 36 cells is comprehensive.

Figure 7-15   *When — Establishing a schedule*

Figure 7-16   *Why — Recognition that your strategies are working*

Each cell of the Framework is primitive because each cell represents an artifact from a single constraint (the perspective) and a single variable (the aspect). A model is a typical artifact used for representing the contents of a cell for any domain. A model based on a single cell is a primitive model. The contents of a primitive model are a series of primitive components. Primitive models are the basis for producing enterprise architectures. If the enterprise is not described using primitive components and primitive models, then the architecture is being compromised.

Reusing components in an enterprise is desirable. One of the first successful commercial components to be reused was Johannes Gutenberg's (1400–1468) move-able-type printing press. Gutenberg's component revolutionized the modern world. Component reuse in an enterprise does not happen by accident. Components must be engineered for reuse.

The primitive nature of each cell in the Framework lends itself to producing normalized and standard interchangeable parts. In addition, the **method of practice** used within the Framework must be a formal, repeatable process. A method of practice is a prescribed way to produce an artifact. Key elements for an enterprise reuse program include:

- An inventory of reusable components
- A repository listing the components and providing search facilities
- Support staff, including someone to maintain the inventory and repository for the components
- Staff to provide training and support for use of the components
- A development methodology that defines opportunities for reuse and harvesting potentially reusable components
- Design standards that ensure consistent component structure, behavior, and appearance
- A measurement program to monitor reuse effectiveness
- An incentive program to encourage individual behavior that promotes reuse

Primitive models are usually easier to understand than composite models. However, you must seek to understand a composite model so that the enterprise can create a desired level of integration. See Figure 7-17.

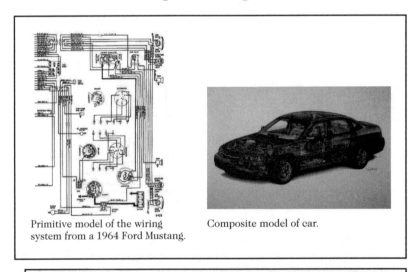

Primitive model of the wiring system from a 1964 Ford Mustang.

Composite model of car.

Figure 7-17   *A primitive and composite design*

Composite models contain components from more than one primitive cell. They are multi-variable models. One of the most famous composite models was drawn in 1861 by Joseph Minard to tell the story of Napoleon's disastrous advance on Moscow.

Napoleon's story was told in Section 5.1. Visualization guru and Yale professor Edward Tufte once called Minard's graphic "one of the finest informational graphics ever produced because of its many layers of metainformation." See Figure 7-18.

Information technology departments still battle with legacy applications. Whereas a legacy application was once the domain of COBOL and mainframes, today legacy applications are surfacing with newer languages, such as Java, C#, and HTML, and running on operating systems such as UNIX and Linux. Legacy applications are characterized by an inability to be readily replaced or altered. *Legacy* has never cared about what language an application was constructed in, or which operating system is used, or even on which hardware platform everything sits.

Legacy needs only an enterprise without primitives and a preponderance of short-term behavior. If an enterprise keeps its models, they are likely to be composite, point-in-time solutions, with no primitive models to support them. Each point-in-time solution is typically optimized at the expense of de-optimizing the architecture of the enterprise.

Many organizations disintegrate, de-optimize, and denormalize the enterprise because they do not understand how the enterprise will survive in the long term. In Section 6.1.1, the Long Now Foundation was described to show how some people are taking long-term thinking and planning to an extreme.

If primitive models were engineered before the composites, and the composites were assembled from the primitives, an enterprise could assemble any type of product or solution at will. Building composites would be like building something with Lego pieces.

If you have all the necessary colors, shapes, and sizes, then when you want a Millennium Falcon...snap, snap, snap, and *voila*. If you change your mind and you want a castle...snap, snap, snap, and *voila*. Just as a Lego set has a finite number of pieces, an enterprise has a finite set of primitives. Even with a limited number of Lego pieces, the number of composites (variations in which the pieces can be combined) can be almost infinite. An enterprise with a fixed set of primitives can create an almost infinite set of variations (or composites) as well.

To reduce the time-to-market for a product, adapt the enterprise to a change, and create a flexible and responsive enterprise, use an enterprise architecture based on primitive models and primitive components.

Primitives are architectural. Primitives can be engineered so they can be used in more than one product. Recognizing whether you are building the enterprise or designing a product is important. A product not created from a set of primitives may become a legacy application rapidly. Legacy applications live in the world of the *functioning enterprise*.

Legacy applications continue to thrive because they are too difficult to change or replace. They disable the enterprise slowly because the enterprise is bound by their constraints. Enterprise architecture using the Zachman Framework is about changing this mode of operation. The Framework is not business as usual.

Collectively, the primitive models that constitute the Framework are comprehensive. From a finite set of primitive models, an organization can compose an almost infinite number of composite views of the enterprise. Each composite view can be used to satisfy any point-in-time requirement.

The knowledge that the enterprise requires both primitives and composites is part of the Framework's neutral foundation.

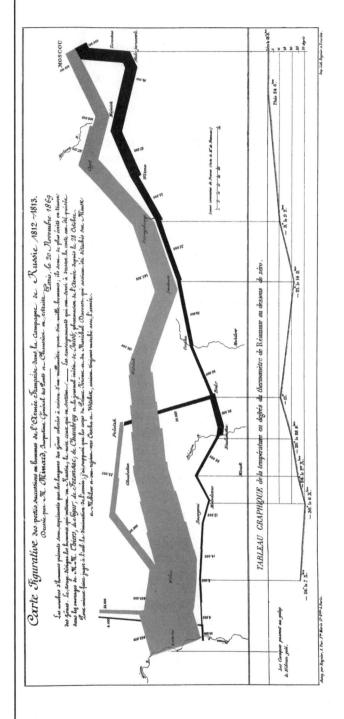

Napoleon's March to Moscow   The War of 1812

This classic of Charles Joseph Minard (1781–1870), the French engineer, shows the terrible fate of Napoleon's army in Russia. Described by E. J. Marey as seeming to defy the pen of the historian by its brutal eloquence, this combination of data map and time-series, drawn in 1861, portrays the devastating losses suffered in Napoleon's Russian campaign of 1812. Beginning at the left on the Polish-Russian border near the Niemen River, the thick band shows the size of the army (422,000 men) as it invaded Russia in June 1812. The width of the band indicates the size of the army at each place on the map. In September, the army reached Moscow, which was by then sacked and deserted, with 100,000 men. The path of Napoleon's retreat from Moscow is depicted by the darker, lower band, which is linked to a temperature scale and dates at the bottom of the chart. It was a bitterly cold winter, and many froze on the march out of Russia. As the graphic shows, the crossing of the Berezina River was a disaster, and the army finally straggled back into Poland with only 10,000 men remaining. Also shown are the movements of auxiliary troops, as they sought to protect the rear and the flank of the advancing army. Minard's graphic tells a rich, coherent story with its multivariate data, far more enlightening than just a single number bouncing along over time. Six variables are plotted: the size of the army, its location on a two-dimensional surface, direction of the army's movement, and temperature on various dates during the retreat from Moscow. It may well be the best statistical graphic ever drawn.

Edward R. Tufte, *The Visual Display of Quantitative Information*   Graphics Press   Box 430   Cheshire, Connecticut   06410

Reprinted by permission, Edward Tufte, The Visual Display of Quantitative Information, Graphics Press, 1983

Figure 7-18   *Composite model of Napoleon's advance and retreat from Russia*

7.2.6 Use *(how)*

The Framework is neutral with respect to any method of practice (such as iterative software development) and technology (such as a programming language or a manufacturer's computer chip). The Framework is based on logic. Therefore, to change the Framework's underlying science and engineering, the mathematics of the logic used for constructing the Framework must change. This statement does not necessarily mean the Framework is perfect, or the Framework is a silver bullet; however, it does mean that the Framework has a very strong foundation.

The Framework is a writing system, a planning tool, and a problem-solving tool. Its characteristics can be summarized as follows:

- Simple to use
- Comprehensive in structure
- Neutral to method of practice and technology
- Ubiquitous

The Framework is relatively *simple* and easy to understand because the Framework is based on logic rather than on a specific method, technology, or need. The Framework addresses the enterprise in its entirety and is *comprehensive*. Any issue can be mapped against the Framework to understand where the issue fits within the context of the enterprise as a whole. Mapping an issue to the Framework means that if you are a developer with an algorithm problem, the design of the algorithm can be placed in one of the cells of the Framework. If you are responsible for an area of the business, you can place your business needs and objectives in one or more of the Framework's cells.

The Framework is a *writing system*. The language of the writing system helps practitioners think about complex concepts and communicate them precisely without using technical words. The Framework can also be a *planning tool* that helps improve decision-making. Because the Framework offers a holistic view of the enterprise, decisions are made in context using the primitive models. Issues can be positioned in the context of the enterprise to present as many alternative solutions as the imagination allows.

The Framework is also a *problem-solving tool*. The aspects of the Framework allow practitioners to simplify and isolate subjects without losing a sense of the complexity of the enterprise as a whole. The Framework is also *neutral* to method of practice and technology. Because the Framework is independent, any methodology, tool, technique, or technology can be mapped against the Framework to understand its implicit trade-offs. Potentially, you can see the holistic view of any decision.

The Framework is *ubiquitous*. The Framework's classification schema is not limited to information technology or business. The Framework allows an enterprise to create a holistic contextual understanding of itself. The Framework is a tool that is used to help with thinking, reasoning, and communicating. The tool can be beneficial to technical and non-technical practitioners alike in dealing with the complexities and dynamics of the Information Age enterprise.

The Framework has a semantic structure based on logic. The Framework was not created to fill a specific need, but with the ubiquitous understanding of the commonality in building any type of complex product or service. Similar to Extreme Programming, mentioned in Section 6.2.4, the Framework has a set of values, principles, and practices to guide the practitioner.

461

POSITIONING

If you decide to build a house…

You may start out by thinking about the size of the house. You may think of the number of rooms and their spatial relationships. In this thought process, you are a *planner*. You may then decide to seek out a certified architect. The architect will listen to your needs and create a set of architectural drawings. The architect is the *owner* because she conceptually depicts the final product in a drawing. (You, too, are the *owner* because you are viewing your house with these conceptual architectural drawings.)

Once you approve the architectural drawings, the architect creates a set of formal prints that used to be called blueprints. The architect is now the *designer*. At this point, you may seek a general contractor to build your house from the prints. The general contractor is the *builder*. The *builder* creates a set of designs to construct the house based on the prints and includes desired materials and topography.

The general contractor is responsible for hiring the *subcontractors*, the people that actually build the house. Some *subcontractors* specialize in one type of job, such as framing, building cabinets, or laying carpet. Each *subcontractor* works in an out-of-context view of the project by focusing on individual specializations or tasks. Prior to the *subcontractor*, you the *planner*, the *owner*, the *designer*, and the *builder* all took a contextual view of the project, looking at the house as a whole.

Even though you were the *planner*, you may work with the *owner* to tweak the architectural drawings (and become an *owner*). You may approve the *designer's* prints (and become the *designer*). You may work with the *builder* to make sure the kitchen window receives the morning light (and become the *builder*). You may also check the spackling of the *subcontractor* (and become the *subcontractor*). The perspective is just a viewpoint and not a person. A person is free to work or participate in any of the perspectives.

Each perspective views the final house in a different way—an idea, a drawing, a plan, a design, a component (such as a deck, wiring, and plumbing system). The work products of each perspective should be aligned with the work products of the preceding perspective, so that in the end, the final house is the house you planned.

7.2.7 Purpose *(why)*

The Framework includes a set of values, principles, and practices to produce an enterprise architecture.

Values

Enterprise architecture and use of the Zachman Framework for Enterprise Architecture require an emotional investment. Doing anything well takes time and energy. Enterprise architecture is no exception. Producing artifacts that fully describe an enterprise exposes not only the organization's façade but also the enterprise's core—its people.

The artifacts of the enterprise reflect the knowledge, aptitude, creativity, culture, politics, inhibitions, foresight, narrow-mindedness, and open-mindedness of potentially every individual.

Because enterprise architecture requires a personal investment, a set of values is associated with the Framework and with the practice of working with the Framework. The values include the desire to:

- Improve communication
- Seek simplicity
- Receive constant feedback
- Proceed with courage
- Exhibit humility
- Survive

Use of the Framework requires open *communication*. From the most senior executive to the most junior *subcontractor*, positive things can happen only if everybody shares the same roadmap. The Framework encourages *simplicity* by requiring you to think about a subject and reason at a primitive level. The simpler something is, the easier it is to understand.

The only way an enterprise can produce something reasonable is to seek constant *feedback*. The alignment of the perspectives and the aspects allows constant coherent feedback of concepts and progress forward and backward through the Framework.

The Framework encourages you to commit to recording ideas and designs at an excruciating level of detail. The more detail that is recorded, the more a practitioner exposes his personal knowledge and skill. Detail allows a body of work to be criticized. Making the effort to record something in detail takes *courage*.

Clearly no one knows everything about everything, especially in commercial or government organizations—this includes authors of textbooks on enterprise architecture. Therefore, individuals who document, model, or design the enterprise often need to seek the advice or council of others. The practitioner of the Framework shows *humility* in order to seek help.

The reason for undertaking and practicing the art and engineering skills of enterprise architecture is the desire to *survive*. Surviving provides the opportunity to succeed and enjoy the wonders of a career and a life outside of work.

Principles

Establishing a set of principles is an essential element for creating a sustained set of artifacts for an enterprise architecture. Key principles for applying the Framework include:

- Providing a *functioning enterprise* is the primary goal
- Producing quality artifacts is mandatory
- Embracing change is desirable
- Producing artifacts at an appropriate level of detail is important
- Aligning and integrating the enterprise is critical
- Reducing time-to-market improves an organization

- Reusing as many artifacts as possible is prudent
- Maximizing the enterprise and all its investments is beneficial for every-one involved in the enterprise

Any enterprise must function to survive in both the short and long term. Creating a usable *functioning enterprise* is the primary concern and goal of enterprise architecture. Every deliverable produced for the Framework should be of the highest *quality* in order to achieve the desired results and maintain a flexible architecture.

Producing a set of artifacts that cannot be maintained or synchronized with the enterprise defeats the purpose of enterprise architecture. Every artifact must be *changeable* and adaptable. The enterprise is not static—its artifacts should not be either. The practitioners of the enterprise must recognize change is inevitable.

The concept of excruciating levels of detail are further explored in Section 7.4. However, every artifact produced by the enterprise must provide an *appropriate level of detail* to answer any possible question from the user of that artifact.

The thoughts and ideas communicated between the perspectives of the Framework should be realized in the *functioning enterprise*—this is *alignment*. When each aspect aligns with each other for each perspective, the artifacts and *functioning enterprise* of the Framework are *integrated*.

The practice of enterprise architecture should be used to expedite the ability to bring new products or services to the marketplace. The purpose of understanding each primitive at an excruciating level of detail is to *reduce the time-to-market* and improve the overall quality of the *functioning enterprise*.

Leveraging *reuse* of artifacts, designs, models, and components of the enterprise is cost effective, prudent, and highly desirable. Money, time, and effort are necessary to operate an organization. Each has a limit. Every resource that the enterprise has should be used judiciously. An enterprise architecture should not produce artifacts that have no value or whose quality renders them worthless. Artifacts that are purposeful and complete aid the enterprise in making good decisions regarding the investment of resources.

Practices

The use of the Framework is ubiquitous; no single set of practices is common to all endeavors. However, the following practices should apply in most cases:

- Take the holistic view.
- Minimize assumptions.
- Understand your mental filters, biases, and viewpoint (perspective).
- Identify the *things* you need—*what*.
- Identify the *process* required to move forward—*how*.
- Identify the *connectivity* required for performing each task—*where*.
- Identify the *people* or team that can support you—*who*.
- Identify the triggers that incite action and the *timeliness* to complete something—*when*.
- Identify the *motivation* for doing it all—*why*.

Performing enterprise architecture may at times require a Herculean effort to get things done. The Zachman Framework provides a tool to tame, if not conquer, the monsters of the enterprise—the marketplace, the environment, technology, and even the enterprise itself.

A TIP

Often the number of artifacts needed for each primitive and composite in the Framework can seem overwhelming. The need to create documents, documentation, models, diagrams, and designs can at times seem insurmountable. If this ever happens, start by producing a list. This textbook has made ample use of this technique. Creating a list is often quick and easy to do.

A list can be numbered or bulleted. The items in the list can be a single word, a phrase, a sentence, or a paragraph. A list can be direct and detailed. An appropriate list can articulate and communicate everything that is necessary. A list can be fun to produce. Lists are easy to change.

Lists can be used for planning any activity in the Framework and for creating any primitive or composite:

- *Try one today*!

7.2.8 Key Terms

forward engineering   reverse engineering
method of practice

7.2.9 Review Questions

1. What part of the Framework indicates the primitive units for measuring the actions of the enterprise? What do these measures include?

2. How could using the Zachman Framework have helped alleviate the problem that occurred at AT&T when the organization designed an application to provide the monthly bill for customers?

3. Explain the difference between a primitive model and a composite model.

4. Explain how the six aspects help simplify the complexity of the enterprise.

5. What is the difference between architecting the enterprise and designing an implementation?

6. Why should an enterprise architecture be based on primitive models and primitive components?

7. Explain the difference between recording the enterprise architecture using forward engineering and reverse engineering using the Zachman Framework.

SECTION 7.3 WHAT THE WORLD NEEDS NOW—ENTERPRISE GOVERNANCE

QUESTIONS TO CONTEMPLATE

1. What is the purpose of specifying the laws and rules of the Framework?
2. Where should you start creating artifacts for each row?
3. How does the Framework put food on the table?

7.3.1 Introduction

All activities, whether simple or complex, require you to know a method of practice. For example, when performing open-heart surgery, it is best to use a procedure proven to work, or to pilot a procedure before trying it out on a live patient. Activities requiring a greater amount of education and training often have a greater need for rules of practice. Most occupations are rooted in science—even the teenaged cashier at McDonald's is governed by the science of civics. Civics mandates that the cashier follow the laws, rules, and guidelines of McDonald's or face disciplinary action. The practice of a given science is composed of methods of practice, which require discipline.

Modern-day organizations, regardless of size, require vast areas of knowledge and expertise to survive and compete. It is difficult to find one person to operate a large endeavor who has the necessary knowledge and expertise in all disciplines. Even if such a person could be found, it would be unlikely that person would have enough time to dedicate to the practice of each discipline.

In many organizations, executive management can see only a high-level view of the enterprise. Many executives depend on all the practitioners and specialists who work together to keep the operation running. Fortunately, every individual can play an important role in helping to make an enterprise successful.

Accurate and timely information is a precursor to both small and large enterprises that require vast amounts of knowledge. Some enterprises require large quantities of knowledge only in one or two areas of specialization and have little use for knowledge outside of those areas. A small church in Avon, Illinois does not need to know what a large petrol-chemical company does off the Shetland Islands in the North Sea. A professional pharmaceutical association may care little about growing grapes in the south of France for Martell Cognac—unless someone determines that brandy is a cure for a life-threatening disease.

Regardless of the number of areas of interest or specialization, the Zachman Framework for Enterprise Architecture is a classification schema used to help organize, manage, and think about each domain in the enterprise. The Framework helps practitioners align and integrate the knowledge and areas of specialization within the enterprise. Maintaining well-organized information helps each enterprise manage change and improve responsiveness.

The Ancient Egyptians were probably one of the first civilized communities to formalize a set of professional practices. Based on their accomplishments in building the Great Pyramid at Giza, the Ancient Egyptians probably created and mastered six major disciplines:

- Accounting and law (*what*)—helped the Pharaoh know how much was being spent and helped ensure his absolute authority.
- Industrial engineering (*how*)—kept each building practice uniform.
- Civil engineering (*where*)—allowed each building location to be properly built and prepared.
- Personnel management (*who*)—made sure the right people were hired for the right jobs.
- Scheduling (*when*)—enabled the right things to show up in the right places at the right time.
- Industrial psychology (*why*)—meant workers were positively motivated to perform quality work.

The Zachman Framework embodies the sciences and disciplines created by and since the Ancient Egyptians. As a basic operating principle, the Framework includes the need to gather sufficient information to help answer the six interrogatives: *what, how, where, who, when,* and *why*. In addition, the Framework sets in place all the necessary viewpoints for areas of specialization—these perspectives are the *planner, owner, designer, builder, subcontractor,* and *functioning enterprise.*

Visually, the Framework is a modern-day hieroglyphic. The hieroglyphic is quite sophisticated and incorporates all the principles of a writing system. The writing system of the Framework, like all writing systems, is governed by a set of laws and rules to help promote teaching and application of use.

Chapter 1 outlined how writing systems helped create linguistics, the science of communication, which is governed by a set of laws and rules. A set of terminology is associated with the Framework. The terminology is the linguistics of the Framework. To discuss the Framework with others and use it as a practice, you should understand the Framework's vocabulary and laws. Many of the terms are self-evident and the laws are based on logic and common sense.

The Framework is part of management science and establishes a discipline. Laws and rules of practice help govern the discipline. All laws are grounded in science and may not be changed without the science changing; on the other hand, rules establish methods of practice for the science and may change as advancements or new ideas become established.

This section presents and defines the Framework's terminology. Each law presented is named and accompanied by applicable rules, postulates, theorems, corollaries, and comments. Rules help influence and constrain behavior; postulates are propositions that should be accepted as truth to provide a basis for logical reasoning; theorems are ideas that can be demonstrated to be true; corollaries are propositions based on the theorem being correct; and comments are, well, comments.

7.3.2 Terminology *(what)*

The *what* column of the Framework defines all the things of interest to an enterprise. To facilitate communication, the things of interest within a domain need to be cataloged and defined. The domain establishes the boundary or area of interest. If the Framework is the enterprise, these are the things of interest:

- **The Zachman Framework for Enterprise Architecture**—the formal name of a classification schema used to organize an enterprise's artifacts and help facilitate thinking, reasoning, and communicating among the participants of the enterprise.
- **Framework**—the informal name for the Zachman Framework for Enterprise Architecture.
- **Classification schema**—a system of organization. The Framework is a two-dimensional classification schema. A three-dimensional classification schema known as Zachman DNA (Zachman Depth iNtegrating Architecture) is presented in Chapter 8.
- **Enterprise architecture**—the ability to understand and reason the continual needs of integration, alignment, change, and responsiveness of the business to technology and the marketplace through persistent artifacts.
- **Framework subset**—a picture of the Framework showing less than the full classification schema. The full classification schema has six rows and six columns. A Framework subset does not show all the rows and columns.

Figure 7-19 illustrates the previous list.

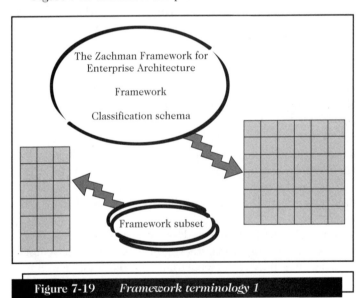

Figure 7-19 *Framework terminology 1*

- **Enterprise**—a group of people organized for a particular purpose to produce a product or provide a service.
- **Domain**—an area of interest with well-defined boundaries. A domain may contain other domains. An enterprise is the highest level of domain. A domain whose scope is less than that of the enterprise is often used in conjunction with a Peer Framework.

- **Architecture**—in the context of the Framework, represents the collective designs of each perspective when modeled at a normalized and primitive level (see definitions for *normalized* and *primitive model* for additional explanations).
- **Method of practice**—a descriptive approach to creating a *functioning enterprise*. A method of practice may be influenced by or related to a domain, standards body, legislative mandate, personal preference, or experience. Examples of methods of practice include: the Rational Unified Process in information technology, Montessori in education, Q in social sciences, Delphi surveys as an aid to build consensus, straight line (for depreciation) in accounting, and vaccination in the medical profession. An enterprise or domain may require many methods of practice to support the enterprise or domain.
- **Practitioner**—anyone who contributes to an artifact in the enterprise.

Figure 7-20 illustrates the previous list.

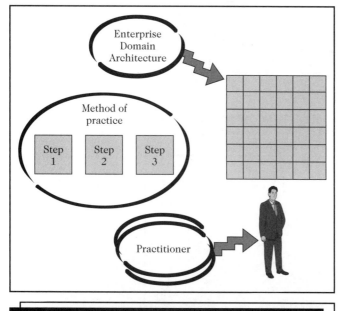

Figure 7-20   *Framework terminology 2*

- **Row**—one of the dimensions of the classification schema. The row is a horizontal plane on the Framework (*y*-axis).
- **Perspectives**—the six viewpoints of the Framework. Each viewpoint is represented by a single row.
- **Perspective**—a single viewpoint of the Framework
- **Perspective alias**—general classification of the type of generic deliverables produced for a row. The alias is associated with the domain. For example, the perspective alias of an *owner* might be a *conceptual model*; the perspective alias of a *designer* might be a *logical model*.

- **Context**—situation or orientation that aids in understanding an issue or topic. The context may come from something outside the actual domain of interest.
- **Contextual view**—perspective that considers the complete problem area relative to a single perspective.
- **Out-of-context view**—perspective that considers only a subset of the complete problem area relative to a single perspective. Out-of-context view is typically attributed to the *subcontractor* perspective during the construction of each part of the entire product or service.

Figures 7-21, 7-22, 7-23, and 7-24 illustrate the previous list.

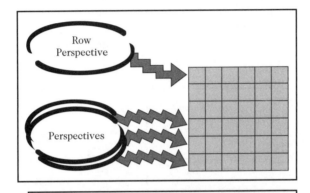

Figure 7-21   *Framework terminology 3a*

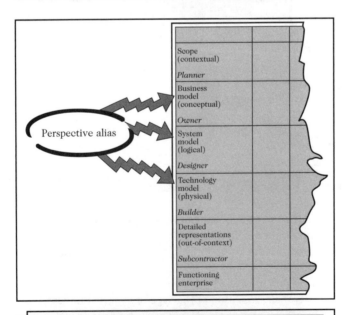

Figure 7-22   *Framework terminology 3b*

Figure 7-23   *Framework terminology 3c*

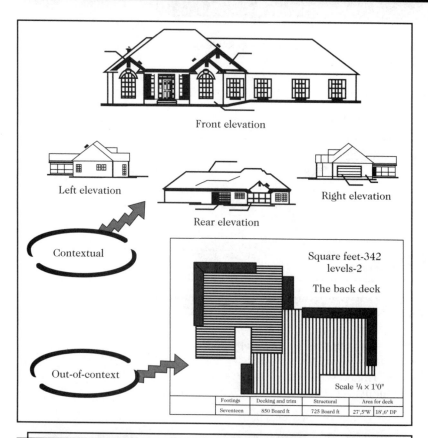

Figure 7-24   *Framework terminology 3d*

- **Planner**—the first of the six perspectives
- **Row 1**—a synonym for the *planner*
- **R1**—a shorthand synonym for the *planner*
- **Scope**—a generic deliverable for the *planner*

Figure 7-25 illustrates the previous list.

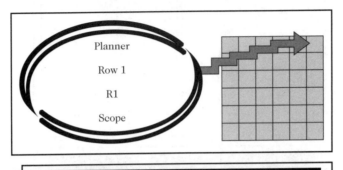

- **Owner**—the second of the six perspectives
- **Row 2**—a synonym for the *owner*
- **R2**—a shorthand synonym for the *owner*
- **Conceptual model**—a generic deliverable for the *owner*

Figure 7-26 illustrates the previous list.

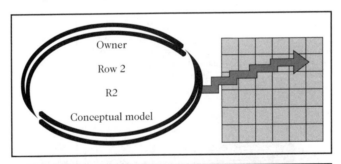

- **Designer**—the third of the six perspectives
- **Row 3**—a synonym for the *designer*
- **R3**—a shorthand synonym for the *designer*
- **Logical model**—a generic deliverable for the *designer*

Figure 7-27 illustrates the previous list.

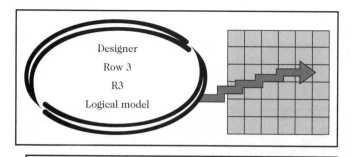

Figure 7-27   *Framework terminology 6*

- **Builder**—the fourth of the six perspectives
- **Row 4**—a synonym for the *builder*
- **R4**—a shorthand synonym for the *builder*
- **Physical model**—a generic deliverable for the *builder*

Figure 7-28 illustrates the previous list.

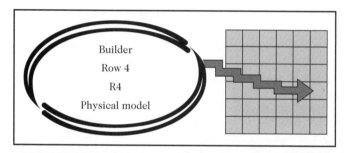

Figure 7-28   *Framework terminology 7*

473

- **Subcontractor**—the fifth of the six perspectives
- **Row 5**—a synonym for the *subcontractor*
- **R5**—a shorthand synonym for the *subcontractor*
- **Detailed representation**—a generic deliverable for the *subcontractor*

Figure 7-29 illustrates the previous list.

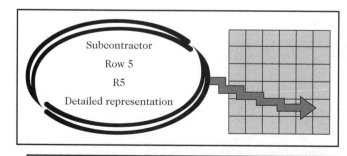

Figure 7-29   *Framework terminology 8*

- **Functioning enterprise**—the final perspective
- **Row 6**—a synonym for the *functioning enterprise*
- **R6**—a shorthand synonym for the *functioning enterprise*
- **The system**—a generic deliverable for the *functioning enterprise*

Figure 7-30 illustrates the previous list.

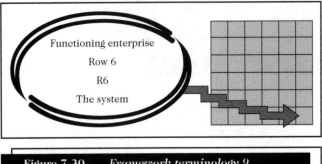

Figure 7-30   *Framework terminology 9*

- **Transformation**—the process of analysis used to move from one perspective to another
- **R*p*T*p*+1**—an example of the shorthand notation for transformation (See Section 7.4.2)
- **R*p*T*p*+1C*m***—another form of the shorthand notation for transformation (See Section 7.4.2)

Figure 7-31 illustrates the previous list.

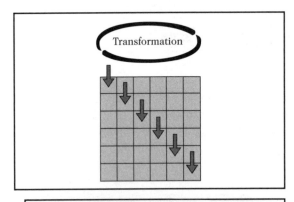

Figure 7-31   *Framework terminology 10*

- **Column**—one of the dimensions on the classification schema, the column is a vertical plane on the Framework (*x*-axis)
- **Aspects**—the six interrogatives of the Framework, where each interrogative is represented by a single column
- **Aspect**—a single interrogative of the Framework

- **Interrogatives**—the six primary ways to ask a question in the English language
- **Aspect alias**—a generic topic for a column

Figures 7-32 and 7-33 illustrate the previous list.

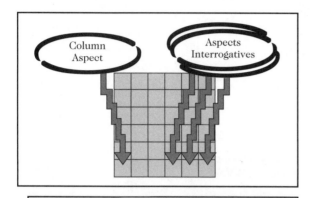

Figure 7-32   *Framework terminology 11a*

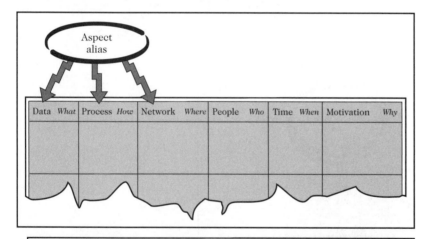

Figure 7-33   *Framework terminology 11b*

- **What**—the first of the six aspects
- **Column 1**—a synonym for *what*
- **C1**—a shorthand synonym for *what*
- **Thing**—a generic topic for *what*

Figure 7-34 illustrates the previous list.

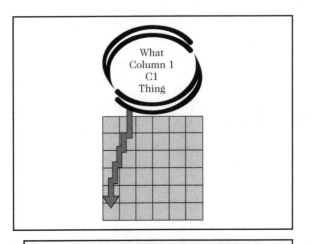

Figure 7-34   *Framework terminology 12*

- **How**—the second of the six aspects
- **Column 2**—a synonym for *how*
- **C2**—a shorthand synonym for *how*
- **Process**—a generic topic for *how*

Figure 7-35 illustrates the previous list.

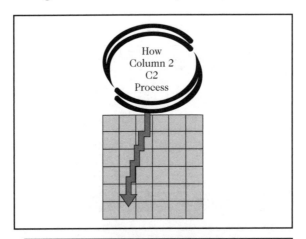

Figure 7-35   *Framework terminology 13*

- **Where**—the third of the six aspects
- **Column 3**—a synonym for *where*
- **C3**—a shorthand synonym for *where*
- **Network**—a generic topic for *where*

Figure 7-36 illustrates the previous list.

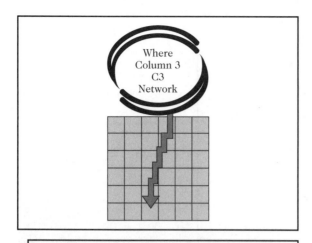

Figure 7-36   *Framework terminology 14*

- **Who**—the fourth of the six aspects
- **Column 4**—a synonym for *who*
- **C4**—a shorthand synonym for *who*
- **People**—a generic topic for *who*

Figure 7-37 illustrates the previous list.

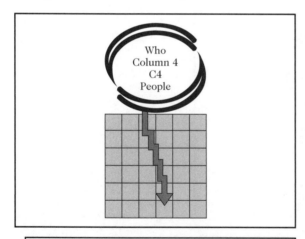

Figure 7-37   *Framework terminology 15*

- **When**—the fifth of the six aspects
- **Column 5**—a synonym for *when*
- **C5**—a shorthand synonym for *when*
- **Time**—a generic topic for *when*

Figure 7-38 illustrates the previous list.

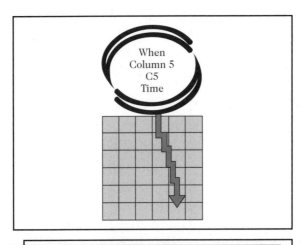

Figure 7-38   *Framework terminology 16*

- **Why**—the final aspect
- **Column 6**—a synonym for *why*
- **C6**—a shorthand synonym for *why*
- **Motivation**—a generic topic for *why*

Figure 7-39 illustrates the previous list.

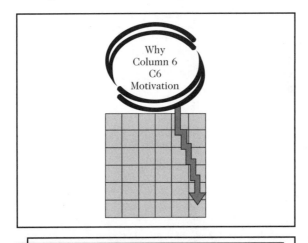

Figure 7-39   *Framework terminology 17*

- **Cell**—the six perspectives and six aspects create 36 intersections. The two-dimensional Framework is a classification schema consisting of 36 cells.
- **Artifact**—a formal representation of a primitive or composite. An artifact may use any type of medium, including print, video, or audio, or it can be transmitted verbally. The chosen media may contain a formal notation, an informal notation, pictures, diagrams, or models.

- **Persistent artifact**—an artifact that can be reused verbatim to communicate concepts, thoughts, designs, and ideas. Persistent artifacts are explicit in nature.
- **Verbal artifact**—a non-persistent form used to communicate what would otherwise be contained in a persistent artifact. Verbal artifacts are more difficult to factually validate or recall. Verbal artifacts are implicit in nature.
- **Assumption**—a decision to produce an artifact based on unproven or non-validated data, information, or knowledge.
- **Descriptive representation**—a synonym for a persistent artifact
- **Model**—a specific type of artifact that is usually produced using a formal descriptive notation. A model can contain just text, or text accompanied by a diagram.
- **Normalized architectural artifacts**—a collection of persistent artifacts where each is primitive in nature and based on one of the cells of the Framework.

Figures 7-40 and 7-41 illustrate the previous list.

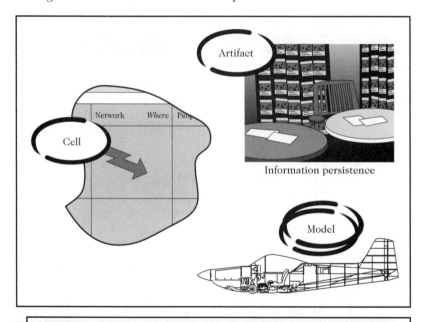

Figure 7-40   *Framework terminology 18a*

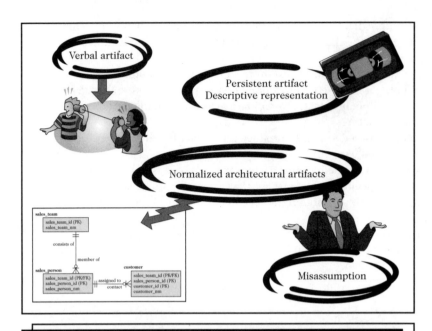

Figure 7-41   Framework terminology 18b

- **Primitive model**—the lowest level of representation for an artifact. A primitive is the intersection of a single perspective with a single aspect.
- **Composite model**—the representation of an artifact that is not primitive. A composite is an artifact that includes representations from more than one cell.
- **Normalization**—the idea that for a single perspective, a single fact is modeled in only one place. Therefore, the same fact may occur (and probably will occur) for multiple perspectives.
- **Denormalization**—the idea that for a single perspective, a single fact is modeled in more than one place.

Figure 7-42 illustrates the previous list.

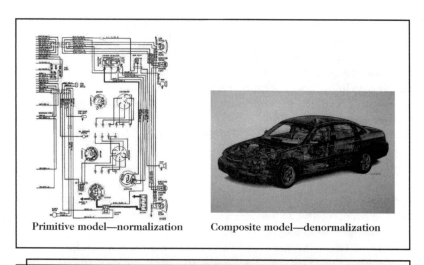

Primitive model—normalization   Composite model—denormalization

Figure 7-42   Framework terminology 19

- **Icon**—a visual representation of a sample primitive model appearing in each cell of the Framework
- **Noun/verb**—indicates a thing (noun) or action (verb). The noun/verb is also known as a primitive component. Each cell is illustrated with its basic noun-verb-noun structure for the primitive model.
- **Primitive component**—the basic three-part structure of a primitive model, normally represented in the form of a noun-verb-noun.

Figure 7-43 illustrates the previous list.

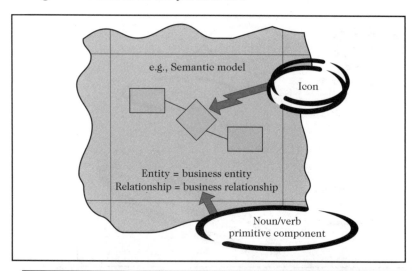

Figure 7-43   Framework terminology 20

- **Sliver**—the representation of completeness for a primitive artifact. A sliver has two dimensions: scope and detail.
- **Scope sliver**—the representation of how much of the full scope has been represented in an artifact.
- **Detail sliver**—the representation of the level of detail found in an artifact
- **Horizontal integration**—the continuity between artifacts from multiple cells across a single row
- **Vertical integration**—the continuity between artifacts from multiple cells along a single column
- **Enterprise wide integration**—the continuity across the scope of the enterprise within every cell
- **Comprehensive**—the complete set of six perspectives and the complete set of six aspects relative to a description of the enterprise
- **Excruciating level of detail**—the contents of an artifact being complete in all respects. Often excruciating level of detail is subjective and its completeness is determined by the perspective of the artifact and its recipient.
- **Excruciating detail**—a synonym for excruciating level of detail
- **Abstraction**—a representation of a real thing. An abstraction is the result of the intersection between one or more perspectives and one or more aspects. There may be more than one possible abstraction for each intersection. Experience, domain knowledge, and descriptive technique all influence the abstraction of choice. In this textbook, an abstraction generally refers to the intersection of one perspective and one aspect.

Figures 7-44 and 7-45 illustrate the previous list.

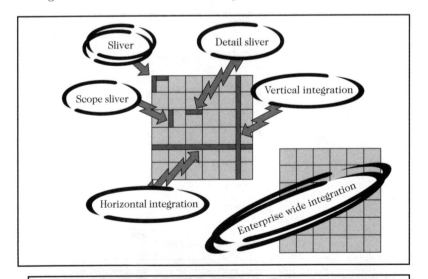

Figure 7-44   *Framework terminology 21a*

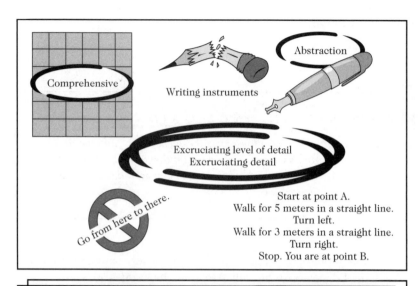

Comprehensive

Writing instruments

Abstraction

Excruciating level of detail
Excruciating detail

Go from here to there.

Start at point A.
Walk for 5 meters in a straight line.
Turn left.
Walk for 3 meters in a straight line.
Turn right.
Stop. You are at point B.

Figure 7-45   *Framework terminology 21b*

- **Peer Framework**—an additional Framework often used to divide a domain, or keep dissimilar domains of a shared enterprise separated.

Figure 7-46 illustrates the Peer Framework.

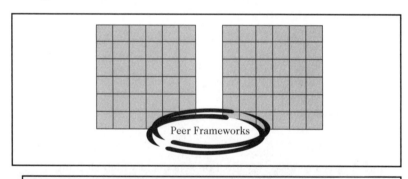

Peer Frameworks

Figure 7-46   *Framework terminology 22*

The Framework's terms and definitions provide the vocabulary for describing all the major concepts of the Framework. Now that you have reviewed the terms and definitions, you are ready to examine the Framework's laws.

7.3.3 I Fought the Law and the Law Won *(why)*

A S   E I N S T E I N   O N C E   S A I D...

One reason why mathematics enjoys special esteem, above all other sciences, is that its laws are absolutely certain and indisputable, while those of other sciences are to some extent debatable and in constant danger of being overthrown by newly discovered facts.

A practitioner who disobeys the Framework's laws impedes communication and the ability to teach the Framework uniformly. Violating the Framework's laws implies the Zachman Framework is not being used appropriately.

The eleven laws of the Zachman Framework are titled as follows:

- Law 1—*Classification*
- Law 2—*Structure*
- Law 3—*Use*
- Law 4—*Domain*
- Law 5—*Naming*
- Law 6—*Perspectives*
- Law 7—*Aspects*
- Law 8—*Abstraction*
- Law 9—*Detail*
- Law 10—*Navigation*
- Law 11—*Communication*

Law 1—*Classification*

- The Framework is a generic classification schema in which all things of interest to the enterprise can be classified.
- The Framework can classify the descriptive representations of anything.
- The Framework can analyze anything relative to its architectural composition.
- The Framework is recursive and can analyze its own architectural composition.
- The Framework is inert.
- The primitive artifacts of the Framework are always normalized.
- An artifact is considered either primitive or composite.

Law 2—*Structure*

- The Framework contains six rows.
- The Framework's physical sequence of the six rows must not be rearranged.

- The physical sequence of the six rows is: *planner, owner, designer, builder, subcontractor,* and *functioning enterprise.*
- Additional rows must not be added to the Framework.
- The rows are known collectively as perspectives.
- The Framework contains six columns.
- The Framework's physical sequence of the six columns must not be rearranged.
- The physical sequence of the six columns is: *what, how, where, who, when,* and *why.*
- Additional columns must not be added to the Framework.
- The columns are known collectively as aspects.
- The intersection of a row and a column creates a cell.

Law 3—*Use*

- The Framework is presented only in a two-dimensional matrix. The six rows represent the *y*-axis. The six columns represent the *x*-axis.
- The Framework presents a methodology because the Framework's logic asserts a series of primitive and composite deliverables.
- Each primitive deliverable is unique and does not contain overlapping concepts.

Law 4—*Domain*

- An enterprise is made up of one or more domains.
- A domain may contain other domains.
- A domain must have at least one defined scope.
- A domain must have a context.

Law 5—*Naming*

- The formal headings of the Framework's six rows must not be renamed.
- The formal headings of the rows are *planner, owner, designer, builder, subcontractor,* and *functioning enterprise.*
- The formal headings of the Framework's six columns must not be renamed.
- The formal headings of the columns are *what, how, where, who, when,* and *why.*

Law 6—*Perspectives*

- The Framework contains six viewpoints.
- Additional perspectives must not be added.
- Each viewpoint is associated with a single row in the Framework.
- The perspectives have a fixed physical sequence.
- The perspectives do not have a fixed work sequence. Work sequence is governed by a method of practice.
- Each perspective is unique and, therefore, normalized.

Law 7—Aspects

- The Framework contains six interrogatives.
- Other interrogatives must not be added.
- Each interrogative is associated with a single column in the Framework.
- The aspects have a fixed presentation sequence.
- The aspects do not have a fixed work sequence. Work sequence is governed by a method of practice.
- Each aspect is unique and, therefore, normalized.

Law 8—Abstraction

- The intersection of a single row and a single column is represented by a cell.
- Each cell is primitive in nature.
- Two or more primitives combined into a single artifact produce a composite.
- When everything known about a primitive has been recorded in an artifact, the artifact has reached a level of excruciating detail.
- The contents of an artifact are an abstraction.
- A primitive artifact represents an abstraction.
- A composite artifact represents an abstraction.
- There is no single abstraction for a primitive.
- There is no single abstraction for a composite.
- Each primitive is based on a primitive component.
- Each cell creates a specialization of the primitive component.

Law 9—Detail

- Each primitive or composite may be explicit or implicit.
- A persistent artifact is always explicit.
- A verbal artifact is always implicit.
- The absence of knowledge does not imply a cell does not exist.
- All cells yield artifacts.

Law 10—Navigation

- Every cell can be integrated with every other cell in the same row.
- Transformation occurs vertically between rows.
- Navigation between cells occurs vertically up or down a column.
- Navigation between cells occurs horizontally along a row.
- Navigation between cells is not permitted diagonally between rows.

Law 11—Communication

- Vocabulary must be consistent for all Frameworks and all domains within a Framework.

7.3.4 Law Enforcement *(how)*

Some people gamble with laws. The willingness to gamble is based on the probability of not being caught. In the United States, automobile drivers often exceed a road's posted speed limit because they think that police officers will be lenient and not issue a speeding ticket for going a little faster than the designated speed limit.

Many American drivers have determined that the risk of being caught for speeding 1, 2, or even 10 miles per hour over the speed limit is minimal. Drivers statistically perceive that the consequences of breaking the law are worth taking. Drivers rationalize that they can speed thousands of times before they might receive a speeding ticket. Therefore, the resulting cost of the speeding ticket is relatively low when distributed across the cost of all the unpunished speeding offenses.

The consequences for breaking some laws are so dire, however, that the punishment for being caught actually serves to dissuade people from violating the law. The Zachman Framework for Enterprise Architecture contains 11 laws. However, unlike the scenario in George Orwell's book *1984*, Big Brother is not watching.

If the laws of the Framework are broken, there are no statutory fines or mandatory prison sentences. There is not even an official slap on the wrist from the Zachman Institute for Framework Advancement. So what is the motivation for following the laws?

The ability to think, reason, and communicate through simple and complex issues with others in order to create an enterprise that is aligned, flexible, integrated, and responsive is the major reason. Following the Framework's laws helps facilitate all of these things. The laws help determine how to use the Framework to be successful. The laws require you to be disciplined, but, in the end, abiding by the laws means you are less likely to shoot yourself in the foot.

7.3.5 Influencing Behavior *(where)*

The 11 laws help govern the science of the Framework, while the discipline of the Framework is constrained and influenced by a set of rules. As previously stated, all laws are grounded in science and may not be changed without the science changing; on the other hand, rules are used to establish methods of practice for the science and may change as advancements or new ideas become established. Following are the rules of the Framework:

Rules for Law 1—*Classification*

- An artifact is organized based on the perspective and aspect represented.
- The rules are indifferent to the actual subject matter of the cell.

Rules for Law 2—*Structure*

- The primitive component for each intersection of a row and column creates a cell.
- The primitive component for each intersection is unique.
- Each cell is independent of every other cell.

Rules for Law 3—*Use*

- The explicit artifacts produced for each primitive and composite should be governed by an appropriate method of practice for each type of domain. Sample artifacts for information technology projects are given in Section 7.4.6. Sample artifacts and issues for other domains are listed in Appendix B.
- For presentation, discussion, or educational purposes, a subset of the Framework may be presented to help focus on a specific row(s) or column(s) of the Framework. However, the Framework subset should be noted clearly as a subset.
- Artifacts for Rows 1 through 5 are representations of the physical materialization at Row 6.

Rules for Law 4—*Domain*

- The boundaries of a domain should be documented clearly as part of the Row 1 artifacts.
- Peer Frameworks can help remove complexity to understand the enterprise better. A Peer Framework establishes another domain.

Rules for Law 5—*Naming*

- The practitioner may choose an alias for each row heading.
- A row heading alias may not use an alternative definition for the row heading it represents.
- The practitioner may choose an alias for each column heading.
- A column heading alias may not use an alternative definition for the column heading it represents.

Rules for Law 6—*Perspective*

- The perspectives are not job titles, but viewpoints.
- More than one person in an enterprise may share the same viewpoint.
- A single individual may take on more than one viewpoint.
- Row 1 is the best place to start any endeavor.
- Row 6 is the best place to end any endeavor.
- Each row has distinct primary constraints which include:
  Row 1: Financial and regulatory
  Row 2: Policy and usage
  Row 3: Environmental in nature
  Row 4: Available technology or technique
  Row 5: Assembly and integration
  Row 6: Measurement
- Each constraint is not necessarily exclusive to a single perspective.
- Each constraint is fundamental to one of the perspectives.

Rules for Law 7—*Aspect*

- Each aspect is normalized.
- Each aspect should be understood by each perspective.

- There is no universal starting point for an aspect.
- Each column has a distinct focus describing a single independent variable:
  Column 1: Things and their relationships
  Column 2: Processes and their inputs and outputs
  Column 3: Nodes and their links
  Column 4: People and their work
  Column 5: Time and cycle
  Column 6: Ends and means

Rules for Law 8—*Abstraction*

- Each cell contains a sliver.
- The sliver has two dimensions: scope and detail.
- An abstraction for a primitive artifact should be developed and coordinated with the other primitives of the perspective.
- The model of any artifact can be optimized or de-optimized relative to other artifacts, at the risk of increasing entropy in the enterprise.
- Optimization is an issue of choice.
- Optimization may not be possible for every cell of the Framework.
- De-optimizing for performance and flexibility may be advantageous to the enterprise.

Rules for Law 9—*Detail*

- Assumption is curtailed by making everything explicit and recording facts at an excruciating level of detail.
- Detail is particular to a cell, but not particular to a row. In other words, as you move further down the Framework's rows, the artifacts of the cells do not get more detailed. The Framework is not a representation of a process decomposition model.[1]
- Every cell should contain an artifact developed to an excruciating level of detail. Artifacts for a cell could include high-level views, mid-level views, and low-level (excruciating level of detail) views.

Rules for Law 10—*Navigation*

- Only primitive models need to be transformed.
- In the absence of a primitive model, a composite model may be transformed.

Rules for Law 11—*Communication*

- Once a term has been defined within the Framework, the term should not be arbitrarily changed or altered.
- Clear communication exists only when everyone within an enterprise shares a common understanding of the terms of the enterprise.
- Each cell is given context by the perspective and aspect represented.

7.3.6 Postulates, Theorems, Corollaries, and Comments *(when)*

Postulates for Law 1—*Classification*

- Because the Framework is ubiquitous, it can be applied to any enterprise.
- The Framework's classification schema is holistic.
- The Framework does not infer a methodology of use for a given enterprise or domain.
- The Framework does not imply the use of any specific tools, techniques, or technologies for an enterprise or domain.

Theorems for Law 1—*Classification*

- Knowledge is key to achieving competitive advantage.
- The Framework is a classification schema used to help organize, understand, and communicate the enterprise's knowledge.

Corollaries for Law 1—*Classification*

- Enterprise architecture is a specific type of management science used to control and manage every facet of the enterprise.

Postulates for Law 2—*Structure*

- The two-dimensional classification schema of rows and columns helps practitioners establish and document an enterprise.
- An enterprise is explained by the knowledge of that enterprise.
- Knowledge must be understood in the context of the enterprise.

Theorems for Law 3—*Use*

- Moving down the rows from one perspective to the next—*planner* to *owner, owner* to *designer, designer* to *builder, builder* to *subcontractor,* and *subcontractor* to the *functioning enterprise*—indicates a tactic for implementation.
- Moving up the rows from one perspective to the next—*functioning enterprise* to the *subcontractor, subcontractor* to *builder, builder* to *designer, designer* to *owner,* and *owner* to the *planner*—indicates a strategy for implementation.

Corollaries for Law 3—*Use*

- Any method of practice can be mapped to the Framework.
- A method of practice may dictate that work begin anywhere within the Framework. The implication of starting anywhere other than Row 1 and moving to a subsequent row, understanding each primitive at an excruciating level of detail, means that assumptions will be made at the subsequent row.
- The Framework can be used to help improve any method of practice.

- Making an assumption is not always negative. In the end, an assumption may prove to be right, wrong, or immaterial to the outcome.
- When you sign your name on a check or a credit card receipt with a pen, the use of the pen is essentially random and chosen at the time you need to write your name. The choice of pen in this scenario reflects a **late binding** strategy and is flexible because any pen can be used. However, if a designated pen had to be used for signing, the **early binding** strategy creates a restriction. Early binding is often simple to put in place, but may be more difficult to change. In this example, if the designated pen is bound early and runs out of ink, you may not have another choice for signing your name. In general, the earlier you bind things, the less flexibility you have. The later you bind things, the more flexibility you have. Primitive models can help influence late binding strategies in composite models. Typically, products or services of the *functioning enterprise* are some form of composite.
- Any enterprise has the opportunity to be successful in spite of the effort put forward.
- Guessing incorrectly does not always result in a poor outcome.
- The following is a methodological assertion that is quite independent of the Framework logic, but constitutes a suggested rallying point for each row. A rallying point is a stake in the ground for which all other opinions or options can be judged:

  Planner row—begin with the aspect *what*. The artifacts of this cell help define the things of interest—assets, liabilities, supply chains, mandates, and competition. The amount of investment required to achieve a desired end is an artifact of this cell. Finance should help force all the other columns into alignment for this perspective.

  Owner row—begin with the aspect *when*. The establishment of the time frames for any given endeavor should help force all the other columns into alignment for this perspective.

  Designer row—begin with the aspect *how*. The design of the processes should help force the other columns into alignment for this perspective.

  Builder row—begin with the aspect *where*. Solving all the issues of topography, topology, logistics, and connectivity for each location should help force the other columns into alignment for this perspective.

  Subcontractor row—begin with the aspect *who*. Solving the problems of the skill sets required to do any given activity should help force the other columns into alignment for this perspective.

  Functioning enterprise row—begin with the aspect *why*. The running operation is the expression of the motivation of the enterprise. Understanding the motivation to achieve a desired result should help force the other columns into alignment for this perspective.

- When a subset of the Framework is used, the column shorthand notation does not change. Therefore, if only the motivation column is shown in the subset, it is still referred to as Column 6 or C6.

The Zachman Framework for Enterprise Architecture

Postulates for Law 4—*Domain*

- Domains are areas of interest and may have formal or informal boundaries.
- The largest domain is the enterprise.
- A domain is explained by the knowledge in that domain.
- Knowledge must be understood in context of the domain.

Theorems for Law 4—*Domain*

- Anything the participants of the enterprise acknowledge is incorporated immediately into a domain.
- A method of practice handles a domain in a series of steps or phases. Each step or phase establishes its own scope.
- A domain has 36 primitive cells.

Corollaries for Law 4—*Domain*

- Within the boundaries of the enterprise, the enterprise's owners and participants are permitted to establish each domain of interest.
- If multiple domains are created within any one enterprise, integration among the Frameworks is realized only by engineering for it or by happenstance.

Comments for Law 4—*Domain*

- Documenting what is outside of the domain often adds clarity to the exact boundary of the domain.
- Documenting items of interest about an external domain can be accomplished by creating a list. Adding structural definitions requires assistance from the responsible external enterprise (e.g., business, government, or organization).

Comments for Law 5—*Naming*

- An alias is used as an alternative word, not an alternative meaning.
- The generic deliverables for the perspectives aliases in information technology are:

  Scope—for the perspective *planner*
  Conceptual model—for the perspective *owner*
  Logical model—for the perspective *designer*
  Physical model—for the perspective *builder*
  Detailed representations—for the perspective *subcontractor*
  The system—for the perspective *functioning enterprise*

- The generic deliverables for the aspect aliases in information technology are:

  Data—for the aspect *what*
  Process—for the aspect *how*
  Network—for the aspect *where*
  People—for the aspect *who*

Time—for the aspect *when*
Motivation—for the aspect *why*

Theorems for Law 6—*Perspective*

- When fully understood and realized, the *owner's* perspective matches the materialization of the *functioning enterprise*.

Comments for Law 6—*Perspective*

- Each perspective is a view of the physical materialization of the product or service in the *functioning enterprise*.
- Each perspective provides a unique way a problem or solution can be viewed. For example:

  The *planner* views the *functioning enterprise* in generalities. The *planner* helps to establish the universe of discourse—the background, scope, and purpose of the *functioning enterprise*.

  The *owner* views the *functioning enterprise* in terms of how the product or service is to be used.

  The *designer* views the *functioning enterprise* as all the necessary details of what is needed to make the *functioning enterprise* a reality.

  The *builder* views the *functioning enterprise* in terms of how the *functioning enterprise* can be constructed.

  The *subcontractor* views small portions of the *functioning enterprise*. Each portion is a piece of the product or service that is being constructed.

  The *functioning enterprise* is the view of what has actually been materialized.

Corollaries for Law 7—*Aspect*

- The word *which* is not considered an interrogative.

Comments for Law 7—*Aspect*

- Each interrogative provides a way to state a question. For example:

  What are the things of interest to the *functioning enterprise*?
  How will the *functioning enterprise* operate?
  Where are the locations for the *functioning enterprise*?
  Who is needed to operate the *functioning enterprise*?
  When will things happen in the *functioning enterprise*?
  Why do things happen in a certain way within the *functioning enterprise*?

Postulates for Law 8—*Abstraction*

- Each primitive can be referred to with a shorthand notation. For example:

  R1C1—the intersection of Row 1 (*planner*) and Column 1 (*what*)
  R1C2—the intersection of Row 1 (*planner*) and Column 2 (*how*)

493

R1C3—the intersection of Row 1 (*planner*) and Column 3 (*where*)
R1C4—the intersection of Row 1 (*planner*) and Column 4 (*who*)
R1C5—the intersection of Row 1 (*planner*) and Column 5 (*when*)
R1C6—the intersection of Row 1 (*planner*) and Column 6 (*why*)

- Each composite can be referred to with a shorthand notation. For example:

R2C1-2—the intersection of Row 2 (*owner*) and Columns 1 and 2 (*what* and *how*)
R2C1-2-3—the intersection of Row 2 (*owner*) and Columns 1, 2 and 3 (*what*, *how*, and *where*)
R2C1-2-3-4—the intersection of Row 2 (*owner*) and Columns 1, 2, 3, and 4 (*what*, *how*, *where*, and *who*)
R2C1-2-3-4-5—the intersection of Row 2 (*owner*) and Columns 1, 2, 3, 4, and 5 (*what*, *how*, *where*, *who*, and *when*)
R2C1-2-3-4-5-6—the intersection of Row 2 (*owner*) and Columns 1, 2, 3, 4, 5, and 6 (*what*, *how*, *where*, *who*, *when*, and *why*)

Theorems for Law 8—*Abstraction*

- An excruciating level of detail is achieved when a practitioner can demonstrate that all knowable terms and facts have been made explicit for an artifact.
- Each technique used to produce an artifact is a method of practice and is governed by its own set of rules. For example, a R3C1 (Row 3 and Column 1) primitive artifact may use an entity/relationship diagram (ERD). ERDs are governed by a set of formal rules. An R4C1-2 (Row 4, Columns 1 and 2) composite artifact may use a UML class diagram. UML class diagrams are governed by a set of formal rules.

Corollaries for Law 8—*Abstraction*

- The basic *ingredient* of all artifacts is the establishment of nouns and verbs that form the terms and facts used to describe something. In the Framework, the form is usually arranged as noun-verb-noun and is called a primitive component. Each aspect uses a specialized form of the noun-verb-noun structure:

What—thing-relationship-thing
How—process-output/input-process
Where—node-link-node
Who—people-work-people
When—time-cycle-time
Why—ends-means-ends

Comments for Law 8—*Abstraction*

- Two people with the same information can create different abstractions for a primitive or a composite based on their experiences, biases, mental filters, and culture. For example, to describe a zoo, one person might create a representation called *animal* to represent all the zoo's animals.

Another person might create separate representations for *lions* and *tigers* and *bears*. Oh my...[2] Both solutions accomplish the objective, but both use different techniques or abstractions.

- An artifact that is complete at an excruciating level of detail might be difficult to use when attempting to create a general understanding. A higher-level abstraction with less detail is often necessary. In many businesses, people use the phrase, *Let me explain the process from the 50,000-foot level*. The phrase implies that at ground level, you can see many details—bees flying, leaves on a tree, the color of someone's eyes. At 50,000 feet above ground level, you lose many of the details—you are limited to seeing only major features such as lakes, rivers, and urban areas.
- Before something can be used, it has to be constructed. Before a product or service can be constructed, the product or service has to be thought about and designed. This fact applies to every product or service, from the simplest to the most complex.
- A sliver for a cell may range from 0 percent (non-existent) to 100 percent (complete).
- The term *abstraction* is not a synonym for the term *cell*. The term abstraction refers to an artifact for a cell.

Comments for Law 9—*Detail*

- Artifacts for any cell that are deemed to contain less than an excruciating level of detail may be useful only for planning and scoping activities.

7.3.7 Eating (*who*)

Since the time of the first organization, leaders have struggled to overcome obstacles standing in the way of achieving the group's goals and objectives. The hunting parties of early civilized man had to overcome obstacles similar to those faced by today's large corporations. The early hunting parties had to understand:

- *What* materials and tools were required to hunt
- *How* the hunt was to be accomplished
- *Where* the hunting was to be done
- *Who* would participate in the hunt
- *When* the hunt would begin and end
- *Why* hunting was important—the need to eat

Modern corporations are in business to provide products or services. Each corporation must understand:

- *What* materials and tools are required to be in business
- *How* the business operates
- *Where* the business is carried out
- *Who* participates in the business
- When the business begins and ends each operating cycle
- *Why* business remains important—the need to eat

Failure to be successful is generally not an option for the survival of any enterprise, including the following types:

- For-profit organization
- Nonprofit organization
- Chess club
- Choir
- Benevolent association
- Government agency
- School
- Homeowners' association
- Karate club
- Gymnasium
- Foundation
- Family farm
- Trio of authors

Every enterprise carves out its desired place—from the smallest enterprises involving one person to the largest enterprises, such as the Chinese government, involving over 1 billion people. The scale of the enterprise may differ, but the Framework's structure of classifying knowledge remains identical.

Most enterprises require time, money (or something to barter with), and effort to achieve a *functioning enterprise*. Time, money, and effort are often limited resources and should not be squandered. Each requires discipline to manage properly. When choosing to organize knowledge according to the Framework, the laws of the Framework help make using the Framework consistent. Consistent use of the Framework elevates the successful use of the Framework. Consistent use also helps reach the overall goals and objectives of the enterprise—like all disciplines, practice makes perfect.

7.3.8 Key Terms

aspect alias	functioning enterprise
cell	horizontal integration
classification schema	icon
column	late binding
comprehensive	normalized architectural artifacts
conceptual model	out-of-context view
context	Peer Framework
contextual view	perspective alias
descriptive representation	practitioner
detail sliver	primitive component
detailed representation	row
domain	scope
early binding	scope sliver
enterprise wide integration	sliver
excruciating detail	transformation
excruciating level of detail	vertical integration
Framework subset	

7.3.9 Review Questions

1. Explain what is included in the Framework hieroglyphic. Why must you understand the terminology associated with the Framework in order to practice the discipline?
2. What is the difference between a law and a rule?
3. What is the motivation for following the laws of the Framework? Explain what is implied if the practitioner does not follow the laws of the Framework.
4. Why might someone new to the Framework find the comments for Law 3 especially helpful, even though there is no required starting point for using the Framework?
5. Explain how the Framework can assist executive management in knowing what it needs to know to keep the enterprise successful.
6. Give some examples that illustrate how the Framework's structure can be used to organize the knowledge for an enterprise of any size.

SECTION 7.4 WHERE TO PAY ATTENTION— THE DEVIL IS IN THE DETAILS

> ## QUESTIONS TO CONTEMPLATE
>
> 1. Why is understanding the target audience imperative to producing an artifact with an excruciating level of detail?
> 2. Where is analysis and design performed relative to the rows of the Framework?
> 3. How might a bias influence an abstraction?

7.4.1 Introduction

The Zachman Framework has a rigid set of laws and rules, but is also flexible. The Framework does not dictate which perspectives or aspects need to be addressed first or in what order. It does not mandate the production of every primitive model, nor require that every assumption be fleshed out and every thought made explicit to an excruciating level of detail. However, the Framework's laws and rules are highly suggestive in how to achieve a *functioning enterprise* that is:

- Aligned
- Flexible
- Responsive
- Integrated
- Interoperable
- Quick to market
- Quality oriented
- Adaptable

Thomas Hobson (1544–1631) was an English livery keeper who is believed to be the originator of the phrase "Hobson's choice." Hobson required that customers who wanted to ride a horse would take either the horse nearest the stable door or none at all. Hobson's choice is the perception of offering someone an array of choices when, in reality, there is *this one*, or nothing.

The Framework is a tool for thinking, reasoning, and communicating. As a tool, the Framework is not about limiting choice. In fact, the purpose of promoting thought, reasoning, and communication is to open the realm of possible choices. Even an enterprise that needs to make only one decision should be able to improve its decision-making when the question can be placed and understood in the context of the entire enterprise.

Most *functioning enterprises* require some level of thinking, reasoning, and communicating. In Part II, many issues regarding each cell of the Framework are discussed. In this section, some of the mechanics for working with any cell are explored.

Unlike Hobson's choice, the Framework is designed to remove limitations. Whether your enterprise is a zoo, a mine, a pancake restaurant, a medical facility, an accounting firm, an information technology department dedicated to using antiquated techniques, or an information technology department focused on the Internet, distributed computing, and object orientation, the Framework is not *Hobson's choice*.

7.4.2 Sitting Down *(where)*

You have been asked to write a cookbook. Despite your culinary expertise, you decide to start with a few basic recipes. The first recipe you are tackling is named *Les Bulles d'Eau*. As far as you know, the recipe has been in your family for generations, but has never been formally recorded. The recipe has been passed down verbally as a form of tribal knowledge. With pen in hand, you sit down and write:

Boil water.

Impressed with your own ability to skillfully articulate what has to be done, you move on to the next recipe.

Does the recipe for *Les Bulles d'Eau* have an excruciating level of detail? Creating artifacts at an excruciating level of detail is one of the most difficult parts of creating an enterprise architecture. How much detail is the right amount of detail? Ultimately, the required amount of detail is governed by the method of practice, the domain, and the experience and knowledge of the practitioner.

For example, would everyone who follows the recipe for *Les Bulles d'Eau* know when the water has reached its boiling point? Would the cookbook's reader know how to place the water in a pot, heat it, and recognize that the water is not boiling when:

- Bubbles are starting to stick to the bottom of the pot. At this point, the water's temperature is about 160°F.
- Bubbles are starting to rise to the top of the pot. At this point, the water's temperature is around 180°F.
- Water is starting to move slowly about the pot. At this point, the water's temperature is around 200°F.

The water is boiling when:

- The water bubbles vigorously, releasing drops that may land out of the pot. At this point, the water's temperature is between 211°F and 212°F.
- 212°F is the exact temperature of the boiling point.

For all of these temperatures to be accurate, the cook must be attempting to boil water at an altitude less than 1,000 feet above sea level. In Breckenridge, Colorado, water evaporates before it reaches 212°F.

You know that several of your recipes require boiled water, so you decide to place the details about how to detect boiling water in an appendix.

But when you review the descriptions of how to know when water is boiling, you wonder:

- Will the cook know what type of pot to use?
- Will the cook put enough water in the pot?
- Will the cook put too much water in the pot?
- Will the cook leave the pot unattended on the heat source?
- What will the cook use for a heat source?
- Where will the cook get the water?
- Will the cook know not to use contaminated water?
- Will the cook need to make a pot?
- Will the cook know not to use a flammable pot?
- Where will the cook be—in a kitchen, hiking in a forest, roaming in a desert, or on an ice cap in the Arctic Circle?
- What if the cook tries to boil water while driving in a car? That would be dangerous. Do I need to put a cautionary notice in the book?
- What if the cook is a five-year-old child?
- Can the cook read and understand what is being read?
- What if the cook is a fragile man who needs to use both hands to hold a walking cane?
- Will the cook try to test the water's temperature by placing a finger in the water?
- Will the cook keep away from the steam?
- What if the cook gets scalded? Do I need to include medical procedures?
- Will the cook know to turn off or put out the heat source afterward?

After writing the first recipe, you decide to give up. The amount of implied details involved in *Les Bulles d'Eau* is overwhelming. The next recipe calls for diced onions and that requires using a knife—yikes...way too risky. You decide to shelve the project.

The amount of excruciating detail required depends on the domain and the product or service in the *functioning enterprise*. You would hope someone who is designing a dialysis machine does not get overwhelmed by the amount of detail required to make the machine work properly.

Obviously, the more information someone communicates formally, the less chance for a mistake in the final product or service. If the *planner* leaves out some details, the *owner* is forced to make assumptions, or simply ignore what is not known. If the *owner* leaves out some details, the *designer* is forced to make assumptions, or simply ignore what is not known. If the *designer* leaves out some details, the *builder* is forced to make assumptions, or simply ignore what is not known. If the *builder* leaves out some details, the *subcontractor* is forced to simply make it up.

TOO COMPLEX?

Authors Raphael Malveau and Thomas Mowbray in *Software Architect Bootcamp* write, "These contrary notions can be summarized in terms of the principle of pragmatism. We side with the pragmatists...because most software systems are too complex to model completely."

When software is too complex to model, how can you tell someone what you want? We live with legacy applications because people shift the responsibility to create software to the last person in the line, the *subcontractor*. If something is too complex to model, why is it not too complex to code? Who are these pragmatists?

A lack of excruciating detail contributes to failed software and indicates laziness on the part of the enterprise's workers.

The devil is in the details and in American culture, it is morally acceptable *to pass the buck*, which means to shift responsibility. The *planner* shifts responsibility for detail to the *owner*, who, in turn, shifts responsibility for detail to the *designer*, and so on, until the *subcontractor* is involved. The *subcontractor* will then decide to:

- Seek out what has not been detailed
- Decide without advice how something should be done
- Not bother constructing something

When the *subcontractor* fills in the gaps left implicit by the other perspectives, the *subcontractor* can guess right or wrong. In either case, should the *subcontractor* be left to guess?

Most, if not all, enterprises require an implied level of knowledge to help maintain the enterprise. If you produce a diagram or write text, regardless of the subject material, you assume that someone can understand the diagram's notation or the language of the text.

Creating an artifact written to an excruciating level of detail implies that the artifact's target audience has a minimum level of knowledge. Each enterprise should determine that minimum level of knowledge. The contents of an artifact should accommodate the minimum level of knowledge, and the excruciating level of detail should provide the target audience with the answer to any question relative to the perspective, aspect, and domain.

Therefore, when writing a cookbook that includes basic recipes, such as *Les Bulles d'Eau*, you may need to assume a minimum level of knowledge (or education) for the intended audience. Other assumptions about the audience include:

- Having a certain level of literacy
- Being morally responsible
- Understanding basic first aid
- Understanding how to seek additional medical help

- Familiarity with the layout of a modern kitchen
- Familiarity with the operation of modern kitchen appliances and facilities

Writing to an excruciating level of detail demands that you understand and make explicit your intended audience. However, writing to an excruciating level of detail does not mean that the artifact has to be written for everyone.

Accepted Norms and Standards

In addition, achieving an excruciating level of detail does not imply that every piece of information must be in a single place. When building a timber-framed house, you use nails to attach two pieces of wood. Typically, architectural prints (blueprints) do not show where each nail should be placed. The building industry, through its standards and accepted methods of practice, has established the appropriate number of nails and distance between nails for attaching wood.

Most IT departments have standards. When designing an application, it is not usually necessary to incorporate or directly reference the coding standards in the design. The *subcontractor* uses both the design document and the coding standards document to create a program. For example, standards may include suggested spacing between words, placement of a semi-colon (;) or brace ({ or }), or use of constructors or deconstructors in a computer program—the artifact.

Much of the information placed in an artifact is based on the domain. The diagram of a house on Earth may not need to indicate where each nail should be placed, but the International Space Station diagram does need to indicate where each nut and bolt must be placed.

When details for an artifact are included within a set of standards, the standards do not necessarily need to be placed in the artifact. The same applies for any conventions or accepted norms. However, conventions and accepted norms should be documented for reference.

Too Much Detail, too Little Detail, or Just Right

The image of singer and songwriter John Lennon (1940–1980) is well known by many people. With a few squiggles, an image can be rendered that identifies the artist. Figure 7-47 shows such an image. The other images in Figure 7-47 show Lennon's face in increasing detail. To portray Lennon, a quick sketch can be drawn in a matter of seconds, or a more elaborate drawing can be rendered, taking many hours to complete.

Figure 7-47   *Part I — How much detail?*

501

When producing an artifact, the excruciating level of detail should represent the minimum amount of complete information. Therefore, if a few squiggles contain everything you need to know, then do not bother to add detail. On the other hand, a house drawn with a few squiggles, as shown in Figure 7-48, is insufficient to start building a house. Detail is dependent on the domain and relevant to the practitioner.

Figure 7-48   *Part II — How much detail?*

7.4.3 Transformation *(how)*

Each perspective in the Framework is a viewpoint of the *functioning enterprise*:

- The *planner* articulates the *functioning enterprise* through scope.
- The *owner* articulates the *functioning enterprise* through conceptual design.
- The *designer* articulates the *functioning enterprise* through logical design.
- The *builder* articulates the *functioning enterprise* through physical design.
- The *subcontractor* articulates the *functioning enterprise* as the individually constructed components.
- The *functioning enterprise* is viewed differently by the users of the enterprise and by those that envisioned and constructed it.

The Framework recognizes that each perspective has a unique set of constraints relative to the *functioning enterprise*. The Framework also recognizes that each perspective uses terminology, techniques, tools, and communication vehicles that are not necessarily understood or used by the other perspectives.

Therefore, between each perspective is a transformation. The transformation is not a mechanism of adding more detail. In an ideal situation, each perspective produces artifacts to an excruciating level of detail. The transformation translates what is mandated by a previous row. Transformation is a process of analysis.

You analyze something to come to a comprehensive understanding of the subject. If the subject already exists, analyzing produces an *as-is* (current state) portrayal. If the subject is something desired, the analysis produces a *to-be* (end state) portrayal of the subject. The concepts of current and end states are discussed in Chapter 2.

TRANSFORMATION SHORTHAND

The shorthand for a row is Rn, where n is a number from 1 to 6. For example, R1, R2, R3, R4, R5, and R6. R1 is the *planner* perspective and R6 is the *functioning enterprise* perspective.

The shorthand for a column is Cm, where m is also a number from 1 to 6. For example, C1, C2, C3, C4, C5, and C6. C1 is the *what* aspect and C6 is the *why* aspect.

The shorthand for a row and column intersection is $RnCm$. Although n and m are numbers from 1 to 6, n and m do not need to have the same value at the same time. For example, R1C1, R3C2, R5C3, etc. R1C1 is the intersection of the *planner* perspective and the *what* aspect. R3C2 is the intersection of the *designer* perspective and the *how* aspect.

The transformation shorthand for top-down or forward engineering is $RpTp+1$, where p is a number from 0 to 5. Whereas, the domain value for n is 1 to 6, the domain value for p is 0 to 5. For example, the transformation shorthand is:

R0T1—Row 0 transforming to Row 1
R1T2—Row 1 transforming to Row 2
R2T3—Row 2 transforming to Row 3
R3T4—Row 3 transforming to Row 4
R4T5—Row 4 transforming to Row 5
R5T6—Row 5 transforming to Row 6

In addition, a column can be specified in the transformation shorthand as follows—$RpTp+1Cm$, where p is a number from zero to five and m is still a number from one to six. For example:

R0T1C6—Row 0 transforming to Row 1 for just Column 6
R1T2C5—Row 1 transforming to Row 2 for just Column 5
R2T3C4—Row 2 transforming to Row 3 for just Column 4
R3T4C3—Row 3 transforming to Row 4 for just Column 3
R4T5C2—Row 4 transforming to Row 5 for just Column 2
R5T6C1—Row 5 transforming to Row 6 for just Column 1

In the Framework, the transformation between rows is often a combination of a current state and end state analysis process. The rows of the Framework represent a design effort. The work between the rows is an analysis effort. Working through the Framework, the pattern of alternation between analysis and design is:

- R0T1—Perform analysis for the scope-oriented artifacts for the *planner's* requirements.
- R1—Create the *planner's* scope-oriented artifacts.
- R1T2—Perform analysis of the scope-oriented artifacts for the *owner's* requirements.
- R2—Create the *owner's* conceptual artifacts.
- R2T3—Perform analysis of the conceptual design artifacts for the *designer's* requirements.
- R3—Create the *designer's* logical design artifacts.
- R3T4—Perform analysis of the logical design artifacts for the *builder's* requirements.
- R4—Create the *builder's* physical design artifacts.
- R4T5—Perform analysis of the physical design artifacts for the *subcontractor's* requirements.
- R5—Create the *subcontractor's* descriptive representation artifacts.
- R5T6—Perform analysis of the descriptive representation artifacts for the *functioning enterprise's* requirements.
- R6—The materialized *functioning enterprise*.
- R6T1—Perform analysis of the *functioning enterprise* as a feedback mechanism into the Framework. The Framework's feedback mechanism is a causal loop.

The designation R0 (Row 0) is not an indication of another row on the Framework. Rather, R0 indicates that the analysis is not based on an existing *functioning enterprise*, which would be R6. R0T1 states that the analysis performed to determine scope is not based on what is currently known. R0T1 implies that new information is being sought.

From R0T1 to R6T1, the Framework switches attention between analysis and design as you progress through the perspectives. The alternation is maintained for bottom-up or reverse engineering efforts. In other words, in R6T5, you analyze the *functioning enterprise* so that the *subcontractor* can create the descriptive representations.

The sequence of analysis followed by design means that first you create an understanding, then you design or construct. Part of the analysis transformation process is gathering all the necessary techniques, standards, rules, and disciplines for completing the subsequent perspective.

For example, suppose the *planner* decides the organization needs to expand and enter the competitive gravitational-powered kumquat market. The *planner* creates a list of things necessary to enter the marketplace. The lists are based on answering the questions: *what, how, where, who, when,* and *why*. The *planner's* lists are analyzed and transformed by the *owner*, who creates a conceptual model for each aspect. See Figure 7-49.

- This is the *subcontractor*
- Who wrote an application for a gravitational-powered kumquat
- That could be integrated into the *functioning enterprise*
- That went through the dealer
- That enabled contracts
- That alerted manufacturing
- That checked with accounting
- That contacted shipping
- That sent the delivery
- That sealed the process
- That brought kudos from the *owner*
- Who congratulated the *designer*
- Who acknowledged the *builder*
- Who patted the *subcontractor* on the back
- And all because the *planner* was explicit from the start

Figure 7-49   Kudos

The *owner's* conceptual model is analyzed and transformed by the *designer*, who creates a logical model of each aspect. The *builder* then performs an analysis and transforms the *designer's* model into a model of how the organization will produce the gravitational-powered kumquats and operate in the marketplace. The *subcontractor* analyzes and transforms the physical design and builds each component, or sets in place everything that is necessary for the *functioning* enterprise to operate.

From the *planner* to the *subcontractor*, nobody is actually operating in the *functioning enterprise*; each of these perspectives has only a viewpoint of the *functioning enterprise*. The *planner, owner, designer, builder,* and *subcontractor* deal with representations of the real thing—such as a gravitational-powered kumquat. A description, picture, identification number, and a model are all examples of abstractions for articulating real things. Abstractions let you think, reason, and communicate about something real without having to experience the real thing.

If any of the people who created the lists and artifacts for Rows 1, 2, 3, 4, and 5 do something with the real thing in the *functioning enterprise*, they no longer experience the real thing as a representation of their analysis or design perspective. Instead, they are experiencing the real thing from the perspective of the *functioning enterprise*. This is why the perspectives are viewpoints and not job titles—because people can and do change perspectives.

Later on, if someone alters the design, they return to the appropriate design perspective (Row 1, 2, 3, 4, or 5). However, before the design is refined, a transformation takes place. Because the information being fed into the transformation is mandated from another perspective, the transformation inherits information from the previous perspective.

The output of the transformation process may appear in a form that cannot be understood by the participants of the previous perspective, but the mappings (the outcome of the analysis) from how to get from one perspective to another should be understood, or better yet, documented.

Remember that the perspectives are not directly aligned with job titles; the perspectives are based on the type of viewpoint. Therefore, both a corporate CEO and a programmer can choose to work at any perspective, provided they understand the purpose of the viewpoint, its terminology, methods of practice, and techniques.

Transformations can be made mentally, or formalized as an additional set of artifacts. Some transformations can be automated, such as a computer program that is compiled into an executable application program. The compiler creates the transformation between notation written and understood by a programmer to the notation understood by a computer.

7.4.4 Bias *(when)*

Everyone is different and differences create individual biases. Personal biases are based on influences, including when and where you were born, the type of education you received, and, potentially, how well you have liked this book. Biases may cause people to try and solve the same problem in different ways.

Needing to design a writing tool for its astronauts to write in space, NASA spent millions of dollars developing a ballpoint pen capable of writing in extreme temperatures and operating in an environment without gravity. Naturally, the Russian space agency faced the same problem for its cosmonauts. However, the Russians saved time and money by simply providing their cosmonauts with ordinary pencils. The agencies faced the same problem, and both provided different solutions.

Even though the Framework prescribes a comprehensive set of primitive models, there is no single primitive model for any problem. The primitive model or artifact for every cell is going to be the result of information at hand and individual biases. The Framework prescribes the types of deliverables, but not the exact content of the deliverables.

The primitives help focus attention on a particular perspective and aspect. The abstraction of the primitive is based on the biases of individuals, such as:

- A business enterprise may need to deal with customers, vendors, and suppliers. One solution a *designer* may choose for modeling these terms in the *what* aspect might be to create a diagram with three boxes representing the concept of a customer, vendor, and supplier. However, an alternative abstraction might be to create a single box called *party*. See Figure 7-50. The style is a personal preference.

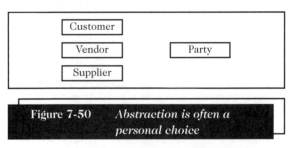

Figure 7-50   *Abstraction is often a personal choice*

- Most computer languages have syntax for looping. A loop is designed to repeat a set of instructions until a certain condition has been met. Most computer languages have one type of syntax that tests a condition at the top of the loop and a separate syntax to test a condition at the bottom of the loop. See Figure 7-51. The type of loop used is often based on the biases of the *subcontractor*.

```
while (count <= 4)
{
        cout << "n/Enter a number: ";
        cin >> num;
        cout << "The number entered is " << num;
        count++
}
```
Loop testing at the top of the statement

```
do
{
        cout << "n/Enter a number: ";
        cin >> num;
        cout << "The number entered is " << num;
        count++
}
while (count <= 4)
```
Loop testing at the bottom of the statement

Figure 7-51   *Sample loops written in C/C++*

- One *owner* may choose to describe all of the organization's connectivity needs between distribution facilities together, while another *owner* may choose to separate connectivity models based on local laws and export/import restrictions, thereby creating separate Peer Frameworks based on geography and politics. See Figure 7-52. If Peer Frameworks are used, integration across the enterprise can occur only if it is specifically engineered.

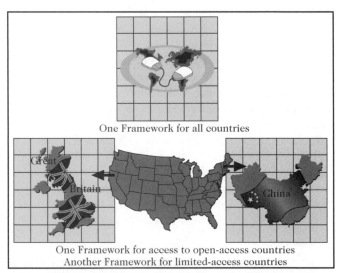

One Framework for all countries

One Framework for access to open-access countries
Another Framework for limited-access countries

Figure 7-52   *Peer Frameworks created to handle disparate export markets*

Workflow in an organization might be modeled by one *builder* based on individuals. Another *builder* may choose to model the organization by the general roles people play, regardless of how many roles a single individual might play. See Figure 7-53.

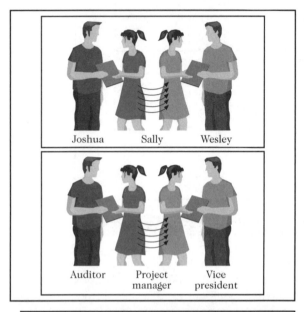

Figure 7-53   *Common workflows by named people and role*

- Schedules typically contain a series of tasks to be performed. Schedules are usually invoked synchronously or asynchronously within an organization. At the end of a synchronous schedule, a notification of completion is sent to the person or process that triggered the schedule. The completion message usually indicates whether the tasks were performed successfully. An asynchronous schedule is not required to notify its originator of completion. Depending on the *planner's* preferences, a schedule may be specified as synchronous or asynchronous, or left unspecified. If left unspecified, an assumption is made by the other perspectives. See Figure 7-54.
- One *functioning enterprise* may allow its customers to pay only with cash. Another *functioning enterprise* may allow its customers to pay only with checks and credit cards. Both *functioning enterprises* accumulate revenue on their balance sheets in the same way. See Figure 7-55.

Working through a solution cell by cell (or primitive by primitive) helps factor a topic to its simplest contextual form. Having representation of each primitive allows complex composites to be built that are understood at the *primitive* (root) level. When or if a problem arises, problem analysis, root cause analysis, or systems thinking can all be made easier because the primitive is known, and the composite is a derivative of multiple primitives. See Figure 7-56.

Figure 7-54 *Synchronous: Return message; asynchronous: No return message*

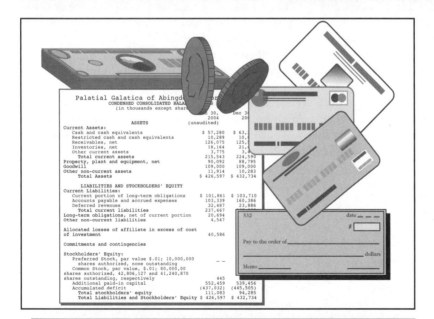

Figure 7-55 *Strategies for payment acceptance*

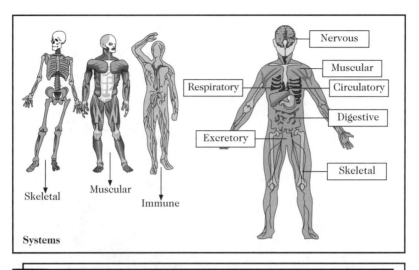

| Nervous |
| Muscular |
| Circulatory |
| Digestive |
| Skeletal |

Respiratory

Excretory

Skeletal   Muscular

Immune

Systems

Figure 7-56   *Composite model and its primitives*

7.4.5 Risky Business *(what)*

Any artifact can be mapped to the Framework. An artifact is either primitive or composite in nature. A primitive artifact addresses only issues and designs relative to one perspective and one aspect. Primitive artifacts are normalized: one fact or concept in one place. If an artifact is not primitive, then the artifact is composite. A composite artifact addresses more than one perspective, more than one aspect, or potentially, multiple perspectives and multiple aspects.

If six primitives have been produced for a single perspective, then, collectively, the artifacts are comprehensive. At an excruciating level of detail, a comprehensive artifact contains everything that you need to know about an issue or design for the domain. Comprehensive artifacts are normalized artifacts.

PRIMITIVE ARTIFACTS AND NORMALIZATION

The structure of the Framework governs what is considered to be a primitive artifact. If an artifact is primitive, then by the laws of the Framework, the artifact is normalized. However, only the artifact itself is considered normalized. The content of the artifact may not necessarily be normalized.

For example, a data model may contain a denormalized entity called *party* with the following attributes:

Entity Name:

PARTY

(continued)

Attribute Names:

PARTY_NAME—a non-unique identifier for each tuple (a row or record). There could be multiple John Smiths

MAIDEN_NAME—an attribute to hold the unmarried name of a person

BIRTH_DATE—a date field is not atomic. A date normally contains three pieces of information: a month, a day, and a year. In information technology, something that is atomic is at its lowest level of composition without losing meaning.

Figure 7-57 illustrates a denormalized design.

Party

party_name
maiden_name
birth_date

Figure 7-57   *Denormalized design*

A normalized version of the data model would be:

Entity Name:

PARTY

Attribute Names:

PARTY_ID—a unique identifier for each Party
BIRTH_MONTH—the Party's month of birth
BIRTH_DAY—the Party's day of birth
BIRTH_YEAR—the Party's year of birth

Entity Name:

PARTY_NAME

Attribute Names:

PARTY_ID—a unique identifier for each Party
NAME—the Party's name
NAME_TYPE—the type of name for the Party, e.g., legal, maiden, alias, former, given, etc.

Figure 7-58 illustrates a normalized design.

(continued)

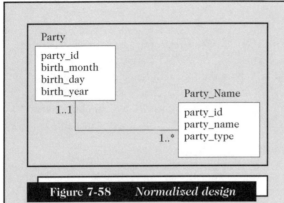

Figure 7-58   _Normalized design_

An artifact can be considered normalized even when the artifact's contents are denormalized. The normalization of the artifact is relative to the perspective and the aspect. Content normalization is relative to the method of practice, but typically follows having only _one of something in one place_. In Figure 7-57, a person's name could occur multiple times.

Having a primitive artifact does not guarantee the production of a worthwhile or valid deliverable. Conversely, a composite artifact produced without a primitive does not guarantee a worthless or invalid deliverable. The purpose of the Framework is to help you think through a problem, create a solution, and then communicate the solution.

Understanding the Framework's structure regarding the nature and purpose of a primitive artifact can help a practitioner simplify a problem, thereby helping to create a logical structure for the practitioner to create a solution. The Framework is a tool for thinking, reasoning, and communicating. The Framework does not do the work of architecture. The Framework is inert, but does help guide the work of architecture.

Primitive artifacts are architectural and imply normalized knowledge. Normalization helps partition a problem into a logical, organized, and practical form. When change is required—and all business organizations require change to survive—the normalized (primitive) artifacts can accommodate and implement change at a faster rate. In business, regardless of financial assets, organizations that can change the fastest have the best chance to remain in business.

If you do not need to remain in business, you do not need primitive artifacts, and you do not need to take an enterprise architecture approach to your _functioning enterprise_.

The use of the Zachman Framework for Enterprise Architecture prescribes, but does not mandate, producing primitives before composites. For most enterprises, being able to manage risk is critical. The Framework helps promote making everything primitive, explicit, and at an excruciating level of detail. When things are composite, left assumed, or implicit, the Framework helps promote understanding of the level of risk to an enterprise.

7.4.6 Analysis Paralysis *(why)*

Producing a series of artifacts for an enterprise does not necessarily create analysis paralysis. Analysis paralysis is an antipattern in which an enterprise never completes a design to build a *functioning enterprise* because it is afraid it may have left something out.

Here are some examples of information technology artifacts mapped to the Framework:

Figures 7-59, 7-60, 7-61, 7-62, 7-63, and 7-64 illustrate Row 1 artifacts.

NOTATION

Many of the following models use the Unified Modeling Language (UML) notation. Each model is a sample of a model type that can be used to create a primitive or composite model. A stereotype is a feature of UML and is used on several of the sample models. The stereotype is indicated by the French quotation marks called guillemets (« and »). The purpose of a stereotype is to extend the capabilities of UML.

Examples of the stereotypes used are «FACT» to indicate a Fact entity and «ELH» to represent an entity in an entity life history model.

In addition, many of the symbols used in the UML models are notated.

- Customers
- Orders
- Products
- Markets
- Tornadoes
- Threats
- Processes

Figure 7-59   *Row 1, Column 1 (R1C1) — Sample list*

- Invent products
- Design products
- Produce products
- Develop markets
- Store finished goods

Figure 7-60   *Row 1, Column 2 (R1C2) — Sample list*

- Los Angeles (area)
- Chicago (area)
- Orlando (area)
- Seattle (area)
- Mobile facilities

Figure 7-61 *Row 1, Column 3 (R1C3) — Sample list*

- Research and development
- Manufacturing
- Material
- Marketing
- Accounting
- Vendors
- Customers

Figure 7-62 *Row 1, Column 4 (R1C4) — Sample list*

Event	Cycle
IPO	Economic cycle
Commit	Engineering cycle
Order (purchase)	Acquisition cycle
Release	Manufacturing cycle
Prospect	Sell cycle
Announcement	Product cycle
Order (customer)	Order cycle
Close	Accounting cycle
April 15	Tax cycle

Figure 7-63 *Row 1, Column 5 (R1C5) — Sample list*

- To be best
- To be cheapest
- To be most responsive
- To be cost effective
- To be first to market
- To be the lowest-cost producer
- To be a full service provider
- To be profitable
- To be bigger
- To be international
- To be ethical and moral
- To be environmentally sensitive

Figure 7-64 *Row 1, Column 6 (R1C6) — Sample list*

Figures 7-65, 7-66, 7-67, 7-68, 7-69, and 7-70 illustrate Row 2 artifacts.

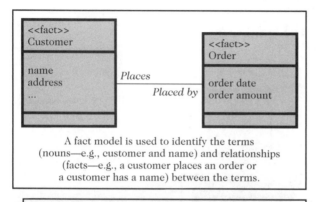

A fact model is used to identify the terms (nouns—e.g., customer and name) and relationships (facts—e.g., a customer places an order or a customer has a name) between the terms.

Figure 7-65   *Row 2, Column 1 (R2C1) — A fact model*

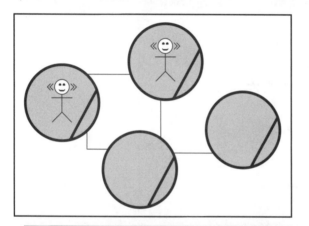

Figure 7-66   *Row 2, Column 2 (R2C2) — A business object model*

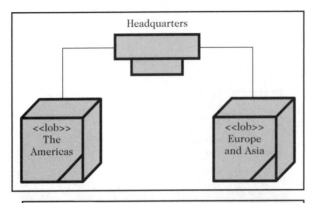

Figure 7-67 *Row 2, Column 3 (R2C3) —*
Business channels model

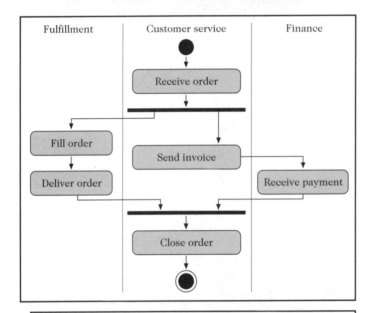

Figure 7-68 *Row 2, Column 4 (R2C4) — Workflow*

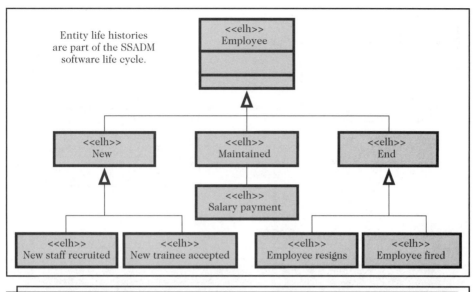

Entity life histories are part of the SSADM software life cycle.

<<elh>>
Employee

<<elh>>
New

<<elh>>
Maintained

<<elh>>
End

<<elh>>
Salary payment

<<elh>>
New staff recruited

<<elh>>
New trainee accepted

<<elh>>
Employee resigns

<<elh>>
Employee fired

Figure 7-69   *Row 2, Column 5 (R2C5) — An entity life history model*

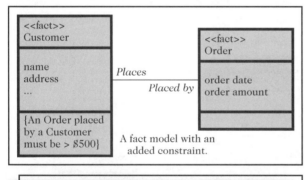

<<fact>>
Customer

name
address
...

{An Order placed by a Customer must be > $500}

Places

Placed by

<<fact>>
Order

order date
order amount

A fact model with an added constraint.

Figure 7-70   *Row 2, Column 6 (R2C6) —*
A fact model with constraints

Figures 7-71, 7-72, 7-73, 7-74, 7-75, and 7-76 illustrate Row 3 artifacts.

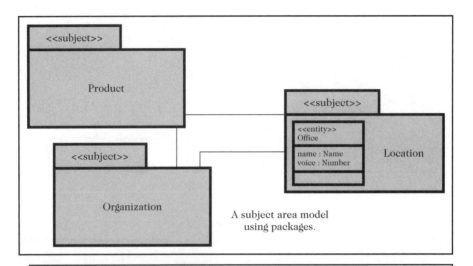

A subject area model
using packages.

Figure 7-71   Row 3, Column 1 (R3C1) — A subject area model

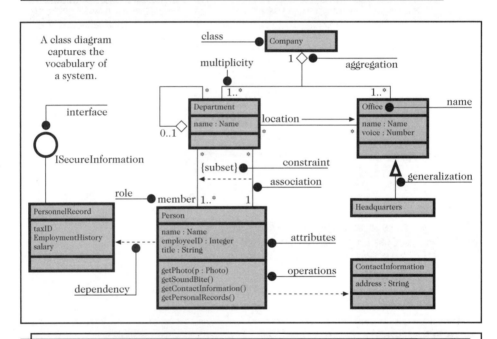

Figure 7-72   Row 3, Column 2 (R3C2) — A class diagram

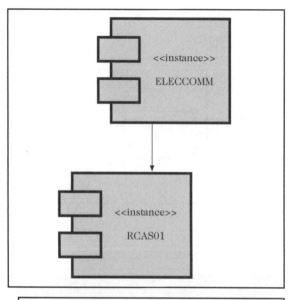

Figure 7-73   *Row 3, Column 3 (R3C3) —*
A distribution model

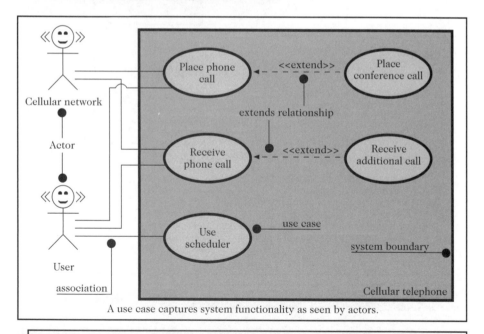

A use case captures system functionality as seen by actors.

Figure 7-74   *Row 3, Column 4 (R3C4) — A use case*

The Zachman Framework for Enterprise Architecture

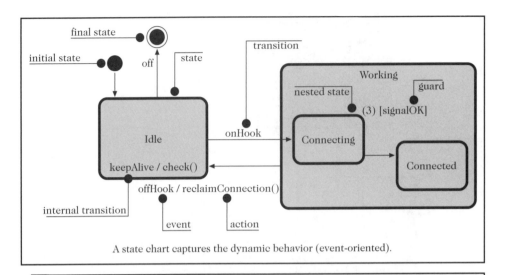

A state chart captures the dynamic behavior (event-oriented).

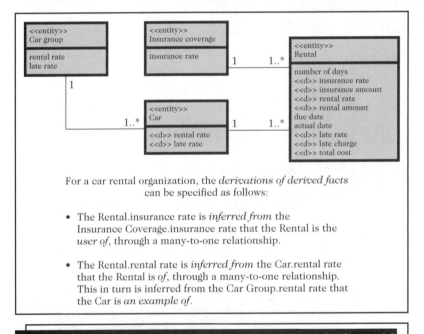

For a car rental organization, the *derivations of derived facts* can be specified as follows:

- The Rental.insurance rate is *inferred from* the Insurance Coverage.insurance rate that the Rental is the *user of*, through a many-to-one relationship.

- The Rental.rental rate is *inferred from* the Car.rental rate that the Rental is *of*, through a many-to-one relationship. This in turn is inferred from the Car Group.rental rate that the Car is *an example of*.

Figures 7-77, 7-78, 7-79, 7-80, 7-81, and 7-82 illustrate Row 4 artifacts.

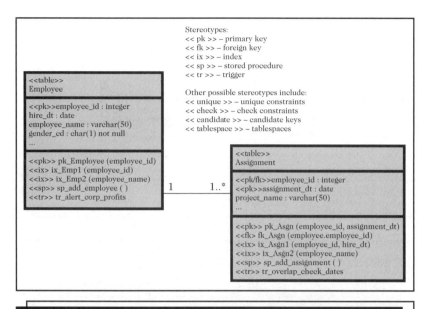

Stereotypes:
<< pk >> – primary key
<< fk >> – foreign key
<< ix >> – index
<< sp >> – stored procedure
<< tr >> – trigger

Other possible stereotypes include:
<< unique >> – unique constraints
<< check >> – check constraints
<< candidate >> – candidate keys
<< tablespace >> – tablespaces

Figure 7-77   *Row 4, Column 1 (R4C1) — Database tables*

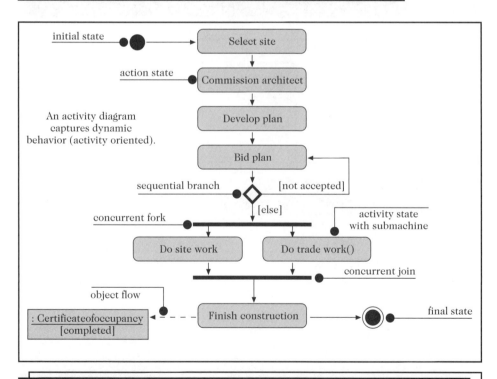

Figure 7-78   *Row 4, Column 2 (R4C2) — An activity diagram*

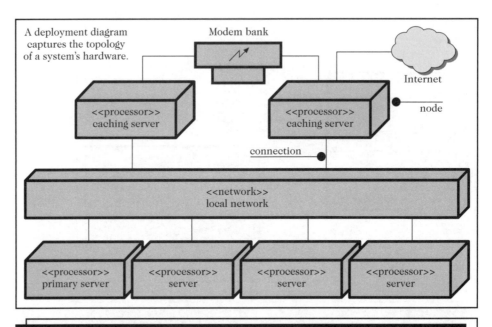

A deployment diagram captures the topology of a system's hardware.

Modem bank

Internet

node

<<processor>>
caching server

<<processor>>
caching server

connection

<<network>>
local network

<<processor>>
primary server

<<processor>>
server

<<processor>>
server

<<processor>>
server

Figure 7-79   *Row 4, Column 3 (R4C3) — A deployment diagram*

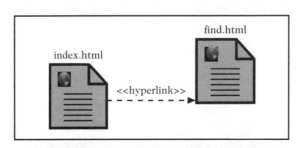

index.html

find.html

<<hyperlink>>

Figure 7-80   *Row 4, Column 4 (R4C4) —*
A user interface model

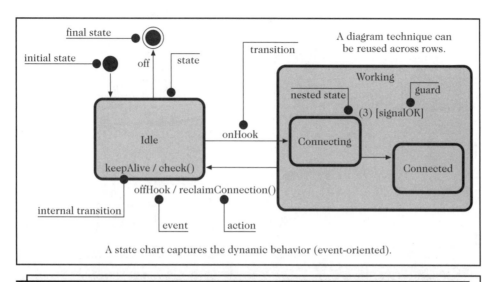

A state chart captures the dynamic behavior (event-oriented).

Figure 7-81 *Row 4, Column 5 (R4C5) — A state chart*

The Object Constraint Language (OCL) is an:
- Expression language
- Modeling language
- Formal language

OCL has syntax to include:
- Preconditions
- Postconditions   Context: LoyaltyProgram
- Invariants   Inv: customer->forAll (age >= 18)

Figure 7-82 *Row 4, Column 6 (R4C6) — Object Constraint Language*

Figures 7-83, 7-84, 7-85, 7-86, 7-87, and 7-88 illustrate Row 5 artifacts.

```
create table party
(party_id              number              not null,
 party_name            varchar(40)         not null,
 party_birth_date      date                not null);


create unique index party_ix on party
(party_id);
```

Figure 7-83 *Row 5, Column 1 (R5C1) — Database creation script*

Figure 7-84   *Row 5, Column 2 (R5C2) — A component diagram*

Figure 7-85   *Row 5, Column 3 (R5C3) — Assembling a network*

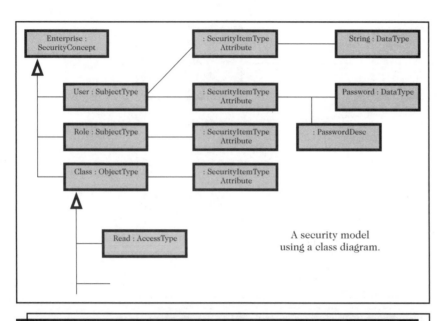

A security model
using a class diagram.

Figure 7-86   *Row 5, Column 4 (R5C4) — A security model*

```
0 * * * * /etc/reset.cgi
0 0 * * * /etc/resetlogs.cgi
30 4 31 12 * /etc/yearend.cgi
0 12 * * 1 /etc/everymondayatnoon.cgi
```

The Unix operating system has a scheduler called
Crontab. The scheduler can execute a command at a
specific date and time.

The first five fields are used to set the execution
date and time:

- **MINUTE**   (0–59)
- **HOUR**   (0–23)
- **DAYOFMONTH**   (1–31)
- **MONTHOFYEAR** (1–12)
- **DAYOFWEEK**   (0–6)   0 = Sun

The asterisk is a wild card, meaning that any value
will be matched.

Figure 7-87   *Row 5, Column 5 (R5C5) — A schedule*

The Zachman Framework for Enterprise Architecture

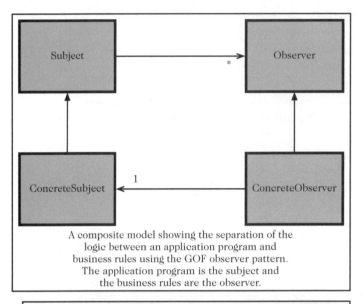

A composite model showing the separation of the logic between an application program and business rules using the GOF observer pattern. The application program is the subject and the business rules are the observer.

7.4.7 For Fate Has Left Him Indestructible *(who)*

Captain Scarlet was the name of a 1967 British television series. The plot began with a *slight* blunder on behalf of Spectrum agent Captain Black. He destroyed a Martian city (on planet Mars). This event greatly upset the once peaceful Martians who were known as the Mysterons. The Mysterons were an invisible race, who also had the power to regenerate things. They quickly rebuilt their city. The Mysterons sought revenge and vowed to slowly destroy the Earth.

Captain Scarlet was one of their first victims. The Mysterons killed him in a car accident and regenerated his body for their use. Even after being under their control, Captain Scarlet suffered a second death—the result of a shootout with Captain Blue. He fell several hundred meters from a poorly designed parking lot. From that moment, Captain Scarlet lost his Mysteron influence, but was now able to regenerate and recover himself from any fatal accident within a few hours.

Colonel White, the leader of Spectrum, instantly recognized the benefits of having someone indestructible on his team. Captain Scarlet became Spectrum's most valuable agent and served Spectrum well, battling the Mysterons during the show's 32 episodes.

Captain Scarlet was indestructible, but his indestructibility did not mean he was always functioning. He still needed time to regenerate from a fatal wound before being ready to fight again. For Spectrum, a regenerating agent meant having an agent who was:

- *Aligned* to any need of the organization to produce a quality result
- *Flexible* to undertake any new type of mission
- *Responsive* to the organization's needs

- *Integrated* with the other agents—Captain Scarlet always needed their help
- *Interoperable* to work in any location
- Quick-to-market to save the day
- Quality oriented because he knew what Spectrum demanded of him
- Adaptable to the situation of any given episode

The qualities of an indestructible agent align to the pursuit of enterprise architecture. One of the objectives of enterprise architecture is to create an indestructible enterprise. In a competitive marketplace, each enterprise is likely to become wounded. The ability to regenerate is, therefore, critical.

In Section 7.3.5, a list of proposed rallying points for each perspective was presented:

- *Planner*—begins with the aspect *what*.
- *Owner*—begins with the aspect *when*.
- *Designer*—begins with the aspect *how*.
- *Builder*—begins with the aspect *where*.
- *Subcontractor*—begins with the aspect *who*.
- *Functioning enterprise*—begins with the aspect *why*.

Chapters 2 through 6 contain six sections. Each section starts with a different interrogative. Each starting point is followed by the other interrogatives in a mixed sequence. This pattern is used to illustrate that a complete story can be painted from any starting point and threaded in an appropriate way.

The starting points in each section and the proposed rallying points are ways to orient a set of biases. The rallying point does not mean complete this particular interrogative before moving on to the next interrogative. In reality, all six interrogatives may be worked on at exactly the same time by different teams. Information about one primitive artifact can be shared with another practitioner working on a different primitive artifact.

The iterative flow of information helps prevent or curtail gaps, assumptions, and implicit details. Independent of a method of practice, the proposed rallying points are viewed as ubiquitous ways for the perspectives to create a unification point to make sure all the details are:

- Aligned
- Flexible
- Responsive
- Integrated
- Interoperable
- Quick-to-market
- Quality oriented
- Adaptable

An indestructible enterprise is not one that is impervious to pain or problems, but one that has the right people produce the right artifacts to handle unforeseen circumstances.

7.4.8 Review Questions

1. How does the example of the recipe *Les Bulles d'Eau* illustrate the most difficult part of performing architecture?
2. Explain the meaning of the phrase *excruciating level of detail*. How do you know what level of detail is the right level of detail for the artifacts?
3. What is meant by transformation in the Framework?
4. Explain how the story about the indestructible Captain Scarlet aligns to the result of an iterative flow of information enabled by use of the Framework.
5. Give some examples of how personal biases can be reflected in the primitive model.
6. How can understanding the Framework's structure help simplify a problem?

SECTION 7.5 HOW THINGS TAKE SHAPE

528

QUESTIONS TO CONTEMPLATE

1. How does cell integration provide continuity for the enterprise?
2. How does the Framework help organize what a business needs to do to comply with a mandate for change?

7.5.1 Introduction

If everything lasted forever and was always built perfectly, if competition did not exist, if governments never passed any new laws, if nature did not constrain our environment, if only...Change is a constant—an oxymoron. Whether change is welcomed, expected, desired, or unforeseen, change affects all of us in some way.

TO QUOTE JOHN ZACHMAN...

Today, we tend not to manage change with a scalpel; we manage change with an axe!

An underlying precept of the Zachman Framework is that every enterprise would like to be in a position to maximize its choice in responding to a need or an opportunity to change. The change an enterprise is faced with may be minor or complex. The change can be cosmetic. The change can even be for the fun of it.

Engineered solutions that form the architecture, especially those accompanied by a comprehensive set of normalized architectural artifacts, help the enterprise facilitate change by keeping the enterprise responsive, flexible, aligned, and prepared for the next succession of changes.

The term legacy application has a negative connotation. The contextual meaning of legacy is that the enterprise is burdened and forced to perform or operate in a less than satisfactory mode. Most business and government organizations could classify a significant amount of their operations as legacy. Legacy impedes an organization's ability to survive and change in the way it desires.

TO QUOTE JOHN ZACHMAN...

Enterprises are embroiled in a state of mega-lega.[3] Architectural approaches must be adopted by any enterprise seeking refuge.

Imagine that you work for a company called Palatial Galactica of Abingdon, Incorporated, otherwise known by its employees as PalGal. Everything is going well. In fact, you think everything is finally under control. One morning, you take a drink of your morning beverage and read a dozen or so new e-mails. You open an e-mail from Camille in the legal department. She forwarded you a notice from the U.S. Federal Trade Commission. See Figure 7-89.

You finish reading the business alert from the FTC and take one last sip from your cup. *Change* just hit your desk! You smile to yourself. You pick up the telephone and dial Camille's extension.

7.5.2 Preliminaries (how)

This particular notice from the FTC, referencing the GLB Act, does not affect every business organization. However, a government body at the federal, state, or local level will pass some form of *mandated* legislation that causes an organization to change or investigate the need to change.

The cause of change is not the sole privilege of government, but this particular FTC notice is genuine and illustrates how the classification schema of the Framework can be used to work through a problem or issue in an enterprise.

FTC Business Alert
To: Palatial Galactica of Abingdon
From: Federal Trade Commission—Bureau of Consumer Protection—Office of Consumer and Business Education
Subject: Safeguarding customers' personal information

Many financial institutions' transactions with customers involve the collection of personal information: name, address, and phone number; bank and credit card account numbers; income and credit histories; and Social Security numbers. The Gramm-Leach-Bliley (GLB) Act, a Federal law, requires that financial institutions take steps to ensure the security and confidentiality of this kind of customer data.

Now, as part of its implementation of the GLB Act, the Federal Trade Commission (FTC) is issuing a rule requiring financial institutions under its jurisdiction to safeguard customer records and information.

The Safeguards Rule applies to individuals or organizations that are significantly engaged in providing financial products or services to consumers, including check-cashing businesses, data processors, mortgage brokers, non-bank lenders, personal property, or real estate appraisers and retailers that issue credit cards to consumers.

According to the Safeguards Rule, financial institutions must develop a written information security plan that describes their program to protect customer information. All programs must be appropriate to the financial institution's size and complexity, the nature and scope of its activities, and the sensitivity of the customer information at issue. Covered financial institutions must:

- Designate the employee or employees to coordinate the safeguards.
- Identify and assess the risks to customer information in each relevant area of the company's operation, and evaluate the effectiveness of current safeguards for controlling these risks.
- Design a safeguards program and detail the plans to monitor it.
- Select appropriate service providers and require them (by contract) to implement the safeguards.
- Evaluate the program and explain adjustments in light of changes to its business arrangements or the results of its security tests.

Experts suggest that three areas of operation present special challenges and risks to information security: employee training and management; information systems, including network and software design, information processing, storage, transmission and retrieval; and security management, including the prevention, detection and response to attacks, intrusions or other system failures. The Rule requires financial institutions to pay special attention to these areas.

The Safeguards Rule is available at the FTC's Web site. To find out whether your company is considered a financial institution, check section 313.3(k) of the Commission's Privacy Rule and related materials.

The FTC works for the consumer to prevent fraudulent, deceptive, and unfair business practices in the marketplace and to provide information to help consumers spot, stop, and avoid them. To file a complaint or to get free information on consumer issues, visit the FTC Web site or call the FTC's toll-free number. The FTC enters Internet, telemarketing, identity theft, and other fraud-related complaints into Consumer Sentinel, a secure, online database available to hundreds of civil and criminal law enforcement agencies in the U.S. and abroad.

Figure 7-89   *The FTC Business Alert for the GLB Act*

Back at work, your telephone conversation with Camille has ended. You have arranged a meeting with her in 90 minutes. You have decided to conduct a preliminary investigation into the act by using the FTC's Internet address. You discover that on November 12, 1999, President Bill Clinton (b. 1946) signed the GLB Act (Public Law 106–102) into law. The final rulings and the FTC's safeguard rulings took quite a while to finalize, and now, financial institutions affected by the law have 12 months to comply.

Your PDA beeps—the alarm for your meeting with Camille. The two of you sit down in a conference room and Camille begins to explain some of the legal aspects of the law. "The GLB Act requires companies like ours to give consumers privacy notices that explain our information-sharing practices. In turn, the consumer has the right to ask us to limit some, but not all, sharing of their information," Camille began.

This meeting is the first of many meetings that take place in the company about the act. This particular meeting provides some background information for you about the act, and according to the laws and rules of the Framework, you place yourself at Row 1—the *planner* row. Interested in determining the scope of the challenge, you start making lists.

PLACEMENT

Placement at a given row is not dependent on a job title or a specific individual. The perspective is constrained by a set of guidelines and objectives. Placement in a row is based on the characteristics you are adopting physically. During a conversation, it is possible to change perspective dynamically or to oscillate between perspectives.

Camille started her discussion by talking about *opting-out* and *pretexting*. These terms are unfamiliar to you. As a practitioner of the Framework, you recognize that obtaining definitions is a vital first step in determining the domain of a problem. You let Camille speak freely, but you organize your notes based on the six interrogatives. Under *what*, you list opt-out and pretexting and then ask for some preliminary definitions.

Camille tells you:

Opting-out refers to the customer's right to say "no" with regard to the information we share with certain third parties. By law, we must provide customers with a privacy notice that explains how they can say "no."

For example, PalGal currently gives customers a choice of contacting us either by using a toll-free telephone number, or by returning a pre-printed, return-addressed form from a letter previously sent by our company. If we forced our customers to write a letter, the federal government would judge that we were not offering a reasonable way for our customers to opt-out.

The privacy notice explains to our customers that they have a right to say "no" to sharing some types of information, such as a credit report or application information, with one of our financial affiliates. As you know, an affiliate can be an organization that is controlled by another company, by PalGal, or under common control with PalGal and another.

Our customers actually have most of these rights under a different law, the Fair Credit Reporting Act. The GLB Act does not give our customers the right to opt-out of all the information we may have about them. For example, a customer cannot opt-out if:

- *We want to share information with an outside company that provides essential services, like data processing or account services.*
- *We are legally required to disclose the consumer's information.*
- *We want to share customer data with an outside service provider that markets our products and services.*

Pretexting is the practice of obtaining customer information for financial institutions under false pretenses. When thinking of their personal assets, many people think of their home, car, or the money they have in their bank accounts. However, social security numbers and credit card numbers are assets too.

People who obtain this information under false pretenses are known as pretexters. Pretexters try to sell a person's information so someone else can try to get credit under that person's name, steal their assets, or use the information to investigate or sue that person.

You diligently write down everything Camille is telling you. It then crosses your mind that you should have already known all of this. You make a note to check if these terms and definitions are already available on the corporate intranet for everyone to review. You also consider the possibility that PalGal might need to provide some additional education for its employees.

As the conversation with Camille ends, you summarize a set of next steps:

- Develop a complete understanding of the opportunity.[4] By getting all the departments involved, we can fully understand the scope of this issue—*planner*.
- Determine exactly which customer information is affected—*what*.
- Determine exactly which business processes and IT processes are affected—*how*.

- Determine exactly which locations and connectivity means are affected—*where*.
- Determine exactly which organizations and workflows are affected—*who*.
- Determine exactly when everything must be put in place—*when*.
- Determine exactly if we need to adjust any business goals and objectives and if we need to create new policies or rules—*why*.

The GLB Act applies to organizations offering financial products or services to individuals. Examples of products and services include loans, financial advice, investment advice, and insurance. The Federal Trade Commission has authority to enforce the law with respect to any organization offering such a product or service when the organization is not already under the jurisdiction of the federal banking agencies, the Securities and Exchange Commission, the Commodity Futures Trading Commission, and state insurance authorities.

Some of the organizations that come under FTC jurisdiction for purposes of the GLB Act are non-bank mortgage lenders, loan brokers, some financial or investment advisers, tax preparers, providers of real estate settlement services, and debt collectors. At the same time, the FTC's regulation applies only to companies that are *significantly engaged* in such financial activities.

TO QUOTE JOHN ZACHMAN...

The argument that the business is too big and complex to do architecture is a red herring. EVERY business is big and complex.

7.5.3 To Be or Not To Be, As Is the Question *(why)*

The following week, PalGal's chief operating officer (COO) called a meeting of her top executives. The COO used the meeting as an official kickoff for the company-wide project to comply with the GLB Act. The COO told her executives:

Our organization is subject to the jurisdiction of the Federal Trade Commission, and, therefore, we must implement an information security program in accordance with the law and rules associated with the Gramm-Leach-Bliley Act. The act is going to have a ripple effect throughout the company as we implement our new policies and procedures. Every part of our business will be affected.

I need everyone to cooperate and work as a team. If we need additional resources, we can pull them in. The FTC's Final Rule has been published in the Federal Register, which means we have less than one year to complete the program. However, the ruling does provide a grace period for some of our service contracts with nonaffiliated third parties.

The grace period grandfathers our need to comply with those companies for two years. Our legal department will be sending a memorandum to everyone regarding a summary of all our existing contracts.

The COO then explains what the organization needs to do:

In order to set up our information security program, we will need a lot of documentation. The FTC will require us to keep the documentation readily accessible. I would imagine that our corporate intranet is a good place to keep the documentation, but I will leave it up to your people to decide what is best.

Our documentation must outline at an excruciating level of detail the administrative, technical, and physical safeguards that are appropriate to our organization's size, complexity, nature and scope of activities, and the sensitivity of any customer information at issue.

The bottom line is that our information security program must:

- *Ensure the security and confidentiality of customer information.*
- *Protect us and our customers against any anticipated threats or hazards related to the integrity and security of the covered information.*
- *Protect us against unauthorized access to or use of the covered information that could result in substantial harm or inconvenience to any of our customers.*

Therefore, in order for us to develop, implement, and maintain an information security program, we shall:

- *Designate or hire someone to coordinate the information security program.*
- *Reasonably identify foreseeable internal and external risks to the security, confidentiality, and integrity of our customer information that could result in the unauthorized disclosure, misuse, alteration, destruction, or compromise of the information in some form. We also need to assess the sufficiency of any existing safeguards already in place to control these risks. At minimum, our risk assessment should include the consideration of risks in such operational areas as:*

  - *Employee training and human resource programs*
  - *IT systems, including the network, software design, processing, storage, transmission, archival, and data disposal systems*
  - *Operational processes needed to detect, prevent, and respond to any attack, intrusion, or other type of system failure*
  - *Design and implementation of information safeguards to control the risks we identify through our risk assessment*
  - *Operational processes needed to regularly test and monitor the effectiveness of our safeguards' key controls, systems, and procedures*

Okay Tinne, this is certainly in your area. We will need to oversee our service providers. We will need to take reasonable steps to select and retain service providers that are capable of maintaining appropriate safeguards for the customer information at issue. We will also need to require our service providers to implement and maintain such safeguards by contract.

I will need to be kept up to date with the program. I want to be kept apprised of our testing and monitoring results. Feedback to the senior management team will help us evaluate and adjust the information security program as we see necessary.

I want to send out a mass broadcast to all of our customers to let them know we are actively moving on this program and that we have their best interests in mind.

At this point in the meeting, the COO begins to wrap up and set some action items in place:

Over the next week or so, we will have some more meetings to discuss exactly how this program is going to take shape. Let us get some of our business analysts and modelers involved. I know that over the past several years, we have been fully documenting all our designs in accordance with Zachman.

I am still not as fluent as I should be with all the Framework's fundamentals, but I know many of our managers have been able to benefit from all the collective artifacts. The analysts and modelers can document the owner's perspective.

As a starting point, we must determine what artifacts we have cataloged. I know we use the intranet as the basis of our corporate repository. Therefore, everyone should have immediate access to everything. Although everyone in the organization works hard, I know we are not perfect.

We probably have some artifacts that have been misplaced, overlooked, or not completed. Any missing artifacts or those found to be less than our customary standard, especially if they are relevant to the information security program, must be completed.

The management team must review our current artifacts. The artifacts represent our current (as-is) state. As we start to define our target functioning enterprise, we will have established an end (to-be) state. The management team will organize a gap analysis to determine how best to proceed, what needs to be done, and what steps or phases might be needed to create an implementation.

The information security program is obviously important to us; we are probably already complying with a number of key aspects of the act, but we need to know which ones. Understanding our current state is critical in planning our transition to the end state. We do not have unlimited funds, so we need to make prudent decisions as we move toward our new end state.

We know the program is going to have a major impact on our IT department, but the program is also going to affect the business side of the house too. Security is one area that is going to need constant revision in the future. We do not know what other laws or rules might be mandated. We also do not know what future programs we might want to initiate ourselves.

Taking an engineered approach to our security programs now will help us in the future. If we understand and document each of the normalized *architectural artifacts, we can maintain our flexibility and be quick-to-market. We have one year to comply with this program. However, I would like to see us complete the information security program in five months.*

Any questions?

One of the newest members of the management team inquires about cookies. The COO is unaware that a cookie is a term used to describe a small text file placed on a person's computer hard disk by a Web server, and that a cookie is used to transmit information back to the server that originally placed it on the hard disk. The COO, believing the employee was being trivial and arrogant, barks that not every senior management meeting is going to be catered.

The question is clarified by another member of the executive team, who informs the COO that any personal information captured through an Internet cookie is subject to the GLB Act. The COO then makes this point:

Many of our business solutions involve technology. Some of our business solutions seem to involve technologies of which I am not aware. Cookies, for example, may very well affect some of the policies and procedures that we articulate from the 'owner' perspective. Therefore, as we perform our analysis to transition from our current state to our end state, we need to review the impact of everything from a top-down and a bottom-up approach.

A top-down or forward engineering approach using the Framework starts with the *planner* and then transitions a design to the *owner*. The transition then progresses from the *owner* to the *designer*, to the *builder*, to the *subcontractor*, and finally to the *functioning enterprise*.

A bottom-up or reverse engineering approach using the Framework starts with the *functioning enterprise* and transitions backward, one perspective at a time toward the *planner*.

In adopting a bottom-up approach, the COO hopes to determine if any of the current implementation choices now affect the business as a whole. In general, senior managers do not care about the specifics of computer languages for applications, or hardware platforms. However, some technologies, such as the Internet, intranet, and cookies, do become important for senior management to know.

As technology and society become more intertwined and legislative laws begin to explicitly reference types of technologies, *planners* and *owners* can no longer remain indifferent to the technology.

TO QUOTE JOHN ZACHMAN...

Artifacts are not merely documentation. Artifacts have intrinsic value in their own right. They are enterprise assets and must be maintained as such. In fact, they are the *knowledge base* of the enterprise, the enterprise definition.

Up until the late 1990s, senior managers could describe a business problem or need and not worry much about its implementation. Whether the solution used a lead pencil or a computer, the problem could be described with indifference to the physical solution. Today, the Internet and mass electronic commerce are not allowing the *owner* to be completely removed from an awareness of technology solutions.

7.5.4 Getting from Here to There *(when)*

During the meeting, the COO ordered a *mass broadcast to be sent to all of our customers to let them know we are actively moving on this program and that we have their best interests in mind*. As the requirement moved from the *owner* to the *designer* and down through the *subcontractor*, the mechanics to perform a mass broadcast were changed and *de-optimized*. See Figure 7-90.

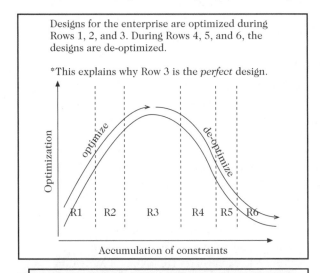

Designs for the enterprise are optimized during Rows 1, 2, and 3. During Rows 4, 5, and 6, the designs are de-optimized.

*This explains why Row 3 is the *perfect* design.

Figure 7-90   *Optimizing and de-optimizing*

The request to produce a single mass broadcast to all customers was viewed as impractical based on the organization's currently available hardware and network resources. The *designer* and *builder* came up with a solution to include a message on the customer's next bill, which was built physically by the *subcontractors*. If a customer was not active during the current billing cycle, a letter was produced and mailed based on the customer's geographic region.

The mailing was based geographically to optimize postage discount rates. The country was split into four geographic regions, and each region was processed at 10 p.m. on a Sunday night when PalGal's hardware and network usage was minimal.

In Figure 7-90, the curve illustrates the tendency for the *planner* and *owner* to think of solutions in an increasing mode of vertical optimization. As the *designer* takes over, the optimization continues, but starts to taper off as the *designer* completes his artifacts. The constraints of technology or logistics force the *builder* to further de-optimize the *designer's* artifacts.

Although the *builder* may include techniques for improving performance or throughput, the designs are de-optimizations relative to the *owner's* design. In the case of the mass broadcast, the solution was efficient, but nonetheless was a de-optimization of the original solution.

7.5.5 All Is Not Known *(who)*

PalGal knew they needed someone to coordinate the information security program. The organization structure of the end state revealed a need for the security administrator to be a senior level manager position. The organization created a chief security officer (CSO) role at the senior vice president level within the enterprise.

The CSO's responsibilities would include managing the policies and procedures associated with the GLB Act and all homeland security. The position would require a small staff. The scope of homeland security would include all security issues related to technology and the enterprise's premises and employees.

The CSO would also be responsible for evaluating each business partner's security capabilities. In addition, the role would be expanded to help employees who travel abroad on business with potential security needs for various countries.

The growth of Internet viruses, the need to protect the rights of individuals, and the terrorist attacks on September 11, 2001 confirmed the organization's belief that security was no longer something the organization could treat with a cavalier attitude. Security had become a necessity, and PalGal determined that security affected everything.

Senior executives knew the scope of the position, but did not know all the details that would be included in actually performing the job. They wanted the new CSO to help define the position.

Scope and detail are concepts that can be mapped to the Framework. The executives were comfortable that they had done a good job outlining the job's purpose. Therefore, the executives considered the scope sliver to be reasonably complete. Each cell in the Framework also has a y-axis and an x-axis. Instead of the axes being perspective and aspect, the axes represent slivers—a scope sliver and a detail sliver. See Figure 7-91. However, the executives believed the detail sliver needed lots of work. The executives also realized that, as the sliver's detail is uncovered and documented, the scope of the job may change too. Therefore, they did not consider the scope sliver to be 100 percent complete.

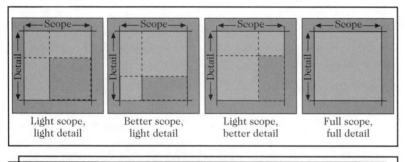

Figure 7-91   *Slivers*

Adding a new executive would affect PalGal's organizational structure; the human resource department had to recognize the job function and the candidate's basic skill set. The human resource department had to find and hire such a person.

The department would need to know:

- *What* skills were needed
- *How* to find a qualified person
- *Where* the person would work
- *Who* the person would work with and report to
- *When* the hiring needed to be finalized
- *Why* the organization needed such a person

Office space would need to be found for the CSO and the CSO's staff. Computer equipment would need to be ordered. Reporting responsibilities would need to be clarified. The job function could not be readily integrated into the enterprise until the job was better defined and the CSO had a better understanding of the roles, activities, and responsibilities.

There are slivers associated with each perspective of the CSO's job function. At each row, the slivers need to be integrated horizontally with the enterprise. Horizontal integration provides continuity between artifacts from multiple cells across a single row. So too, the slivers for each aspect need to be integrated vertically within the enterprise. Vertical integration provides continuity between artifacts from multiple cells along a single column. Once everything has been integrated across the Framework, the

539

enterprise is said to have continuity across the scope of the enterprise within every cell and has reached a state of enterprise-wide integration.

7.5.6 Getting the Point Across *(where)*

It may seem that one of the points of establishing a normalized set of architectural artifacts is to produce an optimized solution. The concept of vertical optimization and de-optimization is illustrated in Figure 7-90. As more constraints are added to solve the problem, de-optimization may be forced upon the participants of the perspective.

TO QUOTE JOHN ZACHMAN...

Do not measure the *infrastructure people* using the same criteria as you measure *results people*, or you will not get infrastructure.

Optimization and de-optimization also occur horizontally across all the cells of a single row. For example, you could have one team of people design and develop the best road surface—one that would never wear out. Another team of people could design and develop the best tire for a wheel—one that would never wear out. Both designs could be viewed as optimized.

However, the tire is placed on a wheel and affixed to a car, which then drives on the road. As a result, the ride might be awful, the tire might actually cause the road surface to crack, or the road surface might cause the tire to break and fall apart.

When designing a road surface and a tire, it is best to consider a problem holistically rather than independent of its operating environment. The reasonable solution is to design a tire that is not as resilient as the road surface and will wear out naturally with use. The key is to design the tire artifacts independently of the road surface.

Therefore, it is best to de-optimize the tire in order to have a better performing solution. De-optimization will occur based on time, cost, and effort. De-optimization is a desirable choice when viewed contextually as part of the whole. In other words, only seek to de-optimize a primitive design when knowledge about the other primitives is known and understood.

Normalized architectural artifacts are independent artifacts. However, they are not produced without considering their dependency on other artifacts. Normalized architectural artifacts lead to additional implementation choices and improved ways of knowing where or how to de-optimize.

EFFICIENCY

The ability to respond and change the enterprise should be part of the efficiency and optimization evaluation conducted by an enterprise to evaluate choices and reach a solution.

In his book *Slack*, Tom DeMarco uses the tile game to illustrate efficiency. The basic game has 15 tiles, with room for 16. The empty space allows the tiles to be moved with the objective to get the numbers into an ascending or descending sequence.

However, in business terms, an empty space is viewed as wasted space. Seeking efficiency, a business would place another tile in the empty position and maximize the use of all available space. See Figure 7-92.

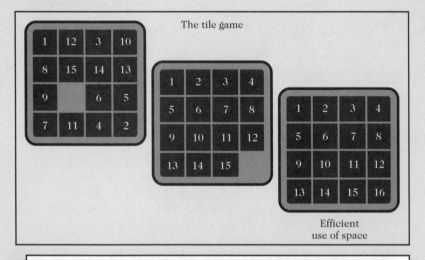

Figure 7-92   *Being too efficient*

If everything is being used efficiently and there is no space to move, there is no space to change. When you cannot change, you cannot respond, and in business, that often means becoming less competitive. What was once considered an efficient mode transforms from being a benefit to a liability. This affect is one of the major causes of a legacy environment or application.

Therefore, if change is constant, the ability to change should be part of the determination of what is considered optimized and efficient. If something is optimized, but cannot be readily changed, it should not be regarded as optimized. Additionally, if something is efficient, but cannot be readily changed, it should not be regarded as efficient.

7.5.7 Contextual Relationships *(what)*

As you and the other team members of PalGal start to design solutions, one area someone in the company researches is **enterprise application integration (EAI)**. EAI is one of the fastest-growing segments in IT vendor software. EAI solutions help glue together disparate and stovepipe systems. In other words, EAI is a software solution used to resolve the legacy problem.

Because you understand how PalGal has taken an approach to produce a comprehensive set of normalized architectural artifacts, you understand the short-term relief EAI offers. You also understand the trade-offs between short-term relief and long-term recovery. You understand that new solutions for solving the GLB Act must come from an architected approach.

TO QUOTE JOHN ZACHMAN...

There is only one game in town...architecture.

One company that PalGal reviewed was Stylus Systems, in Bangalore, India, which offers services such as porting legacy applications to the Web and enterprise application integration. It states that:

> *Unless there is a universal computer system, or technology stops evolving, there will always be a need for IT integration. Integration has been a solution to the business problem of connecting dissimilar systems for many years. In the last year or so, it [integration] has gained growing acceptance as the prerequisite for CRM, Supply Chain Management, and other e-Business initiatives. In the past, integration has been avoided because it was viewed as difficult, costly, and often hard to justify with realistic return on investment (ROI) estimates...The business benefits provided by integration are now more easily justified.*

Because of your knowledge of enterprise architecture using the Zachman Framework, you realize the fallacy in this statement. Companies create legacy systems because they think only about the current implementation. Companies think and act in the short term. Enterprise application integration is difficult because the problem EAI tries to solve was created out of chaos.

You have understood and seen how focusing on independent cells and establishing the contextual relationships between the cells provide a native way to create integration. One major problem many companies discover is that the EAI solution often becomes legacy too—and, therefore, another part of the problem.

Figure 7-93 shows the independence of a single cell in the Framework. That cell is given context by integration with the:

- Cell directly above it in the same column

- Cell directly below it in the same column
- Other cells in the same row

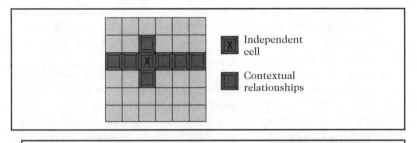

Independent cell

Contextual relationships

Figure 7-93 *Independent and contextual cell*

7.5.8 Key Term

enterprise application integration (EAI)

7.5.9 Review Questions

1. Explain the difference between a top-down and a bottom-up approach using the Framework.
2. Why was the *builder* in the PalGal case forced to de-optimize the *owner's* artifacts? What effect, if any, did the vertical de-optimization have on the solution?
3. What is the difference between a scope sliver and a detail sliver? How did PalGal use slivers to define the CSO's job function in order to assure integration of the artifacts?

4. How do legacy applications affect the enterprise's ability to respond to change?
5. In the PalGal case, why was it important to obtain definitions during the first discussion of the legislative mandate?
6. What example was used to describe horizontal optimization? How does this example illustrate the importance of viewing a problem holistically rather than as a single part?

SECTION 7.6 WHO WANTS IN

QUESTIONS TO CONTEMPLATE

1. Does the physical presentation of an artifact matter?
2. What is the difference between architecture and design?
3. Are there drawbacks to short-term implementations?

7.6.1 Introduction

Architecting, designing, modeling, and diagramming are techniques used to produce descriptive representations of something real. They are abstractions of a materialized *functioning enterprise*. Each descriptive representation is an artifact. Whether an artifact contains an architecture, a design, a model, or a diagram, it is still an artifact of design.

In IT, regardless of whether you are creating or documenting a software architecture, a technology architecture, or an information architecture, you are creating a form of design. Whether you are creating a process model, a class model, or a data model, you are creating a design. Whether you are writing a database creation script, a program written in Java, or a script for a scheduler, you are creating a design.

The Framework helps to classify the designs of the enterprise. You can use the classification schema of enterprise architecture to distinguish between primitive designs and composite designs. The designs create a baseline for managing change. Enterprise architecture focuses on artifacts that are central to creating a design. Enterprise architecture is about design—the designs of the enterprise used to create a *functioning enterprise*.

Without a *functioning enterprise*, the enterprise is not truly viable. No matter how efficient or dysfunctional the enterprise is, having an operational product or service is a necessity. If the *functioning enterprise* is a necessity, then everything about the *functioning enterprise* must be cared for, or else the *functioning enterprise* will surely perish.

The Zachman Framework contains 30 primitive cells, which can be used to describe the *functioning enterprise*. If each cell contains a primitive artifact, an infinite number of composite artifacts can be produced.

The laws and rules of the Zachman Framework do not mandate which primitive artifacts an enterprise should build. The laws and rules of the Zachman Framework do not mandate which type of composite artifacts an enterprise should build. If the artifacts are not mandated, how does the Framework help with design?

- Use of the Framework helps the practitioner identify all the primitives the enterprise should recognize.
- Primitives that are recognized can be made explicit.
- Each explicit artifact can be described to various levels of excruciating detail.
- Anything not made explicit is left implicit.
- Anything that is implicit is subject to assumption.
- You can choose what you want to assume.
- Choice gives you the ability to manage risk.
- Managing risk gives you freedom.

The Framework helps with design because the Framework can help clarify to the enterprise what is perceived to be important and what is perceived to be unnecessary. Having a good grasp on the enterprise's perceptions provides freedom and momentum. When you are free to make choices and manage risks, your chances to succeed are improved. Normally, when risks are identified, a plan can be established to help mitigate the risk. A risk mitigation plan positions the enterprise to be proactive instead of reactive.

A risk can be viewed in two dimensions:

- The likelihood of the risk being realized
- The impact should the risk be realized

Assessing risk factors against each dimension can be qualified with simple high, medium, and low scores. For example, the likelihood of the computer network failing could be low, but the impact might be high because all operations could cease. On the other hand, the likelihood that the office-supplied coffee will taste bad might be high, but the impact is low because you do not drink the office-supplied coffee.

Assessing risk and creating a risk mitigation plan are essential to an organization that wants to manage change. The COO from PalGal, in the previous section, might make this statement regarding the issue of risk taking: "In our organization, we perceive that the time, cost, and effort required to make all our artifacts explicit is less than the time, cost, and effort we would incur as a result of making assumptions about them."

7.6.2 Methodology and Technology Independent *(who)*

The Framework is methodology independent. This means the Framework does not provide a notation to produce an artifact, nor does the Framework illustrate the mechanics for how to produce an artifact.

The advantage of the Framework's methodology independence is that the best (or worst) practices of any discipline's notation and method can be used with the Framework. The Framework describes the purpose of an artifact relative to the perspective and aspect, but not relative to the physical appearance of the artifact.

Because the Framework is neutral to methodology, the Framework does not force you to start or end at any particular location. The Framework is indifferent to one person working on all the cells, or hundreds of people working on just one cell. In many ways, the Framework helps visualize how everyone has an opportunity to help design the enterprise.

The Framework is technology independent also. In other words, the Framework can be applied to *functioning enterprises* that are either manual or automated. The tools used to produce any artifact or *functioning enterprise* do not have a direct dependence on the use of the Framework.

The neutrality to method and technology makes the Framework a viable tool for thinking, reasoning, and communicating about any subject matter. However, the practitioners of the enterprise must actually perform the work of creating the artifacts and mapping them to the Framework.

7.6.3 The Paradox *(when)*

Scott Ambler in his book *Agile Modeling* states, "Focus on software, not documentation...your primary goal is to develop software, not documentation...create it [documentation] only if it is absolutely essential to your effort." Without question, Ambler's focus is on the effort toward short-term implementation because enterprises are volatile entities—people continuously come and go. The paradox is that short-term implementation creates the illusion of an agile enterprise.[5] Short-term implementation often creates only a temporary relief to the enterprise, whereas a long-term implementation strategy using enterprise architecture makes the enterprise truly agile.

In the same book, Ambler states: "Accept the fact that change happens. Revel in it. Change is one of the things that makes software development exciting." However, Ambler is really focusing on change that occurs during the creation of something (while a project is still active), not the type of change that happens after something has been created (possibly one year after the project was implemented). Many software developers enjoy software development (writing new programs), but passionately hate software maintenance (modifying an existing program).

Object-oriented and agile methodologists like Ambler and Martin Fowler, author of *UML Distilled*, promote the creation of Row 1, 2, 3, and 4 artifacts only to promote their abandonment once the subcontractor has completed Row 5 artifacts—the code. Many modern methodologists promote managing change directly from application code.

An application program is normally written as a specific solution for an implementation need. Many organizations have tens of thousands of programs and millions of lines of software code. Many organizations have no idea what programs they have. Many organizations do not even have source code that matches the operational version in the *functioning enterprise*.

The enterprise can never guarantee that the person who wrote a program is going to be around to maintain the program. In addition, most organizations cannot provide a complete inventory of the programs they have installed. You might ask yourself, how easy can change be incorporated into an enterprise that tries to manage the enterprise exclusively through *subcontractor* artifacts?

If an *owner* stated, "I want to expand our operations into Canada. We'll need to handle foreign addresses." The *owner* might need the following questions addressed:

- Which databases, programs, platforms are affected—*what*
- How do you go about finding every place that needs to be changed—*how*
- Where is everything located, or how are things communicated—*where*
- Which organizations, workflows, or screens will be affected—*who*
- Will foreign addresses affect any automated schedules—*when*
- What are the rules for accepting and presenting a foreign address—*why*

Object-oriented applications develop objects based on real-world objects. Object-oriented applications use a technique called encapsulation to help mitigate the effects of change. However, encapsulation often only works well on small isolated changes. Developing objects without maintaining artifacts from the *planner*, *owner*, *designer*, and *builder* coerces the enterprise into sustaining the shape and form of the real-world object.

Initially when an object-oriented application is written, the code mirrors the real-world object; soon the real-world object is forced to mirror the code. Object-oriented and agile methods do not mitigate the legacy problem. Without recognizing that the enterprise needs to be engineered before the enterprise is implemented, the habit of creating *legacy applications* remains intact. Because change is inevitable, each needed change should be engineered before the change becomes a part of the implementation.

Overall, object-oriented design and development, as well as agile modeling techniques, are good approaches for developing software. Both can be incorporated or mapped to the Framework. Many object-oriented artifacts are composite artifacts, while agile modeling is strictly a method of practice. In an engineered solution to produce an architecture, object-oriented artifacts need to be supported by primitive artifacts. Agile modeling needs to recognize the long-term benefits of maintaining models. Both approaches can be applied in an enterprise architecture solution.

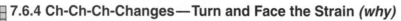

7.6.4 Ch-Ch-Ch-Changes—Turn and Face the Strain *(why)*

Change can be quite exciting. From the standpoint of the practitioner who works on artifacts for the *designer*, *builder*, or *subcontractor* perspective, creating a design that is indifferent to change can be a rewarding goal. A design that is indifferent to change can help materialize a functioning enterprise that is indifferent to change. An enterprise that becomes indifferent to change is a versatile enterprise.

Section 6.6.7 discussed what it means to be defensive. Here is an example of a defensive data model. See Figure 7-94.

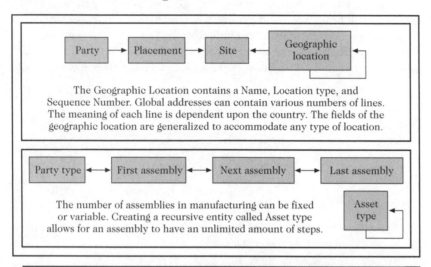

Figure 7-94　*Defensive design*

7.6.5 No Sweat *(how)*

Information persistence is a method of practice used by companies, such as Steelcase (see Section 1.2.1), to keep a visual display of designs on the wall where product development teams work. Designs are kept on display around a room so that team members can learn about what they are trying to put together. See Figure 7-95.

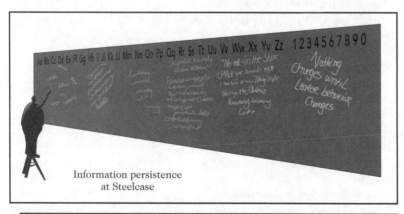

Figure 7-95　*Information persistence*

The Zachman Framework for Enterprise Architecture

Modeling should not be conducted in a vacuum. Receiving input and ideas and providing constant feedback help evolve the modeling artifacts. Information persistence is a collaborative technique used by teams to help produce detailed and well-defined descriptive representations. The collaborative artifacts can come from any perspective, primitive, or composite and can be used as a step toward effectively producing a *functioning enterprise*. Collaboration allows business and IT specialists to explore the requirements and needs of the enterprise.

Collaboration and information persistence require shared space in which the artifacts can emerge. For many organizations, the simplest and cheapest form of shared space is a wall. From caves and pyramids to classrooms and offices, walls have been used as a primary surface to communicate collectively. The concepts communicated using information persistence are often complex; however, the tools used to create the persistent information are often simple. Basic tools include:

- Post-It notes
- 3 × 5 cards
- Pens
- Markers
- Poster paper
- Tacks
- Tape
- Digital camera and printer

When producing a diagram or a model, a general set of guidelines can be applied to enhance the visual meaning of the artifact.

7.6.6 Style *(what)*

A diagram has three basic elements: a regularly or irregularly shaped blob, a line, and a label. Diagrams use a myriad of blobs including boxes, ovals, circles, clouds, and stickmen. Notations often give these shapes names, such as object, class, entity, and use case. Lines are connectors on diagrams and can represent associations, dependencies, and transitions between states. Labels identify names, roles, and constraints.

In general:

- Minimize crossing lines on a diagram.
- Use straight lines instead of diagonal or curved lines.
- Use consistent sizes for each blob.
- Incorporate only blobs, lines, and labels that add value.
- Use popular notations.
- Be consistent in your use of a notation.
- If a diagram becomes too large, split the diagram into several smaller ones.
- Use white space to make the diagram visually appealing.
- Diagrams are easier to read in a top/down, left/right flow. The diagram should be laid out accordingly.
- Place notes on the diagram to mitigate any assumptions or enhance an explanation.
- Indicate anything that is unknown.

- Use consistent names.
- Define every blob or line on the diagram.

Remember that to see is to know. To *not* see is to guess.

7.6.7 Architecture and Design *(where)*

Architecture is design, but there is a subtle difference between an architecture and a design. Figure 7-96 illustrates a sample data architecture. Figure 7-97 illustrates a sample data design.

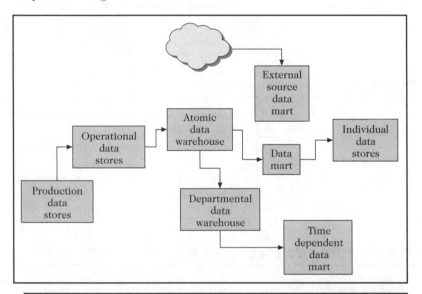

Figure 7-96   *Data architecture*

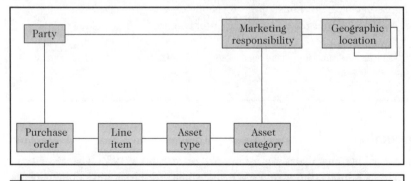

Figure 7-97   *Data design*

The data architecture shows a framework or a shell in which a more detailed design can be made. For example, a room may have walls, a floor, a ceiling, a window, and a door. These items tend to be fixed and can be regarded as the architecture of the room. The type of furniture used in the room and the placement of the furniture can be considered design. The design of the furniture has to fit within the bounds of the architecture.

In Figure 7-96, the data architecture provides a similar structure to that of a room. Each database can be designed specifically, but it should fit within the data architecture.

7.6.8 Key Term

information persistence

7.6.9 Review Questions

1. How does the Framework help you with design?
2. Why is a risk mitigation plan important to the enterprise?
3. What are the two dimensions of assessing a risk?
4. What are the three basic elements of a diagram? Explain their significance.
5. What are the advantages of having a neutral framework?
6. Are architecture and design the same thing? Why or why not?

SECTION 7.7 WHY ZACHMAN

QUESTIONS TO CONTEMPLATE

1. What are some of the responsibilities of a chief enterprise architect?
2. What causes scrap and rework, and what problem does this cause for the enterprise?
3. What benefits has the Department of Veterans Affairs realized from using the Zachman Framework?

7.7.1 Introduction

The Department of Veterans Affairs was established on March 15, 1989. The agency succeeded the Veterans Administration and has responsibility for providing federal benefits to veterans and their dependents. The agency is headed by the Secretary of Veterans Affairs. The agency is the second largest of the 14 cabinet departments and operates nationwide programs of healthcare, financial assistance, and national cemeteries.

In a letter that was published with the Department of Veterans Affairs *Enterprise Architecture: Strategy, Governance, & Implementation* guide, John Zachman commented to The Honorable Anthony Principi, Secretary of Veterans Affairs in Washington D.C., that he was impressed by the department's realization that enterprise architecture is actually a business issue, not a technical issue. He also commented about the work being "insightful, coherent, comprehensive, and innovative." He went on to say the work was "a tribute to the clarity of vision and understanding that can only result from intense communication."

Zachman informed Secretary Principi that the role of the information technology community in an enterprise is not simply to build and run systems, unlike Ambler, who says, "Focus on software..." (See Section 7.6.3.) The narrow view undertaken by most IT departments leads to disintegration and stovepipe applications.

As Zachman sees it, the mission of the information technology department is to engineer and manufacture the enterprise so that the enterprise is aligned with the intent of general management. The engineered and manufactured enterprise should be flexible, adaptable, interoperable, integrated, lean, and responsive to the customers and stakeholders of the enterprise.

The purpose of **enterprise engineering and manufacturing** is to provide structure, rigor, and discipline to create the operational products or services of the enterprise. Enterprise architecture is an essential part of engineering the enterprise before the enterprise is manufactured. Enterprise engineering and manufacturing combine a mindset, a philosophy, and a discipline to deliver something coherent that meets the needs of enterprise management. Enterprise architecture is an important initiative to minimize **scrap and rework** and to avoid legacy applications.

Zachman has stated that the long-term objectives of enterprise engineering and manufacturing are to make every cell of the Framework explicit. Each cell represents a primitive artifact, which when integrated enterprise wide—horizontally across each row and vertically down each column—at an excruciating level of detail constitutes an inventory of reusable components from which the enterprise can be assembled-to-order.

In Zachman's letter to the Department of Veterans Affairs, he offered some advice to Secretary Principi to help with institutionalizing enterprise architecture:

- Enterprise architecture is a new way of life.
- Enterprise architecture is not a quick fix.
- Enterprise architecture is not a project.
- Enterprise architecture is a process.
- Enterprise architecture is different from the Industrial Age of the past.
- Enterprise architecture is the Information Age of the present.
- Do not underestimate the difficulty and complexity of engineering and manufacturing the most complex object yet conceived by humankind—the enterprise.
- Enterprise architecture takes time and determination.
- Enterprise architecture is a revolution in thinking, a discipline, and an engineering process.
- Enterprise architecture as a change agent takes time and perseverance.
- Things will have to be implemented periodically, so you have to accept some risk of scrap and rework, but build that risk and cost into the short-term strategy.
- Set realistic expectations.
- Make executive education and technical training a continuous process.
- Do not assume anything.

551

- Long-term issues are easily forgotten in the short-term stresses of daily life.
- There is still much to learn and discover and many opportunities to create advantage and value.
- Do not get discouraged.

7.7.2 Simple *(why)*

In 2002, Secretary Principi managed a budget of approximately $51 billion. Allocation of funds included:

- Compensation and pension
- Education and training
- Medical care
- Research
- Home loan assistance
- Insurance
- National cemeteries
- Employees
- Enterprise architecture

THEN AND NOW

The Veterans Administration was created by Executive Order 5398, signed by President Herbert Hoover (1874–1964) on July 21, 1930. At that time, there were 54 hospitals, 4.7 million living veterans, and 31,600 employees.

In 2002:

- Approximately 2.7 million veterans received disability compensation or pension.
- Approximately 579,000 surviving spouses, children, and parents of deceased veterans also received benefits.

Since 1944, when the first GI Bill began, more than 20.9 million veterans, service members, and family members have received $75 billion in GI Bill benefits for education and training. By 2002, the number of GI Bill recipients included:

- 7.8 million veterans from World War II
- 2.4 million veterans from the Korean War
- 8.2 million post-Korean and Vietnam-era veterans and active-duty service personnel

In 2001, the agency helped pay for the education or training of approximately:

- 292,000 veterans and active-duty personnel
- 82,300 reservists and National Guardsmen
- 47,000 survivors of veterans

The agency wants to be the leader in enterprise architecture within the federal government. It continuously benchmarks the quality and delivery of its services. The department intends to use innovative means coupled with technology to help deliver a high level of services to American veterans and their families.

In adopting an enterprise architecture approach, the agency defined a set of principles and goals to help set direction on issues, such as the promotion of interoperability, open systems, public access, information technology security, compliance with the Government Paperwork Elimination Act, and end-user satisfaction.

The agency supported the initiative with a complete inventory of agency information resources, personnel, equipment, and funds devoted to information resource management and information technology, at an appropriate level of detail.

The main principles the agency established for enterprise architecture include:

- Develop applications that are designed to be interoperable, portable, and scalable across networks of heterogeneous hardware, software, and telecommunications platforms.
- Meet the agency's information technology needs by seeking cost-effective solutions. Prior to acquiring new information technology resources, the agency would determine what could be shared and reused by investigating all resources (intra-agency and interagency) within the federal system.
- Establish a level of security for all applications that is commensurate to the risk and magnitude of the harm resulting from the loss, misuse, unauthorized access to, or modification of the information stored or flowing through the applications.

The Department of Veterans Affairs was drawn to the simplicity of the Zachman Framework. The agency grasped the power of understanding the enterprise by the six interrogatives: *what*, *how*, *where*, *who*, *when*, and *why*. The agency realized that the primitive components tied to an aspect were valid for all perspectives of the same aspect:

- *What*—thing-relationship-thing
- *How*—process-output/input-process
- *Where*—node-link-node
- *Who*—people-work-people
- *When*—time-cycle-time
- *Why*—ends-means-ends

The agency realized the primitive components provided continuity as they modeled current state and end states for each perspective. Although the representations in the artifacts were different for each perspective within an aspect, the primitive components provided a consistent focus for validating and assisting in artifact transformations between the rows.

7.7.3 Comprehensive *(what)*

The agency understood that although the Framework's representation appears to be a matrix, the Framework is actually a classification schema. The classification schema is a normalized classification, not a matrix.

Many companies repeat the same activities or tasks over and over. The agency was no exception. Because the Framework was normalized, the agency believed it would be in a better position to manage and minimize any redundant work efforts.

The agency used a variety of criteria in the selection of its enterprise architecture framework. Among the decisive factors were the requirements that the framework should be:

- Understandable
- Usable in the short term
- Endurable with long-term value
- Complete and comprehensive, leading to improved service to veterans
- Credible and able to meet federal requirements
- Supportive of a high-performance enterprise architecture
- Capable of allowing strategic linkage of program goals and business goals to information technology
- Able to accommodate clearly defined program rules and business rules
- Scalable, extendible, and flexible

By using the Framework, the agency plans to derive the following benefits:

- Improved information technology budget management and efficiencies
- Increased responsiveness to changing program, business, and information technology conditions
- Improved communication between program, business, and information technology that contributes to alignment necessary to achieve the agency's mission
- Improved data sharing to those who have a need
- Fully documented and effective corporate repository
- Standardized technology and data across the agency

7.7.4 Evergreen *(where)*

To produce and maintain the Department of Veterans Affairs' enterprise architecture, the agency is using an evergreening process. **Evergreening** is an open, collaborative process philosophy that involves continuous improvement of enterprise architecture (or any discipline or project) through stakeholder involvement and improving practices. The evergreen process is consistent with continuous changes occurring within an enterprise and thus its architecture.

The agency's stakeholders include the chief enterprise architects and chief information officers. In addition, program and business stakeholders from each administration and staff office, veterans' service organizations, suppliers, federal agencies, and information technology staff are also included.

Only through continuous evolution, or evergreening, can the agency's enterprise architecture initiative best ensure that program, business, and information technology decisions continue to support the mission, goals, and program and business needs. The agency tightly manages the cycle of evergreening and publication of the enterprise architecture. The cycle is repeated often enough to reflect changes, but infrequently enough so unnecessary burdens are avoided. See Figure 7-98. Publication of Veterans Affairs enterprise architecture occurs as needed.

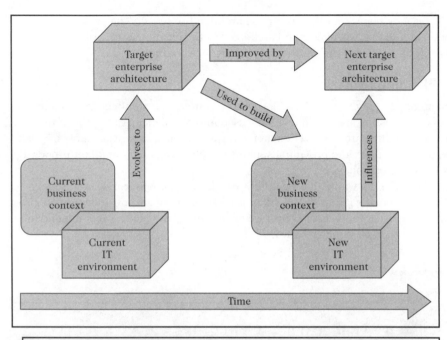

Target enterprise architecture

Improved by

Next target enterprise architecture

Used to build

Evolves to

Influences

Current business context

Current IT environment

New business context

New IT environment

Time

Figure 7-98 *Department of Veterans Affairs architectural improvement cycle*

The agency sees its enterprise architecture as overarching—thereby, the agency purposely takes an enterprise-wide view of the enterprise. Quality improvement initiatives are used for continuous improvement for all processes, programs, businesses, technology, and the enterprise architecture itself. Whenever an opportunity (a problem) is identified, quality improvement initiatives are planned and implemented.

Enterprise architecture does not occur in a vacuum. Enterprise architecture is created by people and for people. Periodically, the agency finds it necessary to revisit its vision and objectives and re-energize and redirect the enterprise architecture. As part of the agency's strategic planning process, the enterprise architecture is reviewed to ensure:

- The current state architecture accurately reflects the current status of the Veterans Affairs' information technology infrastructure.
- The end state architecture accurately reflects the program and business vision of the enterprise and appropriate technology advances.
- The tactics and strategies reflect the prevailing priorities of the enterprise and the resources that will be realistically available.
- Security architecture accurately reflects current security policies and controls.

The assessment of the enterprise architecture could generate a series of necessary updates and corresponding changes in sequencing plan projects. The current state architecture is maintained to reflect actions taken to:

- Implement the enterprise architecture sequencing plan
- Upgrade the agency's legacy applications as the organization modernizes

The agency hopes that the enterprise architecture reflects the evolution of the department and that the evolution is reflected in the current state artifacts, end state artifacts, and both the short-term and long-term strategies.

7.7.5 Planning *(when)*

As the agency began to build the artifacts of the enterprise architecture, the current state of each existing application was assessed for compliance against the enterprise architecture of the enterprise. The chief enterprise architect is responsible for making recommendations and providing support to help bring non-compliant proposals or projects into compliance.

In cases where a waiver has been requested, the chief enterprise architect is required to respond with an independent assessment of operational, economic, productivity, and other impacts of granting such a waiver, and make a recommendation to the information technology board.

BEING PRAGMATIC IS PRAGMATIC

Pragmatism in business and government demands that the enterprise allows for special instances or exceptions. A level of 100 percent purity, 100 percent perfection, or 100 percent compliance may not be achievable, though it can still be a goal.

The chief enterprise architect understands that a waiver to the enterprise architecture does not mean the Zachman Framework has to be abandoned. The project can still move forward using the Framework; however, the artifacts are just not integrated into the artifacts of the enterprise domain. The artifacts are controlled through a Peer Framework.

Within the agency, the following types of enterprise architecture reviews are conducted:

- *Program or business alignment assessment*—Determines if a proposed project aligns with the agency's strategic plans, values, goals, and objectives. The goal of the review is to ensure that the expected outcomes of the project are aligned to the high-level enterprise architecture requirements and the program or business.
- *Program or business, and technical case solution*—Examines a proposed solution, at a high level, to determine the impact to the organization's information technology environment. The goal of the review is to ensure that the proposed solution supports both the program or business and the technical architecture.
- *Sequencing plan assessment*—The sequencing plan incorporates the strategies and tactics of the agency. The assessment helps determine

whether the proposed investment is consistent with the sequence and priorities in the enterprise architecture and information technology plans. The goal of the review is to ensure progress toward the end state architecture.

- *Architecture alignment assessment*—Determines if the architecture of a proposed solution complies with the enterprise standards (including security), the enterprise architecture, and the agency's project methodologies. The goal of this review is to ensure enterprise architecture compliance with information technology projects, as well as assess project management and organizational change concerns.
- *Security architecture assessment*—Determines if a proposed solution is compliant with the agency's standards and policies to ensure confidentiality, integrity, and availability.
- *Post-implementation assessment*—Compares the performance promised in the initial proposal, program or business case and requirements to actual performance of the application in production. The return-on-investment (ROI) is evaluated to validate the estimated benefit. In addition to the ROI, the net-present-value (NPV) or internal-rate-of-return (IRR) may also be calculated.

7.7.6 End State *(how)*

Starting with the enterprise's mission, the end state enterprise architecture describes the agency's desired end state. The end state architecture illustrates the future capabilities and technologies that result from design enhancements to support the changing program and business needs.

The end state architecture for Veterans Affairs is determined by outside forces, such as legislation, office of management and budget policy, and veteran demographic changes. It is also determined by industry trends, such as technology, housing, education, and healthcare, as well as internal agency program and business units identifying and cataloging which major program and business processes will be new or different in the future.

An integral part of the process to create an end state is conducting a gap analysis that helps define the sequencing plans (strategies and tactics) to implement the changes. The transition from the current state to the end state architecture involves many groups in the agency.

Using its enterprise architecture governance process, the agency uses representation from the information technology, program, and business communities. The governance process also includes technical activities, such as migration planning, configuration management, change control, and considerations for project management and organizational change management.

Artifacts used in the planning process become artifacts in the agency's enterprise architecture repository at the appropriate level of excruciating detail. The process of maintaining and refining the artifacts is iterative. To maintain the alignment of the end state architecture and associated transitional processes that move the organization forward, the agency continuously:

- Interprets emerging laws and regulations
- Assesses changing veterans' needs

- Evaluates agency program and business objectives
- Evaluates emerging technologies
- Aligns veterans' needs, agency program and business objectives, and information technology initiatives
- Gains concurrence across the veteran service community
- Supports *out-of-the-box* thinking about how the agency can better serve the needs of veterans

7.7.7 One Voice *(who)*

The approach the agency is taking to develop and deploy an enterprise architecture repository is to create performance metrics, measure results, and implement course corrections as needed. The first step is to begin the process of identifying suitable architectural artifact forms and tools for creation and maintenance, then identify a repository tool and platform to store and manage all the architectural artifacts.

The following three processes are used:

- Tying the repository population activities to the governance process
- Building a comprehensive set of normalized architectural artifacts for the Framework
- Maintaining the current state of the agency's existing application portfolio

The agency actively retrofits existing application portfolios into the repository to maintain an accurate picture of its current state inventory. The retrofitting involves a myriad of processes, activities, and tasks due to the diversity of the agency and its information technology portfolio. Factors that contribute to the variation in techniques include the application's age, size, technology base, and utilization.

The chief enterprise architect establishes schedules for completing the enterprise architecture artifacts for all of the agency's information technology. Specific content requirements and delivery schedules for each information technology vary. The infrastructure and application manager, *owner*, or stakeholder is responsible for completing, or at least collaborating with others to create, the enterprise architecture artifacts. The artifacts are created in accordance with the standards, requirements, and tools approved and provided by the chief enterprise architect.

The intention of the agency's processes is to document both the end state enterprise architecture (through a process of forward engineering) and the current state enterprise architecture (through a process of reverse engineering). The chief enterprise architect determines the primitive and composite enterprise architecture artifacts. The chief enterprise architect also decides what constitutes an appropriate level of excruciating detail for each cell in the Zachman Framework.

For the Department of Veterans Affairs, the answer to the question, "Why Zachman" is the power of the classification schema—a roadmap. See Figure 7-99.

Figure 7-99   Lost?

7.7.8 Key Terms

enterprise engineering and manufacturing
evergreening

scrap and rework

7.7.9 Review Questions

1. Explain why enterprise architecture is an essential part of engineering the enterprise.
2. Why would the Department of Veterans Affairs agency benefit from modeling the current state and end state for each perspective? What are some of the benefits the agency hopes to gain from using the Framework?
3. Explain what is meant by the evergreening process. How does this organization believe the evergreening process will assist it in being successful with its enterprise architecture initiative?
4. What happens in this organization when the artifact being produced does not comply with the enterprise architecture of the enterprise?
5. What are some of the forces that determine the end state architecture? Why is it important to record the transitional process of moving from current state to end state? Where does the agency record this information?
6. Identify some of the responsibilities of the chief enterprise architect for the Veterans Affairs agency.

7.8 SYNTHESIS AND CHAPTER SUMMARY

Enterprise architecture is a huge topic. Enterprise architecture has only one boundary—the domain of the enterprise. The enterprise is holistic and can be documented by the enterprise's explicit normalized architectural artifacts. In the end, enterprise architecture is not about leading or succeeding with technology. Enterprise architecture is about leading and succeeding with knowledge.

Unfortunately, most enterprises are beyond the scope of a single individual to fully comprehend, understand, and appreciate. A typical business enterprise contains executives, managers, accountants, planners, production controllers, line workers, janitors, cafeteria workers, programmers, sales staff, marketing staff, suppliers, vendors, and customers. The list can be extensive; the list can be unique for each enterprise.

Depending on your own personal knowledge and role in an enterprise, you will be constrained by looking at things in a certain way. Being constrained does not necessarily limit your abilities to contemplate something. On the one hand, your education, upbringing, disposition, social environment, goals in life, and experiences do shape and constrain how you view a situation or issue. However, these constraints can help you be consistent, maintain a direction, be practical, and stay focused.

Sometimes a constraint is going to be imposed upon you. For example, the laws of nature—it is difficult to circumvent the gravitational pull of the Earth, or the rising and setting of the sun each day. However, speeding down a side street in your Porsche 911 and ignoring the speed limit is a constraint that you are free to ignore. The constraint is likely to be substituted by other constraints that can plague your mind, such as the risk of injuring a passerby or yourself, or being caught by a law officer.

Constraints mold your point of view. Because viewpoints are governed by the individual, and each individual is unique, it is possible that all viewpoints are unique. However, viewpoints can be generalized and classified. In the Zachman Framework for Enterprise Architecture, viewpoints are classified as the *planner*, *owner*, *designer*, *builder*, *subcontractor*, and *functioning enterprise* (but you already knew that). This classification does not preclude your ability to think uniquely, but instead provides a general clustering based on observing how complex things have been built over the past several thousand years.

Whiz-kids are notorious for ripping apart a complex object, seeing how it works, and then putting it back together again. Perhaps in order to understand, they have a need to create or re-create. Apple Computer founder Steven Wozniak (b. 1950) was such a kid (and adult). However, Wozniak was often able to improve the complex object during reassembly. The Framework helps classify and organize decomposed parts in order to construct a *whole*.

The ability to improve the whole during reconstruction is assisted by creating normalized architectural artifacts. By themselves, primitive artifacts are independent of the whole and can be assessed and understood as independent artifacts. When primitive artifacts are combined with other primitive artifacts, composites are formed. A composite is an implementation of the primitives.

If you had 100 Lego blocks of various shapes and colors in front of you, what could you build? You are constrained only (there is that word again) by your imagination. The combinations are, for all practical purposes, limitless. However, once you have assembled the blocks into some structure, you have what you have. You are now forced to see the blocks in a limited way.

If you disassemble the blocks and start again, you can build something completely different. You can decide to use all or only a portion of the blocks available to you. Each time you do this, you start the construction exercise with the same primitive parts. Each time, the assembly or composite is an implementation choice.

To create another implementation choice (to change) is typically easier when you start with the primitive as opposed to the composite. The primitive provides the highest level of flexibility relative to your personal constraints.

The fundamentals of any given domain are classified in the Framework as *what*, *how*, *where*, *who*, *when*, and *why* (but you already knew that too). This classification does not preclude your ability to think uniquely, but provides a general separation clustering based on the six interrogatives of the English language.

The Framework's classification schema of perspectives and aspects is:

- Simple to use
- Comprehensive in structure
- A writing system
- A planning tool
- A problem-solving tool
- Neutral to method of practice and technology
- Ubiquitous

See Figure 7-100.

Here's your benefits list...

- Simple
- Comprehensive
- Planning tool
- Writing system
- Problem-solving
- Neutral
- Ubiquitous

Figure 7-100   *Benefits list*

Simple

The Framework is simple and easy to understand. The Framework is not technical; the Framework is purely logical. The Framework contains six perspectives and six aspects. Both technical and non-technical people can be readily taught to understand the Framework's structure.

Comprehensive

The Framework is comprehensive and addresses the enterprise in its entirety. Any issues can be mapped against the Framework to understand where they fit within the context of the enterprise as a whole.

A Writing System

The Framework is a writing system, a hieroglyphic, and a language. The Framework helps you think and reason about complex concepts and communicate those complex concepts precisely to others.

A Planning Tool

The Framework is a planning tool that can be used to help you make better choices. Being aware of and taking a holistic view means you are never making choices in a vacuum. You can position issues in the context of the enterprise and have the opportunity to see a total range of alternatives.

A Problem-Solving Tool

The Framework is a problem-solving tool. The Framework organizes artifacts based on the intersection of a perspective and an aspect. Each aspect helps simplify and isolate simple variables without losing sense of the complexity of the enterprise as a whole.

Neutral

The Framework is neutral to any tool or methodology. Any tool or methodology can be mapped against the Framework to understand the implicit trade-offs. Therefore, you can determine the capabilities of the tool or methodology.

The Framework is also neutral to other architectural frameworks. Other frameworks mentioned earlier in this chapter included: C4ISR, RM-ODP, and P1471. In addition, other frameworks include Domain Analysis and Microsoft Solutions Framework. Each framework can be used in a project and then mapped to the Zachman Framework to understand its implicit trade-offs.

Ubiquitous

The Framework is ubiquitous. Any domain can be applied to the Framework. Any extent of knowledge can be used with the Framework. The Framework can be used *explicitly* in its entirety. The Framework can be used *implicitly* in its entirety also. The Framework can cover any topic, at any level of articulation.

7.8.1 Level of Importance

Which is more important: *what, how, where, who, when,* or *why*? The question is somewhat rhetorical. You may establish a level of importance, but to the Framework, each aspect is equally important. The presentation sequence—*what, how, where, who, when,* and *why*—is just a presentation sequence; the sequence is important only for communicating the Framework's structure.

What if we asked the same question relative to the perspectives: *planner, owner, designer, builder, subcontractor,* and *functioning enterprise.* Which is more important? Again, the Framework is indifferent to the importance of each perspective. After all, the Framework is inert. However, as a practitioner of the Framework, you should establish your own level of importance for each perspective.

Suggested guidance for establishing a level of importance for each perspective is as follows: first, the *functioning enterprise.* Out of all six rows, this is the only row that represents the real thing. The *functioning enterprise* is the materialization of the enterprise. Regardless of any of the artifacts produced in accordance with the other perspectives, whatever the *functioning enterprise* can do is the boundary of what the *functioning enterprise* can do. The *functioning enterprise* is the system and the system is the *functioning enterprise*. Your ability to control and change the system is your direct ability to control and change the enterprise.

The *functioning enterprise* should be perceived as the most important perspective. The next most important perspective should be the *owner's* perspective because the *functioning enterprise* should mirror what the *owner* wants as closely as possible.

The next most important perspective is the *planner*. The *planner* defines the domain of the enterprise and controls the boundaries within and choices from which the *owner* works. The next most important perspective is the *designer*. The *designer* details and refines most of the constraints from which the *functioning enterprise* operates. Next is the *builder's* perspective. The *builder* determines the exact *what*, *how*, *where*, *who*, *when*, and *why* of materializing the *functioning enterprise*. Finally, the *subcontractor* is the one who actually puts the whole thing together. The *functioning enterprise* is what the *subcontractor* constructs and assembles.

In the end, the real importance is to *eat*. If nothing works and your enterprise goes the way of Enron, Webvan, IXL, WorldCom, and countless other failed enterprises and you end up with no job, where are you going to get your next meal?

Do everything you can to make your enterprise survive. In today's business environment, surviving means being able to adapt to change and reduce your time-to-market. The Framework is a tool for helping you and your enterprise survive. Enjoy your lunch!

7.8.2 Recursive

Part II of this textbook covered each perspective while focusing on some key issues relative to the perspective. In Chapter 2—Science, the *planner* focused on the underlying sciences of creating a solution or solving a problem. In Chapter 3—Commerce, the *owner* focused on the need to take ownership and lead. In Chapter 4—Psychology, the *designer* focused on the interplay among the members of the enterprise. In Chapter 5—Technology in Commerce, the *builder* focused on the topography of making the solution viable. In Chapter 6—Systems Development, the *subcontractor* focused on the skill level and artistic ability of the individual. In Chapter 7—The Zachman Framework for Enterprise Architecture, the *functioning enterprise* focused on the Framework and how any assumptions within the enterprise, coupled with implicit and explicit primitive and composite artifacts, shape the products and services of the enterprise.

Many of the focus areas are, in general terms, applicable to the other perspectives. The recursive nature of the Framework forecasts this. The implementation of the Framework discussed in Chapter 8—The Dynamical Framework, exploits the recursive nature of the Framework by visualizing several extensions known as Zachman DNA.

7.8.3 It Ain't Getting Any Easier

Even though many of the products we use in our daily lives are highly complex, their user interfaces make the products relatively easy to use. For example, a compact disc containing 700 megabytes of your favorite MP3s playing on your personal listening device provides an interface where you do not need to know:

- How the player works
- How to make a compact disc
- The actual format of an MP3 file
- How the MP3 files were burned onto the disc
- How you actually fit 700 megabytes on a disc

For many people, product usage is actually getting easier. However, product or service creation is getting more difficult. For example, consider how you perform the following tasks:

- Build a pyramid
- Build a Gothic cathedral
- Build an atomic bomb
- Construct a town
- Land a man on the moon
- Build an airplane
- Create a software application

Trial and error is one approach—an antipattern. Trial and error is the preferred method for many information technology departments. Soon, this technique will not be tolerated. The U.S. and Canadian government's movement to adopt an enterprise architecture approach to IT initiatives will ripple throughout private and public organizations in time.

As knowledge increases, our ability to create things that are more complex also increases. Because of man's desire to fly, the hot air balloon was created; simple gliders followed. Then, in 1903, the Wright Brothers completed the first engine-powered flight in the Outer Banks of North Carolina. By the beginning of World War I, airplanes had been turned into machines of war. By the 1950s, aircraft begat spacecraft as man was taken beyond the atmosphere of the Earth. Missions to the moon, Mars, the galaxy—reusable spacecraft all extend the complexity of being able to fly.

To quote John Zachman:

"When things get so complex that you cannot remember how it works, you have to write it down." This is the basis for architecture.

"When you want to change how it works, you start with what you have written down." This is the use of architecture.

"The key to dealing with complexity and change is architecture." The tool for dealing with complexity and change is the Zachman Framework for Enterprise Architecture.

However, please remember, in order to use the Framework, you do not have to produce artifacts for every cell in the Framework. You do not have to produce any primitive artifacts. The use of the Framework does not force you to work in a specific way. The Framework can work with rigid formal methods. The Framework can work easily with agile methods. However, if you find your enterprise floundering or failing, you can:

- Increase the scope of the domain of interest to become the entire enterprise
- Document each artifact to a level of excruciating detail
- Drive out assumptions
- Make things explicit
- Describe at a primitive level
- Align the perspectives
- Align the aspects

Then, your enterprise can potentially do more. So go ahead and create a chain of impact that will outlive you. In the words of Pharaoh Sethi, "So let it be written. So let it be done."[6]

7.9 CHAPTER ACTIVITIES

7.9.1 Discussion Topics

1. Discuss the difference between the conceptual view and the contextual view of the enterprise. Give examples of each.
2. Describe the viewpoints of the *planner*, *owner*, *designer*, *builder*, *subcontractor*, and the *functioning enterprise*.
3. Describe the importance of defining the primitives of the enterprise.
4. How does the Framework help simplify the complexity of the enterprise?
5. Discuss the difference between primitives and composites and explain the importance of each.
6. How does the Zachman Framework facilitate reuse?
7. Why is an implementation considered to be a point-in-time solution? What effect can point-in-time solutions have on optimization of the enterprise?
8. Discuss the characteristics of the Framework, and explain how this tool can help the enterprise adapt and respond more quickly to the marketplace.
9. Explain how the enterprise's artifacts expose the organization's core.
10. Discuss the importance of having a set of principles for applying the Framework.
11. Compare and contrast narrow and broad boundaries for the enterprise domain. How is analysis affected?
12. How do enterprise boundaries affect integration, interoperability, and reusability?
13. During the first of many PalGal meetings about the GLB Act, you placed yourself at Row 1 of the Framework. Why is this an appropriate choice for this particular example?
14. Why do you think it is important for information technology professionals to understand both technology and business requirements?
15. Explain why you must first understand the terminology of the Framework before you can follow the laws of the Framework. Discuss how knowing the terminology of the Framework facilitates communication between information technology professionals and senior management.
16. Discuss how becoming familiar with the laws and rules of the Framework, including the postulates, theorems, corollaries, and comments, can assist you in creating an enterprise architecture.
17. Explain how transformation shorthand aids the practitioner in analyzing a subject and understanding movement from current state to an end state. How does this process help create a better understanding prior to design or construction?
18. Can the Framework still benefit organizations that do not follow the guidelines of producing primitives before composites? Why or why not?
19. Discuss why there is no single primitive model for any problem even though the Framework prescribes a comprehensive set of primitive models.
20. Explain how vertical and horizontal integration can add constraints and force de-optimization of an original need.
21. Discuss why enterprise architecture is a business issue, not a technical issue.
22. Discuss how building normalized architectural artifacts can improve the entire enterprise.
23. Although the Framework is indifferent as to the importance of each perspective, the practitioner of the Framework should establish a level of importance to each perspective. Discuss the level of importance of each perspective for the practitioner.

7.9.2 Critical Thinking

1. Write a one to two-page paper summarizing your understanding of the need to use architecture to manage complexity and change in the enterprise.
2. Create a new set of names for each of the perspectives and aspects. Then, in small groups determine how your unique names aid or hinder a discussion of enterprise architecture.
3. Using the Internet, find an example that illustrates why senior management can no longer remain indifferent to technology. Write a short paper that describes your example. Explain why you believe the statement regarding senior management and technology to be true.
4. With a partner, choose one aspect and discuss its meaning. Be ready to provide an example of that aspect and explain your understanding of that particular interrogative to the class.
5. Using recent magazines or the Internet, find an article that illustrates how an organization changed its approach toward security. After reading the article and using the Framework, explain in a one-page paper some of the things that are not known, as well as some of the things the organization needed to know in the context of the Framework.
6. In a small group, compare and contrast the three categories of perspectives (principle, empirical, and certifiable). Discuss your understanding of the significance of each category. Be prepared to report your findings to the class.

567

Endnotes

[1] A process decomposition model is a description technique where each level describes in more detail what is required or needed. The highest level contains the least amount of information and the lowest level contains the greatest amount of information.

[2] The reference to *lions* and *tigers* and *bears. Oh my*...is made to the 1939 movie, *The Wizard of Oz*.

[3] Mega-lega is a term coined by John Zachman to emphasize the vastness of the legacy problem within an enterprise.

[4] In business, all problems tend to be called opportunities.

[5] An agile enterprise releases software frequently; however, the paradox is that the software corrects existing problems frequently, without providing new features.

[6] From the 1956 movie, *The Ten Commandments*. Pharaoh Sethi was played by Sir Cedric Hardwicke (1896–1964).

PART 2

IMPLEMENTING THE
FRAMEWORK

"It is hard enough to remember my opinions, without also remembering my reasons for them."

— *Friedrich Nietzsche (1844–1900), Philosopher*

INTRODUCTION

No matter how challenging or complicated things can get, hopefully, we can find something to laugh about...

570

CHAPTER 8

DYNAMICAL FRAMEWORK

"It takes less time to do a thing right than explain why you did it wrong."
— *Henry Wadsworth Longfellow (1807–1882), Poet*

LEARNING OBJECTIVES

After completing Chapter 8, you will be able to:

1. Discuss a variety of software development life cycles from which IT professionals may choose.
2. Discuss how Zachman DNA assists in producing the descriptive representations of an enterprise architecture.
3. Explain how fractal mathematics and chaos relate to the Zachman Framework.
4. Give several examples of chaos experienced by businesses.
5. Describe what is meant by *Zachman Depth iNtegrating Architecture*.
6. Describe the main processes involved in a system development life cycle.
7. Compare a variety of system development life cycles.
8. Understand the goal of Zachman DNA.
9. Give examples of several attractors in complex systems.
10. Explain what attractors reveal about the overall quality of a computer system.
11. Discuss what the *x*, *y*, and *z*-axes of Zachman DNA represent.
12. Explain how *sciences* are applied to Zachman DNA by the IT department.
13. Explain the meaning of the phrase *sensitive dependence on initial conditions*.
14. Explain the difference between a primary science and a secondary science, as related to Zachman DNA.
15. Understand that Zachman DNA contains the *building blocks of business life*.
16. Understand how metrics are incorporated in Zachman DNA.
17. Describe an embedded Framework.

8.1 INTRODUCTION

The purpose of enterprise architecture is to produce a set of **descriptive representations**, **artifacts**, or **models** for the enterprise with the intent of handling **chaos**. In business, chaos often includes the need to embrace change, align business units, stay flexible, and be responsive.

Companies go through a myriad of chaotic situations daily. These situations may range from corporate mergers and acquisitions to strategic alignments; initiating new products or services to retiring old products or services; and hiring new people to firing those no longer needed. People calling in sick, taking vacation, or requesting a leave of absence also add to the daily chaos. The marketplace changes, new laws are enacted, competition stiffens, and corporate accounting practices get challenged. Amid all this chaos, how do executives find the extra time needed to meet with analysts from Wall Street?

The list of stimuli to chaos is endless, and responses to this list always seem to be...*We need it yesterday*. The intellectual capital and body of knowledge in a corporation are remarkable. People engaged by the business have to handle everything from cleaning restrooms and making coffee to balancing the general ledger, making strategic decisions, and writing software.

Writing software is complex. See Figure 8-1. Apart from the physical act of writing computer code, many other activities, disciplines, and sciences are required. An incomplete list of requirements includes:

- Project management
- Project administration
- Program management office
- Testing
- Change management
- Version control
- Involvement from users, customers, and stakeholders
- Principles
- Methodologies
- Techniques

Figure 8-1   *Developing complex software: A warning sign!*

Traditionally, the Zachman Framework for Enterprise Architecture has been described as a two-dimensional schema in a six-by-six arrangement. Each cell depicts a primitive model, which is a descriptive representation. The cells on the sixth row describe the *functioning enterprise*. The Framework further implies the need for enterprise-wide integration—achieving continuity across the scope of the enterprise within any and every cell.

Chapter 7 states that models integrated enterprise-wide are engineered to remove discontinuity across the entire enterprise. Removing discontinuity means there is no conceptual redundancy, and the models are normalized conceptually. In other words, concepts show up only once. Models are synthesized and concepts are harmonized. There are no incongruities, discontinuities, dissonance, or misfits. Each model is optimized.

How do you put a process around the Zachman Framework? To answer that question, the authors turned to the body of knowledge on **fractals**, **chaos theory**, molecular DNA, and **system development life cycles**. The authors' work led to the creation of **Zachman DNA** or *Zachman Depth iNtegrating Architecture*. Zachman DNA is an extension of the Framework used to handle all the sciences involved in producing an enterprise architecture. This chapter explores the premise and background of Zachman DNA.

SECTION 8.2 FRACTALS

Fractal:

A geometric pattern that is repeated at ever smaller scales to produce irregular shapes and surfaces that cannot be represented by classical geometry. Fractals are used especially in computer modeling of irregular patterns and structures in nature.[1]

8.2.1 Background

Benoît Mandelbrot (b. 1924) was born in Warsaw, Poland. In 1936, his family immigrated to France, where his uncle, Szolem Mandelbrot (1899–1983), a professor of mathematics at the Collège de France, took responsibility for his education. In 1945, his uncle introduced him to *Mémoire sur l'itération des fonctions rationnelles*. Gaston Julia (1893–1978) wrote the publication in 1918. In the 199-page mathematical masterpiece, Julia described *the set J(f) of those z in C for which the nth iterate f(z) stays bounded as n tends to infinity*.

Mandelbrot did not like Julia's paper, but returned to the document nearly 30 years later while working with his own theories at IBM. Mandelbrot joined IBM in 1958. He became an expert in processes with unusual statistical properties and geometric features. His work later culminated in his well-known and highly admired contributions to fractal geometry.

A LIFE OF LEARNING

Mandelbrot's academic career is quite extensive. Prior to joining IBM in 1958, he received a diploma from L'École Polytechnique, Paris, in 1947, a master's degree in aeronautics from the California Institute of Technology in 1948, and a philosophy degree in mathematical sciences from the University of Paris in 1952.

From 1949 to 1957, Mandelbrot worked at the Centre National de la Recherché Scientific. He also worked as a professor of mathematics in Geneva from 1955 to 1957 and at L'École Polytechnique from 1957 to 1958.

Mandelbrot became professor of mathematics at Yale University in 1987. He is an Abraham Robinson Professor of Mathematical Sciences and an IBM Fellow Emeritus at the IBM Thomas J. Watson Research Center, and Professor of the Practice of Mathematics at Harvard.

He has been Institute lecturer at the Massachusetts Institute of Technology and Professor of the Practice of Mathematics at Harvard. He has been a Visiting Professor at various institutions, including Harvard—first of economics, later of applied mathematics, then of mathematics; Yale University for engineering; the Albert Einstein College of Medicine for physiology; and the University of Paris-Sud for mathematics. He has also served as Professeur de l'Académie des Sciences de l'École Polytechnique.

Mandelbrot has received numerous awards and honorary doctorates including: the Barnard Medal for Meritorious Service to Science in 1985; the Franklin Medal for Signal and Eminent Service in Science in 1986; the Alexander von Humboldt Prize in 1988; the Charles Proteus Steinmetz Medal in 1988; the Science for Art Prize in 1988; the Harvey Prize for Science and Technology in 1989; the Nevada Medal in 1991; the Wolf Prize in Physics in 1993; and the Honda Prize in 1994.

Mandelbrot is also a member of the American Academy of Arts and Sciences, the National Academy of Sciences, and the European Academy.

Mandelbrot's 1967 article, *How long is the coast of Britain?* published in Science magazine, has been described as a turning point in science and mathematics, with a high spreading rate to other fields of human experience. In the article, he used the longitude of Britain's coast as an example to illustrate that a coastline does not have a determinable length. Mandelbrot pointed out that Britain's longitude is relative to the resolution of measurement or scale. The article concluded that Britain's coastline is infinite in length.

The coastline discussion helped provide an explanation for many non-Euclid[2] figures and natural phenomena, such as rivers, clouds, plants, mountain ranges, galaxies, population growth, hurricanes, electronic noise, and chaotic **attractors**. Mandelbrot had uncovered that the shapes of rivers, clouds, plants, etc. share a unifying principle: their general patterns repeat in different scales within the same object. In other words, the object is *self-similar*. See Figure 8-2.

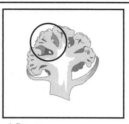

You'll notice the self-similarity of the cauliflower...
that means a cauliflower is a fractal.

Later that evening...

But Mom...I did eat one more piece.
Don't you know cauliflower is a fractal?

Figure 8-2   *Fractals have self-similar patterns*

In the mid-1970s, Mandelbrot coined the word *fractal* (from the Latin word *fractus*, meaning fractured, broken) to label objects, shapes, or behaviors having properties of self-similarity at all levels of magnification, or across all times, the dimensions of which are greater than one but smaller than two, but cannot be expressed as integers.

Fractal mathematics is applied in diverse domains including economics, linguistics, meteorology, demography, and computers. Fractals have moved into the arts, not only advancing some aesthetic principles in fine arts, but also contributing to the study of sound and music theory. Computers are used frequently to diagram complex iterative processes associated with fractal geometry.

Mandelbrot first put forward his ideas on fractals in 1977 with the book *Les objets fractals: forme, hasard et dimension*, or *Fractals: form, chance, and dimension,* if you need help with your French. A follow-up book was published in 1983— *The Fractal Geometry of Nature*.

8.2.2 Key Terms

artifact	fractal
attractor	model
chaos	system development life cycle
chaos theory	Zachman DNA
descriptive representation	

8.2.3 Review Questions

1. Explain the purpose of enterprise architecture.
2. Why is it advantageous for an enterprise to integrate models enterprise wide?
3. What are some of the activities, disciplines, and sciences required to write software?
4. What are the primary bodies of knowledge that led to the creation of Zachman DNA?
5. What characteristics do fractals have in common?
6. Provide three examples of where fractal mathematics is used today.

SECTION 8.3 CHAOS

Chaos:

A dynamical system that has a sensitive dependence on its initial conditions.[3]

8.3.1 Background

Like fractals, chaos has been found in all branches of science; in fact, most scientists now think that chaos is the rule in nature—not the exception. Harold Agnew, a former apprentice to Robert Oppenheimer, had flown over Hiroshima, Japan with the 509th bombardment group on an instrument plane accompanying the Enola Gay. In September 1970, Agnew became the third director of the Los Alamos National Laboratory, succeeding Oppenheimer and Norris Bradbury (1909–1997). He oversaw groundbreaking work in the laboratory's various divisions.

Agnew employed over 100 physicists and mathematicians in the theoretical division. One of the more eccentric scientists was Mitchell Feigenbaum (b. 1944). At one point, Feigenbaum found the normal 24-hour day too constraining and began self-experimenting on a 26-hour day. His other research topics were not considered norms either. He contemplated about turbulence in liquids and gases. He considered whether time glides smoothly, or if it is prone to take the occasional discrete hop. He thought about the eye's ability to see consistent colors and forms. He deliberated about clouds.

Feigenbaum was the first person to prove chaos was not a quirk of mathematics, but a universal property of nonlinear feedback systems. His work provided the first significant theoretical evidence that chaos exists in many real-world situations.

Around the same time Mandelbrot was trying to conjure up a name for the shape of a cloud, Feigenbaum was trying to understand the fuzziness, details, structure, and unpredictability of clouds. Feigenbaum was working on chaos.

In Chapter 3, the children's nursery rhyme, *For want of a nail*, was used to illustrate the term *sensitive dependence on initial conditions*, which is a characteristic of chaos theory. Chaos theory is the qualitative study of unstable **aperiodic behavior** in deterministic nonlinear **dynamical systems**. *Probably not an easy thing to say if you are intoxicated.*

A dynamical system is a simplified model for time-varying behavior of an actual system. Aperiodic behavior is the behavior that occurs when no variable describing the state of the system undergoes a regular repetition of values.

Aperiodic behavior never repeats and continues to manifest the effects of any small agitation. Predicting the future state in a given system that is aperiodic is impossible. Human history illustrates aperiodic behavior by observing the rise and fall of civilizations. No patterns of events repeat exactly.

Slight variations in patterns within the context of enterprise architecture result in the consistent failure to deliver computer software on time and on budget, meeting the expectations of users. For example, applying a requirement to an application based on hearsay, without communicating the requirement to the processes in the system development life cycle, may cause slight variations. In this scenario, an application developer might be heard to say, "Okay, no problem, I'll *slide* that into the code tomorrow; it's not a big deal."

In business, many corporations use an AVO form or *avoid verbal orders*. The form annotates what a customer or internal department requires. In addition, the form's name emphasizes policy and culture—namely, avoid doing anything that is not written down. In IT, writing things down for record keeping is not mandated.

IDEAS ABOUT FRACTALS AND CHAOS

The following people have completed studies using ideas about fractals and chaos:

- Mitchell Feigenbaum—who studied dynamic systems in physics
- Aristid Lindermayer—who studied plant growth
- Edward Lorenz—who studied weather and population
- Robert May—who studied population dynamics
- Benoît Mandelbrot—who studied non-Euclid figures
- Hans Meinhardt and Martin Klingler—who studied patterns on seashells
- James Murray—who studied fur markings in mammals
- Toru Nakamori—who studied coral formation
- T. A. Whitten and L. M. Sander—who studied chemical buildup in the presence of electricity
- John Zachman—who studied complex engineering and manufacturing and produced the Zachman Framework for Enterprise Architecture
- Neal Fishman, Warren Selkow, and Carol O'Rourke—who studied science organized around the Framework and created Zachman DNA

8.3.2 Key Terms

aperiodic behavior   I   dynamical system

8.3.2 Review Questions

1. Mandelbrot and Feigenbaum were two individuals who were known for *thinking outside the box*. What did they study and how do these topics relate to the Framework?

2. What is the result of aperiodic behavior in businesses?
3. What is a dynamical system?
4. What types of problems do written instructions and written records help an organization avoid?

SECTION 8.4 DNA

DNA:

> *A nucleic acid that carries the genetic information in the cell and is capable of self-replication and synthesis of RNA. DNA consists of two long chains of nucleotides twisted into a double helix and joined by hydrogen bonds between the complementary bases adenine and thymine or cytosine and guanine. The sequence of nucleotides determines individual hereditary characteristics.*[4]

8.4.1 Background

The molecule deoxyribonucleic acid, or DNA as it is more commonly known, contains the genetic blueprint for a cell and determines every characteristic of a living organism—the building blocks of life. DNA carries the information needed to direct protein synthesis and **replication**. Protein synthesis is the production of proteins needed by the cell for its activities and development. Replication is the process by which DNA copies itself for each descendant cell, passing on the information needed for protein synthesis.

Molecular DNA provides a building block to *human life*; Zachman DNA provides a building block to *enterprise life*. See Figure 8-3.

Between 1951 and 1953, American biochemist James Watson (b. 1928) and British biophysicist Francis Crick (b. 1916) worked out the double helix structure of the DNA molecule while performing research at the University of Cambridge Cavendish Laboratory in Cambridge, England.

Watson's and Crick's work was aided by X-ray diffraction pictures of DNA taken by Maurice Wilkins (b. 1916) and Rosalind Franklin (1920–1957). In 1962, Crick, Watson, and Wilkins received the Nobel Prize for their pioneering work on the structure of the DNA molecule. Had Franklin lived and been a man, her name probably would have appeared on the Nobel Prize too.

Watson and Crick determined that DNA looks like two threads twisted around each other, held together by bridges between the strands. The geometric shape of DNA forms a double helix. DNA's double helix resembles a spiral staircase with many individual steps linking each helix.

In most cellular organisms, DNA is organized on chromosomes located in the nucleus of the cell. English scientist Robert Hooke (1635–1703) first observed cells in 1665. While examining a piece of cork using a crude microscope, he noted the rows of tiny boxes that made up the dead wood's tissue. Hooke coined the term cell because the boxes reminded him of the small cells in monasteries that are occupied by monks like Abbot Suger.

The human body contains an estimated 20 to 30 trillion cells, a quantity far greater than the number of cells in the Framework. Each human cell is a model of independence and self-containment. Despite individuality, these cells are able to join, communicate, and coordinate.

Human cells organize into specialized groups called tissues. Tendons and bones are composed of connective tissue, whereas skin and mucous membranes use epithelial tissue. Different tissue types assemble into organs, such as the brain, stomach, and heart. Organs can be grouped into systems such as the digestive, circulatory, or nervous systems. Assembled organ systems form the human body.

Each cell is subject to physical forces. Cells have a form of architecture called **tensegrity**, which enables them to withstand battering by a variety of mechanical stresses, such as the pressure of blood flowing around cells. Tensegrity stabilizes cells by evenly distributing mechanical stresses to the cytoskeleton and other cell components.

Millions of times per second cells commit suicide in the human body, as part of the normal cycle of cellular replacement. This action helps stave off disease. If a mutation builds up within a cell, the cell usually self-destructs. If a mutated cell fails to self-destruct, it may divide and spread to form a growth called a tumor. Unregulated growth by rogue cells can be cancerous and threaten healthy tissue.

A microscopic structure within a cell that carries DNA molecules is the chromosome—the hereditary material that influences the development and characteristics of each organism. Humans have 23 pairs of chromosomes. The chromosomes of each pair contain genes corresponding to inherited characteristics. Each pair of chromosomes is different from the other pairs of chromosomes in the same cell. Females have two copies of the X chromosome, while males have one X chromosome and one Y chromosome.

Scientists number these chromosome pairs according to size—the largest is chromosome 1 and the smallest is chromosome 23. There are certain types of health problems associated with errors in human chromosomes. In a process called nondisjunction, paired members of chromosomes fail to separate from one another during meiosis. Nondisjunction can lead to a condition known as Down's syndrome,[5] in which a person inherits three copies of chromosome 21. Another condition that may result from nondisjunction is Turner syndrome, a disorder in which a female inherits only a single X chromosome.

Genetic errors occur if part of a chromosome is either missing or duplicated. Chromosomes sometimes undergo changes called translocations, in which part of one chromosome breaks off and attaches to another chromosome. A type of leukemia, called chronic myelogenic leukemia, is a translocation involving chromosomes 9 and 22.

Chromosomes consist chiefly of proteins and DNA. A sequence of bases along a DNA strand that codes for the production of a protein is a gene. Genes occupy precise locations on the chromosome. Genes are basic units of heredity found in a cell. Genes determine the physical characteristics that an organism inherits, such as the shape of a leaf on a tree, markings on an animal, and the color of human hair. The information encoded within the DNA structure of a gene directs the manufacture of proteins, which carry out all life-supporting activities within a cell.

The activities or processes within a cell usually work as designed, but when they fail, ill health usually arises. A similar result occurs in computer software development where the activities or processes are called system development life cycles. IT managers hope the life cycle works as designed. However, often when the life cycle fails, a software project typically dies.

8.4.2 Key Terms

replication

| tensegrity

8.4.3 Review Questions

1. What often happens when a system development life cycle does not work as designed?
2. What is the purpose of tensegrity in the cells of the human body?
3. How many cells are contained in the Zachman Framework?
4. Cells are self-contained and independent, but are able to show what other characteristics?

SECTION 8.5 SYSTEM DEVELOPMENT LIFE CYCLES

System development life cycle:

> *Any logical process used by a systems analyst to develop an information system, including requirements, validation, training, and user ownership.*
>
> *An SDLC should result in a high quality system that meets or exceeds customer expectations, within time and cost estimates, works effectively and efficiently in the current and planned information technology infrastructure, and is cheap to maintain and cost effective to enhance.*[6]

8.5.1 Background

System development life cycles (SDLCs) consist of defined activities or processes to be completed over a period of time for the purpose of developing software applications or applying changes to existing software applications. In either case, the software may be bespoke or **COTS**.

The main processes encompassed in an SDLC include: analyzing how a business user's needs are currently being met; designing a new application, or modifying an existing application to meet new business needs; developing an application based on the design; and implementing the completed application.

Many SDLCs are based on a systematic approach to solving problems called **scientific management**. Frederick Taylor (1856–1915) originated the approach in 1911. Taylor recommended the following steps for solving problems:

- Define the problem.
- Identify alternative solutions.
- Evaluate alternatives.
- Select alternatives to implement.
- Implement selected alternative solution.

The first computer business systems were developed in the late 1950s. The systems provided basic accounting functionality and included applications such as payroll, general ledger, accounts receivable, and accounts payable. The systems were batch oriented and contained relatively few lines of code. Businesses did not attempt to integrate the systems; each stood alone and dealt with separate flat files. The standalone systems were labeled *stovepipes*.

Most applications were not well documented or well designed. Many people referred to the style of code used in the computer programs as *spaghetti code* because the coding style was unstructured and looked a mess. The code was hard to follow and even harder to maintain.

By the 1970s, the structured revolution to systems development began. The structured approach established a top-down process to application development, meaning the structure applied was orderly and stepped. The process would always start at the first step and continue to the next subsequent step. Each step was completed until implementation was achieved. The structured approach tried to enhance communication and simplify the maintenance process.

The initial formal SDLC method introduced by Winston Royce in 1970 was known as the **waterfall method**. Waterfall methods typically include the following steps:

- Feasibility study
- Requirements definition
- System specifications
- System design
- Program design and development
- System test
- Conversion
- Maintenance

OTHER STRUCTURED TECHNIQUES

- Demarco—Tom Demarco, 1978
- Gane and Sarson—Chris Gane and Sally Sarson, 1977
- Jackson Structured Design—Michael Jackson (not the singer), 1975
- Myers—Glenford Myers, 1978
- Page-Jones—Meilir Page-Jones, 1988
- Warnier-Orr—J.D. Warnier and Ken Orr, 1974
- Yourdon and Constantine—Ed Yourdon and Larry Constantine, 1979

The next step in the evolution of applications development was the automation of structured tools into a **toolkit**. The toolkit name was coined because the various automated tools were not integrated. They were just a mishmash collection, or bag, of tools. Organizations purchased these tools one at a time, choosing tools to fit specific development methodologies.

The 1980s introduced CASE technology. CASE stands for computer-aided software engineering. Some **CASE tools** integrate the entire SDLC process, while others specialize in certain areas. The specialized tools are known as upper-CASE and lower-CASE tools. Upper-CASE tools specialize in planning and requirements gathering, while lower-CASE tools specialize in design and coding. Depending on the sophistication of the CASE tool, the tool may be capable of forward engineering, reverse engineering, and **round tripping**.

The waterfall method is often criticized as being a *one-way street, with no turning back*. For example, after the specifications have been completed, the design can begin; but once the design begins, the specification step is normally not reentered. Each step is *frozen* as it becomes completed. Waterfall methods are sometimes referred to as traditional, classic, or conventional methods.

In 1981, Barry Boehm developed the **incremental model**. With the incremental model, the overall architecture for the application is developed initially. The application is broken down into implemental increments. Each increment has its own complete life cycle, usually the waterfall method. Increments may be built serially or in parallel, depending on the nature of the dependencies among releases and on availability of resources. Each increment adds additional or improved functionality to the application.

In 1987, Boehm introduced the **spiral life cycle**, combining elements of the waterfall along with an emphasis on the use of risk management techniques. Its chief distinguishing feature is risk avoidance, rather than being document, code, or release driven.

The spiral life cycle is diagrammed as a sequence of cycles. See Figure 8-4. Boehm summarizes the benefits of the spiral life cycle model as:

> *The primary advantage of the spiral model is that its range of options allows it to accommodate the best features of existing software process models, while its risk-driven approach helps it to avoid most of their difficulties. In appropriate situations, the spiral model becomes equivalent to one of the existing process models. In other situations, it provides guidance on the best mix of existing approaches to be applied to a given project.*

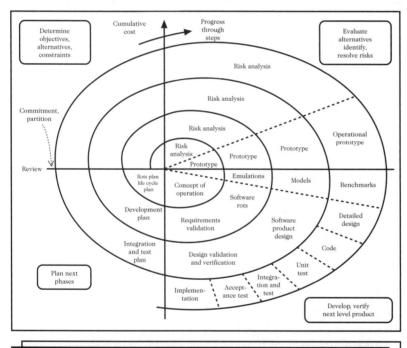

Figure 8-4   *Spiral model*

Evolutionary life cycle methods, which are also referred to as evolutionary prototyping, prototyping/simulation, rapid delivery, evolutionary delivery cycle, or rapid application development (RAD), accommodate incremental development using experience from earlier increments to help define requirements for subsequent increments.

Increments are developed sequentially rather than in parallel. Within each incremental development cycle, there are repeating progressions of analysis, design, code, test, and implementation, followed by operations and maintenance. During the operations and maintenance stages for an increment, feedback from customers may cause a reiteration of some steps of development for an increment, resulting in the re-release of the increment.

From a business user's point of view, the application evolves as each increment is delivered over a period of time. From an IT point of view, clarified requirements at the beginning of the project help dictate the initial increment, and the requirements for each development cycle are clarified through the experience of prior increments.

Object-oriented (OO) methods became popular in the 1990s. The Booch Method was introduced in the book *Object-Oriented Analysis and Design*, by Grady Booch. James Rumbaugh was part of a team at General Electric that developed a popular OO methodology called Object Modeling Technique (OMT). Another major OO methodologist was a Swede named Ivar Jacobson, who developed the Objectory methodology at Ericsson.

In the mid-1990s, Rumbaugh and Jacobson joined Booch at Rational Software[7] to unify their methodologies. They soon became known as the three amigos. Their first success was a notation called the Unified Modeling Language (UML). UML was adopted by the Object Management Group, a recognized standards body, as the defacto OO modeling notation. The three amigos followed up UML with a popular SDLC called RUP, the Rational Unified Process.

RUP focuses on six areas:

- Iterating software development
- Managing requirements
- Promoting component-based architectures
- Using visual modeling software
- Verifying software quality
- Controlling changes to software

The RUP has nine workflows and four phases. See Figure 8-5.

Some people regard the methods mentioned so far as heavyweight or monumental methods. Today, many people are turning to **agile life cycles** for application development. Agile methods are people oriented rather than process oriented. As Martin Fowler, chief scientist at ThoughtWorks, states, "They [agile methods] explicitly make a point of trying to work with people's nature rather than against them, and they emphasize that software development should be an enjoyable activity."

Agile techniques and methods include:

- Extreme programming
- Crystal
- Adaptive software development
- Scrum
- Feature-driven development
- Dynamic system development method
- Agile modeling

Despite the vast array of life cycles from which to choose, most software development remains a chaotic activity, characterized by the phrase *code and fix*. IT professionals find it hard to stick to a method, which is why many larger software projects fail. The reason there are so many methods to choose from is that nobody has found the right homogeneous remedy.

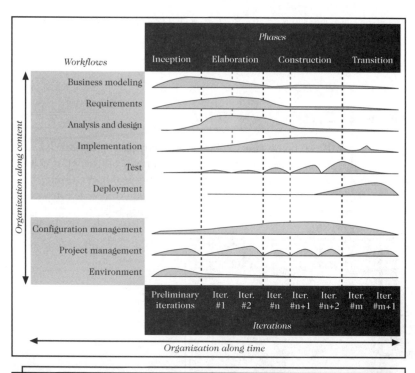

Workflows

Phases: Inception, Elaboration, Construction, Transition

Business modeling
Requirements
Analysis and design
Implementation
Test
Deployment

Configuration management
Project management
Environment

Organization along content

Preliminary iterations | Iter. #1 | Iter. #2 | Iter. #n | Iter. #n+1 | Iter. #n+2 | Iter. #m | Iter. #m+1

Iterations

Organization along time

Figure 8-5   Rational Unified Process

Many commercial life cycles are marketed as customizable, meaning that each IT department or project picks the elements of interest. How can IT professionals be sure they have chosen the right set of steps, activities, or processes for a project? The authors believe one answer to that question is the use of Zachman DNA.

8.5.2 Key Terms

agile life cycle	round tripping
CASE tool	scientific management
COTS	spiral life cycle
evolutionary life cycle method	toolkit
incremental model	waterfall method

8.5.3 Review Questions

1. Describe a system development life cycle.
2. List the steps recommended for solving problems using the scientific management technique originated by Frederick Taylor.
3. When were the first computer business systems developed and for what purpose?
4. What is the meaning of the term *toolkit* in relation to applications development?

5. When was CASE technology introduced and what do the initials represent?

6. Describe the difference between heavyweight application development methods and agile methods.

SECTION 8.6 ZACHMAN DNA

Waclaw Sierpinski (1882–1969) is a famous Polish mathematician who introduced his *carpet* to the world in 1916. Sierpinski's carpet is not a physical carpet; it is a fractal. The carpet's pattern continues infinitely, so the carpet is not even something that can be drawn completely. The carpet is the object you would have if you were able to continue removing its center squares forever. See Figure 8-6.

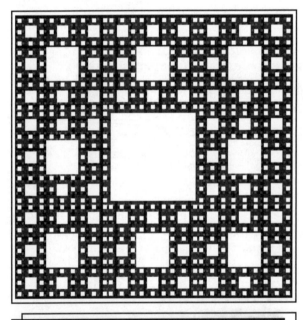

Figure 8-6   *Sierpinski's carpet*

Sierpinski, and other mathematicians of his time, tried to understand the finer points of dimension. The true purpose of his construction was to create a universal object that could contain any closed and bounded one-dimensional object that could exist in the plane.

From Sierpinski's carpet, Austrian mathematician Karl Menger (1902–1985) developed a spatial counterpart in 1926, named the Menger sponge. See Figure 8-7. Although it looks like a three-dimensional object, the sponge is actually a 2.73-dimensional fractal. Another interesting aspect of the Menger sponge is that the lattice has an infinite surface area and zero volume.

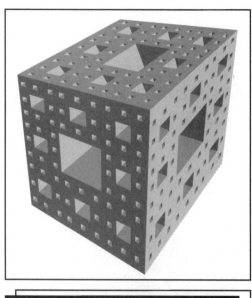

As a fractal, the Zachman Framework has many self-similar patterns. Each row looks like any other row; each column looks like any other column; and each cell looks like any other cell. The Framework can appear as a stack of self-similar Peer Frameworks. Chapter 7 discusses Peer Frameworks.

The Zachman Framework was always good at explaining the descriptive representations of the enterprise, but did little to suggest how to incorporate a process to create the descriptive representations. The Framework has always been described as methodology and technology independent, so the Framework never needed to directly address the problems associated with actually *doing the work* of planning, architecture, design, coding, testing, and implementation.

Borrowing from Menger's ideas, the authors applied additional dimensions to the two-dimensional Zachman Framework. The resulting work gave way to a structure known as Zachman DNA. In the same way, the two-dimensional Framework helps describe the types of descriptive representations an enterprise needs. The three-dimensional Framework helps authenticate any SDLC used in the creation of the descriptive representations. Figure 8-8 shows that each cell in the Zachman DNA contains an entire six-by-six Framework. Potentially, each cell within a cell contains another six-by-six Framework.

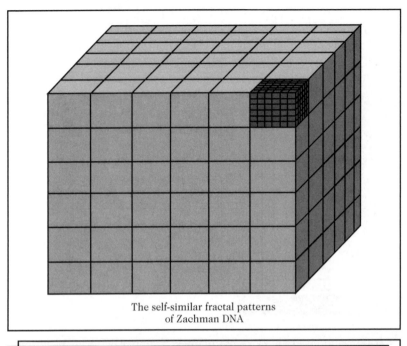

The self-similar fractal patterns
of Zachman DNA

Figure 8-8   *The self-similar fractal patterns of Zachman DNA*

Zachman DNA first originated on September 9, 2000. To help explain the concepts of Zachman DNA and authenticate an SDLC, analogies are drawn using fractals, chaos theory, and molecular DNA.

Fractals reveal a structure in chaos. An attractor is the key to uncovering the structure of chaos and is "A set of physical properties toward which a system tends to evolve, regardless of the starting conditions of the system."[8]

8.6.1 Attractors

There is a game called the chaos game. The game resembles a dot-to-dot drawing, only you do not join the dots with lines. Instead, you plot point after point, according to the game's rules. You begin by drawing three dots as points of a triangle—it does not have to be an equilateral triangle. Then you place a fourth dot anywhere inside the triangle as a starting point. You will need one additional piece of equipment, namely a die.

Roll the die. If the top facing number is a 1 or a 2, draw another dot halfway from the starting point to the first dot. If the number is a 3 or 4, draw a dot halfway from the starting point to the second dot. When the die shows a 5 or 6, draw a dot halfway to the third dot.

The new dot becomes the new starting point. You should repeat the process of rolling the die and plotting a new point until you are bored silly. As long as your dots are fine enough, the game never ends. After several hours, a pattern begins to emerge. The pattern was uncovered originally by Sierpinski. This one is called the Sierpinski triangle. See Figure 8-9.

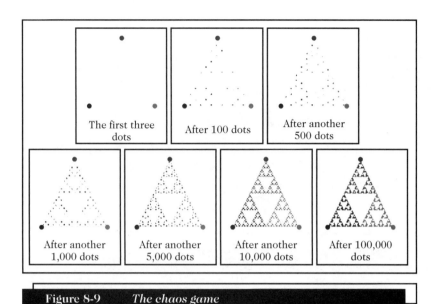

The first three dots	After 100 dots	After another 500 dots

After another 1,000 dots	After another 5,000 dots	After another 10,000 dots	After 100,000 dots

Figure 8-9   *The chaos game*

The initial decision of where to place the first starting point does not really matter. What actually happens is that the points are pulled toward an attractor. This type of attractor is called a strange attractor. Zachman DNA also has strange attractors that can help govern what actually happens in software development.

SOMETHING TO TRY AT HOME

Alternatively, you can use Sierpinski's carpet in the chaos game. Here are the rules for creating the carpet:

1. Select eight vertices, four being the corners of a square and four the midpoints of the edges of the square.
2. Randomly select one of these points and call its coordinates (x, y).
3. Randomly select a vertex and draw a point between (x, y) and the vertex such that the distance from the new point to the vertex is one third of the distance from the previous point to the vertex.
4. Redefine (x, y) to be the coordinates of the new point and repeat the last step.

In Chapter 3, Lorenz's butterfly effect described cause and effect by *sensitive dependence on initial conditions*. The butterfly effect is an attractor. See Figure 8-10.

Dynamical Framework

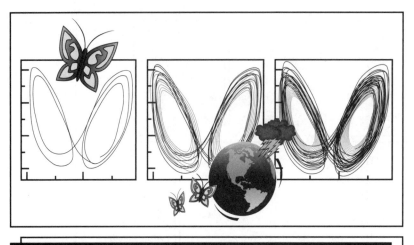

Figure 8-10   *The Lorenz attractor: The butterfly effect*

Lorenz assumed originally that a small event, such as the flap of a butterfly's wing, could have no significant effect on its surroundings. However, even a small difference extended over a long period of time can produce a large effect. The way the difference affects the outcome can be very sensitive to small changes. It is possible that the air turbulence created by the page you turned a few moments ago will prevent a tornado in Wichita, Kansas next summer.

590

THANK YOU MR. PRESIDENT

For many people, just catching a glimpse of the U.S. President is an enjoyable moment. Actually shaking the President's hand creates a memory that lasts a lifetime. On March 11, 2002, two-and-a-half-year-old Sean Franklin met the President and shook his hand. Unfortunately, Sean might be a little too young to retain clear distinct memories of the occasion.

The reason Sean met the President was because his father, Thomas E. Franklin, had taken one of the most instantly recognizable photographs. Franklin, a reporter for the Bergen Record newspaper in New Jersey, had captured three firefighters raising an American flag at Ground Zero. That photograph helped revive a nation's shattered spirit.

On March 11, 2002, the President unveiled a U.S. postage stamp commemorating the heroism of rescue workers on September 11, 2001. See Figure 8-11. This stamp is one of the first to sell for more than its face value by the United States Post Office. Selling for 45 cents, 34 cents was allocated to postage, 3 cents for administrative costs, and 8 cents to be distributed to the families of rescue

(continued)

workers killed or injured permanently during the attack on the World Trade Center in Manhattan.

Figure 8-11   *First-class heroes: Firefighters Daniel McWilliams, George Johnson, and William Eisengrein*

At 7:59 a.m. on September 11, American Airlines Flight 11, carrying 92 people, left Logan International Airport in Boston, Massachusetts, bound for Los Angeles, California. Forty-six minutes later, it was the first of two planes to crash into the World Trade Center. Behind the day's catastrophic events was Saudi-born Osama bin Laden.

Today, his name stands for terror worldwide. He held a deep-rooted hatred against the western world, especially the United States, and set out to threaten the western world's very existence. He was responsible for the deaths of thousands of innocent civilians.

Bin Laden felt Islam was threatened when the Soviet Union troops invaded Afghanistan in December, 1979. His passion compelled him to take up the Islamic cause. He left Saudi Arabia and traveled to Pakistan to meet with members of Jamaate Islami and got an insight into the dark lives of the Afghan Muslims. He vowed to fight. His radicalism had been fueled.

He collected funds from many sources and funneled the money to the Mujahideen fighters. He made repeated trips to Pakistan and regularly financed

(continued)

591

operations. In 1982, he made his first foray into Afghanistan. He took with him construction machinery and handed the equipment to the Mujahideen. Gradually, he involved himself in actual battles. Slowly, he began to grow in popularity among the Mujahideen.

The American Central Intelligence Agency (CIA) had a major role in training Bin Laden. Concerned by the widening reign of communism, it actively supported the Taliban against the Soviet troops. The support included supplying Stinger anti-aircraft missiles.

The Soviets invaded Afghanistan during Christmas 1979 to support the Afghan Communist government. However, many Afghani factions rose up against the government and the Soviet Union, uniting together to fight. When the Soviets left Afghanistan in 1990, the Communist government fell apart. Civil war took place because the victors started turning on each other. The Taliban took over governmental control of the country.

In 1978, the Communist party had taken over the governmental control in Afghanistan. The Communist rise to power resulted in a young man, who would not be born for another 22 years, shaking the hand of the President of the United States of America—*a sensitive dependence on initial conditions.*

The Zachman Framework illustrates that the operational components (the *functioning enterprise*—Row 6) of a computer system consist of more than just computer programs. The holistic view of a computer system includes the data (*what*), programs (*how*), connectivity mechanisms including hardware and networks (*where*), people (*who*), schedules (*when*), and motivation including business rules (*why*).

The holistic view of a computer system is a group of interacting parts (from the *what, how, where, who, when,* and *why* columns) functioning as a whole, but still distinguishable from each other by recognizable boundaries.

The boundary for data includes databases and file systems. For programs, the boundary is the embedded logic and exposed interfaces. The boundary for the connectivity components includes buildings, hardware, networks, and middleware. For people, the boundary includes organizations, security, and workflow. The boundary for schedules includes schedules of both business and system events. For motivation, the boundary includes business rules, service agreements, strategies, and tactics.

The purpose and usefulness of a computer system depend on the nature and arrangement of the parts. The arrangement may change if parts are added, removed, or otherwise rearranged within the computer system.

Even when focused on a single interrogative such as *how*, a series of programs can be connected into various configurations[9] the resultant system no longer solely exhibits the collective logic of the programs. Instead, additional behaviors result. This is an **emergent system property**. Unexpected features or bugs are not always isolated to an individual program.

Emergence is the appearance of a property or feature not previously observed as a functional characteristic of the system. Generally, higher-level properties are emergent. For example, a car is an emergent property of its interconnected parts. The car disappears if the parts are disassembled and placed in a heap.

Executing a set of programs in a particular sequence to achieve a desired result restricts the behavior of the system, confining it to a smaller volume of its **phase space**. When programs are governed externally by parameters, including arguments, messages, triggers, reference files, and reference tables, the instantiation for this type of self-organizing system can be problematical. Extensive testing is often necessary to find all behaviors.

A phase space is the total number of behavioral combinations available to the system. A single coin has two states—heads and tails. The number of possible states increases rapidly with complexity. One hundred coins can be arranged in over 1,000,000,000,000,000,000,000,000,000,000 different ways.

BYTES

Kilobyte	1,000
Megabyte	1,000,000
Gigabyte	1,000,000,000
Terabyte	1,000,000,000,000
Petabyte	1,000,000,000,000,000
Exabyte	1,000,000,000,000,000,000
Yettabyte	1,000,000,000,000,000,000,000
Zettabyte	1,000,000,000,000,000,000,000,000→*The Greeks stopped here*
Lottabyte	1,000,000,000,000,000,000,000,000,000→*Suggested by IBM*
Itbytes	1,000,000,000,000,000,000,000,000,000,000→*Being silly*
Vampirebyte	1,000,000,000,000,000,000,000,000,000,000,000→*Being clever*

Each coin can be viewed as a separate parameter or dimension in the system. A single arrangement is equivalent to specifying 100 binary digits; each binary digit for each coin indicates a 1 for heads and a 0 for tails. A system has one dimension of phase space for each variable that can change. An attractor governs a system moving around its phase space.

The attractor is the preferred position for the system, such that if the system is started from another state, it evolves until it arrives at the attractor and stays there in the absence of other factors. Outside of a computer system, an attractor can be a point like the center of a bowl containing a ball, a regular path such as a planetary orbit, a complex series of states like the metabolism of a cell, or an infinite sequence, which is called a strange attractor. See Figure 8-12.

All attractors specify a restricted volume of phase space. The larger area of phase space leading to an attractor is called its basin of attraction. The ratio of the volume of the basin to the volume of the attractor is used as a measure of the degree of self-organization present.

Computer systems are drawn to an attractor. Complex computer systems can have many attractors, such as **drag**, **weight**, **thrust**, **lift**, **scope**, **detail**, **time**, **cost**,

people, **intrusion**, **convention**, and **history**. Each of these attractors is represented in Zachman DNA.

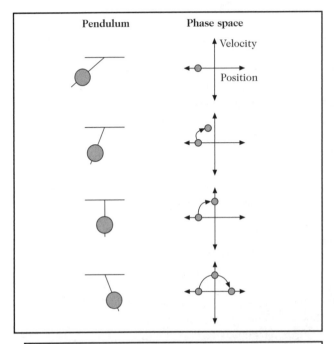

Figure 8-12 *Pendulum behavior and associated phase space diagrams*

Drag, Weight, Thrust, and Lift

The attractors drag, weight, thrust, and lift are mechanisms that are always present and need to be balanced for a corporation to survive. See Figure 8-13. Mechanisms could include: a procedure, an activity, and a verbal authorization or direction.

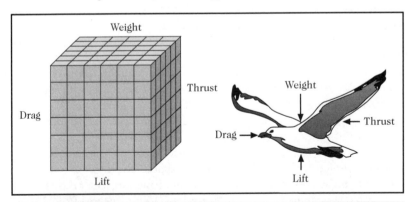

Figure 8-13 *Attractors: drag, weight, thrust, and lift*

Drag constitutes mechanisms that inhibit forward momentum. For example, throughput on a computer is limited to the technology employed. This includes the amount of memory, the types and size of cache, rotation speed of hard drives, and the types and bandwidth of the network. Unless changed in some way, the deployed technology will eventually limit corporate growth and flexibility.

Weight constitutes the burdens of performing certain duties that ordinarily would not be done. For example, a public corporation in the U.S. has to file a 10-Q report with the Securities and Exchange Commission (SEC) every quarter. Unless mandated to do so, a corporation would not voluntarily expend the time, cost, and energy to produce the report.

Thrust constitutes mechanisms that promote forward movement. Rightsizing a deployed application can provide necessary movement for a corporation. An application that is deployed using Microsoft Windows XP on an Intel platform is not as scaleable as an SMP or MPP[10] Unix environment. The UNIX environment does not scale as well as a Z class IBM mainframe computer. If the capacity of the hardware limits order taking or distribution of product through a warehouse, the hardware has the adverse effect of causing drag.

Lift constitutes mechanisms that are enablers. For example, a person's productivity improves when provided with the correct tools to accomplish a task or an activity in an appropriate work environment.

Scope and Detail

Scope sets a boundary. Many activities are so large they must be broken down into manageable parts. See Figure 8-14. In IT, this approach is called iterative or incremental development. Each part is a sliver of the whole, and each part has a scope. The scope determines how much work is to be undertaken. When the cumulative scope is not 100 percent of the whole, there is a chance that some needed feature is going to be missing and inhibit the corporation from being agile, competitive, or profitable.

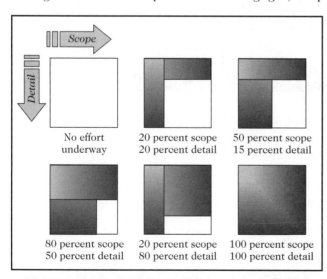

Figure 8-14   *Attractors: scope and detail*

Detail is the depth at which something is known. The detail is relative to the scope and indicates the explicit level of knowledge known and recorded about the work at hand. If the detail is less than 100 percent of the scope, either the undocumented detail is implied to be known, or it is assumed someone can determine the missing information when needed.[11] Assumptions and implicit knowledge are not always negatives, but they constitute a level of risk to the enterprise.

Together, scope and detail are indications of risk because the organization does not have either the features it needs or the quantified information to appropriate quality or knowledge.

Time, Cost, People, Intrusion, Convention, and History

Time provides an opportunity to accomplish something. Cost is a willingness to accept a financial burden. People are the available human resources. Intrusions are situations or conditions over which the business has no control. History provides an opportunity to learn. Convention is a guide to moving an activity forward. See Figure 8-15.

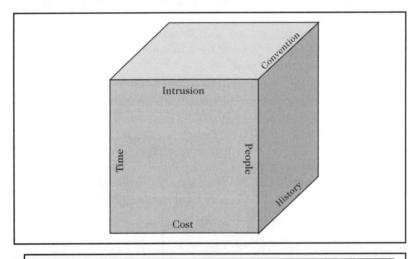

Figure 8-15 *Attractors: time, cost, people, intrusion, convention, and history*

All the attractors are in the context of the *x*, *y*, and *z*-axes of Zachman DNA. The axes are labeled **aspect**, **perspective**, and **science**. Aspect represents the interrogatives, a technique for breaking the whole into constituent primitive parts. Perspective is a biased way of viewing something. Science is a specific specialty.

Examples of context for an aspect, perspective, and science include information technology and education. Aspects in IT include data for *what* (Column 1), process for *how* (Column 2), network for *where* (Column 3), organization for *who* (Column 4), schedule for *when* (Column 5), and strategy for *why* (Column 6). For education, they include textbooks for *what*, pedagogy for *how*, classroom for *where*, teaching staff and students for *who*, school calendar for *when*, and contributing members of society for *why*.

Perspectives in IT include scope for *planner* (Row 1), enterprise model for *owner* (Row 2), system model for *designer* (Row 3), technology model for *builder* (Row 4), detailed representations for *subcontractor* (Row 5), and computer application for *functioning enterprise* (Row 6). For education, they include school district for *planner*, superintendent for *owner*, principal for *designer*, department chair for *builder*, teacher for *subcontractor*, and the act of teaching for *functioning enterprise*.

Sciences in IT include project management (Depth 1) and project administration (Depth 2). For education, they include education standards by grade and fundraising.

Investigating the form and dynamics of the attractors can reveal many things about the overall quality of a computer system and drive what type of metrics should be used to produce measurements.

8.6.2 Measurements

The surface structures of cancer cells are crinkly and wrinkly. The convoluted structures of cancer display fractal properties, which vary markedly during the different stages of the cancer cell's growth.

The medical science field employs fractal geometry to help detect the initial presence of cancer cells in the body. With the aid of computers, mathematical pictures can be obtained, revealing whether or not cells are becoming cancerous. The computer is able to measure the fractal structure of the cells. If cells are too fractal, it spells trouble, and there is something wrong with those particular cells.

The fractal dimension of cancerous material is higher than that of healthy cells. This breakthrough can be leveraged in helping diagnose breast cancer in women, using magnetic resonance imaging when mammography is not effective. Researchers focus on developing robust dimension estimates to improve discrimination between benign and malignant breast masses.

Cancer cells are not the only fractals in our bodies. Fractured bones are fractal, and so is our heartbeat. Most people's heartbeats seem regular and rhythmic, but when the structure of timing is examined in *excruciating detail*, the beat is revealed as slightly fractal. The fact that our heartbeats are not regular and always contain tiny variations is quite important. The fine time-scale variation reduces the wear and tear on the heart dramatically. Extreme and arrhythmic fractal behavior can be indicative of heart disease.

These types of discoveries have helped develop other new ideas in business. Engineers have been able to design railroad car wheels that last longer, and scientists have been able to optimize the orbits of satellites.

Because Zachman DNA is a fractal, it has the ability to help direct measurements based on the attractors: drag, weight, thrust, lift, scope, detail, time, cost, people, intrusion, convention, and history. Applying measurements can help determine healthy *Zachman* cells from unhealthy *Zachman* cells.

There is a crisis in software development. Schedules and costs are often wrong. IT departments cannot keep up with the demand for new or modified software. If software is implemented before the project is cancelled, the delivered quality is often poor.

Many IT departments do not keep measurements from past projects. They are unable to learn proactively from previous experiences. Experiences are retained typically as tribal knowledge, which is discussed in Chapter 4. Tribal knowledge has the propensity to deteriorate quickly as people leave or move around the organization.

Capers Jones' 1997 book, *Applied Software Measurement: Assuring Productivity and Quality*, illustrates that the bigger the software project, the harder it falls. The probability of failure only goes up as the project gets bigger. See Figure 8-16.

Function points	Probability of termination prior to project completion
100	6 %
1,000	17 %
10,000	45 %
100,000	80 %

Figure 8-16   *Function points*

In the late 1970s, IBM wanted to develop a way to estimate effort in developing software independent of the programming language used to construct the application. Allan Albrecht, an IBM employee, was charged with developing a new approach. The result was the **function point** technique. Albrecht's ideas were presented initially at the IBM Application Development Symposium in Monterey, California in October 1979.

Function points are a measure of the size of computer applications and the projects that build them. Function points measure functionality by objectively measuring functional requirements, independent of any computer language, development methodology, technology, or capability of the project team used to develop the application.

Function points are not a perfect measure of the effort needed to develop an application, nor of the business value an application will produce once operational. However, function points can be useful factors that contribute to measuring effort and value. For example, a 3,000-square foot house is usually less expensive to build than a 6,000-square foot house. However, attributes like marble bathrooms, tile floors, and gold-plated fixtures might actually make the smaller house more expensive. Other factors, including location and number of bedrooms, might also make the smaller house more valuable as a residence.

To illustrate this concept of scale, see Figure 8-17. Often, IT managers apply the same methodology to build both small and large systems. Larger systems, by sheer size, are more complex. Complex systems need defined approaches and descriptive representations to help make them manageable. For example, the average doghouse can be assembled without any forethought. A quick trip to the local hardware store to buy some two-by-fours, plywood, a few shingles, nails, blue paint, and a stencil kit to write Fido's name neatly on the front is almost the hard part. The same technique cannot be applied to building a house or a downtown skyscraper. Large structures cannot be built adequately on a trial and error basis.

If mankind is capable of sending a man to and from the moon, building 110-story skyscrapers, laying communication cables across the bed of the Atlantic Ocean, and building computer chips exceeding 110 gigahertz, why are IT departments unable to *throw a few lines of code together* that work? The answer is discipline. Most complicated initiatives are governed by procedures, methods, and adequately trained personnel. This is not always the case in IT.

Most commercial enterprises have **mission critical systems**. A mission critical system is one that is crucial to the daily operation of the business. Companies are free to let any employee or consultant touch production code. A company can let a trainee programmer make a change to a core system and have the change implemented without testing. The modified code can severely hinder the company.

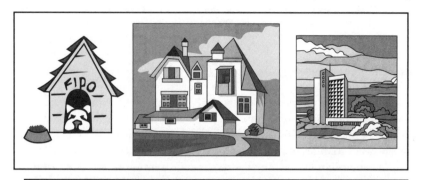

Figure 8-17   *Scale can cause inherent problems*

In 1982, Fisher Controls, an industrial valve manufacturer, lost one million dollars when a programmer made a change to a COBOL language production program and did not test the program. The programmer had left out a period. A dot. A one million dollar dot. A building architect is not allowed to build a skyscraper as a first project. Architects serve an extensive apprenticeship before being trusted to develop such an undertaking. In contrast, many IT professionals do not experience a disciplined work environment.

Although many IT departments find it hard to stick with an SDLC, the impetus to use one is a physiological one of being afraid. IT departments are *afraid* of building the wrong product, producing a product of inferior quality, delivering the project late, having employees spend over 80 hours at the office each week, letting down management and customers, and not having any fun. If we could read the *writing on the wall*, it would say, *Be afraid...be very afraid*. See Figure 8-18.

Figure 8-18   *The writing on the wall*

Dynamical Framework

Managing activities without feedback just makes the task of managing harder. *If you can't measure it, you can't manage it; and if you can't manage it, you can't evaluate it; and if you can't evaluate it, you can't value it; and if you can't value it, you can't understand it; and if you can't understand it, you're simply hosed.* Then again, determining what *it* is, is a good starting point. Having measurements just makes the task of managing easier.

A **measurement** is the result of applying a metric in which the result has been given context by a unit of measure. A **metric** is an algorithm or expression of something to be accumulated. The metric may also specify how the something is to be accumulated. A **unit of measure** is both an amount quantifying something as a value of 1 and a designation applied to a number to understand what the number represents.

An example of a unit of measure is 1 second. A metric using 1 second as a unit of measure is: how long does it take to complete a 26.2-mile marathon. The algorithm is $(x \div y) = z$, where x is 26.2, y is the average speed of the runner, and z is the elapsed duration in seconds. For British runner Paula Radcliffe (b. 1973), the fastest female marathon runner, the measurement was 8,238 seconds on October 13, 2002. Additionally, the duration can be converted into hours, minutes, and seconds: 2 hours, 17 minutes, and 18 seconds.

A metric requires a unit of measure. By using the Framework, the highest level of abstraction for a unit of measure can be surmised. The unit of measure is primitive and undefined in terms of numbers. The unit of measure is not typical at this level because it is entirely out of context and scope and devoid of content. It is short-lived.

The abstract unit of measure for each column in the Framework is:

- Column 1, *what*—Thing and its definition→Inventory
- Column 2, *how*—Work→Yield
- Column 3, *where*—Location→Capacity
- Column 4, *who*—Function→Performance
- Column 5, *when*—Time→Duration
- Column 6, *why*—Desire→State

Every other thought, statement, reason, definition, expression, and number become dependent upon these six primitive units of measure.

The primitive unit of measure is not a metric or a statistic. The primitive unit of measure is unreal and unusable until placed in context and scope. In addition, the primitive unit of measure must be tied to one or more other primitive units of measure, as defined in the other columns, forming a compound. Therefore, to have a metric, both a context and a scope are required. A compound is the result of viewing two or more primitives together at the same time. When using a compound, the underlying primitives may not be readily apparent or identifiable. The whole (the compound) may hide or obscure the parts (the primitives).

The primitive unit of measure is also absent of history or predication. The primitive unit of measure can be expressed only in terms of the present, and as soon as the primitive unit of measure is expressed, it may become incorrect. This concept is true for all primitive units of measure.

Often, an enterprise may not know exactly what to measure. The primitive units of measure provide a starting point to identify the types of metrics that should be established. The attractors of Zachman DNA and the primitive units of measure of the Framework help provide a vehicle to develop metrics. Starting with the attractors—time, cost, people, intrusion, convention, and history, metrics can be formulated to govern the processes for any type of procedure. In other words, these metrics are associated with metrics for **process management**.[12]

The attractor labeled time is associated with the unit of measure *time*. The attractor labeled cost is associated with *thing*, people are associated with *function*, intrusion with *location*, history with *desire*, and convention with *work*. Process metrics based on these attractors are given context when applied to a specific domain, such as information technology, enterprise, and product.

Scope and detail are metrics associated with **entropy**. In this particular case, the entropy deals with the probability and degree of disorder and disorganization that occur within a project that does not drive out assumptions and leaves appropriate project details implicit. In other words, entropy is associated with metrics for **risk management**.[13]

When the scope and detail are not known to the fullest extent, entropy occurs. Some degree of entropy is normal. The underlying processes supporting the Framework cell may exacerbate the entropy when measured by the process metrics. Processes cannot compensate for what you do not know, but a deficient process can make matters worse. At best, the processes have a neutral effect on entropy. The lower the level of entropy, the more likely the project is proceeding in an adequate manner.

Opposite states of entropy are illustrated in Figure 8-19.

Low entropy (good)	High entropy (bad)
• Large proportion of energy available for doing work	• Small proportion of energy available for doing work
• Order, high degree of organization, meticulous sorting, or separation	• Disorder, disorganization, thorough mix
• Preordained outcomes, high probability of a selected event	• Equally probable events, low probability of a selected event
• Uniform distribution	• Highly uneven distribution
• Near certainty, high reliability	• Great uncertainty
• Non-randomness, accurate forecasts	• Randomness or unpredictability
• Narrowly constrained choice, few possible outcomes	• Free to choose from a wide variety of options, many possible outcomes
• Small diversity	• Large diversity
• Little or no surprise	• Great surprise
• Much information	• Little information
• Large amount of information used to specify state of system	• Small amount of information used to specify state of system
• High accuracy of data	• Low accuracy of data

Figure 8-19   *Entropy*

Risk associated with a set of descriptive representations on a row of Zachman DNA is inherited automatically by each subsequent row. In other words, what you do not know on one row remains unknown on the next row, and the likelihood of making incorrect decisions increases. The cost of correcting defects grows exponentially from one row to the next.

I WISH YOU COULD TELL ME WHAT IT WAS YOU WANTED

Joey decided he needed a new vehicle. He went to a local dealership and explained what he was looking for to the salesperson. The salesperson said, "What you need is a truck," and brought out a truck to show Joey.

"Oh wait," said Joey, "I forgot to tell you. I need to be able to seat six people."

"Not a problem," said the salesperson. The salesperson returned the truck to its original parking space and brought a king-cab version of the truck for Joey to consider.

"Hmmmm. I'm sorry, my wife, she will be driving it too, and she likes a stick-shift," Joey now informed the salesperson.

"Not a problem," said the salesperson, but sounded the words "gee whiz" underneath his breath and came back with a king-cab, stick-shift truck for Joey to view.

"One more thing I forgot to mention...there are no roads where I need to use this vehicle," responded Joey with a smile.

The salesperson started to lose his patience. He returned the truck and politely told Joey, "I do not sell helicopters."

No transaction was completed.

In developing software, customers (end-users) and IT project teams go around in circles like this. Sometimes these circles take years and result in the project being cancelled. While important to iterate on a process, placing appropriate time constraints on a project is important too. The project team must either deliver something early on or acknowledge that the team is unable to deliver what is needed.

Figure 4-4 from Chapter 4 illustrated the principles of drag, weight, thrust, and lift in keeping an airplane moving in the air. The following attractors—drag, weight, thrust, and lift—provide the same type of mechanics for the Framework. These attractors, when placed in the context of a specific domain, are associated with **asset management**.[14] Asset management is affected by the underlying entropy, which is affected by the underlying processes.

Because Zachman DNA contains self-similar properties of scale associated with fractals, all the attractors scale too. The scaling attractors affect asset management, risk management, and process management. See Figure 8-20.

The business world is complex and demands the need for a business to reinvent itself periodically to stay alive and competitive. An impact on the types of metrics gathered as an enterprise grows, shrinks, or otherwise changes potentially requires certain measurements be added, dropped, or refined. A goal of Zachman DNA is to help simplify the complexity of software development to make chaos as manageable as possible.

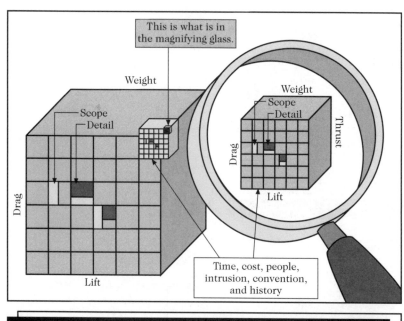

Figure 8-20   *Scaling attractors*

Any organization implementing a metric program hopes the correct type of measurements are captured and reported. These measurements should be delivered in a timely fashion to someone who can understand and interpret the information at an appropriate level. Once a metric has been captured, a number of things can happen.

For example, the measurement could be discarded and not presented to anyone in the organization for review. The measurement could be delivered for review, but then ignored completely and not reviewed—in this case, it is as though the measurement had never been produced. Alternatively, the measurements may be reviewed, but may not provide insight for actions to be taken; this can happen because the wrong types of metrics are taken, or the measurements are not presented in a coherent manner. These are symptoms of a dysfunctional organization.

When measurements are used to take action, the result is either negative or positive feedback. Feedback is often stated as a feedback loop and modeled in a circular fashion, emphasizing the *loop*. Although circular, the loop is linear. See Figure 8-21. In reality, feedback comes from many places and tends to be nonlinear and more chaotic to handle, as shown in Figure 8-22.

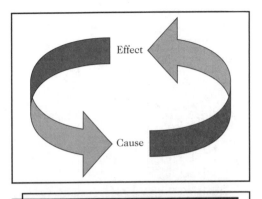

Figure 8-21   *Linear feedback loop*

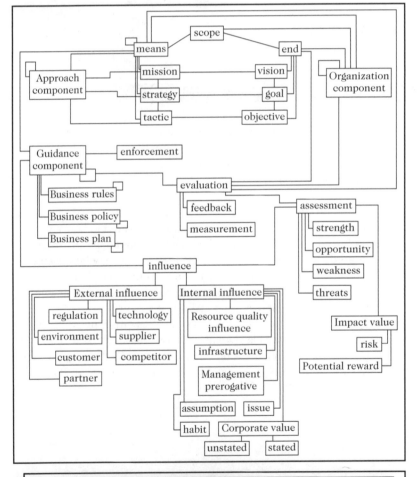

Figure 8-22   *Nonlinear feedback loop: a picture of the process of making a nonlinear feedback model is itself a nonlinear feedback process*

Positive feedback is information returned to a process, which reinforces and encourages the original results. The intent is to keep things going, or to try to get more of the same results. An increase in sales would cause management to keep pushing for an even greater number of sales in the next reporting period. An uncontrolled positive feedback loop contributes to a process's eventual demise. Applying negative feedback to maintain a process helps control wild looping behaviors.

In many ways, negative feedback, despite its name, is deemed preferable. Negative feedback leads to adaptive and goal-seeking behavior. The goal may be self-determined, fixed, or evolving, and the adaptive behavior seeks to sustain a given level. Negative feedback influences the process to produce a result opposite of a previous result.

Metrics, measurements, and feedback govern behavior and influence the features of an application. A heuristic philosophy in the spacecraft industry is: *If you can't analyze it, don't build it*. However, most business organizations do not go to that extreme. The heuristic philosophy is: *The level of energy spent gathering a measurement should not exceed the business value gathered from acquiring a measurement*.

Zachman DNA can be used as a dashboard for monitoring all aspects of the enterprise. Asset management provides a macro viewpoint for measurements using the attractors drag, weight, thrust, and lift to influence metrics. Process management provides a micro viewpoint for measurements using the attractors time, cost, people, intrusion, convention, and history to influence metrics. Risk management covers the middle ground for measurements using the attractors scope and detail to influence metrics.

Using Zachman DNA as a dashboard allows a person to gauge the current state of an enterprise. The current state provides feedback to the enterprise on its current course. Given a state or situation, the enterprise can apply appropriate behavior in response to what it sees on the dashboard. See Figure 8-23.

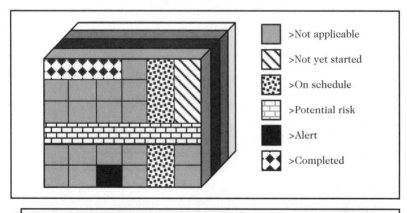

>Not applicable

>Not yet started

>On schedule

>Potential risk

>Alert

>Completed

Figure 8-23 *Using Zachman DNA as a dashboard*

Ultimately, each enterprise determines how much energy will be expended to control chaos. One purpose of Zachman DNA is to help enterprises find an appropriate balance between the expenditure of time, resources, logistics, and the enterprise's exposure to risk.

8.6.3 Getting Your Arms around the Chaos

The word dynamical implies force, energy, motion, or change. A dynamical system is anything that moves, changes, or evolves in time. Very few enterprises are static and stable. Zachman DNA is a framework of a dynamical system. Zachman DNA is designed to encompass all that is known, all that is known to be unknown, and all that is unknown about the unknown.

The dynamical system in Zachman DNA is dissipative. All enterprises are affected by dissipative internal and external influences, such as government regulation, people, resources, standards, and culture. Each influence has the effect of applying a certain degree of drag or weight to the dynamical system that is the enterprise. The drag or weight in a dynamical system causes chaos.

Chaos theory attempts a qualitative study of a dynamical system by concentrating on behavior that is unstable or aperiodic. The observation is that chaos produces nonlinear systems. Nonlinear means the output is not directly proportional to input. In other words, change in one variable does not produce a proportional change or reaction in the related variables.

Over time, a linear process that is charted appears smooth and regular, whereas nonlinear ones may be regular at first, but often change to erratic-looking lines on a chart. Linear processes change smoothly and in proportion to a stimulus. In contrast, change in a nonlinear system is often much greater than the stimulus. See Figure 8-24. Mathematically, a linear relationship can be expressed as a simple equation where the variables appear only to the power of 1: $x = 2y + z$.

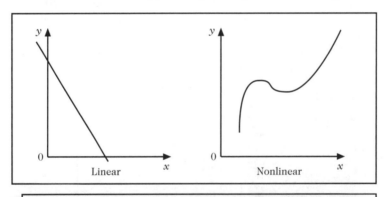

| Figure 8-24 | *In linear systems, variables are simply and directly related* |

Nonlinear relationships involve powers other than one. Here is a nonlinear equation: $A = 3B2 + 4C3$. Such equations are much harder to analyze and frequently need the help of a computer to understand.

If chaos concentrates on behavior, the single biggest behavior problem in software development is *people*. People do a wonderful job of creating chaos. Different types of human behavior can be quantified readily, such as the eel, backstabber, and Essene, as mentioned in Chapter 4. When these behaviors get used is not easily predicted. As quantum physicist Niels Bohr once said, "Prediction is very hard...especially regarding the future."

Most SDLCs place emphasis on the process. When the SDLC fails, IT professionals proclaim the process is lousy. Humans distance themselves from the process and find no fault in how they participated...*I did my part. I did what I was supposed to do. It was the process. It was no good.*

If the emphasis of an SDLC was placed on people, continual reviews of the project team would be necessary to establish the current behaviors. A project team would not progress in a straight line—a linear march to success. The project team would have its highs and lows; the team would have its productive days and nonproductive days; the team would get some things wrong and have to rework portions that were thought completed. In essence, the SDLC needs to be adaptive based on human behavior.

Many SDLCs also attempt to optimize process. The Software Engineering Institute's Capability Maturity Model, mentioned in Chapter 2, strives for an optimized IT project. Very few companies are able to reach Level 5—optimized. Many enterprises would also find it cost prohibitive to achieve Level 5 optimization.

An adaptive SDLC should focus on both the psychology of the project team and the processes required to accomplish the task at hand. The SDLC would allow continual adaptation to produce desired results. In an ideal situation, only six simple steps are required to produce software: plan, analyze, design, code, test, and implement.

Many factors affect the ease by which software is built, but only one makes it truly difficult—human behavior. Human behavior is responsible for much of the chaos in software development. The behavior shows itself in being undisciplined and unfocused. Other negative behaviors include lack of appropriate knowledge, hidden agendas, and passive aggressive resistance.

Human behavior is one of the variables contributing to chaos experienced by project teams. The attractors of Zachman DNA help classify the boundaries in which chaos is experienced after a specific context has been established. The context in Zachman DNA is controlled by the axes aspect, perspective, and science. These are the x, y, and z-axes—they are self-similar and scalable.

8.6.4 Biologically Speaking

The x, y, and z-axes of Zachman DNA represent aspect, perspective, and science. As previously mentioned, the six aspects are *what, how, where, who, when,* and *why*; or data, process, network, people, time, and motivation. The six perspectives are the *planner, owner, designer, builder, subcontractor,* and the *functioning enterprise.*

The number of z coordinates for science is not pre-defined. An IT department specifies the number and types of sciences assigned to Zachman DNA. As previously mentioned in Chapter 2, not all sciences are natural sciences. A science can be viewed as a "methodological activity, discipline, or study,"[15] or "an accumulated and established knowledge, which has been systematized and formulated with reference to the discovery of general truths or the operation of general laws; knowledge classified and made available in work, life, or the search for truth; comprehensive, profound, or philosophical knowledge."[16]

Collectively, the aspect, perspective, and science represent the *body* for a species. Our analogy uses a human being. See Figure 8-25. In Zachman DNA, the aspect, perspective, and science represent the *body of knowledge*. The body of knowledge is applied to a specific field or species for context, such as software for business, medicine, politics, engineering, and manufacturing.

The human body	Zachman DNA
Body: the species	Body of knowledge: The x, y, and z-axes; aspect, perspective, and sciences
System: e.g., the nervous system	System: A group of associated z-axis sciences
Organ: e.g., the brain	Organ: An individual z-axis science
Tissue: connective or epithelial	Tissue: A single row or a single column. Tissues contain six cells
Cell	Cell: The intersection of an aspect, perspective, and science
Chromosome	Chromosome: Each z-axis science has one chromosome in each cell
Molecular DNA	DNA: Six DNA strands make up a chromosome
Gene	Gene: 36 genes make up a single strand of DNA
Tensegrity: structural strength of a cell	Primitive models: Structural strength of a Framework cell

Figure 8-25   Analogy

Examples of sciences for the z-axis in software development for a commercial business include:

- Project management
- Project administration
- Testing
- Methodology
- Principles
- Standards
- Stakeholder involvement
- User involvement
- Change control
- Version control

Each individual science is an *organ*. Associated organs form a *system*. For example, the organs called project management and project administration form a system. Likewise, the organs called change control and version control form another system. A single row or a single column of an organ is *tissue*. Tissues are comprised of six cells. An organ always has 36 cells. See Figure 8-26.

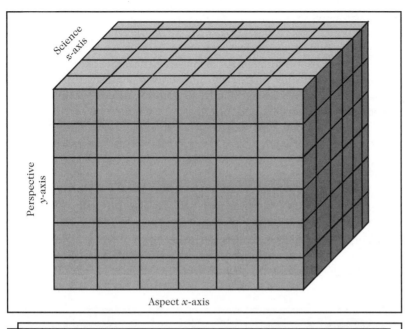

Science
z-axis

Perspective
y-axis

Aspect x-axis

Figure 8-26   *Three dimensions*

Residing in each cell are a series of *chromosomes*. Each chromosome is a six-by-six-by-six cube. This is an **embedded Framework**. Instead of having just X and Y chromosomes, Zachman DNA has X, Y, and Z chromosomes. Each letter is associated with an axis. The axes of the chromosome are again labeled: aspect, perspective, and science.

The six aspects remain *what, how, where, who, when*, and *why*; or data, process, network, people, time, and strategy. The perspectives remain the *planner, owner, designer, builder, subcontractor*, and the *functioning enterprise*. However, a single chromosome, which represents an individual science, uses the same labels as the aspect for its axis: *what, how, where, who, when*, and *why*.

A chromosome is made up of six *DNA* strands, and each DNA strand is made up of 36 *genes*. Everything in Zachman DNA has an *x, y*, and *z*-axis. Therefore, everything can be given a contextual meaning. The embedded Framework could go on infinitely and represents a self-similar trait of a fractal because the structure looks the same, regardless of scale.

The cells, tissues, organs, systems, and body contain the descriptive representations at various levels of abstraction. Examples of descriptive representations for cells include use cases, class models, entity-relationship diagrams, and distributed network architectures.

A row tissue's descriptive representations are contextual for the *planner*, conceptual for the *owner*, logical for the *designer*, physical for the *builder*, out of context for the *subcontractor*, and operational for the *functioning enterprise*. A column tissue's descriptive representations are things of interest for *what*, processes for *how*, connectivity for *where*, people for *who*, timing for *when*, and motivation for *why*.

The name for the organs' descriptive representations is based on the science. When the science changes on the z-axis, its name changes too. The name of the system depends on the associated sciences on the z-axis. The body's descriptive representations are known collectivity as the enterprise's body of knowledge.[17] For example, in IT, three organ sciences might be version control, change control, and configuration management. Collectively, the three organs form a system that might be called release management.

A strand of Zachman DNA contains the genetic blueprint for a cell. The blueprint determines every characteristic of a living enterprise—the building blocks of *business life*. DNA carries the information needed to direct productivity, culminating in new or modified applications. Productivity and quality are needed by the cell for its activities and development. Quality is the process by which DNA transforms itself for each descendant cell, passing on the information needed for productivity and quality.

Molecular DNA strands are held together by bridges. A similar concept is used in Zachman DNA. Zachman DNA bridges emphasize the horizontal, vertical, and depth integration required for alignment and communication. See Figure 8-27, which shows the double helix of DNA. Zachman DNA uses a similar concept to illustrate the need for integration.

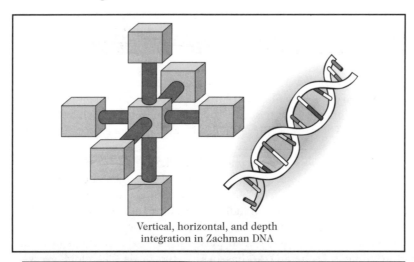

Vertical, horizontal, and depth
integration in Zachman DNA

Figure 8-27   *The double helix of molecular DNA is held together by bridges*

As previously stated, the human body contains an estimated 20 to 30 trillion cells. The exact number of cells in Zachman DNA is dependent on the number of sciences represented. The basic formula is $(6 \times 6 \times s)$, where s represents the number of sciences. Despite the individuality of each cell, cells integrate through horizontal, vertical, and depth integration to join, communicate, coordinate, and form compounds with other cells.

Each cell is subject to physical forces and chaos. In biology, tensegrity is the structural strength of the cell. In enterprise architecture, primitive models represent the structural strength of the cells in the Framework. Each cell has some form of structural design: conceptual, logical, and physical.[18] The robustness (abstractness, scalability, reliability, security, and adaptability) of the architecture enables the cell to withstand battering by a variety of chaotic stresses, such as changing legislation, entering new markets, or increasing transactional throughput from several thousand per day to hundreds of millions per day.

Frequent cell replacement is a normal function of the human body. A cell's descriptive representations are replaced frequently in the Framework as a normal function of business change. Change is constant in business. Every change moves the business from a current state to a new end state. The concepts of changing state were discussed in Chapter 2.

In the human body, cell replacement helps stave off disease. Initiatives by an enterprise to replace descriptive representations as a course of action to accommodate desired changes help keep enterprises in the business of business—many types of enterprises need to continually stave off competition. Typically, enterprises continually change an existing way of performing business to increase revenue, decrease costs, meet new regulatory rules, and remain competitive.

When mutated cells in a human body fail to self-destruct, the result may lead to a serious health issue. The health of the business is threatened when individuals decide to *do their own thing*—not producing the appropriate deliverables, not providing the appropriate quality of deliverables, developing a negative attitude, and making assumptions. The disease or damage caused may remain localized in the enterprise, within a single project or department, or potentially spread and both infect and affect the entire business.

The result of some paper shredding in November 2001 by a few employees of Enron, an energy company based in Houston, Texas, with the participation of a few senior accountants from the accounting firm Arthur Andersen, led to the downfall of both corporations. The impact even affected an IT consulting company called Accenture that, prior to August 2000, was part of the Andersen accounting firm. The lives of over 100,000 employees were affected because a few individuals decided to *do their own thing*.

Nondisjunction is a process that occurs in the human body due to abnormalities associated with chromosomes. Nondisjunction happens in a business too. Businesses consistently fail to react in a timely fashion to external influences. For example, companies end up with five or six purchase order systems; companies maintain core systems that remain nonintegrated; one department does not know what another department is doing; and companies fail outright to deliver operational software.

Each condition is traceable to the chromosomes in Zachman DNA. By mapping the activities of an enterprise to Zachman DNA, an enterprise can readily identify gaps in its activities. If desired, an enterprise can then choose to change the way it functions.

Genes in a human body identify the traits of a person and direct the manufacture of proteins. The genes in Zachman DNA help identify the granular levels of work activities and the characteristic traits in the enterprise for each cell in the Framework. The sides of a gene are labeled so you can measure the work activities. When something is measured…it can be managed and changed.

Supplying an unending amount of time, money, and people to a need will probably never produce a solution. Conversely, restricting the amount of time, money, and people too tightly will probably never yield a solution either. The appropriate balance of time, money, and people achieves the work at hand. Nevertheless, you can bet in business, there will always be *too little time*, *too little money*, and *too few people* for a project.

There are hundreds of different SDLCs and methodologies in information technology. The right one may never be invented, but enterprises will always need to keep refining the processes because the demands for new software to be delivered in shorter periods force evolution. The labels of the gene are time, cost, people, intrusion, convention, and history.

The label *intrusion* represents situations or conditions the business encounters, but over which the business has no control. The intrusions *intrude* into the business' operating space. Examples of intrusion are competition, changing technology, new legislation or regulation, poor economic conditions, vendors, suppliers, and laws of nature.

The label *history* represents the foundation upon which the present predicament was built. Since nothing happens in a vacuum, events over time tend to define subsequent moments in time. History is how we got here in terms of corporate history, corporate culture, and the people who got you where you are.

To some degree, history determines the course of action available without implementing some form of change. Unless an alteration is made to resources or direction, history weighs heavily upon how the enterprise moves forward. The inability to move forward is a literal meaning to the term *legacy system*. The legacy is that of traveling in a particular direction with particular people in a particular pattern and the inability to change the situation. To move forward, the enterprise must alter itself specifically.

The label *convention* represents the normal or regular way of moving forward. All enterprises move forward typically in relatively predictable ways. An enterprise's operations either wind up or wind down, grow or shrink, specialize or diversify.

Decision-making in a company often follows convention. For example, if the company wants to buy a new mainframe computer, the person in charge will probably buy a model from IBM. If the company wants to buy a desktop operating system, the person in charge will probably buy an operating system from Microsoft (even though the Linux operating system is obtainable free of charge). People play things safe in the business world to protect their jobs. Conventions are extensions of the past that carry through the present and tend to force us into a particular future direction.

The gene in Zachman DNA is drawn as a cube—a box. There is a saying that for new ideas one should *try to think outside the box*. The labels on the gene box provide insight into knowing if your thoughts are indeed outside the box, or if the solution already available is within the box. The traits of an enterprise are established in the gene. To think outside the box is the starting point to changing the traits.

Think about the gene box as having concrete, brick, or glass walls. Concrete walls are thick, impenetrable, and difficult to break through. Brick walls offer opportunities for partial views by knocking a few bricks out of the way. Glass walls represent a potentially daunting perspective. While it may be easy to see what is desirable, the act of getting through the wall to achieve it may not be easy.

To understand each gene box in Zachman DNA, take measurements and look all around. *Measurements* can be taken by inventorying the people, time, and money in the enterprise. *Looking down* provides a solid appreciation of the simple fact that this particular moment is the product of your history. No one and no enterprise starts fully grown and complete. *Looking up* provides a full measure of the self-imposed convention ceiling within the enterprise. Ceilings are like Tinker Bell exercises; *anything is possible if you believe.*

If ceilings are perceived as solid and limiting, they will be. If ceilings are perceived as moveable, shapeable, sizeable, and even removeable—they can be. When *looking out*, if the walls are made of concrete, burrow back into your history and come up somewhere else. If the walls are perceived as brick, start by removing some of the bricks to get a clearer picture of what is going on outside. If the walls are glass, decide whether you like it better inside, or if you have the guts to deal with shards and jagged pieces on your way toward your new and challenging future.

As stated in Chapter 1, by learning and understanding each cell in the Framework, you will have the ability to reason why things work and why things fail. More importantly, you will have the ability to help prevent or minimize failure. The *diet* is knowledge. The *cause and prevention of disease* involve the ability to communicate and understand the basics of science, humanity, business, and technology. These are the primary ingredients for a happy and healthy business life.

8.6.5 Key Terms

aspect	measurement
asset management	metric
convention	mission critical systems
cost	people
detail	perspective
drag	phase space
embedded Framework	process management
emergence	risk management
emergent system property	science
entropy	scope
function point	thrust
history	time
intrusion	unit of measure
lift	weight

8.6.6 Review Questions

The following questions relate to section 8.6:

1. What do Sierpinski's carpet, the Menger sponge, and Zachman DNA have in common?
2. Why is Zachman DNA a fractal?
3. The two-dimensional Zachman Framework helps describe the types of descriptive representations an enterprise needs. What does the three-dimensional Framework help accomplish?

The following questions relate to section 8.6.1:

1. Explain what is included in the holistic view of a computer system.
2. What does the chaos game illustrate, related to software development?
3. List several attractors used in Zachman DNA.
4. Describe something in your classroom that has emergent properties.

The following questions relate to section 8.6.2:

1. Explain how Zachman DNA can help direct measurements to determine if *Zachman* cells are healthy.
2. What is a function point?
3. Explain what is meant by entropy in the context of project management.
4. What is the difference between negative feedback and positive feedback?
5. What is one purpose of Zachman DNA?
6. What is the difference between a unit of measure, metric, and measurement?

The following questions relate to section 8.6.3:

1. What is a dynamical system?
2. Explain the difference between linear and nonlinear.
3. In an ideal world, what are the seven steps needed to produce software?
4. What is the one factor that makes software development very difficult and why?

The following questions relate to section 8.6.4:

1. What formal labels are applied to the x, y, and z-axes of Zachman DNA?
2. Explain what the x, y, and z-axes of Zachman DNA represent.
3. Who specifies the number and types of sciences assigned to Zachman DNA?
4. What purpose do the bridges of Zachman DNA serve?
5. Provide examples of sciences for the z-axis.

SECTION 8.7 SCIENCE: THE Z-AXIS

The z-axis creates the third dimension of Zachman DNA called science. The z-axis adds process to the Zachman Framework. The third dimension adds a visual representation of integrated activities used to successfully produce the descriptive representations.

8.7.1 Science

The system development life cycle is noted along Zachman DNA's z-axis. Chapter 7 discussed the axes' aspect and perspective. Their use in Zachman DNA remains the same as their use in the two-dimensional Zachman Framework.

The following sample list of sciences can be plotted on the z-axis:

- Project management
- Project administration
- Configuration management
- Change management
- Version control
- Testing[19]
- Metrics
- Actor[20] involvement
- Methodologies
- Standards
- Principles

The sciences listed are explained later in this section.

Each science produces a distinct set of descriptive representations for the Framework. Each science participates in the enterprise-wide integration for horizontal, vertical, and depth integration. The number and types of sciences on the z-axis are dependent on the project team using Zachman DNA. The z-axis is the only variable axis on the Framework.

Pictorially, the first science listed is the primary science. In other words, the first science listed is the focus of the project team. All the other secondary sciences are positioned to support the primary science. The descriptive representations of the primary science are the primary descriptive representations. The descriptive representations of the other sciences are secondary descriptive representations.

The mechanics of producing the descriptive representations for a science are the Frameworks embedded in each cell. The embedded Frameworks contain the genes, DNA, and chromosomes. The embedded Frameworks are also integrated throughout the enterprise.

One of the major insights garnered by mapping the sciences on the z-axis is the necessity to apply a science through every aspect of the primary science. Therefore, if you are interested in producing computer software, you can see that testing needs to occur in every column or aspect and in every row or perspective. This explains the need to integrate all the cells horizontally, vertically, and in depth. See Figure 8-28.

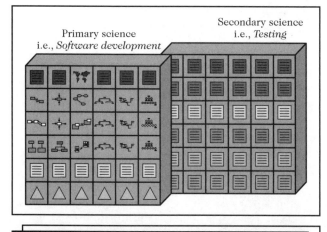

Figure 8-28   *Primary and secondary segments*

Traditional methods for producing software test only computer programs. Zachman DNA highlights the need to test every document, every database, every network, every workflow, every schedule, and every rule. In fact, every single aspect, perspective, and science needs to be tested. The same applies to metrics, standards, principles, and project management. Zachman DNA makes enterprise-wide integration obvious.

Any SDLC can be mapped to Zachman DNA. It is not necessarily important that every SDLC produces something for every cell. If an SDLC is not producing a descriptive representation for a cell, it means that knowledge regarding that cell is being left implicit. Understanding this simple fact allows a project team to manage the project's risk associated with having incomplete detail.

Incomplete detail may or may not be a problem. If it is a problem, the SDLC can be adjusted to produce a descriptive representation, a plan to mitigate potential problems can be established, or you can pinpoint the blame when the project fails because the SDLC was once again *inadequate*.[21]

WHAT IS YOUR UNIT OF MEASURE

Outside it had been a beautiful sunny day, but inside NASA's Jet Propulsion Laboratory, a storm was just brewing. For nine months, the 125 million dollar Mars Climate Orbiter had been dashing through space and chitchatting to NASA in metric units of measure. However, the engineers on the ground were replying with imperial units of measure.

The miscommunication caused the spacecraft to enter the Martian atmosphere a little too low and way too fast. Whoops.

A spokesperson for Lockheed Martin Astronautics, prime contractor for the Mars-bound spacecraft, said at a news conference that it was up to the company's engineers to assure the metric system used in one computer program was compatible with the imperial system used in another computer program. The simple conversion check was not done.

The Mars Climate Orbiter was launched December 11, 1998. During its nine months in space, the spacecraft's rockets were fired 12–14 times per week to compensate for the slow twist caused by the sun's heat. Engineers were calculating the size of each rocket firing using feet per second of thrust, a value based on the imperial measure of feet and inches. However, the spacecraft's computer interpreted the instructions in Newtons per second, a metric measure of thrust. The difference is 1.3 meters a second.

Art Stephenson, director of the Marshall Spaceflight Center and head of a NASA *what-went-wrong-this-time* team, said, "Each time there was a rocket firing, the error built up. The mathematical mismatch was a little thing that could have been fixed easily if it had been detected. Sometimes the little things can come back and really make a difference."

Yes, it seems so.

The following is a candidate set of sciences for a software development project.

Project Management

The goal of project management is to assure a project produces an appropriate set of deliverables with the highest possible quality and the lowest possible cost to meet the needs and expectations of the project's customer. Project management attempts to obtain efficiency by organizing (roles and responsibilities), planning, monitoring and reporting, controlling, and correcting the building activities.

A project is a unique and temporary endeavor consisting of a set of activities aimed to achieve a specific objective by creating, changing, or improving a product. Often the project manager's greatest challenge is dealing with limited resources available to the project. The limited resources are time, money, and people.

Project management activities consist of establishing a suitable, healthy work environment conducive to starting and completing all necessary activities associated with the project. The activities include putting in place an appropriate organizational structure, allocating resources available when required, anticipating and solving problems as soon as possible, obtaining quiet and comfortable rooms, and minimizing influences and pressures from outside parties. The project manager has to adapt the work environment when needed so that all associated resources work efficiently.

The project manager is responsible for planning activities necessary to build the product. The plan's work breakdown structure defines and organizes activities necessary to build the product. The project manager must also control the execution of the plan and accommodate any changes that occur to the project during its life span.

Project Administration

Project administration is adjunct to the project management science. Project administration handles records management, time collection reporting, office management, audit reporting, and tool identification.

Configuration Management

Configuration management is a process used to identify and define products that constitute an application or system. The products may consist of all forms of descriptive representations, including artifacts, models, programs, and schedules. Other products may include hardware and firmware.

Configuration management seeks to maintain alignment of all application products throughout the life cycle by tracking versions and changes to the releasable product. Configuration management is responsible for recording and reporting the status of products and verifying the completeness and correctness of each releasable product.

Change Management

Change management seeks to provide an organized, systematic approach to track changes in software, hardware, firmware, tools, and other resources. Change management handles requests for new projects, applications, or processes. Change management also handles requests for modifying existing application functionality and for handling changes associated with correcting defects.

Change management records and prioritizes descriptive requirements of change. The need for a change might be initiated by: an external source, such as a customer or regulatory body; an internal source seeking to correct a defect; a third-party software vendor requiring or supplying maintenance patches for software; or a competitive need to upgrade the environment's hardware or network.

Change management is responsible for prioritizing the queue for changes. Changes associated with KTLO (keep the lights on) are normally given the highest priority. KTLO is an expression meaning that the business cannot operate without the system. These types of systems are mission critical.

Version Control

Version control is used to organize, manage, and protect software assets to support configuration management. Version control manages the incremental changes of every component used in an application. Version control simplifies the task of restoring previous versions of software to a development, test, or production environment.

Version control provides methods to check items into and out of a repository. This type of control helps ensure two people are not trying to work on the same activity at the same time. Unless of course, that is what you desire.[22]

Testing

Testing involves the evaluation of an application or system under controlled conditions, including normal and abnormal. There are numerous types of tests that can be performed. Testing types include:

- Unit
- System
- Acceptance
- Regression
- Black box
- White box
- Parallel
- Disaster recovery
- Failover
- Compatibility
- Performance
- Scalability
- Reliability
- Volume
- Stress

The purpose of testing is to determine the overall quality of the application or system. In addition to the number of defects found, the stability and reliability of the application determine the quality. Other attributes that affect the quality of an application include ease of configuration, ease of installation, flexibility to accept change, and scalability across hardware platforms.

Quality must be designed into an application. Testing does not produce quality; testing verifies quality. Testing intentionally attempts to make things go wrong. Observations determine if things happened as they should. Organizations vary considerably in how responsibility is assigned for testing and quality assurance.

Metrics

Collecting objective information about the current state of a software product, project, or process allows managers and practitioners to make timely and appropriate decisions. Metrics are applied to track an enterprise's progress towards its goals. Metrics can also be applied to assess the impact of changes.

Collecting data just to say you have it, or just because you are able to apply a metric, is an easy way to lose sight of why metrics are being applied. According to metrics guru Howard Rubin, up to 80 percent of software metric initiatives fail. When establishing a metrics program, pay attention to the following:

- Management needs to actively support measurement capture.
- Measuring too much data too soon can kill a metrics initiative. If people cannot efficiently analyze the volume of information, they tune out psychologically and ignore the data.
- The converse of measuring too little too late can also kill a metrics initiative. If people are not getting enough useful information, they may conclude the metrics effort is not worthwhile.
- Not measuring the right things either causes people to ignore the information captured, or lures them into making incorrect assumptions or decisions.
- Metric definitions should be precise to avoid practitioners interpreting the information as they see fit. Symptoms of vague or ambiguous metric definitions are trends showing erratic behavior. Erratic behavior is exhibited when individuals do not measure, report, or chart results in the same way. Many companies find it hard to define what constitutes a *change* to software. When this happens, IT departments are unable to show the value of their efforts for the change as it correlates to the business value.
- Metrics should be used to understand how software is built. The measurements obtained permit informed decisions to be made regarding the impact of changes. When metrics include the evaluation of individual team members, there is a propensity to report incorrect statistics. However, peer pressure can be used to both minimize incorrect reporting and provide an important incentive to improve quality. Salespeople are used to having their performance measured—IT personnel are not. Until everyone in an organization is held accountable, the enterprise will be disparate and suffer.
- Appropriately distribute the measurements. All metrics associated with an individual or a project team should be sharable. Senior management should be able to select which metrics it wants to view. Individuals should also use measurements to judge and correct themselves, thereby improving their personal software process.
- Metrics should be used to create understanding. They can also be used as a weapon (threat) or *carrot* (promissory reward) to motivate people. Measurements are neither virtuous nor evil. Measurements are neutral and are simply informative. Organizations that learn by understanding metrics and measurements are in a position to instill quality as a cultural behavior.
- Collect data only that will be used. People may collect data diligently and report it as requested, yet they never see evidence that the data is being used for anything. This leads to dysfunctional behavior.
- Practitioners should be trained in the metrics program so they have a clear understanding of expectations. Fear of measurement is a sign that the objectives and intent of the metrics program need to be better communicated. If people do not understand the metrics and have not been

trained in how to perform them, they will not collect reliable data at the right times.

- Correctly interpreting the measurements is vital. A measurement trend that jumps in an undesirable direction can cause a quick response to get the measurement back on track. Those who do not want to hear bad news may ignore a measurement trend that warns of serious problems. For example, if the number of defects in software continues to increase despite quality improvement efforts, the project team might conclude that the quality improvements are doing more harm than good and be lured back to the old ways of working. In reality, what may be happening is the improved software testing techniques might be doing a better job of finding the defects that are located within the application—this would be a good thing.

For an enterprise to improve the quality of its products, services, software, accounting practices, and people, it must determine what needs to be measured and then use the results to help educate everyone in the corporation. In the book *Out of the Crisis*, Deming (1900–1993) asserts, "A company cannot buy its way into quality—it must be led into quality by top management."

Actor Involvement

The term **actor** is an alternative word for a *user*. According to Ronald Ross, an expert on business rules, data modeling, and methodologies, the term *actor* suggests someone whose own activity or role is integral to understanding and doing the work, whereas the term *user* suggests an outside beneficiary of information system services whose own work and interactions are beyond our scope.

Numerous actors participate in software development. Their generic roles include customer, stakeholder, sponsor, auditor, controller, comptroller, developer, data administrator, database administrator, analyst, architect, and manager.

At some point during the software development process, these actors need to interact. Each actor has a specific need and the level of involvement will vary. In general, actors are agents of action and their participation causes something to happen. For an actor to cause something to happen, that individual must be able to grant permission and provide direction.

Methodologies

Indigenous to every software project is its process. The process is the methodology by which the project is brought to fruition. Normally, a methodology is a set of repeatable processes adopted by an enterprise or project.

Different types of software projects may require different types of methodologies. Various project types include:

- Enterprise resource planning
- Enterprise architecture determination
- Re-engineering projects
- Rapid application development projects
- Product selection
- Component configuration projects

- Conversion projects
- Maintenance projects
- Component integration projects
- Development projects
- Client/server changeover projects
- Internet enablement projects

When a software project does not use a formal methodology, the default is called *on-the-fly* methodology.

In 1492, Christopher Columbus (1451–1506) set out from Palos in Spain on the Santa Maria, accompanied by two other vessels, the Nina and the Pinta. When Columbus started his journey, he wanted to find a shorter trade route to India. However, he did not know where he was going or how long it would take. When he finally got *there*, he did not know where he was, and when he returned home to King Ferdinand and Queen Isabella, he could not tell them where he had been.

A methodology attempts to mitigate the types of problems Columbus experienced. A methodology helps map out where you want to go and how to recognize your endpoints. When you finally proclaim victory, the methodology helps you state your accomplishments—even if the result was less than what you had hoped.

Standards

Standards come in three varieties: mandates, policies, and guidelines. The difference between the varieties is the level of enforcement. A *mandate* standard must be followed. No relief or exemption is provided. Refusing to follow a mandate may result in probation, losing you job, being fined, or even receiving a jail sentence.

A *policy* standard specifies a preferred way of performing an activity and dictates how to make a deliverable conform to an acceptable level. Typically, a policy connotes rules for deviation.

A *guideline* standard is a preferred way of performing an activity and dictates how to make a deliverable conform to an acceptable level, but yields to an individual or group to make the final appropriate decisions.

Mandated, policy, and guideline standards are formal and written. Some standards are not recorded and are only communicated verbally. These standards are informal or cultural. Punishment for not adhering to informal or cultural standards is unpredictable. The enforcement levels for defacto and proprietary standards are governed by the enterprise.

A defacto standard is an accepted norm but is not typically enforced. Proprietary standards are usually mandated because a perceived advantage is placed on them by an enterprise.

Standards reflect adopted agreements on products, practices, and operations by:

- An enterprise
- Globally by recognized national or international industrial bodies such as the American National Standards Institute (ANSI), International Standards Organization (ISO), and the Institute of Electrical and Electronic Engineers (IEEE)
- Professional associations such as the Project Management Institute (PMI) and the Object Management Group (OMG)

- Trade unions such as the International Brotherhood of Electrical Workers (IBEW) and the National Education Association (NEA)
- Trade associations such as the Software and Information Industry Association (SIIA) and the American Bankers Association (ABA)
- Governmental entities at local, state, or federal levels

Principles

Principles reflect preferred approaches to solving a problem or task. The following principles could be adopted by an enterprise for software development:

- Software should be loosely coupled to make future substitutions easier as new technologies become available.
- Software deployments should demonstrate early wins—proving value promotes ongoing managerial support. In other words, financial funding for the project continues.
- Software should be produced as economically as possible—keeping costs to a minimum. Most enterprises have limited resources.
- Keep the end user in mind. Just because software was difficult to write, the application should not be difficult to use. End users prefer natural naming and intuitive tools.

8.7.2 Key Term

actor (non-UML use)

8.7.3 Review Questions

1. Which one of the axes of the Framework is a variable and why?
2. How does the use of metrics benefit the enterprise?
3. How does Zachman DNA make obvious the fact that testing is needed in every column or aspect, as well as in every row or perspective?
4. Explain the term *actor* in relation to software development.
5. If an SDLC is not producing a descriptive representation for a cell, what is the result? Explain if this is problematic for the organization.

SECTION 8.8 EMBEDDED FRAMEWORK

Each cell contains an embedded Framework or chromosome. The chromosome is a schema with six columns, six rows, and six depths. The columns are labeled *what, how, where, who, when,* and *why*. The rows are labeled the *planner, owner, designer, builder, subcontractor,* and *functioning enterprise*. The depths are also conveniently labeled *what, how, where, who, when,* and *why*.

Chromosomes

In Zachman DNA, each chromosome relates to a single science and each gene occupies precise locations on the chromosome. This pattern is consistent throughout the Framework. In general, any type of recurring pattern promoting a consistent, reusable, and understandable solution in a given context is advantageous. In software development, a pattern that promotes *goodness* is simply known as a pattern; a pattern that is perceived to promote *badness* is called an **antipattern**.

Examples of good patterns in software development include the *Gang of Four* design patterns,[23] analysis patterns, business patterns, and Zachman DNA. Examples of antipatterns include: analysis paralysis, spaghetti code, stovepipe systems, and waterfall life cycles. Most antipatterns were, at one time or another, perceived as good patterns. As new techniques or technologies became available, they became obsolete and most became harmful to the well-being of the enterprise.

The chromosome contains six DNA strands. Each DNA strand contains 36 genes. See Figure 8-29. The DNA strand provides a minimal holistic view of how something is accomplished. For example, if a developer is writing a program or modifying some existing code within the Framework's schema, the developer is operating on Row 5, the *subcontractor* view, and Column 2, the *how* or process aspect. The developer will be influenced or constrained by the sciences associated with the activity of programming.

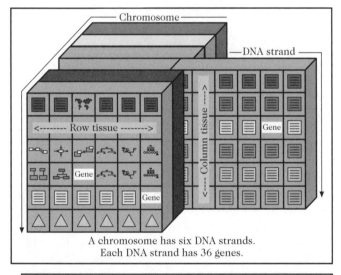

A chromosome has six DNA strands.
Each DNA strand has 36 genes.

Figure 8-29 *Chromosome cube*

The sciences influencing or constraining the developer include the same set provided in the section *Science: The Z-Axis*. For each science, the developer has a chromosome, which is made of DNA strands and genes.

Analogies help communicate and explain new ideas. Because of the fractal nature of Zachman DNA, at all levels of scale, everything looks like a square or a cube. The names and labels associated with the analogies play an important part in defining the fractal level being discussed.

The *planner* perspective (Row 1) of an organ (an organ was previously defined as being an individual science on the *z*-axis of Zachman DNA) addresses issues similar to the *planner* perspective (Row 1) of the chromosome. In essence, only the domain has changed. The *planner* perspective of an organ plans at the enterprise level, and the *planner* perspective of a chromosome plans at the process level of the particular embedded Framework.

The *planner* associated with the organ focuses on the descriptive representations associated with the completed activities of Row 1. The *planner* associated with the chromosome focuses on planning activities to produce the descriptive representations. The intersection of each aspect, perspective, and science associated with an organ contains a chromosome—an embedded Framework.

This means the *planner* (Row 1) of the organ has a chromosome with activities associated with planning. The *owner* (Row 2) of the organ has a chromosome with activities also associated with its own planning. Applying the same logic to every row, every row has a set with planning activities. This means every row has a set of *owner* (Row 2) activities, *designer* (Row 3) activities, *builder* (Row 4) activities, *subcontractor* (Row 5) activities, and activities associated with the final outcome (Row 6). The result is an embedded Framework within each cell. The embedded Framework has been called a chromosome.

Coding

The developer of a computer program expects to deliver source code that can be compiled cleanly and assembled into an executable program. The developer's program probably contains a series of algorithms that when executed produce a desired result. The developer probably witnessed the desired result during a unit test.

The developer will write the computer program in a given language. It may be Java, COBOL, C++, Smalltalk, Korn Shell, or Visual Basic. There are hundreds of computer languages from which a developer can choose. Potentially the developer could even use one he wrote himself. How does a developer choose a language? Typically, an enterprise uses several computer languages. It is normal for a single application to be written in several languages. For example, an Internet application will probably use Java, JSP, HTML, XML, SQL, and CGI.

Each computer language has a general purpose. The general purpose is probably governed by a set of standards that the enterprise has dictated. In addition, the enterprise has probably set a standard limiting which computer languages can be used based on licensing costs and the perceived cost of maintenance for altering a program written in a given language. If a program is written in a language that most people are unfamiliar with, the cost to maintain that program can become prohibitive and potentially inhibit the application from being changed because no one understands how to read or fix the program.

Therefore, the developer is constrained by the organ *standards*. The standards are likely to govern not only language selection, but also appropriate styles of code. The standards may also dictate appropriate development tools and documentation styles. Other sciences influencing the developer include testing, project management, project administration, and version control.

Prior to writing a computer program, the developer needs to plan (Row 1 of the chromosome) how to approach the programming task. The approach is broken into the interrogatives *what*, *how*, *where*, *who*, *when*, and *why*. The developer needs to understand what needs to be delivered (Row 2 of the chromosome). The developer then determines what has to be done (Row 3 of the chromosome) and then makes any adjustments based on the environment in which he is working (Row 4 of the chromosome). Then, the programming can actually be done (Row 5 of the chromosome). Finally, when the developer has completed the activity, the computer program will need to be formally delivered (Row 6 of the chromosome).

The interrogatives of the chromosome describe:

- Things that need to be produced—*what*
- Processes needed to produce the things—*how*
- Connectivity required to accommodate the processes—*where*
- People who need to get involved—*who*
- Sequencing of events and any pre-conditions (*a priori*) or post-conditions (*a posteriori*) that need to occur to accommodate the processes—*when*
- Understanding constraints for producing a quality product—*why*

A single chromosome exists only in one intersection of an organ's aspect, perspective, and science. The activities associated with programming involve many chromosomes. Each chromosome has a set of inputs from a previous row and a set of outputs for the successive row. The methodology chosen by the project team may require an iterative or incremental approach to program construction whereby the output of a chromosome will, at some point, feed back into itself as an input. See Figure 8-30.

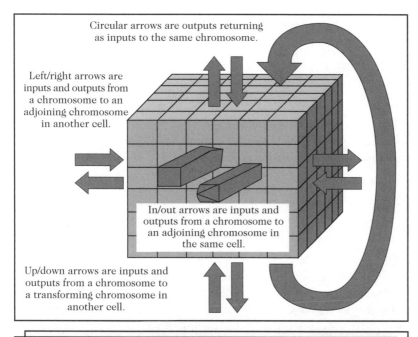

Figure 8-30   *Chromosome inputs and outputs*

Each gene, each DNA strand, and each chromosome needs to be horizontally, vertically, and depth integrated to produce a coherent method.

8.8.1 Sensitivity

A computer program may be prone to sensitivity of initial conditions at the time of execution. The unit test environment is usually different from the system test environment. Both environments are usually different from the operational or production environment.

You might think using a computer can help resolve problems associated with sensitivity to initial conditions and provide better information for feedback loops. In reality, computers just extend a grace period until the uncertainty expands to a greater magnitude. Computer programs are examples of sensitivity to initial conditions.

All computers use the binary system (zeroes and ones)—from handheld devices, to laptops and desktops, to midrange, to supercomputers and mainframes. However, not all computers and not all software interpret numbers (zeroes and ones) the same way.

A common programming language for database access is SQL, pronounced sequel,[24] which stands for structured query language. Donald Chamberlain and Raymond Boyce from IBM invented SQL in the 1970s. The standard bodies, ANSI and ISO, control the rules for database vendors that comply with the SQL standard.

Each of the following databases complies with the ANSI and ISO SQL standards:

- Unisql
- Sybase
- SQL Server
- OpenIngres
- DB2 UDB
- Access
- Oracle
- SQL Anywhere
- Teradata

To highlight the inaccuracy of computers, the following equation was executed on each database: $(x \div y) = z$. Substituting 10.4 for x and 6.3 for y, the following SQL was constructed and executed on each database:

- Select 10.4 / 6.3 from a_table_with_one_row;

The results were as follows:

Unisql	1.6
Sybase	1.650793
SQL Server	1.650793
OpenIngres	1.65079365
DB2 UDB (mainframe version)	1.650793650793
DB2 UDB (Unix version)	1.650793650793650793650793650793650793650793650793650793650793650793650793650793650793650793650793650793
Access	1.65079365079365
Oracle	1.6507937
SQL Anywhere	1.651
Teradata	1.7

Although the equation was specified the same way (Select 10.4 / 6.3 from a_table_with_one_row;) in each SQL dialect, the results varied by techniques of precision, truncation, and rounding—each producing a close approximation for the answer. Even when the equation was forced to produce a result of only four decimal places, the results varied. This technique is known as casting.

- DB2 UDB   <DECIMAL (10.4 / 6.3, 7,4)>   1.6507
- Sybase   <CONVERT (DECIMAL(7,4), 10.4 / 6.3)>   1.6507
- Access   <FORMAT (10.4 / 6.3, '###.####')>   1.6508
- Teradata   <(10.4 / 6.3) (DECIMAL(7,4))>   1.7000

Although we think of a computer as calculating with accuracy to a certain number of decimal places, the real accuracy is something different. The result is governed by the combination of hardware platform, operating system, and computer software.

An advantage of an enterprise having a database's SQL comply with ANSI and ISO standards is to *theoretically* allow the enterprise to swap in or out a database from an application, without requiring the application to be rewritten. However, if a financial institution calculates interest payments using SQL, substituting databases can lead to the same result, a monetary gain, or a monetary loss. It would probably take many hours of investigation to find out that the balance sheet was affected through the sensitivity to initial conditions.

MANAGING CHANGE

German scientist Hermann Oberth (1894–1989) proposed an observatory in space in 1923. Scientific instruments were installed on early rockets, balloons, and satellites in the late 1940s and produced enough exciting information to hint at how much remained to be discovered.

In 1962, a National Academy of Sciences study group recommended the development of a large space telescope as a long-range goal for NASA's space program. Similar groups repeated these recommendations in 1965 and 1969.

The first two successful NASA satellites designed for observing the stars were launched in 1968 and in 1972. The satellites' success supported the need for a larger, more powerful optical space telescope. In 1973, NASA scientists established a basic design for such a telescope and its instruments. The European Space Agency got involved with the project in 1975.

As part of a funding request, NASA presented the Hubble Space Telescope's (HST)[25] job description to the U.S. Congress:

- Explore the solar system.
- Measure the age and size of the universe.
- Search for our cosmic roots.
- Chart the evolution of the universe.
- Unlock the mysteries of galaxies, stars, planets, and life itself.

(continued)

627

Congress approved funding for the project in 1977. Two primary companies were contracted to build the HST by the Marshall Space Flight Center in Huntsville, Alabama. Perkin-Elmer Corporation in Danbury, Connecticut and Lockheed Missiles and Space Company of Sunnyvale, California were the two companies chosen.

Perkin-Elmer was selected to develop the optical system and guidance sensors. The company is now called Hughes Danbury Optical Systems, Inc. Lockheed was selected to produce the protective outer shroud and the support systems for the telescope, as well as to assemble the finished product.

NASA decided building the primary mirror was a challenging and crucial part of the program and elected to build a backup copy. The Eastman Kodak Company (Rochester, New York) was selected to build the backup mirror.

Construction and assembly of the space telescope was a painstaking process, and the assembly of the entire telescope was completed in 1985. HST was launched in 1990, after a four-year delay because of the Space Shuttle Challenger disaster. Engineers used the interim period to subject the telescope to intensive testing and evaluation, assuring the greatest possible reliability.

HST's power was calculated to be 10 times better than any telescope on Earth and was poised to open a new era in astronomy. Within a few months, a flaw was discovered in Hubble's main mirror, significantly reducing the telescope's ability to focus.

The focusing defect was due to spherical aberration, an optical distortion caused by an incorrectly shaped mirror. The mirror was too flat near the edge by about one-fiftieth the width of a human hair. Instead of being focused into a sharp point, light collected by the mirror was spread over a larger area in a fuzzy halo. Images of objects, such as stars, planets, and galaxies, were blurred.

Kodak had used a more traditional method for grinding its mirror. Because Kodak used different equipment for monitoring and testing the mirror during fabrication, that mirror did not have the optical flaw that was built unknowingly into the Perkin-Elmer mirror.

As the space telescope was constructed and launched, the Kodak backup mirror sat in its shipping crate in Danbury. It was impounded eventually, along with other materials relating to the investigation of the mirror flaw on Hubble.

The Kodak mirror proved invaluable because it was used in tests to find out exactly what went wrong with the fabrication of the primary mirror aboard HST. Ultimately, the problem was traced to equipment that was not calibrated properly.

No practical way existed for NASA to swap out the good mirror for the flawed mirror in space. The best alternative solution was to construct corrective optics that fixed the flaw, much the same way a pair of glasses corrects the vision of a near-sighted person.

The corrective optics were installed on Hubble by shuttle astronauts in 1993, and the telescope has been at the forefront of astronomy ever since.

Although the task proved technically challenging, the task was less difficult than predicted because NASA had always planned to service the telescope in space. Engineers designed HST so astronauts could easily change failed parts or

(continued)

update the telescope with advanced instrumentation. Instruments were designed like dresser drawers: they could be pulled out and replaced with others of the same size.

Not only has HST advanced science's understanding of the universe, the telescope has made direct contributions to other sciences. During 1994, a new non-surgical breast biopsy technique was developed using imaging charge coupled devices originally developed for HST's imaging spectrograph. The biopsy technique enables doctors to precisely locate and extract sample tissue from a suspicious lump in a woman's breast using a needle, instead of a scalpel.

The HST was designed to work in orbit for 15 years. The Next Generation Space Telescope (NGST) is being designed and may be launched in 2008.

HST's real eye-opener is its ability to see into the past. Because light takes a finite amount of time to travel across space, approximately 300,000 km every second, everything in the universe is seen as it was in the past. For example, we see the sun, as it was just over eight minutes ago; the nearest star from four years in the past; and the Andromeda Galaxy as it was two million years ago.

No matter how disciplined the testing, bugs seem inescapable. Backup and disaster recovery mechanisms are only useful if they can be deployed. Designing something that can be changed readily is worth its weight in gold. Come to think of it, in space, gold would be weightless. Hmmmm.

8.8.2 Key Term

antipattern

8.8.3 Review Questions

1. How many cells are contained in a Zachman DNA chromosome?
2. Provide an example of a pattern and an antipattern.
3. What are the interrogatives of the chromosome described?
4. How might a program using SQL be sensitive to initial conditions?

8.9 SYNTHESIS AND CHAPTER SUMMARY

Sun Tzu's 2,500-year-old[26] guidebook to warfare, *The Art of War*, says, "There is no invariable strategic advantage, no invariable position, which can be relied upon at all times." Warfare is an extreme example of human turbulence. In both warfare and software development, there are no foolproof methods for dealing with change.

There are no fixed or reliable strategies. However, several ideas exist to help think through complex changing situations. They include:

- Theories dealing with chaos and complexity
- Systems thinking and complex adaptive systems theory
- Family dynamics
- Organizational development
- Eastern mystical thought
- Zachman Framework and Zachman DNA

The list does not involve simple ideas and concepts. Ken Blanchard has not yet penned the journeyman's guide to *The One Minute Change Manager*. The business world is chaotic and conditions are turbulent. Many specialized skills are required to make the enterprise operable due to the complexity of the business environment.

Organizations have to deal with governments at all levels: local, state, and federal. Organizations must compete with other businesses for sales; deal with suppliers and vendors; understand how to apply technology; and deal with the laws of nature. Not surprisingly, IT departments inherit all these complex issues, in addition to adding several of their own, including how to handle the myriad of personalities. Underlying the complexity is the need to constantly change something: planning for change, figuring out what to change, applying change, and mitigating change.

Zachman DNA is a framework used to view an enterprise holistically from the most macro of views down to the microscopic level. Zachman DNA builds on the Zachman Framework to identify not only the descriptive representations of an enterprise, but also the processes to produce the descriptive representations and ultimately the operational portions of the enterprise. The Zachman Framework and Zachman DNA are powerful communication and reasoning tools, which facilitate the handling of complexity and change in all environments.

Zachman DNA is a tool that encourages thought leadership, provides blueprints for systems thinking, and places a framework around *business* chaos. Business is not going to get simpler. Business models and business strategies highlight the complexities involved in sustaining a competitive business stance. It is clear that enterprises must adapt to business environments at ever-increasing speeds. In nature, only the strong survive. This statement in business is not necessarily true. All too often, those who *arrive* have the best fighting chance to survive. Those enterprises that are best equipped to manage complexity and manage change are the enterprises that will survive.

In Chapter 3, systems thinking was introduced. The opposite approach to systems thinking is *reductionist thinking*. Zachman DNA embraces both concepts, promoting the study of objects in isolation and in the whole. In the late 1940s, building on the studies of communication, computation, and game theory, and also the work of John von Neumann (1903–1957) and Norbert Weiner (1894–1964), scientists began seeking a holistic view to solving problems.

Scientists realized if they wanted to understand a frog, they would need to learn about the world in which frogs live—ponds, lily pads, fish, and flies. If IT professionals, especially architects, modelers, and designers, want to understand business software, they need to learn about the world in which business software lives—the enterprise: business, government, competition, technology, nature, vendors, and suppliers. In almost every field, systems thinking has proven to be an effective tool. As a tool, systems thinking focuses on the *interaction* between the pieces, in terms of control, communication, and feedback. Understanding systems thinking is fundamental to any study of change.

The rate of change is increasing. An IT department juggles many variables, including technology and people. Software development is a complex environment. A prediction of the outcome of a software development initiative is uncertain—it is nonlinear. IT departments are less robotic and more like hurricanes, families, and anthills. IT departments that are adaptive in interacting with the environment have the highest potential to succeed. Adaptive IT departments take in and dissipate energy. They learn in one way or another—it is a form of preservation.

Scientists have traditionally tried to simplify things to study them. For instance, a scientist might try to approximate the mass of a mountain by imagining a pyramid of equal size. Unfortunately, few things in nature are truly that simple. In recent years, scientists have found ways to mimic and study the real complexity of natural structures, such as ferns, mountains, and the rings of Saturn, as well as chaotic surges in the power grid, financial stock markets, and interactions within families.

Chaos theory has risen from a variety of sources, including quantum mechanics, probability, systems thinking, and the study of communication. Chaos theory focuses on how complexity is generated, especially in iterative processes, in which the output of one phase is the input of the next phase.

Within the Framework, this happens when development iterates within a cell, across cells to create a composite, or from one row to another in a transformation. Chaos tries to discern what is theoretically predictable and what is fundamentally unpredictable, no matter how much we know about the present. Chaos provides a powerful new way of thinking about complex change. Zachman DNA facilitates this type of thinking for managing complex change.

A flock of birds flying high in the sky has no idea it is flying in a *V* formation. As such, ants do not know how to make an anthill. Anthills emerge from the much simpler interactions of the ants. There is no one individual that decides which way the stock market will go. Activity on the stock market emerges from millions of decisions made by stockholders. An organization's leaders make decisions, yet the organization's actual behavior can surprise its leaders. The organization can seem to resist its leaders, even when it does not seem that anyone in particular is resisting. John Holland, Ph.D. of the University of Michigan states, "The control of a complex adaptive system tends to be highly dispersed."

When plotted on a graph, solutions to linear equations make a straight line. Changes are proportional. Change one variable and other variables change with it. For example, by increasing a plant's capacity by a small amount, production output, payroll, and the consumption of raw materials rise. Changes are smooth and continuous.

Nonlinear equations do not produce a line on a graph, but instead produce weird clouds, rills, and whirlpools. Changes can be sudden, paradoxical, and chaotic. Increasing a plant's capacity by a small amount could as easily cause production output to double or fall drastically. Managers and methodologists try to keep things linear. However, the enterprise we live in is complex and tends to be nonlinear.

In such a complex, nonlinear space, the possibilities for the future are unpredictable—fortunately, they are not infinite. Future possibilities of a healthcare system include mergers, liquidation, growth, and even transformation of parts of it into office buildings, insurance organizations, or substance abuse clinics. It is far less likely that a healthcare system will turn into a Mercedes 190D, Luke Skywalker, or a Häagen-Dazs ice cream bar. The possibility space for the enterprise's future consists of the cloud of outcomes that have more than a remote probability of happening.

No matter how much information we have regarding a complex interaction, we cannot predict its outcome. Unpredictability is why testing output from each cell in the Framework is important. However, we can gather enough information and analyze it: we can determine which of the initial conditions are important to the outcome.

A landing airplane has little sensitivity to whether the runway is asphalt or concrete, but a lot of sensitivity to the presence of ice on the wings or wind shear in the descent path. The programming language Java has little sensitivity to whether an exclamation point precedes an equal sign, but the outcome could cripple the company financially. (!= means *not equal*, == means *equal*, = means *assign*). For an IT department, the nursery rhyme used in Chapter 3 could be rewritten as:

> For want of a comment, the business rule was lost;
> For want of a business rule, the test was lost;
> For want of a test, the system was lost;
> For want of a system, the customer was lost;
> For want of the customer, the business was lost!

Feedback loop cycles influence actions. There are two types of feedback: positive and negative. The words positive and negative have nothing to do with whether the outcome is good or bad. A stock market crash is an example of a positive feedback loop. A thermostat, which keeps a room at a pleasant temperature, provides a negative feedback loop.

A positive feedback loop reinforces itself at each turn: a falling market in Tokyo causes London stockholders to sell, which causes New York stockholders to panic, and so forth. A negative loop folds back on itself, each turn countering the previous one: a thermostat responds to a cool room by turning on the heater, the heater warms the room, the thermostat responds to the warm room by turning off the heater, the room cools, and so on, around and around. Homeostasis is our body's way of keeping itself at an optimal temperature and chemical balance. Homeostasis is a complex web of negative feedback loops. Shock is another example of a positive feedback loop.

Positive and negative feedbacks exist in enterprises. Quality control is a negative feedback loop: a mistake or problem results in an improvement to the system, which prevents future mistakes. Labor trouble, a divorce, or an addiction is usually the result of a positive feedback loop: each step in the process pushes the next one further from the optimal, feeds it, and magnifies it.

In IT, this phenomenon is seen by the skipping of Zachman Row 1 (*planner*), Row 2 (*owner*), Row 3 (*designer*), and Row 4 (*builder*) activities, and jumping straight into Row 5 (*subcontractor*) to perform the *necessary*[27] programming activities to make changes.

The fundamental nature of change is fractal. This means that the nature of change is fundamentally the same at different scales, in the same way that a slice through a small piece of a cauliflower looks identical to a slice through the whole cauliflower. Observations about feedback and chaotic unpredictability apply equally well to families, communities, organizations, industries, and nations.

Paradoxically, questions of scale are of great importance in attempting change. For instance, debate over family values has raged on the U.S. political landscape since the Reagan era. Certainly, our national laws and policies can be better or worse in their influence on values, but it is equally clear that no federal legislation fundamentally changes our values. Values are not generated at that scale. They are generated at the scale of church, community, family, and school.

Attempting to solve a problem at the wrong scale makes it more difficult. Most pollution problems, for instance, need to be solved over entire bioregions. Trade problems have a global nature, while many health problems are fundamentally local and community based. Software development has levels of scale too. Some features impact the entire enterprise, while other changes may only help a specific individual.

Lao Tzu's *Tao Te Ching* is mysterious from its first sentence, "The way of which we can speak is not the true way," to the book's last sentence, "The path of the wise is to act for others, not to compete." The book forms the basis of philosophical Taoism. Whereas Confucianism focused on practical, hierarchical, relationships, rules, and duty, Taoism focuses on the evocative, the paradoxical, and the nature of chaos and change.

Taoism's assumptions and themes show wisdom about the nature of change. This includes the interrelated, systemic nature of things—the way strength arises from weakness, and vice versa; how a retreat can be an advance, and an advance a defeat; the paradoxical nature of knowledge; and the importance of true listening. Another quote from *Tao Te Ching* states, "The wise one constantly has no set mind; he takes the mind of the common people as his mind."

In dealing with complexity and change, IT departments need to be adaptable, they need to communicate, and they need to be able to reason effectively regarding any given situation or requirement. IT departments need to deliver software products at ever-increasing speeds—toward a zero delivery time. The software needs to meet the needs and expectations of its users. The software must be cost effective and must be changeable. Though it cannot be declared a *silver bullet*, Zachman DNA is a framework that enables these things to happen.

8.10 CHAPTER ACTIVITIES

8.10.1 Discussion Topics

1. Typical chaotic business situations include the need to embrace change, align business units, stay flexible, and be responsive. Give some explicit examples of these four different types of chaos in this week's business news.

2. Describe the similarities of a fractal and Zachman DNA.

3. How do the cells in Zachman DNA resemble the cells of the human body?

4. What are the goals of Zachman DNA?

5. Like the human body's cells, the cells of Zachman DNA are also susceptible to physical forces. In a business environment, what physical forces affect the cells of Zachman DNA?

6. Describe the main processes that an SDLC encompasses.

7. The SDLC known as the waterfall method typically includes what steps? Why is this initial formal SDLC method sometimes criticized?

8. Compare and contrast the different SDLCs that were discussed in the chapter.

9. Explain why software development remains a chaotic activity.

10. Discuss how fractal mathematics and chaos relate to Zachman DNA.

11. Discuss why there is a crisis in software development.

12. Explain why the additional dimension of the two-dimensional Zachman Framework can enable IT professionals to be sure they have chosen the right set of steps, activities, or processes for a project.

13. What is the purpose of enterprise architecture?

14. How does Zachman DNA assist in producing an enterprise architecture?

15. Discuss the meaning of the phrase *sensitive dependence on initial conditions* and how that might relate to the enterprise.

16. How does the interaction of the parts of a computer system affect its usefulness?

17. Explain the boundaries within the holistic view of a computer system.

18. What does the form and dynamics of attractors reveal about the overall quality of a computer system?

19. Explain what sciences might be applied to Zachman DNA by an IT department and why.

20. Explain why Zachman DNA contains the building blocks of business life.

21. Describe the equivalent of human cell replacement in Zachman DNA.

22. Discuss how human behavior can contribute to chaos in a project.

23. Explain how an embedded Framework can contain another embedded Framework.

24. Discuss the dependencies among asset management, risk management, and process management.

25. Explain the difference between a primary descriptive representation and a secondary descriptive representation.

26. What is the purpose of capturing a metric?

27. What was one of Christopher Columbus' problems?

28. How is it possible for each row to have a *planner*, *owner*, *designer*, *builder*, and *subcontractor*?

29. Who benefits by making it easy to modify computer software and why?

8.10.2 Critical Thinking

1. Complex systems can have many attractors, such as drag, weight, thrust, lift, scope, detail, time, cost, people, intrusion, convention, and history. Write a one to two-page paper describing each attractor and explain what makes each an attractor.

2. Research how fractals and chaos have been applied to financial stock markets. Create an electronic presentation describing your findings.

3. Explain what is meant by horizontal, vertical, and depth integration by creating a scenario of a typical problem.

4. Create a simplistic sketch of a human body. Place the following labels on the body in an appropriate area: organ, system, cell, tissue, chromosome, DNA, and gene. Correlate the business equivalents with each body part.

5. In a short paper, describe what is meant by a robust architecture. How does the enterprise benefit from such an architecture?

6. Compare and contrast the pros and cons of a process-oriented SDLC versus a people-oriented SDLC.

7. Research and write a one-page paper describing how IT departments use metrics.

8. Explain what is meant by *thinking outside of the box.*

9. For your favorite hobby, what sciences would you list on the *z*-axis and why?

10. Illustrate *sensitivity on initial conditions* by writing a nursery rhyme that starts, "For want of some handed in homework…"

11. What is meant by context and why is it important?

12. On the Internet, research an SDLC and document its approach to software development.

13. Create an electronic presentation that illustrates several types of design or architectural patterns.

14. If a scope sliver is 80 percent and the detail sliver is 80 percent, in a short paper, explain what type of risks the project might face.

15. Imagine you are an IT project manager for a payroll system. What cells would you mandate and what cells would you ignore? Present your arguments in front of the class.

16. Imagine you are an IT project manager for medical equipment software used in an ICU (intensive care unit). What cells would you mandate and what cells would you ignore? Present your arguments in front of the class.

635

Endnotes

[1] The American Heritage Dictionary of the English Language, Fourth Edition.

[2] Euclid of Alexandria (325 BCE–265 BCE), a prominent mathematician of antiquity is best known for his treatise on mathematics, *The Elements.* The long lasting nature of *The Elements* makes Euclid the leading mathematics teacher of all time. Euclid figures include straight lines, triangles, circles, etc. They are all regularly formed shapes.

[3] The American Heritage Dictionary of the English Language, Fourth Edition.

[4] The American Heritage Dictionary of the English Language, Fourth Edition.

[5] Sometimes referred to as Downs syndrome.

[6] *The Free On-line Dictionary of Computing.*

[7] In 2003, IBM acquired Rational Software for $2.1 billion.

[8] The American Heritage Dictionary of the English Language, Fourth Edition.

[9] Varying configurations occur because of conditional looping, if-then-else logic, case statements, branch conditions, triggers, overloading, system events, etc.

10SMP is an acronym for Symmetric Multiprocessor, and MPP is an acronym for Massively Parallel Processor. An SMP system shares resources such as memory, operating system, and hard drives. An MPP system has separate nodes, and each node consists of one or more processors separating local memory, operating system, and hard drives.

11Usually in a state of panic and when it is too late.

12Process management involves monitoring, measuring, controlling, and continuous improvement of the activities that make up the software life cycle.

13Risk management involves maintaining enterprise stability by anticipating and planning for potential problems.

14Asset management involves overseeing the physical and intellectual property of an organization.

15The American Heritage Dictionary of the English Language, Fourth Edition.

16Webster's Revised Unabridged Dictionary, 1998.

17The more descriptive representations an enterprise produces, the more effective the long-term corporate memory. Descriptive representations also benefit the intellectual capital of the workers.

18Today, computer programs are perceived as the last step of design activity and not a coding activity. The *coding* is actually done by the compilers and linkers.

19There are multiple types and techniques of testing; each one could be broken out into a separate science (for example, unit testing, acceptance testing, and regression testing).

20Examples of actors include a stakeholder, user, customer, executive, and sponsor.

21Pinpointing the shortcomings of an SDLC is a human behavior problem. The SDLC could have been modified.

22At least one Fortune 500 company has an application where two developers code the same program. Once each program is written, they are both tested. If the test results are different, the one that looks *more right* is kept and the other program is discarded. If both programs produce the same result, the quicker one is kept, and the slower one is discarded.

23The Gang of Four are the authors Erich Gamma, Richard Helm, Ralph Johnson, and John Vlissides. The four collaborated on the book *Design Patterns*, published in 1994.

24SQL was originally named SEQUEL, but IBM was not able to trademark that name, so it abbreviated it to SQL, but the name sequel stuck. Some people do call the language *ess-que-ell*. SEQUEL was an acronym for structured English query language.

25The Hubble Space Telescope was named after Edwin P. Hubble (1889–1953). Hubble was a staff astronomer at Carnegie Institution's Mount Wilson Observatory, California.

26An approximation.

27Without the context of output from the previous rows, it would be difficult to understand what is *necessary* or even *right*.

APPENDIX A—BIOGRAPHY OF JOHN ARTHUR ZACHMAN

"The rare scholars who are nomads-by-choice are essential to the intellectual welfare of the settled disciplines."

— *Dr. Benoît Mandelbrot (b.1924), Mathematician*

John Arthur Zachman was born in Toledo, Ohio on December 16, 1934, and grew up in the Midwest. After graduating from high school in 1953 and a brief stint working for Capital Airlines at Chicago's Midway Airport, Zachman was awarded a Naval Reserve Officers Training Corps scholarship and attended Northwestern University in Evanston, Illinois until 1957, when he became a commissioned ensign in the U.S. Navy and began to develop his leadership skills. He eventually left the Navy to work as a salesperson for International Business Machines (IBM) in Chicago, where he focused on orchestrating support for his clients.

During his 26-year career at IBM, John Zachman made significant contributions to IBM's information planning methodology, *Business Systems Planning*. He was directly influenced by Dewey Walker, IBM manager of architecture in the late 1960s, and by the works of Robert Anthony, Jay Forrester, and Sherman Blumenthal. According to Zachman, their works form the basis for most of the current architectural thinking about information systems. Based on these works and the theories of Peter Drucker and Alvin Toffler, Zachman developed his views on information strategy and enterprise architecture. His innovation involves separating independent variables to provide the architectural ability to dynamically create and change the enterprise in very short periods of time. This insight forms the basis of the six columns of the Zachman architectural Framework.

Around 1980, Zachman began formalizing his thoughts about the Framework. He published his first paper on the subject, "A Framework for Information Systems Architecture," in the *IBM Systems Journal* in 1987. (See Appendix E.) A follow-up paper co-written with John Sowa was published in1993 in the same journal. The Framework for Enterprise Architecture is now widely accepted as the definitive work in the field of enterprise architecture.

In 1996, John started the Zachman Institute for Framework Advancement (ZIFA) as an educational vehicle for the Framework, which he makes freely available. (Although the Framework is copyrighted, Zachman has placed the Framework into the public domain.) As the world's leading expert on enterprise architecture, he also operates his own education and consulting business, Zachman International, for which he conducts seminars worldwide on the use and implementation of the Framework, communicating the purpose and logic of the Framework with clarity and enthusiasm.

Part of the message that John shares with his customers includes:

The way the world is evolving and operating determines the way individuals respond. By necessity, this response is actually the opposite way individuals should respond. Everyone is running out of time. As the rate of change gets more complex, there is less and less time to deal with that change. People respond to change in the short-term and make quick decisions, while putting off worrying about the long-term effects. The result is that people increasingly do things in shorter and shorter timeframes, when realistically individuals should be doing things from a longer and longer standpoint. People tend to think that the long-term approach takes too long and costs too much. If individuals took more of an architectural approach, time and cost could actually be reduced immeasurably.

John Zachman currently is a Fellow for the College of Business Administration at the University of North Texas, and serves on advisory boards, including those for Boston University's Institute for Leading in a Dynamic Economy (BUILDE); Data Resource Management Program at the University of Washington; and Data Administration Management Association (DAMA) International.

For the federal standards bureau, NIST (National Institute of Standards and Technology), John chaired a panel on planning, development and maintenance tools, and methods integration. In addition, John has served on the board of councilors for the School of Library and Information Management at the University of Southern California. He served as special advisor to the School of Library and Information Management at Emporia State University in Kansas, and on the Advisory Council to the School of Library and Information Management at Dominican University in California. He is a member of the Information Resource Management Advisory Council of the Smithsonian Institution in Washington D.C.

Zachman is a concepts integrator who does not believe he has all the answers, but tries to understand how everything must be integrated. He says, "I picture myself sitting in the middle, collecting all the technology ideas and the strategy ideas, and then putting everything into a structure." Beginning with his career in the U.S. Navy and through his endeavors as an entrepreneur, Zachman has retained the role of a *damage control officer*.

Additional Resources

For those students interested in learning more about the life and times of John A. Zachman, additional resources have been provided in the Instructor's Manual associated with this textbook and can also be downloaded in PDF format from our Web site at *www.eabook.info*.

APPENDIX B—USES OF THE FRAMEWORK OUTSIDE OF INFORMATION TECHNOLOGY

"My work is a game, a very serious game."

— *Maurits C. Escher (1898–1972), Artist*

This appendix presents five case studies to show how the Zachman Framework can be used outside of information technology. Each case study contains a completed Framework. Each cell in each Framework illustrates a portion of the topics of interest, relative to the case study type and the perspectives and aspects of the Framework.

The five case studies are:

- A school district with a focus on the classroom as part of the *functioning enterprise*
- A mineral mine with a focus on mine management as part of the *functioning enterprise*
- A restaurant with a focus on the menu as part of the *functioning enterprise*
- A zoo with a focus on the care of tigers as part of the *functioning enterprise*
- A business operation with a focus on acquiring, allocating, and spending money as part of the *functioning enterprise*

Each case study demonstrates that the enterprise requires a *planner*, *owner*, *designer*, *builder*, and *subcontractor* to make the *functioning enterprise* a reality. In addition, each perspective needs to resolve some details relative to the aspects: *what*, *how*, *where*, *who*, *when*, and *why*.

Each sample Framework contains a domain that is a subset of the enterprise domain. Therefore, each represented domain is a scope sliver of the enterprise. The content of each cell is a description of the types of knowledge that should be made explicit. Therefore, each description is incomplete; the sample represents a detail sliver. Slivers are discussed in Chapter 7.

Many independent slivers can be developed for an enterprise domain. However, to achieve an enterprise architecture, the slivers must be integrated and aligned. Eventually, an organization should work toward a complete set of integrated and aligned scope and detail slivers.

In the restaurant Framework, other domains could be added, such as food procurement, food disposal, accounting and reporting, hiring, and equipment maintenance. Each domain should be developed, integrated, and aligned with the enterprise. Similar expansions can be made to each Framework scenario.

The samples illustrate what type of information is appropriate for each cell. If organizations develop independent slivers, later efforts to integrate and align may seem overly complex. In part, this is the value of the Framework—the Framework, as a tool, helps individuals and organizations better manage complexity through thought, reasoning, and communication. Enterprises are complex. When you can handle complexity, you have reached a place of opportunity most organizations cannot begin to contemplate.

B.1 Case Study — A School Classroom

The case study in Table B-1 focuses on a classroom in a public school. From the district's superintendent to the teacher, each public servant is interested in the education and welfare of the student.

	What (Things)	How (Processes)	Where (Locations)	Who (People)	When (Time)	Why (Motivation)
Planner	Approved curriculum	Approved subject (teaching) delivery	Delivery techniques such as person-to-person and television-to-person	Staffing skills for full-time educators and substitute teachers	School calendar	Federal, state, and local mandates
Owner	Material composition of classroom contents	Delivery according to student needs	Location of intra- and inter-school facilities	Teacher workflow	Teaching schedule (daily, weekly, semester)	Scholastic achievement targets
Designer	Optimal material composition	Optimal delivery of course plan	Preferred location of teaching activities	Teacher and student ratios	Student and teacher interaction	Grading rules and guidelines
Builder	Practical material composition	Course plan based on enrollment and facilities	Realistic location for activities	Class assignments to remove overlaps and conflicts	Teacher assignments	Teacher rules and guidelines
Subcontractor	Arrange classroom things	Lesson plan	Location of classroom materials	Security needs	Attendance and dismissal	Strategy and tactics for teaching based on plan, location, time of day, and students
Functioning Enterprise	Books	Montessori or individual-ization	Classroom	Students and teachers	Timetable	Prepare students to be contributing members of society

Table B-1   *Framework for a School Classroom*

B.2 Case Study — A Mine

The case study in Table B-2 focuses on mining ore. The mine's owners are interested in the quantity and quality of the ore being extracted and maintaining the safety of their employees.

The following Framework was populated with the help of Adriaan Vorster. Vorster is the Director: Rautegniek at the Rand Afrikaans University in South Africa.

	What (Things)	How (Processes)	Where (Locations)	Who (People)	When (Time)	Why (Motivation)
Planner	List of the production deliverables	List of processes the business performs	List of locations where the business operates	List of users, groups, and units of the business	List of business events and cycles	List of business goals and strategies
Owner	Production require-ments and deliverables	Mining and support services	Mining and support network	Organization chart	Master production schedule	Business plan
Designer	Logical production require-ments and deliverable model	Business processes required to manage the ore body focused on the customer	Distributed systems model for ventilation, water, ore electricity transport, etc.	Strategic structure (production teams and targets)	Ore processing schedule	Statutory and mining rules and regulations
Builder	Needs for the infra-structure to establish a production environment	Business processes required to manage the ore body focused on the miner	Ore movement and storage	Determination of the work team struc-ture (capa-bility and competency requirements)	Develop-ment and mining schedules	Rules applicable to specific task and environment
Subcontractor	Machines, material, consum-ables, equipment, transport mecha-nisms, and products	Extraction processes based on geology, rock engineering, survey, and sampling processes	Allowance of ventilation, heat, humidity, illumination, and commu-nication for the miners in the mine	Work teams such as mine planners, geologists, surveyors, and engineers	Determine priorities of mining schedule subject to operational constraints	Miner safety rules
Functioning Enterprise	Raw ore and products	Activity	Equipped workplace	Team member	Execution schedule	Product quantity and quality goals and objectives

Table B-2	*Framework for a Mine*

B.3 Case Study — A Restaurant Specializing in Pancakes and Waffles

The case study in Table B-3 focuses on the menu at a pancake and waffle house that is open 24 hours a day. The restaurant's proprietors are interested in offering good food at reasonable prices in order to encourage a devoted clientele.

	What (Things)	How (Processes)	Where (Locations)	Who (People)	When (Time)	Why (Motivation)
Planner	Things of interest to run a restaurant	Processes needed to run a restaurant	Locations of all suppliers and vendors with delivery mechanisms	Job skills for running a business	Greeting customers, serving customers, receiving payment	Strategies for keeping customers happy and encouraging their repeat business
Owner	List of menu items and ingredients	Recipe for each menu item	Workstations and storage locations	Kitchen staff organization	State change of each recipe	Food handling laws and regulations
Designer	Refining knowledge of ingredients to include freshness and prices	Optimal process of food preparation	Spatial design of kitchen including equipment and maneuverability of staff	Workflow of receiving the order to serving the food	State changes for server	Rules for preparation of food
Builder	Menu design	Food preparation based on equipment	Venting, heating, cooling of equipment	Courtesy training	Customer awareness	Rules for operating the kitchen equipment
Subcontractor	Print menu and write daily specials on a whiteboard	Prepare each food item and final meal assembly	Workstation equipment for food preparation	Cash register management and operation	Shift schedule	Rules for personal cleanliness
Functioning Enterprise	Food items	Delivery of food to table	Dining table	Customers	Speed of service based on the busyness of restaurant	Hoping the customer says, "See you tomorrow."

Table B-3 *Framework for a Restaurant*

642

B.4 Case Study — A Large Metropolitan Zoo

The case study in Table B-4 focuses on Sumatran tigers at a zoo. The zookeepers are interested in the safety of both the animals and the visitors.

	What (Things)	How (Processes)	Where (Locations)	Who (People)	When (Time)	Why (Motivation)
Planner	List of animals and their needs	Animal acquisition; animal transportation	Location of suppliers, zoo, and quarantine facilities	Customer base	Feeding logistics	Preservation and education
Owner	Specific animal needs, materials for education	Medical, cleaning, security procedures	Parking; visitor transportation means	On-hours and off-hours staffing needs	Feeding and care needs by species	Safety policies
Designer	Organization of animal inventory	Trash disposal	Viewing routes	Preferred route for public education (workflow)	Viewing times	Visitor rules—no tapping on glass
Builder	Specific items and needs for each species	Emergency Exit procedures	Distance between visitor and animal	Tools for handling (interfacing) with animals	Sick animal attention	Laws for animal safety
Subcontractor	Raw meat, water, vitamins	Visitor and animal food preparation	Enclosure construction	Work teams	Employee and animal needs schedules	Handling rules
Functioning Enterprise	Sumatran tigers	Feeding and caring	Visitor enclosures and animal enclosures	Animal caretakers and visitors	Feeding schedule	Safety and education

Table B-4   *Framework for a Zoo*

B.5 Case Study — Spending Money to Make Money

Most business operations are required to acquire, allocate, and spend money in order to stay in business. This Framework focuses on the part of the enterprise that is focused on money.

	What (Things)	How (Processes)	Where (Locations)	Who (People)	When (Time)	Why (Motivation)
Planner	Sources of money	List of business endeavors	List of locations for business transactions	Staffing requirements	Fiscal calendar, order initiation, product or service delivery	Maintain a profitable company that contributes to the communities it serves
Owner	Determination of funds for each investment	Determination of product and infrastructure processes	Supply chain and connectivity mechanisms	Reporting structure	Critical path for logistical planning	Legislative mandates and business plan
Designer	Allocation of resources	Optimal design of all business processes	Communication infrastructure	Roles and responsibilities	Gantt chart for sequencing activities	Efficiency
Builder	Authorize spending of allocated resources	Actual business processes	Selection of technology for all connectivity	Task assignment	Production schedules	Profitability
Subcontractor	Accounting of resources	Assemble products or services	Assemble connectivity mechanisms	Individuals assigned to work	Timed work schedule	Individuals making a living
Functioning Enterprise	Formal record-keeping	Just-in-time manufacturing	Supply chain	Value chain	Sequencing	Quantity, quality, and profitability

Table B-5   *Framework for a Financial Business*

APPENDIX C—MAPPING INFORMATION TECHNOLOGY CAREERS TO THE ZACHMAN FRAMEWORK

"Don't you wish there were a knob on the TV to turn up the intelligence? There's one marked *Brightness*, but it doesn't work."

— *(Leo) Gallagher (b. 1947), Comedian (sledge-o-matic)*

"The principal tools of production today are not machinery and equipment, but the ideas and talents of the people. Today, the intellectual capital of the scientist, the machinist, and the programmer is the critical resource, so the possessors of the intellectual tools of production—people—will come to exercise effective power."

— *James Belasco (b. 1936), Professor, author, management consultant and Ralph Stayer (b. 1943), CEO, author*

Table C-1 illustrates a variety of IT job titles and careers with sample placement in the Framework. These sample careers cover a wide spectrum including management, architecture, data, software, hardware, and support services. Actual tasks and responsibilities for each job title may vary by employer and, therefore, the mappings may change slightly.

The Framework can help you focus on key relationships between people, the organization, technology, and information, no matter where the job titles are placed on the classification schema.

	What (Things)	How (Processes)	Where (Locations)	Who (People)	When (Time)	Why (Motivation)
Planner	Data Administrator	Business Analyst	Logistics Analyst, Hardware Analyst, Communication Analyst	Business Analyst	Data Administrator, Business Analyst	Information Architect, Software Architect, Technology Architect, Business Analyst
Owner	Data Administrator, Information Architect	Business Analyst, Systems Analyst, Software Architect	Technology Architect, Network Architect, Business Analyst	Business Analyst, Systems Analyst, Information Architect	Data Administrator, Information Architect, Systems Analyst	Information Architect, Software Architect, Technology Architect, Business Analyst
Designer	Data Administrator, Information Architect, Database Administrator	Business Analyst, Systems Analyst, Software Architect	Technology Architect, Network Architect	Business Analyst, Systems Analyst, Information Architect, Software Architect, Security Administrator	Data Administrator, Information Architect, Systems Analyst	Information Architect, Software Architect, Technology Architect, Business Analyst, Systems Analyst
Builder	Data Administrator, Information Architect, Database Administrator, Data Warehouse Architect	Programmer, Software Tester, Web Designer, Data Warehouse Architect	Network Engineer, Systems Administrator, Network Administrator, Systems Programmer, Middleware Programmer	Business Analyst, Systems Analyst, Information Architect, Software Architect, Security Administrator, Web Designer	Web Designer, Data Administrator, Information Architect, Systems Analyst, Software Architect	Web Designer, Information Architect, Software Architect, Technology Architect, Business Analyst, Systems Analyst, Programmer Analyst
Subcontractor	Database Administrator, Information Architect, Data Warehouse Architect, Tester	Programmer, Software Tester, Webmaster, Data Warehouse Architect, Tester	Network Engineer, Systems Administrator, Network Administrator, Systems Programmer, Middleware Programmer, Tester	Programmer, Security Administrator, Webmaster, Tester	Programmer, Webmaster, Tester	Programmer, Database Administrator, Webmaster, Tester
Functioning System	Database Administrator, Tech Support	Configuration Manager, Tech Support	Systems Administrator, Network Administrator, Tech Support	Security Administrator, Tech Support	Systems Administrator, Tech Support	Programmer, Database Administrator, Tech Support

Table C-1	Information Technology Careers

Note: The job title, Data Administrator, includes Data Analyst and Data Modeler activities.

APPENDIX D—THOUGHTS FROM OTHERS REGARDING THE ZACHMAN FRAMEWORK

"In the business world, the rearview mirror is always clearer than the windshield."
— *Warren Buffett (b. 1930), Investor*

The following comments are from friends and colleagues, who have shared thoughts and opinions about their use and experiences with the Zachman Framework.

Leon Kappelman Ph.D.

Leon Kappelman Ph.D.
Dallas, Texas
Farrington Professor of Information Systems
Director of Information Systems Research Center
College of Business—University of North Texas

In one form or another, the alignment of information and technology with the rest of the enterprise has been near the top of IT management's key concerns every year since the late 1960s. Most have not been able to achieve it, and, sadly, little net value is created by IT spending in the vast majority of enterprises.

The Zachman Framework provides the conceptualization and the grammar for the revolution in thinking and communication needed to achieve that alignment. Moreover, the Framework's reliance on capturing knowledge about the enterprise in the form of normalized primitives may significantly reduce the cycle of buy and scrap that has plagued computing since ENIAC.

IT lives in the lower left-hand corner of the Framework, but enterprise management lives in the upper-right corner. Close that communication gap and you are on the road to real alignment in the Information Age.

Adriaan Vorster

Adriaan Vorster
Johannesburg, South Africa
Director: Rautegniek
Rand Afrikaans University

Any feature or complex attribute can be mapped to the Zachman Framework. The Framework is neutral and does not need to be defended. The Framework is comprehensive, complete, and can address primitives at every level of the enterprise. It is not technology, application, situation, problem, domain, fashion, methodology, ego, or religion specific.

The Framework is implicit in every object or subject. You may ignore the Framework, but that does not make the Framework go away. The Framework and the constituent parts, primitives, patterns, models, and architecture still exist. The fact that these parts may not have been made explicit says more about the often-silent assumptions that have been made than the analysis that was performed.

The Framework is the only way to move from enterprise alchemy to enterprise engineering. The Framework is not limited to the information technology domain. It is an enterprise framework. Now think about *your* enterprise—not the place where you work—your own personal enterprise. The Framework is *that* capable.

Cindy Walker

Cindy Walker
Falls Church, Virginia
President
WalkerBurr, Incorporated

As an information management consultant, I help large corporations and federal government agencies improve information asset management. Organizations seek WalkerBurr's help because they continually experience higher costs, decreases in productivity, and failed application development projects. Organizational problems are often attributed to storing redundant information, inability to share information across the enterprise, and poor data quality.

I use the Zachman Framework extensively in my client engagements. It is a powerful tool not only for producing an architecture for the entire enterprise, but also for analyzing components of the enterprise and addressing individual problems. For example, I have used the Framework to address complex issues related to information security, information sharing, strategic planning, information systems planning and development, performance measurement, data stewardship, and data quality.

Allan Kolber

Allan Kolber
East Brunswick, New Jersey
Principal Enterprise Architect
ConcentrX, LLC

A large Mexican manufacturing corporation with many divisions, companies, and interrelationships needed to rebuild its entire infrastructure to respond to competitive changes brought on by deregulation. The rebuild involved massive changes to both business processes and IT applications.

As part of the proposed rebuild solution, corporate management accepted the idea of first architecting the new vision. Because the company's business management had little experience with IT, I taught the Zachman Framework to both business and IT management. The Framework was accepted by all and allowed management across the enterprise to communicate with each other about the entire architecture, relative to the perspectives, aspects, and cells of the Framework.

For the first time, business management was able to understand the necessity and purpose of each IT activity. At the same time, IT personnel were better able to understand where the business was headed and what was needed to support the business. The new initiatives became the basis for higher quality development and increased reuse. IT personnel experienced an easier time enhancing and maintaining the applications they built. The company gained long-term strategic benefits.

Sung Kun Kim

Sung Kun Kim
Seoul, Korea
Professor, Information Systems
Chung-Ang University

The Zachman Framework, with two dimensions of perspective and aspect, is handy for representing the structural view of the enterprise. With the additional depth dimension, the Framework is handier for representing the heuristic view of how to run the enterprise.

Burton Parker

Burton Parker
Arlington, Virginia
Principal
Paladin Integration Engineering

I focus on Column 1—*data*—soup to nuts. As a consultant, I have been helped immeasurably with my engagements by using the Zachman Framework. For example, my involvement may require me to be:

- An operational database administrator—addressing Row 5, Column 1 issues
- A physical design database administrator—addressing Row 4, Column 1 issues
- A logical data modeler—addressing Row 3, Column 1 issues
- A conceptual data designer—addressing Row 2, Column 1 issues
- A data planner—addressing Row 1, Column 1 issues

The Framework has helped open my eyes to the full scope of the issues related to enterprise data management. For Column 1 and every other column, the Framework provides an excellent roadmap for managing the artifacts of the enterprise. The Framework allows me to be a proactive participant in the organization.

Donald Chapin

Donald Chapin
London, England
Business Language and Rules Consultant
Business Semantics Limited

Personally, the insights I have garnered from the Framework have improved my clarity of thought, given me a greater ability to give logical reasons for the conclusions I reach, and enabled a greater ability to communicate my work in an unambiguous fashion.

I specialize in Row 2, and to aid communication, I always state deliverables for a project in terms of the Framework's cells. For example, this deliverable deals with issues or designs for R2C1 and R2C6; or while talking, I might say, we will need to table these items (temporarily set aside) and readdress them in Rows 3 and 4. Being able to discuss anything in terms of its position in the Framework is a great way to gain the full benefit of the Framework as a thinking and communication tool.

George Brundage

George Brundage
Washington, D.C.
Chief Enterprise Architect
U.S. Department of the Treasury

The U.S. federal government incorporated the Zachman Framework into its Federal Enterprise Architecture Framework (FEAF) for interagency projects in 1999. Since that time, the Framework has been incorporated into many federal agency enterprise architecture efforts.

The Framework is the most widely known tool of its kind and was included in the FEAF primarily for that reason. The Framework is sophisticated and, at the same time, simple and clear-cut. Without the Framework, I do not believe the U.S. government would have a clear idea of the aspects (columns) of information technology.

John Zachman is a positive force behind enterprise architecture and gives people the confidence to try to change things for the better. The logic supporting his Framework is powerful. He participates freely in discussions involving large numbers of industry and government personnel. He has helped to stimulate enterprise architecture throughout the U.S. government.

650

Markus Schacher

Markus Schacher
Zurich, Switzerland
KnowBody
KnowGravity, Incorporated

The Zachman Framework gives an enterprise a bird's-eye view on its business and systems instead of a huge set of frog's-eye views. The Framework is necessary for investigating the business prior to any IT-related activities. Otherwise, from my experiences, you will end up with some cool applications that do not really support the (money-producing) business.

I consider an empty Framework to be a checklist for information that is available (explicit) and unavailable (implicit) to the project. I recommend starting any project by focusing on what information is unavailable, and then evaluating the risk of not making that information explicit. I define the tasks needed to make the implicit explicit by prioritizing the tasks needed according to the perceived risks.

Michael Eulenberg

Michael Eulenberg
Seattle, Washington
Business Architect
Owl Mountain

No organization can do everything at once. Documenting an entire enterprise using the Zachman Framework shows all the possibilities, allowing management to pick what needs to be done first. Basing information technology implementations directly on business strategy means that every project contributes to the ends defined in advance by the business.

The Framework's *why* column suggests work in Row 1 to develop the business strategies that support the business goals. This helps prevent the situation of management asking at the end of an IT project, "Why did we do this?"

My primary use of the Framework is as a communication tool. I often place a copy of the Framework on a table between a client and me to determine where we are in a project. Sometimes a client thinks we are doing design work at Row 2, but the team is actually doing design work at Row 4. The Framework helps us sort out exactly what we are doing and what we should be doing.

Marcio Rocha

Marcio Rocha
São Paulo, Brazil
Database Administrator
Data Tribune

Performance tuning a database is critical to my ability to add value. In reality, I have to tune the enterprise. To coin a phrase from the author, Thomas Merton, "No database is an island." I have to work closely with everyone in the enterprise to accomplish my job. The Framework is how I've learned to approach every problem.

Prakash Rao

651

Prakash C. Rao
Vienna, Virginia
Vice President
Metadata Management Corporation Limited

Capital assets are enablers for creating wealth. You also need mechanisms that draw upon or use the capital asset in some manner to produce something useful. The Zachman Framework is a capital asset that represents a collection of understanding of how the enterprise works and how it should work.

We use the Framework in my own company and have used it with clients who hire us. Not too long ago, one of our clients that used the Framework was able to merge the capabilities, features, roles, information exchanges, location relationships, and data needs of two large existing global information systems into the specification of a single integrated system in a short period of time—even with all the office politics.

The Framework enabled us to present clear specifications and a conscious merger of the various global applications, while allowing all the stakeholders to be actively involved in the decisions that were made to put together the specification.

Robert Rencher

Robert Rencher
Seattle, Washington
Senior Systems Engineer, eBusiness Infrastructure
The Boeing Company

Companies like ours benefit from enterprise architecture in much the same way that organized people benefit from address books, to-do lists, personal inventories, task lists, contact lists, and plans. Organized companies can find many ways to benefit from the Zachman Framework—creating roadmaps to move the enterprise forward, reengineering business processes, and taking advantage of new technology to gain competitive advantage.

Simon Seow

Simon Seow
Selangor, Malaysia
Managing Director
Info Spec (Singapore) Private Limited

The Zachman Framework has allowed me to quickly grasp any given situation and ask the right questions. Outside of receiving a solid general education, there are few things in life that have a wide and lasting payback for the effort you take in learning the subject—the Framework is one of the subjects that will pay you back continually.

The Framework has helped me drastically cut down on the time I need to get a quick grasp of a business or technical situation. This has translated into spending less time with individual clients, while at the same time, I can charge a higher fee. I now service more clients during the course of a year...and my revenues are way up.

TJ Cope

TJ Cope
Dayton, Ohio
Consulting Software Engineer
LexisNexis

The Zachman Framework is essential for my understanding of the many decisions I make, am involved in making, or that I learn have been made each day. Placing a decision in terms of the perspectives and aspects of the Framework provides an initial context. The context allows me to think about how a decision fits with other decisions I have placed in the same cell.

As I begin to develop confidence with how each decision fits into the enterprise, I can look for ways to integrate that decision with other rows and columns. I find that many of the questions I need to ask are answered when I navigate the question in the context of the Framework. Through this scrutiny, I can confidently include a decision in the categorization of my business world.

Thomas Hokel

Thomas Hokel
Breckenridge, Colorado
President
The Enterprise Framework Group

Prior to being exposed to the Zachman Framework, I used traditional information engineering methodologies coupled with information architecture and Kaplan and Norton's Balanced Scorecard concepts to achieve enterprise integration.

However, traditional information engineering methods tend to ignore Rows 1 and 2, or at least blur the lines between conceptual business models and logical system models. Most of the U.S. federal government architecture frameworks (e.g., FEAF, TEAF, and C4ISR) keep getting closer to (i.e., stealing concepts from) the Zachman Framework, so they would be practically non-existent for use as a substitute.

Carla Marques Pereira

Carla Marques Pereira
Lisbon, Portugal
Student
Lisbon Technical University

Identifying and understanding the architecture of its own enterprise should be a fundamental desire for any organization that wants to be competitive. The Zachman Framework provides a structured way for any organization to achieve the necessary knowledge about itself using the rows and columns.

The Framework's structure grounds the enterprise's architecture as a process. The Framework helps govern the architectural process with the dependency, coherence, and traceability needed for an enterprise to manage change.

The thesis for my master's degree at the Technical Superior Institute of the Lisbon Technical University in Portugal is models representing architectural components. I am focusing on the coherence and dependency mechanisms among different models for each of the Framework's cells. Each of the models used is based on the Unified Modeling Language (UML). My work addresses integration between neighborhood cells, specifically for coherence, dependency, and version control.

653

Per Strand

Per Strand
Copenhagen, Denmark
CEO
Strand and Donslund A/S

Many projects start with an end date and a fixed budget. Only after these two items have been established do we try to figure out what the users need. In many cases, the deadlines and budget do not allow us to complete every document.

Using the Zachman Framework, we can effectively communicate what we can and cannot do. When we can communicate to managers and executives what we are not addressing, the entire enterprise can come together to manage risk. The Framework is our key to identifying and proactively managing risk.

Cheryl Estep

Cheryl Estep
Alamo, California
Senior Business Requirements Analyst (retired)
ChevronTexaco Corporation

I specialized in meeting facilitation. The Zachman Framework helped me ensure everyone talked effectively to each other. Using personality typing and the Framework, I was able to facilitate productive meetings.

Karen Lopez

Karen Lopez
Toronto, Canada
Principal Consultant
InfoAdvisors

We have been using the Zachman Framework in the Canadian Information Processing Society for several years to classify our products and services. The Framework helped us identify conflicting understandings among our board members. We are now able to address disconnects and enhance our product and service offerings.

APPENDIX E—THE
ORIGINAL PAPER

"How wonderful it is that nobody need wait a single moment before starting to improve the world."

— *Anne Frank (1929–1945), World War II Holocaust victim*

John Zachman's original paper decribing the Zachman Framework was published in the *IBM Systems Journal*, Volume 26, Number 3 in 1987. It was subsequently republished in the same magazine, Volume 38, Numbers 2 and 3 in 1999. The paper has also been published in other publications, such as *The ZIFA Letter*, Volume 1 Number 1 in 1996 and the *Data Management Handbook*, 1993. In the 1980s, enterprise architecture was often called information systems architecture— hence the title of the paper.

E.1 A Framework for Information Systems Architecture

> With increasing size and complexity of the implementation of information systems, it is necessary to use some logical construct (or architecture) for defining and controlling the interfaces and the integration of all of the components of the system. This paper defines information systems architecture by creating a descriptive framework from disciplines quite independent of information systems, then by analogy, specifies information systems architecture based upon the neutral objective framework. Also, some preliminary conclusions are drawn about the implications of the resultant descriptive framework. The discussion is limited to architecture and does not include a strategic planning methodology.

The subject of information systems architecture is beginning to receive considerable attention. The increased scope of design and levels of complexity of information systems implementations are forcing the use of some logical construct (or architecture) for defining and controlling the interfaces and the integration of all of the components of the system. In 1960, this issue was not at all significant because the technology itself did not provide for either breadth in scope or depth in complexity in information systems. The inherent limitations of the then-available 4K machines, for example, constrained design and necessitated suboptimal approaches for automating a business.

Current technology is rapidly removing both conceptual and financial constraints. It is not hard to speculate about, if not realize, very large, very complex systems implementations, extending in scope and complexity to encompass an entire enterprise. One can delineate readily the merits of the large, complex, enterprise-oriented approaches. Such systems allow flexibility in managing business changes and coherency in the management of business resources. However, there also is merit in the more traditional, smaller, suboptimal systems design approach. Such systems are relatively economical, implemented quickly, and easier to design and manage.

In either case, since the technology permits *distributing* large amounts of computing facilities in small packages to remote locations, some kind of structure (or architecture) is imperative because decentralization without structure is chaos. Therefore, to keep the business from *dis*integrating, the concept of information systems architecture is becoming less an option and more a necessity for establishing some order and control in the investment of information systems resources. The cost involved and the success of the business depending increasingly on its information systems require a disciplined approach to the management of those systems.

On the assumption that an understanding of information systems architecture is important to the development of a disciplined approach, the question that naturally arises is, "What, in fact, is information systems architecture?" Unfortunately, among the proponents of information systems architecture, there seems to be little consistency in concepts or in specifications of *architecture*, to the extent that the words *information systems architecture* are already losing their meaning! Furthermore, it probably is not reasonable to expect reconciliation or commonality of definition to emerge from the professional data processing community itself. The emotional commitment associated with vested interests almost demands a neutral, unbiased, independent source as a prerequisite for any acceptable work in this area.

In any event, it likely will be necessary to develop some kind of framework for rationalizing the various architectural concepts and specifications in order to provide for clarity of professional communication, to allow for improving and integrating development methodologies and tools, and to establish credibility and confidence in the investment of systems resources.

Although information systems architecture is related to strategy, both information strategy and business strategy, this paper deliberately limits itself to architecture and should not be construed as presenting a strategic planning methodology.

The development of a business strategy and its linkage to information systems strategies, which ultimately manifest themselves in architectural expression, is an important subject to pursue, but it is quite independent of the subject of this work, which is defining a framework for information systems architecture.

E.1.1 Derivation of the Architectural Concept

In searching for an objective, independent basis upon which to develop a framework for information systems architecture, it seems only logical to look to the field of classical architecture itself. In so doing, it is possible to learn from the thousand or so years of experience that have been accumulated in that field. Definition of the deliverables, i.e., the work product, of a classical architect can lead to the specification of analogous information systems architectural products and, in so doing, can help to classify our concepts and specifications.

With this objective in mind, that is discovering the analogous information systems architectural representations, the following is an examination of the classical architect's deliverables produced in the process of constructing a building.

Bubble Charts

The first architectural deliverable created by the architect is a conceptual representation, a *bubble chart*, which depicts, in gross terms, the size, shape, spatial relationships, and basic intent of the final structure. This bubble chart results from the initial conversations between the architect and prospective owner. A sample of such an initial conversation follows:

I would like to build a building.

What kind of building do you have in mind? Do you plan to sleep in it? Eat in it? Work in it?
Well, I would like to sleep in it.

Oh, you want to build a house?
Yes, I would like a house.

How large a house do you have in mind?
Well, my lot size is 100 feet by 300 feet.

Then you want a house about 50 feet by 100 feet?
Yes, that is about right.

How many bedrooms do you need?
Well, I have two children, so I would like three bedrooms.

Note that each question serves to pose a constraint (the lot size) or identify a requirement (the number of bedrooms) in order to establish the *ballpark*, or approximate conditions, within which any design will take place. From the above dialogue, the architect can depict what the owner has in mind in the form of a series of *bubbles*, each bubble representing a room, its gross size, shape, spatial relationship, etc. See Figure E-1.

657

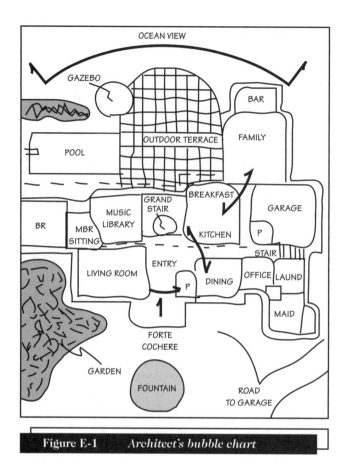

Figure E-1   Architect's bubble chart

The architect prepares this bubble chart for two reasons. First, the prospective owner must express what he or she has in mind that will serve as a foundation or basis for the architect's actual design work. Second, the architect must convince the owner that the owner's desires are understood well enough so that the owner *will* pay for the creative work to follow and, in effect, initiate the project.

Having established a basic understanding with the prospective owner, the architect produces the next set of architectural deliverables, which are called architect's drawings.

Architect's Drawings

The architect's drawings are a transcription of the *owner's* perceptual requirements, a depiction of the final product from the *owner's* perspective.

The drawings include horizontal sections (floor plans), vertical sections (cutaways), and pictorial representations depicting the artistic motif of the final structure. The purpose of these drawings is to enable the owner to relate to them and to agree or disagree: "That is exactly what I had in mind!" or "Make the following modifications."

The drawings can be very detailed; however, they are normally developed only to the level of detail required for the prospective *owner* to understand and approve the design.

Once the *owner* agrees that the architect has captured what he or she has in mind and further agrees to pay the price for continuing the project, the architect produces the next set of architectural deliverables, which are called the architect's plans.

Architect's Plans

The architect's plans are the translation of the *owner's* perceptions/requirements into a product. The plans are a *designer's* representation of the final product (as opposed to an *owner's* representation, which is embodied in the *drawings*). The *designer's* representation (plans) puts an explicit specification around the material composition of the final product.

The plans are composed of 16 categories of detailed representations, including site work, electrical system, masonry, wood structure, etc. They describe material relationships in the form of diagrams (drawings) as well as bills of materials. These plans are the final deliverables prepared by the architect and ultimately become the official *record* of the finished structure.

The architect's plans are prepared to serve as a basis for negotiation with a general contractor. The owner takes the plans to a contractor and says, "Build me one of these." If the contractor builds *one of these*, which is represented in the architect's plans, the *owner* knows that there is a high probability of getting the desired product, as depicted in the architect's drawings.

As a result of the negotiations between the *owner* and general contractor, the plans may be modified because of cost/price and other considerations, but they finally serve to represent what is committed to construction.

Contractor's Plans

At this point, the contractor redraws the architect's plans to produce the contractor's plans, representing the *builder's* perspective. Such plans are prepared because complex engineering products are not normally built in a day. Some phased approach is required which, in the case of a building, may comprise first some site work, next the foundation, then the first floor, and so on, until the building is completed. Furthermore, the contractor may have technology constraints. Either the tool technology or the process technology may constrain his ability to produce precisely what the architect designed. In either case, the contractor will have to design a reasonable facsimile, which can be produced and satisfies the requirements. These technology constraints, plus the natural constraints requiring phased construction, are reflected in the contractor's plans, which serve to direct the actual construction activity.

Shop Plans

Other representations, short of the final structure itself, are prepared by subcontractors. These representations are called shop plans and are drawings of parts or subsections that are an out-of-context specification of what actually will be fabricated or assembled. The drawings, architect's plans, and contractor's plans are in context because the owner, architect, and contractor are all concerned with the entirety of the structure, whereas the *subcontractors'* representations are concerned with components or parts of the total structure. These shop plans might even serve as patterns for a quantity of identical parts to be fabricated for the project.

The Building

In the case of producing a building, the final representation is the physical building itself.

In summary, there is a set of *architectural* representations that are produced during the process of constructing a building. The set is given in Figure E-2.

Representation	Nature/Purpose
Bubble charts	• Provide basic concepts for building • Show gross sizing, shape, spatial relationships • Allow architect/*owner* mutual understanding • Initiate project
Architect's drawings	• Show how the *owner* sees the final building • Include floor plans, cutaways, and pictures • Demonstrate the architect/*owner* agreement on the building • Establish contract
Architect's plans	• Show how the *designer* sees the final building • Translate the *owner's* view into a product • Include 16 categories of detailed drawings • Provide a basis for negotiation with general contractor
Contractor's plans	• Show how the *builder* sees the final building • Reflect the architect's plans constrained by laws of nature and available technology • Include a description of *how to build it* • Direct construction activities
Shop plans	• Show *subcontractor's* design of a part or section • Provide a detailed standalone model • Specify what should be constructed • Show a patterm
Buildings	• Represent the physical buildings

Figure E-2   *Architectural representations for constructing a building*

E.1.2 A Generic Set of Architectural Representations

Now that we have specified the set of architectural representations produced during the process of constructing a building, it becomes apparent that this set of *architectures* may be generic to the process of building any complex engineering product. A cursory examination of military airframe manufacturing appears to validate this hypothesis as follows:

- Concepts equals *bubble charts* (ballpark view). The airframe manufacturers begin with some *concepts*, which are specifications for the *ballpark* in which they intend to manufacture. For example, concepts for the final product indicating that it will fly so high, so fast, so far, for such and such purpose, with so many people, etc. are formulated to establish its gross size, shape, and performance.

- Work *breakdown structure* equals *architect's drawings* (*owner's* view). The work breakdown structure is the *owner's perspective*. The government requires that the manufacturer specify the work to be accomplished in terms of the components/systems against which costs are accrued and schedules are managed. In this fashion, the government controls the manufacturer in the production of the product.

- *Engineering design* equals *architect's plans* (*designer's* view). Engineering, the designer, translates the work breakdown structure into a physical product. The resultant *engineering design* is composed of drawings and bills of materials.

- *Manufacturing engineering bill of materials* equals *contractor's plans* (*builder's* view). Manufacturing engineering, the *builder*, applies the laws of nature and technology constraints to the engineering design to describe how to build the product (i.e., inside out, bottom up) and to ensure that everything designed is actually producible.

- *Assembly and fabrication drawings* equals shop *plans* (detail view). Assembly and fabrication drawings are the instructions to the shop floor personnel on how they are to assemble/fabricate the pieces or parts as standalone entities.

- *Machine tool representation* (machine view). Because manufacturing uses computer-controlled equipment to produce some parts, it inserts an additional representation of the final piece or part, short of the physical part itself. This representation is a *Program* (i.e., *numerical code program*) that is a machine language representation.

- *Airplane* equals *building* (finished product). The final representation is the actual, physical item itself.

In any case, there appear to be conceptual equivalents in the manufacturing industry for the architectural representations of the construction industry. This equivalency would strengthen the argument that an analogous set of architectural representations is likely to be produced during the process of building any complex engineering product, including an *information system.*

Before identifying the information systems analogs, it is useful to make some general observations regarding architecture.

First, there appear to be three fundamental architectural representations, one for each *player in the game*—that is, the *owner*, the *designer*, and the *builder*. The *owner* has in mind a product that will serve some purpose. The architect transcribes this perception of a product into the owner's perspective. Next, the architect translates this representation into a physical product, the designer's perspective. The *builder* then applies the constraints of the laws of nature and available technology to make the product producible, which is the *builder's* perspective.

Preceding these three fundamental representations, a gross representation of size, shape, and scope is created to establish the *ballpark* within which all of the ensuing architectural activities will take place.

661

Succeeding the three fundamental representations are the detailed out-of-context representations, which technically could be considered architectures because they are representations short of being the final physical product. However, they are somewhat less interesting *architecturally*, since they do not depict the final product in total and are more oriented to the actual implementation activities. Nonetheless, they are included in this discussion for the purpose of ensuring a comprehensive framework.

A significant observation regarding these architectural representations is that each has a different *nature* from the others. They are not merely a set of representations, each of which displays a level of detail greater than the previous one. Level of detail is an independent variable, varying *within* any one architectural representation. For example, the *designer's* representation (i.e., architect's plans) is not merely a succeeding, increasing level of detail of the *owner's* representation (i.e., architect's drawings). It is different in *nature*, in content, in semantics, and so on, representing a different perspective. The level of detail of the *designer's* representation (i.e., plans) is variable and quite independent of the level of detail of the *owner's* representation (i.e., drawings).

In the same fashion, each of the architectural representations differs from the others in *essence*, not merely in level of detail.

Given this description of the perspectives (i.e., *owner's* perspective, *designer's* perspective, *builder's* perspective, etc.) of architectural representation produced over the process of building a complex engineering product, it is relatively straightforward to identify the analogs in the information systems area, since information systems are also *complex engineering products*. Figure E-3 identifies those information systems analogs, along with the building and airplane equivalents.

Generic	Buildings	Airplanes	Information systems
Ballpark	Bubble charts	Concepts	Scope/objectives
Owner's representation	Architect's drawings	Work breakdown structure	Model of the business
Designer's representation	Architect's plans	Engineering design/ bill of materials	Model of the information system
Builder's representation	Contractor's plans	Manufacturing engineering design/ bill of materials	Technology model
Out-of-context representation	Shop plans	Assembly/ fabrication drawings	Detailed description
Machine language representation	Not applicable	Numerical code programs	Machine language description
Product	Building	Airplane	Information system

Figure E-3 *Architectural representations in engineering*

Different Types of Descriptions for the Same Product

Before the idea regarding the different perspectives (and therefore the different architectural representations produced over the process of building complex engineering products) is developed further, it is necessary to introduce a second, entirely different idea. Specifically, there exist different types of descriptions oriented to different aspects of the object being described. Figure E-4 characterizes three such types of descriptions, one of which is oriented to the material of the product, another to its function, and the third to the relative location of its components.

	Description I	Description II	Description III
Orientation	Material	Function	Location
Focus	Structure	Transform	Flow
Description	*What* the thing is made of	*How* the thing works	*Where* the flows (connections) exist
Example	Bill of materials	Function specifications	Drawings
Descriptive models	Part-relationship-part	Input-process-output	Site-link-site

Figure E-4   *Three types of descriptions for the same product*

In spite of the fact that each of the descriptions may be describing the same product, each of them is unique and stands alone because each serves quite different purposes. Furthermore, none of the descriptions says anything explicitly about any of the other descriptions. Only assumptions can be made from one about the contents of another. For example, a bill of materials exists independently of, and is clearly different from, functional specifications or drawings. Looking at a bill of materials tells nothing about functional specifications or drawings (relative locations of components). Only assumptions can be made about function or location, depending upon how descriptively named the parts are in the bill of materials. Similarly, the functional specifications say nothing explicit about the bill of materials or functional specifications.

In short, each of the different descriptions has been prepared for a different reason, each stands alone, and each is different from the others, even though all the descriptions may pertain to the same object and, therefore, are inextricably related to one another.

The *description* row of Figure E-4 suggests that there likely are additional descriptions not characterized in the table as the material description addresses *what*, the functional description addresses *how*, and the location description addresses *where*. The implications are that there must be at least *who*, *when*, and *why* descriptions as well. Discussion of these additional types of descriptions is reserved for the future, since using only three different descriptions introduces considerable complexity into the subject of information systems architecture at this time. Therefore, the remainder of this paper will be limited to the three types of descriptions contained in Figure E-4. For future reference, Figure E-5 is included and contains a preliminary, Figure E-4 type of characterization of the additional descriptive types related to people (*who*), time (*when*), and motivation (*why*).

	Description IV	Description V	Description VI
Orientation	People	Time	Purpose
Focus	Responsibility	Dynamics	Motivation
Description	*Who* is doing what	*When* the events take place	*Why* choices are made
Example	Organization chart	Production schedule	Objectives hierarchy
Descriptive model	Organization-reporting-organization	Event-cycle-event	Objective-precedent-objective

Figure E-5 *Possible characterization of additional types of descriptions*

As was the case with the earlier idea regarding the different perspectives of the different participants in the architecture process, once again, it is straightforward to identify the information systems analogs for the elements of the second idea—that is, the different types of descriptions for the same object, as follows:

- Functional description—In information systems terms, this would likely be called a process (or a functional) model, and the descriptive representation would be called the same as the general case, *input-process-output*.

- Material description—Generally speaking, the material description describes the *stuff the thing is made of*, which, in the case of information systems, is data. Therefore, in information systems terms, the analog for the material description would be a data model, and in the data vernacular, *part-relationship-part* would become *entity-relationship-entity*. The data model is the equivalent of the bill of materials for the information systems product.

- Location description—In information systems, this would likely be called the network model, in which the focus is on the flows (connections) between the various components. In the information systems network vernacular, *site-link-site* would become *node-line-node*.

Therefore, the rows of Figure E-6, which constitute the analogs in information systems for the more generic types of descriptions, could be added to Figure E-4.

664

	Description I—material	Description II—function	Description III—location
Information systems analog	Data model	Process model	Network model
IT descriptive model	Entity-relationship-entity	Input-process-output	Node-line-node

Figure E-6 *Information systems analogs for the different types of descriptions*

The Framework

Two ideas have been discussed thus far:

- There is a set of architectural representations produced over the process of building a complex engineering product, representing the different perspectives of the different participants.

- The same product can be described for different purposes and in different ways, resulting in different types of descriptions.

The combination of the two ideas suggests that for every different type of description, there are different perspectives (and actually different representations) for each of the different participants. For example, for the material (or data) description, there are the *owner's* representation, the *designer's* representation, the *builder's* representation, etc. For the functional (or process) description, there are the *owner's* representation, the *designer's* representation, the *builder's* representation, etc. For the location (or geographic) description, there are also the *owner's* representation, the *designer's* representation, the *builder's* representation, etc.

Figure E-7 illustrates the total set of different perspectives for each type of description. Note that because the intent is to depict a framework for *information systems* architecture, all the information systems analog names from Figures E-3, E-4, and E-6 have been used in Figure E-7 in place of the more generic manufacturing or construction names. Also, the machine language perspective in Figure E-3 has been omitted, merely because it is not as interesting as the others from an *architectural* point of view.

The one single factor that makes this framework extremely interesting is the fact that each element on either axis of the matrix is explicitly differentiable from all other elements on that one axis. That is, the model of the business (*owner's* perspective) is different from the model of the information system (*designer's* perspective), and so on. (Remember from earlier discussions that these representations are not merely successive levels of increasing detail, but are actually *different* representations—different in content, in meaning, in motivation, in use, etc.) Also, the data description column (entity-relationship-entity) is different from the process description column (input-process-output) and so on. Because each of the elements on either axis is explicitly different from the others, it is possible to define *precisely* what belongs in each cell, and, further, each cell in the matrix will be explicitly different from all the other cells.

	Data description ■ Entity □ Relation	Process description ■ Process □ Input/Output	Network description ■ Node □ Link
Scope description (Ballpark view)	List of entities important to the business ■ Entity = class of business entity	List of processes the business performs ■ Process = class of business process	List of locations in which the business operates ■ Node = business location
Model of the enterprise (Owner's view)	e.g., Entity relationship diagram ■ Entity = business entity □ Relation = business rule	e.g., Functional flow diagram ■ Process = business process □ I/O = business resources	e.g., Logistic network ■ Node = business unit □ Link = business relationship flow
Model of the information system (Designer's view)	e.g., Data model ■ Entity = data entity □ Relation = data relationship	e.g., Data flow diagram ■ Process = application function □ I/O = user views set as data elements	e.g., Distributed systems architecture ■ Node = access □ Link = connection
Technology model (Builder's view)	e.g., Data design ■ Entity = Data □ Relation = Pointer key	e.g., Structure chart ■ Process = computer function □ I/O = screen device formats	e.g., Systems architecture ■ Node = hardware/ system software □ Link = specification
Detailed description (Subcontractor's view)	e.g., Database description ■ Entity = field □ Relation = addresses	e.g., Program ■ Process = language requirements □ I/O = control block	e.g., Network architecture ■ Node = addresses □ Link = protocols
Actual system	Data	Function	Communications

Figure E-7 *Framework for Information Systems Architecture*

E.1.3 Architectural Representations for Describing the Data

To illustrate how each cell differs from all of the others, examine the data description column of Figure E-7. Even though each cell in the column is descriptive type I relating to data, and the descriptive model is *entity-relationship-entity*, the meanings of *entity* and *relationship* change with the different perspectives of the participants in the architecture process. The only exception is the scope description (ballpark) cell, in which entity is defined the same as entity in the model of the business cell. This ballpark perspective is merely a very high level of aggregation, which is being used like the architect's *bubble charts* to establish the gross size and scope of the data strategy, leading to the decision regarding investment of data processing resources in managing data.

Scope/Description (Ballpark Perspective)—Data Column

The scope description cell in the data description column of Figure E-7 could be expected to be a list of all the things that are important to the business and, therefore, that the business manages.

Figure E-8 is an example of an architectural representation in the data description column from the scope description perspective.

• Product	• Policies and procedures
• Part	• Legal requirements
• Supplies	• General ledger accounts
• Equipment	• Accounts payable
• Employee	• Accounts receivable
• Customer	• Long-term debt
• Supplier	• Marketplace
• Competitor	• Promotion
• Building and real estate	• Purchase order
• Objectives	• Customer order
• Job	• Production order
• Organization unit	• Shipment

Figure E-8   *Sample entities*

This representation would be a list of *things* (i.e., material-grammatically, nouns) as opposed to a list of *actions* (i.e., processes-grammatically, verbs). A list of actions (verbs) could be expected in the next column, process description. The list of things (material) in the data description column would be called *entities* in data vernacular.

Since this architectural representation is at the scope description row, one could also expect that the entities (*things*) would likely be entity *classes*—that is, higher levels of aggregations—because the decision being made as a result of this representation would be one of scope, not one of design. A selection would be made of the entity class or classes in which to invest actual information technology (IT) resources for data *inventory* management purposes.

667

Further, in this cell, one might not expect to be definitive about the relationship between entities. The scope decision would constitute overlaying the business values on the total range of possibilities to identify a subset of entity classes for implementation, which is consistent with the resources available for investing in information systems—specifically, in this case, the management of the selected class (or classes) of data. Furthermore, it is useful to start with the total list of entities because, at times, the entities that are not selected are as significant as those that are selected.

The strategy/resource investment decision is made by understanding the values/strategies of the business, which can be done by using various data-gathering/analytical techniques. The decision is made by overlaying the analytical conclusions on the total list of business entities in the scope description cell and thereby selecting the subset of business entities in which to actually invest data processing resources. Since this appendix is intended to define architecture, not to describe strategy methodologies, nothing further will be said about strategic planning, except to point out that similar kinds of decisions have to be made relative to every other scope description cell. That is, out of the total list of business processes, the business likely does not have enough data processing resources to automate all the processes. Therefore, a decision will have to be made to select a subset in which to invest data processing resources for actual automation. By the same token, out of the total list of locations in which the business operates, it probably does not have enough data processing resources to put hardware and software in every location. Again, decisions will have to be made in selecting a subset of locations in which to actually install hardware and software.

These are the strategy/resource investment decisions that are supported by the scope description cells in the top row of Figure E-7. Although they are inextricably related, the probability is that each decision will have to be addressed independently of the others. Discussion now continues on the Framework, particularly the data description column of Figure E-7.

Model of the Business (*Owner's* Perspective)—Data Description Column

Since this model (or description) appears in the data description column, the descriptive model will be *entity-relationship-entity*, and when owners (users) describe the business and say *entity*, what they have in mind are *business* entities.

For example, when *owners* (users) specify an entity such as *employee*, what they have in mind would be real beings—that is, flesh and blood employees who work for the business. That meaning of *employee* is entirely different from the one used in the information systems model (the *designer's* perspective), in which *employee* would refer to a record on a machine, which also happens to be called *employee*, however conceptually and entirely different it is. (This *data* entity, as opposed to *business* entity, would be found in the cell directly below.) Figure E-9 is an example of a model of a *business*, oriented to data.

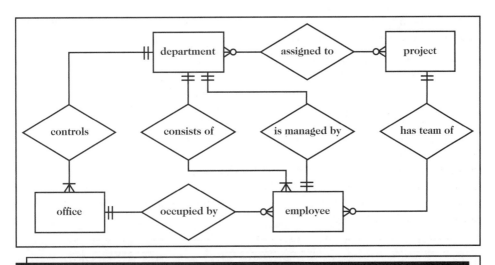

Figure E-9   *Business model*

Further, when *owners*, describing a business, specify a relationship between the entities, what they have in mind would be the business rule or strategy that relates one entity to another entity. A business rule or strategy, for example, might be, *In this business we ship this product from that warehouse only*. An entirely different rule would be, *In this business, we ship this product from any warehouse*. These are business rules, not data relationships, such as would be expected in the model of the information system (*designer's* perspective) in the cell below the model of the business, shown in Figure E-9.

Finding good, *real-life* examples that illustrate crisply each of the architectural representations is difficult. There are two reasons for this difficulty. First, when the real-life representations were being developed, no framework existed to clearly define and differentiate one representation from the others. Therefore, many real-life illustrations are a mixture of representations, both conceptually (e.g., business entities and data entities get mixed together) and physically (e.g., entities and inputs/outputs—that is, user views from the process description column of Figure E-7—get mixed together). Second, real-life examples are hard to understand because it is not always clear what model, or cell, the author had in mind when developing the representation.

This difficulty is illustrated in Figure E-9. It is clear that this model is describing *data*, not *process*, but the question is, did the author have in mind a description of a *business* or a description of an *information system*? In this case, it is likely that the description is of a business because of the existence of the *many-to-many* relationships. In real life, there are lots of *many-to-many* relationships, but the database management concepts that are popular today require that the *many-to-many* relationships be resolved in order to run on a machine. Therefore, *artificial* entities have to be created to resolve the *many-to-many* relationships, and the model in Figure E-9 would have to be *normalized* before it could be a legitimate model of an information system. In any case, since the model in Figure E-9 is not *normalized*, by today's standards, at least, it is clearly a model of a business as opposed to a model of an information system.

Model of an Information System (*Designer's* Perspective)—Data Description Column

Once again, since the model of the information system is in the data description column of the Framework, the descriptive model used is *entity-relationship-entity*. But from the *designer's* perspective, the meaning of *entity* would change to that of a record on a machine, and relationship would change to that of a data relationship. Clearly, the example in Figure E-10 is a model of an information system, not a model of a business, because of the existence of *artificial* entities, specifically the *department_project* entity (resulting from the concatenation of department and project), which is not a real-life item, but something in an information system, created in the process of translating the business description into an information systems *product*. In the data design vernacular, this example of Figure E-10 would likely be called a data model.

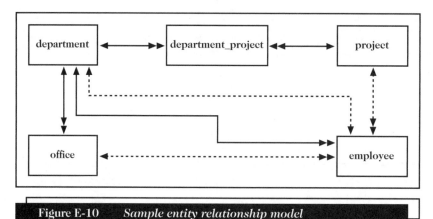

Figure E-10   *Sample entity relationship model*

Technology Model (*Builder's* Perspective)—Data Description Column

As in the previously described cells, the descriptive model in the *builder's* cell is *entity-relationship-entity*, and what could be expected is the physical implementation or data design for the conceptual model of the information system.

In the technology model, the laws of nature and technology constraints are being applied. A decision is made to use Oracle, IBM's DB2 UDB, or XYZ, and depending on the choice, the meaning of entity and relationship change. In the case of a hierarchical database like IBM's IMS, entity means *segment* and relationship means *pointer*. In the case of Oracle and DB2 UDB, entity means *row* and relationship means *key*, etc. Figure E-11 is an example of an architectural representation of the technology model (*builder's* perspective) in the data description column of the Framework.

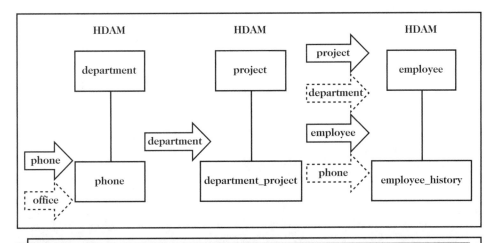

Detailed Description (Out-of-Context Perspective)—Data Description Column

The descriptive model is *entity-relationship-entity* in the detailed description cell. This cell is analogous to the *subcontractor's* out-of-context descriptions. What could be expected is Data Definition Language. An example might be an IMS DBDGEN in which the entities are specifications of the *fields* and relationships are specifications of the *addresses*. An example is shown in Figure E-12.

This description is *compiled* to produce the machine language representation (relative addressing—not shown in the figure), which is further *link-edited* to produce the actual physical data (absolute addressing) residing in the machine. It is clear that real-life examples can be found to illustrate all of the architectural representations for the various viewpoints or perspectives that are created for the data (or material) description of the information system.

Although actual samples (figures) for each of the remaining cells are available, no attempt will be made to include them in this paper. Let it be sufficient merely to describe how the meanings of the descriptive model terms change in the remaining two columns as the representations shift from perspective to perspective.

```
IMS DBDGEN sample statements

DBD
        NAME=STDCDBP,           Database description name             X
        ACCESS=HDAM,            Hierarchical direct                  X
        RMNAME=(DLZHDC10,       Randomizing routine phasename        X
        3,                      Root anchor points per block         X
        100,                    Root address area hi relative block  X
        600)                    Insert bytes limit for RAA           X

Dataset
        DD1=STDCDBC,            Filename                             X
        DEVICE=3380,            Disk device                          X
        BLOCK=(2048),           VSAM control internal size           X
        SCAN=2                  Number cylinders scan for insert space X

SEGM
        NAME=STSCCST,           Segment name for employee name/address X
        PARENT=0,               It is a root segment                 X
        BYTES=106,              Data length                          X
        POINTER=TWIN            Physical twin forward only           X

Field
        NAME=(STQCCNO,SEQ,U),   Unique key field (employee number)   X
        BYTES=6,                Field length                         X
        START=1,                Where it starts in segment           X
        TYPE=C                  Alphanumeric data                    X
```

Figure E-12   *Sample DL/I physical model*

E.1.4 Architectural Representations for Describing the Process

The descriptive model for describing the process is *input-process-output*, and, as in the case of the data description column, each of the representations in the different cells in the process description column of Figure E-7 has different meanings associated with *input*, *process*, and *output*.

At the scope description (ballpark perspective) cell, *process* would mean business process. It would likely be some process *class*, a relatively high level of aggregation, as the decision being made from the scope description cell is the selection of some subset of the appropriate business processes in which to invest some finite amount of information systems resources for actual automation purposes. Further, in making the scope decision, it is unnecessary to be definitive about the input and output linkages between the functions by overlaying the business values against the total range of automation possibilities. Therefore, just a list of business processes would be expected in this cell representation.

In the model of the business (*owner's* perspective) in the process description column, an example might be a functional flow diagram in which *process* would be a *business* process (not an information systems process) and inputs and outputs would be business resources such as people, cash, material, product, etc.

In the model of the information system (*designer's* perspective) for the process description column, an example would be a data flow diagram in which processes are information systems (application) processes (not business processes) and the inputs/outputs are *user views*—some aggregations of data elements that flow into and out of the application processes, connecting them in some sequential fashion.

672

(Note that this does not preclude depicting manual functions that are introduced as part of the information system.)

Proceeding to the technology model (*builder's* perspective)—process description column, we see that the meaning of *input-process-output* changes once again. In applying the physical constraints of the technology chosen for implementation—for example: hard drives versus DVD drives, Web-based transaction monitor versus non-Web-based transaction monitor, C++ versus Java; WAP devices versus personal computers, etc.—the builder's perception of a process becomes a computer function, and inputs and outputs are device formats. The predictable example would be a structure chart and screen/device formats.

For the detailed description (out-of-context) cell, the example is a *program* in which *process* is a language statement and the inputs and outputs are control blocks.

The program is compiled to produce object code, the machine language representation (not shown in Figure E-7), which, in turn, is assembled to produce running instructions for the actual, physical system.

Again, it is clear that examples can be found for every descriptive representation for the process description column, as well as for the data description column.

E.1.5 Architectural Representations for Describing the Network

The descriptive model for the network set of architectural representations in the network description column of Figure E-7 is *node-line-node*.

From the scope description (ballpark) perspective, what could be expected is a list of locations in which the business operates. Therefore, *node* would mean business location, likely at a high level of aggregation—that is, showing little detail about the *contents* of the location. The locations might even be arranged on a map, a geographical construct. If lines were shown, they would probably merely indicate where there are communication or logistics connections between the locations. The purpose served, once again, is the strategy/resource investment decision in which the main decision is to select the subset of locations in which to actually locate technology (hardware/software).

The *owner*, in describing the business—that is, producing the model of the business as related to the network (or the connectivity characteristics of the business)—would perceive the *nodes* to be business units, an aggregation of business resources (people, facilities, responsibilities, etc.) at some geographical location. The lines would represent logistics connections or flows, probably including communication linkages, but even more basically, would represent the distribution structure or logistics network along which communication takes place.

In the model of the information system (the *designer's* perspective) for the network description, the information system designer would perceive the node to be some IT function, like a processor, storage unit, or access point. This would be a conceptual representation, independent of specific technology that would be introduced in the *builder's* cell. The line, from a *designer's* standpoint, would be a communication line at the conceptual level, such as a leased line, dial-up service, or U.S. mail. This cell would serve the purpose of making the *distributed systems* decisions—that is, specifying where the IT facilities would be installed, which of them would be connected, and by what type of connection.

673

The technology constraints would be introduced in the technology model (the *builder's* perspective). This cell would depict physical hardware and software—for example, a mainframe processor, WAP device, personal computer, Linux operating system, or TCP/IP at the nodes, and Synchronous Data Link Control (SDLC), bisynchronous communications, 56K baud, etc. for the lines.

In the detailed description (out-of-context) cell, the nodes would be addresses, and the lines would be protocols.

In summary, although actual pictures have not been included in the paper, examples could be presented to illustrate every hypothetical architectural representation postulated by the relationship among the various architectural perspectives and the different types of descriptions.

E.1.6 Conclusions

When the question is asked, "What is information systems architecture?" the answer is, "There is no information systems architecture, but a set of them!" Architecture is relative. What you think architecture is depends on what you are doing. For an example, see Figure E-13.

If you are a:	Then you probably think architecture is a:
Programmer	Structure chart
Database administrator	Data design
Analyst	Data flow diagram
Planner	Combination of entity/relationship diagrams or functional flow diagrams
Communications manager	Business logistics infrastructure or distributed systems architecture
Operations manager	System architecture
Network administrator	Network architecture
Program support representative	Detailed data and program descriptions
Computer designer	Machine language
President	Entity classes, process classes, or map

Figure E-13   *Sample detailed description*

We are having difficulties communicating with one another about information systems architecture because a *set* of architectural representations exists, instead of a *single* architecture. One is not right and another wrong. The architectures are different. They are additive and complementary. There are reasons for electing to expend the resources for developing each architectural representation. And there are risks associated with not developing any one of the architectural representations.

Research is being done to create more explicit definitions for each of the architectural representations in this Framework, to understand the design issues, the reasons for developing each representation, the risks associated with not developing any one, and the *tool* implications of each cell.

E.1.7 Summary

In summary, by studying fields of endeavor external to the information systems community, specifically those professions involved in producing complex engineering products (e.g., architecture/construction, manufacturing, etc.), it is possible to hypothesize by analogy a set of architectural representations for information systems.

The resultant *framework for information systems architecture* could prove quite valuable for:

- Improving professional communication within the information systems community
- Understanding the reasons for and risks of not developing any one architectural representation
- Placing a wide variety of tools and/or methodologies in relation to one another
- Developing improved approaches (including methodologies and tools) to produce each of the architectural representations, as well as possibly rethinking the nature of the classic *application development process*, as we know it today

What WHERE WHO

HOW WHEN

Why

AFTERWORD

The authors would like to acknowledge the assistance of John Zachman in the preparation of this textbook. John graciously reviewed our textbook, chapter by chapter.

He allowed us to review early manuscripts of his book, *The Zachman Framework for Enterprise Architecture—Primer for Enterprise Engineering and Manufacturing*.

Over the years, John has kindly shared his knowledge and given his friendship. Through personal conversations, conference presentations, and published works, John has provided us with invaluable information. The contents of this book have been both directly and indirectly influenced and adapted from John's teachings and his work.

Each of us has filters; we select what comes in and what goes out. Although we, the authors, have taught and used this subject matter in our professional lives, the concepts and ideas expressed in this textbook are the result of our experiences, perceptions, and understanding. We sincerely hope our message is in alignment with our teacher, John Zachman. Any errors in translation are our own.

GLOSSARY

"Words are meaningless. It is the way they are said that gives them meaning."

— *Unknown*

"It's only words, and words are all I have..."

— *The Bee Gees, pop singing group*

80 hour rule A basis for detailed estimating, planning, and measuring work and performance by requiring a project to be broken down into tasks of 80 contiguous hours or less (work to be concluded in two business weeks)—resulting in a tangible product, work product, or deliverable.

80/20 rule Developed by an Italian economist, Vilfredo Pareto, the management application of this rule states that 20 percent of an effort generates 80 percent of the results. The implication is that 80 percent of the effort produces 20 percent of the results. Therefore, most of the effort extended produces minimal results.

A

Abstraction A representation of the real thing. The representation is the result of an intersection between one or more perspectives and one or more aspects. The intersection can yield multiple abstract representations. The representation can be persisted, verbalized, or just thought.

Acceptance criteria A definition of what is *good enough* that is established in advance and helps determine whether the product being delivered is *good enough*. For example, a development team uses the criteria definition to design correct application functions, and the customer uses the criteria definition to decide whether the application matches what was requested.

Accountability Being held responsible for an assigned action.

Agent of action A person who commands respect and has the tenacity to implement a solution.

Agent of change A person who commands respect and has the drive to create paradigm shifts.

Agile life cycle A people-oriented approach that is responsive to the rapid development of a product.

Alignment A desired end state whereby the owner's desires and the implementations of the enterprise are the same. Alignment is a qualitative objective.

Annual cycle A period of time (one year) in which an organization makes operational decisions.

Aperiodic behavior Behavior that never repeats itself and continues to manifest the effects of any small agitation.

Application program A series of tasks executed on a computer.

Architected Jargon meaning to create a *functioning enterprise* by means of a design that was holistically thought about by a *designer*. The *designer's* design helped provide a framework for the construction work that followed.

Architecture The design of any type of structure whether physical or conceptual, real or virtual. In the context of the Framework, the collective designs of each perspective when modeled at a normalized and primitive level. *See also* Normalized and Primitive model.

Artifact A thing created by a person that is important to an enterprise. Also a formal representation of a primitive or composite. An artifact can use any type of medium including print, video, audio, or verbal communication. The chosen media may contain a formal notation, an informal notation, pictures, diagrams, or models.

Aspect The label for the *x*-axis on the Framework. An aspect represents the six columns of the Framework—*what, how, where, who, when,* and *why*. See *also* Column.

Aspect alias A generic topic for a column, such as data for *what* and process for *how*.

Asset *See* Column 1.

Asset management Overseeing the physical and intellectual property of an organization.

Associated Credit Bureaus of America An organization that allows members to share consumer information, allowing them to better handle risk.

Assumption A decision to produce an artifact based on unproven or non-validated data, information, or knowledge.

Attractor The preferred position for a system that helps uncover the structure of chaos. In Zachman DNA, strange attractors help govern what happens during software development.

Authentication Identity verification.

B

Back office computers Computers that are used for administrative functions that support, but are not directly involved in, business operations.

Back-end A two-part classification system in which companies can separate independent processes. For example, reporting month-end sales is independent from taking an order. Stopping replenishment may be an independent activity in one company, but a dependent activity in another company. The first company then classifies replenishment as a back-end activity, while the second company classifies replenishment as a front-end activity. *See also* Front-end.

Bad debt An expense created when someone buys a product or service on credit and then does not pay the money owed within the required time frame.

Balanced Scorecard An analysis technique that translates the organization's mission and strategies into quantifiable goals, and measures achievement of these goals.

Best practices The belief that a set of techniques can provide optimum benefits when used in an appropriate context.

Beta testing Pre-release version of software where potential users try out the product.

Bill of materials A list of parts in a specific hierarchical sequence, containing the product and every assembly and subassembly, down to the smallest part used.

Bit The smallest unit of data in a computer binary digit.

Bleeding-edge Refers to organizations that are early adopters of new technology, prior to proven reliability and accuracy.

Builder *See* Row 4.

Building process *See* Column 2.

Bursty Describes a Web site that is prone to unpredictable spikes of user traffic.

Business contention A struggle to accomplish an end, involving disagreement or controversy.

Business cycle A set of periodic swings in an economy's pace of demand and production activity.

Business logic Code that shapes what an application can and cannot do, and the parameters within which the application works.

Business model *See* Conceptual model.

Business objective The observable, measurable goal, which states the conditions under which a goal should be achieved and the level of expected performance.

Business requirement A need or desire. Usually refers to the needs of a business that drive the technology.

Butterfly effect Sensitive dependence on initial conditions. Relates to cause and effect where even a minor change in one variable can have a major impact on another variable.

Byte A series of contiguous bits.

C

Capability maturity model (CMM) Five levels of competency used to certify demonstrated competencies of an organization or project. CMM was created by the Software Engineering Institute of Carnegie Melon University.

Capacity planning A process used to determine the appropriate amount of hardware that a project needs.

CASE tool A computer-aided software engineering tool that can assist all facets of the software development life cycle.

Causal loop A closed loop of cause and effect links that show how variables in a system are related.

Cause and effect A situation where one variable affects another variable.

Cell The classification schema of six perspectives and six aspects create 36 primitive intersections in the Framework. Each primitive intersection is known as a cell.

CEO *See* Chief Executive Officer.

Certificate authority An organization that generates and validates secure keys that establish identity across computer networks.

Chain of events A description of each step or stage involved in an outcome.

Change procedure Formal steps for managing any type of alterations in a project.

Chaos Unstable or aperiodic behavior where a change in one variable may not produce a proportional change or reaction in the related variables.

Chaos theory A qualitative study of a dynamic system concentrating on behavior that is unstable or aperiodic.

Chief Executive Officer (CEO) The person who is usually the highest-ranking member of an organization. The person who is responsible for quarterly results.

Chief Information Officer (CIO) The person typically responsible for a company's information systems, which might include technology direction, IT budget, IT quality management, software, hardware, networks, data centers, people, air conditioners, and vendor relationships.

CIO *See* Chief Information Officer.

Classification schema A system of organization.

Classification system A consistent method of labeling and organizing.

Clinger-Cohen Act Public Law 104-106, passed in 1996, intended to improve the productivity, efficiency, and effectiveness of federal programs through the improved acquisition, use, and disposal of IT resources.

Closed loop *See* Causal loop.

CMM *See* Capability maturity model.

Column One of the dimensions on the Zachman Framework's classification schema. The column is a vertical plane on the Framework (x-axis). The Framework contains a total of six columns. Each column represents an interrogative of the English language—*what, how, where, who, when,* and *why*. The columns are also known as aspects. The order of the columns is a presentation sequence and not a sequence of work.

Column 1 The first vertical plane on the Framework. The column or aspect represents the interrogative *what*. The *what* aspect represents things of interest such as material composition and structure. Things of interest to an enterprise are often items that need to be counted like employees, office buildings, and products. Things of interest do not have to be physical objects, for example, they could be a social security number or the status of an item to be delivered. The column is abbreviated as C1.

Column 2 The second vertical plane on the Framework. The column or aspect represents the interrogative *how*. The *how* aspect represents processes including functional specifications and transformations. Processes normally have an input and yield an output. Processes transform an input into an output. For example, the calculation of an individual's payroll tax may use current earnings and tax rate tables to produce monies owed to a taxation authority. The column is abbreviated as C2.

Column 3 The third vertical plane on the Framework. The column or aspect represents the interrogative *where*. The *where* aspect represents networks such as spatial descriptions and information flows. Networks provide the connectivity to communicate across locations no matter how close or far apart. Each location is a node that may have a physical or a virtual link to another node. The column is abbreviated as C3.

Column 4 The fourth vertical plane on the Framework. The column or aspect represents the interrogative *who*. The *who* aspect represents people and includes organizational descriptions and operations. People or organizations are often responsible for work to be performed and are integral in establishing a workflow. The column is abbreviated as C4.

Column 5 The fifth vertical plane on the Framework. The column or aspect represents the interrogative *when*. The *when* aspect represents timing such as life cycles and dynamics. Most business events are triggered by something. An event is a state of the business at a point in time. Timing involves *when* something happens relative to something else. The column is abbreviated as C5.

Column 6 The sixth vertical plane on the Framework. The column or aspect represents the interrogative *why*. The *why* aspect represents motivation such as purpose or targets. Motivation includes items such as goals, objectives, strategies, tactics, and business rules. Each of these things are included in an enterprise's ends and means. The column is abbreviated as C6.

Commercial off-the-shelf (COTS) software Prewritten purchased software, available to any enterprise.

Communication An exchange of thoughts, messages, or information between people or machines.

Competition Companies or people capable of vying for market share in any marketplace.

Componentize The process of organizing complex objects into discrete and manageable segments.

Composite An artifact that includes abstractions (representations) from more than one cell. Two or more relationships between cells of the Framework.

Composite model The representation of an artifact that is not primitive. A composite is an artifact that includes representations from more than one cell. The representations in a composite from multiple cells may be distinguishable or indistinguishable and any relationship between them may be implicitly or explicitly depicted.

Comprehensive The complete set of six perspectives and the six aspects relative to a description of the enterprise.

Compromise An agreement made through mutual concession.

Computer programmer A person capable of creating software.

Conceptual model A representation of the real thing often depicted in a common non-technical language (writing system). In the Framework, conceptual models are associated with the *owner's* perspective—Row 2.

Conceptualize *See* Mental model.

Concurrent development A concept that acknowledges that multiple efforts can occur at the same time for multiple end states.

Connectivity *See* Column 3.

Consensus A collective agreement to move forward or take action even if that action is not the preference of all participating members.

Constraint Something that limits, influences, or controls behavior.

Consumer An individual who purchases goods and services without intending to sell them.

Consumer authentication Identifying an anonymous individual on the Internet, thereby removing anonymity.

Contention Struggle or argument toward an end.

683

Context A situation or orientation that aids in understanding an issue or topic. The context for understanding may come from something outside the actual domain of interest.

Contextual view A perspective that considers the complete problem area relative to a single perspective.

Convention In the context of Zachman DNA, an attractor that represents the normal or regular way of moving forward.

Core dump Copying the contents of random access memory to permanent storage.

Core system A system that is critical to the daily operation of the business.

Corporate culture Attitudes, values, beliefs, and traditions of a corporation.

Corporation Any legal entity that represents a business enterprise.

Cost In the context of Zachman DNA, an attractor that indicates a willingness to accept a financial burden.

COTS software *See* Commercial off-the-shelf software.

CPM *See* Critical path method.

Credit Willingness of a lender to provide the borrower a sum of money because the lender has confidence in a borrower's *ability* and *intention* to fulfill financial obligation.

Critical mass An amount needed to take a course of action. For example, a predetermined number of clients, projects, or revenue needed to support the growth of an organization in a specific area.

Critical path method (CPM) A technique used in project management that predicts the total length of a project, highlighting the longest sequence of dependent tasks that lead to project completion.

Culture The attitudes, values, beliefs, and traditions of an individual, organization, or location.

Culture shock The reaction of an individual unfamiliar with social customs of an organization or location.

Current state The present condition derived from a course of action.

Customer relationship management A system that identifies traits, activities, and situations between a company and those who buy its products or services.

D

Dashmat A pad that creates an acoustic barrier between the engine compartment and the passenger compartment of the Dodge Neon.

Data *See* Column 1.

Data archaeologist One who searches old records, documentation, tapes, and observations to find things of interest.

Data center A location for housing computers with fire and security control systems.

Data modeling A technique for documenting an enterprise's data structures.

Database A collection of interrelated files.

Database server A computer dedicated to managing data and information.

Deliverable A product or work product produced as part of a project.

Demilitarized zone (DMZ) A security perimeter network that can be used to separate an organization's applications from the firewall.

Demographic information Information gathered from a statistical study of the characteristics of a group of people and their behaviors.

Denormalization In the context of the Framework, a composite model where the concepts of multiple cells have been combined without the underlying primitives. In the context of a single Framework cell, a model that allows a fact or behavior to occur in more than one place.

Denormalizing A process for reducing the degree of normalization, usually associated with an intent to improve performance.

Depth iNtegrating Architecture *See* Zachman DNA.

Descriptive representation A synonym for a persistent artifact.

Designer *See* Row 3.

Detail In the context of Zachman DNA, an attractor that indicates the explicit level of knowledge known and recorded about the work at hand.

Detail sliver The representation of the amount of significant information (level of detail) found in an artifact.

Detailed representation *See* Row 5.

Digital certificate An electronic document that contains information about a computer, verifying identification and indicating that the machine belongs to a certain organization.

Digital signature A code that verifies and guarantees the sender's machine is the sender's machine.

Disaster recovery plan A list of actions or the action an organization will take prior to and in the event of a disaster. Part of the business continuity plan.

Dishonored check A check not paid by the bank on which the check is drawn, usually due to insufficient funds available.

DMZ *See* Demilitarized zone.

DNA An acronym normally associated with deoxyribonucleic acid—the double helix, the building block of life. DNA is part of an analogy used to explain Zachman DNA, the building block of the enterprise.

Documentation A testimony of how you believe something to be.

Domain An area of interest with well-defined boundaries. A domain may contain other domains. For example, natural science is an area of interest. Natural science also includes other areas of interest with well-defined boundaries such as physics, chemistry, and biology. In business, General Motors is a single domain enterprise that contains many other domains such as Cadillac, Opel, ACDelco, and Hughes Electronics Corporation. Cadillac itself also contains other domains such as purchasing, and distribution.

Driver A program that interacts with a hardware device or a special type of software.

Dynamical system Anything that evolves, changes, or moves in time.

E

Early binding A strategy or stipulation that creates a restriction for action.

Embedded Framework In the context of Zachman DNA, the six-by-six-by-six cube for each discipline that resides in each cell.

Emergence Appearance of a property or feature not previously observed as a functional characteristic of a system.

Emergent system property An additional behavior resulting from varying configurations occurring due to conditional looping, if-then-else logic, case statements, branch conditions, triggers, overloading, and system events. For example, bugs in a system may not be attributable to one application alone.

Emotional filter A personal mechanism that establishes individual constraints that influence understanding and communication.

Empathic listening The skill of being a good listener, including listening for purpose, main points, evaluation, application, and value.

End A result derived from a course of action.

End state A future condition derived from a course of action.

Enterprise A group of people organized for a particular purpose to produce a product or provide a service.

Enterprise application integration A software solution used to resolve disparate and stovepipe systems.

Enterprise architect A senior designer whose skills blend all forms of IT architecture and disciplines.

Enterprise architecture The ability to understand and to reason the continual needs of integration, alignment, change, and responsiveness of the business to technology and to the marketplace through the development of models and diagrams.

Enterprise Engineering and Manufacturing In developing a software-driven *functioning enterprise*, Row 5 represents the manufacturing and Rows 1 through 4 represent the engineering.

Enterprise resource planning system (ERP) A system to manage every operation of an enterprise value chain to minimize the cost and time of getting products to customers.

Enterprise wide integration The continuity of all knowledge occurring across each perspective and aspect of the Framework.

Entropy An inverse measure of a system's capacity for change. For example, the more entropy, the less the system is capable of changing. Entropy acts as an overall drain on the capability of the system.

Environmental ethics Concerns that affect the choice to conscientiously adhere to sound business practices for one's immediate and extended surroundings.

Environmental physics Conditions that affect an enterprise's ability to conduct business, such as topography, location idiosyncrasies, and weather.

ERP *See* Enterprise resource planning system.

Ethics Rules or standards under which a person or an organization operates.

Event An occurrence, activity, or point in time independent of another occurrence, activity, or point in time.

Event-driven A type of action to be taken or decision to be made as a result of a previous outcome.

Evergreening Jargon used to denote the continuation and possible improvement of a practice or discipline.

Evolutionary life cycle method A method that accommodates incremental development, using experience from earlier increments to help define requirements for subsequent increments.

Excruciating detail *See* Excruciating level of detail.

Excruciating level of detail The contents of an artifact being complete in all respects. Often excruciating level of detail is subjective and its completeness is determined by the perception of the person producing the artifact and the target audience of the artifact. A level achieved when the user of the artifact is satisfied that the contents of the artifact are complete (including explicitness, answers, justifications, and rationale).

Expense Part of the cost of doing business.

Explicit Fully and clearly defined or expressed; readily observable. *See also* Implicit.

External customer An organization or people that can and will buy the products or services of another organization.

External influence A situation for which you have no direct control that requires a course of action.

F

Federated mechanisms A distribution of nodes that have a high degree of local autonomy.

Federated system *See* Heterogeneous database.

Finite Something that can be quantified.

Firewall Software or hardware used to prevent unauthorized access to networks, systems, and Internet/intranet sites.

Five whys An exercise that helps uncover the deeper roots of a problem.

Fortune 1000 An annual list of the 1,000 largest corporations in the U.S., published by *Fortune* magazine. Size is ranked according to metrics such as revenues, market values, and profit.

Forward engineering A direction of work within a given life cycle or methodology where the major sequence of activities is conducted in a manner of composition rather than decomposition.

Fractal A geometric pattern that is repeated in smaller and smaller segments.

Frame A personal image or perspective from which to gather information, make judgments, and determine how best to get things done.

framework A set of assumptions, concepts, values, and practices that constitutes a way of viewing reality. *See also* Framework.

Framework An informal name of the Zachman Framework for Enterprise Architecture.

Framework subset A picture of the Framework showing less than the full classification schema. The full classification schema has six rows and six columns. A Framework subset does not show all the rows and columns.

Front-end A two-part classification system in which companies can separate independent processes. For example, taking an order is independent from waiting for month-end reporting. Stopping replenishment may be an independent activity in one company, but a dependent activity in another company. The result is that the first company classifies replenishment as a back-end activity, while the second company classifies replenishment as a front-end activity. *See also* Back-end.

Function point A measure of the size of computer applications and the projects that build them. For example, function points measure functionality by objectively measuring functional requirements, independent of any computer language, development methodology, technology, or capability of the development project team.

Functional specification A description of how something should work.

Functioning enterprise *See* Row 6.

G

Gantt chart A timeline used in project management that lists activities and dates for start and completion.

Global 2000 companies An annual list of the 2,000 largest corporations in the world, published by *Fortune* magazine. Size is ranked according to metrics such as revenues, market values, and profit.

Global positioning system (GPS) A system made up of satellites, computers, and receivers that can determine a position on Earth.

Goal The purpose toward which an effort is directed, but which cannot be quantitatively measured.

GPS *See* Global positioning system.

Great Depression A long period of unemployment and business failures caused by a stock market crash in the U.S. in 1929.

H

Heterogeneous database A distributed database with local autonomy, where every node in the system has its own local users, applications, and data and connects to other nodes only for additional data.

Hidden agenda A concealed plan or motivation.

History In the context of Zachman DNA, an attractor representing the foundation upon which the present predicament was built, providing an opportunity to learn how you arrived where you are today.

Holiday cycle A period of time (days normally selected by a governing or religious body) in which an organization makes alternative operational decisions.

Holistic view An attempt to take into account all major and possibly all minor elements for a solution in a given domain.

Homogeneous database A distributed database that uses the same database software and has the same applications on each node.

Horizontal integration The continuity of all knowledge occurring across a single perspective of the Framework.

How *See* Column 2.

Human resource manager An individual who works toward matching the needs of people with the needs of the organization.

Human resources A person or persons available to undertake a task within an organization.

I

Icon A visual representation of the type of primitive model appearing in a cell of the Framework.

Implicit Not fully or clearly defined and expressed. Not readily observable. *See also* Explicit.

Incremental model Development that begins with overall architecture and cycles to continuously add or improve functionality.

Industrial engineering Production of goods that considers the elements of design (Row 1, Row 2, Row 3, Row 4, Row 5) and implementation (Row 6), and the management of materials and energy (Column 1), processes (Column 2), location, plant, communication (Column 3), integration of workers (Column 4), business events (Column 5), and strategies and rules (Column 6) within the overall system. This is why the Framework supports engineering and manufacturing of the enterprise.

Industrial psychology Deals with management of workers and problems in the workplace environment.

Infinite Something that cannot be quantified.

Information Data or raw facts with context and perspective.

Information Age The current era, beginning around the late 1960s or early 1970s, during which computers and networks publish, consume, and manipulate information. Transition from the Industrial Age to the Information Age might originate as early as World War II, and could lead to the Age of Knowledge and Understanding.

Information persistence The reinforcement of ideas within a person's consciousness through the visual display of words, symbols, models, and objects.

Information technology The planning, building, and managing of computer hardware, networks, and software.

Infrastructure The necessary components of an enterprise, both tangible and intangible, which help support its productivity. The outsider is often unaware of the infrastructure.

Integrated enterprise solution A new product or service that fits seamlessly into the organization.

Initial public offering An enterprise's first proposal to sell stock to the public.

Intangible Something that cannot be readily defined or be given a monetary value, such as feelings or dedication.

Integration Continuity between artifacts that create a consistent interpretation of the enterprise.

Intellectual capital Knowledge held by an individual regarding menial to complex tasks carried out in the enterprise. Brainpower.

Internal audits Self-directed procedures and standards used for validation and verification of a business' measurements. For example, the internal audit can authenticate accounting practices, inventory, employee hours, and adherence to operating procedures.

Internal customer Within an organization, a person or department that uses or buys the products or services of the organization.

Internal influence A situation that you control and that requires a course of action.

Internet time The indication that something must happen within a few minutes rather than days, weeks, or years.

Interorganizational communication The process of information being transmitted from one organization to another, which encourages alignment and integration of business operations.

Interrogative Six questions of the English language needed to establish a common understanding: *what*, *how*, *where*, *who*, *when*, and *why*. *See also* Column.

Intrusion In the context of DNA, an attractor representing a situation or condition the business encounters, but over which the business has no control, such as new legislation or changing technology.

Intrusion detection system A security device that monitors the network and can detect, log, and stop unauthorized access when a breach occurs.

Inventory The finished and unfinished products, raw materials, and unsold merchandise held by a company.

ISO-9000 Standards that define, establish, and maintain an effective quality

689

system for manufacturing and service industries.

IT outsourcing When a company buys software, hardware, or people services from another company for one or more projects.

J

JAD session *See* Joint application development session.

JIT delivery *See* Just-in-time delivery.

Joint application development (JAD) session A structured and formal meeting of both users and IT professionals to determine the design and requirements of the application.

Joint venture The collection of two or more people or organizations to create an enterprise where involved parties share profit and loss for a specific purpose and duration.

Just in time An inventory control practice for a manufacturing process in which there is little or no manufacturing material inventory on hand at the manufacturing site, thus saving inventory costs for parts, sub parts, and raw materials and improving cash flow.

Just-in-time (JIT) delivery The practice where assembly lines receive frequent deliveries of parts and materials in small lots timed to production, saving the manufacturer inventory carrying costs.

K

Keep the lights on (KTLO) The minimal amount of support and services required to keep an organization operational.

Kludge A make-do, or less than desirable, solution to a problem.

Knowledge Information with guidance for action.

Knowledge management system A system that captures, catalogs, retains, and retrieves data and information with the intent of benefiting decision-making.

Knowledge worker An individual who contributes to the transformation and commerce of information. Peter Drucker introduced the term in his 1959 book, *Landmarks of Tomorrow*.

KTLO *See* Keep the lights on.

L

Late binding A strategy or stipulation that allows flexible action.

Latency A measure of time between actions when seemingly nothing is happening, such as the wait time in a computer system or network.

Leading edge Organizations that adapt quickly to proven new technologies.

Lean manufacturing Reducing the waste from the customer's order to the customer's receipt of that order by eliminating unnecessary steps in the production stream.

Life cycle The formal processes involved from the beginning to end of anything, frequently divided into phases, with specific activities and deliverables produced from those activities.

Life cycle of the project *See* Life cycle.

Lights out A fully automated data center where day-to-day human activity is unnecessary.

Location *See* Column 3.

Logical model A representation of the real thing in an optimal form often depicted in a technical language (writing system). In the Framework, logical models are associated with the *designer's* perspective—Row 3.

Logistics *See* Column 5.

M

Mandate A delegated order that must be followed. The act of giving an authoritative instruction.

Market share The proportion of industry sales of a good or service that is controlled by a company.

Marketplace World of commercial activity that defines and identifies buyers and sellers.

Materials Things needed to make something or accomplish a task.

Materials management Governance to ensure the right thing (Column 1) is getting done in the right place (Column 3) at the right time (Column 5) by the right people (Column 4) for the right reason (Column 6) using the right method (Column 2).

Means The course of action taken to get something done. How the *ends* gets accomplished.

Measurement The result of applying a metric in which the result has been given context by a unit of measure.

Measuring stick A tool to enumerate something of interest.

Mental model Representations in the mind of real or imaginary situations.

Meta A prefix that means *a definition of something* and is used to describe characteristics of the suffix.

Metalinguistics The characteristics of interrelationships between language and other cultural behaviors.

Metamodel Characteristics that describe other models. A model is a specific type of artifact.

Metarule Characteristics that describe rules. Often a rule is a statement made to direct or constrain behavior.

Method of practice An approach taken by a person or organization to create something. A method of practice may be influenced by or related to a domain, standards body, legislative mandate, personal preference, or experience.

Methodology A list of practices, procedures, and rules used by those who work in a discipline.

Metrics The practice of measuring activities.

Mine To analyze to discover facts, patterns, and relationships.

Misassumption A past, present, or future situation taken as truth, with the intent of making a decision based on that truth and later discovering it to be false.

Mission The overall directive for shaping the means to achieve the vision. For example, if your vision is to be the best soft drink seller, your mission might be to provide a range of soft drink products that have an overall preferred taste.

Mission critical Necessary to the daily operation and survival of the business.

Model A specific type of artifact that is usually produced using a formal descriptive notation. A model can contain just text, or text accompanied by a diagram.

Motivation *See* Column 6.

Myers-Briggs Type Indicator A psychological instrument that explains personality differences in scientific and reliable terms, according to Jung's theory of personality preferences.

N

NAT *See* Network address translation.

Network *See* Column 3.

Network address translation (NAT) A protocol that often comes with firewalls and helps secure internal networks by allowing private IP addresses inside an organization to be translated into different legal external public addresses.

Non-repudiation An attribute of a secure system that prevents the sender of a message from claiming a message was not sent.

Normalization The idea that for a single perspective a single fact is only modeled in one place. Therefore, the same fact may occur (and probably will occur) for multiple perspectives.

Normalized Redundancy has been minimized and integrity has been improved.

Normalized architectural artifacts A collection of persistent artifacts where each is primitive in nature and each artifact is based on one of the cells of the Framework.

Noun/verb A thing (noun) or action (verb). The noun/verb is also known as a primitive component. Each cell has a basic noun-verb-noun structure for the primitive model.

O

Objective A statement to reach a desired result through a quantitative measurement.

Object-oriented technique The analysis, design, or solution for a problem that uses a specific approach whose traits include polymorphism and encapsulation.

Opportunity The culmination of the *cosmic forces* (*what, how, where, who, when, and why*), where if some form of action is taken, a favorable outcome is anticipated.

Organic entity Something that changes naturally and is not static.

Organization A corporation, group, body, company, kingdom, etc. that has been formalized and has some structure.

Out of context Considering a subset without inference to that larger set to which it belongs.

Out-of-context view A perspective that considers only a subset of the complete problem area relative to a single perspective. Out-of-context is typically attributed to the *subcontractor* perspective during the construction of each part of the entire product or service.

Owner *See* Row 2.

P

Paradigm The way you view something, or your frame of reference.

Paradigm shift A change from one way of thinking to another.

Passive aggressive resistance Behaviors where negative emotions—especially anger—are expressed indirectly through negative attitudes and resistance to reasonable requests.

Pattern A consistent and recognizable design or form.

Peer Framework An additional Framework often used to divide a domain or to keep dissimilar domains of a shared enterprise separated.

People *See* Column 4.

Perception A person's view of reality, made up of true or false information, personal assumptions, concepts, and values.

Persistent artifact A medium that can be reused verbatim to communicate concepts, thoughts, designs, and ideas. Persistent artifacts are explicit in nature. A persistent artifact in and of itself does not necessary yield truth; it only serves to make something at some level of detail explicit in nature.

Persistent data A fact that outlives the execution of a program and may be stored in a database.

Personality typing A classification system that identifies patterns of how people are alike and different from one another.

Perspective The label for the *y*-axis on the Framework. A term used to represent the six rows of the Framework—*planner, owner, designer, builder, subcontractor,* and *functioning enterprise. See* Row.

Perspective alias A general classification of the type of generic deliverables produced for a row. The alias is associated with the domain.

PERT *See* Program evaluation and review technique.

Phase space Total number of behavioral combinations available to a system.

Physical model A representation of the real thing in a form that can be built and is often depicted in a technical language (writing system). In the Framework, physical models are associated with the *builder's* perspective—Row 4.

PKI *See* Public key infrastructure.

Planner *See* Row 1.

Plugability The ability to add or remove functionality without disrupting the whole, often associated with components because it is difficult to add or remove functionality without dealing with small segments.

Point in time A phrase used frequently to determine validity at a particular moment. The duration of that period depends on the current situation.

Political agenda A list of things to be done based on the biases in order to achieve an outcome where one benefits or perceives satisfaction.

Practitioner Anyone who contributes to an artifact in the enterprise.

Prefabricated To build standardized parts in advance, for easy and rapid assembly of the final product.

Primitive The lowest level of representation of an artifact. An artifact associated exclusively with a primitive is the intersection of a single perspective and a single aspect.

Primitive component The basic three-part structure of a primitive model, normally represented in the form of a noun-verb-noun.

Primitive model The lowest level of representation for an artifact. A primitive is the intersection of a single perspective with a single aspect.

Proactive Being anticipatory and thinking before acting.

Problem space A self-imposed boundary for which an organization desires to create a solution.

Process *See* Column 2.

Process management The monitoring, measuring, controlling, and continuous improvement of the activities in the production of a product or service.

Process model A diagram of a series of actions directed toward achieving a particular result.

Product explosion A term used by manufacturers when determining all the parts required for any one product.

Product implosion A term used by manufacturers when there is a need to identify all the products in which a particular part is used.

Profit The difference between revenue and expenses.

Program evaluation and review technique (PERT) A method of project management that shows the interdependencies among activities required to reach certain events. The technique establishes a feedback loop for every phase of a project.

Project life cycle *See* Life cycle.

Project plan A document describing how a project is organized and the work to be done, including scheduling, resources, and cost.

Prototype A mock-up, substitute, or sample of the real thing developed quickly and improved continuously until involved parties are satisfied. Often in software, due to eagerness and budget, prototypes become the real thing.

Public key infrastructure (PKI) A system where a person's online identity is validated by a digital certificate.

Pushback Resistance to an idea or direct order.

Q

QS-9000 Certified quality system requirements that apply to suppliers of production materials and production or service parts, as well as heat treating, painting, plating, and other finishing services.

Quality control Procedures followed to ensure that defects in goods and services are minimized.

R

Raw materials Things needed and used to make something else.

Real time The latency between a type of action and an outcome, where latency has been reduced to almost zero.

Refactoring Code modification that improves a program's structure and simplifies maintenance over time.

Regulatory body An authority or system of authorities that is given legal rights and responsibilities to mandate.

Relationship A connection that can allow some form of communication.

Replication The process by which Zachman DNA copies itself and passes information on to each descendant cell, providing a building block for enterprise life.

Repository A place to store system models, descriptions and specifications, and other products of an enterprise.

Resources Things that can be procured by and used within the enterprise, such as money, people, and buildings.

Return on investment (ROI) The financial benefit or return an enterprise gets by spending or investing money on a given alternative.

Revenue Actual income.

Reverse engineer The process of taking something apart to see how it works to make improvements. A direction of work within a given life cycle or methodology where the major sequence of activities is conducted backwards.

Risk Anything with the potential to cause harm or have a negative effect on the enterprise.

Risk management Maintaining enterprise stability by anticipating and planning for potential problems.

ROI *See* Return on investment.

Role Something that frames the type of action expected by a person in a particular situation.

Root cause The most basic cause of a problem that can be fixed to prevent reoccurrence of a similar situation in the future.

Row One of the dimensions on the Zachman Framework's classification schema. The row is a horizontal plane on the Framework (*y*-axis). The Framework contains a total of 6 rows. Each row represents a perspective based on general architecture—*planner, owner, designer, builder, subcontractor,* and *functioning enterprise.* A row represents a biased way to view a product or service. The rows are also known as perspectives. The order of the rows is both a presentation sequence and a recommended sequence of work.

Row 1 The first horizontal plane on the Framework. The row represents the *planner* perspective. The *planner* perspective views the boundary and area of concern of a project or enterprise in terms of scope. Scope is delineated by each of the six aspects. The *planner's* deliverable often contains a series of lists in a scope document. The row is abbreviated as R1.

Row 2 The second horizontal plane on the Framework. The row represents the *owner* perspective. The *owner* perspective views the boundary and area of concern of a project or enterprise conceptually. Concepts are delineated by each of the six aspects. The *owner's* deliverable is often a conceptual or business model. The row is abbreviated as R2.

Row 3 The third horizontal plane on the Framework. The row represents the *designer* perspective. The *designer* perspective views the boundary and area of concern of a project or enterprise in optimal or ideal terms. Optimal or ideal terms are delineated by each of the six aspects. The *designer's* deliverable is often a logical model. The row is abbreviated as R3.

Row 4 The fourth horizontal plane on the Framework. The row represents the *builder* perspective. The *builder* perspective views the boundary and area of concern of a project or enterprise in terms of what is feasible. What is feasible is delineated by each of the six aspects. The *builder's* deliverable is often a physical model. The row is abbreviated as R4.

Row 5 The fifth horizontal plane on the Framework. The row represents the *subcontractor* perspective. The *subcontractor* perspective views the boundary and area of concern of a project or enterprise in terms of each component. Each component is further delineated by each of the six aspects. The *subcontractor's* deliverable is often an assembled component such as a computer program or a wired computer network. The row is abbreviated as R5.

Row 6 The sixth horizontal plane on the Framework. The row represents the *functioning enterprise* perspective. The *functioning enterprise* perspective views the boundary and area of concern of a project or enterprise in terms of what is actually in place. What is in place is delineated by each of the six aspects. The *functioning enterprise* is the actual deliverable—the real thing such as the Great Pyramid of Giza, the Cathedral of Chartres, the Boeing 777, an ERP system, a payroll application, or a dry cleaning service. The row is abbreviated as R6.

Rule A statement that governs, constrains, or influences behavior with varying degrees of enforcement.

Rule of use *See* Rule.

S

Scalability The ability to adapt to change, requiring a larger or smaller need, and the capability of taking full advantage of that change.

Scalable *See* Scalability.

Schema A diagrammatic representation of a set of assumptions, concepts, values, and practices that constitutes a way of viewing reality.

Science In the context of Zachman DNA, a specific specialty. For example, in IT, project administration, project management, standards, and version control can be represented on the z-axis of Zachman DNA.

Scientific management A systematic approach to solving problems.

Scope *See* Row 1.

Scope creep When a change for work that has not been accepted formally goes beyond the original boundary and area of concern of a project.

Scope sliver The representation of the undertaking found in an artifact.

Scrap and rework The need to discard a product because the product is incapable of being modified to accommodate change. The product is scrapped and the redesign and reconstruction of the new product is considered to be rework.

SDLC *See* System development life cycle.

Sequential file A storage mechanism where information is accessed one record at a time in a fixed order.

Service level agreement An agreement between a subscriber and a provider specifying that hardware, software, and personnel are available during certain periods, or perform at a certain level in order to avoid penalty.

Shelf life The length of time an item can stay in saleable condition.

Six Sigma A management philosophy, a statistic, and a process that are part of total quality management.

Sliver The representation of completeness for an artifact. A sliver has two dimensions: scope and detail.

Software architect A person who determines the techniques and tools for a programmer to use in the development of an application.

Source code Statements for a computer program written in a nonexecutable form.

Spiral life cycle A development method that combines elements of the waterfall, but focuses on risk management.

Stakeholder A person or organization with a vested interest in a project or situation.

Standard Provides a uniform level of understanding, applicability, and use.

Standish Group The Standish Group International, Inc., a recognized market research and advisory firm.

Statistic Measurement used as a vehicle for comparison.

Strategic advantage A characteristic that creates a favorable situation for the organization within the marketplace.

Strategic imperative A directive to achieve a favorable situation for the organization within the marketplace.

Strategic partner A relationship with an outsider to achieve a favorable situation for the organization within the marketplace and share and leverage knowledge and resources for mutual benefit.

Strategy A course of action to achieve an end that is often supported by a series of tactics.

Subcontractor *See* Row 5.

Sunsetted A condition when technology has been phased out or retired, and the company ceases to find ways to use that technology.

Supplier A company or individual that sells, exchanges, or gives parts or services to another company.

Supply chain Everything necessary to identify and manage the movement of something between two endpoints (the chain). For example, from mining ore to distribution of an automobile, including all the things, processes, locations, people, events, and motivations.

SWOT analysis A technique used for identifying internal strengths and weaknesses and external opportunities and threats of a project.

Synergize When two or more people create a better solution than either of the two or more people could do separately.

System A collection of elements or components that are organized for a common purpose.

System development life cycle (SDLC) An overarching name for any method or practice used in the development of software.

Systems thinker One who has the ability to think or reason beyond what is visually observable.

Systems thinking The process of thinking and reasoning beyond what is visually observable.

T

Tactic An action taken by the organization to execute the strategies to satisfy the objective.

Tangible Something definable, or that can be valued monetarily.

Task model The relationship of projects, activities, tasks, deliverables, and milestones associated with creating an outcome.

Tensegrity Structural strength of cells. In the context of Zachman DNA, primitive models represent the structural strength of the cells in the Framework.

Thing *See* Column 1.

Thinning process Separating to create a simpler maintenance environment.

Thought leader One who respects and listens to the opinions of others and values the voice of experience. A person who is willing and able to share with others and believes in being part of a learning community.

Throughput The amount of work a computer system or a component can do in a certain period of time.

Time *See* Column 5.

Timing *See* Column 5.

Timing coordination *See* Column 5.

Toolkit A collection of automated tools purchased by an organization to fit individual development methodologies.

Topography A detailed and accurate description of a location, place, or region.

Topology The complexity of a computer system resulting from its environment and topography. The physical layout of a network.

Total Quality Management (TQM) A structured, cultural, and comprehensive approach to organizational management based on feedback, with the goal of continuous improvement.

TQM *See* Total Quality Management.

Trade-off An exchange of one thing in return for another.

Trailing-edge Organizations that continue to use older, outdated technologies that may be difficult to maintain and support.

Transformation A process of analysis that translates what is mandated by a previous row in the Framework, often involving a combination of a current state and end state analysis effort.

Trigger The initial starting action of a business event.

U

Unit of measure Quantifies a measurement creating a common understanding; both an amount quantifying something as a value of 1, and a designation applied to a number to understand what the number represents. For example, 1 second.

V

Value chain A sequence of events that maximizes performance and adds wealth to the organization through internal or external operations. Added value may include conversion; movement or placement of goods, products, processes, techniques, or services; and cost-effectiveness.

Vendor A company or individual, which sells parts or services to another company.

Vertical integration The continuity of all knowledge occurring along a single aspect of the Framework.

Virtual private network (VPN) A network that uses the Internet, but does not allow public access to data transmitted through an encrypted tunnel.

Vision An end state desired by an individual or organization.

VPN *See* Virtual private network.

W

Waterfall method A sequential development method that follows a strict order moving from concept to: design, implementation, testing, installation, troubleshooting, and finally, operation and maintenance.

Weekly cycle A period of time (7 calendar days) in which an organization makes an operational decision.

What *See* Column 1.

When *See* Column 5.

Where *See* Column 3.

Who *See* Column 4.

Why *See* Column 6.

Wisdom The integration of intellectual and experiential knowledge transformed into meaning, enabling prudent decisions to be made for the enterprise. A synthesis for the application of data, information, and knowledge.

Z

Zachman DNA An extension that transforms the Zachman Framework into a three-dimensional schema. Within the context of the Framework, DNA is an acronym for Depth iNtegrating Architecture. Zachman DNA combines the architectural representations and the activities, disciplines, and infrastructures required to make a business functional and operational.

Zachman Framework for Enterprise Architecture The formal name of a classification schema used to organize an enterprise's artifacts and help facilitate, thinking, reasoning, and communicating among the participants of the enterprise.

Zero defects A concept created by Philip Crosby during the quality revolution, meaning perfection.

INDEX

location and, 269,
280–281, 284, 292–296,
319–320, 326–327

motivation and, 269–270,
284–285, 286–287,
322, 332–333

people and, 265–266,
281–282, 284, 296–298,
316–317, 330–331

processes and, 267–268,
282–283, 284, 288–292,
318–319, 327

timing and, 264–265,
283–284, 284, 298–299,
321, 331–332

building, at Keane, Inc., 145

building processes. *See*
process(es)

business contention, 186

business cycles, 141, 143

business image, culture and,
226–229

business logic, 209–211

business models, 135

business needs agenda,
244–245

business objectives, 138

business plans, 119–121

business processes. *See*
process(es)

business requirements, 183

business rules, 247–249,
365–366

business-to-business
sites, 392

Butterfly Effect, 114

bytes, 351

C

Cabral, Pedro Alvares, 286

California Air Resources
Board (CARB), 331–332

Capability Maturity Model
(CMM), 87–88

capacity planning, 391
Internet and, 390–393

capital, intellectual, 194

CARB (California Air
Resources Board),
331–332

careers. *See* IT careers

Carnival Cruise Lines, 380

Carter, Marshall, 325

Cascade Engineering,
150–157, 230

business processes at,
152–154

customer focus of, 157

disaster recovery plan
at, 155

location of, 156

organizational structure
at, 156

people at, 211–212

quality certification at,
153–154

timing at, 154–155

CASE tools, 582

causal loops, 313

cause and effect chain, 114

cells, 12
defined, 478
of Framework, 448,
457–460

CEOs (chief executive
officers), 7

certificate authority, 398

certification, 420

chain of events, 114

Chamberlain, Donald, 373

change, 403–414
assembled-to-order
projects and, 410–411

example of process,
528–543

made-to-order projects
and, 409–410

managing, 627–629

provided-from-stock
projects and, 410

as threat to profits, 322

change management, 617

change procedure, 146, 147

changes, failure to record,
319–320

chaos, 572, 576–577
Zachman DNA and,
606–607

chaos theory, 573

Chapel of the Holy Cross
(Sedona, Arizona),
178–180

Chapman, Tom, 323

Charcot, Jean-Martin, 245

Chartres, Cathedral of, 62–73
building processes for, 68

location for building,
63–66

materials for building,
68–71

motivation for building,
66–68

organization for building,
71–72

timing for building, 72–73

chief executive officers
(CEOs), 7

Chief Information Officer
(CIO) Council, 16

Chinese Civil Service, 220

CIO (Chief Information
Officer) Council, 16

classification law, 484
postulates, theorems,
corollaries, and
comments for, 490

rules for, 487

classification schema,
439–441
defined, 468

for personality type,
194–197

classification systems,
100–101
owner's understanding of,
127–128

climate, 37–38

Clinger-Cohen Act, 16

clock, long-term, 404–405

closed corporations, 122

data retention, 381–384
  business continuity
    and, 383
  data management and,
    382–383
  judicial discovery and
    legal liability and,
    383–384
database(s), 370–384
  changes in, 373–378
  data centric approach
    to, 381
  data greenhouse approach
    to, 379–381
  data retention policies
    and, 381–384
  disparity among
    products, 372
  distributed, 378–379
  heterogeneous, 379
  homogeneous, 379
  standards for, 372
  types of, 371–372
database servers, 378
Davidson, Mary Ann, 328
Davis, Ronald, 430–431
de facto standards, 621
Deal, Terrence, 203
defensive data models, 547
deliverables, 43
Delta Airlines, 278
demilitarized zone (DMZ), 401
Deming, Edward, 304
demographic information, 142
denormalization, 266
  defined, 480
Department of Homeland
  Security, 16
Department of Veterans
  Affairs, Framework
  applied to, 550–559
Depth iNtegrating
  Architecture. See
  Zachman DNA (Depth
  iNtegrating Architecture)

descriptive
  representations, 572
  defined, 479
designer's perspective, 10, 11,
  169–251, 450, 472. See
  also perspective(s)
  assets and, 183–184, 207,
    216, 226–229
  bias and, 506
  location and, 187, 211,
    213–214, 243
  motivation and, 221–223,
    245–246
  people and, 186, 214–216,
    243–245
  people and design
    challenges and,
    176–178
  processes and, 184–186,
    193–194, 207–208,
    218–219, 230
  technical and psychological
    challenges and, 172–176
  timing and, 187–191,
    200–201, 220–221
detail, 593, 595–596
  excruciating level of,
    498–502
detail law, 486
  postulates, theorems,
    corollaries, and
    comments for, 495
  rules for, 489
detail slivers, defined, 482
detailed representations,
  defined, 473
DeVries, Pierre, 329–330
digital certificates, 396–399
digital signatures, 398
disaster recovery plans, 155
disciples, 224
disciplines, 41–42
distributed databases, 371,
  378–379
Djoser, King, 49
DMZ (demilitarized zone), 401

DNA, 578–580. See also
  Zachman DNA (Depth
  iNtegrating Architecture)
documentation, 61
Dodge Neon, 152–154
domain, 184
domain(s), defined, 468
domain law, 485
  postulates, theorems,
    corollaries, and
    comments for, 492
  rules for, 488
dominators, 190
Donatello, 345
drag, 593, 594–595
drives, 373
dynamical systems, 576
Dyson, Esther, 319

E

EAI (enterprise application
  integration), 541
eBay, 120
economic priorities, 242
eels (personality type),
  214–215
efficiency, 541
ego, 246
80–hour rule, 146, 147
80/20 rule, 184
Einstein, Albert, 74–75
Eisenhower, Dwight, 96
Electronic Numerical
  Integrator Computer
  (ENIAC), 364–365
Eli Lilly and Company, 421
embedded Framework, 609,
  622–629
  chromosomes and,
    623–624
  coding and, 624–626
  sensitivity and, 626–629
emergence, 592
emergent system property, 592
emotional filters, 181

705

religion and culture and,
230–232

subcontractors and,
357–360, 367–369,
378–379, 386–388,
411–412

technology and, 269

timing, religion and
culture and, 232–233

for Walt Disney Company,
138–139

Lockheed, Oxcart project at,
171–176

logical models, defined, 472

logistics, 48

Long Now Foundation, 404

Lorenz, Edward, 114,
589–590

Lucian, 259

M

Mach, Ernst, 175

Mach number, 175

made-to-order projects,
409–410

Mafia, 123–124

Magic Kingdom, 138–139

malcontents, 190

management, 26
at Keane, Inc., 145

mandate(s), 26

mandated business rules,
247–249

mandated standards, 621

Mandelbrot, Benoit, 573–575

Mandelbrot, Szolem, 573

Manhattan Project, 73–80, 127
building process for,
75–77

location for, 79–80

materials for, 80

motivation for, 79

organization for, 80–81

timing for development of,
77–79

market share, 128

marketplace, 128

Marshall, Barry, 318

Maslow, Abraham, 204, 243

mass production, 85–86

Mata Atlantica rainforest, 286

materials. *See* asset(s)

materials management, 55

Mauchly, John, 365

McCormick, Michelle, 211

means, 115

measurement, 271–285,
597–605

changes and, 282–283

metrics and, 277

organization and, 281–282

planning and, 283–284

rules and, 274–275

standard operating
procedures and,
278–279

standards and, 275–276

statistics and, 277–278

unfavorable comparisons
and, 284–285

units of measure and,
276–277, 279

Zachman DNA and,
597–605

measuring sticks, 216, 217

meetings, 187–191
attendees at, 189–191

stupid questions in,
220–221

types of, 187–188

unscheduled, 236

Meijer Corporation, 208, 387

memory, shortcomings of
depending on, 316–317

Menger, Karl, 586

Menger sponge, 586, 587

mental models, 205, 442

metalingusitics, 19–20

metamodels, 19, 20

metarules, 17

method(s), corporate life
events and, 241–242

method of practice,
defined, 469

methodologies, 6, 43,
313–322, 620–621

change and, 322

elements common to, 314

human memory and,
316–317

incorrect information and,
319–320

information overload and,
318–319

managing body of
knowledge and,
317–318

unrealistic expectations
and, 321

methodology independence
of Framework, 545

metrics, 51, 216–220, 277,
600, 618–620

Michelangelo, 344–345, 347

Microsoft, 328–330, 338
Web services and,
295–296

mining, 382

misassumptions, 61

mission, 124, 205–206

mission critical systems,
598–599

mission statements, 217

mission-critical opera-
tions, 386

Mitchell, John, 440

MMC Communications, 211

mobility of IT workers,
420–421

models, 7, 8, 572
business, 135

conceptual, defined, 472

data, defensive, 547

data modeling and, 375

defined, 479

incremental, 582–583

New York Stock Exchange (NYSE), 117
Newton, Isaac, 27, 51
Next Generation Telescope (NGT), 629
Noble Polymers, 153
nonprofit corporations, 123
normal forms of relations, 375–376
normalization, 266, 446–447, 510–512
    defined, 480
    of relational databases, 376–378
normalized architectural artifacts, defined, 479
North, Oliver, 383
nouns, defined, 481
NYSE (New York Stock Exchange), 117

O

Oberth, Hermann, 627
Object Modeling Technique (OMT), 584
object relational databases, 371
objections, as corporate resistance, 250
objectives, 216, 217
    methodologies and, 314
object-oriented (OO) applications, 546
object-oriented (OO) methods, 16, 584
OBRA (Omnibus Budget Reconciliation Act) (1986), 278, 280, 281–282
obstructionists, 190
ODBC (open database connectivity), 373
offshore corporations, 123
Omnibus Budget Reconciliation Act (OBRA) (1986), 278, 280, 281–282

OMT (Object Modeling Technique), 584
online shopping sites, 392
on-the-fly methodology, 621
OO (object-oriented) applications, 546
OO (object-oriented) methods, 16, 584
open database connectivity (ODBC), 373
Open Systems Interconnection (OSI) model, 399–400
openness, 241
open-source software, 289–291
open-source software license, 290
Oppenheimer, Robert, 77
opportunities, 63
    in SWOT analysis, 221–223
Oracle, 288
organic entities, 371, 388–390
organization. See people
organization charts, 14
organized crime families, 123–124
OSI (Open Systems Interconnection) model, 399–400
out-of-context view, defined, 470
owner's perspective, 10, 11, 126–133, 449, 472. See also perspective(s)
    authority and responsibility and, 126–133
    bias and, 507
    classification system and, 127–128
    in public education, 129–133
Oxcart project, 171–176

P

paradigm(s), 144
paradigm shifts, 264
Pareto's Law, 184
partnerships, 241
    general, 123
passive aggressive resistors, 189–190
patterns, 315
Paulino, Rolando, 184
Peanuts comic strip, 225
peer framework, defined, 483
Pemberton, John, 133
people, 10, 12, 455, 456, 594, 596–597. See also aspects
    for Boeing 777 airplane, 104
    builders and, 265–266, 281–282, 284, 296–298, 316–317, 330–331
    for building Cathedral of Chartres, 71–72
    for building pyramids, 47–49
    of Cascade Engineering, 157
    change and, 412–413
    for Coca-Cola, 137
    corporate life events and, 243–245
    defined, 477
    designers and, 186, 214–216, 243–245
    at Equifax, Inc., 161
    Framework and, 449–452
    gaining support for ideas and, 211–212
    at Keane, Inc., 149
    for Levittown, 84–85
    for Manhattan Project, 80–81
    for Moon landing, 91–93
    for Movie Outpost, 142
    people skills and, 186